NW09000946

British Qualifications

**FOR
REFERENCE ONLY**

WITHDRAWN

British Qualifications

40TH EDITION

A Complete Guide to Professional, Vocational & Academic Qualifications in the United Kingdom

KoganPage

LONDON PHILADELPHIA NEW DELHI

Consultant editor: Elizabeth Holmes

Publisher's note
Every possible effort has been made to ensure that the information contained in this book is accurate at the time of going to press, and the publishers and authors cannot accept responsibility for any errors or omissions, however caused. No responsibility for loss or damage occasioned to any person acting, or refraining from action, as a result of the material in this publication can be accepted by the editor, the publisher or any of the authors.

First published in Great Britain in 1966

Fortieth edition published in Great Britain and the United States in 2010 by Kogan Page Limited

120 Pentonville Road	525 South 4th St, #241	4737/23 Ansari Road
London N1 9JN	Philadelphia PA 19147	Daryaganj
United Kingdom	USA	New Delhi 110002
www.koganpage.com		India

© Kogan Page, 2010

British Library Cataloguing-in-Publication Data

A CIP record for this book is available from the British Library.

ISBN 978 0 7494 5710 5
ISSN 0141-5972

Typeset by AMA DataSet Ltd, Preston
Printed and bound in Great Britain by MPG Books Ltd, Bodmin, Cornwall

UNIVERSITY OF SURREY

Achieve your potential

With a world-class Management degree from the University of Surrey

The University of Surrey's School of Management offers a world-class education, providing degrees which are valued by today's global community.

Overseas delivery

Many of our programmes are available overseas in Germany, Hong Kong, Barbados and Mauritius.

Accreditation

The School holds simultaneous accreditation by the AMBA (Association of MBAs) for the Surrey MBA programme, the AACSB (Association to Advance Collegiate Schools of Business) and by the UNWTO (United Nations World Tourism Organisation) in recognition of the high standard of its teaching and operations.

Academic excellence

With over 40 years of experience in providing management education and with leading academics on its staff, the School seeks to ensure that both research and teaching anticipate, reflect and deliver tomorrow's needs today.

For further information please contact
T: +44 (0)1483 686300
E: somadmissions@surrey.ac.uk
www.surrey.ac.uk/postgraduate/taught/

PUBLISHER'S NOTE

This 40th edition of *British Qualifications* has been considerably revised and updated to reflect the many changes in degree, diploma and certificate courses and to take account of legislative reforms affecting the structure of higher and further education over the past year.

The editor and compilers are most grateful to the academic registrars and the secretaries of the many bodies they have contacted for information and advice. Without their cooperation, the revision and updating of *British Qualifications* would not have been possible.

CONTENTS

Contents

Contents

Contents

Contents

Contents

REFERENCES

Association of MBAs (AMBA) (annual) *AMBA – Financial Times Guide to Business Schools,* AMBA, London

Committee of Vice-Chancellors and Principals (CVCP) (annual) *University Entrance: The official guide,* CVCP, London

Department for Education and Skills (DfES) (2003) *The Future of Higher Education,* The Stationery Office, London [online] http://www.dfes.gov.uk/hegateway/strategy/hestrategy/foreword.shtml

DfES (2004) *Five-Year Strategy for Children and Learners,* DfES, London

Qualifications and Curriculum Authority (QCA) (2004) *New Thinking for Reform: A framework for achievement,* QCA, London (July)

HOW TO USE THIS BOOK

You may find these notes helpful when using the book.

Part 1 presents an overview of the further and higher educational systems currently in operation in the United Kingdom, including a discussion of the major reforms that have taken place over the past year and their impact.

Part 2 takes a look at the teaching establishments whose qualifications are listed in Part 4 of the book, offering an explanation of the different types of institution, their place in the overall system and the levels of qualification that they award.

Part 3 presents a detailed description of vocational qualifications awarded by many of the professional associations included in Part 5, including an explanation of validating, examining and awarding bodies.

Part 4 is a directory of qualifications awarded by universities in the United Kingdom (ordered by university name). There is a brief introduction detailing admission to degree courses, degree structure and the various categories of degree available.

Part 5 is a directory of qualifications awarded by professional, trade and specialist associations in the United Kingdom (ordered by profession / discipline), including certificates, diplomas, NVQs and SVQs. A short introduction explains the functions of professional associations and how to gain membership.

Part 6 describes various bodies involved in the accreditation of colleges in the independent sector of further and higher education.

Part 7 is a list of study associations and learned societies.

Also included (at the beginning of the book) is a list of all abbreviations and designatory letters used throughout *British Qualifications*.

INDEX OF ABBREVIATIONS AND DESIGNATORY LETTERS

AAB	Associate of the Association of Book-keepers
AACB	Associate of the Association of Certified Bookkeepers
AACP	Associate of the Association of Computer Professionals
AAFC	Associate of the Association of Financial Controllers and Administrators
AAIA	Associate of the Association of International Accountants
AAMS	Associate of the Association of Medical Secretaries, Practice Managers, Administrators and Receptionists
AASI	Associate of the Ambulance Service Institute
AASW	Advanced Award in Social Work
AAT	Association of Accounting Technicians
ABC	Awarding Body Consortium
ABDO	Associate of the British Dispensing Opticians
ABE	Association of Business Executives
ABEng	Associate Member of the Association of Building Engineers
ABHA	Associate of the British Hypnotherapy Association
ABIAT	Associate Member of the British Institute of Architectural Technologists
ABIPP	Associate of the British Institute of Professional Photography
ABMA	Associate of the Business Management Association
ABPR	Association of British Picture Restorers
ABRSM	Associated Board of the Royal Schools of Music
ABS	Association of Business Schools
ABSSG	Associate of the British Society of Scientific Glassblowers
ACA	Associate of the Institute of Chartered Accountants in England and Wales
ACA	Associate of the Institute of Chartered Accountants in Ireland
ACB	Association of Certified Bookkeepers
ACC	Accredited Clinical Coders
ACCA	Associate of the Association of Chartered Certified Accountants
ACCA	Association of Chartered Certified Accountants
ACE	Association for Conferences and Events
ACEA	Associate of the Institute of Cost and Executive Accountants
ACertCM	Archbishop of Canterbury's Certificate in Church Music
ACGI	Associate of City and Guilds of London Institute
ACIArb	Associate of the Chartered Institute of Arbitrators
ACIB	Associate of the Chartered Institute of Bankers
ACIBS	Associate of the Chartered Institute of Bankers in Scotland
ACIBSE	Associate of the Chartered Institution of Building Services Engineers
ACIH	Associate of the Chartered Institute of Housing
ACII	Associate of the Chartered Insurance Institute
ACILA	Associate of the Chartered Institute of Loss Adjusters
ACIM	Associate of the Chartered Institute of Marketing
ACIOB	Associate of the Chartered Institute of Building
ACIS	Associate of the Institute of Chartered Secretaries and Administrators
ACIT	Advanced Certificate in International Trade
ACLIP	Certified Affiliate of CILIP
ACMA	Associate of the Chartered Institute of Management Accountants
ACP	Association of Child Psychotherapists
ACP	Associate of the College of Preceptors

ACP	Association of Computer Professionals
ACPM	Associate of the Confederation of Professional Management
ACPP	Associate of the College of Pharmacy Practice
ACT	Associate of the College of Teachers
ACYW	Associate of the Community and Youth Work Association
ADCE	Advanced Diploma in Childcare and Education
ADCM	Archbishop of Canterbury's Diploma in Church Music
AdDipEd	Advanced Diploma in Education
ADI	Approved Driving Instructor
AECI	Association Member of the Institute of Employment Consultants
AEWVH	Association for the Education and Welfare of the Visually Handicapped
AFA	Associate of the Faculty of Actuaries
AFA	Associate of the Institute of Financial Accountants
AFBPsS	Associate Fellow of the British Psychological Society
AFCI	Associate of the Faculty of Commerce and Industry Ltd
AffBMA	Affiliate of the Business Management Association
AffIManf	Affiliate of the Institute of Manufacturing
AffIMI	Affiliate of the Institute of the Motor Industry
AffIMS	Affiliate of the Institute of Management Specialists
AffInstM	Affiliate of the Meat Training Council
AffIP	Affiliate of the Institute of Plumbing
AffProfBTM	Affiliate of Professional Business and Technical Management
AFIMA	Associate Fellow of the Institute of Mathematics and its Applications
AFISOL	Aerodrome Flight Information Service Officer's Licence
AFPC	Advanced Financial Planning Certificate
AFRCSEd	Associate Fellow of Royal College of Surgeons of Edinburgh
AGCL	Associate of the Guild of Cleaners and Launderers
AGI	Associate of the Greek Institute
AGSM	Associate of the Guildhall School of Music and Drama
AHCIMA	Associate of the Hotel and Catering International Management Association
AHFS	Associate of the Council of Health Fitness and Sports Therapists
AHRIM	Associate of the Institute of Health Record Information and Management
AIA	Associate of the Institute of Actuaries
AIA	Association of International Accountants
AIAgrE	Associate of the Institution of Agricultural Engineers
AIAT	Associate of the Institute of Asphalt Technology
AIBCM	Associate of the Institute of British Carriage and Automobile Manufacturers
AIBMS	Associate of the Institute of Biomedical Science
AICB	Associate of the Institute of Certified Book-Keepers
AIChor	Associate of the Benesh Institute of Choreology
AICHT	Associate of the International Council of Holistic Therapists
AICM(Cert)	Associate Member of the Institute of Credit Management
AICS	Associate of the Institution of Chartered Shipbrokers
AICSc	Associate of the Institute of Consumer Sciences Incorporating Home Economics
AIDTA	Associate of the International Dance Teachers' Association
AIE	Associate of the Institute of Electrolysis
AIEM	Associate of the Institute of Executives and Managers
AIExpE	Associate of the Institute of Explosive Engineers
AIFA	Associate of the Institute of Field Archaeologists
AIFBQ	Associate of the International Faculty of Business Qualifications
AIFireE	Associate of the Institution of Fire Engineers
AIFP	Associate of the British International Freight Association

AIGD	Associate of the Institute of Grocery Distribution
AIHort	Associate Member of the Institute of Horticulture
AIIMR	Associate of the Institute of Investment Management and Research
AIIRSM	Associate of the International Institute of Risk and Safety Management
AIL	Associate of the Institute of Linguists
AILAM	Associate of the Institute of Leisure and Amenity Management
AIMBM	Associate of the Institute of Maintenance and Building Management
AIMC	Associate of the Institute of Management Consultancy
AIMgt	Associate of the Institute of Management
AIMIS	Associate of the Institute for the Management of Information Systems
AIMM	Associate of the Institute of Massage and Movement
AInstAM	Associate of the Institute of Administrative Management
AInstBA	Associate of the Institute of Business Administration
AInstBCA	Associate of the Institute of Burial and Cremation Administration
AInstBM	Associate of the Institute of Builders' Merchants
AInstCM	Associate of the Institute of Commercial Management
AInstM	Associate of the Meat Training Council
AInstPkg	Associate of the Institute of Packaging
AInstPM	Associate of the Institute of Professional Managers and Administrators
AInstSMM	Associate of the Institute of Sales and Marketing Management
AInstTA	Associate of the Institute of Transport Administration
AInstTT	Associate Member of the Institute of Travel and Tourism
AIOC	Associate of the Institute of Carpenters
AIOFMS	Associate of the Institute of Financial and Management Studies
AIP	Associate of the Institute of Plumbing
AIQA	Associate of the Institute of Quality Assurance
AIS	Accredited Imaging Scientist
AISOB	Associate of the Incorporated Society of Organ Builders
AISTD	Associate of the Imperial Society of Teachers of Dancing
AISTDDip	Associate Diploma of the Imperial Society of Teachers of Dancing
AITSA	Associate of the Institute of Trading Standards Administration
AIVehE	Associate of the Institute of Vehicle Engineers
AIWSc	Associate Member of the Institute of Wood Science
ALCM	Associate of the London College of Music
ALI	Associate of the Landscape Institute
ALS	Associate of the Linnean Society of London
AMA	Associate of the Museums Association
AMABE	Associate Member of the Association of Business Executives
AMAE	Associate Member of the Academy of Experts
AMASI	Associate Member of the Architecture and Surveying Institute
AMBA	Association of MBAs
AMBA	Non-Teacher Associate Member of the British (Theatrical) Arts
AMBCS	Associate Member of the British Computer Society
AMBII	Associate Member of the British Institute of Innkeeping
AmCAM	Associate of the Communication Advertising and Marketing Education Foundation
AMCT	Associate of the Association of Corporate Treasurers
AMCTHCM	Associate Member of the Confederation of Tourism, Hotel and Catering Management
AMI	Association Montessori Internationale
AMIA	Affiliated Member of the Association of International Accountants
AMIAgrE	Associate Member of the Institution of Agricultural Engineers
AMIAP	Associate Member of the Institution of Analysts and Programmers

AMIAT	Associate Member of the Institute of Asphalt Technology
AMIBC	Associate Member of the Institute of Building Control
AMIBCM	Associate Member of the Institute of British Carriage and Automobile Manufacturers
AMIBE	Associate Member of the Institution of British Engineers
AMIBF	Associate Member of the Institute of British Foundrymen
AMICE	Associate Member of the Institution of Civil Engineers
AMIChemE	Associate Member of the Institution of Chemical Engineers
AMIED	Associate Member of the Institution of Engineering Designers
AMIEE	Associate Member of the Institution of Electrical Engineers
AMIEx	Associate Member of the Institute of Export
AMIHIE	Associate Member of the Institute of Highway Incorporated Engineers
AMIHT	Associate Member of the Institution of Highways and Transportation
AMIIE	Associate Member of the Institution of Incorporated Engineers
AMIIExE	Associate Member of the Institution of Incorporated Executive Engineers
AMIIHTM	Associate Member of the International Institute of Hospitality Tourism & Management
AMIISE	Associate Member of the International Institute of Social Economics
AMIM	Associate Member of the Institute of Materials
AMIManf	Member of the Institute of Manufacturing
AMIMechE	Associate Member of the Institution of Mechanical Engineers
AMIMechIE	Associate Member of the Institution of Mechanical Incorporated Engineers
AMIMI	Associate Member of the Institute of the Motor Industry
AMIMinE	Associate of the Institute of Mining Engineers
AMIMM	Associate Member of the Institution of Mining and Metallurgy
AMIMS	Associate Member of the Institute of Management Specialists
AMInstAEA	Associate Member of the Institute of Automotive Engineer Assessors
AMInstBE	Associate Member of the Institution of British Engineers
AMInstE	Associate Member of the Institute of Energy
AMInstR	Associate Member of the Institute of Refrigeration
AMInstTA	Associate Member of the Institute of Transport Administration
AMIPlantE	Associate Member of the Institution of Plant Engineers
AMIPR	Associate Member of the Institute of Public Relations
AMIPRE	Associate Member of the Incorporated Practitioners in Radio and Electronics
AMIQ	Associate Member of the Institute of Quarrying
AMIQA	Associate Member of the Institute of Quality Assurance
AMIRTE	Associate Member of the Institute of Road Transport Engineers
AMISM	Associate Member of the Institute for Supervision & Management
AMIStrutE	Associate Member of the Institution of Structural Engineers
AMITD	Associate Member of the Institute of Training and Development
AMIVehE	Associate Member of the Institute of Vehicle Engineers
AMNI	Associate Member of the Nautical Institute
AMPA	Associate Member of the Master Photographers Association
AMProfBTM	Associate Member of Professional Business and Technical Management
AMRAeS	Associate Member of the Royal Aeronautical Society
AMRSH	Associate Member of the Royal Society for the Promotion of Health
AMS	Associate of the Institute of Management Services
AMS(Aff)	Affiliate of the Association of Medical Secretaries, Practice Managers, Administrators and Receptionists
AMSE	Associate Member of the Society of Engineers (Inc)
AMSPAR	Association of Medical Secretaries, Practice Managers, Administrators and Receptionists

AMusEd	Associate Diploma in Music Education
AMusLCM	Associate in Music of the London College of Music
AMusTCL	Associate in Music of Trinity College of Music
AMWES	Associate Member of the Women's Engineering Society
ANAEA	Associate of the National Association of Estate Agents
ANCA	Advanced National Certificate in Agriculture
AOP	Association of Photographers
AOR	Association of Reflexologists
APA	Accreditation of Prior Experience
APC	Assessment of Professional Competence
APCS	Associate of the Property Consultants Society
APMI	Associate of the Pensions Management Institute
APMP	Association for Project Management Professional
AQA	Assessment & Qualifications Alliance
ARAD	Associate of the Royal Academy of Dancing
ARAM	Associate of the Royal Academy of Music
ARB	Architects Registration Board
ARCM	Associate of Royal College of Music
ARCO	Associate of the Royal College of Organists
ARCS	Associate of the Royal College of Science
AREC	Associate of the Recruitment and Employment Confederation
ARELS	Association of Recognised English Language Services
ARELS-FELCO	Association of Recognised English Language Teaching Establishments in Britain
ARIBA	Associate of the Royal Institute of British Architects
ARICS	Associate of the Royal Institution of Chartered Surveyors
ARIPHH	Associate of the Royal Institute of Public Health and Hygiene
ARPS	Associate of the Royal Photographic Society
ARSC	Associate of the Royal Society of Chemistry
ARSCM	Associate of the Royal School of Church Music
ARSM	Associate of the Royal School of Mines
AS	Advanced Supplementary level
ASCA	Associate of the Institute of Company Accountants
ASCT	Associate of the Society of Claims Technicians
ASDC	Associate of the Society of Dyers and Colourists
ASE	Associate of the Society of Engineers (Inc)
ASI	Ambulance Service Institute
ASI	Architecture and Surveying Institute
ASIAffil	Affiliate of the Ambulance Service Institute
ASIS	Accredited Senior Imaging Scientist
ASLC	Advanced Secretarial Language Certificate
ASMA	Associate of the Society of Sales Management Administrators Ltd
ASNN	Associate of the Society of Nursery Nursing
AssCI	Associate of the Institute of Commerce
AssociateCIPD	Associate of the Chartered Institute of Personnel and Development
AssociateIEEE	Associate of the Institution of Electrical and Electronics Engineers Incorporated
AssociateIIE	Associate of the Institution of Incorporated Engineers
AssocIMechIE	Associate of the Institution of Mechanical Incorporated Engineers
AssocIPD	Associate of the Institute of Personnel & Development
AssocIPHE	Associate of the Institution of Public Health Engineers
AssocMIWM	Associate Member of the Institute of Wastes Management
AssocTechIIE	Associate Technician of the Institution of Incorporated Engineers
ASTA	Associate of the Swimming Teachers' Association

ASVA	Associate of the Incorporated Society of Valuers and Auctioneers
ATC	Art Teacher's Certificate
ATCL	Associate of Trinity College of Music
ATCLicence	Air Traffic Controller's Licence
ATCLTESOL	Associate Diploma in the Teaching of English to Speakers of Other Languages, Trinity College
ATD	Art Teacher's Diploma
ATI	Associate of the Textile Industry
ATII	Associate of the Chartered Institute of Taxation
ATPL	Airline Transport Pilot's Licence
ATSC	Associate of the Oil and Colour Chemists' Association
ATSC	Associate in the Technology of Surface Coatings
ATT	Association of Taxation Technicians
ATT	Member of the Association of Taxation Technicians
ATTA	Association of Therapy Teachers Associate
ATTF	Association of Therapy Teachers Fellow
ATTM	Association of Therapy Teachers Member
AWeldI	Associate of the Welding Institute
BA	Bachelor of Arts
BA(Econ)	Bachelor of Arts in Economics & Social Studies
BA(Ed)	Bachelor of Arts (Education)
BA(Lan)	Bachelor of Languages
BA(Law)	Bachelor of Arts in Law
BA(Music)	Bachelor of Music
BABTAC	British Association of Beauty Therapy and Cosmetology Ltd
BAC	British Accreditation Council for Independent Further and Higher Education
BAC	British Association for Counselling
BAcc	Bachelor of Accountancy
BACP	British Association for Counselling Psychotherapy
BADA	British Antique Dealers' Association
BADN	British Association of Dental Nurses
BAE	British Association of Electrolysists Ltd
BAGMA	British Agricultural and Garden Machinery Association
BAgr	Bachelor of Agriculture
BAO	Bachelor of Obstetrics
BAP	British Association of Psychotherapists
BArch	Bachelor of Architecture
BASELT	British Association in State English Language Teaching
BBO	British Ballet Organisation
BChD	Bachelor of Dental Surgery
BChir	Bachelor of Surgery
BCL	Bachelor of Civil Law
BCom	Bachelor of Commerce
BCombStuds	Bachelor of Combined Studies
BComm	Bachelor of Communications
BCS	Bachelor of Combined Studies
BCS	British Computer Society
BD	Bachelor of Divinity
BDA	British Dietetic Association
BDes	Bachelor of Design
BDS	Bachelor of Dental Surgery
BEconSc	Bachelor of Economics

BECTU	Broadcasting, Entertainment, Cinematograph and Theatre Union
BEd	Bachelor of Education
BEng	Bachelor of Engineering
BEng and Man	Bachelor of Mechanical Engineering, Manufacture and Management
BER	Board for Engineers' Regulation
BFA	Bachelor of Fine Arts
BFin	Bachelor of Finance
BHA	British Hypnotherapy Association
BHI	British Horological Institute Ltd
BHS	British Horse Society
BHSAI	British Horse Society's Assistant Instructor's Certificate
BHSI	British Horse Society's Instructor's Certificate
BHSII	British Horse Society's Intermediate Instructor's Certificate
BHSIntSM	British Horse Society's Intermediate Stable Manager's Certificate
BHSSM	British Horse Society's Stable Manager's Certificate
BIA	Beauty Industry Authority
BIAT	British Institute of Architectural Technologists
BIBA	Bachelor of International Business Administration
BIE	British Institute of Embalmers
BIFA	British International Freight Association
BIPP	British Institute of Professional Photography
BIS	British Interplanetary Society
BKSTS	British Kinematograph Sound and Television Society
BLD	Bachelor of Landscape Design
BLE	Bachelor of Land Economy
BLEng	Bi-Lingual Engineer
BLib	Bachelor of Librarianship
BLing	Bachelor of Linguistics
BLitt	Bachelor of Letters
BLS	Bachelor of Library Studies
BM	Bachelor of Medicine
BMA	British Medical Association
BM, BCh	Conjoint degree of Bachelor of Medicine, Bachelor of Surgery
BM, BS	Conjoint degree of Bachelor of Medicine, Bachelor of Surgery
BMedBiol	Bachelor of Medical Biology
BMedSci	Bachelor of Medical Sciences
BMedSci(Speech)	Bachelor of Medical Sciences (Speech)
BMet	Bachelor of Metallurgy
BMid	Bachelor of Midwifery
BMidwif	Bachelor of Midwifery
BMSc	Bachelor of Medical Sciences
BMus	Bachelor of Music
BN	Bachelor of Nursing
BNNursing	Bachelor of Nursing, Nursing Studies
BNSc	Bachelor of Nursing
BNurs	Bachelor of Nursing
BOptom	Bachelor of Optometry
BPA	Bachelor of Performing Arts
BPharm	Bachelor of Pharmacy
BPhil	Bachelor of Philosophy
BPhil(Ed)	Bachelor of Philosophy (Education)
BPL	Bachelor of Planning

BSc	Bachelor of Science
BSc(Archit)	Bachelor of Science (Architecture)
BSc(DentSci)	Bachelor of Science in Dental Science
BSc(Econ)	Bachelor of Science in Economics
BSc(MedSci)	Bachelor of Science (Medical Science)
BSc(Social Science)	Bachelor of Science (Social Science)
BSc(Town & Regional Planning)	Bachelor of Science (Town & Regional Planning)
BSc(VetSc)	Bachelor of Science (Veterinary Science)
BScAgr	Bachelor of Science in Agriculture
BScEng	Bachelor of Science in Engineering
BScFor	Bachelor of Science in Forestry
BScTech	Bachelor of Technical Science
BSocSc	Bachelor of Social Science
BSSc	Bachelor of Social Science
BSSG	Member of the British Society of Scientific Glassblowers
BTEC	Business and Technology Education Council
BTech	Bachelor of Technology
BTechEd	Bachelor of Technological Education
BTEC HC	Business and Technology Education Council Higher Certificate
BTEC HD	Business and Technology Education Council Higher Diploma
BTEC HNC	Business and Technology Education Council Higher National Certificate
BTEC HND	Business and Technology Education Council Higher National Diploma
BTechS	Bachelor of Technology Studies
BTh	Bachelor of Theology
BTheol	Bachelor of Theology
BTP	Bachelor of Town Planning
BVC	Bar Vocational Course
BVetMed	Bachelor of Veterinary Medicine
BVMS	Bachelor of Veterinary Medicine
BVM&S	Bachelor of Veterinary Medicine
BVSc	Bachelor of Veterinary Science
C&G	City and Guilds
CA	Member of the Institute of Chartered Accountants of Scotland
CAA	Civil Aviation Authority
CABE	Companion of the Association of Business Executives
CACHE	Council for Awards in Children's Care and Education
CAE	Certificated Automotive Engineer
CAE	Companion of the Academy of Experts
CAM	Communication Advertising and Marketing Education Foundation
CAS	Certification of Accountancy Studies
CASS	Certificate of Applied Social Studies
CAT	Certificate for Accounting Technicians
CAT	College of Advanced Technology
CATS	Postgraduate Qualification by Credit Accumulation and Transfer
CBA	Companion of the British (Theatrical) Arts
CBAE	Companion of the British Academy of Experts
CBIM	Companion of the British Institute of Management
CBiol	Chartered Biologist
CBLC	Certificate in Business Language Competence
CBSSG	Craft Member of the British Society of Scientific Glassblowers
CCETSW	Central Council for Education and Training in Social Work

CChem	Chartered Chemist
CCol	Chartered Colourist
CCST	Certificate of Completion of Specialist Training
CDBA	Certified Doctor of Business Administration
CDipAF	Certified Diploma in Accounting and Finance
CEE	Extended European Command Endorsement
CeFA	Certificate for Financial Advisers
CEM	Certificate in Executive Management
CeMAP	Certificate in Mortgage Advice and Practice
CEng	Chartered Engineer
CertAMed	Certificate in Aviation Medicine
CertArb	Certificate in Arboriculture
CertBibKnowl	Certificate of Bible Knowledge
CertCIH	Chartered Institute of Housing recognised Housing Qualification
CertCM	Certificate of Cash Management
CertDesRCA	Certificate of Designer of the Royal College of Art
CertEd	Certificate in Education
CertEPK	Certificate of Essential Pensions Knowledge
CertHE	Certificate of Higher Education
CertHSAP	Certificate in Health Services Administration Practice
CertHSM	Certificate in Health Services Management
CertMFS	Certificate in the Marketing of Financial Services
CertOccHyg	Certificate in Operational Competence in Comprehensive Occupational Hygiene
CertRP	Certificate in Recruitment Practice
CertTEL	Certificate in the Teaching of European Languages
CertTESOL	Certificate of Teaching of English to Speakers of Other Languages
CertTEYL	Certificate of Teaching of English to Young Learners
CertYCW	Certificate in Youth and Community Work
CETHV	Certificate of Education in Training as Health Visitor
CEYA	Council for Early Years Awards
CFS	Certificate in Financial Services
CFSP	Certificate in Financial Services Practice
CGeol	Chartered Geologist
CGLI	City & Guilds of London Institute
CHARM	Centre for Hazard and Risk Management
ChB	Bachelor of Surgery
CHD	Choral-Training Diploma
ChM	Master of Surgery
CHP	Certificate in Hypnosis and Psychology
CHRIM	Certified Member of the Institute of Health Record Information and Management
CIAgrE	Companion of the Institution of Agricultural Engineers
CIArb	Chartered Institute of Arbitrators
CIB	Chartered Institute of Bankers
CIBM	Corporate Member of the Institute of Builders' Merchants
CIBS	Chartered Institute of Bankers in Scotland
CIBSE	Chartered Institution of Building Services Engineers
CIC	Construction Industry Council
CIEx	Companion of the Institute of Export
CIFE	Conference for Independent Further Education
CIH	Chartered Institute of Housing
CII	Chartered Insurance Institute
CILA	Chartered Institute of Loss Adjusters

CILIP	Chartered Institute of Library and Information Professionals
CIM	Chartered Institute of Marketing
CIMA	Chartered Institute of Management Accountants
CIMediE	Companion of the Institution of Mechanical Engineers
CIMgt	Companion of the Institute of Management
CIOB	Chartered Institute of Building
CIP	Certificate of Institute Practice
CIPD	Chartered Institute of Personnel and Development
CIPFA	Chartered Institute of Public Finance & Accounting
CIPS	Chartered Institute of Purchasing and Supply
CISOB	Counsellor of the Incorporated Society of Organ Builders
CIT	Certificate in Information Technology
CIWEM	Chartered Institution of Water and Environmental Management
CL(ABDO)	Diploma in Contact Lens Practice of the Association of British Dispensing Opticians
CLAC	Commercial Language Assistant Certificate
CLAIT	Computer Literacy & Information Technology
CLC	Council for Licensed Conveyancers
CLE	Limited European Command Endorsement
ClinPsyD	Doctorate in Clinical Psychology
CMA	Certificate in Management Accountancy
CMathFIMA	Fellow of the Institute of Mathematics and its Applications
CMBA	Certified Master of Business Administration
CMBHI	Craft Member of the British Horological Institute
CMC	Certified Management Consultants
CMet	Chartered Meteorologist
CMIWSc	Certified Member of the Institute of Wood Science
CMS	Certificate in Management Studies
CNAA	Council for National Academic Awards
COA	Certificate of Accreditation
COBC	Certificate of Basic Competence
CoEA	Certificate of Educational Achievement
COES	Certificate of Educational Studies
CofE	Church of England
CofS	Church of Scotland
CompBCS	Companion of the British Computer Society
CompIAP	Companion of the Institution of Analysts and Programmers
CompIEE	Companion of the Institution of Electrical Engineers
CompIGasE	Companion of the Institution of Gas Engineers
CompIManf	Companion of the Institute of Manufacturing
CompIMS	Companion of the Institute of Management Specialists
CompIP	Companion of the Institute of Plumbing
CorporateIRRV	Corporate Member of the Institute of Revenues, Rating and Valuation
COSCA	Confederation of Scottish Counselling Agencies
CPA	Chartered Patent Agents
CPC	Certificate of Professional Competence, the Institute of Transport Administration
CPD	Continuing Professional Development
CPE	Common Professional Exam
CPEA	Certificate of Practice in Estate Agency
CPFA	Member of Chartered Institute of Public Finance and Accountancy
CPhys	Chartered Physicist of the Institute of Physics
CPIM	Certificate in Production and Inventory Management

CPL	Commercial Pilot's Licence
CPM	Certified Professional Manager
CPP	Certificate of Pre-school Practice
CPR	Chartered Professional Review
CProfBTM	Companion of Professional Business and Technical Management
CPS	Certificate in Pastoral Studies and Applied Theology
CPSC	Certificate of Proficiency in Survival Craft
CPsychol	Chartered Psychologist, British Psychological Society
CPT	Continuing Professional Training
CPVE	Certificate of Pre-Vocational Training
CRAeS	Companion of the Royal Aeronautical Society
CRAH	Central Register of Advanced Hypnotherapists
CRCW	Church Related Community Workers
CRNCM	Companion of the Royal Northern College of Music
CSCT	Central School for Counselling Training
CSD	Chartered Society of Designers
CSE	Certificate of Secondary Education
CSM	Certificate in Safety Management
CSMGSM	Certificate in Stage Management (Guildhall School of Music and Drama)
CStat	Chartered Statistician
CSYS	Certificate of Sixth Year Studies
CTABRSM	Certificate of Teaching of the Associated Board of the Royal School of Music
CTextATI	Associate of the Textile Institute
CTextFTI	Fellow of the Textile Institute
CTHCM	Confederation of Tourism, Hotel and Catering Management
CVA	Certificated Value Analyst
CVM	Certificated Value Manager
CVT	Certified Vehicle Technologist
DA	Diploma in Anaesthetics
DAdmin	Doctor of Administration
DAES	Diploma in Advanced Educational Studies
DArch	Doctor of Architecture
DAvMed	Diploma in Aviation Medicine
DBA	Doctor of Business Administration
DBE	Diploma in Business Engineering
DBO	Diploma of the British Orthoptic Society
DBS	Diploma in Business Studies
DCC	Diploma of Chelsea College
DCDH	Diploma in Child Dental Health
DCE	Dangerous Cargo Endorsements
DCE	Diploma in Childcare and Education
DCG	Diploma in Careers Guidance
DCH	Diploma in Child Health
DChD	Diploma of Dental Surgery
DChM	Diploma in Chiropodial Medicine, Institute of Chiropodists and Podiatrists
DCHT	Diploma in Community Health in Tropical Countries
DCL	Doctor of Civil Law
DCLF	Diploma in Contact Lens Fitting
DClinPsych	Doctor of Clinical Psychiatry
DCLP	Diploma in Contact Lens Practice
DCR(R)or(T)	Diploma of the College of Radiographers
DD	Doctor of Divinity

DDH(Birm)	Diploma in Dental Health, University of Birmingham
DDOrthRCPSGlas	Diploma in Dental Orthopaedics of the Royal College of Physicians and Surgeons of Glasgow
DDPHRCS(Eng)	Diploma in Dental Public Health, Royal College of Surgeons of England
DDS	Doctor of Dental Surgery
DDSc	Doctor of Dental Science
DEBA	Diploma in European Business Administration
DEdPsy	Doctor of Educational Psychiatry
DEM	Diploma in Executive Management
DEng	Doctor of Engineering
DES	Department of Education and Science (now the Department for Education)
DETR	Department of the Environment, Transport and the Regions
DFin	Doctor of Finance
DFSM	Diploma in Financial Services Management
DGA	Diamond Member of the Gemmological Association and Gem Testing Laboratory of Great Britain
DGDPRCSEng	Diploma in General Dental Practice, Royal College of Surgeons of England
DGM	Diploma in Geriatric Medicine
DGO	Diploma in Obstetrics and Gynaecology
DHC	Doctorate in Healthcare
DHE	Diploma in Horticulture, Royal Botanic Garden, Edinburgh
DHMSA	Diploma in the History of Medicine, Society of Apothecaries of London
DHP	Diploma in Hypnosis and Psychotherapy
DIA	Diploma of Industrial Administration
DIB	Diploma in International Business
DIC	Diploma of Membership of Imperial College of Science and Technology, University of London
DIH	Diploma in Industrial Health
DipABRSM	Diploma of the Associated Board of the Royal Schools of Music
DipAD	Diploma in Art and Design
DipAdvHYP	Diploma in Advanced Hypnotherapy
DipAE	Diploma in Adult Education
DipAgrComm	Diploma in Agricultural Communication
DipArb	Diploma in Arbitration
DipArb	Diploma in Arboriculture
DipArch	Diploma in Architecture
DipASE(CofP)	Graduate Level Specialist Diploma in Advanced Study in Education, College of Preceptors
DipASSc	Diploma in Arts and Social Sciences
DipAT	Diploma in Accounting Technology
DipAvMed	Diploma in Aviation Medicine
DipBA	Diploma in Business Administration
DipBldgCons	Diploma in Building Conservation
DipBMA	Diploma in Business Management
DipCAM	Diploma in the Communication Advertising and Marketing Education Foundation
DipCD	Diploma in Community Development
DipCHM	Diploma in Choir Training, Royal College of Organists
DipClinPath	Diploma in Clinical Pathology
DipCOT	Diploma of the College of Occupational Therapists
DipCP	Diploma of the College of Teachers
DipCT	Diploma in Corporate Treasury Management
DipDerm	Diploma in Dermatology

DipEd	Diploma in Education
DipEF	Diploma in Executive Finance
DipEH	Diploma in Environmental Health
DipEM	Diploma in Environmental Management
DipEMA	Diploma in Executive and Management Accountancy
DipEngLit	Diploma in English Literature
DipFD	Diploma in Funeral Directing, National Association of Funeral Directors
DipFS	Diploma in Financial Services
DipGAI	Diploma of the Guild of Architectural Ironmongers
DipGrTrans	Diploma in Greek Translation
DipGSM	Diploma of the Guildhall School of Music and Drama
DipHE	Diploma of Higher Education
DipHS	Diploma of the Heraldry Society
DipIEB	Diploma of the International Employee Benefits
DipISW	Diploma of the Institute of Social Welfare
DipLE	Diploma in Land Economy
DipLP	Diploma in Legal Practice
DipM	Postgraduate Diploma in Marketing
DipMedAc	Diploma in Medical Acupuncture
DipMetEng	Diploma in Meteorological Engineering
DipMFS	Diploma in the Marketing of Financial Services
DipMth	Diploma in Music Therapy
DipOccH	Diploma in Occupational Health
DipOccHyg	Diploma of Professional Competence in Comprehensive Occupational Hygiene
DipPDTC	Diploma in Professional Dancers Teaching Course
DipPharmMed	Diploma in Pharmaceutical Medicine
DipPhil	Diploma in Philosophy
DipProjMan	Diploma in Project Management
DipPropInv	Diploma in Property Investment
DipRAM	Diploma of the Royal Academy of Music
DipRCM	Diploma of the Royal College of Music
DipRMS	Diploma of the Royal Microscopical Society
DipSc	Diploma in Science
DipSM	Diploma in Safety Management
DipSurv	Diploma in Surveying
DipSW	Diploma in Social Work
DipTCL	Diploma of the Trinity College of Music, London
DipTCR	Diploma in Organ Teaching
DipTESOL	Diploma in Teaching of English to Speakers of Other Languages
DipTHP	Diploma in Therapeutic Hypnosis and Psychotherapy
DipTM	Diploma in Training Management, Institute of Personnel and Development
DipTransIoL	Diploma in Translation, Institute of Linguists
DipUniv	Diploma of the University
DipVen	Diploma in Venereology, Society of Apothecaries of London
DipWCF	Diploma of the Worshipful Company of Farriers
DIS	Diploma in Industrial Studies
DLang	Doctor of Language
DLit(t)	Doctor of Letters or Literature
DLO	Diploma of Laryngology and Otology
DLORCSEng	Diploma in Laryngology and Otology, Royal College of Surgeons of England
DLP	Diploma in Legal Practice
DM	Doctor of Medicine

DMedRehab	Diploma in Medical Rehabilitation
DMedSc	Doctor in Medical Science
DMet	Doctor of Metallurgy
DMJ(Clin) or DMJ(Path)	Diploma in Medical Jurisprudence (Clinical or Pathological), Society of Apothecaries of London
DMRD	Diploma in Medical Radio-Diagnosis
DMRT	Diploma in Radiotherapy
DMS	Diploma in Management Studies
DMU	Diploma in Medical Ultrasound
DMus	Doctor of Music
DMusCantuar	Archbishop of Canterbury's Doctorate in Music
DNSc	Doctor in Nursing Science
DO	Diploma in Ophthalmology
DO	Diploma in Osteopathy
DocEdPsy	Doctorate in Educational Psychology
DOpt	Diploma in Ophthalmic Optics
DOrth	Diploma in Orthoptics
DOrthRCSEdin	Diploma in Orthodontics, Royal College of Surgeons of Edinburgh
DOrthRCSEng	Diplomate in Orthodontics, Royal College of Surgeons of England
DP	Diploma in Psychotherapy
DPA	Diploma in Public Administration
DpBact	Diploma in Bacteriology
DPD(Dund)	Diploma in Public Dentistry, University of Dundee
DPH	Diploma in Public Health
DPharm	Diploma in Pharmacy
DPhil	Diploma in Philosophy
DPHRCSEng	Diploma in Dental Public Health, Royal College of Surgeons of England
DPM	Diploma in Psychological Medicine
DPodM	Diploma in Podiatric Medicine
DProf	Doctor of Professional Studies
DPS	Diploma in Professional Studies
DPSE	Diploma in Pastoral Studies and Applied Theology
DPsychol	Doctor of Psychology
DrAc	Doctor of Acupuncture
Dr(RCA)	Doctor of the Royal College of Art
DRCOG	Diploma of the Royal College of Obstetricians and Gynaecologists
DRDRCSEd	Diploma in Restorative Dentistry, Royal College of Surgeons of Edinburgh
DRE	Diploma in Remedial Electrolysis, Institute of Electrolysis
DRI	Diploma in Radionuclide Imaging
DRSAMD	Diploma in the Royal Scottish Academy of Music and Drama
DSA	Diploma in Secretarial Administration
DSc	Doctor of Science
DSc(Econ)	Doctor of Science (Economics) or in Economics
DSc(Eng)	Doctor of Science (Engineering)
DSc(Social)	Doctor of Science in the Social Sciences
DScEcon	Doctor in the Faculty of Economics and Social Studies
DSCh(Ox)	Diploma in Surgical Chiropody (Oxon), Oxford School of Chiropody and Podiatry
DScTech	Doctor of Technical Science
DSocSc	Doctor of Social Science
DSSc	Doctor of Social Science
DSTA	Diploma Member of the Swimming Teachers' Association
DTCD	Diploma in Tuberculosis and Chest Diseases

DTech	Doctor of Technology
DTI	Department of Trade and Industry
DTMH	Diploma in Tropical Medicine and Hygiene
DTM&H	Diploma in Tropical Medicine and Hygiene
DTp	Department of Transport
DUniv	Doctor of the University
DVetMed	Doctor of Veterinary Medicine
DVM	Doctor of Veterinary Medicine
DVM&S	Doctor of Veterinary Medicine and Surgery
DVS	Doctor of Veterinary Surgery
DVSc	Doctor of Veterinary Science
ECBL	European Certification Board for Logistics
ECDL	European Computer Driving Licence
ECG	Executive Group Committees (of the Board for Engineers Registration)
EDBA	Executive Diploma in Business Accounting
EdD	Doctor of Education
EDH	Efficient Deck Hand
EdPsyD	Doctor of Educational Psychology
EEAC	European Executive Assistant Certificate
EFB	English for Business
EFL	English as a Foreign Language
EHO	Environmental Health Officer
EIS	Educational Institute of Scotland
EITB	Engineering Industry Training Board
EMBA	European Master of Business Administration
EMBS	European Master of Business Sciences
EMFEC	East Midland Further Education Council
EN	Enrolled Nurse
EN(G)	Enrolled Nurse (General)
EN(M)	Enrolled Nurse (Mental)
EN(MH)	Enrolled Nurse (Mental Handicap)
ENB	English National Board
EngC	Engineering Council
EngD	Doctor of Engineering
EngTech	Engineering Technician
ENS	Electronic Navigational System
ESD	Executive Secretary's Diploma
ESOL	English for Speakers of Other Languages
ESSTL	Engineering Services Training Trust Ltd
EurIng	European Engineer
EuroBiol	European Biologist
FABE	Fellow of the Association of Business Executives
FACB	Fellow of the Association of Certified Bookkeepers
FACP	Fellow of the Association of Computer Professionals
FAE	Fellow of the Academy of Experts
FAFC	Fellow of the Association of Financial Controllers and Administrators
FAIA	Fellow of the Association of International Accountants
FAMS	Fellow of the Association of Medical Secretaries, Practice Managers, Administrators and Receptionists
FAPM	Fellow of the Association for Project Management
FASI	Fellow of the Ambulance Service Institute
FASI	Fellow of the Architecture and Surveying Institute

FASP	Fellow of the Association of Sales Personnel
FBA	Fellow of the British Academy
FBA	Fellow of the British (Theatrical) Arts
FBCS	Fellow of the British Computer Society
FBDO	Fellow of the Association of British Dispensing Opticians
FBDO(Hons)	Fellow of the Association of British Dispensing Opticians with Honours Diploma
FBDO(Hons)CL	Fellow of the Association of British Dispensing Opticians with Honours Diploma and Diploma in Contact Lens Practice
FBEI	Fellow of the Institution of Body Engineers
FBEng	Fellow of the Association of Building Engineers
FBHA	Fellow of the British Hypnotherapy Association
FBHI	Fellow of the British Horological Institute
FBHS	Fellow of the British Horse Society
FBID	Fellow of the British Institute of Interior Design
FBIDST	Fellow of the British Institute of Dental and Surgical Technologists
FBIE	Fellow of the British Institute of Embalmers
FBIPP	Fellow of the British Institute of Professional Photography
FBIS	Fellow of the British Interplanetary Society
FBMA	Fellow of the Business Management Association
FBPsS	Fellow of the British Psychological Society
FCA	Fellow of the Institute of Chartered Accountants in England and Wales
FCAM	Fellow of the Communication Advertising and Marketing Education Foundation
FCB	Fellow of the British Association of Communicators in Business Ltd
FCBSI	Fellow of the Chartered Building Societies Institute
FCCA	Fellow of the Association of Chartered Certified Accountants
FCEA	Fellow of the Institute of Cost and Executive Accountants
FCGI	Fellowship, City & Guilds
FChS	Fellow of the Society of Chiropodists and Podiatrists
FCI	Faculty of Commerce and Industry
FCI	Fellow of the Institute of Commerce
FCIArb	Fellow of the Chartered Institute of Arbitrators
FCIB	Fellow of the Chartered Institute of Bankers
FCIBS	Fellow of the Chartered Institute of Bankers in Scotland
FCIBSE	Fellow of the Chartered Institute of Building Services Engineers
FCIH	Fellow of the Chartered Institute of Housing
FCII	Fellow of the Chartered Insurance Institute
FCIJ	Fellow of the Chartered Institute of Journalists
FCILA	Fellow of the Chartered Institute of Loss Adjusters
FCIM	Fellow of the Chartered Institute of Marketing
FCIOB	Fellow of the Chartered Institute of Building
FCIPD	Fellow of the Chartered Institute of Personnel and Development
FCIPS	Fellow of the Chartered Institute of Purchasing and Supply
FCIS	Fellow of the Institute of Chartered Secretaries and Administrators
FCIT	Fellow of the Chartered Institute of Transport
FCLIP	Chartered Fellow of CILIP
FCLS	First Certificate for Legal Secretaries
FCMA	Fellow of the Chartered Institute of Management Accountants
FCMA	Fellow of the Institute of Cost and Management Accountants
FCMC	Fellow Grade Certified Management Consultants
FCOphth	Fellow of the College of Ophthalmology
FCOptom	Fellow of the College of Optometrists
FCoT	Ordinary Fellow of the College of Teachers

FCPM	Fellow of the Confederation of Professional Management
FCPP	Fellow of the College of Pharmacy Practice
FCSP	Fellow of the Chartered Society of Physiotherapy
FCT	Fellow of the Association of Corporate Treasurers
FCoT	Fellow of the College of Teachers
FCTHCM	Fellow of the Confederation of Tourism, Hotel and Catering Management
FCYW	Fellow of the Community and Youth Work Association
FDSRCPSGlas	Fellow in Dental Surgery of the Royal College of Surgeons of Glasgow
FDSRCSEd	Fellow in Dental Surgery of the Royal College of Physicians and Surgeons of Edinburgh
FDSRCSEng	Fellow in Dental Surgery of the Royal College of Surgeons of England
FE	Further Education
FEANI	Fédération Européene d'Associations Nationales d'Ingénieurs
FECI	Fellow of the Institute of Employment Consultants
FEFC	Further Education Funding Council
FEIS	Fellow of the Educational Institute of Scotland
FFA	Fellow of the Faculty of Actuaries
FFA	Fellow of the Institute of Financial Accountants
FFARCSEng	Fellow of the Faculty of Anaesthetists of the Royal College of Surgeons in England
FFARCSIrel	Fellow of the Faculty of Anaesthetists of the Royal College of Surgeons in Ireland
FFAS	Fellow of the Faculty of Architects and Surveyors (Architects)
FFCA	Fellow of the Association of Financial Controllers and Administrators
FFCI	Fellow of the Faculty of Commerce and Industry
FFCS	Fellow of the Faculty of Secretaries
FFHom	Fellow of the Faculty of Homeopathy
FFPHM	Fellow of the Faculty of Public Health Medicine, Royal College of Physicians of London and Edinburgh and Royal College of Physicians and Surgeons of Glasgow
FFPHMIrel	Fellow of the Faculty of Public Health Medicine, Royal College of Physicians of Ireland
FFRRCSIrel	Fellow of the Faculty of Radiologists, Royal College of Surgeons in Ireland
FFS	Fellow of the Faculty of Architects and Surveyors (Surveyors)
FGA	Fellow of the Gemmological Association and Gem Testing Laboratory of Great Britain
FGCL	Fellow of the Guild of Cleaners and Launderers
FGI	Fellow of the Greek Institute
FGSM	Fellow of the Guildhall School of Music and Drama
FHCIMA	Fellow of the Hotel and Catering International Management Association
FHFS	Fellow of the Council of Health, Fitness and Sports Therapists
FHG	Fellow of the Institute of Heraldic and Genealogical Studies
FHRIM	Fellow of the Institute of Health Record Information and Management
FHS	Fellow of the Heraldry Society
FHSM	Fellow of the Institute of Health Services Management
FHT	Federation of Holistic Therapies
FIA	Fellow of the Institute of Actuaries
FIAB	Fellow of the International Association of Book-keepers
FIAEA	Fellow of the Institute of Automotive Engineer Assessors
FIAgrE	Fellow of the Institution of Agricultural Engineers
FIAP	Fellow of the Institution of Analysts and Programmers
FIAT	Fellow of the Institute of Asphalt Technology
FIBA	Fellow of the Institution of Business Agents
FIBC	Fellow of the Institute of Building Control

FIBCM	Fellow of the Institute of British Carriage and Automobile Manufacturers
FIBCO	Fellow of the Institute of Building Control Officers
FIBE	Fellow of the Institution of British Engineers
FIBF	Fellow of the Institute of British Foundrymen
FIBiol	Fellow of the Institute of Biology
FIBM	Fellow of the Institute of Builders' Merchants
FIBMS	Fellow of the Institute of Biomedical Science
FIBMS	Fellow of the Institute of Medical Laboratory Sciences
FICA	Fellow of the Institute of Company Accountants
FICB	Fellow of the Institute of Certified Book-Keepers
FICE	Fellow of the Institution of Civil Engineers
FIChemE	Fellow of the Institution of Chemical Engineers
FIChor	Fellow of the Benesh Institute of Choreology
FICHT	Fellow of the International Council of Holistic Therapies
FICM	Fellow of the Institute of Credit Management
FICorr	Fellow of the Institute of Corrosion
FICS	Fellow of the Institute of Chartered Shipbrokers
FICW	Fellow of the Institute of Clerks of Works of Great Britain Incorporated
FIDTA	Fellow of the International Dance Teachers' Association
FIED	Fellow of the Institution of Engineering Designers
FIEE	Fellow of the Institution of Electrical Engineers
FIEM	Fellow of the Institute of Executives and Managers
FIEx	Fellow of the Institute of Export
FIExpE	Fellow of the Institute of Explosives Engineers
FIFBQ	Fellow of the International Faculty of Business Qualifications
FIFireE	Fellow of the Institution of Fire Engineers
FIFM	Fellow of the Institute of Fisheries Management
FIFST	Fellow of the Institute of Food Science and Technology
FIGasE	Fellow of the Institution of Gas Engineers
FIGD	Fellow of the Institute of Grocery Distribution
FIGeol	Fellow of the Institute of Geologists
FIHEc	Fellow of the Institute of Home Economics Ltd
FIHIE	Fellow of the Institute of Highway Incorporated Engineers
FIHort	Fellow of the Institute of Horticulture
FIHT	Fellow of the Institution of Highways and Transportation
FIIE	Fellow of the Institution of Incorporated Engineers
FIIHTM	Fellow of the International Institute of Hospitality Tourism & Management
FIIM	Fellow of the International Institute of Management
FIIMR	Fellow of the Institute of Investment Management and Research
FIIRSM	Fellow of the International Institute of Risk and Safety Management
FIISE	Fellow of the International Institute of Social Economics
FIISec	Fellow of the International Institute of Security
FIL	Fellow of the Institute of Linguists
FILAM	Fellow of the Institute of Leisure and Amenity Management
FILT	Fellow of the Institute of Logistics and Transport
FIM	Fellow of the Institute of Materials
FIMA	Fellow of the Institute of Mathematics and its Applications
FIManf	Fellow of the Institute of Manufacturing
FIMarE	Fellow of the Institute of Marine Engineers
FIMatM	Fellow of the Institute of Materials Management
FIMBM	Fellow of the Institute of Maintenance and Building Management
FIMechE	Fellow of the Institute of Mechanical Engineers

FIMechIE	Fellow of the Institute of Mechanical Incorporated Engineers
FIMF	Fellow of the Institute of Metal Finishing
FIMgt	Fellow of the Institute of Management
FIMI	Fellow of the Institute of the Motor Industry
FIMIS	Fellow of the Institute for the Management of Information Systems
FIMM	Fellow of the Institute of Massage and Movement
FIMM	Fellow of the Institution of Mining and Metallurgy
FIMM	International Federation of Manual Medicine
FIMS	Fellow of the Institute of Management Specialists
FIMunE	Fellow of the Institution of Municipal Engineers
FInstAEA	Fellow of the Institute of Automotive Engineer Assessors
FInstAM	Fellow of the Institute of Administrative Management
FInstBA	Fellow of the Institute of Business Administration
FInstBCA	Fellow of the Institute of Burial and Cremation Administration
FInstBM	Fellow of the Institute of Builders' Merchants
FInstBRM	Fellow of the Institute of Baths and Recreation Management
FInstCh	Fellow of the Institute of Chiropodists
FInstCM	Fellow of the Institute of Commercial Management
FInstD	Fellow of the Institute of Directors
FInstE	Fellow of the Institute of Energy
FInstLEx	Fellow of the Institute of Legal Executives
FInstMC	Fellow of the Institute of Measurement and Control
FInstNDT	Fellow of the British Institute of Non-Destructive Testing
FInstP	Fellow of the Institute of Physics
FInstPet	Fellow of the Institute of Petroleum
FInstPkg	Fellow of the Institute of Packaging
FInstPM	Fellow of the Institute of Professional Managers and Administrators
FInstPS	Fellow of the Institute of Purchasing and Supply
FInstR	Fellow of the Institute of Refrigeration
FInstSMM	Fellow of the Institute of Sales and Marketing Management
FInstTA	Fellow of the Institute of Transport Administration
FInstTT	Fellow of the Institute of Travel and Tourism
FInstWM	Fellow of the Institute of Wastes Management
FInstWM	Fellowship of the Institute of Wastes Management
FIntMC	Fellow of International Management Centre
FIOC	Fellow of the Institute of Carpenters
FIOM	Fellow of the Institute of Operations Management
FIOP	Fellow of the Institute of Plumbing
FIOP	Fellow of the Institute of Printing
FIOSH	Fellow of the Institution of Occupational Safety and Health
FIPA	Fellow of the Institute of Practitioners in Advertising
FIPD	Fellow of the Institute of Personnel Development
FIPI	Fellow of the Institute of Professional Investigators
FIPlantE	Fellow of the Institution of Plant Engineers
FIPR	Fellow of the Institute of Public Relations
FIQ	Fellow of the Institute of Quarrying
FIQA	Fellow of the Institute of Quality Assurance
FIR	Fellow of the Institute of Population Registration
FIRSE	Fellow of the Institution of Railway Signal Engineers
FIRTE	Fellow of the Institute of Road Transport Engineers
FIS	Fellow of the Institute of Statisticians
FISM	Fellow of the Institute for Supervision & Management

FISOB	Fellow of the Incorporated Society of Organ Builders
FISTC	Fellow of the Institute of Scientific and Technical Communicators
FISTD	Fellow of the Imperial Society of Teachers of Dancing
FIStrucE	Fellow of the Institution of Structural Engineers
FISW	Fellow of the Institute of Social Welfare
FIT	Foundation Insurance Test
FITD	Fellow of the Institute of Training and Development
FITSA	Fellow of the Institute of Trading Standards Administration
FIVehE	Fellow of the Institute of Vehicle Engineers
FIWM	Fellow of the Institute of Wastes Management
FLAW	Foreign Languages at Work
FLCM	Fellow of the London College of Music
FLCSP	Fellow of the London and Counties Society of Physiologists
FLI	Fellow of the Landscape Institute
FLIC	Foreign Languages for Industry and Commerce
FLS	Fellow of the Linnean Society of London
FMA	Fellow of the Museums Association
FMAAT	Fellow Member of the Association of Accounting Technicians
FMPA	Fellow of the Master Photographers Association
FMR	Fellow of the Association of Health Care Information and Medical Records Officers
FMS	Fellow of the Institute of Management Services
FMusEd	Fellowship in Music Education
FN	Fellow of the Nautical Society
FNAEA	Fellow of the National Association of Estate Agents
FNAEAHon	Honoured Fellow of the National Association of Estate Agents
FNCP	Fellow of the National Council of Psychotherapists
FNI	Fellow of the Nautical Institute
FNIMH	Fellow of the National Institute of Medical Herbalists
FPC	Financial Planning Certificate
FPC	Foundation for Psychotherapy and Counselling
FPCS	Fellow of the Property Consultants Society
FPMI	Fellow of the Pensions Management Institute
FPodS	Fellow of the Surgical Faculty of the College of Podiatrists
FProfBTM	Fellow of Professional Business and Technical Management
FRAeS	Fellow of the Royal Aeronautical Society
FRAS	Fellow of the Royal Astronomical Society
FRCA	Fellow of the Royal College of Anaesthetists
FRCGP	Fellow of the Royal College of General Practitioners
FRCM	Fellow of the Royal College of Music
FRCO	Fellow of the Royal College of Organists
FRCO(CHM)	Fellow of the Royal College of Organists (Choir-training Diploma)
FRCOG	Fellow of the Royal College of Obstetricians and Gynaecologists
FRCP	Fellow of the Royal College of Physicians of London
FRCPath	Fellow of the Royal College of Pathologists
FRCPEdin	Fellow of the Royal College of Physicians of Edinburgh
FRCPsych	Fellow of the Royal College of Psychiatrists
FRCR	Fellow of the Royal College of Radiologists
FRCS(Irel)	Fellow of the Royal College of Surgeons in Ireland
FRCSEd	Fellow of the Royal College of Surgeons of Edinburgh
FRCSEd(C/TH)	Fellow of the Royal College of Surgeons of Edinburgh, specialising in Cardiothoracic Surgery

FRCSEd(Orth)	Fellow of the Royal College of Surgeons of Edinburgh, specialising in Orthopaedic Surgery
FRCSEd(SN)	Fellow of the Royal College of Surgeons of Edinburgh, specialising in Surgical Neurology
FRCSEng	Fellow of the Royal College of Surgeons of England
FRCSEng(Oto)	Fellow of the Royal College of Surgeons of England, with Otolaryngology
FRCSGlasg	Fellow of the Royal College of Physicians and Surgeons of Glasgow
FRCVS	Fellow of the Royal College of Veterinary Surgeons
FREC	Fellow of the Recruitment and Employment Confederation
FRHS	Fellow of the Royal Horticultural Society
FRIBA	Fellow of the Royal Institute of British Architects
FRICS	Fellow of the Royal Institution of Chartered Surveyors
FRIN	Fellow of the Royal Institute of Navigation
FRINA	Fellow of the Royal Institution of Naval Architects
FRIPHH	Fellow of the Royal Institution of Public Health and Hygiene
FRNCM	Fellow of the Royal Northern College of Music
FRPharmS	Fellow of the Royal Pharmaceutical Society of Great Britain
FRPS	Fellow of the Royal Photographic Society
FRS	Fellow of the Royal Society
FRSC	Fellow of the Royal Society of Chemistry
FRSCM	Fellow of the Royal School of Church Music
FRSH	Fellow of the Royal Society for the Promotion of Health
FRTPI	Fellow of the Royal Town Planning Institute
FSAPP	Fellow of the Society of Advanced Psychotherapy Practitioners
FSBP	Fellow of the Society of Business Practitioners
FSBT	Fellow of the Society of Teachers in Business Education
FSCT	Fellow of the Society of Claims Technicians
FSDC	Fellow of the Society of Dyers and Colourists
FSE	Fellow of the Society of Engineers (Inc)
FSElec	Fellow of the Society of Electroscience
FSG	Fellow of the Society of Genealogists
FSG(Hon)	Honorary Fellow of the Society of Genealogists
FSGT	Fellow of the Society of Glass Technology
FSIAD	Fellow of the Society of Industrial Artists and Designers
FSMA	Fellow of the Society of Martial Arts
FSMA	Fellow of the Society of Sales Management Administrators Ltd
FSNN	Fellow of the Society of Nursery Nursing
FSS	Fellow of the Royal Statistical Society
FSSCh	Fellow of the British Chiropody and Podiatry Association
FSSF	Fellow of the Society of Shoe Fitters
FSTA	Fellow of the Swimming Teachers' Association
FSVA	Fellow of the Incorporated Society of Valuers and Auctioneers
FTCL	Fellow of the Trinity College of Music
FTI	Fellow of the Textile Institute
FTII	Fellow of the Chartered Institute of Taxation
FTSC	Fellow of the Oil and Colour Chemists' Association
FTSC	Fellow in the Technology of Surface Coatings
FWeldI	Fellow of the Welding Institute
FYDA	Associate Fellowship of the Youth Development Association
GAGTL	Gemmological Association and Gem Testing Laboratory of Great Britain
GAI	Guild of Architectural Ironmongers
GASI	Graduate Member of the Ambulance Service Institute

GBSM	Graduate of the Birmingham School of Music
GCE	General Certificate of Education
GCE A	General Certificate of Education Advanced Level
GCE O	General Certificate of Education Ordinary Level
GCGI	Graduateship, City & Guilds
GCL	Guild of Cleaners and Launderers
GCSE	General Certificate of Secondary Education
GDC	General Dental Council
GIBCM	Graduate of the Institute of British Carriage and Automobile Manufacturers
GIBiol	Graduate of the Institute of Biology
GIEM	Graduate of the Institute of Executives and Managers
GIMA	Graduate of the Institute of Mathematics and its Applications
GIMI	Graduate of the Institute of the Motor Industry
GInstP	Graduate of the Institute of Physics
GIntMC	Graduate of the International Management Centre
GIS	Graduate Imaging Scientist
GLCM	Graduate Diploma of the London College of Music
GMAT	Graduate Management Admissions Test
GMC	General Medical Council
GMDSS	Global Maritime Distress & Safety System
GMInstM	Graduate Member of the Meat Training Council
GMus	Graduate Diploma in Music
GMusRNCM	Graduate in Music of the Royal Northern College of Music
GNSM	Graduate of the Northern School of Music
GNVQ	General National Vocational Qualifications
GradAES	Graduate of the Royal Aeronautical Society
GradBEng	Graduate Member of the Association of Building Engineers
GradBHI	Graduate of the British Horological Institute
GradDip	Graduate Diploma
GradIAP	Graduate of the Institution of Analysts and Programmers
GradIBE	Graduate of the Institution of British Engineers
GradIElecIE	Graduate of the Institution of Electrical and Electronics Incorporated Engineers
GradIIE	Graduate of the Institution of Incorporated Engineers
GradIISec	Graduate of the International Institute of Security
GradIManf	Graduate of the Institute Manufacturing
GradIMF	Graduate of the Institute of Metal Finishing
GradIMS	Graduate of the Institute of Management Specialists
GradInstNDT	Graduate of the British Institute of Non-Destructive Testing
GradInstP	Graduate of the Institute of Physics
GradInstPS	Graduate of the Institute of Purchasing and Supply
GradIOP	Graduate of the Institute of Printing
GradIPD	Graduate of the Institute of Personnel and Development
GradIS	Graduate of the Institute of Statisticians
GradISCA	Graduate of the Institute of Chartered Secretaries and Administrators
GradMechE	Graduate of the Institution of Mechanical Engineers
GradMIWM	Graduate Member of the Institute of Wastes Management
GradRNCM	Graduate of the Royal Northern College of Music
GradRSC	Graduate of the Royal Society of Chemistry
GradSMA	Graduate of the Society of Martial Arts
GradStat	Graduate Statistician
GraduateCIPD	Graduate of the Chartered Institute of Personnel and Development
GraduateIEIE	Graduate of the Institution of Electrical and Electronics Incorporated Engineers

GradWeldI	Graduate of the Welding Institute
GRC	General Readers Certificate
GRC	Grade Related Criteria
GRIC	Graduate Membership of the Royal Institute of Chemistry
GRSC	Graduate of the Royal Society of Chemistry
GRSM	Graduate Diploma of the Royal Manchester School of Music
GRSM(Hons)	Graduate of the Royal Schools of Music
GSMA	Graduate of the Society of Sales Management Administrators Ltd
GSNN	Graduate of the Society of Nursery Nursing
GTC	General Teaching Council
HABIA	Hairdressing and Beauty Industry Authority
HC	Higher Certificate
HCIMA	Hotel and Catering International Management Association
HD	Higher Diploma
HDCR (R) or (T)	Higher Award in Radiodiagnosis or Radiotherapy, College of Radiographers
HEFCE	Higher Education Funding Council for England
HFInstE	Honorary Fellow of the Institute of Energy
HNC	Higher National Certificate
HND	Higher National Diploma
HonASTA	Honorary Associate of the Swimming Teachers' Association
HonDrRCA	Honorary Doctorate of the Royal College of Art
HonFAE	Honorary Fellow of the Academy of Experts
HonFBID	Honorary Fellow of the British Institute of Interior Design
HonFBIPP	Honorary Fellow of the British Institute of Professional Photography
HonFCP	Charter Fellow of the College of Preceptors
HonFEIS	Honorary Fellow of the Educational Institute of Scotland
HonFHCIMA	Honorary Fellow of the Hotel, Catering and Institutional Management Association
HonFHS	Honorary Fellow of the Heraldry Society
HonFIEE	Honorary Fellow of the Institution of Electrical Engineers
HonFIExpE	Honorary Fellow of the Institute of Explosives Engineers
HonFIGasE	Honorary Fellow of the Institution of Gas Engineers
HonFIMarE	Honorary Fellow of the Institute of Marine Engineers
HonFIMechE	Honorary Fellow of the Institution of Mechanical Engineers
HonFIMM	Honorary Fellow of the Institution of Mining and Metallurgy
HonFInstE	Honorary Fellow of the Institute of Energy
HonFInstMC	Honorary Fellow of the Institute of Measurement and Control
HonFInstNDT	Honorary Fellow of the British Institute of Non-Destructive Testing
HonFIQA	Honorary Fellow of the Institute of Quality Assurance
HonFIRSE	Honorary Fellow of the Institution of Railway Signal Engineers
HonFIRTE	Honorary Fellow of the Institute of Road Transport Engineers
HonFPRI	Honorary Fellow of the Plastics and Rubber Institute
HonFRIN	Honorary Fellow of the Royal Institute of Navigation
HonFRINA	Honorary Fellow of the Royal Institution of Naval Architects
HonFRPS	Honorary Fellow of the Royal Photographic Society
HonFSE	Honorary Fellow of the Society of Engineers (Inc)
HonFSGT	Honorary Fellow of the Society of Glass Technology
HonFWeldI	Honorary Fellow of the Welding Institute
HonGSM	Honorary Member of the Guildhall School of Music and Drama
HonMIFM	Honorary Member of the Institute of Fisheries Management
HonMInstNDT	Honorary Member of the British Institute of Non-Destructive Testing
HonMRIN	Honorary Member of the Royal Institute of Navigation
HonMWES	Honorary Member of the Women's Engineering Society

HonRAM	Honorary Member of the Royal Academy of Music
HonRCM	Honorary Member of the Royal College of Music
HonRNCM	Honorary Member of the Royal Northern College of Music
HonRSCM	Honorary Member of the Royal School of Church Music
HSC	Higher School Certificate
HSE	Health & Safety Executive
HTB	Hairdressing Training Board
HTC	Higher Technical Certificate
IAAP	International Association for Analytic Psychology
IAB	International Association of Book-Keepers
IABC	International Association of Business Computing
IAC	Investment Advice Certificate
IAgrE	Institution of Agricultural Engineers
IAP	Institution of Analysts and Programmers
IAQ	Investment Administration Qualification
IAT	Institute of Asphalt Technology
IBA	Institute of Business Administration
IBC	Institute of Building Control
IBE	Institution of British Engineers
IBF	Institute of British Foundrymen
IBMS	Institute of Biomedical Science
ICAEW	Institute of Chartered Accountants in England and Wales
ICAI	Institute of Chartered Accountants in Ireland
ICAS	Institute of Chartered Accountants of Scotland
ICB	Institute of Certified Book-Keepers
ICE	Institution of Civil Engineers
ICEA	Institute of Cost and Executive Accountants
ICG	Institute of Careers Guidance
IChemE	Institution of Chemical Engineers
ICIOB	Incorporated Member of the Chartered Institute of Building
ICM	Institute of Commercial Management
ICM	Institute of Complementary Medicine
ICM	Institute of Credit Management
ICMQ	International Capital Markets Qualification
ICSA	Institute of Chartered Secretaries and Administrators
ICSF	Intermediate Certificate of the Society of Floristry
IDA	Improvement and Development Agency
IDTA	International Dance Teachers' Association Ltd
IED	Institution of Engineering Designers
IEE	Institution of Electrical Engineers
IEM	Institute of Executives and Managers
IEng	Incorporated Engineer
IETTL	Insulation and Environmental Training Trust Ltd
IEx	Institute of Export
IExpE	Institute of Explosives Engineers
IFA	Institute of Field Archaeologists
IFA	Institute of Financial Accountants
IFA	Insurance Foundation Certificate
IFBQ	International Faculty of Business Qualifications
IFM	Institute of Fisheries Management
IFST	Institute of Food Science and Technology (UK)
IHBC	International Health & Beauty Council

IHIE	Institute of Highway Incorporated Engineers
IHort	Institute of Horticulture
IHT	Institute of Highways and Transportation
IIA	Institute of Internal Auditors
IIE	Institution of Incorporated Engineers
IIExE	Institution of Incorporated Executive Engineers
IIHHT	International Institute of Health & Holistic Therapies
IIHTM	International Institute of Hospitality Tourism & Management
IIRSM	International Institute of Risk and Safety Management
ILAM	Institute of Leisure and Amenity Management
ILE	Institution of Lighting Engineers
ILEX	Institute of Legal Executives
ILT	Institute of Logistics and Transport
IMarE	Institute of Marine Engineers
IMBM	Institute of Maintenance and Building Management
IMC	Institute of Management Consultancy
IMechE	Institution of Mechanical Engineers
IMF	Institute of Metal Finishing
IMI	Institute of the Motor Industry
IMIBC	Incorporated Member of the Institute of Building Control
IMInstAEA	Incorporated Member of the Institute of Automotive Engineer Assessors
IMIS	Institute for the Management of Information Systems
IMM	Institution of Mining and Metallurgy
IMS	Institute of Management Specialists
IncMWeldI	Incorporated Member of the Welding Institute
InstAEA	Institute of Automotive Engineer Assessors
InstAM	Institute of Administrative Management
InstBCA	Institute of Burial and Cremation Administration
InstE	Institute of Energy
InstPet	Institute of Petroleum
IOB	Institute of Brewing
IOC	Institute of Carpenters
IoD	Institute of Directors
IOM	Institute of Operations Management
IOP	Institute of Packaging
IOSH	Institution of Occupational Safety and Health
IOTA	Institute of Transport Administration
IPA	Institute of Practitioners in Advertising
IPD	Initial Professional Development
IPD	Institute of Personnel and Development
IPFA	Member of the Chartered Institute of Public Finance and Accountancy
IPlantE	Institution of Plant Engineers
IPR	Incorporated Professional Review
IPR	Institute of Public Relations
IPSM	Institute of Public Service Management
IQ	Institute of Quarrying
IQA	Institute of Quality Assurance
IRMT	International Register of Massage Therapists
IRRV	Corporate Member of the Institute of Revenues, Rating and Valuation
IRRV	Institute of Revenues, Rating and Valuation
IRSE	Institution of Railway Signal Engineers
IRTE	Institute of Road Transport Engineers

ISEB	Information Systems Examinations Board
ISM	Incorporated Society of Musicians
ISM	Institute for Supervision & Management
ISMM	Institute of Sales and Marketing Management
ISRM	Institute of Sport and Recreation Management
ISTD	Imperial Society of Teachers of Dancing
IStructE	Institution of Structural Engineers
ITEC	International Therapy Examination Council
ITIL	IT Infrastructure Library
ITSA	Institute of Trading Standards Administration
IVehE	Institute of the Vehicle Engineers
IVM	Institute of Value Management
IWSc	Institute of Wood Science
JEB	Joint Examination Board
JET	Jewellery, Education and Training
JP	Justice of the Peace
LA	Library Association
LABAC	Licentiate Member of the Association of Business and Administrative Computing
LAE	Licentiate Automotive Engineer
LAEx	Legal Accounts Executive
LAMDA	London Academy of Music and Dramatic Art
LAMRTPI	Legal Associate Member of the Royal Town Planning Institute
LASI	Licentiate of the Ambulance Service Institute
LASI	Licentiate of the Architecture and Surveying Institute
LBEI	Licentiate of the Institution of Body Engineers
LBIDST	Licentiate of the British Institute of Dental and Surgical Technologists
LBIPP	Licentiate of the British Institute of Professional Photography
LCCI	London Chamber of Commerce and Industry
LCCIEB	London Chamber of Commerce and Industry Examinations Board
LCEA	Licentiate of the Association of Cost and Executive Accountants
LCFI	Licentiate of CFI International (Clothing and Footwear Institute)
LCGI	Licentiate, City & Guilds
LCIBSE	Licentiate of the Chartered Institution of Building Services Engineers
LCP	Licentiate of the College of Preceptors
LCSP	London and Counties Society of Physiologists
LCSP(Assoc)	Associate of the London and Counties Society of Physiologists
LCSP(BTh)	Member of the London and Counties Society of Physiologists (Beauty Therapy)
LCSP(Chir)	Member of the London and Counties Society of Physiologists (Chiropody)
LCSP(Phys)	Member of the London and Counties Society of Physiologists (Physical and Manipulative Therapy)
LCT	Licentiate of the College of Teachers
LDS	Licentiate in Dental Surgery
LDSRCPSGlas	Licentiate in Dental Surgery of the Royal College of Physicians and Surgeons of Glasgow
LDSRCSEd	Licentiate in Dental Surgery of the Royal College of Surgeons of Edinburgh
LDSRCSEng	Licentiate in Dental Surgery of the Royal College of Surgeons of England
LFA	Licentiate of the Institute of Financial Accountants
LFCI	Licentiate of the Faculty of Commerce and Industry
LFCS	Licentiate of the Faculty of Secretaries
LFS	Licentiate of the Faculty of Architects and Surveyors (Surveyors)
LGCL	Licentiate of the Guild of Cleaners and Launderers
LGSM	Licentiate of the Guildhall School of Music and Drama

LHCIMA	Licentiate of the Hotel and Catering International Management Association
LHG	Licentiate of the Institute of Heraldic and Genealogical Studies
LI	Landscape Institute
LicentiateCIPD	Licentiate of the Chartered Institute of Personnel and Development
LicIPD	Licentiate of the Institute of Personnel & Development
LicIQA	Licentiate of the Institute of Quality Assurance
LICW	Licentiate of the Institute of Clerks of Works of Great Britain Incorporated
LIDPM	Licentiate of the Institute of Data Processing Management
LIEM	Licentiate of the Institute of Executives and Managers
LIIST	Licentiate of the International Institute of Sports Therapy
LILAM	Licentiate of the Institute of Leisure and Amenity Management
LIM	Licentiate of the Institute of Materials
LIMA	Licentiate of the Institute of Mathematics and its Applications
LIMF	Licentiate of the Institute of Metal Finishing
LIMIS	Licentiate of the Institute for the Management of Information Systems
LInstBCA	Licentiate of the Institute of Burial and Cremation Administration
LInstBM	Licentiate of the Institute of Builders' Merchants
LIOC	Licentiate of the Institute of Carpenters
LIR	Licentiate of the Institute of Population Registration
LISTD	Licentiate of the Imperial Society of Teachers of Dancing
LISTD(Dip)	Licentiate Diploma of the Imperial Society of Teachers of Dancing
LittD	Doctor of Letters
LIWM	Licentiate of the Institute of Wastes Management
LLB	Bachelor of Law
LLCM	Performers Diploma of Licentiateship in Speech, Drama and Public Speaking
LLCM(TD)	Licentiate of the London College of Music and Media (Teachers' Diploma)
LLD	Doctor of Law
LLM	Master of Law
LM	Licentiate in Midwifery
LMIFM	Licentiate Member of the Institute of Fisheries Management
LMInstE	Licentiate Member of the Institute of Energy
LMPA	Licentiate Member of the Master Photographers Association
LMRTPI	Legal Member of the Royal Town Planning Institute
LMSSALond	Licentiate in Medicine, Surgery and Obstetrics & Gynaecology, Society of Apothecaries of London
LMusEd	Licentiate Diploma in Music Education
LMusLCM	Licentiate in Music of the London College of Music
LMusTCL	Licentiate in Music, Trinity College of Music
LNCP	Licentiate of the National Council of Psychotherapists
LPC	Legal Practice Course
LRAD	Licentiate of the Royal Academy of Dancing
LRAM	Licentiate of the Royal Academy of Music
LRCPEdin	Conjoint Diplomas Licentiate of the Royal College of Physicians of Edinburgh
LRCPSGlasg	Conjoint Diplomas Licentiate of the Royal College of Physicians and Surgeons of Glasgow
LRCSEdin	Conjoint Diplomas Licentiate of the Royal College of Surgeons of Edinburgh
LRCSEng	Licentiate of the Royal College of Surgeons in England
LRPS	Licentiate of the Royal Photographic Society
LRSC	Licentiate of the Royal Society of Chemistry
LRSM	Licentiate Diploma of the Royal Schools of Music
LSBP	Licentiate of the Society of Business Practitioners
LSCP(Assoc)	Associate of the London and Counties Society of Physiologists

LTCL	Licentiate of Trinity College of Music
LTh	Licentiate in Theology
LTI	Licentiate of the Textile Industry
LTSC	Licentiate of the Oil and Colour Chemists' Association
LVT	Licentiate Vehicle Technologist
MA	Master of Arts
MA(Architectural)	Master of Arts (Architectural Studies)
MA(Econ)	Master of Arts in Economic and Social Studies
MA(Ed)	Master of Arts in Education
MA(LD)	Master of Arts (Landscape Design)
MA(MUS)	Master of Arts (Music)
MA(RCA)	Master of Arts, Royal College of Art
MA(SocSci)	Master of Arts (Social Science)
MA(Theol)	Master of Arts in Theology
MAAT	Member of the Association of Accounting Technicians
MABAC	Member of the Association of Business and Administrative Computing
MABE	Member of the Association of Business Executives
MAcc	Master of Accountancy
MACP	Member of the Association of Computer Professionals
MAE	Member of the Academy of Experts
MAgr	Master of Agriculture
MAgrSc	Master of Agricultural Science
MAMS	Member of the Association of Medical Secretaries, Practice Managers, Administrators and Receptionists
MAMSA	Managing & Marketing Sales Association Examination Board
MAnimSc	Master of Animal Science
MAO	Master of Obstetrics
MAP	Membership by Assessment of Performance
MAPM	Member of the Association for Project Management
MAppSci	Master of Applied Science
MAQ	Mortgage Advice Qualification
MArAd	Master of Archive Administration
MArb	Master of Arboriculture
MArch	Master of Architecture
MArt/RCA	Master of Arts, Royal College of Art
MasFCI	Master of the Faculty of Commerce and Industry
MASHAM	Management and Administration of Safety and Health at Mines
MASI	Member of the Architecture and Surveying Institute
MBA	Master of Business Administration
MBAE	Member of the British Association of Electrolysists
MB, BCh	Conjoint Degree of Bachelor of Medicine, Bachelor of Surgery
MB, BChir	Conjoint Degree of Bachelor of Medicine, Bachelor of Surgery
MB, BS	Conjoint Degree of Bachelor of Medicine, Bachelor of Surgery
MB, ChB	Conjoint Degree of Bachelor of Medicine, Bachelor of Surgery
MBChA	Member of the British Chiropody and Podiatry Association
MBCO	Member of the British College of Ophthalmic Opticians
MBCS	Member of the British Computer Society
MBEng	Member of the Association of Building Engineers
MBHA	Member of the British Hypnotherapy Association
MBHI	Member of the British Horological Institute
MBIAT	Member of the British Institute of Architectural Technologists
MBID	Member of the British Institute of Interior Design

MBIE	Member of the British Institute of Embalmers
MBII	Member of the British Institute of Innkeeping
MBioc	Master of Biochemistry
MBKS	Member of the British Kinematograph, Sound and Television Society
MBM	Master of Business Management
MBMA	Member of the Business Management Association
MBSc	Master in Business Science
MBSSG	Master of the British Society of Scientific Glassblowers
MCAM	Member of the Communication Advertising and Marketing Education Foundation
MCB	Mastership in Clinical Biochemistry
MCB	Member of the British Association of Communicators in Business
MCBDip	Member of the British Association of Communicators in Business who hold the Association's Certificate and Diploma
MCC	Master of Community Care
MCCDRCS(Eng)	Member of the Royal College of Surgeons of England, Clinical Community Dentistry
MCD	Master of Civic Design
MCDH	Master of Community Dental Health
MCGI	Membership, City & Guilds
MCGPIrel	Member of the Irish College of General Practitioners
MCh	Master of Surgery
MChD	Master of Dental Surgery
MChem	Master of Chemistry
MChemA	Master of Chemical Analysis
MChemPhys	Master of Chemical Physics
MChemPST	Master of Chemistry Polymer Science and Technology
MChir	Master of Surgery
MChOrth	Master of Orthopaedic Surgery
MChS	Member of the Society of Chiropodists and Podiatrists
MCIArb	Member of the Chartered Institute of Arbitrators
MCIBS	Member of the Chartered Institute of Bankers in Scotland
MCIBSE	Member of the Chartered Institution of Building Services Engineers
MCIH	Corporate Member of the Chartered Institute of Housing
MCIJ	Member of the Chartered Institute of Journalists
MCIM	Member of the Chartered Institute of Marketing
MCIOB	Member of the Chartered Institute of Building
MCIPD	Member of the Chartered Institute of Personnel and Development
MCIPS	Member of the Chartered Institute of Purchasing and Supply
MCIT	Member of the Chartered Institute of Transport
MCIWEM	Member of the Chartered Institution of Water and Environmental Management
MCLIP	Chartered Member of CILIP
MCom	Master of Commerce
MCommH	Master of Community Health
MComp	Master of Computer Science
MCOptom	Member of the College of Optometrists
MCoT	Member of the College of Teachers
MCPM	Member of the Confederation of Professional Management
MCPP	Member of the College of Pharmacy Practice
MCQ	Multiple Choice Question paper
MCSD	Member of the Chartered Society of Designers
MCSP	Member of the Chartered Society of Physiotherapy
MCT	Member of the Association of Corporate Treasurers

MCTHCM	Member of the Confederation of Tourism, Hotel and Catering Management
MCYW	Member of the Community and Youth Work Association
MD	Doctor of Medicine
MDA	Master of Defence Administration
MD; ChM	Conjoint Doctorate in Medicine, Doctorate in Surgery
MDCR	Management Diploma of the College of Radiographers
MDent	Master of Dental Science
MDes	Master of Design
MDes(RCA)	Master of Design, Royal College of Art
MDORCPSGlas	Membership of Dental Orthopaedics, Royal College of Physicians and Surgeons of Glasgow
MDra	Master of Drama
MDS	Master of Dental Surgery
MDSc	Master of Dental Science
MEBA	Master of European Business Administration
MECI	Member of the Institute of Employment Consultants
MEd	Master of Education
MEd(EdPsych)	Master of Education (Educational Psychology)
MEdStud	Master of Educational Studies
MEng	Master of Engineering
MEnv	Master of Environmental Studies
MEnvSci	Master of Environmental Science
MESc	Master of Earth Sciences
MFA	Master of Fine Art
MFC	Mastership in Food Control
MFCM	Member of the Faculty of Community Medicine
MFDO	Member of the Faculty of Dispensing Opticians
MFDS	Member of the Faculty of Dental Surgery
MFGDPEng	Membership in General Dental Practice, Royal College of Surgeons of England
MFHom	Member of the Faculty of Homeopathy
MFM	Master of Forensic Medicine
MFPHM	Member of the Faculty of Public Health Medicine, Royal College of Physicians of London and Edinburgh and Royal College of Physicians and Surgeons of Glasgow
MFPHMIrel	Member of the Faculty of Public Health Medicine, Royal College of Physicians of Ireland
MFTCom	Member of the Faculty of Teachers in Commerce
MGDSRCSEd	Membership in General Dental Surgery, Royal College of Surgeons of Edinburgh
MGDSRCSEng	Membership in General Dental Surgery, Royal College of Surgeons of England
MGeog	Master of Geography
MGeol	Master of Geology
MGeophys	Master of Geophysical Sciences
MHCIMA	Member of the Hotel and Catering International Management Association
MHM	Master of Health Management
MHort(RHS)	Master of Horticulture, Royal Horticultural Society
MHSM	Member of the Institute of Health Services Management
MIAB	Member of the International Association of Book-keepers
MIAEA	Member of the Institute of Automotive Engineer Assessors
MIAgrE	Member of the Institution of Agricultural Engineers
MIAP	Member of the Institution of Analysts and Programmers
MIAT	Member of the Institute of Asphalt Technology
MIBC	Member of the Institute of Building Control

MIBCM	Member of the Institute British Carriage and Automobile Manufacturers
MIBCO	Member of the Institution of Building Control Officers
MIBE	Member of the Institution of British Engineers
MIBF	Member of the Institute of British Foundrymen
MIBiol	Member of the Institute of Biology
MIBM	Member of the Institute of Builders' Merchants
MICB	Member of the Institute of Certified Book-Keepers
MICE	Member of the Institute of Civil Engineers
MIChemE	Member of the Institution of Chemical Engineers
MICIIT	Member of the International Council for Holistic Therapies
MICM	Member of the Institute of Credit Management
MICM(Grad)	Graduate Member of the Institute of Credit Management
MICorr	Member of the Institute of Corrosion
MICS	Member of the Institute of Chartered Shipbrokers
MICSc	Corporate Member of the Institute of Consumer Sciences Incorporating Home Economics
MICW	Member of the Institute of Clerks of Works of Great Britain Incorporated
MIDTA	Member of the International Dance Teachers' Association
MIED	Member of the Institution of Engineering Designers
MIEE	Member of the Institution of Electrical Engineers
MIEM	Member of the Institute of Executives and Managers
MIEx	Member of the Institute of Export
MIEx(Grad)	Graduate Member of the Institute of Export
MIExpE	Member of the Institute of Explosives Engineers
MIFA	Member of the Institute of Field Archaeologists
MIFireE	Member of the Institution of Fire Engineers
MIFM	Registered Member of the Institute of Fisheries Management
MIFST	Member of the Institute of Food Science and Technology
MIGasE	Member of the Institution of Gas Engineers
MIGD	Member of the Institute of Grocery Distribution
MIHEc	Member of the Institute of Home Economics
MIHIE	Member of the Institute of Highway Incorporated Engineers
MIHM	Member of the Institute of Healthcare Management
MIHort	Member of the Institute of Horticulture
MIHT	Member of the Institution of Highways and Transportation
MIIA	Member of the Institute of Internal Auditors
MIIE	Member of the Institution of Incorporated Engineers
MIIExE	Member of the Institution of Incorporated Executive Engineers
MIIHTM	Member of the International Institute of Hospitality Tourism & Management
MIIM	Member of the Institute of Industrial Managers
MIIM	Member of the International Institute of Management
MIIRSM	Member of the International Institute of Risk and Safety Management
MIISE	Member of the International Institute of Social Economics
MIISec	Member of the International Institute of Security
MIL	Member of the Institute of Linguists
MILAM	Member of the Institute of Leisure and Amenity Management
MILT	Member of the Institute of Logistics and Transport
MIM	Professional Member of the Institute of Materials
MIMA	Member of the Institute of Mathematics and its Applications
MIManf	Member of the Institute of Manufacturing
MIMarE	Member of the Institute of Marine Engineers
MIMatM	Member of the Institute of Materials Management

MIMBM	Member of the Institute of Maintenance and Building Management
MIMC	Member of the Institute of Management Consultancy
MIMechE	Member of the Institution of Mechanical Engineers
MIMechIE	Member of the Institution of Mechanical Incorporated Engineers
MIMF	Member of the Institute of Metal Finishing
MIMI	Member of the Institute of the Motor Industry
MIMinE	Member of the Institution of Mining Engineers
MIMIS	Member of the Institute for the Management of Information Systems
MIMM	Member of the Institute of Massage and Movement
MIMM	Member of the Institution of Mining and Metallurgy
MIMS	Member of the Institute of Management Specialists
MInstAEA	Member of the Institute of Automotive Engineer Assessors
MInstAM	Member of the Institute of Administrative Management
MInstBA	Member of the Institute of Business Administration
MInstBCA	Member of the Institute of Burial and Cremation Administration
MInstBE	Member of the Institution of British Engineers
MInstBM	Member of the Institute of Builders' Merchants
MInstCF	Master Fitter of the National Institute of Carpet and Floorlayers
MInstChP	Member of the Institute of Chiropodists & Podiatrists
MInstCM	Member of the Institute of Commercial Management
MInstD	Member of the Institute of Directors
MInstE	Member of the Institute of Energy
MInstLEx	Member of the Institute of Legal Executives
MInstMC	Member of the Institute of Measurement and Control
MInstNDT	Member of the British Institute of Non-Destructive Testing
MInstP	Member of the Institute of Physics
MInstPet	Member of the Institute of Petroleum
MInstPkg	Member of the Institute of Packaging
MInstPkg(Dip)	Diploma Member of the Institute of Packaging
MInstPM	Member of the Institute of Professional Managers and Administrators
MInstPS	Corporate Member of the Institute of Purchasing and Supply
MInstPSA	Member of the Institute of Public Service Administrators
MInstR	Member of the Institute of Refrigeration
MInstSMM	Member of the Institute of Sales and Marketing Management
MInstTA	Member of the Institute of Transport Administration
MInstTT	Full Member of the Institute of Travel and Tourism
MInstWM	Member of the Institute of Wastes Management
MIOC	Member of the Institute of Carpenters
MIOFMS	Member of the Institute of Financial and Management Studies
MIOM	Member of the Institute of Operations Management
MIOP	Member of the Institute of Printing
MIOSH	Member of the Institution of Occupational Safety and Health
MIP	Member of the Institute of Plumbing
MIPA	Member of the Institute of Practitioners in Advertising
MIPD	Member of the Institute of Personnel and Development
MIPI	Member of the Institute of Professional Investigators
MIPlantE	Member of the Institution of Plant Engineers
MIPR	Member of the Institute of Public Relations
MIPRE	Member of the Incorporated Practitioners in Radio & Electronics
MIQ	Member of the Institute of Quarrying
MIQA	Member of the Institute of Quality Assurance
MIR	Member of the Institute of Population Registration

MIRRV	Member of the Institute of Revenue, Rating and Valuation
MIRSE	Member of the Institution of Railway Signal Engineers
MIRTE	Member of the Institute of Road Transport Engineering
MISM	Member of the Institute for Supervision & Management
MISOB	Member of the Incorporated Society of Organ Builders
MISTC	Member of the Institute of Scientific and Technical Communicators
MIStrucE	Member of the Institution of Structural Engineers
MISW	Member of the Institute of Social Welfare
MITAI	Member of the Institute of Traffic Accident Investigators
MITSA	Member of the Institute of Trading Standards Administration
MIVehE	Member of the Institute of Vehicle Engineers
MIWM	Member of the Institute of Wastes Management
MIWPC	Member of the Institute of Water Pollution Control
MJur	Master of Jurisprudence
MLA	Master of Landscape Architecture
MLang	Master of Languages
MLangEng	Master of Language Engineering
MLD	Master of Landscape Design
MLE	Master of Land Economy
MLI	Member of the Landscape Institute
MLing	Master of Languages
MLitt	Master of Letters
MLPM	Master of Landscape Planning and Management
MLS	Master of Library Science
MM	Master of Midwifery
MMA	Master of Management and Administration
MMAS	Master of Minimal Access Surgery
MMath	Master of Mathematics
MMedE	Master of Medical Education
MMedSci	Master of Medical Science
MMet	Master of Metallurgy
MML	Master of Modern Languages
MMS	Member of the Institute of Management Services
MMSc	Master of Medical Sciences
MMus	Master of Music
MMus(Comp)	Master of Music (Composition)
MMus(Perf)	Master of Music (Performance)
MMus, RCM	Master of Music, Royal College of Music
MMusArt	Master of Musical Arts
MN	Master of Nursing
MNAEA	Member of the National Association of Estate Agents
MNatSc	Master of Natural Science
MNCP	Member of the National Council of Psychotherapists
MNeuro	Master of Neuroscience
MNI	Member of the Nautical Institute
MNIMH	Member of the National Institute of Medical Herbalists
MNRHP	Full Member of the National Register of Hypnotherapists and Psychotherapists
MNRHP(Eqv)	Full Member (Equivalent) of the National Register of Hypnotherapists and Psychotherapists
MNTB	Merchant Navy Training Board
MObstG	Master of Obstetrics and Gynaecology
MOptom	Master of Optometry

MOrthRCSEng	Membership in Orthodontics, Royal College of Surgeons of England
MPA	Master of Public Administration
MPaedDenRCSEng	Membership in Paediatric Dentistry, Royal College of Surgeons of England
MPC	Master of Palliative Care
MPH	Master of Public Health
MPharm	Master of Pharmacy
MPharmSci	Master of Pharmaceutical Science
MPhil	Master of Philosophy
MPhil(Eng)	Master of Philosophy in Engineering
MPhys	Master of Physics
MPhysGeog	Master of Physical Geography
MPlan	Master of Planning
MPPS	Master of Public Policy Studies
MPRI	Member of the Plastics and Rubber Institute
MProf	Master of Professional Studies
MProfBTM	Member of the Professional Business and Technical Management
MPS	Member of the Pharmaceutical Society of Northern Ireland
MPsychMed	Master of Psychological Medicine
MPsychol	Master of Psychology
MQB	Mining Qualifications Board
MRad	Master of Radiology
MRad; MRad(D)	Master of Radiology (Radiodiagnosis) or (Radiotherapy)
MRAeS	Member of the Royal Aeronautical Society
MRCGP	Member of the Royal College of General Practitioners
MRCOG	Member of the Royal College of Obstetricians and Gynaecologists
MRCP	Member of the Royal College of Physicians of London
MRCP(UK)	Member of the Royal College of Physicians of the United Kingdom
MRCPath	Member of the Royal College of Pathologists
MRCPEdin	Member of the Royal College of Physicians of Edinburgh (superceded by MRCP(UK))
MRCPGlasg	Member of the Royal College of Physicians of Glasgow (superceded by MRCP(UK))
MRCPIrel	Member of the Royal College of Physicians of Ireland
MRCPsych	Member of the Royal College of Psychiatrists
MRCSEd	Member of the Royal College of Surgeons of Edinburgh
MRCSEng	Member of the Royal College of Surgeons of England
MRCVS	Member of the Royal College of Veterinary Surgeons
MRDRCS	Membership in Restorative Dentistry, Royal College of Surgeons of England
MREC	Member of the Recruitment and Employment Confederation
MREHIS	Member of the Royal Environmental Health Institute of Scotland
MRes	Master of Research
MRIN	Member of the Royal Institute of Navigation
MRINA	Member of the Royal Institution of Naval Architects
MRIPHH	Member of the Royal Institute of Public Health and Hygiene
MRPharmS	Member of the Pharmaceutical Society of Great Britain
MRSC	Member of the Royal Society of Chemistry
MRSH	Member of the Royal Society for the Promotion of Health
MRSS	Member of the Royal Statistical Society
MRTPI	Member of the Royal Town Planning Institute
MS	Master of Surgery
MSA	Marine Safety Agency
MSAPP	Member of the Society of Advanced Psychotherapy Practitioners

MSBP	Member of the Society of Business Practitioners
MSBT	Member of the Society of Teachers in Business Education
MSc	Master of Science
MSc(Econ)	Master of Science in Economics
MSc(Ed)	Master of Science in Education
MSc(Eng)	Master of Science in Engineering
MSc(Entr)	Master of Entrepreneurship
MSc(Mgt)	Master of Science in Management
MScD	Master of Dental Science
MScEcon	Master in Faculty of Economic and Social Studies
MSCi	Master of Natural Sciences
MScTech	Master of Technical Science
MSE	Member of Society of Engineers (Inc)
MSF	Member of the SMAE Institute
MSFA	Advanced Financial Planning Certificate
MSIAD	Member of the Society of Industrial Artists and Designers
MSMA	Member of the Society of Martial Arts
MSocSc	Master of Social Science
MSSc	Master of Social Science
MSSc	Master of Surgical Science
MSSCh	Member of the British Chiropody and Podiatry Association
MSSF	Member of the Society of Shoe Fitters
MSt	Master of Studies
MSTA	Member of the Swimming Teachers' Association
MSTI	Certificate of Insurance Work
MSurgDentRCSEng	Membership in Surgical Dentistry, Royal College of Surgeons of England
MSW	Master of Social Work
MTCP	Master of Town and Country Planning
MTD	Master of Transport Design
MTech	Master of Technology
MTh	Master of Theology
MTheol	Master of Theology
MTP	Master of Town Planning
MTPI	Master of Town Planning
MTropMed	Master of Tropical Medicine
MTropPaediatrics	Master of Tropical Paediatrics
MUniv	Master of University (Honorary)
MURP	Master of Urban and Regional Planning
MusB	Bachelor of Music
MusD	Doctor of Music
MVC	Management Verification Consortium
MVM	Master of Veterinary Medicine
MVSc	Master of Veterinary Science
MWeldI	Member of the Welding Institute
MWES	Member of the Women's Engineering Society
MYD	Member of the Youth Development Association
NACOS	National Approval Council for Security Systems
NAEA	National Association of Estate Agents
NAG	National Association of Goldsmiths
NAMCW	National Association for Maternal and Child Welfare
NC	National Certificate
NCA	National Certificate in Agriculture

NCC	National Computing Centre
NCC	Navigational Control Course
NCDT	National Council for Drama Training
NCTJ	National Council for the Training of Journalists
NCVQ	National Council for Vocational Qualifications
ND	Diploma in Naturopathy
NDD	National Diploma in Design
NDF	National Diploma in Forestry
NDH	National Diploma in Horticulture
NDSF	National Diploma of the Society of Floristry
NDT	National Diploma in the Science and Practice of Turfculture and Sports Ground Management
NEBOSH	National Examination Board in Occupational Safety and Health
NEBS	National Examining Board for Supervision & Management
NFTS	National Film and Television School
NICCEA	Northern Ireland Council for the Curriculum, Examinations and Assessment
NID	National Intermediate Diploma
NIM	Northern Institute of Massage
NNEB	National Nursery Examination Board
NRHP	National Register of Hypnotherapists and Psychotherapists
NRHP(Affil)	Affiliate of the National Register of Hypnotherapists and Psychotherapists
NRHP(Assoc)	Associate of the National Register of Hypnotherapists and Psychotherapists
N-SHAP	National School of Hypnosis and Psychotherapy
NTTG	National Textile Training Group
NUJ	National Union of Journalists
NVQ	National Vocational Qualifications
NWRAC	North Western Regional Advisory Council for Further Education
OCR	Oxford, Cambridge & RSA Examinations
ODLQC	Open & Distance Learning Quality Council, formerly CACC, Council for Accreditation of Correspondence Colleges
ONC	Ordinary National Certificate
OND	Ordinary National Diploma
OSCE	Objective Structured Clinical Exam
PBTM	Professional Business and Technical Management
PCN	Personnel Certification in Non-Destructive Testing Ltd
PDP	Professional Development Programme
PESD	Private and Executive Secretary's Diploma, London Chamber of Commerce and Industry
PgC	Postgraduate Certificate
PGCE	Postgraduate Certificate in Education
PGCert	Postgraduate Certificate
PgD	Postgraduate Diploma
PGDip	Postgraduate Diploma
PGDip(Comp)	Postgraduate Diploma in Composition
PGDip(LCM)	Postgraduate Diploma of the London College of Music
PGDip(Perf)	Postgraduate Diploma in Performance
PGDip(RCM)	Postgraduate Diploma of the Royal College of Music
PGDipMin	Postgraduate Diploma in Ministry
PGDipMus	Postgraduate Diploma in Music
PhD	Doctor of Philosophy
PhD(RCA)	Doctor of Philosophy (Royal College of Art)
PIC	Professional Investment Certificate

PIFA	Practitioner of the Institute of Field Archaeologists
PIIA	Practitioner of the Institute of Internal Auditors
PInstNDT	Practitioner of the British Institute of Non-Destructive Testing
PJDip	Professional Jewellers' Diploma
PJGemDip	Professional Jewellers' Gemstone Diploma
PJManDip	Professional Jewellers' Management Diploma
PJValDip	Professional Jewellers' Valuation Diploma
PPL	Private Pilot's Licence
PPRNCM	Professional Performance Diploma of the Royal Northern College of Music
PQS	Professional Qualification Structure
PQSW	Post-Qualifying Award in Social Work
PRCA	Public Relations Consultants Association
PSC	Private Secretary's Certificate
PSD	Private Secretary's Diploma
PTA	Pianoforte Tuners' Association
PVM	Professional in Value Management
QC	Queen's Counsel
QCA	Qualifications and Curriculum Authority
QCG	Qualification in Careers Guidance
QDR	Qualified Dispute Resolver
QICA	Qualification in Computer Auditing
QIS	Qualified Imaging Scientist
QPA	Qualification in Pensions Administration
QPSPA	Qualification in Public Sector Pensions Administration
RA	Royal Academician
RAD	Royal Academy of Dancing
RADA	Royal Academy of Dramatic Art
RAM	Royal Academy of Music
RANA	Royal Animal Nursing Auxiliary
RAS	Royal Astronomical Society
RBS	Royal Ballet School
RC	Roman Catholic
RCM	Royal College of Midwives
RCN	Royal College of Nursing
RCSLT	Royal College of Speech and Language Therapists
RCVS	Royal College of Veterinary Surgeons
REA	Regional Examining Body
REC	Recruitment and Employment Confederation
Ret'dABID	Retired Associate of the British Institute of Interior Design
Ret'dFBID	Retired Fellow of the British Institute of Interior Design
Ret'dMBID	Retired Member of the British Institute of Interior Design
RGN	Registered General Nurse
RHS	Royal Horticultural Society
RHV	Registered Health Visitor
RIBA	Royal Institute of British Architects
RICS	Royal Institution of Chartered Surveyors
RINA	Royal Institution of Naval Architects
RJDip	Diploma for Retail Jewellers
RJGemDip	National Association of Goldsmiths Gemstone Diploma
RM	Registered Midwife
RMN	Registered Mental Nurse
RMS	Royal Microscopical Society

RNMH	Registered Nurse for the Mentally Handicapped
RP	Registered Plumber
RPS	Royal Photographic Society
RSA	Royal Society of Arts
RSBEI	Registered Student of the Institution of Body Engineers
RSC	Royal Society of Chemistry
RSCN	Registered Sick Children's Nurse
RSP	Registered Safety Practitioner
RTO	Recognised Training Organisation
RTPI	Royal Town Planning Institute
SA	Salvation Army Management
SBP	Society of Business Practitioners
SCAA	School Curriculum and Assessment Authority
ScD	Doctor of Science
SCE	Scottish Certificate of Education
SCLS	Second Certificate for Legal Secretaries
SCMT	Ship Captain's Medical Training
SCOTVEC	Scottish Vocational Education Council
SCPL	Senior Commercial Pilot's Licence
SE	Society of Engineers
SEE	Society of Environmental Engineers
SEFIC	Spoken English for Industry and Commerce
SenAWeldI	Senior Associate of the Welding Institute
SEng	Qualified Sales Engineer
SenMWeldI	Senior Member of the Welding Institute
SF	Society of Floristry Ltd
SFA	Securities and Futures Authority
SFInstE	Senior Fellow of the Institute of Energy
SG	Society of Genealogists
SGT	Society of Glass Technology
SHNC	Scottish Higher National Certificate
SHND	Scottish Higher National Diploma
SIEDip	Securities Industry Examination Diploma
SInstPet	Student of the Institute of Petroleum
SITO	Security Industry Training Organisation Ltd
SLC	Secretarial Language Certificate
SLD	Secretarial Language Diploma
SNC	Scottish National Certificate
SND	Scottish National Diploma
SNNEB	Scottish Nursery Nurses Examination Board
SPA	Screen Printing Association
SPRINT	Sport Play and Recreation Industries National Training Executive
SQA	Scottish Qualifications Authority
SRD	State Registered Dietician
SRN	State Registered Nurse
SSC	Secretarial Studies Certificate, London Chamber of Commerce and Industry
STA	Specialist Teacher Assistant (CACHE)
STA	Swimming Teachers' Association
STAT	Society of Teachers of the Alexander Technique
StudentIEE	Student of the Institution of Electrical Engineers
StudentIIE	Student of the Institution of Incorporated Engineers
StudentIMechE	Student of the Institution of Mechanical Engineers

StudIAP   Student of the Institution of Analysts and Programmers
StudIManf   Student Member of the Institute of Manufacturing
StudIMS   Student of the Institute of Management Specialists
StudProfBTM   Student of the Professional Business and Technical Management
StudSE   Student of the Society of Engineers (Inc)
StudSElec   Student of the Society of Electroscience
StudWeldI   Student of the Welding Institute
SVQ   Scottish Vocational Qualification
TC   Technician Certificate
TCA   Technician in Costing and Accounting
TCA   Technician of the Institute of Cost and Executive Accountants
TCert   Teacher's Certificate
TD   Technician Diploma
TDCR   Teacher's Diploma of the College of Radiographers
TechICorr   Technician of the Institute of Corrosion
TechMIWM   Technician Member of the Institute of Wastes Management
TechRICS   Technical Surveyor of the Royal Institution of Chartered Surveyors
TechRMS   Technological Qualification in Microscopy, Royal Microscopical Society
TechRTPI   Technical Member of the Royal Town Planning Institute
TechSP   Technician Safety Practitioner
TechWeldI   Technician of the Welding Institute
TEMOL   Training in Energy Management through Open Learning
TI   Textile Institute
TIMBM   Technician of the Institute of Maintenance and Building Management
TMBA   Teacher Member of the British (Theatrical) Arts
TnIMBM   Technicians of the Institute of Maintenance and Building Management
TOEFL   Test of English as a Foreign Language
TPP   Test of Professional Practice
TVM   Trainer in Value Management
UCAS   Universities and Colleges Admissions Service
UCL   University College London
UEB   United Examining Board
UKCC   United Kingdom Central Council
UKCP   United Kingdom Council for Psychotherapy
UMIST   University of Manchester Institute of Science and Technology
URC   United Reformed Church
VetMB   Bachelor of Veterinary Medicine
VTCT   Vocational Training Charitable Trust
WCMD   Welsh College of Music and Drama
WES   Women's Engineering Society
WJEC   Welsh Joint Education Committee
WMAC   West Midlands Advisory Council for Further Education
WSA   West of Scotland Agricultural College
YHAFHE   Yorkshire and Humberside Association for Further and Higher Education
ZSL   Zoological Society of London

Part 1

Introduction

Since its first publication in 1970, *British Qualifications* has charted a number of fundamental changes in further and higher education provision in the UK. Major advances in technology and more flexible delivery and attendance patterns have created different types of learning opportunity, encouraging an ever more diverse student population to access education at all levels. The range of subjects delivered has grown beyond all recognition. New areas of research have been established and developed into major subject specialisms. Employers and professional bodies have collaborated to develop subject areas aligned to changing industry requirements. Flexibility and choice are the hallmarks of today's system, and anyone new to higher education might well be bewildered by the sheer variety of degree pathways available. The capacity to combine and mix modules and subjects has in fact grown beyond anything that could have been imagined in 1970.

Traditional boundaries between academic and vocational pathways continue to break down, and today most degrees have a vocational slant. Extended industry and professional placements, sponsored research projects, practitioner input and field-based assignments are common features in many degrees, and provide an important link into practice at the early stages of learning. Overall in twenty years, universities have doubled in size and the responsibilities they have taken on have expanded considerably.

Collaboration between further and higher education (HE) institutions has enabled a substantial amount of HE-level provision to be delivered in further education institutions. Clear progression routes have been established for some time.

Considerable breadth of provision is now available in further education. Not only has the sector grown to accommodate sub-degree provision, it has continued to deliver a wide range of pre- and post-18 vocational qualifications, which include technical, occupational and professional awards.

Today, certain types of external qualification cross the boundaries between further and higher education. Several higher education institutions (HEIs) – particularly those that gained university status in the 1990s and more recently in 2005 – deliver advanced professional qualifications and higher national diplomas or certificates awarded by awarding bodies like Edexcel, OCR and SQA. At the same time there has been a significant shift towards further education's involvement in delivery of these types of qualification, and a greater input from private sector colleges.

EDUCATION REFORM

The Higher Education Act 2004 introduced in 2006/07 new student support and tuition fee arrangements. For full-time UK and EU undergraduate students, institutions may charge up to £3,225 (2009/10 figures), and this may influence where individuals choose to study. A review of tuition fees is due to take place in 2009. (Further authoritative, official information about universities and colleges in the UK can be found at the Unistats website, www.unistats.com.)

As well as implementing reforms, the further and higher education sectors contribute to UK economic performance and the delivery of the government's targets, including that of making progress towards a 50 per cent participation rate in higher education in the 18–30 age group although this will not be achieved by 2010 as originally intended.

As part of this shared responsibility a great deal of effort is being made to increase access to and participation in education, particularly among individuals who have not had much involvement in the past. The general availability of modular study programmes and related credit recognition of units, and greater use of ICT and e-learning resources, have done a lot to create more flexible methods of delivery and attendance requirements in further and higher education.

FOUNDATION DEGREES

Foundation degrees (FDs) were established to give people the intermediate technical and professional skills that are in demand from employers, and to provide more flexible and accessible ways of studying. They are a higher level qualification awarded by universities. The qualification can be 'built up' from a range of relevant learning experiences, to allow for extremely flexible and adaptable qualifications that can be 'tailored' by employers to support their workforce and business development needs. They offer opportunities for employment and career advancement. Progression routes include links with associated professional qualifications and/or direct entry to the final year of a relevant Honours-level degree. FDs are offered by universities, colleges and other providers.

The first FDs in 2001 were studied by 4,000 students. In 2009, there were just over 87,000 enrolled on FDs. Around 3,000 FD courses were available in 2009, with a further 900 new courses in development. Foundation degree forward (*fdf*) was established in the 2003 Higher Education White Paper; it is the centre of expertise on Foundation degrees and its website www.fdf.ac.uk/ provides up-to-date information and guidance on all aspects of FDs for students, employers and institutions, including the full range of courses and illustrative case study material.

POLICY AND REGULATION

National priorities for further and higher education are now set by the UK and Scottish parliaments and the Welsh and Northern Ireland assemblies, following devolution in 1999/2000. Policy development, planning and implementation rest with the government departments responsible for each national education brief – the Department for Business, Innovation and Skills (BIS), the Department for Employment and Learning Northern Ireland (DELNI), the Scottish Executive, and the Department for Children, Education, Lifelong Learning and Skills (DCELLS) in Wales.

In England, delivery of further education is subject to external audit and public reporting by the Office for Standards in Education, Children's Services and Schools (Ofsted). National and regional Learning Skills Councils (LSCs) are responsible for funding, and work closely with colleges to plan national and local qualifications provision.

In Scotland, the Scottish Funding Council (SFC) has overall responsibility for planning, funding and quality assurance of further education through its work with Her Majesty's Inspectorate of Education (HMIE).

DCELLS is responsible for planning, funding and promotion of all post-16 education in Wales. Estyn (the Welsh-language acronym for Her Majesty's Inspectorate for Education and Training in Wales, website: www.estyn.gov.uk) is the appointed authority for audit of the quality of provision and related areas.

The Department for Employment and Learning (DELNI) is responsible for planning and funding of further education provision in Northern Ireland. Inspection and audit are undertaken by the Education and Training Inspectorate on behalf of the Department (www.delni.gov.uk, www.etini.gov.uk).

QUALITY ASSURANCE

A degree of convergence does exist in the area of quality assurance of qualifications at Level 3 and below. England, Wales and Northern Ireland share a common qualifications system, and the regulators in each country (listed below) work together in regulating qualifications for use across the three countries. Scotland has a separate qualifications system, although there is close correlation across all four countries, particularly in the area of vocational qualifications.

The following four bodies are responsible for the accreditation and standards of external qualifications and for curriculum and assessment for ages 3–16:

- England: Ofqual: Office of the Qualifications and Examinations Regulator;
- Northern Ireland: Council for Curriculum, Examinations and Assessment (CCEA*);
- Scotland: Scottish Qualifications Authority (SQA*);
- Wales: Department for Children, Education, Lifelong Learning and Skills (DCELLS).

*CCEA is also an Awarding Body for qualifications in Northern Ireland, which include National Qualifications to A level. SQA is also an Awarding Body that develops and validates SQA-branded qualifications including National Qualifications (Access, Intermediate, Higher and Advanced Higher Levels), Higher National Certificates and Diplomas, Scottish Vocational Qualifications and Scottish Professional Awards.

In higher education the responsibility for standards and quality rests firmly with each institution. All institutions work with the independent Quality Assurance Agency for Higher Education (QAA) for England, Northern Ireland, Scotland and Wales. Institutional audits and subject-level reviews have been undertaken by QAA since 2001. It publishes its findings on its website as publicly accessible information; see www.qaa.ac.uk.

Given the scale and diversity of degree provision in the present-day higher education sector, there has been a need to clarify what can reasonably be expected from undergraduate and postgraduate programmes. QAA has responded to this requirement and developed a code of practice for higher education providers, and subject benchmark statements indicating the expected standards of degrees across a range of subjects.

QUALIFICATION FRAMEWORKS

In further response to the breadth and diversity of qualifications available, a number of national qualification frameworks have been introduced. The framework concept is closely associated with greater transparency and comparability between types of qualification, particularly between those that were traditionally classified as academic or vocational. Common characteristics of all frameworks include universal adoption and understanding of qualification titles, and national tariffs of credits that recognize relevant levels of achievement.

The framework for Higher Education Qualifications in England, Wales and Northern Ireland (FHEQ) applies to degrees, diplomas, certificates and other academic awards by higher education providers (Figure 1.1).

The Scottish Credit and Qualification Framework (SCQF) was developed by SQA, the Scottish Executive, QAA (Scottish Office) and Universities for Scotland. It provides an overview of all levels of national and higher qualifications provision in Scotland (Figure 1.2).

The Qualifications and Credit Framework (QCF) is a new framework for recognizing and accrediting qualifications in England, Wales and Northern Ireland. The intention behind the

Figure 1.1   Framework for Higher Education Qualifications in England, Wales and Northern Ireland
Source: www.qaa.ac.uk

reform was to make the system and qualifications offered far more relevant to the needs of employers, with more flexibility for learners. Every unit and qualification in the framework has a credit value (where one credit represents ten hours) and a level between Entry level and level 8. There are three sizes of qualification in the QCF:

Awards: 1–12 credits
Certificates: 13–36 credits
Diplomas: 37 credits or more

This means that each qualification title contains the level (from Entry to level 8), the size (Award/Certificate/Diploma) and the details of the content of the qualification. For a full list of accredited qualifications please visit the National Database of Accredited Qualifications at www.accreditedqualifications.org.uk. This is a fully searchable database of qualifications that are accredited by Ofqual, DCELLS and CCEA.

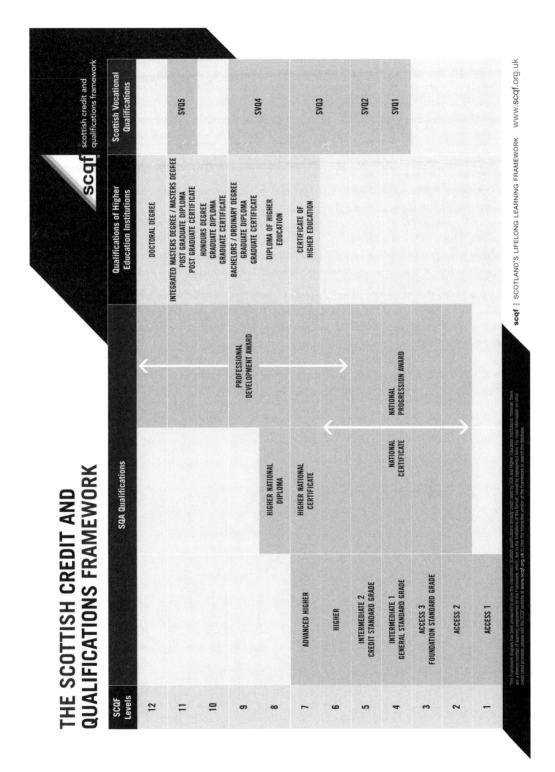

Figure 1.2 Framework for Higher Education Qualifications in Scotland

FUTURE CHALLENGES

Higher education faces some significant challenges in the near future, not least the issue of whether the Government will lift the cap on tuition fees for full-time undergraduates in 2010, and if it does, by how much. In addition, in a speech at the Wellcome Collection Conference Centre in February 2008, then Secretary of State for Innovation, Universities and Skills, John Denham, identified five areas in which English higher education should be world class in the future:

- to be responsible for a disproportionately high share of leading research, and home to leading thinkers in a full range of disciplines;
- maximising the benefits of links to business and public services – both educating the workforce and exploiting the fruits of research and innovation;
- developing international collaboration and top-quality relationships with higher education systems elsewhere in the world;
- teaching to high standards and reaching all those who can benefit;
- making the fullest possible contribution to local and regional development, and to cultural life.

In addition, according to the Higher Education Funding Council for England publication, *Higher Education in England: achievements, challenges and prospects,* higher education will be affected by political and economic trends which are impossible to predict. 'Economic turbulence' and a demographic decline in the age group which produces the majority of full-time undergraduates will both present additional challenges which higher education institutions will have to grapple with. Yet despite the uncertainty in future levels of public spending, higher education is viewed across the political parties as being absolutely crucial to the economic success of the country.

Part 2

Teaching Establishments

The statutory responsibility for the provision of education in the United Kingdom lies with the Department for Children, Schools and Families (DCSF) and the Department for Business, Innovation and Skills (BIS) in England, the Welsh Assembly Government's Department for Children, Education, Lifelong Learning and Skills (DCELLS), the Education Department of the Scottish Government and the Department of Education and Department of Employment and Learning in Northern Ireland. In the United Kingdom the statutory system of public education has three progressive stages: primary education (up to the age of 11 or 12), secondary education (up to age 16), and further education (post-16).

This section briefly describes further and higher provision and the main types of institution.

FURTHER AND HIGHER EDUCATION

'Higher education' is a generic term that broadly defines any course of study leading to a qualification at level 4 and above in the National Qualifications Credit Framework for England, Wales and Northern Ireland, and level 6 and above in the Scottish Credit and Qualifications Framework.

Higher education incorporates study towards a wide range of qualifications including Foundation, undergraduate and postgraduate degrees, certificates and diplomas awarded by individual universities and other higher education institutions (HEIs) with degree-awarding powers.

It can also include study towards general, technical or occupationally-related diplomas and certificates awarded by the large unitary awarding bodies. Unitary awarding bodies are characterized by their breadth of provision, from GNVQ and A levels through to qualifications at level 5 and above in the national frameworks.

The other category that can be characterized as higher education includes post-experience education above level 4 (and level 7 in Scotland). This includes qualifications available from awarding bodies that represent a particular sector, occupation or technical/craft area, and professional institutions that are also approved as awarding bodies.

Higher education can take place in universities and HEIs (which continue to provide the majority of undergraduate and postgraduate courses). It can also take place in colleges of further education. A significant number of colleges deliver parts of, and in some cases entire, Foundation and undergraduate degree courses in agreement with a selected university partner that is responsible for Quality Assurance and final awards.

In general terms, further education is available for students who are over the age of 16 and still in full-time education, and for adults aged 19 and over. Further education provision includes GCSEs, A levels and other types of general and vocational qualifications below level 4 (and level 6 in Scotland) in the National Qualifications Frameworks.

All qualifications are awarded by approved external awarding bodies that include AQA, City & Guilds, Edexcel, LCCI, OCR, OCN and SQA in Scotland. This also includes qualifications below level 4 (level 6 in Scotland) that have a craft or technical focus or are related to an occupation/sector. Readers who want to find out more about approved qualifications below level 4 will find the Qualifications and Curriculum Authority (QCA) 'Accredited Qualifications' website informative (www.accreditedqualifications.org.uk). This is the National Database of Accredited Qualifications (NDAQ) which contains details of all those qualifications which are accredited by the regulators of external qualifications in England (Ofqual), Wales (DCELLS) and Northern Ireland (CCEA).

FURTHER AND HIGHER EDUCATION INSTITUTIONS

England and Wales

There is a wide range of further and higher education establishments, including colleges with various titles. There are also a number of independent specialist establishments, like secretarial and correspondence colleges.

According to latest figures available, there were 120 universities, 49 other education institutions and 444 further education colleges (of which 95 were sixth form colleges) in the UK in 2007/ 2008. Of the Universities, 98 are in England (according to the Open University), 7 are in Wales, 134 are in Scotland and 2 are in Northern Ireland. Courses include those for first and second degrees, certain graduate-equivalent qualifications, and the examinations of the principal professional associations. These institutions also provide courses leading to important qualifications below degree level, such as Foundation degrees, Higher National Diplomas and Certificates, and Diplomas of Higher Education.

On 1 April 1993 further education and sixth-form colleges left local authority control and became independent corporations in a new sector of publicly-funded further education (FE). The sector also includes a small number of designated colleges. FE colleges have diverse titles, including college of technology, college of arts and technology, and regional college. Institutions in the sector are funded by regional Learning and Skills Councils (LSCs). The LSCs have a statutory duty to secure sufficient provision for full-time education for 16–18-year-olds who want such education, and to ensure adequate provision of vocational, academic, access and basic skill courses for adults and part-timers. Most colleges of further education specialize in providing courses which lead to qualifications below degree level, such as A levels and BTEC qualifications. Some offer degree courses, including in many cases the new Foundation degrees.

Students aged 16–18 who have been ordinarily resident in the UK for three years and European Community nationals normally have the right to attend a full-time course without paying tuition fees. Colleges are free to determine fee levels for other students.

Scotland

There are 43 colleges of further education in Scotland which provide a broad mix of courses, many awarded by the Scottish Qualifications Authority (SQA). Most courses of higher education at or near degree level and beyond are provided by the 13 universities, the Open University of Scotland and the 7 other HEIs. These institutions offer a range of vocationally-oriented courses ranging from science, engineering and computing to health care, art and design, music and drama, and teacher training, as well as the more traditional 'academic' courses. All the universities and HEIs are funded by the Scottish Further and Higher Education Funding Council.

Northern Ireland

Responsibility for the further education sector in Northern Ireland rests with the Department for Employment and Learning (DELNI) which directly funds colleges. There are six further education colleges, and these offer a wide range of vocational and non-vocational courses for both full-time and part-time students.

Higher education in Northern Ireland is provided in two universities and two university colleges and is funded by the Northern Ireland Higher Education Council.

Many of the courses in both universities are designed to suit the needs of industry, commerce and the professions. Agricultural, horticultural and food colleges in Northern Ireland are administered through the Department of Agriculture, as in Scotland.

UNIVERSITIES AND HE COLLEGES

Universities are independent self-governing bodies. Although largely financed by the government through the Higher Education Funding Councils in the UK, they do not come under the jurisdiction or control of any government department. They derive their rights and privileges from Royal Charter or Act of Parliament, and any amendment of their charters or statutes is made by the Crown acting through the Privy Council on the application of the universities themselves. The universities alone decide what degrees they award and the conditions on which they be awarded; they alone decide which students to admit and which staff to appoint. However, government policies have started to influence admission criteria, particularly in the area of widening access and participation in higher education by non-traditional students. Student fees set by universities are also subject to strict guidelines set by the government.

Institutions receiving funding from Higher Education Funding Council for England (Source: Higher Education Funding Council for England)

The 19 schools and institutes of the University of London which receive funds directly from the HEFCE are marked *.

Anglia Ruskin University; Aston University; University of Bath; Bath Spa University; University of Bedfordshire; Birkbeck College*; University of Birmingham; University College Birmingham; Birmingham City University; Bishop Grosseteste University College Lincoln; University of Bolton; Arts University College at Bournemouth; Bournemouth University; University of Bradford; University of Brighton; University of Bristol; Brunel University; Buckinghamshire New University; University of Cambridge; Institute of Cancer Research*; Canterbury Christ Church University; University of Central Lancashire; Central School of Speech and Drama*; University of Chester; University of Chichester; City University, London; Conservatoire for Dance and Drama; Courtauld Institute of Art*; Coventry University; Cranfield University; University for the Creative Arts; University of Cumbria; De Montfort University; University of Derby; Durham University; University of East Anglia; University of East London; Edge Hill University; Institute of Education*; University of Essex; University of Exeter; University College Falmouth; University of Gloucestershire; Goldsmiths College*; University of Greenwich; Guildhall School of Music and Drama; Harper Adams University College; University of Hertfordshire; Heythrop College*; University of Huddersfield; University of Hull; Imperial College London; Keele University; University of Kent; King's College London*; Kingston University; Lancaster University; University of Leeds; Leeds College of Music; Leeds Metropolitan University; Leeds, Trinity and All Saints; University of Leicester; University of Lincoln; University of Liverpool; Liverpool Hope University; Liverpool Institute for Performing Arts; Liverpool John Moores University; University College London*; University of London; University of the Arts, London; London Business School*; London School of Economics and Political Science*; London School of Hygiene and Tropical Medicine*; London Metropolitan University; London South Bank University; Loughborough University; University of Manchester; Manchester Metropolitan University; Marjon (University College Plymouth St Mark and St John); Middlesex University; Newcastle University; Newman

University College; University of Northampton; University of Northumbria at Newcastle; Norwich University College of the Arts; University of Nottingham; Nottingham Trent University; The Open University; School of Oriental and African Studies*; University of Oxford; Oxford Brookes University; School of Pharmacy*; University of Plymouth; University of Portsmouth; Queen Mary, University of London*; Ravensbourne College of Design and Communication; University of Reading; Roehampton University; Rose Bruford College; Royal Academy of Music*; Royal Agricultural College; Royal College of Art; Royal College of Music; Royal Holloway, University of London*; Royal Northern College of Music; Royal Veterinary College*; St George's Hospital Medical School*; St Mary's College; University of Salford; University of Sheffield; Sheffield Hallam University; University of Southampton; Southampton Solent University; Staffordshire University; University Campus Suffolk; University of Sunderland; University of Surrey; University of Sussex; University of Teesside; Thames Valley University; Trinity Laban Conservatoire of Music and Dance; University of Warwick; University of the West of England, Bristol; University of Westminster; University of Winchester; University of Wolverhampton; University of Worcester; Writtle College; University of York; York St John University.

Universities receiving funding from the Department for Employment and Learning in Northern Ireland (source: Higher Education Funding Council for England)

Queen's University Belfast; University of Ulster.

Higher Education Institutions receiving funding from the Scottish Further and Higher Education Funding Council for Scotland (Source: Scottish Further and Higher Education Funding Council)

University of Aberdeen; University of Abertay Dundee; University of Dundee; Edinburgh College of Art; Edinburgh Napier University; University of Edinburgh; Glasgow Caledonian University; Glasgow School of Art; University of Glasgow; Heriot-Watt University; The Open University in Scotland; Queen Margaret University, Edinburgh; Robert Gordon University; Royal Scottish Academy of Music and Drama; Scottish Agricultural College; University of St Andrews; University of Stirling; University of Strathclyde; University of the West of Scotland; UHI Millennium Institute.

Institutions receiving funding from the Higher Education Funding Council for Wales (source: Higher Education Funding Council for Wales)

Aberystwyth University; Bangor University; Cardiff University; University of Wales Institute, Cardiff; University of Glamorgan, incorporating Royal Welsh College of Music and Drama; Glyndwr University; University of Wales, Lampeter; University of Wales, Newport; Open University in Wales; Swansea Metropolitan University; Swansea University; Trinity University College; University of Wales.

OTHER HE ORGANIZATIONS

There are a number of other organizations involved in shaping the Higher Education sector, for example the British Academy, the General Medical Council and Research Councils UK. You can find a full list of these organizations on the Universities UK website, www.universitiesuk.ac.uk.

Part 3

Qualifications

INTRODUCTION

Definition of Common Terms

A number of terms are commonly used as synonyms for qualifications, for example, 'examinations' and 'courses'. This can hide important differences of meaning and lead to confusion and misunderstanding. In some contexts it may be important to make these differences explicit in order to guard against exaggerating or diminishing the level of achievement, which is an essential core of the concept of qualification. It is especially important to clarify the difference in meaning between 'examination', 'course' and 'qualification'.

Examination

An examination is a formal test or assessment. It can focus on one or more of the following: knowledge, understanding, skill or competence. An examination may be set as a written test, an oral test, an aural and oral test (eg, a foreign language test) or a practical test. In the past, most forms of external assessment in FE were based on a model of examination dominated by the psychometric model, designed to discriminate between individuals – normative referencing – and took the form of written tests. There was considerable variation in different kinds of written examination, ranging through essays, question and answer, and 'multiple response'. Today, largely as a result of the introduction of National Vocational Qualifications (NVQs), the purpose and format of many examinations have been reappraised, and criterion-referenced examinations that focus on achievement (and in the case of NVQs, competence) are increasingly common. Many forms of assessment are now an integral part of the learning process, with a formative as well as a summative function rather than a separate, terminal, summative function.

Course

A course implies an ordered sequence of teaching or learning over a period of time. A course is governed by regulations or requirements, frequently imposed by an external awarding body and sometimes by the institution providing the course. An important distinguishing feature between different courses is the length of time allocated to study: it can vary from a few days to several years. Some courses offer a terminal award on the basis of course completion, and these courses are set for a given period of time. Other 'set period' courses may prescribe examinations; these can include continuous assessment, terminal testing or a combination of both. In other courses, the programme of study may be accomplished at a faster or slower rate; such courses normally enjoin continuous assessment or a terminal examination, or both. Many courses require attendance at an institution, while distance learning, correspondence courses, and various forms of flexible-learning courses are usually free of these requirements, although some of these courses may require occasional attendance for residential components or face-to-face tutoring. A successful examination result usually confers a qualification or an award.

Qualification

A qualification is normally a certificated endorsement, from a recognized awarding body, that a level or quality of accomplishment has been achieved by an individual. Qualifications are usually conferred on successful completion of an examination, although not all examinations necessarily offer qualifications. An examination may offer an award that is a part-qualification. For example, an NVQ candidate may acquire a unit of competence that is a part-qualification building towards a full statement of competence – an NVQ. A first-year student on an HND course may be required to pass all first-year examinations in order to be permitted to continue into the second year; in a sense, that student is 'qualified' to continue the course but no qualification is awarded. Some award-bearing examinations may be fully recognized and certificated qualifications in themselves (eg, a BTEC HNC) but only part-qualifications for a profession (eg, Chartered Engineer).

Apparent anomalies do exist. Some professional bodies and trade associations award qualifications that are recognized within the profession or association but that are not obtained by examination. They are usually awarded on the basis of experience, and payment of a fee, and denote membership or acceptance. When the body also offers an examination route to the same qualification, successful examinees are usually known as 'graduate members'.

There are a number of accreditation authorities that approve qualifications. There are also many specialist and general validating, examining and awarding bodies that are responsible for the design and assessment of qualifications.

ACCREDITING REGULATORY BODIES

England

Sector Skill Councils

The Alliance of Sector Skills Councils launched in April 2008 is an organization that supports the network of licensed UK Sector Skills Councils (SSCs). These are employer-led, independent organizations that cover specific work sectors across the UK (currently accounting for approximately 90 per cent of the UK workforce). With the influence granted by licences from the governments of England, Scotland, Wales and Northern Ireland, and with private and public funding, this independent network engages with the education and training supply-side, such as universities, colleges, funders and qualifications bodies, to increase productivity at all levels in the workforce. Details are listed in Table 3.1.

Table 3.1 Sector Skill Councils

Asset Skills
Sector: Property services, housing, cleaning sectors and facilities management
Tel: 01392 423399
E-mail: enquiries@assetskills.org
Website: www.assetskills.org

Cogent
Sector: Chemical and pharmaceutical, oil, nuclear, gas, petroleum and polymer industries
Tel: 01925 515200
E-mail: info@cogent-ssc.com
Website: www.cogent-ssc.com

ConstructionSkills
Sector: Construction
Tel: 044 900 4400
E-mail: call.centre@cskills.org
Website: www.cskills.org

Creative & Cultural Skills
Sector: Advertising, crafts, music, performing, heritage, design and arts sectors
Tel: 020 7015 1800
E-mail: info@ccskills.org.uk
Website: www.ccskills.org.uk

Energy & Utility Skills
Sector: Energy, waste and utilities
Tel: 08450 779922
E-mail: enquiries@euskills.co.uk
Website: www.euskills.co.uk

e-skills UK
Sector: Information technology and tele-communications sector
Tel: 020 7963 8920
E-mail: info@e-skills.com
Website: www.e-skills.com *continued*

Table 3.1 *Continued*

Financial Services Skills Council
Sector: Financial services, accountancy and finance
Tel: 08452 573772
E-mail: info@fssc.org.uk
Website: www.fssc.org.uk

GoSkills
Sector: Passenger transport
Tel: 01216 355520
E-mail: info@goskills.org
Website: www.goskills.org

Government Skills
Sector: Central Government
Tel: 0203 300 8977
E-mail: info@government-skills.gsi.gov.uk
Website: www.government-skills.gov.uk

Improve Ltd
Sector: Food and drinks manufacturing and processing
Tel: 08456 440448
E-mail: info@improveltd.co.uk
Website: www.improveltd.co.uk

The Institute of the Motor Industry
Sector: Retail motor industries
Tel: 01992 511521
E-mail: info@motor.org.uk
Website: www.motor.org.uk

Lantra
Sector: Environmental and land-based sectors
Tel: 02476 696996
E-mail: connect@lantra.co.uk
Website: www.lantra.co.uk

Lifelong Learning UK
Sector: Community learning education, FE, HE, libraries, work-based learning and training providers
Tel: 08707 577890
E-mail: enquiries@lluk.org
Website: www.lluk.org

People 1st
Sector: Hospitality, leisure, travel and tourism
Tel: 08700 602550
E-mail: info@people1st.co.uk
Website: www.people1st.co.uk

Proskills UK
Sector: Building products, coatings, extractive and mineral processing, furniture, furnishings and interiors, glass and glazing, glazed ceramics, paper and pulp and printing
Tel: 01235 833844
E-mail: info@proskills.co.uk
Website: www.proskills.co.uk

SEMTA
Sector: Science, engineering and manufacturing technologies
Tel: 0845 643 9001
E-mail: customerservices@semta.org.uk
Website: www.semta.org.uk

Skillfast-UK
Sector: Fashion and textiles
Tel: 01132 399600
E-mail: enquiries@skillfast-uk.org
Website: www.skillfast-uk.org

Skills for Care & Development
Sector: Social care, children, early years and young people's workforces in the UK
Tel: 0113 390 7667
E-mail: info@skillsforcareanddevelopment.org.uk
Website: www.skillsforcareanddevelopment.org.uk

Skills for Health
Sector: UK health
Tel: 01179 221155
E-mail: office@skillsforhealth.org.uk
Website: www.skillsforhealth.org.uk

continued

Table 3.1 *Continued*

Skills for Justice **Sector:** Policing and law enforcement, youth justice, custodial care, community justice, court services, prosecution services and forensic science Tel: 01142 317 375 E-mail: info@skillsforjustice.com Website: www.skillsforjustice.com	**Skillset** **Sector:** TV, film, radio, interactive media, animation, computer games, facilities, photo imaging and publishing Tel: 020 7713 9800 E-mail: info@skillset.org Website: www.skillset.org
Skills for Logistics **Sector:** Freight logistics and wholesaling industries Tel: 01908 313360 E-mail: info@skillsforlogistics.org Website: www.skillsforlogistics.org	**Skillsmart Retail** **Sector:** Retail Tel: 020 7462 5060 E-mail: contactus@skillsmartretail.com Website: www.skillsmartretail.com
SkillsActive **Sector:** Sport and recreation, health and fitness, outdoors, playwork and caravanning industry Tel: 020 7632 2000 E-mail: skills@skillsactive.com Website: www.skillsactive.com	**SummitSkills** **Sector:** Building services engineering Tel: 01908 303960 E-mail: enquiries@summitskills.org.uk Website: www.summitskills.org.uk **The Alliance of Sector Skills Councils (ASSC)** Tel: 08450 725600 E-mail: info@sscalliance.org Website: www.sscalliance.org

The Qualifications and Curriculum Authority (QCA)

83 Piccadilly, London W1J 8QA, Tel: 020 7509 5555, e-mail: info@qca.org.uk

The QCA is a public body, sponsored by the Department for Children, Schools and Families, which performs many functions in England. These include developing and reviewing the national curriculum; working with stakeholders and strategic partners to develop innovative education initiatives; and providing guidance and support. Since December 2008, QCA has also been carrying out the tests and exams support functions of the former National Assessment Agency (NAA), including developing and delivering tests and assessments, ensuring the safe production and administration of national curriculum tests and other assessments, safeguarding the administration of exams in schools and colleges, facilitating good practice within exams offices and offering training and support as well as providing logistical management and ensuring the secure delivery of exam scripts.

During 2009–10, QCA will become the Qualification and Curriculum Development Agency (QCDA) which will have roles in creating, developing and delivering the Government's programmes for the management and reform of qualifications, curriculum and assessment.

Ofqual: Office of the Qualifications and Examinations Regulator

Ofqual is the regulator of qualifications, exams and tests in England, and was created in April 2008. Its main aim is 'to ensure that the whole qualifications system has integrity'. It is responsible for ensuring that the awarding organizations that offer and deliver qualifications have good systems in place, and that they are held to account for their performance; making sure that all qualifications offered by awarding organizations are fair and are comparable with other qualifications; monitoring standards in qualifications, exams and tests, and reporting on their findings, and ensuring that there is fair access to qualifications for all candidates. It also ensures the quality of marking of exams, tests and other assessments to make sure that learners get the results their work deserves, makes sure that the qualifications market provides value for money and meets the needs of learners and employers, and encourages debate about important topics, such as standards of exams and qualifications.

At the time of writing the government is in the process of legislating formally to establish Ofqual as the regulator of qualifications. Until this legislation is passed, Ofqual it will operate as part of QCA and afterwards, the regulator will be accountable to Parliament rather than to government ministers.

Scotland

The Scottish Qualifications Authority (SQA)

Customer Contact Centre, tel 0845 279 1000, fax 0845 213 5000, e-mail customer@sqa.org.uk.

The SQA is the national body for qualifications in Scotland. It is an executive non-departmental public body responsible for the development, accreditation, assessment and certification of all Scottish education and training qualifications other than degrees (and some professional qualifications). Its overall aim is to manage the qualification system below degree level.

At first glance the Scottish qualification system may seem complicated, but the fundamental aim is to provide a learning framework that provides opportunities to all. The SQA are responsible for three types of qualifications: units, courses and Group Awards.

Most SQA-awarded qualifications are made up of a combination of units, but they are qualifications in their own right, representing approximately 40 hours of teaching with additional study. You achieve a unit by passing an assessment.

Courses consist of Standard Grades and six National Courses levels – Access 2 & 3, Intermediate 1 & 2, Higher and Advanced Higher. They are mainly taken at school but some colleges may also offer provision at some levels.

Group Awards qualifications are designed to be taken at college – National Certificates (NCs), Higher National Certificates and Diplomas (HNCs and HNDs) and National Progression Awards (NPAs) – and the workplace: Scottish Vocational Qualifications (SVQs), Professional Development Awards (PDAs) and Customised Awards. A private company or training provider must become an 'approved centre' to deliver SQA qualifications, or work in partnership with a college or training provider.

Standard Grades and National Courses

Standard Grades are generally taken over two years of study in the third and fourth years at secondary school. The courses are made up of different parts, called elements, usually with an exam at the end.

National Courses, with the exception of Access level, are made up of three units plus an external assessment – usually an examination. These can be taken in the fourth, fifth and sixth years at school.

There is a comprehensive appeals system for those who do not perform as well as expected.

About Higher National qualifications

Higher National Certificates (HNCs) and Higher National Diplomas (HNDs) are developed by SQA in partnership with further education colleges, universities, and industry and commerce. They are credible, flexible qualifications that are designed to deliver the skills and knowledge to meet the needs of today's businesses.

National Progression Awards (NPAs)

NPAs are designed to assess a defined set of skills and knowledge in specialist vocational areas. They are mainly used by colleges for short programmes of study.

National Certificates

Primarily aimed at 16–18-year-olds and adults in full-time education, normally at a college. They prepare candidates for employment or further study, by developing a range of skills.

Scottish Vocational Qualifications (SVQs)

SVQs are based on job competence, and recognize the skills and knowledge people need in employment. SVQs can be attained in most occupations and are available for all types and levels of job.

They are primarily delivered to candidates in full-time employment and in the workplace. They are equivalent to NVQs available elsewhere in the UK.

Professional Development Awards (PDAs)

PDAs are qualifications for people who are already in a career and who wish to extend or broaden their skills. In some cases they are designed for people wishing to enter employment. PDAs can be taken at college or the workplace.

Customised Awards

Though these qualifications meet the needs of the majority of organizations, SQA also offers specially designed vocational qualifications at any level to meet an organization's need for skills and expertise.

Scottish Credit and Qualifications Framework

The SQA is a partner in a 'credit' system called the Scottish Credit and Qualifications Framework (SCQF), which helps to quickly make clear the credit value of the multitude of awards available in Scotland.

The framework has 12 levels: from Level 1 for very basic education to Level 12 for doctoral degrees.

More information about SQA and its qualifications can be found at their website www.sqa.org.uk. The Scottish Credit and Qualifications Framework can be found at www.scqf.org.uk.

VALIDATING, EXAMINING AND AWARDING BODIES

A large number of external bodies provide qualifications recognized by accrediting and regulatory bodies. Not all qualifications are available across the entire further education sector: some colleges specialize in particular vocational areas, while others are involved in more general adult education provision. It is therefore important to contact the examining or awarding bodies directly to find which colleges deliver the qualifications desired. However, most colleges deliver courses leading to qualifications awarded by the organizations listed in the following section.

ABC Awards

Robins Wood House, Robins Wood Road, Aspley, Nottingham NG8 3NH, Tel: 0115 854 1616, Fax: 0115 854 1617, e-mail: enquiries_nottingham@abcawards.co.uk, Website: www.abcawards.co.uk

ABC is one of the largest vocational awarding bodies in the United Kingdom with a broad range of qualifications from Entry Level to Level 6, all offering stepping stones to success. Each qualification is assessed in a 'user-friendly' manner and most are delivered in manageable 'bites' of learning. Each qualification is unit-based, enabling centres to select ABC qualifications and units to meet learners' needs. Its operation is supported through its four offices based in Chorley, Nottingham, Reading and Taunton, all providing customer support and a full range of assessment services.

AQA

Stag Hill House, Guildford, Surrey GU2 7XJ, Tel: 01483 506 506, Fax: 01483 300 152, e-mail: mailbox@aqa.org.uk, Website: www.aqa.org.uk

AQA is the largest of the English exam boards currently awarding around 49 per cent of full course GCSEs and 42 per cent of A Levels nationally. As an awarding body AQA offers a broad range of qualifications available through academic or vocational pathways including GCEs, GCSEs, Entry Level Certificates, Basic and Key Skills, Vocationally Related Qualifications and others such as the Diploma, the Extended Project Qualification, and the AQA Baccalaureate among others.

ASDAN

Wainbrook House, Hudds Vale Road, St George, Bristol BS5 7HY, Tel: 0117 9411126, Website: www.asdan.org.uk, e-mail: info@asdan.org.uk

ASDAN is established as a registered charity for 'The advancement of education, by providing opportunities for all learners to develop their personal and social attributes and levels of achievement through ASDAN awards and resources, and the relief of poverty, where poverty inhibits such opportunities for learners.'

ASDAN offers the following qualifications:

- Key Skills (including the Wider Key Skills) Levels 1–4
- Basic Skills (Skills for Life/Adult Literacy and Numeracy/ALAN)
- Certificate in Life Skills (Entry Level) Entry Levels 1–3
- Certificate in Career Planning Levels 1–3

- Certificate of Personal Effectiveness (CoPE) Levels 1 and 2
- Award of Personal Effectiveness (AoPE) Level 1
- Certificate of Personal Effectiveness (CoPE) Level 3
- Personal and Social Development (PSD) Levels 1 and 2
- Personal and Social Development (PSD) Entry 1, 2 and 3
- Volunteering Qualifications Levels 1 to 3
- Employability Entry 2 – Level 3
- Functional Skills
- Personal Progress Entry 1

To find out more about ASDAN visit www.asdan.org.uk

City & Guilds

1 Giltspur Street, London EC1A 9DD, Tel: 020 7294 2800, Fax: 020 7294 2400,
Website: www.cityandguilds.com

City & Guilds is a leading provider of vocational qualifications, awarding over a million certificates every year. Over 50 per cent of all NVQs are awarded by City and Guilds. It offers over 500 qualifications spanning 28 industry areas at all levels from basic skills and pre-entry qualifications to awards that recognize professional achievement at the highest levels.

City & Guilds qualifications are available in over 100 countries through 8,500 centres worldwide and are recognized by employers as proof of the knowledge and skills needed for a wide range of jobs.

Qualifications are available across all areas of industry and commerce and include: agriculture, horticulture and animal care; business and commercial services; computing and information technology; construction and construction services; creative arts; education, training and development; electrical and electronic engineering; hairdressing and beauty services; health and social care; hospitality and catering; leisure and tourism; media and communication; process industries; production and mechanical engineering; retailing, warehousing and sales; science and technology; sport and recreation; textiles, clothing and leather goods; vehicle and transport engineering.

City & Guilds schemes are designed to provide a combination of practical experience and theoretical knowledge. Courses leading to City & Guilds qualifications are run in approved centres, which include schools, colleges of further education, training organizations, companies and adult education institutes. It is possible to study full time, part time, as part of a training scheme, in the evenings, or, where appropriate, through distance learning.

Edexcel Foundation

190 High Holborn, London WC1V 7BH, tel BTEC and NVQ: 0844 576 0026, GCSE: 0844 576 0027, GCE: 0844 576 0025, The Diploma: 0844 576 0028, DiDA and other qualifications: 0844 576 0031, Website: www.edexcel.org.uk

Edexcel is the UK's largest awarding body, operating in over 80 counties and offering a range of international qualifications including GCEs, GCSEs, vocational and business learning and adult literacy and numeracy qualifications that are offered in schools and colleges, through training providers or in the workplace. Edexcel's BTEC qualifications provide a range of widely accessible, high-quality education programmes of study directly related to employment. Edexcel approves nationally recognized qualifications and Certificates of Achievement that equip students both for employment and for further study. These include adult learning qualifications and NVQs. They are delivered through a network of approved centres around the world. It collaborates closely with industry, government and others to ensure that Edexcel programmes serve the interests of individuals, employers and the nations they are taken in.

EDI plc

International House, Siskin Parkway, Middlemarch Business Park, Coventry CV3 4PE, Tel: 08707 202909 (general enquiries), Fax: 02476 516505, e-mail: enquiries@ediplc.com, Website: www.ediplc.com

EDI is an accredited and awarding body offering a wide range of vocational and professional qualifications in the UK and internationally. EDI is accredited to award over 350 vocational qualifications, many of which are available online. Over 1,400 colleges and private training providers are approved to offer EDI qualifications. The EDI website has a qualification search facility found at: www.ediplc.com/Qualifications_Search.asp.

NCFE

Citygate, St James' Boulevard, Newcastle upon Tyne NE1 4JE, tel: 0191 239 8000, fax: 0191 239 8001, e-mail: info@ncfe.org.uk, Website: www.ncfe.org.uk

NCFE is a national awarding body and registered educational charity. It currently offers over 220 nationally accredited qualifications from Entry level up to and including Level 4 as well as NVQs, functional Skills, Diplomas, Apprenticeships and Key Skills. Further qualifications are in development. The NCFE website has a qualifications finder search facility at www.ncfe.org.uk/qualfinder.aspx.

OCR

1 Hills Road, Cambridge, CB1 2EU, Tel: 01223 553998, Fax: 01223 552627, e-mail: general.qualifications@ocr.org.uk, Website: www.ocr.org.uk

OCR is at the forefront of developing qualifications for the 21st century. It offers a range of more than 500 general and vocational qualifications, from GCSEs, A levels and Diplomas to OCR Nationals, NVQs and specialist qualifications. You can find a full index of OCR qualifications here: www.ocr.org.uk/ qualifications/index.html.

Welsh Joint Education Committee

245 Western Avenue, Cardiff CF5 2YX, tel 02920 265000, e-mail info@wjec.co.uk, website www.wjec.co.uk

WJEC is an examining board offering the following major qualifications: General Certificate of Secondary Education (GCSE); Entry Level (EL) and Advanced (A)/Advanced Supplementary (AS) levels and the Welsh Baccalaureate, a new overriding qualification for Wales available at different levels and incorporating GCSEs, A Levels, GNVQs or NVQs. In addition WJEC provides Key Essential Skills and Project and Principal Learning Plans.

JCQ: Joint Council for Qualifications

Veritas House, 125 Finsbury Pavement, London EC2A 1NQ, Tel: 020 7638 4135/4132, Fax: 020 734 4343, e-mail: info@jcq.org.uk, Website: www.jcq.org.uk

The Joint Council for Qualifications (JCQ) was established in 2004 and consists of AQA, City & Guilds, CCEA, Edexcel, OCR, SQA and WJEC, the seven largest providers of qualifications in the UK, offering GCSE, GCE, AEA, Scottish Highers, Entry Level, Vocational and vocationally-related qualifications. The JCQ enables member awarding bodies to act together on a number of issues including providing, wherever possible, common administrative arrangements for the schools and colleges and other providers which offer their qualifications and dealing with the regulators; in responding to proposals and initiatives on assessment and the curriculum.

The National Database of Accredited Qualifications (NDAQ) contains details of qualifications that are accredited by the regulators of external qualifications in England (Ofqual), Wales (DCELLS) and Northern Ireland (CCEA). The website also carries a full alphabetical list of awarding bodies offering qualifications accredited by the regulatory authorities in England, Wales and Northern Ireland. For more information visit www.accreditedqualifications.org.uk.

Part 4

Qualifications Awarded in Universities

ADMISSION TO DEGREE COURSES

Higher Education Institutions (HEIs)

Most institutions have a general requirement for admission to a degree course; special requirements may be in force for particular courses. Requirements are usually expressed in terms of subjects passed at GCE A level and the Higher Grade of the SCE. The universities have a clearing-house to handle applications for university courses, UCAS, www. ucas.ac.uk. All intending students who live in the United Kingdom may obtain information on application procedures from their schools or colleges, or directly from UCAS. The scheme covers all universities and all medical schools. UCAS also has specialist services: the Graduate Teacher Training Registry (GTTR), the UK Postgraduate Application and Statistical Service (UKPASS) and the Conservatoires UK Admissions Service (CUKAS).

HEIs have specific schemes to encourage access and participation in higher education. These can include partnerships with further education colleges that run access to higher education courses.

The Open University

For admission to first-degree courses, no formal educational qualifications are necessary. However, students who have successfully completed one or more years of full-time study at the higher education level (or its equivalent in part-time study) may be eligible for exemption from some credit requirements of the BA degree. The Open University handles its own admissions.

Business Schools

The degrees awarded by the various university business schools are postgraduate and therefore normally require an honours degree as part of their entrance qualification.

AWARDS

The awards made by the universities may be separated into the following categories: first degrees; higher degrees; honorary degrees; first diplomas and certificates; higher diplomas and certificates.

First Degrees

Nomenclature

Various names are given to the first degrees at British universities. At most universities the first degree in Arts is the BA (Bachelor of Arts) degree and the first degree in Science is the BSc (Bachelor of Science) degree. But at the universities of Oxford and Cambridge and at several new universities, the BA is the first degree gained by students in both Arts and Science. In Scotland the first arts degree at three of the four old universities is Master of Arts (MA).

There are numerous variations on the bachelor theme, eg BSc (Econ) (Bachelor of Science in Economics), BCom (Bachelor of Commerce), BSocSc (Bachelor of Social Science), BEng (Bachelor of Engineering), BTech (Bachelor of Technology). The first award in medicine is the joint degrees of MB, ChB (Bachelor of Medicine, Bachelor of Surgery), the designatory letters of which vary from university to university.

Structure of Courses

First-degree courses vary considerably in structure, not only between one university and another but also between faculties in a single university. The degree examination is usually in two sections, Part 1 coming after one or two years of the course and Part II, 'finals', at the end of the course. The first-degree system at some Scottish universities differs substantially from that in English and Welsh universities (see below).

Bachelor Degrees

These degrees, sometimes known as 'ordinary' or 'first' degrees, lead to qualifications such as Bachelor of Arts (BA), Bachelor of Science (BSc) or Bachelor of Medicine (MB).

Each university decides the form and content of its own degree examinations. These vary from university to university.

The first-degree structure in all British universities is based on the Honours degree. Successful candidates in Honours degree examinations are placed in different classes according to their performance, first class being the highest. The other classes given vary from university to university, but the classification most often used is: Class I; Class II (Division 1); Class II (Division 2); Class III. Most graduates who go on to higher academic qualifications, and those entering, for example, the higher grades in the Civil Service or research, normally have an Honours degree of good class.

You can find out more about qualification types in higher education from the Hero website; www.hero.ac.uk.

Number of Subjects Studied

Excluding medicine and dentistry, the broad subject areas are Arts (or Humanities), Social Science, Pure Science and Applied Science. Most students study one main subject selected from one of these areas. It is possible to distinguish many types of degree course according to the number of subjects studied; these types are a variation on three main categories:

- honours course in one to three subjects with or without examinable subsidiary subjects;
- pass or ordinary courses in one to three subjects with or without examinable subsidiary subjects;
- commmon studies for pass and honours in one to three subjects, with or without examinable subsidiary subjects.

Length of Degree Course

First-degree courses may be preceded by a preliminary year, from which students with the appropriate entry qualifications may be exempted. At most universities honours and pass courses in arts, social science, pure and applied science last three or four years, but courses in architecture, dentistry and veterinary medicine usually last five years, and complete qualifying courses in medicine up to six years. Courses in fine arts and pharmacy may last four years; four-year courses exist mainly in double honours schools, especially when they involve foreign languages and a period of study abroad, and in the technological universities, where some courses include a period of integrated industrial training (sandwich courses).

The Scottish First Degree

The distinctive feature of first degrees at some Scottish universities is the Ordinary MA course, which has no counterpart in England and Wales, and the Ordinary BSc course. The function of the Ordinary MA is to provide a broad, general education. Scottish undergraduates are required to show during their first two years of study, over a range of subjects, that they are fit to go on to an honours degree course, which takes a further two years to complete.

Aegrotat Degrees

Candidates who have followed a course for a degree but have been prevented from taking the examinations by illness may be awarded a degree certificate indicating that they were likely to have obtained the degree had they taken the examinations.

Higher Degrees

These comprise:

- some Bachelor's degrees: BPhil, BLitt, etc;
- Master's degrees: MA, MSc, etc;
- Doctor of Philosophy: PhD or DPhil;
- Higher Doctorates: DLitt, DSc, etc.

At Oxford and Cambridge the degree of MA is conferred on any BA of the university without any further course of study or examination after a specified number of years and on payment of a fee. Candidates for a Master's degree at other universities (and at some for the degrees of BPhil, BLitt and BD, which are of equivalent standing) are normally required to have a first degree, although it need not have been obtained in the same university. Master's degrees are taken after one or two years' full-time study. The PhD requires at least two, or more usually three, years of full-time study.

In some universities and faculties students may be selected for a PhD course after an initial year's study or research common to both a PhD and a Master's degree. Candidates for a Master's degree are required either to prepare a thesis for presentation to examiners, who may afterwards question them on it orally, or to take written examination papers; they may be required to do both. All PhD students present a thesis; some may be required to take an examination paper as well. A major development in recent years has been the introduction of MPhil, MSc and similar degrees, awarded at the end of a one- or two-year course in a special topic on the results of a written examination, or a thesis. Higher doctorates are designated on a faculty basis, eg DLitt (Doctor of Letters) and DSc (Doctor of Science). Candidates are usually required to have at least a Master's degree of the awarding university. Senior doctorates are conferred on more mature and established workers, usually on the basis of published contributions to knowledge.

Foundation Degrees

Foundation degrees were established to give people the intermediate technical and professional skills that are in demand from employers and to provide more flexible and accessible ways of studying. Increasing opportunities for employment and career advancement is a priority. Foundation degree content and assessment is therefore designed in consultation with employers. Additional progression routes include links with associated professional qualifications and/ or direct entry to the final year of a relevant Honours level degree.

Provision is available across a range of further education colleges and a number of HEIs.

Honorary Degrees

Most universities confer honorary degrees on persons of distinction in academic and public life, and on others who have rendered service to the university or to the local community. Normally degrees awarded are at least Foundation degree level.

Diplomas and Certificates of Higher Education

Courses for first diplomas and certificates are relatively simple in structure; they usually reach a level lower than that required for the award of a degree. There is usually a carefully defined course in a specialized or vocational subject, lasting one or two years, followed by all candidates. Most courses are full time.

Postgraduate Diplomas and Certificates

Diplomas (eg in public health, social administration, medicine and technology) are awarded either on a full-time, or less often part-time, basis according to the subject and the university. Candidates must usually be graduates or hold equivalent qualifications. Diplomas are awarded after formal courses of instruction and success in written examinations. A Certificate or Diploma in Education is awarded to graduates training to become teachers after one year's full-time study and teaching practice.

Postgraduate Courses

A number of courses for graduates or persons with equivalent qualifications are offered in further education establishments. They include short specialist courses in Management and Business Studies and secretarial courses for graduates.

Business Schools

A Master of Business Administration (MBA) is an internationally recognized postgraduate qualification intended to prepare individuals for middle to senior level general managerial positions. Most programmes contain as their core a number of subjects considered essential for understanding the operations of any enterprise. These are: accounting and finance, operations management, business policy, economics, human resource management, marketing, information systems and strategic planning.

Unlike any other Master's programme, the MBA is not only postgraduate, it is also strongly post experience. A minimum of three years' (often more) work experience at an appropriate level of responsibility is generally expected of applicants. The requirement for a first degree (or equivalent) is sometimes waived for those holding an impressive track record of over five years at managerial level. Approximately one-third of MBA students have an engineering or information technology background. Many undertake the qualification to facilitate change from technical or specialist positions to more generalist ones.

The MBA was conceived originally in the United States at the beginning of the 20th century. Introduced in the United Kingdom in the late 1960s, it did not grow in popularity until the late 1980s. The popularity of this degree in the United Kingdom can be seen in the rapid expansion in the number of providers. There are now over 8,000 graduates each year and the number continues to rise. Welcome though this expansion may be, it calls for vigilance in maintaining quality and standards. To this end, the Association of MBAs (AMBA) operates a system of accreditation.

The accreditation process, which is internationally recognized for all MBA, DBA and Masters in Business and Management (MBM) programmes, measures individual MBA programmes against specific accreditation criteria.

Further information, including a list of accredited MBA programmes, can be obtained from the Association of MBAs, 25 Hosier Lane, London EC1A 9LQ; Tel 020 246 2686, e-mail info@mbaworld.com, Website www.mbaworld.com.

The Association of Business Schools (ABS)

137 Euston Road, London NW1 2AA; Tel 020 7388 0007, Fax 020 7388 0009, E-mail abs@the-abs.org.uk, Website www.the-abs.org.uk

The ABS is the representative body for Management and Business Education. It has all the United Kingdom's leading business schools. The ABS works broadly in three main areas; policy development, promotion and representation and training and development.

The ABS is able to provide general information about the wide range of courses and programmes provided by the United Kingdom's business schools.

First Awards

BA, BEd, BEng, LLB, BSc: with 1st Class, 2nd Class (Divisions 1 and 2), 3rd Class Honours or Pass; or unclassified with or without Distinction.
MEng: awarded to students who successfully complete a course of study which is longer and more demanding than the BEng first degree course in Engineering.
GMus (Graduate Diploma in Music): awarded to those students who complete three years' approved full-time study (or equivalent) in Music and who demonstrate competence in musical performance.
DipHE (Diploma of Higher Education): equivalent in standard and often similar in content to the first two years of an Honours degree course.
Certificates of Higher Education: equivalent to the first year of an Honours degree course.

Higher Awards

MA, MBA, MEd, MSc: for successful completion of an approved postgraduate course of study of 48 weeks' duration (or the part-time equivalent).
MPhil, PhD: for successful completion of approved programmes of supervised research.
DSc, DLitt and DTech: for original and important contributions to knowledge and/or its applications.
Postgraduate Diploma: awarded for the successful completion of an approved postgraduate course of study of 25 weeks' duration (or the part-time equivalent).
Postgraduate Certificate: awarded for the successful completion of postgraduate/post-experience courses of 15 weeks' duration (or the part-time equivalent).

Postgraduate Certificate in Education (PGCE): awarded on completion of a one-year full-time course; candidates must be British graduates or hold another recognized qualification.
Diploma in Professional Studies: available in the fields of education and nursing, health visiting, midwifery and sports coaching. Students normally hold an initial professional qualification. A minimum of two years' experience is normally expected.
Second Bachelor's Degree: Bachelor in Town Planning (BTP).

UNIVERSITY OF ABERDEEN
www.abdn.ac.uk

College of Arts and Social Sciences; www.abdn.ac.uk/about/social-sciences

Aberdeen Business School; www.abdn.ac.uk/business
accountancy, business development, business finance, coaching, economics, enterprise creation, entrepreneurship, finance, innovation, international business, international relations, macroeconomics, management studies, organizational change, property, real estate management; MA(Hons), MBA, MRes, MSc, PgCert, PhD

School of Divinity, History and Philosophy; www.abdn.ac.uk/sdhp
cultural history, divinity, European studies, historical studies, history, history of art, philosophy, religious studies; BD, BTh, DMin, LicTh, MA(Hons), MLitt, MTh, PgDip, PhD

School of Education; www.abdn.ac.uk/education
early childhood studies, music, primary education, professional development; BA(Hons), BEd(Hons), MEd, MPhil, MRes, MSc, Mus(Hons), PGCert, PGDE, PGDip, PhD

School of Language & Literature; www.abdn.ac.uk/sll
Celtic, comparative literature, creative writing, English/literature/language, film and visual culture, French, German and Hispanic studies, Irish–Scottish studies, Latin American studies, linguistics, medieval studies, modern thought, the novel, sociolinguistics; MA, MA(Designated), MA(Hons), MLitt, PhD

School of Law; www.abdn.ac.uk/law
civil, French/German/ Belgian/Spanish law, law (with options in languages, management subjects, music), property law, Roman law; LlB, LlB(Hons), LlM, MPhil, PhD

School of Social Science; www.abdn.ac.uk/socsc
anthropology, gender studies, politics and international relations, social anthropology, ethnology and cultural history, sociology; MA(Designated), MA(Hons), MA Joint or Combined Honours, MLitt, MPhil, MRes, MSc, PGDip, PhD

College of Life Sciences and Medicine; www.abdn.ac.uk/clsm

School of Biological Sciences; www.abdn.ac.uk/biologicalsci
animal ecology, biology, conservation biology, ecology, environmental science, forest conservation, forestry, immunology, marine biology, parasitology, tropical environmental, wildlife management, zoology; BSc(Hons), BSc(Hons, Medical Science), MPhil, MSc, MSc/PGDip, PhD

School of Medical Science; www.abdn.ac.uk/sms
biochemistry, biomedical sciences, biotechnology, genetics, human embryology & development,

immunology, microbiology, molecular biology, neuroscience, pharmacology, physiology, sport & exercise science, sports studies; BSc(Hons), MPhil, MSc, MSc/PGDip, PhD

School of Medicine and Dentistry; www.abdn.ac.uk/medicine-dentistry

dentistry, health science, health studies, medicine,; BDS, BSc, MA, MBChB, MMedSci, MPhil, MSc, PhD

School of Psychology; www.abdn.ac.uk/psychology

patient safety: clinical human factors, psychology, BSc(Hons), MA, MRes, MSc

Rowlet Institute of Nutrition and Health Studies; www.rowletac.uk

health studies/with education; BSc(Hons), MSc, MSc/PgDip, PhD

College of Physical Sciences; www.abdn.ac.uk/cps

School of Engineering; www.abdn.ac.uk/engineering

applied dynamics, chemical engineering, civil engineering, communications & optical engineering, electrical & electronic engineering, environmental hydraulics, mechanical engineering, mechanics of materials, BEng(Hons), BScEng, EnD, MEng, MSc

School of Geosciences; www.abdn.ac.uk/geosciences

Dept of Archaeology; www.abdn.ac.uk/archeology

archaeology with anthropology/Celtic civilisation/history/geography, archaeology of the north; BSc(Hons), MA(Hons), MPhil, PhD

Dept of Geography & the Environment; www.abdn.ac.uk/geography

geography, geoscience, international relations, management studies, marine & coastal resource management, planning, political economy, property, rural surveying, spatial planning; BSc(Hons), MA(Hons), MSc, PgDip/Cert, PhD

Dept of Geology & Petroleum; www.abdn.ac.uk/geology

gas enterprise management, geology, geology and physics, geoscience and geography, integrated petroleum geoscience; BSc(Hons), MA(Hons), MRes, MSc, PgDip/Cert, PhD

School of Natural & Computing Sciences; www.abdn.ac.uk/sncs

Chemistry; www.abdn.ac.uk/chemistry

biomedical materials, chemical science, chemistry, environmental chemistry, materials, medicinal chemistry; BSc(Hons), MChem, MSc, PgDip, PhD

Computing Science; www.csd.abdn.ac.uk/

artificial intelligence, business information systems, computational analysis, computing science, artificial intelligence,business computing/information systems, mathematics, psychology, GIS, computing and e-business/education, information systems and management, knowledge technology, natural language generation; BSc(Hons), MA(Hons), MSc, MSci, PhD

Mathematics; www.maths.abdn.ac.uk/

algebraic/differential geometry, functional analysis, engineering mathematics, mathematics, pure mathematics, relativity theory, topology; BSc(Hons), MA(Hons), MSc, PhD

Physics; www.abdn.ac.uk/physics

natural philosophy, physical sciences, physics, physics with chemistry/geology/philosophy/engineering/mathematics; BSc(Hons), MSc(Hons)

UNIVERSITY OF ABERTAY, DUNDEE
www.abertay.ac.uk

School of Computing & Creative Technologies; www.abertay.ac.uk/studying/schools/ccs

adaptive systems engineering, arts & design, computer arts, computer games/technology, computing & IT, engineering, information technology, networks, sound production, web design & development; BA(Hons), BSc(Hons), DipHE, MProf, MSc/PGDip

Dundee Business School; www.abertay.ac.uk/studying/schools/dbsl

accountancy, business studies, enterprise creation, Europe (law, economy business law), finance, HRM, law, marketing, management, oil and gas accounting, retail marketing, tourism; BA (Hons), Grad Cert, MBA, MSc, PGDip

The School of Contemporary Sciences; www.abertay.ac.uk/studying/schools/ss

bioinformatics, biomedical sciences, biotechnology, built and natural environment, civil engineering, food & consumer studies, food biotechnology, forensic sciences, health sciences, water pollution control; BSc(Hons), DipHE, MSc, MTech, PGDip

The School of Social & Health Sciences; www.abertay.ac.uk/studying/schools/shs

behavioural science, coaching, counselling, criminological studies, forensic psychobiology, media, culture and society, nursing, psychology, sexual/reproductive health, social science, sociology, sport and exercise/management/nutrition/psychology, sports development; BA(Hons), BSc(Hons), Grad Cert, MSc, PGDip

ABERYSTWYTH UNIVERSITY
www.aber.ac.uk

School of Art; www.aber.ac.uk/art
art, art history, fine art, museum and gallery studies; BA(Hons), MA, MPhil, PhD

Institute of Biological, Environmental & Rural Sciences; www.aber,ac.uk/ibers
agriculture, animal science/zoology, biochemistry, biology, conservation/countryside management, environmental science, equine science, genetics, marine and freshwater biology, microbiology, tourism & recreation; BSc(Hons), MPhil, MSc, PhD

Dept of Computer Science; www.aber.ac.uk/cs
artificial intelligence, business information technology, computer graphics, vision and games, internet computing/engineering, mobile computing, open source computing, robotics, software engineering; BEng, BSc(Hons), HND, MEng, MSc, PhD

School of Education & Lifelong Learning; www.aber.ac.uk/sell
education degrees are offered combined with other subjects; BA(Hons), BSc(Hons), MPhil, PGCE, PGD, PhD

Dept of English & Creative Writing; www.aber.ac.uk/en/english
creative writing, English literature, literary studies, postmodern fictions; BA(Hons), MA, PhD

Dept of European Languages; www.aber.ac.uk/eurolangs
French, German, Italian, modern European culture, modern German Studies, romance languages, Spanish; BA(Hons), MA, PhD

Institute of Geography & Earth Sciences; www.ies.aber.ac.uk/
environmental monitoring and analysis/science, geography, GIS and remote sensing, glaciology, human geography, local and regional economic development, physical geography, quaternary environmental change, river basin dynamics; BSc(Hons), MPhil, MRes, MSc, PhD

Dept of History & Welsh History; www.aber.ac.uk/history
economic and social history, European history, medieval and early modern history, modern and contemporary history, politics & modern history, welsh history; BA(Hons), MA, PhD

Dept of Information Studies; www.dis.aber.ac.uk
archive administration, business information, historical and archival studies, information and library studies, information management/systems, records; BA(Hons), BSc(Econ), Dip/Cert, MPhil, MSc(Econ), PhD

Dept of International Politics; www.aber.ac.uk/interpol/en
European politics/ studies, intelligence & strategic studies, intelligence studies, international history, international politics, international history/strategic studies/third world/military history, international relations, modern history & politics; BSc(Econ), MA, MSc, MSc(Econ), PhD

Dept of Law and Criminology; www.aber.ac.uk/law-criminology
business law, criminal law, criminology with applied psychology/law, European law, human rights, law,

law with languages; BA(Hons), BSc(Econ), LlB, LlM, PhD

School of Management and Business; www.aber.ac.uk/en/smb

accounting & finance, business, business economics, business finance, economics, entrepreneurship, international business management, management, marketing; BSc(Econ), MBA, MSc(Econ), PhD

Institute of Mathematical & Physical Sciences; www.aber.ac.uk/en/maps

applied mathematics, statistics, computer science, pure mathematics, physics, planetary and space physics, space science; BSc(Hons), MMath, MPhys, PhD

Dept of Psychology; www.aber.ac.uk/en/psychology

psychology; single Honours or Combined, BSc(Econ), BSc(Hons), PhD

Dept of Sport & Exercise Science; www.aber.ac.uk/sport/exercise

biology & sport science, equine & human sport exercise, sport exercise science, sport & information technology; BSc(Hons), PhD

Dept of Theatre, Film & Television Studies; www.aber.ac.uk/en/tfts

drama & theatre, film & television, film studies, media & communication studies, practising performance, scenography & theatre design, scriptwriting, Welsh medium courses; BA(Hons), MA, MPhil, PhD

Dept of Welsh; www.aber.ac.uk/cymraeg-welsh

Breton, Celtic languages, Celtic studies, Irish and Scottish Gaelic, literature and history of Wales; BA(Hons), MA

ANGLIA RUSKIN UNIVERSITY
www.anglia.co.uk

Faculty of Arts, Law and Social Sciences; www.anglia.co.uken/home/faculties/alss

Dept of English,Communication,Film & Media; www.anglia.ac.uk/ruskin/en/home/faculties/alss/deps/english.media

art, communication, film & media, communication studies, drama, English, English language/language teaching & EFL, English writing, film studies, film, television and theatre writing, publishing, applied linguistics & TESOL, writing; BA(Hons), MPhil, PhD

Anglia Law School; www.anglia.ac.uk/ruskin/en/home/faculties/alss/deps/law

criminology, international business law, law, legal practice, professional legal studies; BA(Hons), LlB, LlD, LlM

Cambridge School of Art; www.anglia.ac.uk/ruskin/en/home/faculties/alss/deps/csoa

children's book illustration, computer games, design and media, fashion design, film, television and theatre, fine art, graphic and web design, illustration, media studies, photography, printmaking; BA(Hons), FdA, MA, MFA

Dept of Humanities & Social Sciences; www.anglia.ac.uk/ruskin/en/home/faculties/alss/deps/hss.

criminology, forensic science and criminology, history, English, philosophy, psychosocial studies, public service, social policy, sociology; BA(Hons), FdA, MPhil, PhD

Dept of Music & Performing Arts; www.anglia.ac.uk/ruskin/en/home/faculties/alss/deps/music

audio technology, contemporary theatre, creative music technology, drama, music, music therapy, performing arts, popular music; BA(Hons), FdADip, MA, MPhil, PhD

Ashcroft International Business School; www.anglia.ac.uk/ruskin/en/home/faculties/aibs

accountancy, business, business economics, business studies, finance, international business law, international management, marketing, tourism management; BA(Hons), BSc(Hons), MA, MBA, MSc

Faculty of Education; www.anglia.co.uk/en/home/faculties/education

childhood studies, cultural services, education, education studies, ESOL, learning through technology, PGCE primary and secondary courses, playwork, primary education/with modern foreign languages, teaching and learning assistants, teaching English (literacy), teaching mathematics (numeracy); BA(Hons), Diplomas, FdA/FdSc Professional Practice, MA, PGCE, UnivCert

Faculty of Health and Social Care; www.anglia/ruskin/en/home/faculties/hsc

children and young people's nursing, community public health nursing, health care, mammographic studies, management and leadership in health and social care, midwifery, nursing (adult, child, learning disabilities, mental health), operating department practice, physiotherapy, public health, radiotherapy & oncology practice, registered nurse (adult, child, learning disabilities, mental health), social work, youth and community work; BSc(Hons), Cambridge FdSc, Cert HE, Dip HE, MSc, PGDip/Cert

Faculty of Science and Technology; www.anglia/ruskin/en/home/faculties/fst

Dept of Built Environment; www.anglia.ac.uk/ruskin/en/home/faculties/fst/departments/builtenv

architecture, architectural technology, building surveying, civil engineering, construction and design, construction management, environmental planning, housing, property and surveying, quantity surveying, real estate management, structural engineering, sustainable construction, town planning; BSc(Hons), FdSc, MSc, PGCert, PGDip

Dept of Computing & Technology; www.anglia.ac.uk/ruskin/en/home/faculties/fst/departments/comptech

animation technology, audio technology, audio, video and music technology, business information systems/technology, computer aided visualisation, computer games, computer networking, computer science, computing, computing and the internet, creative music technology, electronics, forensic computing, information security, information technology, integrated engineering, internet management and web design, internet technology, mechanical engineering, mobile telecommunication, multimedia, new media production technology, on-line design, sustainable design and innovation, web development; BEng(Hons), BSc(Hons), HND

Dept of Optometry and Ophthalmic Dispensing

hearing & audiology, ophthalmic dispensing assistants, ophthalmics, optometric clinic assistants, optometry; BOptom(Hons), BSc(Hons), FdSc, UnivCert

Dept of Psychology

health psychology, psychology, psychology and criminology/music/sociology; BSc(Hons)

Dept of Life Sciences; www.anglia.ac.uk/ruskin/en/home/faculties/fst/departments/lifesciences

animal behaviour, animal welfare, applied biomedical science, biological sciences, cell and molecular biology, coaching science, conservation, DNA analysis, ecology, equine studies, fire investigation, genetics, marine biology, medical biology, microbiology, natural history, sport, health and exercise, sports science, wildlife biology; BSc(Hons), FdSc, MSc, PGDip

---

Degrees validated by Anglia Ruskin University offered at:

COLCHESTER INSTITUTE
www.colchester.ac.uk

Art, design and media

art, fashion textiles, fine art, graphic design, media/video production; BA(Hons), FdA, HNC, MA

Business and management

accountancy, business, e-business, hospitality, logistics & transport, public services, sport, tourism; BA(Hons), DipMan, Foundation degree, HNC, HND, PgDip/Cert

Computing and administration

computing, business administration, systems support, web design; Bsc(Hons), BTEC, Dipl Man, Nat Cert

Construction

brickwork, construction, electrical installations, plumbing, site supervision/management, woodcraft/carpentry/joinery/cabinet making; BSc(Hons), Foundation degree, HNC, NVQs 4 & 5

Education

childhood studies and early years, GCSE (English language, maths, human physiology and health), higher education, numeracy and literacy, teacher training; BA(Hons), Cert in Education, EFT, ESOL, Foundation degree, PGCE, PGCE and CertEd

Engineering

acoustics & noise control, auto/service, repair, welding & fabrication, electronic engineering, mechanical engineering; C&G Certs, Dipl in Acoustics, Foundation degree, HNC

Hairdressing and beauty therapy

aromatherapy, beauty therapy, hairdressing, holistic massage, reflexology; Adv Cert, Dip, NVQs

Health & care

counselling, health, occupational therapy, physiotherapy, social care; BA(Hons), Foundation degree, DipHE

Hospitality and food studies

food & drink service, food preparation & cooking, hospitality supervision; Dips, Nat Dip, NVQs

Music and performing arts

acting, arts business, classical music, dance, instrumental and vocal tuition, jazz and popular music, music education, music technology, musical theatre, performance opportunities, technical theatre, theatre productions; BA(Hons), Foundation degree, MA

ASHRIDGE
www.ashridge.ac.uk

executive coaching, management, organisation consulting, sustainability & responsibility; Doc Orgn Consulting, ExecMBA, MBA, MSc

ASTON UNIVERSITY
www.aston.uk.ac

Aston Business School; www.aston.uk.ac/aston-business-school

accounting, business & management, business computing & IT, business research & consultancy, e-business, economics & management, finance, HRM, international business & management/economics/modern language, international commercial law, investments, IT project management, law, management, administration, marketing, mathematics with economics, operational research & performance management, strategy; BSc(Hons), DBA, Foundation degree, LlB, LlM, MBA, PhD

Centre for Learning, Innovation and Professional Practice; www.aston.uk.ac/clip

curriculum & learning development, learning & teaching, media & learning technologies; Foundation Degree Centre, MA, PG Cert

School of Engineering and Applied Science; www.aston.uk.ac/eas

Chemical Engineering & Applied Chemistry

applied chemistry, biological chemistry, chemical engineering, chemistry

Computer Science

computing science, computing for business, multimedia computing

Electronic Engineering

communications engineering, computer science, electrical & electronic engineering, internet systems

Engineering Systems & Management

construction management/project management

Technology & Enterprise Management

technology & enterprise management

Logistics & Transport Management

logistics, transport management

Mathematics
mathematics, mathematics with computing

Mechanical Engineering & Design
electromechanical engineering, mechanical engineering

Product Design
automotive/ engineering/ industrial/ medical product design, product design & management, sustainable product design; BSc, MChem, MEng, MPhil, MSc, PhD

School of Life and Health Sciences; www.aston.uk.ac/life-health-sciences
applied & human biology, audiology, biomedical science, cell and molecular biology, cognitive neurosciences, health psychology, hearing aid audiology, human biology, infection and immunity, neuroimaging, optometry, pharmacy, psychiatric pharmacy/ therapeutics, psychology; BSc(Hons), GradDip, FD MPharm, MRes, MSc, PGCert/Dip, PhD

School of Languages and Social Sciences; www.aston.uk.ac/ls

Modern Languages & Translation studies
French, German, Spanish, translation studies, international business and modern languages studies course combinations

International Relations, Politics & European Studies
European studies and European language politics: politics with international relations/business/ management

Sociology, International Relations, Politics & European Studies
international relations and business/politics/public policy & management/sociology

English Language
English language, English language and range of subjects for combined honours

Modern Languages & Translation Studies
French, German, Spanish, translation studies, international business and modern languages and numerous subjects for joint honours

Sociology & Public Policy
social sciences, sociology, sociology and business/ computer science/international relations/politics, public policy & management and business/international relations/politics/sociology; BA(Hons), BSc(Hons), MA, MPhil, MRes, MSc, PhD

BANGOR UNIVERSITY
www.bangor.ac.uk

College of Arts and Humanities; www.bangor.ac.uk/cah

Creative Studies & Media; www.bangor.ac.uk/creative.industries
creative studies, creative writing, film, journalism, media studies, theatre

English; www.bangor.ac.uk/english
creative writing, English, English literature, English language, journalism, publishing, theatre studies

History, Welsh History & Archeology; www.bangor.ac.uk/history
archeology, contemporary history, history, medieval & early modern history, Welsh history

School of Linguistics & English Language; www.bangor.ac.uk/linguistics
creative writing, English language, English literature, linguistics

School of Modern Languages; www.bangor.ac.uk/ml
French, German, Italian, Spanish (with another subject)

School of Music; www.bangor.ac.uk/music
music, music technology

Theology & Religious Studies; www.bangor.ac.uk/trs
religious studies, theology, study of religion

School of Welsh
Welsh Centre for Research on Bilingualism; www. bilingualism.bangor.ac.uk

bilingualism; BA(Hons), BD, BMus, Diploma, MA, MMus, MPhil, MTh, PgDip, PhD

College of Business, Social Sciences and Law; www.bangor.ac.uk/cbss

Bangor Business School; www.bangor.ac. uk/business

accounting, banking, business studies, economics, finance, leisure management, management, marketing

School of Social Sciences; www.bangor.ac. uk/so

criminology and criminal justice, health and social care, social policy, social work, social studies, sociology

School of Law; www.bangor.ac.uk/law

law, criminal justice, commercial law, law & devolved goverments; BA(Hons), DBA, HND, LlB, LlM, MA, MBA, MSc, MPhil, PGDip, PhD

College of Education and Lifelong Learning; www.bangor.ac.uk/cell

education, design and technology, secondary education, post-11 learning support studies, early childhood and learning support studies, PGCE primary/secondary lifelong learning; range of subjects (combined studies) offered at BA Degree, Certificate, Diploma, FdA, HNC/HND levels

Academic Development Unit; www.bangor. ac.uk/adu

Welsh for adults; BSc(Hons), EdMed, FdA, MA, MEd, MMusD, MPhil, MTh, PGCE, PhD

College of Natural Sciences; www. bangor.ac.uk/cns

CNS School of Biological Sciences; www. bangor.ac.uk/biology

biology, biomedical science, cancer biology, ecology, molecular biology, zoology, zoology with animal behaviour/animal ecology/conservation/marine zoology; BSc(Hons), Dipl, MA, MBiol, MPhil, MRes, MSc, MZool, PhD

School of Environment, Natural Resources, & Geography; www.bangor.ac.uk/senr

environmental planning and management/science, forest ecosystems, forestry, geography, sustainable development, terrestrial and marine ecology; BA/BSc(Hons), BSc(Hons), MA, MEnvSci, MPhil, MSc, PhD

School of Ocean Sciences; www.bangor.ac. uk/sos

coastal/geological oceanography, marine biology/environmental studies/science/vertebrate zoology, oceanography; BSc(Hons), MMBiol, MMSci, MOcean, MPhil, MSc, PhD

Welsh Institute for Natural Resources; www.bangor.ac.uk/wnr

College of Health & Behavioural Sciences; www.bangor.ac.uk/cohabs

School of Healthcare Sciences; www. bangor.ac.uk/healthcaresciences

health studies, health science, midwifery, nursing, occupational therapy, pharmacology, operating department practice, radiography & allied health professions; BN(Hons), BSc(Hons), BMidw, DipHE, GradCert/Dip, MPhil, PhD,

School of Medical Sciences; www.bangor. ac.uk/sms

behavioural neurology, clinical and functional brain imaging, molecular science for medicine; MSc, PGDip/Cert(HE), PhD

School of Psychology; www.bangor.ac.uk/pschycology

child & language development, clinical & health psychology, neuropsychology, psychology; BSc(Hons), MSc, PhD

School of Sport, Health & Exercise Science; www.bangor.ac.uk/sport

sport science, sport, health and exercise, physical education, exercise science; BSc(Hons), MPhil, MSc, PhD

Institute of Medical & Social Research; www.bangor.ac.uk/imscar

dementia & ageing, health economics, public health; PhD

College of Physical and Applied Sciences; www.bangor.ac.uk/copas

School of Chemistry; www.chemistry. bangor.ac.uk/

analytical chemistry, chemistry, chemistry with bio-molecular sciences, environmental chemistry, marine chemistry, molecular science for medicine; BSc, MChem, MSc, PGDiploma, PhD

School of Electronics; www.eng.bangor.ac. uk/

computer systems engineering, electronic engineering, electronics (hardware systems/software programming), electronics for business (banking and finance/business law/business management), music

technology; BEng(Hons), BSc(Hons), MEng(Hons), MSc, PhD

School of Computer Science; www.cs. bangor.ac.uk

computer science, internet systems and e-commerce, creative technologies, information and communications technology, computer systems engineering, electronic engineering; BA(Hons), BEng(Hons), MEng(Hons), MPhil, MRes, MSc, PhD

UNIVERSITY CENTRE BARNSLEY
www.barnsley.hud.ac.uk

Art & Design
contemporary crafts design/visual arts, interdisciplinary art & design; BA(Hons)

Construction
construction, project management; BSc(Hons), FdSc, HNC

Business
business administration, business management; BA(Hons), FdA, MBA

Computing
animation, digital film, film, multimedia, music and enterprise; BA(Hons), FdSc

Education & Training
early years, education & training, numeracy for teachers, post-compulsory education and training,

professional development; BA(Hons), CertEd, FdA, MA/PGDip/PGCert, PGCE

Human & Health Sciences
health & community studies, holistic therapies, psychological studies, social sciences; BSc(Hons), FdSc

Media & Humanities
history and English, journalism & media production; BA(Hons), FdA

Music
music production & sound recording, popular music and promotion; BA(Hons)

Sciences
Diploma in Professional Studies (resource and waste management)

UNIVERSITY OF BATH
www.bath.ac.uk

Faculty of Engineering and Design; www.bath.ac.uk/engineering

Architecture & Civil Engineering; www. bath.ac.uk/ace

architectural engineering: environmental design, construction management, architecture, civil engineering, conservation of historic buildings/historic gardens & cultural landscapes; BEng, BSc, EngD, MArch, MEng, MPhil, MSc, PGCert, PhD

Chemical Engineering; www.bath.ac.uk/ chem-eng

biochemical engineering, chemical and bioprocess engineering, chemical engineering, environmental

chemical engineering; BEng, EngD, MEng, MPhil, MSc, PhD

Electronic & Electrical Engineering; www. bath.ac.uk/elec-eng

communication engineering, communications, computers, digital communications, electrical & electronic engineering, electrical power engineering, electrical power systems, electronics, mechanical engineering, mechatronics, space science & technology, wireless systems; BEng, EngD, MEng, MPhil, MSc, PhD

Mechanical Engineering; www.bath.ac.uk/ mech-eng

aerospace engineering, automotive engineering, dynamics and control, engineering design, fluid power systems, mechanical and electrical engineering, manufacturing, mechatronics, medical engineering, power transmission & motion control systems, sports engineering, technology management; EngD, MEng, MPhil, MSc, PhD

Faculty of Humanities and Social Science; www.bath.ac.uk/hss

Dept of Economics; www.bath.ac.uk/economics
economics, globalisation & international policy analysis, international development, politics, wellbeing & human development; BSc(Hons), MPhil, MRes, PhD

Dept of Education; www.bath.ac.uk/education
childhood, youth & education studies, coach education, education, sport, sports development, sports performance, TESOL; BA(Hons), EdD, FdSc, MA, MPhil, MRes, PGCE, PhD, ProfPGCE

Dept of European Studies & Modern Languages; www.bath.ac.uk/esml
contemporary European politics, European cinema studies, international politics, international security, interpreting and translating, modern languages & European studies, politics ; BA(Hons), BSc(Hons), MA, MPhil, PGDip, PhD

Dept of Psychology; www.bath.ac.uk/psychology
health psychology, psychology, science, risk and health communication,; BSc(Hons), MPhil, MSc, PhD

Department of Social and Policy Sciences; www.bath.ac.uk/soc-pl
business & community, death & society, European social policy, globalisation & international policy analysis, social policy & administration, social research, social sciences, social work & applied social studies, sociology, wellbeing & human development; BSc, MPhil, MRes, MSc, PhD

Faculty of Science; www.bath.ac.uk

Dept of Biology & Biochemistry; www.bath.ac.uk/bio-sci
biology, biochemistry, biosciences, industrial biotechnology & enterprise, integrated molecular & cellular biology, regenerative medicine; BSc(Hons), MPhil, MRes, PhD

Dept of Chemistry; www.bath.ac.uk/chemistry
chemistry, chemistry for drug discovery; BSc(Hons), MChem, MSci, PhD

Dept of Computer Science; www.bath.ac.uk/comp-sci
advanced computer systems, computer information systems, computer science; BSc(Hons), EngD, MComp, MSc, PhD

Dept of Mathematics; www.bath.ac.uk/math-sci
mathematical biology, mathematical sciences, mathematics, modern applications of mathematics, statistics; BSc(Hons), MMath, MSc, PhD

Dept of Natural Sciences; www.bath.ac.uk/nat-sci
biology, chemistry, pharmacology, physics; BSc(Hons), MSci

Dept of Pharmacy & Pharmacology www.bath.ac.uk/pharmacy
anti-cancer drug design; pharmaceutical practice and therapeutics, pharmacology, pharmacy; MPharm, MPharmacol, PhD

Dept of Physics; www.bath.ac.uk/physics
mathematics and physics, physics, physics with computing; BSc, MSc, MPhil, MPhys, PhD

School of Management; www.bath.ac.uk/management
accounting & finance, action research, education management, international management & modern languages, management; BSc(Hons), DBA, EngD, MBA, MPhil, MRes, MSc, PhD

School for Health; www.bath.ac.uk/health
health practice, healthcare, healthcare informatics, information governance, population health, sport and exercise medicine/science, sports physiotherapy; BSc(Hons), MD, MPhil, MS, PGDip, PhD

Professional Doctorate in Health Division for Lifelong Learning; www.bath.ac.uk/learning-partnerships
range of subjects offered; BA(Hons), BSc(Hons), MA

BATH SPA UNIVERSITY
www.bathspa.ac.uk

Bath School of Art and Design; www. artbathspa.ac.uk

art, ceramics, fine art, graphic communication, interactive multimedia, media communication, textile design studies, fine art; BA(Hons), FdA, MFA, MPhil, PhD

Development and Participation; www. bathspa.ac.uk/schools/development-and-participation

School of Education; www.bathspa.ac.uk/ schools/education

early years education, education studies, FE management, global citizenship, international education, primary education studies, primary education studies for teaching assistants, PGCE (primary (3–11)/ middle years (7–14)/ secondary (11–16); range of subjects), professional studies, TESOL; FD, GradCert, MA/MTeach, PGCE, PGCert/Dip

School of English and Creative Studies; www.ecs.bathspa.ac.uk

broadcasting, creative media practice and broadcast media production, creative writing, English literature, fiction, non-fiction, poetry, performance and script writing, publishing; BA(Hons), MA, PhD

The School of Historical and Cultural Studies; www.bathspa.ac.uk/schools/ historical-and-cultural-studies

contemporary religions, cultural studies, history, Irish studies, media communications, film and screen studies; BA(Hons), MPhil, PhD

Music and the Performing Arts; www. bathspampa.com

commercial music, creative arts, creative music technology, dance, drama, and performing arts, music; BA(Hons), FdA, FdMus, MA, PhD

Science and the Environment; www. ssebathspa.com

biology, development geography, diet and health, environmental science, food nutrition and consumer protection, geography, remote sensing, tourism management; BA(Hons), BA/BSc, BSc(Hons), MPhil, MSc, PhD

School of Social Sciences; www.bathspa.ac. uk/schools/social-science

business and management, health and social care management, health studies, management and management systems, psychology, sociology; BA/ BSc(Hons), BSc(Hons), DipHE, Foundation degree

UNIVERSITY OF BEDFORDSHIRE
www.beds.ac.uk

Faculty of Creative Arts, Technologies & Science; www.beds.ac.uk/departments/ cats

Bedfordshire Institute of Media and the Creative & Performing Arts; www.beds.ac. uk/departments/bm

Div of Art & Design

advertising design, animation, art and design, fashion design, fine art, graphic design, illustration, interior architecture, new media and internet technologies, video art

Div of Journalism & Communication

creative writing, journalism, media arts, media practices, PR, sport journalism

Div of Media Arts & Production

documentary, mass communications, media arts, media, culture and technology/performance/ production, music technology, new media and internet technologies, television production

Div of Performing Arts & English

children's literature & culture, contemporary theatre/ dance and professional practice, education studies, English, English studies, performing arts, theatre studies; BA(Hons), FdA, MA, MRes, PhD

Dept of Computing & Information Systems; www.beds.ac.uk/departments/computing

artificial intelligence, robotics, computer animation/ games development/networking/science/security & forensics, information systems, mobile computing, software engineering; BSc(Hons), FdSc, MSc

Div of Science

biomedical science, biotechnology, biological sciences environmental sciences, forensic science, medical science, nutritional sciences, nutritional therapy; BScHons, FdSc, MSc, PgCert, PgDip

Faculty of Health and Social Sciences; www.beds.ac.uk/departments/ healthsciences

Dept of Acute Health Care; www.beds.ac. uk/departments/acute

Dept of Community Practice

Dept of Midwifery & Child Health

accident and emergency nursing, acute management of patients, advanced nursing studies, practice clinical science, anaesthetic practice, care management, complementary therapy, contraception and sexual health, coronary care, dental nursing, dental practice management, diabetes, health studies, holistic practice, intensive care, learning disabilities, medical education, midwifery, neonatal care, nursing (learning disabilities/mental health), nursing practice (accident and emergency/coronary care/intensive care/neonatal/perioperative critical care/spinal cord injuries), nursing, osteopathy, pain management, palliative care, patient safety, psychosocial intervention, public health, resource management, respiratory, social work, surgical care; BSc(Hons), FdA, FdSc, MSc, PGDip/Cert

Dept of Applied Social Studies; www.beds. ac.uk/departments/appliedsocialstudies

applied social studies, criminology, early years care, health and social care, social work, sociology, systemic leadership and organisation, systemic therapy, young people's services, youth and community studies, youth justice; BSc(Hons), FdA, FdSc, MSc, ProfDoc

Div of Psychology; www.beds.ac.uk/ departments/psychology

applied psychology, counselling and therapies, criminal behaviour, criminology, health psychology, psychology, crime/ criminal behaviour, social psychology; BSc(Hons), CertHE, FdA, MSc, PhD

Bedfordshire & Hertfordshire Postgraduate Medical School; www. beds.ac.uk/departments/bhpms

clinical science/clinical science (diabetes), dental education, medical education, public health, sexual health; MA, MSc, PGDip, PGCert

Institute for Health Research; www.beds. ac.uk/researchir

psychological approach to health & management, public health, research & evaluation; MSc, PhD

Institute of Applied Social Research; www.beds.ac.uk/research/lasr

child & family welfare, crime, vulnerable young people, youth justice; ProfDoc

University of Bedfordshire Business School www.beds.ac.uk/departments/ ubbs

accounting, advertising, air management, sport studies, arts management, beauty therapy and spa management, business decision/management/studies (e-business/finance/business studies/marketing), commercial law, entrepreneurship,event management, finance and business management, football studies, retail management, HRM, information systems, intercultural communication, international business and management/finance and banking/ HRM/tourism, international finance, international tourism management, law/with criminology/management, leisure and business management, logistics and supply chain business management, marketing communications, marketing and business management, marketing, media practices, PR, project management, sport development/management/tourism, strategic leadership and management, travel and tourism; BA(Hons), BSc(Hons), DBA, FdA, LlB, LlM, MA, MBA, MSc

Faculty of Education and Sport; www. beds.ac.uk/departments/ecs

School of Education; www.beds.ac.uk/ departments/schoolofeducation

applied education studies, disability studies, early years education, education studies/practice, mathematics enhancement course/education key stage 2/3 middle years/primary education with Italian, Spanish/secondary, post-compulsory education, qualified teacher status primary education

THE QUEEN'S UNIVERSITY OF BELFAST
www.qub.ac.uk

School of Biological Sciences; www.qub.ac.uk/schools/biological sciences

agricultural biochemistry, biological sciences, ecology, environmental biology, evolution behaviour and environmental economics, food quality, safety and nutrition, genetics, land use & environmental management technology, land environmental sustainability, marine biology, microbiology, molecular biology, rural sustainability, zoology; BSc(Hons), MSc, PGDip, PhD

School of Chemistry and Chemical Engineering; www.ch.qub.ac.uk

chemistry, medicinal chemistry, chemistry with forensic analysis, chemical engineering, chemical enzymology, process engineering; BSc(Hons), MSci, BEng, MEng, MSc, PGDip, PhD

School of Education; www.qub.ac.uk/schools/school of education

applying psychology to education, arts, culture and society, autistic spectrum disorders, coaching and mentoring, education, e-learning, diversity and inclusion, guidance and counselling, initial teacher education, leadership and management in education, management, management and business studies, personal and civic education business and HR, social and community development, TESOL; AdvCertEd, DASE, EdD, MA, MEd, MSc, MSSc, PGCE, PGDip/Cert, UnivCert, BA(Hons)

School of Electronics, Electrical Engineering and Computer Science; www.qub.ac.uk/schools/eeec

business information technology, computer and electronic security, computer games design and development, computer science, computing and infordscapen technology, creative multimedia, educational multimedia, electrical and electronic engineering, electronics, telecommunications, web technology; BEng, BSc, MEng, MSc, MPhil, PhD

School of English; www.qub.ac.uk/schools/SchoolofEnglish

creative writing, English, English language & linguistics, Irish writing, linguistics, medieval studies, modern literary studies, modern poetry, reconceiving the Renaissance; BA(Hons), MA, PhD

School of Geography, Archaeology and Palaeoecology; www.qub.ac.uk/schools/gap

archaeology, dating and chronology, environmental change, geography, landscape, heritage & environment, palaeoecology; BA(Hons), BSc(Hons), MSc, PhD

School of History and Anthropology; www.qub.ac.uk/schools/SchoolofHistoryandAnthroplogy

ancient history, anthropological studies, ethnomusicology, Irish history, modern history, social anthropology, (interdisciplinary arts); BA(Hons), GradDip, MA, MPhil, PhD

School of Languages, Literatures and Performing Arts; www.qub.ac.uk/schools/SchoolofLanguages Literatures andPerformingArts

drama studies, film studies, French studies, German studies, Irish & Celtic studies, Spanish & Portugese studies; BA(Hons), MA, PhD

Queen's University Management School; www.qub.ac.uk/schools/mgt

accounting, accounting & finance, actuarial science and risk management, business economics, economics, finance, management, international business, international business with a modern language, management & information systems, new venture, sustainable management; BSc(Hons), MSc, MScs, eratiMBA, PhD

School of Mathematics and Physics; www.qub.ac.uk/schools /Schoolof MathematicsandPhysics

applied mathematics, computer science and physics, pure mathematics, operational research, statistics, physics with astronomy, physics with medical applications, theoretical physics; BSc(Hons), GradDip, MSc, MSci, PhD

School of Mechanical and Aerospace Engineering; www.qub.ac.uk/schools/SchoolofmechanicalandAerospaceEngineering

aerospace engineering, internal combustion engines, mechanical and manufacturing engineering, product design and development aerospace – integrated aircraft technologies, polymers; BEng, MEng

School of Medicine, Dentistry and Biomedical Sciences; ww.qub.ac.uk/schools/mdbs

biomedical science, clinical dentistry, dentistry, human biology, interprofessional health and social studies, medicine surgery, molecular medicine, mental health, obstetrics, pain science and practice, public health; BCh, BSc(Hons), BDS, DAO, Diploma, MB, MD, MSc

School of Music and Sonic Arts; www.mu.qub.ac.uk

acoustics and psychoacoustics, composition, composition & creative practice, electro-acoustic composition, Irish traditional music, musicology, music technology, performance, sonic arts, sound design, sound engineering; BMus, BSc(Hons), MA, PhD

School of Nursing and Midwifery; www.qub.ac.uk/schools/SchoolofNursingandMidwifery;

nursing sciences – adult branch/children's branch/ learning disability branch /mental health branch, maternal and child health, midwifery sciences, midwifery studies, continuing professional development, evaluation of complex healthcare interventions; BSc(Hons) Diploma, MPhil, PhD, DnursingPractice

School of Pharmacy; www.qub.ac.uk/schools/SchoolofPharmacy

clinical pharmacy, community pharmacy, pharmacist prescribing, pharmacy; MPharm, MSc, PGCert/Dip

School of Planning, Architecture and Civil Engineering; www.qub.ac.uk/schools/SchoolofPlanningArchitectureand CivilEngineering

architecture, civil engineering, durability of structures, environmental engineering, environmental planning, management, construction and project management, spatial regeneration, urban and rural design, water resources; BSc(Hons), MSc, MArch, MPhil, PhD

School of Politics, International Studies and Philosophy; www.qub.ac.uk/schools/SchoolofPoliticsInternationalStudies andPhilosophy

cognitive science, comparative ethnic conflict, Eur opean integration and public policy, gender and society, international politics, international studies, Irish Politics, law with politics, legislative studies and practice, philosophy, political philosophy, politics, politics, economics & philosophy, violence, terrorism and security; BA(Hons), LlB, MA, MRes, MPhil, PhD

School of Psychology; www.psych.qub.ac.uk

atypical child development, child and adolescent psychology, clinical psychology, political psychology, psychology, psychology studies; BSc(Hons), MSc, DocClinPsych, PhD DocEducational

School of Sociology, Social Policy and Social work; www.qub.ac.uk/schools/SchoolofSociologySocialPolicy SocialWork

applied social studies, criminology, gender studies, social policy, social work, social research methods, sociology; BA(Hons), BSW, MA, MSc, DChild Doctorate in Childhood Studies

UNIVERSITY OF BIRMINGHAM
www.bham.ac.uk

College of Arts and Law; www.law.bham.ac.uk

School of Archaeology and Antiquity; www.iaa.bham.ac.uk

archeology, archeology and heritage management, ancient history, Byzantine, Ottoman, and modern Greek, classics and ancient history, classics & the classical world, eastern Mediterranean history, Greece and the Greeks; BA(Hons), MA, MPhil, diploma, PhD

Birmingham Law School; www.about.bham.ac.uk

commercial law, criminal law & criminal justice, European law, international commercial law, English law, law, law with business/ French/German, legal studies (grad dip); LlB, LlM, MPhil/MJur/PhD

English, Drama and American & Canadian Studies; www.weblearn.bham.ac.uk

American studies and film, American literature & film history, business and American studies, applied linguistics, art history and music, creative writing, critical discourse, culture & communication, cultures, drama and theatre arts, English, English language, English linguistics, film studies, history and cultures, intelligence studies, languages, linguistics, literary linguistics, medieval English and history, philosophy, theology and religion, TransAtlantic studies, US foreign policy; BA(Hons), BSc(Hons), MPhil, PhD

School of History and Cultures; www. historycultures.bham.ac.uk
African studies/ with anthropology/ development, ancient & medieval, archaeology and anthropology, Caribbean literature, contemporary history, cultural heritage of Shakespeare's England, early modern history, economic & social history, history, history and social science, history of Christianity, modern European history, modern history, Reformation and early modern studies, Shakespeare, Stratford-upon-Avon and the cultural history of Renaissance England, social research (economic & social history), twentieth century British history, war studies, West Midlands history, world war studies; BA(Hons), MA, MPhil, PGDip, PhD

School of Languages, Cultures, Art History and Music; www.about.bham.ac.uk/colleges/artslaw/lcam
Centre for European Languages & Culture
culture, society & communication, European studies, French, gender studies, German, Hispanic, humanities, Italian, modern European cultures, translation studies
Centre for Modern Languages
Japanese
Dept of History of Art
history of art
Dept of Music
composition, editing, musicology, performance, performance practice

The School of Philosophy, Theology and Religion; www.about.bham.ac.uk/colleges/artslaw/ptr
biblical studies, electronic scholarly editing, global ethics, history of Christianity, inter-religious relations, Islam and Christian–Muslim relations, Islamic studies, Jewish and holocaust studies, patristics and medieval theology, philosophy, philosophy of language and linguistics, philosophy of mind and psychology, philosophy of religion and ethics, pentecostal and charismatic studies, politics and religion, practical theology, Quaker studies, religion and culture, Sikh studies, theology and religion, theology ethics; BA(Hons), BMus, MA, MPhil, PhD

College of Engineering and Physical Sciences; www.about.bham.ac.uk/colleges/eps

School of Chemistry; www.chem.bham.ac.uk
chemical biology, chemistry and/with analytical science/bioorganic chemistry/pharmacy, materials chemistry, molecular processes and theory, molecular synthesis

School of Chemical Engineering; www.eng.bham.ac.uk/chemical
advanced chemical engineering, air pollution management and control, biochemical engineering, chemical engineering, chemical engineering science, chemical and energy engineering, formulation engineering, food safety, hygiene and management

School of Civil Engineering; www.eng.bham.ac.uk/civil
civil engineering, civil and energy engineering, geotechnical engineering, railway systems engineering and integration, road management and engineering, water resources technology and management

School of Computer Science; www.csbham.ac.uk
artificial intelligence, computer science with business software engineering, computer security, electronic and software engineering, intelligent systems engineering, internet software systems, mathematics and computer science, natural computation

School of Electrical, Electronic and Computer Engineering; www.eece.bham.ac.uk
communications engineering (satellite and mobile), communications networks, computer and communications systems engineering, electronic and electrical engineering, electronic and software engineering, electrical and energy engineering, electronic, electrical and computer engineering, embedded systems, interactive digital media, multimedia and interactive computer systems

School of Mathematics; www.mat.bham.ac.uk
analysis, fluid dynamics and multicriteria optimisation, combinatorics, finite group theory, mathematical engineering, mathematical logic, mathematics, mathematics with business management/

psychology/philosophy, mathematics and sport science, pure mathematics and computer science, theoretical physics and applied mathematics

School of Mechanical Engineering; www. eng.bham.ac.uk/mechanical

mechanical engineering, mechanical engineering (biomedical), engineering with business, engineering management, operations management, project management

School of Metallurgy and Materials; www. mat.bham.ac.uk

materials, materials engineering, materials science & technology, materials for sustainable energy technologies, metallurgy, biomaterials, engineered materials for high performance applications/in aerospace and related technologies, science and engineering of materials , sports science and materials technology

School of Physics and Astronomy; www.ph. bham.ac.uk

medical and radiation physics, physics, physics and astrophysics, physics and tehnology of nuclear reactors, physics with nanoscale physics, physics with particle physics and cosmology, theoretical physics, theoretical physics and applied mathematics, radioactive waste management and decommissioning; BEng, BnatSci, BSc(Hons), DEng, MEng, MPhil, MRes, MSc, MSci, PGDip/Cert, PhD

College of Life and Environmental Sciences; www.about.bham.ac.uk/colleges/les

School of Biosciences; www.bioscience. bham.ac.uk

analytical genomics, biochemistry, biology, biotechnology, conservation and utilisation of plant genetic resources, environmental biology, genetics, human biology, microbiology, molecular and cellular biology, molecular mechanistic toxicology, ornithology, plant biology, toxicology, zoology

School of Geography, Earth and Environmental Sciences; www.gees.bham. ac.uk

air pollution management & control, applied meteorology & climatology, earth sciences, economics and geography, enterprise, environment and place, environmental geoscience, environmental health, environmental management, environmental planning, geography, geology and geography, geology, public & environmental health science, river environmental

management, safety & the environment, science of occupational health

School of Psychology; www.psychology. bham.ac.uk

brain imaging and cognitive neuroscience, clinical criminology, clinical psychology, cognition and computational neuroscience, cognitive behaviour therapy, cognitive neuropsychology and rehabilitation, criminological psychology, forensic psychology, neuroscience, psychology

School of Sport and Exercise Sciences; www.sportex.bham.ac.uk

mathematics and sports science, sport and exercise, sports science and materials technology; PG Studentships available, BSc(Hons), Clin, ForenPsyD, MPhil, MRes, MSc, PhD, PsyD, PGDip, PhD, PGDips

College of Medical and Dental Sciences; www.about.bham.ac.uk/colleges/mds

The Five Schools of the College are; Cancer Sciences, Clinical and Experimental Medicine, Dentistry, Health and Population Sciences, Immunity and Infection; biomedical materials science, cancer, cardiovascular sciences, dental hygiene and therapy, dental surgery, dentistry, health sciences, hormones & genes, immunity & infection ,medical science, medicine, medicine and surgery, neuroscience, nursing, physiotherapy; BDS, BMedSci, BSc(Hons), BNurs, DDS, MBChB, MD

College of Social Sciences; www.about. bham.ac.uk/colleges/socialsciences

Birmingham Business School; www. business.bham.ac.uk

accounting and finance, business and American studies, business management, business management with communications, development economics, economic development research and policy, economic policy, economics, environmental and natural resource economics, European business management, geography and urban and regional planning, geography, HRM, international accounting and finance, international business, international economics, international marketing, international money and banking, investments, management, marketing, marketing communications, mathematical economics & statistics, mathematical finance, money, banking & finance, planning, political science, social policy, urban and regional planning, urban and regional studies, urban governance; BSc Economics,

BSc(Hons), Dip, MSc, MBA, DBA, MPhil, PhD PGCert, PGDip, UCert

School of Education; www.education. bham.ac.uk

applied golf management studies, autism, autism spectrum disorders, bilingualism in education, childhood, culture and education, dyslexia studies, education and learning, education for health professionals, educational psychology, English language and literature in education, hearing impairment, inclusion and special educational needs, international studies in education, it and education, leaders and leadership in education, learning and learning contexts, learning difficulties/ disabilities (severe, profound and complex), multisensory impairment (deafblindness), sport, physical education and coaching science, social, emotional and behavioural difficulties, speech and language difficulties, sports coaching, teacher training (early years, general primary, secondary subject courses) – (English, geography, history and citizenship, mathematics, modern foreign languages, physical education, religious education, biology, chemistry, physics), TEFL, visual impairment; AdCert, BA(Hons), BPhil, ChildPsyD, EdD, EdPsychD, MEd, MPhil, PGCE, PGCert/Dip, PhD

School of Government and Society; www. about.bham.ac.uk/colleges/ socialsciences/governmentsociety

aid management, central and east European studies, conflict, security and development, ethnicities and culture, European politics, governance and democratic participation, governance and development management, health services management, health care policy and management, international development, international political economy of development, international relations, international studies, leading public service change and organisational development, local government studies, local policy and politics, media, culture and society, political economy, politics and religion, poverty reduction and development management, public administration, public service commissioning, Russian studies, society and economics, social and political theory, social policy, social research, social work, sociology; BA(Hons), BSc(Hons), GradDip/Cert, MA, MPhil, MSc, PhD

The School of Social Policy (The Health Services Management Centre; Institute of Applied Social Studies); www.hsmc.bham. ac.uk; www.iass.bham.a.uk

health and social care, health care policy and management, improvement, leadership for health services, leading public service change and organisational development, public service commissioning, social policy, social work; MA, MSc, PGDip

---

Degrees validated at the University of Birmingham offered at:

SCHOOL OF EDUCATION, SELLY OAK
www.education.bham.ac.uk

applied golf management studies, autism, bilingualism in education, childhood, culture and education, dyslexia studies, education for health professionals, English language and literature in education, educational psychology, hearing impairment, inclusion and special educational needs, international studies in education, IT and education, leaders and leadership in education, learning and learning contexts, learning difficulties/ multisensory impairment, sports coaching, teacher training – primary courses; early years, general primary/secondary subject courses (English, geography, history and citizenship, mathematics, modern foreign languages, physical education, religious education, biology, chemistry, physics), TEFL, visual impairment; AppEd, BA, ChildPsyD, EdPsychD, MPhil, PhD, PGCE

UNIVERSITY COLLEGE BIRMINGHAM
www.ucb.ac.uk

adventure international tourism management, business enterprise, early childhood studies, entertainment management, food and consumer management food and consumer tourism management, food marketing management, hospitality business management, hospitality management, learning and teaching in vocational subjects, early years marketing, professional studies in childhood, salon business management, spa management with hospitality, sports management, sports therapy, tourism business administration, tourism business management, tourism destination management, travel operations management; BA(Hons), BSc(Hons), FdA Dip HE, FdSc, MA, MSc, PGCE, PGDip/Cert, PgDip/PgCert

BIRMINGHAM CITY UNIVERSITY
www.bcu.ac.uk

Birmingham Institute of Art and Design; www.bcu.ac.uk/bid

animation, animation for game design, architecture, architectural practice administration, art and education, art, health & well-being, art practice and education, contemporary curatorial practice, design, design management, design and visualisation, digital arts in performance, fashion & textiles, fashion design, fashion retail management, fine art, gemmology/horology/jewellery & silversmithing, graphic design, graphic design/illustration/photography/moving image, history of art & design, landscape architecture, landscape studies, textile design, theatre, performance and event design, product design, queer studies in arts and culture, surface design, three dimensional design, visual arts, visual communication, urban design; BA(Hons), BTEC, CertHE/DipHE, HND, MA, MPhil, PgCert/PgDip, PhD

Birmingham City Business School; www.bcu.ac.uk/business-school

accounting, advertising, business and management, business law, business studies, economics, finance, HRM, international business, international marketing, management, marketing, public relations – combined studies in audit management and consultancy, business, business management, education, health, law & social sciences, international human resource management, media & English, performance; BA(Hons), DBA, HND, MBA, MPhil, MSc, PhD

Faculty of Education, Law and Social Sciences; www.bcu.ac.uk/elss

Education & Teacher Training; www.bcu.ac.uk/education

children and integrated professional care, early childhood, early childhood education studies, early years, post-compulsory education and training, primary education, primary education with QTS, secondary education, subject knowledge enhancement in mathematics; BA(Hons), FoundD, FoundC CA, MPhil, PGDip/Cert, PGCE, PhD

The School of Law; www.bcu.ac.uk/law

corporate and business law, international human rights, legal studies, law, law with American legal studies/criminology/legal practice/business law/human rights, legal practice; GradDip, MPhil/PhD, HND, LlB(Hons), PgCert/PgDip/LLM

School of Social Sciences; www.cu.ac.uk/social sciences

criminal investigation, criminology, criminology and security studies, housing practice, integrative counselling and psychotherapy,professional housing studies, psychology, public sociology, social sciences, sociology; BA(Hons), BSc(Hons), CertHE, FdA, MA, MPhil, MSc, PgCert, PgDip, PhD

Faculty of Health; www.bcu.ac.uk/health

advanced health care, advanced practice primary care, appendicular reporting, axial reporting, child care, computed tomography, health and social care, CT head reporting, health and well-being (exercise science/nutrition science/individuals and communities), health promotion and public health, image reporting, integrative counselling intravenous urography, and psychotherapy, management of patients with long term conditions, medical ultrasound, mental health, midwifery, nursing/RN, operating department practice, pain management, perioperative specialist practice, radiography, rehabilitation work (visual impairment), social work, speech and language therapy, strategic leadership, women's health studies advanced practice; BSc(Hons), DipHE, FdA, MPhil, MSc, PgCert, PGDip, PQ, PhjD

Faculty of Performance, Media and English; www.bcu.ac.uk/pme

Birmingham Conservatoire; www.bcu.ac.uk/conservatoire

jazz, digital arts in performance, music, music technology, popular music studies; AdvPGDip, BMus(Hons), HND, MA, MMus, MPhil, PGCert, PhD

Birmingham School of Media; www.bcu.ac.uk/mediacourses

Media and Communication; journalism, media photography, music industries, public relations, radio production

Television, Web and New Media; broadcast journalism, event and exhibition management, international broadcast journalism, media & communication, media enterprise, social media, television & interactive content; BA(Hons), PGDip, MA, MPhil, PhD

Birmingham School of Acting; www.bsa.bcu.ac.uk

acting, community and applied theatre/dance theatre, physical theatre, professional voice practice acting: the British tradition, stage management; BA(Hons), MA, PgDip

School of English; www.lhds.bcu.ac.uk/English

English, English and media/drama/psychology/creative writing, English literature, English language studies, English linguistics, writing, philosophy; BA(Hons), Diploma, MA, MPhil, PhD

Faculty of Technology, Engineering and the Environment; www.bcu.ac.uk/tee-landing

Computing, Telecommunications and Networks: business information technology, computer games technology, computer networks/and security, computer science, computer technology, computing and electronics, electronic engineering, forensic computing, information & communications technology, telecommunications & networks

Digital Media Technology: creative game animation and development, film production and technology, film technology and special effects, multimedia technology, music technology, sound engineering and production, sound & multimedia technology, television technology & production

Engineering Design and Manufacturing Systems: automotive engineering, computer aided automotive design, engineering foundation, management of manufacturing systems, mechanical engineering, motorsports technology

Property Construction and Planning: architectural technology, building surveying, construction management & economics, construction quantity surveying, construction, estate management practice, planning and development, property & construction, quantity surveying, real estate; BSc, HNC, FdSc, MSc, PgCert, PgDip

BISHOP GROSSETESTE COLLEGE
www.bgc.ac.uk

children and youth work, children's services (early childhood/children and youth work), continuing professional development, drama in the community, early childhood studies, education (non-QTS), education studies and art and design /drama/English,/ geography/history/mathematics/music/sport/theology, PGCE in education(primary/secondary), English literature, heritage studies, learning practitioners, primary education with QTS; BA(Hons), FdA, GradDip, MA, PGCE

EAST LANCASHIRE INSTITUTE OF HIGHER EDUCATION AT BLACKBURN COLLEGE
www.blackburn.ac.uk

Vocation qualifications (BTEC, City & Guilds etc) offered in: business, care and health, childhood studies, construction, computing, creative arts, essential studies, hair and beauty, hospitality, motor vehicle, public services

Courses offered at University Centre, Blackburn College: applied psychology – counselling and health, business accounting, business studies, business, care practice, complementary medicine, design (contemporary textiles/graphic communication/illustration and animation/interiors/moving image/new media, digital communication systems, digital media design, early years childcare, educational studies, electrical/electronic engineering, English and history, English language and literary studies, financial services, fine art (integrated media), hospitality management, housing studies, HRM, information and internet technology, journalism, law, law with psychology, marketing, mechanical engineering, neighbourhood management, photographic media, politics and English/ history, public services management, social sciences, sociology and English/history, sustainable construction, sustainable engineering, working with children and young people; BA(Hons, Ord), BEng(Hons, Ord), BSc(Hons, Ord), DMS (validated externally), Foundation degree, HNC, HND, LlB (validated by Lancaster), LlM, MBA, MSc

BOURNEMOUTH UNIVERSITY
www.bournemouth.ac.uk

The Business School; www.business.bournemouth.ac.uk

accounting, business, business law, business studies with economics/enterprise/finance/human resource, management/law/marketing/operations and project management, business & management, economics, entertainment law, finance, finance with risk management, international business studies, international business and management, international business finance, international business management, international business with economics, international commercial law, intellectual property, intellectual property management, law, law and taxation, management, management with marketing/human resources, project management, taxation; BA(Hons), LlB(Hons), LlM, MA, MBA, MPhil, MSc, PhD

School of Conservation Sciences; www.bournemouth.ac.uk/conservation

animal behaviour & welfare, applied architectural stonework and conservation, applied biology, archaeology, archaeological and forensic sciences, arboriculture, archaeology and prehistory, biodiversity conservation, building conservation, crime scene and international investigations, cultural services (libraries/museums), ecology & wildlife conservation, environmental protection & management, environmental forensics, environmental informatics, environmental management, equine behaviour & welfare, field archaeology, forensic anthropology & crime scene investigation, forensic and biological anthropology, forensic & crime scene investigation/ science, forensic archaeology: crime scene and international investigations, forensic science/with forensic archaeology, forensic toxicology, geoinformatics, heritage conservation management, heritage conservation and tourism, human osteoarchaeology, marine & coastal management, marine archaeology, marine ecology, and conservation, maritime archaeology, museum studies, outdoor adventure management, practical archaeology, recovery and identification of human remains, Roman archaeology, timber building conservation, world heritage resource management, zooarchaeology; BSc(Hons), CertHE, FdA, FdSc, MSc, PhD

School of Design, Engineering & Computing; www.dec.bournemouth.ac.uk

3D computer generated imagery: architectural visualisation/modelling and animation/technical illustration, applied art & design, business computing, business information technology, computer aided design – graphics & packaging, computer games design, computer networking, computer security, computing, creative audio technology, design engineering, design visualisation, digital media development, electronics and computer technology, engineering (manufacturing management/mechanical design/ engineering/electrical technology), entertainment technology, forensic computing & security, foundations of clinical psychology, games technology, information technology management, internet communication systems, internet technology, media technology, multimedia business & entrepreneurship, multimedia communication systems, music and sound technology, network systems management, product design, product design innovation, project management, psychology, rapid product development, smart systems and technology, software engineering/management, software product design, sound design technology, sustainable graphics & packaging, sustainable product design, web systems, wireless and mobile networks; BSc(Hons), Foundation degrees, HNC, HND, MA, MPhil, MSc, PhD

School of Health and Social Care; www.bournemouth.ac.uk/hsc

adult nursing, advanced mental health practice, applied biology: health, nutrition, child health nursing, early years, early years: care & education, educational practice, community development, exercise science (health & rehabilitation), leading and developing services, learning disability nursing, mental health nursing, midwifery, occupational therapy, operating department practice, paramedic science, physiotherapy, social work; AdvDip, BA(Hons), BSc(Hons), DipHE, FdA, FdSc, MPhil, PGDip/Cert, PhD, Dr Prof Practice

The Media School; www.media.bournemouth.ac.uk

advertising with marketing communications, communication and media, computer animation arts, computer visualisation and animation, English, film production and cinematography, global computer animation practice, interactive media production, marketing, media production, multimedia, multi-media journalism, music, music technology, performing arts: contemporary theatre performance/dance/music/theatre, photography, photomedia (photography/film and television),popular music, public relations, radio production, scriptwriting for film and television, soundtrack production, television production, video production; BA(Hons), BSc(Hons), FdA, MA, MBA, MPhil, MSc, PhD

School of Services Management; www.bournemouth.ac.uk/servicesmanagement

applied animal management, countryside management, golf and sports turf management, hospitality management, international hospitality and tourism management, international retail marketing, international tourism management, landscape design, leisure marketing, retail management, sports coaching & athlete development, sports development & coaching, sports psychology & coaching sciences, tourism and spa management; BA(Hons), FdA, FdSc/Cert HE, MPhil, MSc, PhD

UNIVERSITY OF BRADFORD
www.bradford.ac.uk

School of Computing, Informatics and Media; www.scim.brad.ac.uk

Computing: advanced computer science, artificial intelligence for games computing, computer science, ICT with business/law/marketing/media/psychology, informatics, information systems, intelligent systems and robotics, internet computing, mobile computing, networks and performance engineering, software development applications, software engineering
Media: digital arts and media, digital and creative enterprise, digital cinema, digital media, digital media and technologies, film studies, informatics, media studies with/cinematics/computer animation/digital imaging/music technology/television/web design, media technology and production, photography for digital media, television production, web design and technology, web technologies
Mathematics: applied mathematics, computational mathematics, informatics, space science
Creative technology: advanced computer animation and special effects, computer animation/and special effects, computer animation and special effects, graphics for games, informatics, interactive systems and video games design, visual computing; BA(Hons), BSc(Hons), MAMSc, FdSc

School of Engineering,Design and Technology; www.eng.brad.ac.uk

advanced materials engineering, automotive design technology, automotive engineering quality improvement, civil & structural engineering, clinical technology, computer aided engineering, e-business technology & management, electrical & electronic engineering, electrical engineering, electrical engineering with power electronics, electromechanical technology, electronic engineering, electronic, telecommunications & internet engineering, engineering and management, information technology management, industrial engineering, manufacturing engineering, manufacturing management, mechanical & automotive engineering, mechanical & vehicle technology, mechanical engineering, medical engineering, personal, mobile & satellite communications, plant and process engineering, product design, technology management, wireless sensor & embedded systems; BEng, BSc, FD, MEng, MPhil, MSc, PhD

School of Health Studies; www.brad.ac.uk/acad/health

cancer care, dementia care, diagnostic radiography, health, wellbeing and social care, midwifery, nursing (adult branch/mental health branch/child branch), nursing practice (acutely ill adult/cancer and palliative care/pain management/tissue viability) nursing studies (adult, child, mental health), occupational therapy, physiotherapy; AdvDip, BSc(Hons), CertHE, DipHE, FD, MSc, MPhil, PGDip/Cert, PhD

School of Life Sciences; www.brad.ac.uk/ acad/lifesci

Div of Archaeological Geographical & Environmental Sciences

archaeological prospection, archaeological sciences, archaeology, bioarchaeology, environmental management, environmental science, forensic and archaeological sciences, forensic archaeology and crime scene investigation, geography, human osteology and palaeopathology, physical and environmental geography; BA, BSc, CertHE,MA, MSc, MPhil, PhD

Div of Biomedical Sciences

applied biomedical science, biomedical science, cancer biology, medical biochemistry, medical cell biology, medical microbiology, pharmacology

Bradford School of Pharmacy

clinical pharmacy, pharmacy, pharmaceutical services and medicines control

Dept of Chemical and Forensic Sciences

chemistry; chemistry for analysis/drug discovery/ medicines development/chemistry with pharmaceutical and forensic science, clinical sciences, forensic sciences, medical sciences

Div of Optometry

optometry; BSc

Institute of Cancer Therapeutics

cancer pharmacology, drug discovery, safety pharmacology; MPhil,MSc, PhD

The School of Lifelong Education and Development; www.brad.ac.uk/admin/ conted/cfa

employability and entrepreneurship, integrated emergency management, regeneration project management, TESOL and applied linguistics, training and development; Foundation degrees, Certs, MA, MSc, PGDip/Cert

The School of Management; www.brad.ac. uk/acad/management

accounting, business studies, finance, financial, business and management studies, HRM, international business and management, law, management, marketing; BA(Hons), BSc(Hons), DBA,LlB, GradDip(-Law), Int Masters MBA, MRes, PhD

The School of Social and International Studies; www.brad.ac.uk/acad/ssis

applied criminal justice,business economics, conflict resolution, creative writing, criminology, development and peace studies, development studies, diversity and social policy, economics, English, financial economics, history, interdisciplinary human studies, international development, international economics, international relations, international relations and security studies, mental health practice, peace studies, philosophy, politics, politics and law, psychology, social policy, social work, sociology; BA(Hons), BSc(Hons), MA, MPhil, PhD, PGDip

Degrees validated by University of Bradford offered at:

BRADFORD COLLEGE
www.bradfordcollege.ac.uk

Art & Design: 3D design (interior design), photography/editorial, advertising and fine art, arts for the creative industries, contemporary surface design and textiles, engineering illustration and digital media, fashion design, fine art, multimedia & design graphic design, photography (editorial, advertising and fine art), visual arts

Accountancy and Law: accountancy, advertising and campaign management marketing, business administration, business (finance), business (human resources management), business management, business studies, financial services, HRM, information technology, international business management, law,

law and legal practice, management, marketing and sales, marketing practice, project management

Interior Design: advanced practices in beauty therapy, beauty therapy management, beauty therapy sciences, creative hairdressing, make-up effects and artistry

Education Studies: culture, ICT citizenship, identity and learning, early years practice, graduate and registered teacher programme early years, inclusive education, leadership & management in education, PGCE primary/French, PGCE secondary (11–18, age ranges) science, physics, chemistry, maths), postcompulsory education and training foundation degree, primary education with qualified teacher status (QTS), supporting and managing learning in education, teaching

Law and Social Welfare: counselling and psychology in community settings, creative practice in community settings, health and social welfare, person centred community development work, public services management, social & community care, social work, supported & community housing, youth and community development

Computing: business computing solutions, computing with software engineering computing (general, ICT systems support, software development), network infrastructure technologies, software applications development

Construction (architecture, quantity surveying and construction management): construction design and management, construction engineering management, electrical, electronic, mechanical and manufacturing engineering, metallurgy and materials

Diet, Nutrition and Health: health-related exercise and fitness, hospitality and travel management, ophthalmic dispensing with management, outdoor adventurous activities, pharmacy, sports coaching, sports science, travel and tourism management; BSc(Hons), CertHE, DipHE, Foundation degrees, HNC, HNDBA(Hons), LlB(Hons), MA, MEd, PGDipCert

UNIVERSITY OF BRIGHTON
www.brighton.ac.uk

Faculty of Arts; www.arts.brighton.ac.uk

School of Architecture and Design, School of Arts and Media, School of Humanities

Architecture and design: architectural design, architecture

English Language & Linguistics: English language, linguistics, media

Fashion & Textiles: textiles/fashion with business studies

Fine Art: critical fine art practice, inclusive arts practice, painting, printmaking, sculpture

History of Art & Design: film and screen studies, history of decorative art and crafts, history of design, culture, history of design and material culture, museum and heritage studies, visual culture

Humanities: applied ethics, conflict, culture, cultural and critical theory, globalisation, histories, histories and cultures, history, humanities and critical studies, literatures, modernity cultures, politics, war

Interiors & Urban Studies: architectural and urban studies, interior architecture, interior design

Learning & Teaching Language: English language teaching studies, media-assisted language teaching, TESOL/TEFL

Literature & Media: broadcast media, creative media, English language, English literature, English studies, media and English literature, Media Studies; radio production, television production,

Performance & Visual Arts: dance performance visual art, music performance visual art theatre performance, visual art

Three Dimensional Design and Materials Practice: 3D design, 3D materials practice, digital music and sound art, moving image, film and screen studies, photography, photography & sound, sustainable design

Visual Communication: arts and design by independent project, digital media arts (lighthouse), graphic design, illustration, sequential design/illustration; BA(Hons), FdSA, Grad Dip, MA, MDes, MFA, MPhil, PGDip/Cert, PhD

Faculty of Education and Sport; www. brighton.ac.uk/fes

Chelsea School; www.brighton.ac.uk/chelsea

education in dance, exercise and health science, exercise physiology, exercise science, fitness, international sport policy, physical education, initial teacher education, physical education with qualified teacher status, sport, sport and exercise science, sport and leisure management, sport coaching /and development, sport, culture and media, sport, culture and society, sport development, sport journalism, sport studies,

School of Education; www.brighton.ac.uk/education

early years care and education, early years professional status, education, learning and development, English literature and education, information technology education, key stage 2/key stage 3 English education/ICT education/mathematics education/key stage 2/key stage 3 science education, design and technology education, mathematics education, PGCE-primary education 5–11 years/3–7 years, art and design/business education/dance/design and technology/English/geography/information technology/mathematics/modern foreign languages/physical education/ religious studies/science/design and technology/information technology/mathematics/science, primary education 3–7 years/5–11 years, post-compulsory education, professional education studies, professional studies in learning and development, professional studies in primary education, religious education, science education, working with young people, youth work

Centre for Learning and Teaching; www.brighton.ac.uk/clt

learning and development; learning and teaching in HE; BA(Hons), BSc(Hons), CertEd, EdD, FdA, MA, MPhil, MPhil/PhD, MSc, PGCert, PGCE, PhD

Faculty of Health and Social Science; www.brighton.ac.uyk/fhss

School of Applied Social Science; www.brighton.ac.uk/sass

applied psychology, community psychology, counselling and psychotherapy, criminology, health and social care, mental health, politics, psychology, psychosocial studies, social policy, social science social work, sociology, substance misuse; BA(Hons), MA, MPhil, MSc, PGDip/Cert, PhD

School of Health Professions; www.brighton.ac.uk/sohs

clinical education, health through occupation, neuromusculoskeletal physiotherapy, occupational therapy, physiotherapy, physiotherapy and education, physiotherapy and management, podiatry, rehabilitation science, sports injury management; BS(Hons), MSc, PGDip/Cert, PhD, Prof Doc

School of Nursing and Midwifery; www.brighton.ac.uk/snm

acute and critical care, acute clinical practice, adult nursing, child nursing, children, family and public health, community specialist practice, health studies

nurse practitioner, mental health and psychosocial care, mental health nursing, midwifery, paramedic practice, professional practice, specialist community public health nursing, supporting long term care; BSc(Hons), FdSc, MPhil, MRes, MSc, PGDip/Cert, PhD

Faculty of Management and Information Sciences; www.brighton.ac.uk/mis

Brighton Business School; www.brighton.ac.uk/bbs

accounting, business administration, business management, business management with finance, business studies, change management, economics, finance, general management, international business, investment, logistics and supply chain management, management, management (entrepreneurship/human resources/public service), personnel and development, professional accounting, public service management; ACCA, BA(Hons), LlB, MBA, MSc

School of Service Management; www.brighton.ac.uk/ssm

culinary arts, food and culinary arts, hospitality and event management, international event management, international event marketing, international hospitality management, international tourism management, international travel management, retail management, retail enterprise, retail marketing, tourism and international development, tourism and social anthropology, travel and tourism management, travel and tourism marketing; BA(Hons), FdA, MA, MSc, PhD

School of Computing, Mathematical and Information Sciences; www.brighton.ac.uk/cmis

business computer systems, business information systems, computer games development, computer science, computer science (games), computing, computing with business, digital media, digital television management and production, e-learning design, enterprise systems, European computing, information management, information management (health), information studies, information systems, interactive technology design, internet and distributed systems, internet computing, internet systems architecture, learning technologies, mathematics, mathematics & computing, mathematics with business, networked systems, software engineering; BA/BSc(Hons), FdSc, MA, MComp, MPhil, MSc, PGDip, PGCert

Faculty of Science and Engineering; www.brighton.ac.uk/scieng

School of Environment and Technology; www.brighton.ac.uk/set

Built Environment: architectural technology, building studies, building surveying, construction management, environmental assessment and management, facilities management, project management for construction, sustainability of the built environment, town planning

Civil Engineering: civil engineering, civil with environmental engineering

Electrical and Electronic Engineering: automotive electronic engineering, computing & communications, digital electronics, electrical and electronic engineering

Environment: environmental geology, environmental hazards, environmental management and assessment, environmental sciences, environment and media studies, GIS and environmental management, sustainability of the built environment, town planning, water and environmental management

Geography: geography, GIS and environmental management

Geology: earth and ocean science, environmental geology, geology

Mechanical, Aeronautical and Automotive Engineering: aeronautical engineering, automotive electronic engineering, automotive engineering, mechanical engineering, mechanical and manufacturing engineering

Product Innovation & Development: product design/product design technology/sports product design/sustainable product design with professional experience; BA/BSc(Hons), BEng(Hons), BSc(Hons), FdSc, FdEng, MEng, MPhil, PGDip/Cert, PhD

School of Pharmacy and Biomolecular Sciences; www.brighton.ac.uk/pharmacy

analytical chemistry with business, applied biomedical science, biological sciences, biomedical science, biomedical science (cellular pathology), bioscience, pharmacy and biomolecular sciences clinical biochemistry/medical microbiology/haematology and transfusion science, ecology and biogeography, clinical pharmacy practice, community pharmaceutical health care, industrial pharmaceutical studies, pharmaceutical and biomedical sciences, pharmaceutical and chemical sciences, pharmacy; BSc(Hons), MSc, MPharmHons, MPhil, MRes, PGDip, PhD

Brighton and Sussex Medical School; www.bsms.ac.uk

cardiology, clinical education, diabetes, health or social care, leadership and management in health care, medicine, nephrology, public health, surgery; BM, BS, MD, MPhil, MSc, PGDip/Cert, PhD

Institute of Postgraduate Medicine

UNIVERSITY OF BRISTOL
www.bris.ac.uk

Faculty of Arts; www.bris.ac.uk/arts

School of Arts; www.bris.ac.uk/arts

Dept of Archaeology; www.bris.ac.uk/archanth;
ancient history, anthropology, archaeological and anthropological sciences

Dept of Drama, Theatre, Film, Television; www.bris.ac.uk/drama
archaeology for screen media, cinema studies, composition of music for film and television, drama, film and television production, performance research

Dept of Music; www.bris.ac.uk/music
British music, composition, composition for film and television, medieval music, music and a modern language, music theory, musicology, performance, Russian music

Dept of Philosophy; www.bris.ac.uk/philosophy
philosophy and French/German/Italian/Portugese/Russian/Spanish/classical studies/English/economics/politics/psychology/mathematics/physics/sociology/law/the history of science; BA(Hons), BSc(Hons), MA, Mlitt, MMus, MSci, PGDip, PhD

School of Humanities; www.bris.ac.uk/humanities

Dept of Classics & Ancient History; www.bris.ac.uk/classics
ancient history, ancient history & archaeology classical studies, classics, history

Dept of English; www.bris.ac.uk/english
English, English and philosophy/classical studies/drama, English literature and community

engagement, modern and contemporary poetry, romanticism, Shakespeare and English literature

Dept of History; www.bris.ac.uk/history
colonialism, contemporary history, histories, peoples, cultures, history, history with study in French, history with study in German, medieval and early modern history, Russian history

Dept of Art History; www.bris.ac.uk/arthistory
art histories and interpretations, history of art

Dept of Theology and Religious Studies; www.bris.ac.uk/thrs
biblical studies, Buddhism and Hinduism, Buddhist studies, interfaith studies, modern theology, New Testament archaeology of early Christianity, philosophy and ethics, reception of the bible: tradition, theology and politics/sociology/philosophy

School of Modern Languages; www.bris.ac.uk/sml
French, German, Hispanic, Portuguese and Latin American studies, Italian, Russian, Russian studies (includes Czech); joint degrees with drama, history of art, music, philosophy and politics, translation, European Literatures, Modern languages, Russian history; BA(Hons), MA, MLitt, MPhil, PGDip, PhD

Faculty of Engineering; www.bris.ac.uk/engineering

Dept of Aerospace Engineering; www.bris.ac.uk/aerospace
aerodynamics and fluid dynamics, aerospace systems design, aerospace/multifunctional composites, dynamics and systems, dynamic applications of bi-stable structures, morphing wings

Dept of Civil Engineering; www.bris.ac.uk/civilengineering
civil engineering, water and environmental management

Dept of Computer Science; www.cs.bris.ac.uk
computer science/and electronic/mathematics, internet technologies with multimedia, machine learning and data mining, security advanced microelectronic systems engineering

Dept of Electrical and Electronic Engineering; www.bris.ac.uk/eeng
aoptical communications, communications and multimedia engineering, communication networks and signal processing, computer science and electronics, electrical and electronic engineering, electronic engineering, electronic and communications engineering, image & video communications, wireless communication systems

Dept of Engineering Mathematics; www.enm.bris.ac.uk
advanced computing (machine learning theme), applied nonlinear mathematics, artificial intelligence, engineering mathematics

Dept of Mechanical Engineering; www.bris.ac.uk/mecheng
design and process engineering, dynamics and control, mechanical engineering, solid mechanics; BSc(Hons), BEng, EngDPGCert MEng, MSc, PhD,

Faculty of Medical and Veterinary Science; www.bris.ac.uk/mvs

Dept of Anatomy; www.bris.ac.uk/anatomy
anatomical science, anatomical science with veterinary anatomy, human musculoskeletal science, neuroscience

Dept of Biochemistry; www.bris.ac.uk/biochemistry
biochemistry, biochemistry with molecular biology and biotechnology, biomedical science research, medical biochemistry, quantitative cell imaging

Dept of Cellular and Molecular; Medicine; www.bris.ac.uk/cellmolmed
cancer biology, immunology, microbiology, medical microbiology, pathology, transfusion and transplantation science, virology

Dept of Clinical Veterinary Science; www.vetschool.bris.ac.uk/
animal behaviour & welfare, meat science and technology, veterinary cellular and molecular science, veterinary nursing and bioveterinary science, veterinary parasitology, veterinary science

Dept of Physiology and Pharmacology; www.bris.ac.uk/phys-pharm
cardiovascular science, cell signalling & cell biology, neuroscience, pharmacology, physiological science; BSc(Hons), BVS, MD, MSc, MSci, PhD

Faculty of Medicine and Dentistry; www.bris.ac.uk/fmd

child and adolescent health, clinical sciences, dental implantology, dental studies (lingual orthodontics), ethics in medicine, medicine, health care ethics and law, molecular neuroscience, obstetrics & gynaecology, oral and dental science, palliative medicine, premedical programme, primary health care, psychiatry, reproduction and development, stem cells and regeneration, social medicine; MB, BDS, BSc(Hons), ChB, ChM, DDS, Diploma, DPDS, MClinDent, MD, MMedEd, MSci, PhD

Faculty of Science; www.bris.ac.uk/science

School of Biological Sciences; www.bris.ac.uk/biology

biology, biology and mathematics, botany, ecological & evolutionary processes, ecology and management of the natural environment, geology and biology, palaeontology and evolution, psychology and zoology, sensory & neurobiology, wildlife biology, zoology

School of Chemistry; www.chm.bris.ac.uk/

chemical physics, inorganic and materials chemistry, law with chemistry, organic and biological chemistry, physical and theoretical chemistry

School of Earth Sciences; www.gly.bris.ac.uk/

archaeological and anthropological sciences, biology, earth system science, earth sciences, environmental geoscience, geology, palaeobiology, science of natural hazards

Dept of Experimental Psychology; www.psychology.psy.bris.ac.uk/

biological psychology, cognition, computational neuroscience, neuropsychology, psychology and zoology, research methods, vision sciences

School of Geographical Sciences; www.ggy.bris.ac.uk/

geography, human geography, physical geography, society and space, science of natural hazards

Dept of Mathematics; www.maths.bris.ac.uk/

applied/pure mathematics, biology and mathematics, economics and mathematics, mathematics, mathematics and computer science/philosophy/physics/statistics, statistics

Dept of Physics; www.phsy.bris.ac.uk/

astrophysics, correlated electron systems, mathematics and physics, micro- and nanostructural materials, nanophysics and soft matter, particle physics, physics, physics with astrophysics, physics and philosophy, quantum photonics, theoretical physics; BSc(Hons), DSc, LlB, MRes, MSci, MSc, PhD, UGCert

Faculty of Social Science and Law; www.bris.ac.uk/fss

advanced clinical audiology, contemporary identities, counselling, deafhood studies, development and security, social policy, social policy and politics/sociology, sociology, sociology and philosophy/theology/politics

Centre for East Asian studies; www.bris.ac.uk/ceas/

East Asian development and the global economy, East Asian studies

Dept of Politics; www.bris.ac.uk/politics

Dept of Sociology; www.bris.ac.uk/sociology

Graduate School of Education; www.bris.ac.uk/education

advanced clinical audiology, economics, economics and econometrics/ finance/ public policy, education, educational research, ethnicity and multiculturalism, European governance, family therapy and systemic practice, gender and international relations, inclusive theory and practice (empowering people with learning disabilities), international development, international relations, international security, management learning and change, nutrition, physical activity and public health, policy research, politics, public policy, quantitative development economics, rehabilitative audiology, sign linguistics, social work, social work with children and young people, social and cultural theory, social science research methods (politics/international relations/sociology), society and space, sociology, strategic management, technology and society

School for Policy Studies; www.bristol.ac.uk/sps

childhood studies, early childhood studies, international health, social policy/and politics/sociology

School of Applied Community and Health Studies; www.bris.ac.uk/sachs

Centre for Deaf Studies

audiology, deaf studies

Dept of Exercise, Nutrition and Health Sciences

nutrition, physical activity and public health

Centre for Hearing & Balance Studies

advanced clinical audiology, rehabilitative audiology

Norah Fry Research Centre

educational psychology, inclusive theory and practice: empowering people with learning disabilities

Centre for Personal and Professional Development

counselling, creative writing for therapeutic purposes

School of Law; www.bris.ac.uk/law

law, law with chemistry, law and French, law and German, socio-legal studies; BA(Hons), BSc(Hons), DSocSci, EdD, LlB, LlD, LlM, MEd, MPhil, MSc, MSci, PCGE, PhD

Degrees validated by University of Bristol offered at:

WESLEY COLLEGE BRISTOL
www.wesley-college-bristol.ac.uk

theological studies, theology and ministry; BA(Hons),
Diplomas and Certificates, MA

UNIVERSITY OF THE WEST OF ENGLAND, BRISTOL;
www.uwe.ac.uk

Bristol Business School; www.uwe.ac.uk/bbs

applied social research, business enterprise, business studies, coaching and mentoring, economics, economics (international business), economics/money, banking and finance, entrepreneurship, finance, finance and global operations, financial management, financial management (health sector/professional learning and development), HRM, international HRM, international management, leadership and management in health and social care, leadership and organisation of public services, management, marketing, marketing communications, social marketing, tourism development; BA(Hons), BSc(Hons), MA, MBA, MSc, PhD

School of Creative Arts; www.uwe.ac.uk/sca

animation, art and visual culture, art, media and design by project, creative practices, design: process, drama, drawing and applied arts, fashion design, fashion/textile design, film studies, fine art, graphic design, journalism, material, media (animation/graphic arts), media and cultural studies, media practice, media: practice and culture, photography; BA(Hons), FdA, MA, MPhil, PhD

Faculty of Environment and Technology; www.uwe.ac.uk/et

School of the Built and Natural Environment; www.uwe.ac.uk/bne

applied social research (built environment), architectural technology and design, architecture, building surveying, built and natural environments, built environment studies/(urban design), change and energy management, civil engineering, community safety and crime prevention, construction/commercial management, construction project management, countryside conservation and management, environmental engineering, environmental management, geography, geography and tourism, housing, housing development and management, integrated catchment management, law for construction professionals, planning, property, property development and planning, property management and investment, quantity surveying and commercial management, real estate, river and coastal engineering, spatial planning, tourism and environmental management, tourism and sustainability, town and country planning, transport planning, urban and rural regeneration, urban design; BArch, BEng(Hons), BSc(Hons), DBEnv, FdSc, HNC, MA, MPlan, MPhil, MSc,PGDip/Cert, PhD

Bristol Institute of Technology; www.uwe.ac.uk/cems

advanced technologies in electronics, aerospace engineering, audio production, business information systems, computer science, digital media, electrical and electronic engineering, games technology, health informatics, information and library management, information technology, IT for business, mathematics and statistics, mechanical engineering, music technology, product design, robotics, software development and the learning society, software engineering, statistics and management science; BEng, BSc(Hons), FdSc, MEng, MPhil, MSc, PGDip/Cert, PhD

Faculty of Health and Life Sciences; www.uwe.ac.uk/hls

School of Life Sciences; www.uwe.ac.uk/hls/ls

applied/biochemistry and molecular biology/biological sciences/biomedical science, (clinical)/genetics/microbiology/physiology and pharmacology, biotechnology, cellular pathology, clinical chemistry, conservation biology, environmental biology/environmental health/science, forensic biology/chemistry/

science, counselling psychology, environmental consultancy, environmental health, forensic genetics, haematology, health psychology, health, safety and the environment, human biology, immunology, medical microbiology, molecular biotechnology, pharmaceutical sciences, psychology, psychology and forensic science/sports biology, science communication, sports biology, sports biomedicine; BSc(Hons), DBMS, MPhil, MSc, PGDip/Cert, PhD, ProfDocs,

School of Health and Social Care; www.hsc. uwe.ac.uk
adult nursing, child and adolescent mental health, childrens nursing, clinical research, community practice, diagnostic imaging, health and social care, leadership and management in health and social care, leadership and organisation of public services, learning disabilities nursing, mental health nursing, mental health/psychosocial interventions, midwifery, music therapy, nuclear medicine, occupational therapy, paramedic science, physiotherapy, public health/specialist community public health, radiotherapy, social work, social work studies (specialist social work with adults), sports therapy and rehabilitation, sports therapy and rehabilitation advanced practice, substance misuse, veterinary physiotherapy, working with children, young people and their families; BSc(Hons) BSc, DipHE, Foundation degrees, MSc, PhD, MPhil, PGCert/Dip, ProfDoc, ResDip

Faculty of Social Sciences and Humanities; www1.uwe.ac.uk/ssh/

Bristol Law School; www.law.uwe.ac.uk
commercial law, criminal justice, criminology, European business law, European and international law, international economic law/human rights/trade law, industrial law, law; LlB, LlM, PhD

School of Education; www.uwe.ac.uk/ssh/ education
applied social research, business and education, drama and education, early childhood studies, early years education, education in professional practice,

English/ psychology, guidance (vocational/educational), HE learning support, initial teacher education, leadership and organisation of public services, mental health nursing, music therapy, PGCE lower primary – early years (3–7)/post-compulsory education and training/secondary art and design/business education/design and technology/English/geography/history/mathematics/modern languages/science/upper primary (7–11), primary education; ASR, BA(Hons), CertEd, DipHE, MA, MPhil, MSc PGCert/Dip, PhD,

School of Languages, Humanities & Social Science
Humanities: English, history, international history with international politics, regional histories
Languages, Linguistic and Area Studies: European business, English language, linguistics, translation, intercultural communication
Social Sciences: criminology, human rights, international relations, peace and conflict studies, politics, philosophy, sociology; BA, MA, PGDip/Cert, PhD

Hartpury College (Associate Faculty); www.hartpury.ac.uk
Animal and Land: agricultural business management, amenity horticultural management, animal behaviour and welfare, animal management, animal science, bioveterinary science, conservation and countryside management
Equine: equine/business management/dental science/performance/sports science
Food and Drink Technology: food and drink manufacturing
Sport: coaching science, golf management, outdoor adventure management, sport and exercise management, sport/events management/studies/business management/coaching performance
Veterinary Nursing; equine veterinary nursing science, veterinary nursing science, veterinary practice management; BA(Hons), BSc(Hons), FdSc, FdA, MA, MSc

BRUNEL UNIVERSITY
www.brunel.ac.uk

School of Arts; www.brunel.ac.uk /about/ acad /sa
contemporary literature and culture/music/performance making, creative writing, digital games theory and design/performance, documentary practice, drama, English, film, games design, journalism, modern drama studies, music, musical composition/

performance, the novel, sonic arts, TV studies; BA(Hons), BMus, MA, MMus, MPhil, PhD

Brunel Law School; www.brunel.ac.uk/about/acad/bls

European and international commercial law, intellectual property/ economic/international economic and trade/international human rights law, public international law and world order; CPE, European Masters in European Affairs, GradDip, LlM, LLB, MPhil, PhD

School of Engineering and Design; www.brunel.ac.uk /about/acad /sed

aeronautics, aerospace engineering, automotive design, aviation engineering, broadcast media design and technology, building services, civil engineering/with sustainability, communication networks engineering, communication systems, computer engineering, computer systems engineering, electrical engineering, electronic/ computer engineering, industrial design and technology, internet engineering, mechanical engineering, microelectronic engineering, mobile computing, motorsport engineering, multimedia technology and design, networked media engineering, pilot studies, product design/engineering, renewable energy systems; BA(Hons), BEng, BSc(Hons), EngD, MEng, MPhil, MSc, PhD

Brunel Business School; www.brunel.ac.uk /about/acad/bbs

business and management, accounting, marketing, business studies, sport sciences, international business, corporate brand management, global supply chain management, HRM, human resource and employment relations, international business management, marketing; BSc, MSc, MBA, PhD

School of Health Sciences and Social Care; www.brunel.ac.uk/about/acad/health

biomedical sciences, biomedical sciences (biochemistry/forensic/genetics/human health/immunology), occupational therapy, physiotherapy, social work, specialist community public health nursing, specialist social work (adults)(children and families), health promotion and public health, neurorehabilitation, occupational health and safety management, occupational therapy, molecular medicine, cancer research, urgent care,vision impairment rehabilitation; BSc, BA, MSc, MA, PGDip, PGCert

School of Information Systems, Computing and Mathematics; www.brunel.ac.uk/about/acad/siscm

artificial intelligence, computational mathematics with modelling, computer science, computing, digital media and games, enterprise systems architecture, financial computing, information and communication technology, information systems (business/e-commerce/human–computer interaction/social web), mathematics, modelling and management of risk, network computing, statistics, systems integration; BSc, MSc, MTech, PhD

School of Social Sciences; www.brunel.ac.uk/about/acad/sss

accounting, anthropology, anthropology and psychology/sociology, business economics/ finance/management, child development and youth, communications, cross-cultural/ evolutionary psychology,studies of globalisation, governance, health, history, international money, international politics, international relations, investment, media and communications, media studies, medical anthropology, politics, psychoanalysis, psychology, public affairs and lobbying, public policy, social and cultural research, sociology; BA, BSc, MRes, MSc, PhD

School of Sport and Education; www.brunel.ac.uk/about/acad/sse

contemporary education, information and communication technology, mathematics, PGCert (secondary) English, physical education, science (primary with QTS, sport and exercise psychology, human performance, sport psychology), secondary education (physical education), sport sciences (coaching/human performance/management of sport development/physical education and youth sport), youth and community studies/work; BA, BSc, EdD, MA, MPhil, MSc, PGCert, PhD

University Specialist Research Institutes offer postgraduate degree opportunities

UNIVERSITY OF BUCKINGHAM
www.buckingham.ac.uk

Buckingham Business School; www. buckingham.ac.uk/business/about/bbs

accounting, business, business enterprise, communication, communication studies, economics, finance, financial management, information systems, management, marketing, media communications, service management; BSc(Econ)(Hons), BSc(Hons), CMS, MBA, MSc/Diploma

Dept of Education; www.beds.ac.uk/ departments/schoolofeducation/ education
Teacher Training; independent PGCE, PGCE with QTS, educational leadership; MEd

School of Humanities; www. buckingham.ac.uk/humanities

Dept of Economics & International Studies; www.beds.ac.uk/international
biography, business journalism, business, communication studies, economics, EFL, English literature, EFL/ESL, English studies/for teaching, French, global affairs, history, information systems, international business and trade, international studies, journalism, law, media, media studies/communication, military history, politics, psychology, security and intelligence studies, Spanish, TESOL; BA(Hons), BSc(Econ)Hons, DPhil, MA, MPhil, MSc

Buckingham School of Law; www. buckingham.ac.uk/law
access to law, common law, international and commercial law, law; Certificate, Diploma, LlB, LlM

School of Medicine; www.buckingham. ac.uk/medicine
graduate entry/postgraduate schools general internal medicine; Clinical MD, MBBS, MSc

School of Science; www.buckingham. ac.uk/science
applied computing, computing, innovative computing; BSc, Cert Comp, MSc, PGDip, Phd

Psychology; www.buckingham.ac.uk/ psychology
cognition & perception, developmental/educational/ music psychology; BSc(Hons), MPhil, MSc, PhD

Clore Laboratory
diabetes, obesity and metabolic research, bioinformatics; DPhil, MPhil, MSc

BUCKINGHAMSHIRE NEW UNIVERSITY
www.bucks.ac.uk

Faculty of Creativity and Culture; www. bucks.ac.uk/PDF/creativityandculture

School of Arts & Media; www.bucks.ac.uk/ about/structure/academic.schools/ arts.media
American literature, creative writing, drama, English literature, film, journalism, post colonial literature, script writing, televison drama

School of Music, Entertainment, and the Moving Image; www.bucks.ac.uk/about/ structure/academic.schools/ music.entertainment.image
commercial music, film & televison production, intellectual property law, music and entertainment/ art management, music management

School of Design & Craft; www.bucks.ac. uk/about/structure/academic.schools/ design.and-craft
art & design, ceramics and glass, furniture conservation/restoration/decorative/art/technology/design &

craft/contemporary design, jewellery, metalwork, product design, silversmithing, spatial design

School of Visual and Communication Arts; www.bucks.ac.uk/about/structure/ academic.schools/ visual.communication.arts
advertising, digital animation, digital/fine art/imaging, garden design, graphic design, illustration, interactive design, photographic arts, printmaking, textile & fashion design/fashion products; BA(Hons), BSc(Hons), FDA, MA, MPhil, PGDip, PhD

Faculty of Enterprise and Innovation; www.bucks.ac.uk/PDF/enterprise and innovation

School of Business & Management; www. bucks.ac.uk/about/structure/ academic.schools/business-management
accounting, advertising management, animal behaviour and welfare, business management, digital media communication, e-business, entrepreneurship,

equine behaviour, finance, HRM, international business, local government, management studies, marketing/communication, PR, project management, retail management, sports management, tourism management;

School of Computing & Advanced Technology; www.bucks.ac.uk/about/structure/academic.schools/computing.technology

3D AutoCAD, business information technology, computing, digital animation, digital games, e-business systems, internet & web design, mobile computing, multimedia technology, network security & management, programming, project planning, telecommunications & network management, web graphics, web page/site design

School of Human Sciences & Law; www.bucks.ac.uk/about/structure/academic.schools/human.sciences.and.law

business law, cognitive behavioural therapy, criminological psychology, international commercial law, criminology, law, police studies with criminal investigation/psychology, psychology, sports psychology, psychosociological studies, renal care

School of Sport, Leisure & Travel; www.bucks.ac.uk/about/structure/academic.schools/sport.leisure.travel

air transport, commercial pilot/training, airline & airport management, coaching, corporate events, dance, event and festival/ golf club/international football business management, international tourist/management, managing safety, pit safety training, security & disaster management, sports management, tourism, web applications; BA(Hons), BSc(Hons), Certs, DMS, Grad Dip, FD, HNC, HND, LlB(Hons), LlM, MA, MBA, MCommunMan, MSc, PhD,FD

Faculty of Society and Health; www.bucks.ac.uk/pdf/societyandhealth

School of Community Health, Education & Social Care; www.bucks.ac.uk/about/structure/academic.schools/health.education.society

adolescent in society, care in epilepsy, childhood obesity, community health care/nursing (children/district nursing/mental health), counselling, education (nursing, midwifery, health visiting), ethnographies, health & social care, risk, leadership & management, learning & teaching in HE, mental health, nurse prescribing, practice development (community development/community health & social care/early years/education/mental health/social work/children & young people/primary education/public health), primary education, qualified teacher programme, recovery & social inclusion, self harm & suicide, sexual health, social work, health visiting/school nursing, population health, teaching & learning in primary school, working with children & young people; BSc(Hons), FD, PGDip

School of Continuing & Advanced Practice; www.bucks.ac.uk/about/structure/academic.schools/continuing.advanced.practice

advanced nurse practioner, advanced practice/respiratory care, cancer & palliative care, critical care, counselling; BSc(Hons), Diploma, MSc

School of Pre-registration Nursing; www.bucks.ac.uk/about/structure/academic.schools/pre-registration.nursing

biophysiology of the child and neonate, nursing (child/mental health/adult); BSc(Hons)

UNIVERSITY OF CAMBRIDGE
www.cam.ac.uk

School of Arts and Humanities; www.csah.cam.ac.uk

Faculty of Architecture and History of Art; www.aha.cam.ac.uk

architecture, environmental design, design in the built environment, history of art, medieval art and architecture, Renaissance art & architecture, 20th-century art & theory, western & non-western cultural exchange; BA, MPhil, MSt, PhD

Faculty of Asian & Middle Eastern Studies; www.ames.cam.ac.uk

Chinese studies, Hebrew and Aramaic studies, Japanese studies, Middle Eastern and Islamic studies; BA, MPhil, PhD

Faculty of Classics; www.classics.cam.ac.uk

art and archaeology, classics, Greek and Latin literature, history, philology and linguistics, philosophy; BA, MPhil, PGCE

Faculty of Divinity; www.divinity.cam.ac.uk

biblical studies, church history, historical and systematic theology, religious studies and the philosophy of religion; BA, MPhil, PhD, PGDip

Faculty of English; www.english.cam.ac.uk

American literature, Anglo-Saxon, Norse & Celtic, English & applied linguistics, English literature, European languages and literatures, English studies: criticism and culture/18th-century and romantic studies; language for literature; BA, MLitt, MPhil, PhD

Faculty of Modern and Medieval Languages; www.mml.cam.ac.uk

Depts of French, German & Dutch, Italian, Spanish and Portuguese, European literature, Linguistics, Modern Greek, neo-Latin, Russian studies, screen & media cultures, Slavonic studies; BA, MPhil, PhDE

Faculty of Music; www.mus.cam.ac.uk

ethnomusicology, historical musicology, music/with education studies, analysis, practical musicianship, tonal compositions and analysis and repertoire, musical composition, science and music; BA, MPhil, PhD

Faculty of Philosophy; www.phil.cam.ac.uk

ethics, experimental psychology, history of philosophy, logic, metaphysics, philosophy of science, political philosophy; BA, MPhil, PhD

School of Humanities and Social Science; www.cshss.cam.ac.uk

Faculty of Archaeology and Anthropology; www.archanthcam.ac

archaeological heritage & museum, archaeology, archaeology of the Americas, biological anthropology, Egyptian archaeology, European prehistory, human evolutionary studies, medieval archaeology, Mesopotamian archaeology, palaeolithic and mesolithic archaeology, social anthropology, south Asian archaeology; BA, MPhil, PhD

Faculty of Economics; www.econ.cam.ac.uk

asset pricing, behavioural economics, British industrialisation, economics of networks, economics of poor countries, industrial organisation, microeconomics, politics, quantitative methods; BA, Diploma, MPhil, PhD

Faculty of Education; www.educ.cam.ac.uk

arts culture and education, child and adolescent counselling, citizenship and well-being in schools, critical approaches to children's literature, education, educational leadership and school improvement, inclusive and special psychology and education, mathematics, PGCE; early years, primary, secondary, second language education; BA, MEd, PGCE, PGDip/Cert, PhD

Faculty of History; www.hist.cam.ac.uk

American history, British political and constitutional history, economic history, European history, extra-European history, medieval history, political thought; BA, MPhil, PhD

Faculty of Law; www.law.cam.ac.uk

criminological research, criminology, international law, law, legal studies, large range of legal topics at Master level; BA, Diploma, LLD, LLM, MLitt, MPhil, PhD

Institute of Criminology; www.crim.cam.ac.uk

applied criminology, penology and management, applied criminology and police management; MPhil, MSt, PhD

Faculty of Politics, Psychology, Sociology and International Studies; www.ppsis.cam.ac.uk

Politics and International Studies; www.ppsis.cam.ac.uk

history of political thought, international relations, modern world politics, the political theorists, politics, representative democracy; BA, MPhil, MSt, PhD

Dept of Psychology

psychology, social and developmental psychology

Dept of Sociology

sociology, modern society and global transformations; BA, MPhil, PhD

Centre for Family Research

bioethics & the family, early social development & the family, genetics, health & families, non-traditional families; MPhil, PhD

History and Philosophy of Science; www.hps.cam.ac.uk

history, philosophy and sociology of science, technology and medicine; BA, MPhil, PhD

Land Economy; www.landecon.cam.ac.uk

environmental policy, land economy, planning, growth and regeneration, real estate finance; BA, MPhil, PhD

Centre of Latin American Studies; www.latin-america. cam.ac.uk

economic issues in contemporary Latin America, history of South American external relations, Latin American Literary culture/film and visual arts, race and ethnicity/anthropology/sociology and politics in Latin America; MPhil, PhD

Centre of African Studies; www.africa.cam.ac.uk

African studies; MPhil

Centre of South Asian Studies

modern South Asian studies; MPhil

Development Studies Committee; www.devstudies. cam.ac.uk

development studies

School of Biological Sciences; www.cam. ac.uk/sbs

Faculty of Biology; www.cam.ac.uk

agriculture, biochemistry, biotechnology and pharmacological industries, experimental psychology, genetics, genomes and gene products, health, integrated functional systems, pathology, pharmacology, physiology, development and neuroscience, plant sciences, zoology; BA, MPhil, PhD

Faculty of Veterinary Medicine

Department of Veterinary Medicine; www.vet.cam.ac. uk/

Clinical Course: veterinary science, preclinical course; MPhil, VetMB

Wellcome Trust Centre for Stem Cell Research; www.cscr.cam.ac.uk

stem cell biology; PhD

Wellcome Trust/Cancer Research UK Gurdon InstituteTechnolog; www.gurdon. cam.ac.uk

cellular and molecular biology, developmental, cell and cancer biology; PhD

PostDoc School of Technology; www. tech.ac.uk

Faculty of Engineering; www.eng.cam.ac. uk

engineering (aerospace & aerothermal, civil, electrical & electronic, engineering for sustainable development, environmental, industrial systems, information & computer, instrument & control, manufacture and management, manufacturing, mechanical, structural); BA(Hons), MEng, MPhil, PhD

Faculty of Business & Management (Judge Business School); www.jbs.cam.ac.uk

business & management economics, energy & environment, finance & accounting, information systems, international business, management science & operations, organisational analysis

Computer Laboratory; www.clcam.ac.uk

advanced computer science, computer science, computer speech, text and internet technology; BA, MPhil, PhD

Department of Chemical Engineering & Biotechnology; www.ceb.cam.ac.uk

advanced chemical engineering, bioscience enterprise, biotechnology, chemical engineering; BA/ MEng, MPhil, PhD

Cambridge Programme for Sustainability Leadership; www.cpi.cam.ac.uk

cross-sector partnership, sustainable business, sustainability leadership MSt, PGCert

School of Physical Sciences; www.cam. ac.uk/about/physsci

Faculty of Earth Sciences & Geography; www.esg.cam.ac.uk

conservation leadership, earth sciences, environment, geography, geological science, minerals science, society & development; BA, MPhil, PhD

Scott Polar Research Institute; www.spri. cam.ac.uk

glaciology, polar studies; MPhil, PhD

Faculty of Mathematics; www.maths.cam. ac.uk

applied mathematics and theoretical physics, computational bilology, mathematics, mathematics with physics, pure mathematics and mathematical statistics, statistical science; BA, MPhil, PhD

Statistical Laboratory Faculty of Physics & Chemistry; www.statslab.cam.ac.uk

astronomy, astrophysics, materials science and metallurgy, nanoscience & technology, physical, theoretical inorganic, organic chemistry, physics; BA, MPhil, MSci, PhD

School of Clinical Medicine; www. medschlca.ac.uk

Dept of Clinical Biochemistry (Metabolic Research Laboratories); www.clbc.cam.ac. uk
biomedical research, diabetes, molecular cell biology of membrane traffic pathways, obesity and other related endocrine and metabolic disorders; PhD

Dept of Clinical Neurosciences (Cambridge Centre for Brain Repair; Neurology Unit; Neurosurgery; Wolfson Brain Imaging Centre); www.neurosciences.medschl.am. ac.uk
cognitive brain science, dementia, genetics of multiple sclerosis, glial cell biology unit, haemorrhagic stroke, hydrocephalus, memory and semantics group, movement disorders, stroke research; MB/ PhD

Dept of Haematology; www.haem.cam.ac. uk
transfusion medicine diagnostics development; PhD

Dept of Medical Genetics; www.cimr.cam. ac.uk/medgen
eye diseases, genetics of inflammatory disorders, juvenile diabetes, neurological anaesthesia, brain mapping, clinical gerontology, clinical pharmacology, developmental psychiatry, obstetrics & gynaecology, oncology, orthopaedic research, paediatrics, psychiatry, public health & primary care – general practice & primary care, radiology, renal medicine, surgery; BChir, MB, MD, PhD

CAMBRIDGE INTERNATIONAL COLLEGE
www.cambridgecollege.ac.uk

business and economics, financial management, marketing and management, human resource administration; BA, Diplomas

CANTERBURY CHRIST CHURCH UNIVERSITY
www.canterbury.ac.uk

Faculty of Arts and Humanities; www. canterbury.ac.uk/arts-humanities
access to music, American studies, applied linguistics, art, commercial music, digital media, English, English language and communication/language studies, film, radio and television studies, film production, fine and applied arts, history, history with archaeology, media, media and cultural studies, multimedia journalism, music, music production, music technology, performing arts, religious studies, theology, visual art; BA(Hons), BA/BSc, Foundation Degree, MA, MMus, MPhil/PhD, PGDip

Faculty of Business and Management; www.canterbury.ac.uk/business-management

The Business School; www.canterbury.ac. uk/business-management/business-school
accounting and finance, advertising management, business & management, business management, business studies, culinary business, economics, entrepreneurship, human resources management, logistics, management studies, managerial finance, marketing, music industry management, retail management

Centre for Leadership & Management; www.canterbury.ac.uk/business-management/CLMD
coaching, leadership development, organisational development, personal effectiveness, project management, recruitment and selection; BSc(Hons), MA, MBA, MPhil/PhD, MSc, PGDip/Cert

Faculty of Education; www.cantebury.ac. uk/ education

childhood studies, early childhood studies, early years, early years professional status, early years studies, educational studies, enabling learning, inclusion and institutional development, leadership and management for learning, lifelong learning, literacy and learning, religion in education,school development, teaching skills for life – numeracy, literacy/ ESOL

PGCE; primary teaching, 7–14, 11–16 (iteach), 11–18, 14–19, post-compulsory primary education

ICT research; post-compulsory education, post graduate initial teacher education, primary education, professional development; BA(Hons), EdD, EYPS, FDA, MA, MPhil/PhD

Faculty of Health and Social Care; www. canterbury.ac.uk/health/home

Department of Allied Health Professions; www.canterbury.ac.uk/health/allied-health-professions

advanced occupational therapy practice, clinical reporting, diagnostic radiography, health and social care, medical imaging, occupational therapy, radiography, speech language therapy

Centre for Health and Social Care Research; www. canterbury.ac.uk/health/health-social-care-research

Dementia Services Development Centre South East; www.dementiacentre.canterbury.ac.uk/
mental health, public health

Dept of Family, Health and Well-being; www.canterbury.ac.uk/health

dance movement, health and social care, health studies (health promotion, public health, maternal and child health, practice based play therapy), health-wellbeing-family, interprofessional health & social care (health promotion and public health), midwifery, nursing, psychotherapy

Department of Nursing and Applied Clinical Studies; www.canterbury.ac.uk/ health/nursing-applied-clinical-studies

adult nursing, advancing nursing practice, cancer care, cardiac nursing, clinical judgement and decision making, cultural diversity, ethics of health care delivery. gerontology and dementia related studies, interprofessional education and academic development, interprofessional health & social care, nursing competence, practice development, practice

education, public and community health, workforce analysis and development

Department of Social Work, Community and Mental Health; www.canterbury.ac.uk/ health/social-work-community-mental-health

children and families, health and social care, mental health and learning disabilities, nursing studies (mental health nursing), social work, specialist social work with adults/in mental health services, young children, their families and carers; Adv Dip, BSc(Hons), DipHE, Foundation Degree, GradCert, MA, MPhil/PhD, MRes, MSc

Faculty of Social and Applied Sciences; www.canterbury.ac.uk/social applied-science

Dept of Applied Psychology; www. canterbury.ac.uk/social-applied-sciences/ aspd

applied social & psychological development, clinical psychology, cognitive behavioural therapy and psychological wellbeing practice, psychology

Dept of Applied Social Science; www. canterbury.ac.uk/social-applied-sciences

global governance, global politics, politics and governance, politics and international relations, sociology and social science

Dept of Computing; www.canterbury.ac. uk/social-applied-sciences/computing

business computing, computing, cybercrime forensics, forensic computing

The Department of Law and Criminal Justice Studies; www.canterbury.ac.uk/ social-applied-sciences/crime-and-policing

applied criminology, crime and policing, crime and policing studies, forensic investigation, police studies, policing

Dept of Geographical and Life Sciences; www.canterbury.ac.uk/social-applied-sciences/geographical-and-life-sciences

animal science, biosciences, ecology and conservation, environmental biology, environmental science, geography, integrated science, urban and regional studies

Dept of Sports Science, Tourism and Leisure; www.canterbury.ac.uk/social-applied-sciences/sport-science-tourism-and-leisure

event management, sport and exercise science, sport and exercise psychology, sport and leisure management, sport science, tourism and leisure studies, tourism management

CARDIFF UNIVERSITY
www.cardiff.ac.uk

Welsh School of Architecture; www.cardiff.ac.uk/archi

architecture, environmental designs of buildings, sustainable energy and environment, urban design, BSc, DipProfStudies, MA, MArch, MPhil, MSc, PhD

School of Biosciences; www.cardiff.ac.uk/bios

biochemistry, biology, biomedical science – anatomy/neuroscience/physiology, biophotonics, biotechnology, ecology, genetics, microbiology, molecular biology, zoology; BSc(Hons), MRes, MSc, PhD

Cardiff Business School; www.cardiff.ac.uk/carbs

accounting, banking, business economics, business management – human resources/international/logistics & operations/marketing, economics, finance, financial economics, HRM, international economics, international transport, lean operations, management studies,marine policy, marketing, port and shipping management, public /policy, strategic marketing; BSc, BScEcon, MBA, MPA, MSc, PhD

School of Chemistry

chemical biology, chemistry, chemistry with physics/industrial experience, heterogeneous catalysis and surface science, inorganic chemistry, organic synthesis, physical organic chemistry, solid state and materials chemistry, theoretical and computational chemistry; BSc, MChem, MPhil, PhD

School of City & Regional Planning; www.cardiff.ac.uk/c/plan

city & regional planning, geography (human) & planning, geography, international planning, regeneration studies, sustainability, planning and environmental policy, transport, urban design; BSc, MSc, PhD

School of Computer Science; www.cardiff.cs.cf.ac.uk

computer science, information systems/computer vision and computer graphics/knowledge and information systems/distributed and mobile systems/computing/computer systems engineering, strategic information systems, information security and privacy; BSc, MSc, PhD

School of Dentistry; www.cardiff.ac.uk/dentl

dental surgery, dental therapy & hygiene, implantology, oral diseases, orthodontics, tissue engineering; BDS, BSc(Hons), MClinDent, MD, MPhil, MSc, PhD

School of Earth and Ocean Sciences; www.cardiff.ac.uk/earth

earth sciences, environmental geoscience/hydrogeology, exploration and resource geology, geobiology, geology, marine geography; BSc, MESc, MPhil, MSc, PhD

School of Engineering; www.cardiff.ac.uk/engin

architectural/civil/environmental/clinical engineering, communication engineering and signal processing, computer systems/electrical and electronic engineering, electronic and communications/environmental/water/geoenvironmental/integrated engineering, mechanical/medical/orthopaedic/structural engineering, sustainable energy and environment; BEng, EngD, MEng, MPhil, MSc, PhD

School of English, Communication & Philosophy; www.cardiff.ac.uk/encap

applied linguistics, communication, creative writing, critical and cultural theory/criticism, English language/literature, ethics and social philosophy, forensic linguistics, language and communication, philosophy; BA, Diploma, MA/Dip, MPhil, PhD

School of European Studies; www.cardiff.ac.uk/euros

European/European Union studies, international relations, political theory, languages, law, politics translation studies; BA, BScEcon, LlB, MA, MScEcon, MPhil, PhD

School of Healthcare Studies; www.cardiff.ac.uk/sohcs

healthcare science, intra & perioperative practice, medical illustration, neurorehabilitation, neuro-musculoskeletal physiotherapy, occupation & health, occupational therapy, operating department practice, physiotherapy, radiography, radiotherapy & oncology, sports physiotherapy, surgical care practice; CertHE, DipHE, MPhil, MSc, PGDip/Cert, PhD

School of History and Archaeology; www.cardiff.ac.uk/hisar

ancient and medieval warfare, ancient history, archaeology, care of collections, conservation/ of objects, early Celtic studies, early medieval society and culture, European neolithic, history and archaeology of the Greek and Roman world, history, Byzantine studies, medieval British studies/history, Welsh history; BA, BSc, MA, MPhil, MSc, PhD

Journalism Media and Cultural Studies; www.cardiff.ac.uk/jomec

film & media, international journalism/journalism, political communications, science, media and communication; BA, MA, MPhil, MSc, PGDip, PhD

School of Law; www.law.cf.ac.uk

canon law, commercial law, European legal studies, human rights, medical practice, law, law & criminology/politics/sociology/French/German/Welsh, social care law; LlB, LlM, MPhil, PhD

Centre for Lifelong Learning

languages, business & management, computer studies, law, science & environment, social studies

School of Mathematics; www.cardiff.ac.uk/maths

analysis, computing in the physical sciences, fluid dynamics, mathematics/& its applications, numerical analysis, operational research and statistics, statistical mechanics; BSc, MMath, MPhil, MSc, PhD

Manufacturing Engineering Centre

industrial engineering and systems engineering, manufacturing engineering; MPhil, PhD

School of Medicine; www.cardiff.ac.uk/medic

advanced surgical practice, bioinformatics, child health, critical care, dermatology, diabetes, geriatric medicine, intensive care medicine, learning disabilities, public health, medical genetics, medicine, obstetrics & gynaecology, occupational health, oncology, paediatrics, pain management, palliative medicine, primary care & public health, psychiatry, therapeutics, wound healing; MBBCh, MD, MPH, MPhil, MSc/PGDip/Cert, PhD

School of Music; www.cardiff.ac.uk/music

composition, ethnomusicology, music, musicology, performance studies; BA/BMus, MA, MMus, PhD

School of Nursing & Midwifery Studies; www.cardiff.ac.uk/sonims

adult nursing, advanced practice, children's nursing, community public health nursing, health studies, independent prescribing, mental health, non-medical prescribing, nursing children and young people with cancer; BMid, BN, BSc(Hons), DipHE, DNurs, DocProf, MPhil, MSc, PGDip/Cert, PhD

School of Optometry & Vision Sciences; www.cardiff.ac.uk/optom

clinical investigation, vision sciences, optometry, visual neuroscience and molecular biology; BSc, MPhil, PhD

School of Pharmacy; www.cardiff.ac.uk/phrmy

clinical pharmacy, clinical research, community pharmacy, independent prescribing for pharmacists and nurses, pharmaceutical medicine, pharmacy; Dipl, MPharm, MPhil, MSc, PhD,

School of Physics and Astronomy; www.cardiff.ac.uk/astro

astrophysics, biophotonics, physics, medical physics, theoretical and computational physics; BSc, MPhil, MPhys, PhD

Postgraduate Medical and Dental Education

dental education, general practice, hospital practice, medical education

School of Psychology; www.cardiff.ac.uk/psych

clinical psychology, educational psychology, psychology; BSc, DEdPsych, DClinPsych, GradDip, PhD

School of Religious and Theological Studies; www.cardiff.ac.uk/relig

chaplaincy studies, Christian doctrine/ethics, church history, religious & theological studies; BA, DipD, MA, MPhil, MTh, PhPG

School of Social Sciences; www.cardiff.ac.uk/socsci

criminal justice, criminology, social sciences, education, equality and diversity, social policy, social science research methods, sociology; BA, BSc, DHS, DSW, EdD, MA, MSc, PGCE

School of Welsh; www.cardiff.ac.uk/welsh

Welsh, Welsh ethnological studies, Welsh history; BA, MA, PhD

UNIVERSITY OF CENTRAL LANCASHIRE
www.uclan.ac.uk

Faculty of Arts, Humanities and Social Sciences; www.uclan.ac.uk/ahss

School of Creative & Performing Arts; www.uclan.ac.uk/ahss/creative.performing.arts

acting; contemporary theatre and performance, dance, music practice/production/theatre, performance and teaching, fine art, contemporary visual arts, drawing and image making, site and archive interventions, brand promotion, creative fashion knit, digital design for fashion, eastern fashion, fashion design, fashion promotion, marketing management, retail management (fashion), styling; BA(Hons), MA, MBA, MPhil, PGCert/Dip, PhD, UniCert

Northern School of Design; www.uclan.ac.uk/ahss/design

3D design, advertising, animation, antiques, ceramics, children's book illustration, computer games, consumer product design, contemporary visual arts, design, digital graphics, food styling, games design, graphic design, illustration, interior design, product design, textiles; BA(Hons), BSc(Hons), MA, PGDip/Cert, MPhil, PhD

School of Education and Social Sciences; www.uclan.ac.uk/ahss/education.social.sciences

Criminology: criminal justice, law and criminology
Deaf Studies: British sign language/English interpreting & translation/communication, deaf studies, support work, education/post-compulsory, learning in healthcare practice
History: contemporary visual arts, history, history of medicine and education, history of popular culture, labour history, local history, family and community history, modern world history, museums and heritage, North America and South Asia

Social Sciences: ethnicity & human rights, politics, religion, culture & society, sociology; BA(Hons), BSc(Hons), MA, Mhil, PGCE, PhD, UnivCert

School of Journalism, Media and Communication; www.uclan.ac.uk/ahss/journalism.media.communication

American studies, broadcast/community/international/magazine/sports/online journalism, English and theatre studies, English language and literature, film and media studies, TV screenwriting, film theory and documentary practice, infographics, interactive digital media/production, media, modern & contemporary literature, news graphics, play writing, publishing, rhetoric, web & multimedia, writing for children; BSc(Hons), BA(Hons), MA, MPhil, PGDip, PGCert, PhD

Lancashire Law School; www.uclan.ac.uk/ahss/lancashire.law.school

advanced legal practice, bioethics and medical law, employment law, European commercial law, forensic and legal medicine, human rights, international business law, law, criminology, information and converging technologies, medical law and bioethics; BA(Hons), BA/BSc, LlB, LLM, MA, MPhil, PGDip

School of Languages and International Studies; www.uclan.ac.uk/ahss/languages.and.international/

Asia Pacific studies, Arabic, Chinese, French/business French, German/business German, TESOL with applied linguistics; BA(Hons), MPhil, PhD

Faculty of Health and Social Care; www.uclan.ac.uk/health

School of Dentistry, & Institute for Postgraduate Dental Education; www.uclan.ac.uk/health/schools/dentistry.at.uclan/

aesthetic dental implantology, clinical periodontology, dental surgery, endodontology, oral surgery, orthodontic therapy, restorative cosmetic dentistry; BDS, CertHE, MSc

School of Nursing and Care Science; www.uclan.ac.uk/health/schools/school.of.nursing/

professional practice – adult nursing, children's nursing, mental health nursing, professional practice – acute, operative and critical care, children, family and community health, complementary therapies, continuing and long-term care, counselling and psychological therapies, emergency and unscheduled care, mental health, pre-hospital care; Advanced Certificate, BSc(Hons), Grad Certi, MPhil, MSc, PGDip, PhD

School of Public Health and Clinical Sciences; www.uclan.ac.uk/health/schools/sphcs/

applied public health, asymptomatic/cervical screening, epidemiology and statistics, exercise referral, general practice, group leadership in primary care, gynaecological care, hazard analysis, health and social care (clinical imaging), health improvement, health informatics, health promotion within sexual health, health protection, health service management, health training, rheumatoid arthritis, maternal and infant nutrition, men's sexual health, midwifery, neonatal care/practice, occupational therapy, ophthalmology, pain management, physiotherapy, public health informatics, rehabilitation studies, rheumatoid arthritis, sexually transmitted infections, sport, health and fitness, sports therapy, substance use, working with people with acquired brain injury; AdvCert, BSc(Hons), DipHE, FdA, FdSc, MA, MPhil, MSc, PGDip/Cert, PhD

School of Social Work; www.uclan.ac.uk/health/schools/school.of.social.work/

care, community and citizenship, child health and social care, safeguarding children, social policy, social work; BA(Hons), MA, PGCert

Faculty of Management; www.uclan.ac.uk/management

Lancashire Business School; www.uclan.ac.uk/lbs

accounting, business, business administration, business and management/marketing, business information management/project management/studies/systems, communication management, economics, financial management, HRM, international finance, investment, logistics and supply chain management, marketing, operations, PR, retail management, sustainable business; BA(Hons), DBA, MA, MBA, MSC, PGDip/Cert

School of Sport, Tourism and the Outdoors; www.uclan.ac.uk/management/ssto

leisure (management), sport/management, sports coaching/development/event management/PR studies; BA(Hons), FdA, MA/PGDip/PGCert

Faculty of Science and Technology; www.uclan.ac.uk/sc.tech

School of Built and Natural Environment; www.uclan.ac.uk/scitech/built.natural.environment/

architecture, architectural conservation, building services, building surveying, construction/law/management/project management, environmental hazards, environmental management, facilities management, geography, project management, quantity surveying, sustainable engineering, sustainable waste management, urban, utilities management; BA(Hons), BSc(Hons), FdSc, BEng, MSc, PGDip/Cert

School of Computing, Engineering and Physical Sciences; www.uclan.ac.uk/scitech/computing.engineering.physical

Computing: computer games, computer network, forensic computing, information systems, internet software development, mobile interactive technology, multimedia development, systems management
Software Engineering: agile software projects, computing, database systems, interaction design, multimedia computing, network computing
Motor Sports & Electronic Engineering: computer aided engineering, digital signal & image processing, computer engineering, electronic design automation, electronic engineering, motor sports/engineering, robotics and mechatronics
Physics & Maths: astronomy, astrophysics, computational physics, mathematical physics, mathematics,

physics; BEng(Hons), BSc(Hons), FdSc, MEng(Hons), MPhil, MSc, PhD

School of Forensic and Investigative Sciences; www.uclan.ac.uk/scitech/ forensic.investigative/

archaeology, chemistry, fire engineering/leadership studies/investigation/safety/engineering, forensic chemistry/genetics, police and criminal investigation, risk management; BA(Hons), BEng, BSc(Hons), FdSc, MPhil, PhD

School of Pharmacy and Pharmaceutical Sciences; www.uclan.ac.uk/scitech/ pharmacy

biological sciences, biomedical science, cancer biology and therapy, independent prescribing, pharmacy, physiology and pharmacology, supplementary prescribing; BSc(Hons), MPharm, MSc, PGDip/Cert, PhD

School of Psychology; www.uclan.ac.uk/ scitech/psychology/

applied psychology, forensic psychology, health psychology, neuropsychology or sport psychology, forensic psychology, psychology; BSc(Hons), Grad-Dip, MSc

UNIVERSITY OF CHESTER
www.chester.ac.uk

Dept of Biological Sciences; www.chester.ac.uk/biology

animal behaviour, animal/zoo management, biomedical sciences, biology, diabetes management, forensic biology, human nutrition, nutrition dietetics, public health nutrition; BSc, MSc, PhD

Dept of Business; www.chester.ac.uk/ business (Chester Business School)

business administration/management/studies, information systems, international business, finance, HRM, management, marketing, tourism management; BA(Hons), BA/BSc, FdA, MBA, MPhil, PhD

Computer Science and Information Systems; www.chester.ac.uk/csis

agile development, computer studies, computing, artificial intelligence, emergent systems, e-learning, mobile computing and multimedia based music promotion; BSc(Hons), MPhil, PhD

Centre for Exercise and Nutrition Science; www.chester.ac.uk/cens

cardiovascular rehabilitation, exercise and nutrition science, weight management; MSc, PhD

Centre for Public Health Research; www.chester.ac.uk/cphr

public health, research methods; MSc

Centre for Science Communication

Centre for Research into Sport and Society; www.chester.ac.uk/scicom

sociology of sport and exercise; MSc, PhD

Education & Children's Services; www.chester.ac.uk/education

children and young education studies, early childhood studies, continuing professional development, early years practice, education, secondary/primary/early years, teaching assistance, working with children, young people and families; BA(Hons), BEd, EdD, FdA, MA, MEd, PGCE

English; www.chester.ac.uk/english

creative writing, English, English language, 19th-century literature and culture; BA, MA, PhD

Fine Art; www.chester.ac.uk/fine.art

art and design, fine art, graphic design, photography; BA(Hons), MA, MSc

Geography and Development Studies; www.chester.ac.uk/geography

geography, international development studies, natural hazard management; BA(Hons), MA, MSc, PhD

Health and Social Care; www.chester.ac.uk/health

community and child health, mental health and learning disability, midwifery and reproductive health, professional development and allied health care, pre-registration nursing, social work; BA(Hons), BSc(Hons), MA, MSc, PGCert, PhD

History and Archaeology; www.chester.ac.uk/departments/history-and-archeology

archaeology, military history; BA(Hons), MA, MPhil, PhD

Languages; www.chester.ac.uk/languages

European languages and cultures, French, German and Spanish; BA(Hons), MA, PGCert/Dip

Law; www.chester.ac.uk/law

law, law(combined), law with journalism or criminology; BA(Hons), LlB, LlM

Leadership and Management; www.chester. ac.uk/

MBA, MSc

Marketing, Tourism & Events Management; www.chester.ac.uk/events

Mathematics; www.chester.ac.uk/ mathematics

applied statistics, computational applied mathematics, mathematics; BSc(Hons), MPhil, PhD

New Technology Initiative; www.chester.ac. uk/nti

health informatics, music technology & creative industries

Sport & Exercise Sciences; www.chester.ac. uk/sport

sport and exercise sciences/sociology, sports coaching and fitness, sports development, sports sciences; BA(Hons), BSc(Hons), FD, MPhil, PhD

Social & Communication Studies; www. chester.ac.uk/scs

clinical counselling, communication studies, counselling skills/studies/supervision, crime and justice, criminology, politics, psychological trauma, PR, sociology; BA(Hons), BSc(Hons), MA, PhD

Theology & Religious Studies; www.chester. ac.uk/trs

Christian youth, community evangelism, Muslim youth work, religious studies, theology; BA(Hons), BTh, Dip HE, FdA, MA, MPhil, MTh, PhD

UNIVERSITY OF CHICHESTER
www.chiuni.ac.uk

Faculty of Business, Arts & The Humanities; www.chiuni.ac.uk/ Faculties.cfm

applied language studies, dance, drama, English, fine art, history, media, music, performing arts, theology

School of Enterprise, Management and Leadership

accounting, business studies, event management, finance, HRM, IT management for business, marketing, tourism management; BA(Hons), FD, MA, MPhil, PhD

Faculty of Sport, Education & Social Sciences; www.chiuni.ac.uk/Faculties. cfm#sportEducation

continuing professional development, international CPD, teacher education; graduate teacher programme; primary PGCE, primary undergraduate, secondary physical education PGCE, physical education, secondary PGCE

Childhood and Youth: childhood studies, education, mathematics education, teaching and learning support, teaching assistants

Psychology and Counselling: social work and social care; sport; adventure education, physical education, sports, exercise and health sciences; BA(Hons), BSc(Hons), FD, GradDip/Cert, MAPGCE, MSc, MSW, TESOL

CITY UNIVERSITY LONDON
www.city.ac.uk

School of of Arts; www.city.ac.uk/arts

Centre for Adult Education; www.city.ac.uk/cae

creative industries, music events management and production; FD

Cultural Policy and Management; www.city.ac.uk/cpm

culture, policy and management, cultural leadership programme, creative industries; FD, MA

Faculty of Journalism; www.city.ac.uk/journalism

broadcast/television/investigative/magazine/newspaper/science/international/journalism, creative writing, electronic publishing, journalism, political campaigning and reporting, publishing studies; BA(Hons), MA, MSc, PhD

Centre for Language Studies; www.city.ac.uk/languages

Dept of Music; www.city.ac.uk/music

film music and multimedia studies, mediterranean and middle eastern music studies, music composition (electroacoustic/instrumental and vocal), music performance studies, musicology/ethnomusicology, popular music studies; BMus, DMA, MA, MMA, MPhil, PhD

Centre for Translation Studies; www.city.ac.uk/

audiovisual translation, legal translation, principles and practice of translation, translation skills; Dip, MA, PG Cert

Cass Business School; www.cass.city.ac.uk

Faculty of Actuarial Science and Insurance; www.cass.city.ac.uk/facact

actuarial management, actuarial science, insurance

Faculty of Finance; www.cass.city.ac.uk/facfin

accounting, corporate finance, econometrics, investment & risk management, mathematical finance

Faculty of Management; www.cass.city.ac.uk/facmana

accounting and finance, actuarial management, actuarial science, banking and international finance, business studies, energy, trade & finance, European business, finance and investment, financial mathematics, investment analysis and insurance, investment management, international accounting & finance, management, mathematical trading, quantitative finance, real estate, real estate finance and investment, shipping, supply chain and energy courses; BSc(Hons), MBA, MEb, MPhil, MSc, PGDip, PhD

School of Engineering and Mathematical Sciences; www.city.ac.uk/sems

aeronautical engineering, air safety management, air transport engineering, air transport operations/and management, air transport management, aircraft maintenance management, analysis and design of structures for hazards, architecture, automotive & motorsport engineering, aviation management, biomedical engineering, civil engineering, civil engineering structures, clinical engineering with healthcare technology management, computer science, computer systems engineering, construction management, electrical engineering, energy and environmental technology and economics, energy and the environment, energy engineering, finance and risk, information engineering, maritime operations, mathematical science, mathematics & finance, mechanical & automotive engineering, mechanical engineering, media communication systems, multimedia and internet systems, multimedia & internet systems engineering, power systems and energy management, professional civil engineering, project management, statistics, surveying, systems and control, telecommunications, telecommunications and networks, telecommunications, electrical and electronic engineering; BEng, BSc(Hons), MEng, MMath, MPhil, MSc, PgDip, PhD

Centre for Mathematical Science; www.city.ac.uk/sems/mathematics

School of Community and Health Sciences; www.city.ac.uk/communityandhealth

adult nursing, anatomy, applied biological sciences, biochemistry, genetics, microbiology, nutrition, pathophysiology, pharmacology, physiology

City EHealth Research Centre; Education Development Unit;

interdisciplinary studies in professional practice

Investigative, Security and Police Sciences; www.city.ac.uk/cisps/pdp

applied investigation, economic crime and fraud investigation, intelligence and security, policing

Language and Communication; www.city.ac.uk/lcs

human communication, joint professional practice, speech & language therapy,

Mental Health and Learning Disabilities; www.city.ac.uk/sonm/nursing/mental-health-nursing

mental health nursing

Midwifery and Child Health; www.city.ac.uk/sonm/midwifery-child-health

child health, midwifery

Optometry and Visual Science; www.city.ac.uk/optometry

advanced/ophthalmic dispensing, applied vision research, imaging and instrumentation, optometry, visual neuroscience, visual psychophysics and perception

Public Health, Primary Care and Food Policy; www.city.ac.uk/communityandhealth/phpcfp

education, food policy, practice development, primary care (district nursing, practice nursing), public health, specialist nursing (health visiting, school nursing)

Radiography; www.city.ac.uk/radiography

nuclear medicine technology, radiography (oncology/diagnostic imaging); BSc(Hons), FD, GradDipCert, MSc, PhD

School of Informatics; www.soi.city.ac.uk

Centre for Health Informatics; www.soi.city.ac.uk/organisation/chi

health care technologies, health informatics

Centre for Human Computer Interaction Design; www-hcid.soi.city.ac.uk

human centred systems

Centre for Software Reliability; www.csr.city.ac.uk

fundamental issues for safety critical systems, modelling, software dependability (particularly safety and reliability), software fault tolerance, software metrics and quality assurance

Department of Computing; www.soi.city.ac.uk

artificial intelligence, business computing systems, computer science, electronic publishing, games technology, health informatics, human computer interaction, information management in the cultural sector, information systems, library science, music technology, software development, software engineering; BSc(Hons), MA, MSc

School of Social Sciences; www.city.ac.uk/social

Department of Economics; www.city.ac.uk/economics

accountancy, business economics, economics, economic evaluation in health care, economic regulation and competition, financial economics, health economics, international business economics, international politics, international politics and sociology

Department of International Politics; www.city.ac.uk/intpol

Department of Psychology; www.city.ac.uk/psychology

counselling psychology, clinical supervision, health psychology, organisational psychology/ organisational behaviour, psychology, psychology/psychology and health, specialist educational intervention

Dept of Sociology; www.city.ac.uk/sociology

criminology, global migration, human rights, international communications and development, media communication systems, media studies, international politics, race and ethnicity, refugee studies, social research methods, sociology, surveillance studies; BEng, BSc(Hons), DPsych, GradDip/Cert, MA, MSc, PhD, ProfDoc

Degrees validated by City University offered at:

GUILDHALL SCHOOL OF MUSIC & DRAMA
www.gsmd.ac.uk

acting, costume supervision, music, music composition, music therapy, stage management; BA(Hons), MA, MMA/DMA, MMP, MMus, PGDipls

LABAN
www.laban.org

choreography, dance, dance studies; BA(Hons), MA, MPhil, MSc, PGDipls, PhD

SCHOOL OF PSYCHOTHERAPY & COUNSELLING PSYCHOLOGY AT REGENT'S COLLEGE
www.spc.ac.uk

counselling, psychology, psychotherapy; DCounsPsy, MA, MPhil/PhD, PGDip

THE CITY LAW SCHOOL
www.city.ac.uk/law

UK and European law; BVC, DipLaw, LlB, LlM, LPC, MA, MJur, MSc, PhD

The School of Social Sciences; www.city.ac. uk/social

economics, international politics, pyschology, sociology; BSc, DPsych, DSc, Grad Cert, LlB, MA, MSc, PhD,

THE NORDOFF-ROBBINS MUSIC THERAPY CENTRE
www.nordoff-robbins.org.uk

music therapy; MMusTherapy, PGDipl

COVENTRY UNIVERSITY
www.coventry.ac.uk

Coventry School of Art & Design; www.coventry.ac.uk/artanddesign

Dept of Design & Visual Arts
fashion, fine art, graphic design, illustration

Dept of Industrial Design
automotive/bike/boat/computer-aided product/consumer product/transport/industrial product/sports product/sustainable transport/toy/transport/vehicle design

Dept of Media & Communication
advertising, culture, English, journalism, media, media production, photography

Dept of Performing Arts
dance theatre, e-music, music, music technology, professional practice

School of Lifelong Learning; www.coventry.ac.uk/SOLL
advanced management techniques, enterprise & global entrepreneurship, leadership career development, management practice, multimedia & technology, project management

Faculty of Business, Environment & Society; www.coventry.ac.uk/bes

Coventry University Business School; www.coventry.ac.uk/bes/bus
accountancy, advertising, business, administration/ decision management/economics/management/ mathematics studies, design & business, disaster management, economics, emergency planning & management, engineering/project management, enterprise & entrepreneurship, environmental/European business management, finance, HRM, information technology, international business/law/

management/marketing/sport management/tourism management, investment, law & business, leisure management, logistics, management information systems, management for construction, marketing, risk & disaster/sport business management, strategic marketing, supply chain management

Coventry University Law School; www. coventry.ac.uk/besl/aw

diplomacy/change & global/employment/global development/international business/international law, law

Department of Geography, Environment & Disaster Management; www.coventry.ac. uk/ged

climate change, disaster management & emergency planning/engineering, reconstruction & development, emergency planning & management, environmental management, geography, global sustainability, natural hazards/tourism, risk & disaster management

School of International Studies & Social Science; www.coventry.ac.uk/bes/isss

community & social action, criminology/psychology, global security, history, history politics, international crime & global security, international relations, politics, sociology, terrorism

Faculty of Engineering & Computing; www.coventry.ac.uk/ engineeringandcomputing

aerospace systems engineering/technology, architectural design technology/engineering, architecture, automotive engineering/design, aviation management, avionics technology, building/services engineering/surveying, business decision management/ information systems/technology, civil engineering/ design, computer hardware & software, computers, networking & communications technology, construction/management, control engineering, creative computing, digital forensics & system security/media production, e-commerce, electrical systems/electronic engineering, engine design & development/performance/business management/mathematics/project management, enterprise systems development,

ethical hacking & network security, European construction engineering, business management/engineering studies/industrial entrepreneurship/information technology management/logistics, financial mathematics, forensic computing, games technology, health informatics, information & systems architecture, internet & enterprise computing, IT, logistics, management, manufacturing systems engineering, mathematical sciences, mathematics, computing/statistics, mechanical engineering/design, micro-electronics & wireless systems, modelling simulation & control, motorsport & motorcycle/powertrain engineering, multimedia/network & mobile computing, operational communications, structural engineering/ with architecture, supply chain management, vehicle dynamics, vehicle structures & safety, virtual engineering

Faculty of Health & Life Sciences; www. coventry.ac.uk/hls

Dept of Clinical Psychology

clinical psychology

Dept of Nursing, Midwifery & Health Care

adult/children & young people nursing, contemporary healthcare (cancer care for teenagers & young adults), health studies, learning disability/mental health nursing, midwifery, paramedic science, social & health care management

Dept of Physiotherapy & Dietetics

acupuncture, dietetics, manual therapy, neurological physiotherapy, physiotherapy, sports nutrition

Dept of Psychology

applied forensic studies, applied/clinical/forensic psychology, crime, health psychology, parapsychology, psychology, criminology, reading development, sociology, sport psychology

Dept of Social & Community Studies

applied community & social studies/health & social care, mental health studies, practice education, social & healthcare management, social work, youth work BA(Hons), BEng(Hon), BSc(Hons), DClinP, FdA, FdSc, HNC, HND, LLB, LLM, MA, MBA, MDes, MEng, MPhil, MSc, PGCert, PGDip, PhD

CRANFIELD UNIVERSITY
www.cranfield.ac.uk

School of Applied Sciences; www.cranfield.ac.uk/sas

manufacturing, materials, natural resources, sustainble systems; EngD, MPhil, MSc, MTech, PhD

Cranfield Defence and Security; www.cranfield.ac.uk/cds

acquisition and logistics, defence chemistry, humanitarian resilience, materials science and engineering, ordnace testing and technology, security and resilience; EngD, MSc, PGDip/Cert, PhD

School of Engineering; www.cranfield.ac.uk/soe

aerospace engineering/science, air transport, applied mechanics, automotive engineering, power and propulsion, process and systems engineering, systems engineering and human factors; EngD, MSc, PhD

Cranfield Health; www.cranfield.ac.uk/health

bioinformatics, bioscience and diagnostics, environment and health, food quality, health care ops management, smart materials, translation medicine; DM, MSc

Cranfield School of Management; www.cranfield.ac.uk/som

business performance, complex systems, economics, enterprise, entrepreneurship, executive development, finance and accounting, information systems, logistics and supply chain management, management development, management knowledge and strategic change, marketing and sales management, operations management, organization studies, praxis, programme and project management, strategic management; DBA, MBA, MSc, PhD

UNIVERSITY OF CUMBRIA
www.cumbria.ac.uk

Faculty of the Arts; www.cumbria.ac.uk/about us/faculties/faculty of the arts

School of Media and Performing Arts

games design, media production, multimedia design and digital animation, music, performing arts, scriptwriting

School of Art and Design

ceramics, crafts, drawing, fine art, furniture, graphic design, illustration, jewellery, metalwork, photography

School of Humanities

American studies, art, contemporary culture, creative writing, drama, English language/literature, film studies, geography, history; BA(Hons), DipHE, MA, MPhil, PhD, TESOL

Faculty of Business, Social Sciences and Sport; www.cumbria.ac.uk/aboutus/faculties/facultyofbsss

School of Applied Social Sciences

applied psychology, counselling, policing and criminal justice studies, social science, youth and community development; AdvUnivDip, BA(Hons), BSc(Hons), DipHE, PdAMA, PdSc, PgDip/Cert

Faculty of Education; www.cumbria.ac.uk/aboutus/faculties/education

graduate teacher programme, mathematics development for teachers, science additional specialism programme, student associates scheme, subject knowledge enhancement; FD, BA/BSc(Hons), GTS, PGCE

Faculty of Science and Natural Resources; www.cumbria.ac.uk/aboutus/faculties/facultyofscienceandnaturalresources

National School of Forestry

forest and woodland management/ecosystem management, forestry

School of Outdoor Studies

adventure, environment, integrated land management, studies, recreation management, sustainable rural recreation, wildlife

School of Construction, Engineering & Technology

applied chemistry, applied science and technology, construction management, engineering, environmental engineering, forensic science, mechanical engineering, renewable energy, sustainable engineering; BA(Hons), BEng(Hons), BSc(Hons), FdEd, FdSc, MA, MSc, PGDip

Faculty of Health, Medical Science & Social Care; www.cumbria.ac.uk/about us/faculties/facultyofhealth

School of Nursing & Nidwifery

community and public health nursing, family planning and sexual healthcare, learning disabilities nursing and children's nursing, medical imaging science; radiography, medical imaging, mental health nursing, midwifery, nurse practitioner, occupational therapy, physiotherapy, public health and complementary therapy; BSc(Hons), CPD, DipHE, FdSc, MSc, PGC, PGD, PhD, Rad

DEMONTFORD UNIVERSITY
www.dmu.ac.uk

Faculty of Art and Design; www.dmu.ac. uk/faculties/art.and.design

architecture, dance, design, fashion, fine art, graphics design, media studies, photography, product design, textiles; BA(Hons), BArch(Hons), BSc(Hons), DipHE, FoundStud, MA, MA/MSc, MPhil, PGDip, PhD

Faculty of Business and Law; www.dmu. ac.uk/faculties/business.and.law

advertising, business, economics, finance, HRM, law, leadership, marketing, public policy; BA(Hons), BSc(Hons), DipHE, GDL/CPE, HND, LlBHons, LLM, LPC, MA, MPhil, MBA, MSc, PGDip/Cert, PhD

Faculty of Health and Life Sciences; www.dmu.ac.uk/faculties/his

audiology, biomedical science, criminology, dental tech, enviroment, forensic science, human community, psychology, social work, youth work; BA(Hons), BSc(Hons), DipHE, FdA, MA, MPharm(Hons), MSc, PGDip, RSHDip

Faculty of Humanities; www.dmu.ac.uk/ faculties/humanities

arts management, creative writing, dance, drama, education, English, history, international relations, journalism, media studies, music; BA(Hons), MA, PGDip

Faculty of Technology (Computer Science and Engineering); www.dmu.ac. uk/faculties/technology

audio recording/technology, business information technology, computers, computers/security/science, creative technology, digital video, electronic engineering, electronic games, electronics, engineering design, forensic computing, info/commtech, mechatronics, media production/technology, mutilmedia computing, music, music technology, radio, software engineering; BEng, BSc(Hons), HND, MPhil, MSc, PGDip, PhD

UNIVERSITY OF DERBY
www.derby.ac.uk

Faculty of Art, Design, and Technology; www.derby.ac.uk/adt

American studies, applied art, architecture, commercial photographic fashion, creative writing, film/TV, history, media, motorsport, music and medical technologies, product design, textiles, theatre, visual commerce; BA(Hons), MDes, PhD, Univ Cert/Dip

Faculty of Business, Computing and Law; www.derby.ac.uk/bcl

computing/forensics, games networks, HRM, leadership, marketing, maths, purchasing & supply; BA(Hons), BSc(Hons), FD, LlBHons, LlM, MA, MPharm, MPhil/PhD, MSc, PGdip/Cert

Faculty of Education, Health and Sciences; www.derby.ac.uk/ehs

biological science, education studies, geography and environmental science, mental health, nursing studies, occupational therapy, pyschology, public health, sports and exercise, teacher education; Adv Dip, BA(Hons), BEd, BSc(Hons), EdD, FdA, HNC/HND, jtHons, MA, MSC, PGCert/Dip, PGCE, PhD, Univ Cert/Dip

DONCASTER BUSINESS SCHOOL
www.don.ac.uk/dbs

acting, building services engineering, business, construction, creative arts, criminology, dance/theatre, early years education, engineering, English, fashion, fine art, graphic design, HRM, information and communication technology, marketing, moving image, music/music technology, purchasing, script writing, social science, sport and leisure, textiles; CIM, CIPD, CIPS, FdA, FdSc, HND/HNCBA(Hons), MA, MBA, MSc, PGCE, PGCert, ProfCertEd

UNIVERSITY OF DUNDEE
www.dundee.ac.uk

College of Art, Sciences and Engineering; www.dundee.ac.uk/case

School of Architecture; www.architecture.dundee.ac.uk
architecture, advanced sustainability of the built environment

School of Computing; www.computing.dundee.ac.uk
applied computing, artificial intelligence, business intelligence, computing, e-commerce, design ethnography, information technology, interactive media design, international business, vision and imaging

Duncan of Jordanstone College of Art and Design; www.djcad.dundee.ac.uk
animation, art and design, art and digital film, art philosophy, design – graphic/interior and environmental/innovative product/interactive media/jewellery and metal/textile, exhibitions, fine art, illustration, media arts and imaging

School of Engineering, Physics and Mathematics; www.dundee.ac.uk/eps
applied physics, civil engineering/and management, concrete design and environmental management, electronic engineering and electrical engineering/microcomputer systems/management, electronic engineering and physics, mathematics, mechanical engineering & mechatronics, physics, renewable engineering; BA(Ord/Hons), BEng, BSc, CertHE, DipHE, MArch, MEng, MRes, MSc, MSci, PhD

College of Arts and Social Sciences; www.dundee.ac.uk/artsoc

School of Accounting & Finance; www.dundee.ac.ukaccountancy
accountancy, finance, business management, international accountancy, international finance, Islamic accounting and finance, strategic financial management

Continuing Education; www.dundee.ac.uk/conted

School of Education, Social Work and Community Education; www.dundee.ac.uk/eswce
Teaching; community education (learning & development), education, educational psychology, PGDE primary/secondary, primary education, teaching qualification (further education/higher education), social work

Interdisciplinary Disability Research Institute (IDRIS)

Institute for Research and Innovation in Social Services (IRISS)

School of Humanities; www.dundee.ac.uk/humanities

Centre for Archive and Information Studies; www.dundee.ac.uk/cias
archives and records management/information rights, family and local history

Communication and Language Studies; www.dundee. ac.uk/language studies

English; www.dundee.ac.uk/English

English, English studies English and film studies

History; www.dundee.ac.uk/history

early America, European history Greater Britain in the twentieth century, history, Scottish history, urban and cultural history

Institute for Transatlantic, European and American Studies; www.dundee.ac.uk/iteas

American studies, contemporary European studies, transatlantic studies

Philosophy; www.dundee.ac.uk/philosophy

European philosophy, philosophy

Politics; www.dundee.ac.uk/politics

European politics, geopolitics and international relations, international relations and politics

School of Law; www.dundee.ac.uk/law

commercial and international commercial law, company law and corporate governance, criminal justice and evidence, English law, environmental law, European law, family law, healthcare law and ethics, human rights, property, contract, tort & delict private international law, public international law, public law, Scottish law

Graduate School of Natural Resources Law, Policy and Management; www.dundee.ac. uk/postgradschool

Centre for Energy, Petroleum and Mineral Law and Policy

energy law and policy, international and comparative nuclear law and policy, international dispute resolution and management, mineral law and policy, natural resources law and policy

UNESCO Centre for Water Law, Policy and Science

international water management, water law, water governance and conflict resolution

School of Psychology; www.dundee.ac.uk/psychology

psychological research methods, psychological therapy in primary care, psychology

School of Social and Environmental Sciences; www.dundee.ac.uk/social science

Economic Studies: business economics with marketing, economics, financial economics, spatial economics and development, numerous joint degrees with economics, energy studies, international business

Environmental Science: environmental science/with geography, hydrosphere, ecosphere, cryosphere, lithosphere

Geography: applied population and welfare geography, environmental management, environmental sustainability, European urban conservation, geography and planning and the distance learning programme in community regeneration, international urban conservation and in spatial planning, remote sensing, social research methods, sustainable catchment management, town and regional planning MA(Hons), MLitt/MSc, MSc, LlB, LlM, PhD, PGCert

College of Life Sciences; www.lifesci. dundee.ac.uk

Taught courses; anatomical sciences, biochemistry & physiological sciences, biological chemistry, biomedical sciences, biomolecular drug discovery, crops for the future, drug design and mechanisms, drug discovery, environmental biology, environmental biology conversion, forensic anthropology, forensic art, human anatomy, medical art, microbiology, molecular biology, molecular genetics, neuroscience, pharmacology, physiological sciences, physiology, sports biomedicine, zoology

School of Research

Centre for Anatomy and Human Identification; www. lifesci.dundee.ac.uk/CAHId

Div of Biological Chemistry and Drug Discovery; www. lifesci.dundee.ac.uk/bcdd

Biological Services (CLS); www.lifesci.dundee.ac.uk/ biolservices

Div of Cell and Developmental Biology; www.lifesci. dundee.ac.uk/cdb

Div of Cell Biology and Immunology; www.lifesci. dundee.ac.uk/cbi

CRUK Nucleic Acid Structure Research Group; www. lifesci.dundee.ac.uk/nasg

gene regulation and expression

Molecular and Environmental Microbiology; www. lifesci.dundee.ac.uk/mmb

Div of Molecular Medicine; www.lifesci.dundee.ac.uk/ mm

Div of Molecular Physiology; www.lifesci.dundee.ac. uk/mp

MRC Protein Phosphorylation Unit; www.lifesci. dundee.ac.uk/mrccpu

Div of Plant Sciences; www.lifesci.dundee.ac.uk/pl

Div of Signal Transduction Therapy; www.lifesci.
dundee.ac.uk/dstt
TMRC Research Lab
BSc(Hons), MRes, MSc, PhD

*College of Medicine, Dentistry and
Nursing; www.dundee.ac.uk/cmdn*

**School of Dentistry; www.dundee.ac.uk/
dentalschool**
dentistry, oral health science, prosthodontics

**School of Nursing and Midwifery; www.
dundee.ac.uk/medden**
advanced practice nursing and palliative care, child
nursing and midwifery, health nursing, infection
prevention and control, nursing, nursing and
midwifery

**School of Medicine; www.dundee.ac.uk/
medschool**
anaesthesia, cardiovascular lung biology, health
skills, immunology, medical science, medicine,
molecular medicine, neuroscience, oncology, orthopaedic and trauma surgery, orthopaedic and rehabilitation technology, primary care, psychiatry cognitive behavioural psychotherapy, psychological
therapy in primary care, public heath, surgery;
BDS, BHealthN, BM, BMSc, BN, BSc, DDSc, DipCert,
MA, MBChB, MChOrth, MD, MDSc, MFM, MMAS,
MMSc, MNurs, MPH, MPhil, MSc, MSSc

Biomedical Research Institute

Div of Clinical & Population Sciences & Education

Centre for Primary Care & Population Research

Dental Health Services & Research Unit (DHSRU)

Institute for Health Skills & Education

Dundee Epidemiology and Biostatistics Unit

**Institute of Cardiovascular Research Centre for
Neuroscience**

Centre for Oncology & Molecular Medicine

DURHAM UNIVERSITY
www.dur.ac.uk

*Faculty of Arts and Humanities; www.
dur.ac.uk /arts.humanities*

**Dept of Classics and Ancient History; www.
dur.ac.uk/classics**
ancient epic/historiography/philosophy, ancient history, ancient history and archaeology, classical past,
classical tradition, classics, Greece, Rome and the
Near East

**Dept of English Studies; www.dur.ac.uk/
english.studies**
English literary studies, English literature, medieval
and renaissance literary studies, romantic and Victorian literary studies, poetry, 20th-century literary
studies

Dept of History; www.dur.ac.uk/history
history, medieval history, early modern history,
modern history, research methods (economic and
social history)

Dept of Music; www.dur.ac.uk/music
music (ethnomusicology/composition/electroacoustic
studies/performance/brass band studies), musicology

**Dept of Modern Languages and Cultures;
www.dur.ac.uk/mlac**
applied language studies (TESOL), Arabic, Arabic/
English translation and interpreting, culture and
medieval and renaissance studies, French, German,
Hispanic studies, Italian, the photographic image,
seventeenth-century studies, translation studies

**Dept of Philosophy; www.dur.ac.uk/
philosophy**
history and philosophy of science and medicine,
philosophy, philosophy, politics and economics
(PPE), philosophy and politics/ psychology, theol-
ogy/English literature/education studies

**Dept of Theology and Religion; www.dur.
ac.uk/theology.religion**
biblical studies, Christian theology, religion and
society, theology, theology and philosophy, theology
and religion; BA(Hons), GDip, MA, MLitt, MMus,
MTh, PhD

Faculty of Science; www.dur.ac.uk/ science.faculty

School of Biological and Biomedical Sciences; www.dur.ac.uk/biological. sciences

biology, biomedical sciences, cell biology, ecology, evolution & behaviour, molecular biology and biochemistry, natural sciences, zoology

Dept of Chemistry; www.dur.ac.uk/ chemisry

bio-organic chemistry, catalysis, organometallic, coordination and supramolecular chemistry, chemistry, collisions and reaction dynamics, inorganic materials synthesis and characterization, photonic and electronic materials, physical organic chemistry, polymer chemistry, structural chemistry, synthetic methodology, theoretical chemistry and simulation

Dept of Engineering and Computer Science; www.dur.ac.uk/ecs/computing.science

advanced software engineering, civil/electronic/ mechanical engineering, communications engineering, computer science, design, manufacturing and management, internet and distributed systems technologies, internet systems and e-business, new and renewable energy, software engineering, software engineering management

Dept of Earth Sciences; www.dur.ac.uk/ earth.sciences

earth science, environmental, geology, geophysics, geosciences

Dept of Mathematical Sciences; www.dur. ac.uk/mathematical.sciences

biomathematics, elementary particle theory, mathematical sciences

Dept of Physics; www.dur.ac.uk/physics

elementary particle theory, physics, physics and astronomy, theoretical physics

Dept of Psychology; www.dur.ac.uk/ psyhology

cognitive neuroscience, developmental psychopathology, developmental psychology, psychology, psychology (applied); BA(Hons), BEng, BSc(Hons), MA, MChem, MEng, MMath, MPhil, MPhys, MSc, MSci, PhD

Faculty of Social Science and Health; www.dur.ac.uk /science.health

School of Applied Social Sciences; www. dur.ac.uk/sass

crime, violence and abuse, criminology, economy and society and sport, health and policy, innovative research methodologies, policy, professions and communities, social policy, social work, social work and community and youth work, sociology, sport, sport and community and youth work

Dept of Anthropology; www.dur.ac.uk/ anthropology

anthropology, development anthropology, evolutionary anthropology, health and human sciences, human sciences, medical anthropology, research methods (anthropology), socio-cultural anthropology

Dept of Archeology; www.dur.ac.uk/ archeology

archeology and ancient civilizations, conservation of archaeological and museum objects, museums and artefacts studies, palaeopathology (human)

Durham Business School; www.dur.ac.uk/ dbs

business, business finance, economics, economics, business economics accounting, decision science, entrepreneurship, finance, HRM and organisational behaviour, international banking, international money, investment, marketing psychology, public management, strategy and organisation

School of Education; www.dur.ac.uk/ education

educational assessment, education studies, history of art, PGCE primary/secondary, practice of education, primary education, research methods (education),

Dept of Geography; www.dur.ac.uk/ geography

geography

School of Government and International affairs; www.dur.ac.uk/sgia

Arab world studies, international relations, international studies, Islamic finance, politics, politics (European studies), politics and sociology/economics/philosophy; BA(Hons), DBA, EdD, MA, MA(Ed), MBA, MSc, PGCE, PGCert, PhD

Faculty of Social Science and Health; www.dur.ac.uk/science.health

Dept of Anthropology; www.dur.ac.uk/anthroplogy

anthropological medicine, anthropology, biological anthropology, development anthropology, evolutionary anthropology, health and human sciences, human sciences, medical anthropology, research methods (anthropology), sociocultural anthropology

School of Applied Social Sciences; www.dur.ac.uk/sass

criminology, community and youth work, education studies – sociology, managing community practice, social research methods, social work/with children and young people, their families and carers, sociology, sociology and anthropology/law/politics, sport; BA(Hons), BSc(Hons), MA, MProf, MSc, PhD/MPhil, PGDip/Cert

Durham Business School; www.dur.ac.uk/dbs

accounting, business, corporate and international finance, economics, enterprise management, finance, financial management, HRM, management, international banking and finance, international money, investment, Islamic finance, marketing

School of Education; www.dur.ac.uk/education

education (primary/secondary), educational assessment, education studies, history of art, practice of education, primary education, research methods

Dept of Geography; www.dur.ac.uk/geography

geography, human geography, physical geography

School of Government and International Affairs; www.dur.ac.uk/sgia

international relations, international studies, Islamic finance, politics/European studies, politics and sociology/economics/philosophy

Durham Law School; www.dur.ac.uk

European trade & commercial law, international trade & commercial law, law

School of Medicine & Health; www.dur.ac.uk/school.health

clinical management, health research methods, history and philosophy of science, interdisciplinary mental health, medical education, phase 1 medicine, public policy and health; BA(Hons), BA(Ed), BSc(Ed), BSc(Hons), Cert Leg Stud, DBA, EdD, LlB, LlM, MA, MBA, MBBS, MEd, MMus, MPhil, MProf, MSc, PGCert, PGCert/Dip, PGCE, PhD

Degrees validated by Durham University offered at:

CRAMNER HALL, ST JOHN'S COLLEGE
www.cranmerhall.com

theology and ministry; BA, Certificate MADMinistry, Diploma

NATIONAL TRAINING CENTRE FOR SCIENTIFIC SUPPORT TO CRIME INVESTIGATION
www.forensic-training.police.uk

Diplomas

NEW COLLEGE DURHAM
www.newdur.ac.uk

administration, business, graphic design, management, podiatry, social work; BA(Hons), BSc(Hons), Foundation degrees, HND

ROYAL ACADEMY OF DANCE
www.rad.org.uk

ballet education, ballet teaching studies, Benesh, dance education, movement notation; BA(Hons), Dip/CertHE

USHAW COLLEGE
www.ushaw.ac.uk

theology and ministry; BA, Certs, Dipls, MA, PGCerts/Dips

UNIVERSITY OF EAST ANGLIA
www.uea.ac.uk

Faculty of Arts and Humanities; www. uea.ac.uk/hum

American Studies; www.uea.ac.uk/ams
American studies, American literature, and American history

School of World Art Studies; www.uea.ac.uk/art
ancient art and African art, art history, contemporary art, cultural heritage and museology, history of art (world art), medieval and Renaissance European art

School of Film & Television Studies; www.uea.ac.uk/ftv
authorship and reception, British and American cinema, film and television studies, gender and representation, genre, media studies, silent cinema, stardom, television studies

School of History; www.uea.ac.uk/his
early modern history, history, history and politics, landscape history, medieval history, modern history

School of Literature and Creative Writing; www.uea.ac.uk/lit
comparative literature and literary translation, creative writing, cultural studies, drama, scriptwriting and performance, English, English and American literature, English literature, intellectual and social history, literary history, literary theory, literature and history, popular culture, translation studies, women's writings

School of Language and Communication Studies; www.uea.ac.uk/lcs
cross cultural communication and linguistics, French, media, Spanish, translation

School of Music; www.uea.ac.uk/mus
electroacoustic music and musicology, music, music and technology, music with mathematics

School of Political, Social and International Studies; www.uea.ac.uk/psi
culture, literature and politics, European studies with politics, international relations and cultural politics, international relations and politics, international studies, philosophy and politics, philosophy, politics and economics, politics, social and political theory, society, culture and media; BA(Hons), MA, MMus, MPhil, PGDip, PhD

Faculty of Health; www.uea.ac.uk/foh

School of Allied Health Professions; www.uea.ac.uk/ahp
biological, psychological and social determinants of health and disease, complex interventions for long-term conditions, individuals' health decisions and behaviour, education for lifelong professional and practice development, occupational therapy, physiotherapy, potential benefits of new interventions, speech and language therapy,

School of Medicine, Health Policy & Practice; www.uea.ac.uk/med
clinical education, clinical psychology, cognitive behaviour therapy, health economics, health sciences,

health research cognitive behavourial therapy, medicine, primary care mental health

School of Nursing and Midwifery; www.uea.ac.uk/nam

acute, critical and emergency practice, community healthcare practice, midwifery practice, nursing practice, nurse practitioner (advanced practice), policy, planning and leadership for health professionals, pre-registration (midwifery, nursing, operating department practice, paramedic)

Institute of Biomedical and Clinical Science; www.uea.ac.uk/foh/research/Institutes/biomed

infection and immunity, nutrition and healthy ageing

Health and Social Science Research Institute; www.uea.ac.uk/foh/research/Institutes/hss

economics, medical statistics, mental health and psychological sciences, public health and health services research, stroke and rehabilitation shared decision making

Education in Health Institute; www.uea.ac.uk/foh/research/Institutes/educationinhealth

BA(Hons), BSc(Hons), ClinPsyD, DipHE, Foundation degrees, MBBS, MClinEd, MD, MHeaRes, MPhil, MSc, PGDip, PhD

Faculty of Science; www.uea.ac.uk/sci

School of Biological Science; www.uea.ac.uk/bio

applied ecology, applied ecology and conservation, biochemistry and ecology, biological sciences, biomedicine, biotechnology for a sustainable future, computational biology, ecology, conservation and project administration, plant genetics and crop improvement

School of Chemical Science; www.uea.ac.uk/che

advanced organic chemistry, analytical science, biological and medicinal chemistry, chemical physics, chemical sciences chemistry, environmental chemistry, forensic science, pharmaceutical chemistry

School of Computing Science; www.uea.ac.uk

actuarial sciences, applied computing science, business/information systems, business statistics, computational biology, computer graphics, computer systems engineering, computing for business, computing science, games development,

geoinformatics, imaging and multimedia, knowledge discovery and data mining, software engineering, strategic information systems

School of Environmental Sciences; www.uea.ac.uk/env

applied ecology, environmental social science, climate atmospheric sciences, climate science, environmental assessment and management, environmental chemistry, environmental earth sciences, environmental geography and international development, environmental geophysics, environmental sciences, geophysical sciences, meteorology & oceanography

School of Mathematics; www.uea.ac.uk/mth

mathematics, mathematics with economics/management studies/statistics/computing business statistics

School of Pharmacy; www.uea.ac.uk/pha

general pharmacy practice, pharmacy; BSc(Hons), GradDip, MPhil, MSc, MSci, PGDip, PhD

Faculty of Social Sciences; www.uea.ac.uk/ssf

School of Economics; www.uea.ac.uk/eco

business economics, business finance and economics, economics with economic psychology, environmental economics, experimental economics, finance and economics, industrial economics, international business economics, international business finance and economics, media economics, politics, philosophy and economics

School of Education and Lifelong Learning; www.uea.ac.uk/edu

adult literacy, advanced educational practice, counselling, counselling focusing-orientated psychotherapy, early childhood studies, education, focusing and experiential psychotherapy, lifelong learning and development: international perspectives, mathematics education, PGCE primary /secondary teacher training, teacher education (teacher training)

School of International Development; www.uea.ac.uk/dev

climate change, conflict, governance and international development, cultural heritage and international development, development economics, development practice, development studies, education and development, environment and international development, gender analysis of international development, globalisation and international development, international development, international development and business, international development with social anthropology and politics/economics/ environment and society, international relations and development studies, international social development, media and international development, rural development, theatre and development

Norwich Law School; www.uea.ac.uk/law

employment law, European legal systems, information, technology and intellectual property law, international commercial and business law, international competition law and policy, international trade law, law, law with American law, law with French law and language, legal studies, media law, policy and practice

Norwich Business School; www.uea.ac.uk/nbs

accounting and finance/management, business management, chain management, international accounting and financial, international HRM, management, marketing, strategic information systems, strategic supply

School of Social Work and Psychology; www.uea.ac.uk/swp

child and family research/ psychology, psychology, social work; BA(Hons), BSc(Hons), CPE/Dip, DEd, GradDip, LlBHons, LLM, MA, MA/DipSW, MBA, MPhil, MRes, MSc, MScEd, PGCert, PGDip, PhD

Degrees validated by University of East Anglia offered by:

CITY COLLEGE NORWICH
www.ccn.ac.uk

business computing, business management, child care and education, early childhood studies, engineering (civil, electrical, electronic, mechanical), English, financial services: insurance/retail, health and exercise, health studies, hospitality management, hospitality tourism, interactive media, leisure and events management, licensed retail, psychology, social work, teaching assistants; BA(Hons), BSc(Hons), FdA, FdSc, HNC, HND

OTLEY COLLEGE
www.otleycollege.ac.uk

foundation degrees in animal care, conservation, ecosystems, equine performance, landscape and garden design

UNIVERSITY OF EAST LONDON
www.uel.ac.uk

School of Architecture and the Visual Arts; www.uel.ac.uk/ava

animation, architecture, design, digital; BA(Hons), BSc/BA, FdA, Grad Cert, MA, MArch, MPhil, MSc, PgC, PhD, ProfDoc

School of Combined Honours; www.uel.ac.uk/combined

range of subjects for which combined honours courses are conducted

School of Computing, Information Technology and Engineering; www.uel.ac.uk/cite

built environment, civil engineering & construction, computing, design materials, electrical & electronic engineering, GIS, information systems, multimedia, product research, software, surveying, sustainability; BA/BEng(Hons), BA/BSc, BSc(Hons), MPhil, MSc, PhD, ProfDoc

Royal Docks Business School; www.uel.ac.uk/businessaccounting

banks, business finance, economics, European business, events management, finance, HRM, management studies, marketing, music industry; BA(Hons), DBA, HND, LlB, MA, MBA, MPhil, MSc, PGDip, PhD

Cass School of Education; www.uel.ac.uk/education

early childhood, education, internation education, language and education, teacher training, teaching, teaching assistants, youth and community work; BA(Hons), EdD, FdA,MA, PGCE, PGDip, ProfDoc, UnivCert

School of Health and Bioscience; www.uel.ac.uk/hal

biochemistry, biomedical science, conservation and ecology, forensic science, health studies, microbiology, pharmacology, physiotherapy, podiatory, sports science; BA(Hons), BSc(Hons), FdSc, MPhil, MSc, PGCert, PhD, ProfDoc

School of Law; www.uel.ac.uk/law

criminal justice, criminology, human rights, international law, Islamic law, refugees studies, terrorism; BA(Hons), BSc(Hons), LlB, LlM, MSc, PostGDips

School of Psychology; www.uel.ac.uk/psychology

counselling, mentoring, pysychology, psychosocial studies; BA(Hons), BSc(Hons), ClinPSyD, FdA, GradDip/Cert, MA, MSc, ProfDoc, UnivCert

School of Humanities and Social Sciences; www.uel.ac.uk/hsocialsciences

cultural and information technology industries, film studies, literature, media studies, music, professional writing, social policy, social work; BA(Hons), BMus, BSc(Hons), FdA, GradDip/Cert, MA, ProfDoc, UnivCert

---

THE UNIVERSITY OF EDINBURGH
www.ed.ac.uk

College of Humanities and Social Sciences; www.hss.ed.ac.uk

School of Arts, Culture and the Environment; www.ed.ac.uk/schools-departments/arts-culture-environment

architecture, architectural facilities/project management, the city; architectural history, architecture in creative and cultural environments, composition, criticism, curating, fine art, history of art, landscape architecture, modern art: history, music, music informatics, music and medicine and music psychology, music technology, musical acoustics, musicology, organology, Scottish art, sustainable design, urban design

The Business School; www.business-school.ed.ac.uk

accountancy, accounting and finance, business studies, economics, entrepreneurship and innovation, international business, management science, marketing, public management, work and employment

School of Divinity; www.div.ed.ac.uk

divinity, ethics, ministry, philosophy & theology, religious studies, world Christianity

School of Economics; www.ed.ac.uk/schools-departments/economics

asset pricing, corporate finance, economics and accounting/economic history/law/mathematics/politics/sociology/statistics/environmental studies/management science/law/social policy, international money and finance

School of Health in Social Science; www.ed.ac.uk/schools-departments/health

advancing nursing practice, applied psychology for children and young people, clinical psychology, counselling, global health, medical sciences, nursing studies, psychotherapy, public policy

School of History, Classics and Archaeology; www.shc.ed.ac.uk

ancient & medieval history, ancient mediterranean civilisations, archaeology, architectural history, architectural history & archaeology, Celtic, Celtic & Scottish history, classical archaeology, classics, economic & social history, environmental archaeology, Greek, history, politics & economic & social history, social anthropology, Scottish ethnology, social history

School of Law; www.law.ed.ac.uk

(includes) administrative/civil/commercial/company/competition/contract/criminal/environmental law, banking and finance law, contract law in Europe, criminology, data protection and information privacy, EC competition law, international law of the sea, international private law, international tax law

School of Literatures, Languages and Cultures; www.ed.ac.uk/schools-departments/literatures-languages-cultures

Asian studies, Celtic and Scottish studies, comparative literature, English literature, European theatre, film studies, Islamic and Middle Eastern studies, literature and transatlanticism, medieval studies, translation studies, word and music studies

Moray House School of Education; www.education.ed.ac.uk

additional support for learning, applied sport science, community education, dance science & education, design & technology, e-learning, education, inclusive & special education, language – theory, practice & literacy, language teaching, management of training & development, outdoor education, performance psychology, physical education, primary education, sport & recreation business management, sport & recreation management, TESOL, university teaching

School of Philosophy, Psychology and Language Science; www.ppls.ed.ac.uk

ancient philosophy, artificial intelligence and philosophy/psychology, cognitive science, English language, history & theory of psychology, human cognitive neuropsychology, linguistics, philosophy, psychology, psychology of individual differences, research ethics & political philosophy; BA(Arch), BD, BEd(Hons), BMedSci, BMus, BN, BSc(Hons), DD, DLitt, DMus, DClinPyschol, EdD, LlM, MA, MA(Hons), MBA, MLA, MPhil/PhD, MSc, MTeach, MTh/Sc, PGDipCert, PGDE

College of Medicine and Veterinary Medicine; www.ed.ac.uk/schools-departments/medicine-vet-medicine;

anaesthesia practice, applied animal behaviour and welfare, dental primary care, medical electives, medical sciences, medicine, oral health science, oral surgery, orthodontics, paediatric dentistry, prosthodontics, public health research, transfusion, transplantation and tissue banking, veterinary medicine and surgery

School of Clinical Sciences and Community Health; www.ed.ac.uk/schools-departments/clinical-sciences

clinical and surgical sciences, community health sciences, medical and radiological sciences, reproductive and developmental sciences

School of Biomedical Sciences; www.bsms.mvm.ed.ac.uk

cognitive and neural systems, infectious diseases, integrative physiology, neurogeneration, pathway medicine

School of Molecular and Clinical Medicine; www.mcm.ed.ac.uk

clinical brain services, clinical neurosciences, molecular medicine, pathology, pyschiatry

The Royal (Dick) School of Veterinary Studies; www.ed.ac.uk/schools-departments/vet applied animal

College of Science and Engineering; www.scieng.ed.ac.uk

School of Biological Sciences; www.ed.ac.uk/schools-departments/biology

biochemistry, biodiversity and taxonomy of plants, bioinformatics, biological sciences with management, biotechnology, developmental/evolutionary/ medical biology/ molecular/reproductive biology, drug discovery and translational biology, ecological science, quantitative genetics and genome analysis

School of Chemistry; www.chem.ed.ac.uk

chemical physics, chemistry, chemistry with environmental & sustainable chemistry, chemistry with materials chemistry, medicinal and biological chemistry,

School of Engineering; www.see.ed.ac.uk

Chemical Engineering: chemical engineering with environmental engineering/management
Civil and Environmental Engineering: civil engineering, civil and environmental engineering/construction management, NDT and construction management, silos and granular solids, structural engineering with architecture, structural and fire safety engineering, structures and fire safety
Electronics and Electrical Engineering: digital communications, electrical engineering, electrical engineering with renewable energy, electrical and mechanical engineering, electronics, electronics and computer science/bioelectronics, electronics and electrical engineering (communications), electronics and

electrical engineering with management, electronics and software engineering, energy conversion and storage, energy delivery, integrated micro and nano systems, operation and control, power electronics renewable energy, restructuring and regulation

Mechanical Engineering: advanced materials applications, electrical and mechanical engineering, fluid and particle dynamics, manufacturing and process optimization, materials and processes, mechanical engineering with management, mechanical engineering with renewable energy, micro- nano- and chemomechanics

Institute for Energy Systems: environmental mitigation, energy delivery, renewable energy, restructuring and regulation

General Engineering

School for Informatics; www.inf.ed.ac.uk

artificial intelligence, cognitive science, computational linguistics, computational physics, computer science, electronics and software engineering/computer science, informatics, mind and language music technology, software engineering,

Centre for Intelligent Systems and Their Applications; Institute for Adaptive and Neural Computation; Institute for Communicating and Collaborative Systems; Institute for Computing Systems Architecture; Institute of Perception, Action and Behaviour; e-Science Institute; Laboratory for Foundations of Computer Science; Informatics Life-Sciences Institute

School of Geosciences; www.geos.ed.ac.uk

Ecological Sciences: appraisal and development (petroleum, hydrocarbons), carbon capture & storage, carbon management, ecological economics, ecological science (conservation and ecological management/environmental science/management), ecological science (forestry), environment and development, environment, protection and management, environmental sustainability, exploration geophysics, geographical information science, geoscience for subsurface exploration, integrated resource management, interactions of organisms with their physical and biological environment, principles and practice of managing ecological systems

Earth Science: environmental geoscience, geography, geography and archaeology/economic & social history/economics/politics/social anthropology/social policy/sociology/environmental studies, geology, geophysics, meteorology, physical geography

School of Mathematics; www.maths.ed.ac.uk

applied mathematics, financial mathematics, mathematics, mathematics & statistics/management/physics/music/artificial intelligence/computer science/philosophy, operational research, pure mathematics

School of Physics and Astronomy; www.ph.ed.ac.uk

astrophysics, chemical physics, computational physics, distributed scientific computing, geophysics physics and computer/mathematics/meteorology/music, high performance computing, mathematical physics, physics; BEng, BSc, MChem, MChemPhys, MEarthSci, MEng, MInf, MPhil, MPhys, MS, MSc, MSci, PGDip, PhD

UNIVERSITY OF ESSEX
www.essex.ac.uk

Faculty of Humanities and Comparative Studies; www.essex.ac.uk/hcs

History of Art: art and curatorial practices, art and film and contemporary art, art history and theory, critical management and curating, gallery studies and critical curating, history of art and modern languages/literature/film studies, Latin American art, theory and criticism

East 15: acting, acting and contemporary theatre/stage combat, acting for TV, film and radio, community theatre, filmmaking, physical theatre, technical theatre studies, theatre arts, theatre directing, world performance

History: American history, British and European history, contemporary history, digital history, historical studies, history, history with film studies, local, community and family history modern history, researching history in Britain, social and cultural history

Department of Literature, Film, and Theatre Studies

comparative literature, creative writing, drama/and literature, English language and/with modern myth, English literature, English and United States literature, literature and film studies/history of art/sociology/philosophy/history, literature and myth, literature, and the unconscious, wild writing: literature, science and the environment

Philosophy: continental philosophy and health care ethics/law, ethics, politics and public policy, philosophy and film/history/literature/politics/ sociology, philosophy and/with modern languages/law/human rights, philosophy and psychoanalysis, philosophy, politics and economics, philosophy, politics and environmental issues, philosophy, sociology and the environment

International Academy: numerous cross-departmental courses; BA(Hons), CertHE, Dip/MA, FdA, MA, MFA, MPhil, PGCert, PhD

Faculty of Social Sciences; www.essex.ac.uk/ss

Dept of Economics; www.essex.ac.uk/economics

accounting and financial economics, applied economics and data analysis, business economics, economics, economics with French/German/Italian/Spanish/Portuguese, economics with mathematics, financial economics, international economics, management, management economics, mathematics and economics, philosophy, politics and economics, politics/accounting/history and economics

Dept of Government; www.essex.ac.uk/government

European integration/politics, global and comparative politics, government, ideology and discourse analysis, international development, international relations and media, international relations and politics, philosophy, politics and economics, political behaviour, political economy, political theory, politics, politics and law, politics and sociology, politics with human rights, public opinion and polling

Dept of Languages and Linguistics; www.essex.ac.uk/linguistics

applied linguistics, English, English language, English language and literature/sociolinguistics, French, German, Italian, linguistics, and teaching, Portuguese, Spanish

Dept of Sociology; www.essex.ac.uk/sociology

criminology, criminology and American studies, criminology with social psychology/the media/American studies, gender, culture and society media, culture and society, migration and citizenship, psychology/history/literature/philosophy/human rights, social sciences, sociology, sociology –

humanities, sociology with management/politics/social; BA(Hons), BSc(Hons), Diploma, GradDip, MA, MPhil, MRes, MSc, PGDip, PhD, ProcDoc

Faculty of Law and Management; www.essex.ac.uk/lm

Essex Business School; www.essex.ac.uk/ebs

Centre for Global Accountability; Centre for Entrepreneurship Research; Essex Finance Centre; Essex Management Centre

accounting, accounting & finance, banking, business, corporate governance, creative industry management, entrepreneurship, entrepreneurship and innovation, financial engineering and risk management, financial management/management, finance, international accounting, international finance, international management, international small business management, investment, management, management psychology, management studies, marketing and society, organisation studies and HRM

Human Rights Centre; www.essex.ac.uk/humanrightscentre

Human rights and cultural diversity/research methods, human rights and public law, international human rights law, Latin American studies and human rights, law/philosophy/sociology, politics with human rights, theory and practice of human rights

School of Law; www.essex.ac.uk/law

English and French laws, European business law, European Union law, EU law and comparative legal studies, health care law and human rights, information technology, media and e-commerce, international human rights/and humanitarian law, international trade law, law, law and philosophy/human rights/politics, UK human rights and public law; BA(Hons), BSc(Hons), DocProg, LlM, LLB, MPhil, MSc, PhD

Faculty of Science and Engineering; www.essex.ac

Dept of Biological Sciences; www.essex.ac.uk/bs

biochemistry, biological sciences, biology, biodiversity and conservation, biomedical science, biotechnology, biotechnology: future crops for food and biofuels, cardiac rehabilitation, ecology, environmental governance: natural world, environmental resource management, genetics, marine and freshwater biology, mathematics and biology, molecular medicine, natural environment and society, science and society, sports and exercise science, sports science and biology

School of Computer Science and Electronic Engineering; www.essex.ac.uk/csee

computer games, computer networks, computer science, computer systems engineering, computers and electronics, electronic engineering, information and communication technology, software engineering, telecommunication engineering

School of Health and Human Sciences; www.essex.ac.uk /hss

adult nursing, health and human sciences, health studies, health studies and sociology, mental health nursing, occupational therapy, oral health sciences, physiotherapy, social psychology and sociology, speech and language therapy

Department of Mathematical Sciences; www.essex.ac.uk/maths

accounting and mathematics, discrete mathematics and its applications, economics and mathematics, finance and mathematics, management with mathematics, mathematics, mathematics, cryptography & network security, mathematics and biomathematics, mathematics for secondary teaching, mathematics with computing, operational research and computer science, statistics and operational research/data analysis/econometrics/computer science

Dept of Psychology; www.essex.ac.uk/ psychology

cognitive psychology, cognitive neuropsychology, cognitive neuroscience, neuropsychology, neuropsychology and development perception and social and health psychology, psychology, research methods in psychology, social psychology and sociology; BA(Hons), BEng, BSc(Hons), Grad Dip, MA, MPhil, MRes, MSc, PGDip, PhD, ProfDoc

Degrees validated by the University of Essex offered at:

WRITTLE COLLEGE
www.writtle.ac.uk

agriculture, business, conservation, countryside, design, engineering, equine, food, horticulture, management, sport, vet nursing; BA(Hons), BSc(Hons), CertMS, Certs, DipMS, FDAs, Higher Certs, MA, MBA, MSc,

UNIVERSITY OF EXETER
www.exeter.ac.uk

School of Arts, Languages and Literature; www.sall.exeter.ac.uk

arts, drama, English, film studies, medieval studies, modern languages, sexuality and gender; BA(Hons), MA, MPhil, PhD

School of Bioscience; www.bioscience. exeter.ac.uk

biological and medicinal chemistry, biological sciences, biology, conservation biology and ecology, evolution, molecular biology, zoology; BSc(Hons), MPhil, MSc, PgDip/Cert, PhD

University of Exeter Business School; www. business-school.exeter.ac.uk

accounting, finance, business (economics, management studies), IT management, marketing,

leadership, tourism; BA(Hons), MBA, MPhil, MSc, PGDip/Cert, PhD

School of Education and Lifelong Learning; www.education.exeter.ac.uk

childhood and youth studies, educational studies, engineering and education, sports science and education, psychology and education; BA(Hons), EdD, MEd, MPhil, MSc, PGCE PhD

School of Engineering, Computing and Mathematics; www.secam.exeter.ac.uk

civil, environmental, electronic, computer, mechanical, materials engineering, engineering and management, mathematics; BSc(Hons), BEng, MEng, MSc, MPhil, PhD

School of Geography, Archeology, and Earth Resources; www.sogaer.exeter.ac.uk

geography, archeology, earth resources, geology, mining engineering, renewable; BA(Hons), BSc(Hons), MA, MPhil, MRes, PGDip, PhD

School of Humanities and Social Sciences; www.huss.exeter.ac.uk

Arab and Islamic studies, classics and ancient history, history, politics, sociology and philosophy, theology; BA(Hons), MA,MPhil, MRes, PhD

School of Law; www.law.exeter.ac.uk

European law, international studies, law, politics and law; BA(Hons), LlB, LlM, MA, MPhil, MRes, PhD

Peninsula College of Medicine and Dentistry; www.pms.exeter.ac.uk

biochemical and clinical sciences, clinical education, dentistry, health service resources medicine, surgery; BClinM, BDS, BMMS, MPhil, MD/MS, PhD, MSc

School of Physics; www.newton.ex.ac.uk

astronomy, medical imaging, physics; BSc(Hons), MPhys, PhD

School of Psychology; www.psychologyexeter.ac.uk

animal behaviour, biology, psychology, sports exercise science; BA(Hons), BSc(Hons), DocCinicalPsychology, MSc, PhD

School of Sport and Health Sciences; www.ssstsexeter.ac.uk

exercise, human biosciences, physiology, sports science; BSc(Hons), MPhil, MSc, PhD

Degrees validated by University of Exeter offered at:

UCP MARJON-UNIVERSITY COLLEGE PLYMOUTH ST MARK & ST JOHN
www.ucpmarjon.ac.uk

children, youth & community, drama & theatre arts, education & teacher training, English language, literature and writing, live music, media, outdoor, sociology, speech and language therapy, sport, health, coaching and PE; BA(Hons), BA/BSc, BEd, FdA church college certs; GTP, MA, MEd, MPhil, PGCE

UNIVERSITY COLLEGE FALMOUTH (INC DARTINGTON COLLEGE OF ARTS)
www.falmouth.ac.uk

3D design, advertising, art & performance, choreography, contemporary crafts, creative events management, creative music technology, dance, digital animation, English with creative writing, fashion design, film, fine art, garden design, graphic design, illustration, interior design, journalism, media studies, music, photography, popular music, PR, radio production, screen & media performance, spatial, sportswear design, textile design, theatre (design and production, directing, performance, writing), writing; BA(Hons), FdA, MA, MPhil, PGDip, PhD

UNIVERSITY OF GLAMORGAN
www.glam.ac.uk

Cardiff School of Creative and Cultural Industries; www.ccc.glam.ac.uk

art and design, drama and music, film studies, media and communications; BA(Hons), FdA, MA, MPhil

Faculty of Health, Sport and Science; www.hesas.glam.ac.uk

biology, chemistry, chiropractic, clinical physiology, coaching, forensic science and police studies, geology, geography, environment, midwifery, nursing, sports health and exercise; BA(Hons), BSc(Hons), BN,

FoundCerts, HEDip, HNC, HND, MA, MPhil, MSC/ PGD/, PGC, PhD

Faculty of Advanced Technology; www. fat.glam.ac.uk

built environment, computing, engineering (aerospace, computer systems, electrical and electronic, mechanical), mathematics, technology; BEng(Hons), BSc, BSc(Hons), CertHE, DipHE, HNC, HND, MEng

Glamorgan Business School; www.bus. glam.ac.uk

accounting, business, business management, executive courses, HRM, leisure and sport management, logistics, tourism events management, supply chain management, transport; ACCA, BA(Hons), BSc(Hons), DBA, DocLC, FdA, MBA, MPhil, MSc

Faculty of Humanities and Social Sciences; www.hass.glam.ac.uk

adolescence, childhood, community regeneration, creative writing, criminology, early years, education and careers, English, history, humanities, languages, law, psychology, public services, sociology, TESOL; BA(Hons), BA/BSc, BSc(Hons), DocPublServ, FCert, FdA, GradDip law, LlB(Hons), LlM/PhD/PgD, MA/ PDip/Cert, MSc, PGD/PGC

The Centre for Lifelong Learning; www. cell.glam.ac.uk

astronomy, business courses, community courses, community regeneration, communication technology, craft and design, creative industries, environmental studies, information, languages, social sciences; BA(Hons), BSc(Hons), FdA, GCert/Dip/MA/MSc

---

UNIVERSITY OF GLASGOW
www.gla.ac.uk

Faculty of Arts; www.gla.ac.uk/faculties/ arts

archaeology, arts & media informatics, Celtic civilisation/studies, classics, comparative literature, Czech, English/English literature, film & television studies, French, German, Greek, Hispanic studies, history, history of art, Italian, Latin, liberal arts, literature, music, philosophy, Polish, Russian, Scottish literature, Slavonic studies, Spanish, theatre studies, theology & religious studies; BD(Min), BMus, DLitt, MA, MAHons, MLitt, MPhil, MTh, PhD

Faculty of Biomedical and Life Sciences; www.gla.ac.uk /faculties/fbls

anatomy, biochemistry, biomedical sciences, biotechnology, genetics, immunology, marine & freshwater biology, medical biochemistry, microbiology, molecular and cellular biology, neuroscience, parasitology, pharmacology, physiology, plant science, sports medicine, virology, zoology, animal biology, biology, biomolecular sciences, human biology, infection biology, sports science; BSc(Hons), MRes, MSc, MSci, PhD

Faculty of Education; www.gla.ac.uk/ faculties/education

childhood practice, community development, music, primary education – with teaching qualifications, religious and philosophical education, technological education, technology and management; BA(Hons), BTechEd, BTechS, EdD, MA, MA(Hons), MEd, MLitt, MSc, MusicBEd, PhD

Faculty of Engineering; www.gla.ac.uk/ faculties/engineering

aerospace engineering, architecture, avionics, biomedical engineering, civil engineering, electrical & electronics engineering, marine engineering, mechanical engineering, microcircuits, nautical science, naval architecture, ocean engineering, product design engineering, software engineering, video engineering; BEng, BSc, EngD, MEng, MSc, PGDip, PhD

Faculty of Law, Business and Social Sciences; www.gla.ac.uk/faculties/lbss

law with European legal studies, central and east European studies, economics, economic and social history, management politics, sociology, urban studies; BAcc, BSc, LlB, MA, MAcc, MFin, MRes, MSc, PhD, MMedicalLaw

Glagow Business School; www.gla.ac.uk/ faculties/business

accounting, finance, banking, international finance, management, management with real estate, strategic marketing; MAcc, MBA, MFin, MSc, PhD

Faculty of Medicine; www.gla.ac.uk/medicine

Medical School; www.gla.ac.uk/departments/medicine

behavioural science, clinical practice, disability and rehabilitation, ethics and law, gender and ethnic background, human biology, human disease, medical science, medicine, palliative medicine and the care of the dying, public health, therapeutics and management; B(MedSci), MBChB, MD, MML, MMLE, MPC, MPH, PhD

Dental School; www.gla.ac.uk/departments/dentalschool

biomedical sciences, clinical dental science, clinical medical science, dentistry, patient management and health; BDS, BSc(Dent Sc), DDS, MSc, PhD

Nursing; www.gla.ac.uk/departments/nursing

clinical nursing practice, critical care nursing, health studies in nursing, integrated biomedical & life sciences, nursing and health studies, nursing and integrated biomedical and life sciences, pathology and human diseases, specialist medical nursing, specialist surgical nursing; BN, BN(Hons), RegNurse, Postgraduate; MSc(MedSci), PGC, PGDip, PhD

Faculty of Science; www.gla.ac.uk/undergraduate/degrees/science

anatomy, astronomy, biochemistry, biological sciences, biomedical sciences, biotechnology, chemical physics, chemistry, chemistry with forensic/medicinal chemistry, computing science, computing science & physiology (neuroinformatics), earth science, electronic & software engineering, environmental biogeochemistry/chemistry/geography, genetics, geography, immunology, marine & freshwater biology, mathematical sciences, mathematics/applied mathematics, medical biochemistry, microbiology, mobile software engineering, molecular & cellular biology, neuroscience, parasitology, pharmacology, physics/theoretical physics, physics with astrophysics, physiology, sports science, nutrition, plant science, psychology, software engineering, sports medicine, statistics, virology, zoology; BSc(Hons), BSc(designated), MSc, MSci, PhD, MRes, PGDip

Faculty of Veterinary Science; www.gla.ac.uk/vet

anatomy, animal husbandry, biomolecular sciences and physiology; microbiology, pathology, parasitology and pharmacology; BSc, BSc(Vet Sci), BVMS, MVPH, PhD

GLASGOW CALEDONIAN UNIVERSITY
www.caledonian.ac.uk

School of the Built & Natural Environment; www.caledonian.ac.uk/bne

building surveying, construction management, environmental civil engineering/management and planning, fire risk engineering, interior design, property management & valuation, quantity surveying; BSc/BEng, BSc(Hons), MSc, MPhil, PhD

Caledonian School of Business; www.caledonian.ac.uk/cbs

accounting, cultural business, fashion, finance, innovation and enterprise marketing, people management and leadership, public policy studies, retailing, risk; BA/BA(Hons), MRes, PhD

School of Engineering and Computing; www.caledonian.ac.uk/sec

3D computer animation, applied graphics technology, audio technology with multimedia/electronics, computer engineering, computer games (design, software development), computing (information, web systems development), digital security and ethical hacking, electrical power, electronics/engineering, graphic design for digital media, information technology management, manufacturing systems, mechanical & power plant systems/mechanical electronic systems engineering, mechatronics, multimedia visualisation with product design, networking & systems support, telecommunications engineering; BA/BA(Hons), BEng/BEng(Hons), BSc/BSc(Hons), DipHE, MA/PGD, MSc/PGD, PhD

School of Health and Social Care; www.caledonian.ac.uk/shsc

occupational therapy, physyiotherapy, podiatric medicine and surgery, radiography, social work; BSc(Hons), GradCert, MPhil, MSc, PgC/D, PhD, ProfDoc,

School of Life Sciences; www.caledonian.ac.uk/sls

biochemistry, biological and medical sciences, dietetics, food science, forensics, microbiology, molecular biology, nutrition, optometry, pharmacology, physiology, psychology, vision sciences; BSc, BSc(Hons), DipHE, DPsych, MSc, OpthDisp, PGD/C, PhD

School of Law and Social Sciences; www.caledonian.ac.uk/sls

business law, criminology, law, legal studies, international law, law and IT, Islamic and ME law, women in the law; BA(Hons), LlB, LlM, MSc, PGD/C, PhD

School of Nursing, Midwifery, and Community Health; www.caledonian.ac.uk/nmch

adult, child, mental health or learning disabilities, community health, midwifery, nursing studies, operating department practices, overseas nursing, public health, sexual health; BA/BA(Hons), BMidwifery, BN, BSc/BSc(Hons), DipN, MPhil, MSc, PGDip, PhD

THE GLASGOW SCHOOL OF ART
www.gsa.ac.uk

environmental art, fine art, fine art photography, historical and critical studies, interior design, printmaking, product design, product design engineering, silversmithing and jewellery, textiles and visual communication; BA(Hons), BEng, DipArch, MA, MArch, MDes, MEng, MPhil, MRes, PhD

UNIVERSITY OF GLOUCESTERSHIRE
www.glos.ac.uk

The Business School; www.glos.ac.uk/faculties/bus

accounting, advertising, business management, business marketing, computing, events management, finance, hospitality management, HRM, international marketing, international business strategy, marketing, marketing management, music and media management

Faculty of Education, Humanities and Sciences; www.glos.ac.uk/ehs

animal biology, biology, biosciences, communications, creative writing, education, education leadership, educational admin & management, English language/literature, geography, international business strategy, landscape architecture, language, marketing, music and media management, philosophy and ethics, psychology, religion, return to teaching, sociology, teacher training; BA/BA(Hons), BEd, BSc/BSc(Hons), Cert HE, Foundation degrees, MA, MEd, MPhil, MSc, PGCE

Faculty of Media, Art, and Communication; www.glos.ac.uk/faculties/mac

advertising, animation, digital film production, drawing, editorial and advertising, fine art, graphics, illustration, interactive media, painting, photography, photojournalism, popular music, printmaking, sculpture, television production, textiles; BA/BA(Hons), BSc/BSc(Hons), MA, MPhil, MSc, PGCert, PGDip, PhD

Faculty of Sport, Health and Social Care; www.glos.ac.uk/faculties/shsc

applied health studies, applied sport and exercise studies, child care, children & young people, community care with vulnerable adults, community health studies, exercise and health sciences, health & social practice, health and wellbeing, integrated youth practice, mental health sports (coaching, development, fitness), non-medical prescribing, performing arts, playwork, social work, social work with adults, sports coaching, sports development/education/therapy/strength and conditioning, theology, youth & community work, youth studies, youth work; BA/BA(Hons), BSc/BSc(Hons), DipSW,

Postgraduate; MA, MPhil, MRes, MSc, PGCert, PGDip, PhD

UNIVERSITY OF GREENWICH
www.gre.ac.uk

School of Architecture and Construction; www.gre.ac.uk/schools/arc

advertising, architecture, building studies, building surveying, construction, digital design, estate management, fine art, garden design, graphic design, health and environment, landscape architecture, landscape management, occupational safety, photography, quantity surveying, real estate, visual art and communication; BA(Hons), BSc(Hons), Certs, Dip, HNC, HND, MA, MSc, MPhil, PGDip, PhD

Business Information Technology and Enterprise (BITE); www.gre.ac.uk/schools/bite

information age education, information and communication technology, information technology, management for business, project management; BA(Hons), BSc(Hons), HND

Business School; www.gre.ac.uk/schools/business

accounting, audit & assurance services, banking, business, business administration, business entrepreneurship and innovation, business in Europe, business logistics & transport management, business management, business psychology, business studies, China international business, economics, events management, finance, financial information systems, HRM, international business, marketing, public service management, purchasing & supply chain management, tourism management; BA(Hons), BSc(Hons), Certs, DBA, Foundation degrees, HNC, HND, MA, MBA, MSc, PGDip, PhD

School of Computing & Mathematical Science; www.gre.ac.uk/schools/cms

business computing, business information systems, business information technology, computer science, computer security & forensics, computer systems & networking, computing (with games development, multimedia), digital animation & production, digital film production, digital television & interactive media, embedded computer systems, film & television production, financial mathematics, internet computing, mathematics & computing, mathematics for decision science, mathematics, statistics & computing, mobile computing & communications, software engineering, software engineering, web business systems, web technologies; BSc(Hons), FDSc, MA, MEng/BEng, MPhil, MSc, PhD

School of Education and Training; www.gre.ac.uk/schools/education

childhood studies, design and technology with QTS, education, education and training, physical education and sport, primary education with QTS, secondary education, secondary education studies, teaching and training, youth and community studies; BA(Hons), BELT, Cert, DipHE, EdD, Foundation degree, MA, MPhil, MSc, PGCert/Dip, PhD

School of Engineering; www.gre.ac.uk/schools/engineering

civil engineering, communications systems engineering, computer networking, electrical and electronic engineering, engineering management, games and entertainment systems, information and communications technology, information technology management, marine engineering, mechanical engineering, software engineering; BEng(Hons), BSc(Hons), HNC, HND, MEng, MSc

Greenwich Maritime Institute; www.gre.ac.uk/schools/gmi

maritime history, maritime management, maritime policy; MA, MBA, MPhil, PhD

School of Health and Social Care; www.gre.ac.uk/schools/health

child protection, clinical practice, counselling, health, learning disabilities management, mental health work, midwifery, nursing, professional practice, psychology, public health, social work and social care, speech and language therapy, therapeutic counselling; BA(Hons), BSc(Hons), DipHE, Foundation degrees, GradDips, MA, MPhil, PGCert, PhD

School of Humanities and Social Sciences; www.gre.ac.uk/schools/humanities

creative industries, creative writing, criminal psychology, criminology, drama, English, film studies, history, humanities, journalism and PR, justice and legal studies, language and culture, law, media and creative arts, media and communication, media writing, modern languages (Chinese, English, French, German, Italian, Japanese, Spanish), philosophy, politics, sociology, TESOL English language teaching; BSc(Hons), BA(Hons), FD, LlB, MA, MPhil, MSc, PGCert, PGDip, PhD

Medway School of Pharmacy; www.gre.ac. uk/schools/studying/index/html

medicine management, pharmacy practice; BSc(Hons), FdMM, FdPP, MPharm, MSc, PGCert/Dip

Natural Resources Institute; www.gre.ac. uk/schools/nri

development studies, ecology and global change management, food safety, natural resources; BSc(Hons), MPhil, MSc, PhD

School of Science; www.gre.ac.uk/schools/ science

animal and equine studies, biomedical, bioscience, biotechnology, chemistry, forensic science, environmental science, geography, human nutrition, international agriculture, pharmaceutical science, sport science, sustainability; BSc(Hons), HNC, HND, MPhil, MSc, PGDip, PhD

GRIMSBY INSTITUTE OF FURTHER AND HIGHER EDUCATION
www.grimsby.ac.uk

access, animal care, business & law, computing, construction, creative arts, electrical/electronics engineering, hair & beauty, health & child care, humanities & science, manufacturing & logistics, mechanical engineering, media & writing, refrigeration, sports & fitness, teacher education, travel & tourism; BA(Hons), BSc(Hons), FdA, FdEd, FdSc, HEdDip, HNC, HND, MA, MBA, MSc, PGCE

HARPER ADAMS UNIVERSITY COLLEGE
www.harper-adams.ac.uk

agricultural and engineering, agriculture, animals, business & management, business management, countryside management, engineering, environment, food, food studies, land & estate management, marketing, tourism, veterinary nursing; BSc(Hons), FdSc, MBA, MSc, PGDip/Cert

HERRIOT-WATT UNIVERSITY
www.hw.ac.uk

School of the Built Environment; www.hw. ac.uk/sbe

Architectural Engineering: architectural design architectural facilities management, architectural project management
Civil and Structural Engineering: civil engineering, structural engineering
Construction Management & Surveying: building surveying, construction project management, planning and property development, quantity surveying, real estate management/investment and finance
Urban Studies: environmental engineering, building conservation, housing and regeneration, urban and regional planning, urban studies/regeneration and real estate development, water resources and catchment development
BSc(Hons,Ord), BEng, MEng, MRes, MSc, PGDip/Cert, PhD

School of Mathematical and Computer Sciences; www.macs.hw.ac.uk

actuarial mathematics, actuarial science, advanced internet applications, applied mathematical sciences, artificial intelligence, computer science, computer systems management, creative software systems, financial mathematics, human computer interaction, information systems, information technology (business/software systems), intelligent web technology, internet systems, mathematics, mathematical, statistical and actuarial sciences, mathematics with computer, mathematics with finance, mobile and handheld applications, multimedia systems, quantitative risk management, software engineering, statistical modelling, statistics, web entrepreneurship; BSc(Hons), MEng, MMath, MRes, MSc, PGDip/Cert, PhD

School of Engineering and Physical Sciences; www.eps.hw.ac.uk

Chemistry: biochemistry, computational chemistry, forensic science, materials chemistry, materials for sustainable and renewable energies, nanotechnology forensic materials, pharmaceutical chemistry

Chemical Engineering: bioprocessing, chemical engineering with energy engineering/environmental management/pharmaceutical chemistry, nanotechnology and microsystems, sustainability engineering, sustainable process management

Physics: chemical physics, computational physics, energy science and technology, engineering physics, mathematical physics, nano-science, nanotechnology and microsystems, photonics, photonics and optoelectronic devices, physics with environmental science/electronic engineering

Electrical, Electronic and Computer Engineering: computer vision and robotics, computing and electronics, electrical and electronic engineering, embedded systems, information technology, information technology (embedded systems/mobile communications, applied systems), microsystems engineering, mobile communications, photonics and optoelectronic devices, renewable energy and distributed generation), sustainability engineering, system level integration, vision, image and signal processing

Mechanical Engineering: automotive engineering, creative 3D digital technologies, design and management energy engineering, forensic materials, materials for sustainable and renewable energies, mechanical engineering, renewable energy and distributed generation, renewable energy engineering, robotics and cybertronics

BEng, BSc(Ord,Hons), EngD, MChem, MEng, MPhil, MPhys, PhD

School of Life Sciences; www.hw.ac.uk/sls

Applied Psychology: applied psychology (forensic science), psychology, psychology for business, psychology with human health, psychology with management

Biological Sciences: biological sciences (cell and molecular biology/food science/human health/microbiology), biology, microbiology

Brewing and Distilling

Sport and Exercise Science: sport and exercise science with psychology

Food Science: food science, food science safety and health, technology and food science

Marine Science: applied marine biology, climate change: managing the marine environment/impacts and mitigation, environmental analysis and assessment, marine biodiversity and biotechnology, marine resource development and protection

BSc(Hons), MSc/Cert/Dip, PGDip, PhD

School of Management and Languages; www.hw.ac.uk/sml

Accountancy: accountancy and business law/finance, business and finance, finance and business law, finance international accounting and finance

Management: business management with HRM/with international marketing, international fashion marketing, international management, logistics and supply chain management, management, management with business law, management with enterprise, management with human resource management, management with marketing, management with operations management, maritime logistics and supply chain management, strategic project management

Languages and Intercultural Studies: Arabic–English translating and conference interpreting, Arabic–English translation and computer-assisted translation tools, applied languages and translating (French/German) (French/Spanish) (German/Spanish), Chinese–English translating and conference interpreting/computer-assisted translation tools, French as main language, German as main language, international management and languages, interpreting studies & skills (British sign language/English), languages (interpreting and translating) (French/German) (French/Spanish) (German/Spanish), Spanish as main language, translation and computer-assisted translation tools

BA(Hons,Ord), GradDip, MA(Hons), MSc

Heriot Watt Institute of Petroleum Engineering; www.pet.hw.ac.uk

geomechanics and rock physics, geoscience for subsurface exploration appraisal and development, hydrates, petroleum engineering, renewable energy development, reservoir evaluation and management, uncertainty quantification; MPhil, MSc, PhD

School of Textiles and Design; www.tex.hw.ac.uk

design for textiles (fashion interior art), fashion, fashion communication, fashion marketing and retailing, fashion menswear, fashion technology, fashion womenswear, fashion and textiles design, fashion and textiles innovation and new applications, fashion and textiles management; BA, BSc(Hons,Ord), MA, MSc

Edinburgh Business School; www.ebs.hw.ac.uk

accounting, alliances and partnerships, competitive strategy, consumer behaviour, corporate governance, credit risk management, derivatives, developing effective managers and leaders, economics, employee relations, employee resourcing, finance, financial risk management/development leadership, human resource development, human resource management and strategic planning, marketing, marketing research, organisational behaviour, project management, project management strategic planning, strategic risk management; DBA, MBA, MSc

Degrees validated by Heriot-Watt University offered at:

EDINBURGH COLLEGE OF ART
www.eca.ac.uk

architecture, art & design, fine art, landscape architecture, sculpture, tapestry, visual culture studies and communication; BAArch, BA(Comb), BSc(Hons, Ord), MAHons, MPhil, MSc, PhD

UNIVERSITY OF HERTFORDSHIRE
www.herts.ac.uk

School of Aerospace, Automotive and Design Engineering; www.herts.ac.uk/courses/schools.of.study/.automotive.and.design.engineering

aerospace/ engineering/technology, airport operations, automotive engineering, aviation logistics, mechanical engineering, motorsport/technology, pilot studies; BEng, BSc, BSc(Hons), MEng, MPhil, MSc, PGC, PgD, PhD

School of Art and Design; www.herts.ac.uk/schools.of.study/courses /art.and.design

3D modelling and prototyping, art and design, art therapy, contemporary applied arts, fashion, fine art, graphic design, illustration, industrial design, interior and spatial design, product design; BA(Hons), BSc(Hons), MA, MPhil, PGC, PGD, PhD, UnivFdn Cert

School of Business; www.herts.ac.uk/schools.of.study/courses/business

accounting, bus adminstration, economics, events management, finance, human resources, international business, investment management, marketing, modern languages, tourism; BA/BSc, BA(Hons), BSc, DBA, DMan, MA, MBA, MPhil, MSc, PGC, PGD, PhD,

School of Computer Science; www.herts.ac.uk/courses/schools.of .study/computer.science

artificial intelligence, business computing networks, computer science, distributed systems, entertainment systems, information technology, mobile computing, mutimedia technology, networks, robotics, secure computing systems, software engineering; BSc(Hons), MEng, MPhil, MSc, PGC, PGD, PhD

School of Education; www.herts.ac.uk/courses/schools.of.study/education

deaf children education, early years, education studies, leading learning, learning support, primary education, secondary education, work-related learning; BA(Hons), BEd, EdD, FdA, MA, MPhil, PGC, PGCE, PGD, PhD

School of Electronic, Communication and Electrical Engineering; www.herts.ac.uk/ courses/schools.of.study/electronic-communication-and-electrical-engineering

audio, computer and network technology, computer engineering/systems and computer engineering, digital broadcast, digital communications and electronics/forensic/rights technology/electrical and electronic engineering, games and graphics hardware technology, internet technology and e-media technology, multimedia technology, video and digital broadcast engineering; BEng, EngD, MEng, MPhil, MSc, PhD

School of Film, Music and Media; www.herts.ac.uk/courses/schools.of.study/ film-music-and-media

2D, 3D digital animation, 3D games, art, entertainment, film, media practices, multimedia design, music, music composition and technology, music and entertainment industry management, photography, screen cultures and media business, sound design technology, television documentary; BA(Hons), BSc(Hons), MA, MPhil, MSc, PGD, PhD, Univ FoundationCert

School of Health and Emergency Professions; www.herts.ac.uk/courses/ schools.of.study/health-and-emergency-professions

diagnostic imaging/radiography, dietetics, emergency management, health research, oncology, paramedic science, physiotherapy, radiation sciences, radiotherapy, sport and exercise rehabilitation, ultrasound; BSc(Hons), DHRes, Foundation degree, MPhil, MSc, PGC, PGD, PhD

School of Humanities; www.herts.ac.uk/ courses/schools.of.study/humanities

acting & screen performance, creative writing, English language & communication/language teaching/ literature, film, French, history, journalism, media cultures, new media publishing, philosophy, Spanish; BA(Hons), MA, MPhil, PGC, PGD, PhD

School of Law; www.herts.ac.uk/courses/ schools.of.study/law

commercial law, criminal justice, e-commerce law, international law, legal practice, maritime law; BSc(Hons), Diploma, LlB(Hons), LlM, MPhil, PGD, PhD

School of Life Sciences; www.herts.ac.uk/ courses/schools.of.study/life.sciences

biochemistry, bioinformatics, biomedical science, environmental management, exercise science, genetics, geography, molecular biology, pharmaceutical science, pharmacology, physiology, sport, sports studies, sports therapy, water and environmental management; AIEMA, BSc/BSc(Hons), MSc, PGC, PGD

School of Nursing and Midwifery; www. herts.ac.uk/courses/schools.of.study/ nursing-and-midwifery/

child welfare and protection, clinical nursing, critical care, diabetes care, emergency nursing, family health, infection prevention and control, mid-tissue viability, midwifery and women's health, nursing (learning disability) and social work, oncology nursing, supportive immunology; BSc/BSc(Hons), DipHE, DipHE Nursing, MSc, NVQs, PGDip/PGCert

School of Pharmacy; www.herts.ac.uk/ courses/schools.of.study/pharmacy

advancing pharmacy practice, medicinal chemistry, pharmacy; MPharm, MPhil, MSc, PGC, PGD, PhD

School of Physics, Astronomy and Mathematics; www.herts.ac.uk/courses/ schools.of.study/ physics.astronomy.and.mathematics

astrophysics, computing mathematics, financial market analysis, financial maths, mathematics, physics, scientific computing; BSc(Hons), MPhil, MSc, PhD

School of Medicine; www.herts.ac.uk/ courses/schools.of.study/ postgraduate.medicine

child health, dermatology skills and treatment, health law and ethics, health and medical education, mental health practice, medical practice, psychiatric practice, western medical acupuncture; MD, MSc, PGC, PGD

School of Psychology; www.herts.ac.uk/ courses/schools-of-study/psychology

business psychology, cognitive neuropsychology, psychology, clinical, health, occupational, organisational psychology; BSc(Hons), DClinPsy, MSc, PGD

School of Social, Community and Health Studies; www.herts.ac.uk/courses/schools-of-study/social-community-and-health-studies

applied criminology, cognitive behavioural therapy, therapeutic counselling, counselling, disability, mental health studies, mental health (primary care), psychotherapy, social work; BSc/BSc(Hons), MA, MPhil, MSc, PGC, PGD, PhD, Post-Qualifying Awards

Degrees validated by the University of Hertfordshire offered at:

HERTFORD REGIONAL COLLEGE
www.hrc.ac.uk

academic and continuing education, business, children care and health, computing, construction engineering and technology, creative arts and industries, hair and beauty, inclusive learning, leisure tourism and catering; DipMS, FD, PCGE/PCCET

NORTH HERTFORDSHIRE COLLEGE
www.nhc.ac.uk

art design and creative studies, beauty, business, early years, finance, HRM, ITfor multimedia, internet, management, performing arts, social and child care, sport, teacher training, travel and tourism; BA(Hons), BSc, C&G, Foundation degrees, national and higher diplomas, NVQs

OAKLANDS COLLEGE
www.oaklands.ac.uk

animal care, art, beauty, business, construction, engineering, fashion design, health and social care, horticulture, hospitality and catering, landscape design, media, music, performing arts, retail, sports studies; C&G, Dips/Certs, FD Dips, HNC, HND, Nat Dips NVQs

WEST HERTS COLLEGE
www.westherts.ac.uk

accounting, advertising, art & design, beauty, business & management, care & early years, construction, counselling, crafts, electrical installation, ESOL, floristry, forensic science, hairdressing, holistic therapies, hospitality and catering, information technology, literacy and numeracy, marketing, media & photography, motor vehicle, performing arts and music, public services, retail, sign language, sport, teaching & training, travel; BA(Hons), BTEC, C&G, College Cert/Dips, Nat Dips, NVQs

THE UNIVERSITY OF HUDDERSFIELD
www2.hud.ac.uk.sas

School of Applied Sciences; www2.hud.ac.uk/sas air

analytical chemistry, biochemistry, biology (molecular and cellular), chemical engineering, chemistry, food science, forensic and analytical science, health, hospitality and events management, human biology, leisure management, logistics/management, medical biochemistry, medical biology, medical genetics, microbial sciences, nutrition, pharmaceuticals, pharmacy, public health, supply chain management, tourism, transport; BA(Hons), BSc(Hons), HND, MA, MChem, MPharm, MSc, MSci, PhD

School of Art, Design and Architecture; www2.hud.ac.uk/ada

3D design, advertising, animation, architectural technology, architecture, art, communication design, construction, costume with textiles, design, digital media, exhibition and retail design, fashion, fashion and textiles buying/management/retailing, fashion design with marketing/production, fine art and

105

contemporary arts, graphic design, graphics, illustration, interior design, media and promotion, multimedia design/games, photography, product design, project management, property development, surface/transport design, textile design and crafts, transport design; BA(Hons), BSc(Hons), CerHE, DipHE, FdA, FdSc, MA, MArch, MSc

Business School; www2.hud.ac.uk/uhbs

accountancy, advertising, brand management, business administration/information management/law & management/project management, business studies, corporate administration, direct marketing, entrepreneurship, environmental management, European business/legal studies, financial services, finance, global business, hospitality management, HRM, information systems, international business, marketing, journalism, law, law (commercial, international), leadership, legal practice, logistics management, management studies, marketing communications, marketing, media relations, PR, retail, risk, disaster and environmental management, small businesses, social entrepreneurship, sports marketing/ promotion, strategic change management; BA(Hons), FdA, GradDipLaw, HND, LlB(Hons), LlM, MBA, MSc, PGCE, PGDip, PGDip/Cert

School of Computing and Engineering; www2.hud.ac.uk/ce

audio systems, automotive design/engineering/systems design and analysis/technology, computer-aided design/engineering, computer control systems, computer-based system design, computer systems, computing, digital media, electronic and communication engineering, electrical engineering, electronic design, energy engineering, engineering and technology management, engineering design: information systems, manufacturing engineering, mechanical and automotive engineering, motorsport engineering/technology, music technology, popular music production, product innovation, software development; BEng(Hons), HNC, HND, MEng, MSc, PhD, UniFdCert

School of Education and Professional Development; www2.hud.ac.uk/edu

business education, childhood studies, early childhood studies, early years, guidance, international education, post-compulsory education and training, religion and education, youth and community work; BA(Hons), CertEd, FdA, MA, PGradDip/Cert, PSCE

Human and Health Sciences; www2.hud.ac.uk/hhs

applied therapeutic counselling, behavioural sciences, child welfare & safeguarding, cognitive behavioural, community nursing practice, counselling studies, criminal justice, criminology, exercise, physical activity and health, health and community studies, holistic therapies, mental health studies, midwifery, nursing, occupational therapy, operating department practice, perioperative practice, physiotherapy, podiatry, police studies, primary health care, psychological studies, psychotherapy, public health, public management, social sciences, social work, sociology, sports; DipHE, MA, MSc, PGDip, PhD

Music, Humanities and Media; www2.hud.ac.uk/mhm

British sign language, Chinese (Mandarin), drama, English (language, literature, and creative writing), history, humanities, media and journalism, modern languages, music, music technology, performance, politics, popular music, sociology, technical theatre; BA(Hons), FdA, MA, MPhil, PdF, PhD

UNIVERSITY OF HULL
www.hull.ac.uk

Faculty of Arts and Social Sciences; www.hull.ac.uk/fass

American studies, anthropology, computer music, creative writing, criminology, dance, digital media, drama, economics, English literature, English, film studies, forensic science, French, gender studies, geography, German, globalisation and governance, history of art, Italian, jazz and pop music, law (common, international, business, French, European), media studies, medieval/military European history, music/technology, philosophy, politics, psychology, social policy, social work, sociology, Spanish law, theatre, theology, war and security studies, web design; BA(Hons), BMus, BSc(Hons), LlB, LLM, MA, MEd, MMus, MPhil, MR/MRes, PGD/C, PhD

The Hull University Business School; www.hull.ac.uk/hubs

accounting, business, business economics, business management, international business, logistics, supply chain, transport; BA(Hons), BSc(Hons), MBA, MPhil, MRes, MSc, PhD

Faculty of Health and Social Care; www.hull.ac.uk/fhsc

child care, community mental health, community nursing, learning disabilities, mental health, midwifery, nursing – childhealth, operating department practice, primary care and social care, professional studies, public health; Adv Diploma, BSc(Hons), FD, MPhil, MRes, PhD

The Hull York Medical School; www.hyms.ac.uk

anatomy, cancer, cardiovascular medicine, child health, clinical sciences, clinical techniques and skills, dermatology, evidence-based decision making, gastrointestinal medicine, immunology, life sciences, managing resources, medicine, mental health, metabolic and renal medicine, pathology, person-centred care, population health and medicine, reproduction, respiration, surgery; BSc, MBBS, MPhil, MSc/Dip/Cert, PGCert/Dip, PhD

The Institute for Learning; www.2.hull.ac.uk/ifl

early childhood education & care, educational studies, e-learning, HE, inclusive education,learning and teaching, primary teaching, young people, social and behavioural studies, social and community studies; BA, EdD, FD, GradCert, MA, MEd, MPhil, MSc, PGCE, PhD

Postgraduate Medical Institute; www2.hull.ac.uk/pgmi

cancer, cardiology, cardio-vascular-respiratory medicine, clinical psychology, community medicine and rehabilitation, diabetes, obstetrics and gynaecology, oncology, psychiatry, respiratory medicine, vascular surgery; MD, MPhil, PhD

Faculty of Science; www.hull.ac.uk/science

acquatic zoology, applied physics, astrophysics, biology, biomedical science, chemistry, coastal marine biology, computer-aided engineering, computer and business informatics, computer science/software development/systems engineering, ecology, electronic engineering, engineering & logistics automatic control, environmental sciences, geography, human biology, information technology, laser science, marine & freshwater biology, mechanical engineering, medical engineering, medical product design, molecular medicine, nanotechnology, ornithology, pharmaceutical science, philosophy, physics, product innovation, psychology, toxology; BA, BEng, BSc, BSc/MEng, MPhil, MPhys, MPhysGeog, MRes, MSc, PhD

Degrees validated by the University of Hull offered at:

BISHOP BURTON COLLEGE
www.bishopburton.ac.uk

animal management, applied animal behaviour, applied science, art & design, business management, countryside and environmental conservation, early years, equine, floristry, food, garden design and horticulture, planning and development, public services, sport, teacher training, travel and tourism; BA(Hons), BSc(Hons), BSc(Ord), BTECExtel, FD, FdSc, HNC, MSc, PGCE

DONCASTER COLLEGE
www.don.ac.uk

administration, animation and games, building services, construction, counselling, criminology, dance/theatre, early years, engineering business, English, fashion & textiles, film & TV, fine art, graphic design, ICT, illustration, law, music/music technology, script writing, social science, sport & leisure; BA(Hons), BSc, BSc(Hons), FD, HNC, HND, MA, MSc, NVQs, PCE, PGCe

IMPERIAL COLLEGE, LONDON
www3.imperial.ac.uk

Faculty of Engineering; www3. engineering.imperial.ac.uk

aeronautics, aerospace, bioengineering, chemical engineering & chemical technology, civil & environmental engineering, computing, earth science & engineering, electrical & electronic engineering, geology, geophysics, geoscience, materials, mechanical engineering, nuclear engineering mechanics, soil; BEng, MA, MEng, MSc, MSci, PhD

Faculty of Medicine; www1.medicine. imperial.ac.uk

medicine, electives biomedical science, cancer biology, cardiorespiratory nursing, clinical research, experimental neuroscience, human molecular, genomic med, infection management, immunology course, integrative neuroscience course, medical science, medical ultrasound, medicine, modern epidemiology, molecular biology & path virus, molecular medicine, pharm & translational allergy, physiology & drug discovery, public health, reproductive biology, surgical science/technology/education, translational med adult critical care; BSc, CAS, MBBS, MEd, MPH, MRes, MSc, MSci, PhD

Imperial College Business School; www3.imperial.ac.uk/business-school

accounting, actuarial finance, business economics/strategy, entrepreneurship, financial management, finance, health economics/service, HRM, innovation management, international business, international health management, management, marketing, organisational behaviour, project management, risk management and financial engineering; BSc, MBA, MSc, PhD

Dept of Humanities; www3.imperial.ac.uk/humanities

controversies and ethical dilemmas in science and technology, creative writing, European history

1870–1989, foreign languages (French, German, Italian, Mandarin Chinese and Spanish), history of medicine, history of science, history of science, technology and medicine, global history of twentieth century things, music and western civilization, music technology, philosophy, politics, science communication, translation; MPhil, MSc, PhD

Faculty of Natural Sciences; www3. imperial.ac.uk/naturalsciences

Chemistry: catalysis and advanced materials, chemical biology of health and disease, chemistry and management/medicinal chemistry/molecular physics, chemistry with French/German/Spanish for science, green chemistry: energy and the environment, nanomaterials, nanostructured materials and devices, plastic chemical biology, synthetic chemistry, theoretical and experimental physical chemistry

Life Sciences: biochemistry, biology, biology with French/German/Spanish for science, biology with management/microbiology, bioimaging sciences, biomedical physical, biomedical science, biotechnology, ecology and environmental biology, microbiology, plant biology, zoology

Mathematics: applied mathematics, computational methods for aeronautics, flow management and fluid-structure, mathematics and finance, pure mathematics

Physics: applied photonics, astrophysics, condensed matter theory, controlled quantum dynamics, experimental solid state physics, high energy physics, optics and photonics, photonics, physics, physics with theoretical physics with studies in musical performance, plastic electronic materials, plasma physics, quantum fields and fundamental forces, quantum optics and laser science, space and atmospheric physics, theoretical physics, theory and simulation of materials; BSc, MRes, MSci, PhD

KEELE UNIVERSITY
www.keele.ac.uk

Faculty of Health; www.keele.ac.uk/facs/health

School of Medicine; www.keele.ac.uk/depts/ms

biomedical engineering, cell and tissue engineering, foundation medical practice, geriatric medicine, medical education, medical science/(ethics)/(surgery), medicine, surgery

School of Pharmacy; www.keele.ac.uk/schools/pharm

advanced professional practice, clinical (hospital) pharmacy, community pharmacy, prescribing studies

Nursing and Midwifery; www.keele.ac.uk/depts/ns

acute care, adult nursing, childrens nursing, clinical practice, critical care, end of life care, generic route, high dependency care, learning disability nursing, long term conditions, maternal and infant health, midwifery, operating dept practice, pre-registsration – mental health nursing, rheumatology nursing

School of Health and Rehabilitation; www.keele.ac.uk/depts/pt

applied clinical anatomy, health science, neurological rehabilitation, neuromusculoskeletal healthcare, osteopathy, pain science management physiotherapy

Faculty of Humanities and Social Sciences; www.keele.ac.uk/facs/humass

Keele Management School; www.keele.ac.uk/schools/ems

accounting and finance, actuarial science, business administration, business economics, economics, finance, finance and IT/management, HRM, industrial relations, international business, leadership and management, management, management and IT, management science, marketing; MA, MBA, MSc, PGCert, PGDip, Univ Cert,

School of Humanities; www.keele.ac.uk/schools/hums

American studies: American literature and Culture, English and American literature, US history and politics; MPhil, MRes, PhD
English: creative writing, film studies, English and American literatures, humanities, Victorian Studies
English Language Unit

History: early modern history, history, local and public history, medieval history, modern history
Media, Communication & Culture: cultural history, cultural theory, environment and cyberculture, film studies, globalisation, media studies, moving and still image production
Modern Languages: French, German, Japanese, Russian, Spanish, TEFOL, TESOL
Music: creative music technology, film music analysis, music, music technology, popular music, performance, composition

Keele Law School; www.keele.ac.uk/depts/law

child care law and practice, contract law, crime, equity and trusts, gender, sexuality and human rights, human rights, globalisation and justice, land law, medical ethics and law, law, law with politics/criminology, law of the EU, social science research in law
Politics, International Relations and Philosophy: diplomatic studies, environmental politics, European politics and culture, global security, globalisation and justice, human rights, international relations, philosophy, politics

School of Public Policy and Professional Practice; www.keele.ac.uk/schools/pppp

Education: creative and critical practice, educational leadership, educational studies, management & learning, PGCE (English, geography, informationa and communication technology, mathematics, modern foreign languages, science, social sciences)
Gerontology: gerontology
Health Policy and Professional Practice: health executive, health services management
Social work: ageing, community and society, families, health, rehabilitation and well-being, psychology, social work
Criminology: criminology
Sociology: changing families/changing households, culture, family, community and society, family studies, health and society, risk and society gerontology, self, gender and consumption, social, cultural and post colonial research, social inclusion and exclusion, sociology of the body, sociology of work, transnational communities, women, identity and global activism

BA, BSc, DLitt, Diploma/Grad Dip Law, EdD, LlB, LLM, MA, MBA, MRes, MSc, PGCE, PGDip/Cert, PhD

Faculty of Natural Siences; www.keele. ac.uk/facs/sci/

School of Computing and Mathematics; www.scm.keele.ac.uk
actuarial science, computer science, creative computing, finance and IT, information systems, IT and management, IT management for business, mathematics (pure, applied, statistics), project management, smart systems, web technologies

School of Life Sciences; www. keele.ac.uk/ depts/bi
biochemistry, biology, biomedical science, European scientific research training, human biology, molecular parasitology and vector biology, neuroscience

School of Physical and Geographical sciences; www.keele.ac.uk/schools/dps/
Chemistry: analytical, materials & surface chemistry, analytical & spectroscopic research, bioinorganic chemistry of aluminium and silicon, chemical ecology group, chemistry, green chemistry and clean energy, integrated macromolecular structure, medicinal chemistry, organic and medicinal chemistry, photochemistry, porous materials, solid state and computational chemistry, zeolite research
Earth Sciences and Geography: applied environmental science, earth system science, environment and sustainability, environmental geology, forensic geophysics, geography, geology, geoscience, human geography, physical geography
Forensic Science: forensic science
Physics and Astrophysics: astrophysics, electromagnetism, nuclear physics, optics, quantum mechanics, quantum physics of atoms and molecules, statistical mechanics and solid state physics, thermodynamics

School of Psychology; www.keele.ac.uk/ depts/ps
applied psychology, clinical psychology, counselling, counselling psychology, psychological research methods/(music), psychology; BA, BSc, DClinPsy, DSc, MGeoscience, MRes, MSc, PGCert, PGDip, PhD

UNIVERSITY OF KENT
www.kent.ac.uk

Faculty of Humanities; www.kent.ac.uk/ humanities

Kent School of Architecture; www.kent.ac. uk/architecture
European architecture, urban design

School of Arts; www.kent.ac.uk/arts
drama & theatre studies, film studies, history & philosophy of art, music technology

School of English; www.kent.ac.uk/english
colonial and post-colonial research, creative writing, gender, long 18th-century poetry, sexuality and writing

School of European Culture & Languages; www.kent.ac.uk/secl
classical and archeological studies, comparative literature, French, German, Hispanic studies, history of archeology, Italian, language and linguistic studies, modern European literature, philosophy, religious studies

School of History; www.kent.ac.uk/history
American studies, history of science, technology & medicine, medieval and modern studies, propaganda & war; BA(Hons), BSc(Hons), MA, MArch, MDram, MPhil, PhD

Faculty of Science, Technology and Medical Studies; www.kent.ac.uk/stms

Dept of Bioscience; www.kent.ac.uk/bio
biochemistry, biological/medical science, biology, forensic science

School of Computing; www.sc.kent.ac.uk/
artificial intelligence, computing & business accounting/business information, computing science, IT, web computing

School of Electronics and Digital Arts; www.kent.ac.uk/eda
electronic & computer systems, multimedia technology, web computing

School of Mathematics, Statistics & Actuarial Science; www.kent.ac.uk/IMS

actuarial science, business/finance mathematics, pure/applied maths, statistics

Medway School of Pharmacy; www.kent.ac.uk/msp

medicine management, pharmaceutical practice, pharmacy

School of Physical Sciences; www.kent.ac.uk/physical-sciences

astrophysics, forensic chemistry/science, physics, space science

Centre for Biomedical Informatics; Centre for Nueroscience and Cognitive Systems

BA(Hons), BEng, BSc(Hons), DClinPsych, MD, MRes, MPhil, MSc, Msurg, PCert, PDip, PhD,

Faculty of Social Sciences; www.kent.ac.uk/socsci

School of Anthropology and Conservation; www.kent.ac.uk/sac

anthropology (social/biological/medical), biodiversity conservation and management, conservation biology, environmental anthropology, ethnicity, ethnobotany, evolution and human behaviour, international trade and wildlife, nationalism and identity, tourism, visual anthropology, wildlife conservation; BA(Hons), BSc(Hons), MA, MSc, PhD

Kent Business School; www.kent.ac.uk/kbs

accounting, business administration, employment relations, finance, HRM, international business, management science, marketing management, operational research, sustainability management, value chain management; BA(Hons), BBA, BSc(Hons), MBA, MEBA, MPhil MSc

School of Economics; www.kent.ac.uk/economics

agricultural economics, applied environmental economics, econometrics, economics, finance, financial economics, international development, international finance; BSc(Hons), MPhil, PhD

Kent Law School; www.kent.ac.uk/law

English, French, German, Spanish or Italian law, European legal studies, law; BA(Hons), LlB, LlM, MPhil, PhD

Centre for Journalism; www.kent.ac.uk/journalism

journalism; BA(Hons)

School of Politics and International Relations; www.kent.ac.uk/politics

comparative federalism, conflict, peace & security, European studies, human rights, international conflict analysis, international law, international relations, international security, politics, security and terrorism; BA(Hons), MA, MPhil, PhD

Dept of Psychology; www.kent.ac.uk/psychology

applied psychology, cognitive psychology/neuropsychology, forensic psychology, group processes and intergroup relations, psychology, social psychology; BSc(Hons), MPhil, MSc, PhD

School of Social Policy, Sociology and Social Research; www.kent.ac.uk/sspssr

British & American policy studies, criminal justice studies, criminology, cultural studies, environmental social science, health & social care, health services, intellectual & development disabilities, mental health and social care, migration studies, political sociology, public sector management, social policy, social work, sociology, urban studies; BA(Hons), BSc(Hons), Certificate and Diplomas, MA, MPhil, MSc, PhD

Centre for Sports Studies; www.kent.ac.uk/sports-studies

exercise & fitness science, exercise professionals, health & fitness, rehabilitation, sport therapy, sports, sports & exercise management; BA, BSc, BSc(Hons), MA

KINGSTON UNIVERSITY
www.kingston.ac.uk

Faculty of Art, Design and Architecture; www.kingston.ac.uk/faculties/#design

architecture, art and design, art and design history, art and space, art history, arts market, building surveying, communication design, contemporary design, curating, design, design: product+space, design studies, fashion, film design and 3D, filmmaking, fine art (painting, sculpture, intermedia, print), games development, garden design, graphic design, historic building conservation, illustration and animation, interior design, landscape architecture/planning, landscape and urbanism, learning & teaching in higher education, mfa15 computer generated imagery, motion graphics, museum and gallery studies, photography, planning and sustainability, product and furniture design, production design for film and television, property planning and development, quantity surveying consultancy, real estate management, residential property, sustainability for built environment practice, sustainable place making and urban design, user experience design, visual and material culture, visual effects; BA(Hons), FdA, FDA, FdSc, MA, MSc, PGCert/Dip

Faculty of Arts and Social Sciences; www.fass.kingson.ac.uk

applied/business/financial economics, applied child psychology, applied econometrics, child centred interprofessional practice, children's special educational needs, classical theatre, composing for film and television, continuing professional development, creative writing, criminology, dance, development economics, developmental psychology, drama, early years: education and childcare/management and leadership/teaching, economics, electroacoustic composition, English, English language and communication, English language teaching, English literature, film studies, French, history, history (early modern/European/international/local/modern/modern British/early British), human rights, international economics, international politics, international relations, journalism, magazine journalism, making plays, media and cultural studies, media practice, music, music education, music performance, music technology, performance and screen studies, poetry, politics, primary teaching, production of popular music, psychology, publishing, secondary teaching, sociology, Spanish, television and new broadcasting media, writing fiction/travel/children's literature

Faculty of Law & Business; www.business.kingston.ac.uk

accounting and finance, business, business administration, business management, business informatics, business information management/technology, business operations management, business studies, business systems management, business and finance/law administration/professional administration/professional administration/accounting/business information management/law, business and law administration, business with law, creative economy, employment law and business law, HRM,

international business with French or Spanish/law, international business with law, international law, law, law with criminology, marketing & strategy, strategic innovation, strategy, marketing & entrepreneurship; BA(Hons), BSc(Hons), DBA, FdA, Grad Dip Law,HND, LlM, MA, MBA, MSC, PhD

Faculty of Computing, Information Systems and Mathematics; www.cism.kingston.ac.uk

actuarial mathematics, biomedical informatics, computer graphics and digital imaging/games programming/communications, computer science, computer vision image analysis, cyber security and computer forensics, electronic commerce, embedded systems, financial mathematics, games technology, health informatics, informatics, information systems, IT for e-business, IT support, mathematical sciences, mathematics, medical statistics, medical technologies, mobile computing, networking and data communications, network and information security, software engineering, statistics, user interaction design, web development; BSc(Hons), FdSc, HND, MComp, MPhil, MSc, PhD

Faculty of Engineering; www.engineering.kingston.ac.uk

advanced industrial and manufacturing systems, advanced product design engineering, aerospace engineering, aircraft engineering, astronautics and space technology, automotive engineering, aviation studies for commercial pilot training, civil engineering, construction engineering/management, construction management and construction, engineering projects & systems management, management in construction, mechanical engineering, mechatronic systems, motorcycle engineering, motorsport engineering, renewable energy engineering, sustainable concrete structures; BEng, BSc(Hons), FdSc, HND, MEng, MSc, PhD

Faculty of Health & Social Care Sciences; www.healthcare.kingston.ac.uk

adult nursing, advanced practice, biomedical science, clinical practice, healthcare practice, long term condition, maternal and child health, medical imaging, mental health studies, midwifery/registered midwife, oncology practice, paramedic science, physiotherapy, radiography, rehabilitation, social care, social work, social work postgraduate, specialist professional child and family studies/community care/education and training in human services/education and training in human services; BSc(Hons), DipHE, FdSc, MREs, MPhil, MSc, MSw, PGCert/Dip, PhD

Faculty of Science; www.kingston.ac.uk/ science

acupuncture, applied chemistry, applied and environmental geology, biochemistry, biology, biomedical science, chemistry, cell and molecular biology, communication system, computer graphics technology, computing, earth systems science, environmental management/science/studies, exercise, nutrition and

health, forensic biology, forensic chemistry/science, forensic science, gemmology and applied mineralogy, geography, geology/applied and environmental, geospatial investigation, GIS, health and medical sciences, human biology, human geography media technology, medical biochemistry/chemistry, nutrition, paramedic sciences, pharmaceutical science, pharmacology, pharmacy, pharmacy services, sports analysis and coaching, sports science, television and video technology; BSc(Hons), FdSc, MPharm, MPhil, MSc, PhD

LANCASTER UNIVERSITY
www.lancs.ac.uk

Faculty of Arts and Social Sciences; www.lancs.ac.uk/fass/faculties

European Languages and Cultures; www.lancs.ac.uk/fass/eurolang

European languages/studies, German, Italian, modern languages, romantic & Victorian literature

Applied Social Science; www.lancs.ac.uk/fass/appsocsci

criminological research, criminology, social work

Educational Research; www.lancs.ac.uk/fass/edres

education, gender and women's studies and education, psychology in education, religious studies

English and Creative Writing; www.lancs.ac.uk/fass/english

English language, English language in the media, linguistics, literature, sociolinguistics

History; www.lancs.ac.uk/fass/history

historical research, historical studies, local and regional history, modern European history

Institute for Cultural Research

cultural research, cultural studies and popular music, English literature, film studies, literary studies or media

Lancaster Institute for the Contemporary Arts; www.lancs.ac.uk/fass/licr

contemporary arts, fine art, innovation & design, music, music technology, sustainability, theatre studies

School of Law; www.lancs.ac.uk/fass/law

bioethics,medical law, European legal studies, humanitarian law, international business & corporate law,

international human rights, international law, law and criminology, management & law ethics, terrorism law

Philosophy; www.lancs.ac.uk/fass/philosophy

anthropology of religion, ethics, combined philosophy, philosophy and religion

Politics & International Relations; www.lancs.ac.uk/fass/politics

conflict, globalisation, international law/relations, peace studies, politics, security and war, strategic studies

Religious Studies; www.lancs.ac.uk/fass/relig

anthropology of religion, ethics, philosophy and religion, religious studies

Sociology; www.lancs.ac.uk/fass/sociology

gender and women's studies, organisation studies, social history, sociology; BA(Hons), BSc(Hons), LlB, LlM, MA, MPhil, MSc, PGD, PhD

School of Health and Medicine; www.lancs.ac.uk/shm/faculties

Biomedical & Health Sciences; www.lancs.ac.uk/shm/bls

biochemistry/with biomedicine or genetics, medical statistics, cell biology, clinical psychology, learning disabilities, life care, premedical studies, public mental health

Medicine; www.lancs.ac.uk/shm/med

basic biomedical research, medical education, medical statistics and epidemiology, medicine, sociology of medicine; BSc(Hons), CertHE, DClinPsych, MBChB, MBiomed, MD, MHospice leadership, MPhil, MRes, MSc, PgDip/Cert, PhD

Lancaster University Management School; www.lums.lancs.ac.uk

accounting, banking, business studies, economics, European management, finance, HR,information technology, international business (economics), logistics & supply chain management, management & law/ organisational change, management science & operations/analytics, money, operational research, project management; BA(Hons), BBA, BSc(Hons), LlM, MBA, MPhil, MRes, MSc, PhD

Faculty of Science and Technology; www.lancs.ac.uk/shm/sci-tech/faculties

Biological Sciences

biology, biophotonics, conservation biology, ecology/ and the environment, environmental biology, environmental science

Communications Systems; www.dcs.lancs.ac.uk

communications, computer science, critical software engineering, distributed systems engineering, human–computer interaction, information and communication systems, information technology and media, intelligent and robotic systems, mobile broadband engineering, social network techniques, telecommunications

Engineering; www.engineering.lancs.ac.uk

computer/mechanical/mechatronic/nuclear/sustainable/safety engineering

Environmental Science; www.lec.lancs.ac.uk

earth science, energy and the environment, environmental chemistry/science

Geography

earth science, economics, geography, geography (environmental change/North America), human physical geography

Lancaster Environment Centre; www.lec.lancs.ac.uk

conservation science, ecology/and the environment, environment and development/biochemical toxicology, environmental informatics/pollution and protection/science/and technology, plant sciences, resource and environmental management, science of the environment, sustainable water management, volcanology and geological hazards

Mathematics and Statistics; www.maths.lancs.ac.uk

applied social statistics, computer science and mathematics, environmental mathematics, mathematics, mathematics and philosophy/statistics/psychology, medical statistics, statistics

Natural Sciences; www.naturalsci.lancs.ac.uk

combined science, combined technology, natural sciences

Physics; www.lancs.ac.uk/depts/physics

astrophysics, cosmology, biomedical physics, physics, space science, theoretical physics/with mathematics

Psychology; www.psych.lancs.ac.uk

development psychology, psychology, psychology of advertising, social pscychology; BEng(Hons), BSc(Hons), MChem, MEng(Hons), MPhil, MPhys(Hons), MRes, MSc, MSci(Hons), PGDip, PhD

Degrees validated by Lancaster University offered at:

BLACKPOOL AND THE FYLDE COLLEGE
www.blackpool.ac.uk

art, art, design and performing arts, business, management and IT, catering, computing and automotive, construction, engineering, hair, beauty and related therapies, health, care and early years, hospitality and food production, media and performance, sport and leisure, tourism, travel; BA(Hons), BSc/(Hons)

EDGEHILL COLLEGE OF HIGHER EDUCATION
www.edgehill.ac.uk

Faculty of Education; www.edgehill.ac. uk/education

primary education, creative art, design & technology/ secondary education with QTS/Science and PE; science key stage 2/3/secondary education with QTS, secondary physical education, secondary science

Business, Psychology, Post-compulsory Education and Training

14–19 education, business education, enterprise education, further education leadership and management, lifelong learning and skills, PCTE, post-compulsory education and training, psychology; BA(Hons), BSc(Hons), CertHE, Foundation degrees, PGCE, MA, MTL

Faculty of Health; www.edgehill.ac.uk/ health

Nursing

advanced practice, behaviour analysis and intervention, case management, clinical education, cognitive behavioural therapies/psychotherapy, complementary therapies, counselling, health & social care practice, health and social wellbeing, health and social care, health research and evaluation, health sciences, integrated practice (early years and children), management and supervision of offenders, midwifery, nutrition and health, operating dept practice, orthopaedics, otorhinolaryngology, paramedic science, person centred support, playwork, positive behaviour support, public health, respiratory practice/disease management, substance misuse interventions, support for families and communities, trauma, women's health, working with vulnerable adults; BSc(Hons), Dip/CertHE, FDA, FdSc, MCh, MPhil, MSc, PhD

Faculty of Arts and Science

Business School; www.edgehill.ac.uk/ business

accountancy, business and management, communications, computing (business information technology management), control and embedded systems, information systems or systems and software, engineering management, information technology, international business marketing, internet computing, leisure and tourism management, management development, teaching information technology, web development

Dept of English and History; www.edgehill. ac.uk/history

Chinese studies, creative writing, English, English language, English literature, film production, film studies, history, history and culture

Law & Criminology; www.edgehill.ac.uk/ law

criminology and criminal justice/law, international sports regulation, law, law with management

Media; www.edgehill.ac.uk/media

animation, film and television production, journalism, media with advertising, film and television or music and sound, PR, television production management

Dept of Natural, Geographical and Applied Sciences; www.edgehill.ac.uk/ngas

biogeography, biology, conservation management, environmental science, geography, geology, geotourism, human geography, laboratory operations management, physical geography

Performing Arts; www.edgehill.ac.uk/ performingart

applied drama and creativity, dance, design for performance, drama/ physical and visual theatre/ music and sound/drama, physical theatre and dance, theatre; BA(Hons), BSc(Hons), FdA, FdSc, Llb, LlBHons, MA, MBA, MSc, PhD

UNIVERSITY OF LEEDS
www.leeds.ac.uk

Faculty of Arts; www.leeds.ac.uk/arts

School of English; www.leeds.ac.uk/english

American literature and culture, English language, English renaissance literature, medieval English literature, post-colonial literary and cultural studies, theatre and development studies, theatre making, theatre studies, 20th-century literature, Victorian literature

School of History; www.leeds.ac.uk/history

18th-century studies, history, international history and politics, medieval history, modern history

School of Humanities; www.leeds.ac.uk/humanites

classical studies, development studies, health care ethics, history and philosophy of science, pastoral studies, philosophy, mind and knowledge, philosophy of physics, religion/theology and public life, religious studies, science communication, theology,

Institute for Colonial and Post-colonial Studies; www.leeds.ac.uk/icps

postcolonial literary and cultural studies, postcolonial literary and cultural studies – race and resistance, world cinema

School of Modern Languages and Cultures; www.leeds.ac.uk/smlc

Arabic & Middle Eastern studies, East Asian studies, French, German, Italian, linguistics and phonetics, modern languages and cultures, professional language & intercultural studies, Russian and Slavonic studies, Spanish, Portuguese and Latin American studies; BA(Hons), MA, MPhil, PgDip, PhD

Faculty of Biological Studies; www.fbs.leeds.ac.uk

biochemistry, biological identification and conservation biology, bioscience, biotechnology,/physiology, infection & immunity or plant science, medical biochemistry, medical microbiology, medical sciences, microbiology with immunology/virology, molecular biology, neuroscience, pharmacology, physiology, sport and exercise sciences, zoology; BSc(Hons), MRes, MSc, PhD

Faculty of Business; www.fbs.leeds.ac.uk

Leeds University Business School; www.leeds.ac.uk/lbs

accounting, advertising and design/marketing, banking, business economics, computing and management, corporate communications and PR, diversity management, economics, finance, financial economics, financial mathematics, HRM, international business/finance/marketing management, manufacturing leadership marketing, transport studies; BSc(Hons), ExecMBA, MA, MBA, MPhil, MSc, PhD

Faculty of Education, Social Sciences & Law; www.essl.leeds.ac.uk

School of Education; www.ed.leeds.ac.uk

childhood studies, clinical education, deaf education, educational assessment, ICT, lifelong learning, mathematics education, PGCE biology/chemistry/English/mathematics/modern foreign languages/physics, children with learning difficulties/developmental disorders, science education, special educational needs, teaching, teaching English (TESOL) for young learners/studies/teacher education,

School of Law; www.law.eeds.ac.uk

banking and finance law, criminal law and criminal justice, criminological research, criminology, European human rights law, European law/and society, international and comparative criminal justice, law, policing

School of Politics and International Studies; www.leeds.ac.uk/polis

British politics (parliamentary studies), conflict, development and security, democratic studies, development studies/and disability/education/ gender, European parliamentary studies, European defence and security, European politics, international development/political economy/relations/studies, politics, terrorism and security, union public policy/union and development studies

School of Sociology and Social Policy; www.sociology.leeds.ac.uk

criminal justice and policing programmes, disability/and special education/ethnicity and racism/health and illness/social policy/gender, disability studies, gender and culture, gender and technology/

management, gender, sexuality and queer theory, interdisciplinary social policy, public policy, racism and ethnicity studies, social policy/and crime, social science, sociology; BA(Hons), LLM, MA, MEd, MPhil, MSc, PGCert, PGCE, PhD

Faculty of Engineering; www. engineering.leeds.ac.uk

School of Civil Engineering; www. engineering.leeds.ac.uk/civil

architectural engineering, civil and environmental engineering/structural engineering/with construction management, environmental engineering, infrastructure asset engineering and management, project management, sustainable waste management

School of Computing; www.engineering. leeds.ac.uk/comp

artificial intelligence, cognitive science, computer science, computing/ for business/and management

School of Electronic and Electrical Engineering; www.engineering.leeds.ac. uk/elec

advanced electronic devices, computational fluid mechanics, electrical engineering, electronic and communications engineering, electronics and computer engineering, mechatronics and robotics, music, multimedia and electronics, nanoelectronics and nanomechanics, nanomaterials, nanoscale science and technology, renewable energy systems

School of Mechanical Engineering; www. engineering.leeds.ac.uk/mech

aeronautical and aerospace engineering, automotive engineering, combustion and energy, mechanical engineering, mechatronics and robotics, medical engineering, oilfield corrosion engineering

School of Process, Environmental and Materials Engineering; www.engineering. leeds.ac.uk/speme

chemical and energy engineering/materials engineering/minerals engineering/pharmaceutical engineering, chemical engineering, energy and environmental engineering, fire and explosion, mining and quarry engineering, petroleum engineering

Aviation and Aerospace Engineering

aeronautical and aerospace engineering, aviation technology and management, aviation technology with pilot studies

Product Design

product design

Electronics and Communication Engineering

broadband wireless and optical communications, communications engineering, modern digital and RF wireless communications, RF and microwave design for wireless systems

Process Engineering

chemical engineering, energy and environment, fire and explosion engineering, minerals and waste planning and operations, pharmaceutical science and engineering, pharmaceutical technology & quality assurance; BEng, MEng, MSc, MSc(Eng), MPhil, PhD

Faculty of the Environment; www.leeds. ac.uk/foe

School of Earth & Environment; www.see. leeds.ac.uk

engineering geology, environment and business/environmental sustainability, environmental geochemistry/geology/management, exploration geophysics, geochemistry, geological/geophysical sciences, hydrogeology, physics of the earth & atmosphere, sustainability (transport/business environment and corporate responsibility/environmental consultancy and project management/environment & development/ environmental politics & policy), transport planning

School of Geography; www.geog.leeds.ac. uk

catchment dynamics, geography, geography with transport planning, geography–geology, GIS, global change and the biosphere, human geography, social and cultural geography

Institute for Transport Studies; www.its. leeds.ac.uk

economics with transport studies, environment and transport planning, geography with transport, management with transport, planning, transport economics,engineering/environment

Earth & Biosphere Institute; www.earth. leeds.ac.uk/ebi

global change and the biosphere; BA(Hons), BSc(Hons), MA, MGeol, MGeophys, MRes, MSc, DGCert/Dip, PhD

Faculty of Mathematics and Physical Science; www.maps.leeds.ac.uk

School of Chemistry; www.chemistry.leeds.ac.uk

chemical biology, chemical process, colour and imaging science, chemistry/with analytical chemistry/colour science, medicinal chemistry, polymer and surface coatings; chemistry with colour science, colour and imaging science, design and colour technology, printing, packaging and graphics, polymer and surface coatings science and technology

School of Food Science and Nutrition; www.food.leeds.ac.uk

food biotechnology, food quality assurance, food science, nutrition

School of Physics and Astronomy; www.physics.leeds.ac.uk

astrophysics, nanotechnology, physics, medical physics, quantum technologies, theoretical physics

School of Mathematics; www.amsta.ac.uk

actuarial/applied/financial mathematics, mathematics, mathematics with finance, pure mathematics, statistics, statistics with applications to finance

Self-organising Molecular Systems

nanotechnology; BSc(Hons), MChem, MMath, MNatSci, MPhil, MPhys, MSc, PhD

Faculty of Health and Medicine; www.leeds.ac.uk/medhealth

Leeds Dental Institute; www.leeds.ac.uk/dental

clinical dentistry, dental hygiene, dental nursing, dental surgery, dental technology, dental therapy

Leeds Institute of Medical Education; www.leeds.ac.uk/medicine/lime

child health, clinical embryology/psychology, health informatics/management, planning and policy, hospital management, medical physics, medicine, nutrition, obesity and health, patient safety and clinical risk management, primary care education/care, psychiatry, psychoanalytic observational studies, public health, statistical epidemiology, systematic family therapy

School of Healthcare; www.lhealthcare.leeds.ac.uk/

acute healthcare, addiction studies, adult/child/mental health/learning disabilities nursing, audiology, cancer care, cardiology, child health studies, cardiology, treatment of substance misuse, counselling, infection control, integrative counselling, medicines management in primary care, midwifery, neonatal care, nursing studies, nursing, palliative care, pharmacy practice, psychotherapy, radiography, social work

School of Medicine; www/leeds.ac.uk/medicine

child health, clinical psychology, clinical risk management, family therapy, health informatics/management, hospital management, medical physics, medicine, nutrition, obesity and health, primary health care, psychiatry, public health, surgery

School of Psychological Sciences; www.psych.leeds.ac.uk

biological psychology, cognitive psychology, health and social psychology; BHSc, BSc(Hons), CPD, DClinPsych, GradDip, MA, MBChB, MD, MMedSci, MPH, MPsycObs, MSc, PGDip/Cert, PhD

Faculty of Performance, Visual Arts and Communication; www.leeds.ac.uk/pvac

Institute of Communication Sudies; www.ics.leeds.ac.uk

broadcast journalism, cinema and photography, communications studies, international communications, journalism, media industries, new media TV production

School of Design; wwwdesign.leeds.ac.uk

textile and performance clothing, advertising/art and design, design and colour technology/technology management, fashion design, graphic and communication design, textile innovation and branding

School of Fine Art, History of Art and Cutural Studies; www.leeds.ac.uk/fine-art

art gallery and museum studies, art history with museum studies, cultural studies, fine art, history of art

School of Music; www.ics.leeds.ac.uk/music

composition, music, music performance, music technology, musicology, performance, popular and world music

School of Performance & Cultural Industries; www.ics.leeds.ac.uk/paci

choreography, culture, creativity and entrepreneurship, dance, managing performance, performance culture, theatre and performance, writing for performance and publication; BA(Hons), Grad Dip, MFA, BMus, BSc(Hons), MA, MMus, MSc, PhD

Degrees validated by University of Leeds offered at:

ASKHAM BRYAN COLLEGE
www.askham-bryan.ac.uk

animal management, business & IT, countryside & environment, crafts & leisure, engineering, plant and construction, equine, floristry, food, forestry & arboriculture, horticulture, landscape, sports, surface & greenkeeping; BA(Hons), BSc(Hons), C&G level 3, Nat Dips, NVQs 2&3

COLLEGE OF THE RESURRECTION
www.mirfield.org.uk

theology & pastoral studies; BA(Hons), DipHE, MA, MPhil, PGDip, PhD

LEEDS COLLEGE OF ART & DESIGN
www.leeds-art.ac.ukfashion

advertising, digital film, fine art, furniture making, games and animation, graphic design, interior design, photography, printed textiles & surface pattern design, visual communication; BA(Hons), Foundation degrees, HNC, National Diploma

LEEDS COLLEGE OF MUSIC
www.lcm.ac.uk

commercial music production & recording, jazz, music production, music and sound production for the moving image, musicology, performance, popular music studies; BA (Hons), FD, MA, PGDip

LEEDS TRINITY & ALL SAINTS
www.leedstrinity.ac.uk

Faculty of Arts and Social Sciences; www.leedstrinity.ac.uk/departments/ fass

English, history, literature and spirituality, psychology, sport, health, leisure and nutrition, theology & religious studies, Victorian studies; BA(Hons), BSc(Hons), MA, MSc, PGCE

Faculty of Education

Catholic education, children, young people & families, early years, initial teacher training, PGCE programmes, primary education, secondary education, teaching assistants; BA(Hons), FD, MA, PGCert, PGCE

Faculty of Media, Business & Marketing; www.leedstrinity.ac.uk/departments/ FMBN

broadcast journalism, business and enterprise/ finance/management, business studies, business with law/with marketing, film and television studies, journalism, management, marketing, media and marketing, journalism, public communications, PR, sports journalism; BA(Hons), MA/PGDip, MB

NORTHERN SCHOOL OF CONTEMPORARY DANCE
www.nscd.ac.ukdance

BPA(Hons)

YORK ST JOHN COLLEGE
www.yorksj.ac.uk

Faculty of Arts

Faculty of Education & Theology

Faculty of Health & Life Sciences

York St John Business School

American studies, business management, counselling studies, creative writing, dance, education studies, English language & linguistics/literature, exercise instruction, film & television production, film studies, fine arts, healthcare practice, history, information technology, languages, media, music/ production, occupational therapy, physical education & sports coaching, physiotherapy, primary education, product design, psychology, sport, society & development, sports science & injury management, supporting learning, theatre, theology & ministry/ religious studies, visual impairment, working with children and young people; BA(Hons), BHSc, BSc(Hons), FD, MA, MSc, PGDip/Cert

LEEDS METROPOLITAN UNIVERSITY
www.leedsmet.ac.uk

Faculty of Arts & Society; www.leedsmet. ac.uk/as

The Leeds School of Architecture, Landscape & Design; www.lmu.ac.uk/as/ald
architecture, design, garden art, interior/landscape architecture/planning, urban design

School of the Built Environment; www.lmu.ac.uk/as/benv
building surveying, commercial management, construction law, construction operations/project management, facilities management, heritage planning, housing studies, human geography, planning law & practice, project management, quantity surveying, town & regional/country planning

The Leeds School of Contemporary Art & Graphic Design; www.lmu.ac.uk/as/cagd
curating contemporary art, contemporary fine art practices, fine art, graphic arts & design

School of Cultural Studies; www.lmu.ac.uk/as/cs
contemporary literatures, English, English literature, history, media & popular culture, politics, screen media

Film, Television, and Performing Arts; www.lmu.ac.uk/as/ftpa
animation, art, events, film and moving image production, playwork, performance/works, screenwriting (fiction)

School of Social Science; www.lmu.ac.uk/as/sss
criminology, politics, psychology & society, social sciences, sociology, working with young people, youth work & community development; BA(Hons), BSc(Hons), DipHE, FdAA, GradCert, MPhil, MRes, MSc, PGDip

Faculty of Business and Law; www.leedsmet.ac.uk/lbs

Leeds Business School; www.leedsmet.ac.uk/lbs/business
accounting, advertising, business, business studies, economics for business, HRM, international business/communication, journalism, management, marketing, PR, public administration, purchasing and supply

Leeds Law School; www.leedsmet.ac.uk/lbs/law
law, law with criminology, legal practice

Leeds School of Accountancy and Financial Services; www.leedsmet.ac.uk/lbs/accfin
accounting & finance, international trade & finance; BA(Hons), HND, LlB(Hons), LlM, MA, MSc, PGDip/Cert

Faculty of Health; www.leedsmet.ac.uk/ health
applied psychology, art psychotherapy, biomedical sciences, health care, public health nursing, health sciences, men's health, mental health, nurse practitioner studies, nursing (adult health/mental healt/ district nursing, learning disabilities, practice nursing, community children's nursing), occupational therapy, osteopathy, physiotherapy, psychology and criminology/sport & exercise, public health.nutrition, safety, health & environmental management, social work, speech & language therapy, sport and exercise therapy, therapeutic counselling; BA(Hons), BSc(Hons), CertHE, HNC, MA, MSc, PGDip/Cert, Prof Dip

Carnegie Faculty of Sport & Education; www.leedsmet.ac.uk/carnegie
childhood, early childhood education, physical education, sport pedagogy, primary education, secondary physical education, sport & exercise science, sport business management, sports coaching/development/performance; BA(Hons), BSc(Hons), FdSc, MSc, PGCE, PGCert/Dip/MA, PhD

Faculty of Innovation & Technology; www.leedsmet.ac.uk/inn
business information systems, computer animation/forensics, creative technology, digital imaging & creative visualisation, digital video & special effects, games design, green computing, information management/systems/studies, mobile & distributed computer networks, multimedia & entertainment, music production/ technology, photographic journalism, professional computing, sound design, web applications development; BSc(Hons), HND, MA, MSc, PGCertt/Dip

Leslie Silver International Foundation; www.leedsmet.ac.uk/international
business & EFL/global development/international relations/& marketing/tourism management, destination management, English language teaching and materials development, English language teaching methodology, events management, French/German/Spanish & business, global development & international relations/political economy, global development/international relations/marketing/public relations, international festivals management, international foundation studies, languages with international business/language studies, peace & conflict resolution, peace and conflict resolution/development in global societies,peace studies & politics/international relations, retail business administration, sports event management; Adv Dip, BA/BA(Hons), HND, MA, MSc, PGCert/Dip, PhD

UNIVERSITY OF LEICESTER
www.le.ac.uk

College of the Humanities and Law, Centre for American Studies; www.le.ac. uk/hi/centres/amstudies
American studies, English, English literary research, governance and democracy, history, humanities, international relations, modern literature, new media, society

School of Archaeology & Ancient History; www.le.ac.uk/ar
ancient history, archaeology, classical Mediterranean, geography, historical archaeology, history, landscape history

School of English; www.le.ac.uk/ee
American studies/history, English, English literary research, humanities, modern literature and creative writing, Victorian studies

Dept of History of Art and Film Studies; www.le.ac.uk/arthistory
the country house in art, film studies and the visual arts, history of art, history and literature media

School of Historical Studies; www.le.ac. uk/hi
contemporary history, English local history, history, history and politics/international relations/ancient history, urbanisation

121

School of Law; www.le.ac.uk/law

law (European Union/ international), law with French law, European law and integration, human rights

School of Modern Languages; www.le.ac.uk/ml

European studies, French, German, Italian, modern language studies, Spanish

Museum Studies; www.le.ac.uk /ms

art museum and gallery studies, digital heritage, interpretive studies, learning and visitor studies; BA(Hons), BSc(Hons), LlB, LlM, MA/GradDip, MPhil, PhD

College of Science and Engineering; www2.le.ac.uk/colleges/science

Dept of Chemistry; www.le.ac.uk/ch

chemical biology, chemistry, forensic science, green chemistry, pharmaceutical chemistry

Dept of Computer Science; www.cs.le.ac.uk

advanced computational methods/distributed systems/software engineering, computers with management, computing, software engineering for financial services, web applications and services

Dept of Engineering; www2.le.ac.uk/departments/engineering

advanced control and dynamics, advanced engineering, aerospace engineering, communications and electronic engineering, control and signal processing, electrical engineering, embedded systems and control engineering, general engineering, information and communication engineering, mechanical engineering, software and electronic engineering

Dept of Geography; www.le.ac.uk/geography

environmental informatics, geography, geology, GIS, global environmental change, human geography, physical geography, sustainable management of natural resources

Dept of Geology; www2.le.ac.uk/departments/geology

applied and environmental geology, crustal processes, geology, geophysics, geophysics/borehole, palaeobiology

Centre for Interdisciplinary Science; www2.le.ac.uk/departments/interdisciplinary-science

communication science, complex systems, evolution, laboratory science, mathematics for science, nanoscale frontiers, sustainable livelihoods in Africa, virtual worlds

Dept of Mathematics; www2.le.ac.uk/departments/mathematics

actuarial science, computational mathematics, financial mathematics, mathematical modelling in biology, mathematics/ and computation

Dept of Physics and Astronomy; www2.le.ac.uk/departments/physics-and-astronomy

astronomy, astrophysics, condensed matter physics, physics, physics with nanotechnology/astrophysics/space science and technology/planetary science, space projects & instrumentation, space science; BA(Hons), BSc(Hons), BEng/MEng, MA, MChem, MComp, MGeol, MMath, MPhil, MPhys, MSc, MSci, PGDip, PhD

College of Medicine, Biological Sciences and Psychology; www2.le.ac.uk/colleges/medbiopsych

School of Biological Sciences; www.le.ac.uk/lbs

biochemistry, bioinformatics, biology, cell physiology & pharmacology, genetics, medical biochemistry/genetics/physiology/microbiology, microbiology, molecular biology, molecular genetics, pharmacology/biological sciences, physiology, zoology

School of Medicine, Leicester Medical School; www.le.ac.uk/sm/le

cancer studies and molecular medicine, cardiovascular sciences, health sciences, infection, medical and social care education, molecular pathology, molecular toxicology, pain management, primary care research, social science applied to health, child and adolescent mental health

School of Psychology; www.le.ac.uk/pc

clinical psychology, forensic psychology, psychological research methods, psychology; DocClinPsych, BSc, MBChB, MBioSci, MD, MSc, PostgradDip/Cert, PhD

College of the Social Sciences Beyond Distance Research Alliance; www.le.ac.uk/departments/beyond-distance-research-alliance

design for e-learning: institutional embedding, assessment & disciplines: developing e-tivities research, delivering university curricula: knowledge, learning and innovation gains, e-learning knowledge sharing, greening of e-learning, second environment advanced learning, 5-stage model and e-tivities in learning, globalization and communications, new media & society/governance & teaching, workbased learners in further education, e-learning and learning technologies, wiki environment

Dept of Criminology; www.le.ac.uk/criminology

applied/clinical criminology, criminology, terrorism, security and policing

Dept of Economics; www.le.ac.uk/ec

banking and finance, business economics, economics, business analysis and finance, financial economics, money, public sector economics

Dept of Education; www.le.ac.uk/education

international education, learning and teaching education leadership, teaching assistants

The Centre for Labour Market Studies; www2.le.ac.uk/departments/clms

development management and globalisation, high performance work practices, HRD and performance management, HRM, industrial relations and HR, international HR and globalisation, organisational and employee development, people management, skills and performance, workplace learning

School of Management; www.le.ac.uk/ulsm

accounting, finance, management, management studies, marketing, MBA

Dept of Media & Communication; www.le.ac.uk/mc

communications, communications democracy, communication research, mass communications, media & society/psychology/English as a foreign language

Dept of Politics and International Relations; www.le.ac.uk/politics

American foreign policy/studies, contemporary history, diplomatic studies, European studies, international relations/and world order, international security studies, management studies with politics, political research, politics

Dept of Sociology; www.le.ac.uk/sociology

contemporary sociology, criminology/communications media and society, psychology with sociology, social research, sociology; BA(Hons), DocSocSci, EdD, Foundation degrees, MA, MBA, MPhil, MSc, PGCE, PGDip/Cert, PhD

Degrees validated by the University of Leicester offered at:

NEWMAN COLLEGE OF HIGHER EDUCATION
www.newman.ac.uk

art & design, counselling, creative arts, creative writing, drama, early years, education studies, English, English literature, history, information technology, local history and heritage, management studies, media and communication, philosophy, theology, religion and ethics, psychology, religious education, social and applied psychology, sports studies, working with children, young people and families, youth and community work; BA/BSc(Hons), Foundation degrees, MA, MPhil, PGCE, PhD

UNIVERSITY OF LINCOLN
www.lincoln.ac.uk

Faculty of Agriculture, Food and Animal Science; www.lincoln.ac.uk/afas

agriculture and environment, bioveterinary science, clinical/animal behaviour and welfare, commercial horticulture, conservation biology, equine science/sports science, food manufacture, food science, management & welfare; BSc, FdSc, MPhil, MSc, PhD

123

Faculty of Art, Architecture & Design; www.lincoln.ac.uk/aad

animation, architecture, art & design, conservation of historic objects, restoration, construction project management, contemporary lens media, design/for exhibition & museums, development and regeneration planning, fashion studies, graphic design, illustration, interactive design, interior design, product design, urban design; BA(Hons), BArch, Grad Dip, MA, March, MPhil, PhD

Faculty of Business & Law; www.lincoln.ac.uk /bl

accountancy, advertising, branding, business administration/management/studies, engineering management, European business/marketing, finance, HRM, international business/management studies/marketing strategy/tourism, law, law and business/criminology, marketing, PR, tourism/recreation; BA(Hons), BSc(Hons), LlB(Hons), LlM, MA, MBA, MPhil, MRes, MSc, PhD

Faculty of Health, Life & Social Sciences; www.lincoln.ac.uk/hlsc

acupuncture, biomedical science, child studies, clinical psychology, criminology/and international relations/politics, forensic science, golf science, health & social care, health science, herbal medicine, human nutrition, international relations and politics/social policy, nursing, psychology, social anthropology, social policy/ and management, social science, social work, sport & exercise science, sport development and coaching, child studies; BA(Hons), BSc(Hons), CertHE, DClinPsy, MA, MClinRes, MPhil, PGCert, PhD

Faculty of Media, Humanities and Technology; www.lincoln.ac.uk/mht

advertising, audio production, community journalism/radio, computer games production, computer information systems, computer science, computing, creative writing, culture and communications, dance, digital imaging and photography, documentary production, drama/and media, film & television, games, journalism, cultural studies, media, culture & communications, media production/technology, PR, public & community history, theatre and consciousness, web technology, war and international human rights; BA(Hons), BS(Hons), FdA, MA, MComp, MPhil, MRes, MSc, PhD

Centre for Educational Research & Development; www.lincoln.ac.uk/cerd
EdD, PhD

School of Theology & Ministry Studies; www.lincoln.ac.uk/home/theology
theology; BA(Hons), Cert/Dip Theology, MA

Degrees validated by the University of Lincoln offered at:

EAST RIDING COLLEGE
www.eastridingcollege.ac.uk

access to higher education, applied digital media, art, design and media, business and administration, construction, early childhood policy and practice, early years, education and training, hair and beauty, health and social care, hospitality and catering, information technology, motor vehicle and engineering, music, public services, sport and recreation, travel and tourism; BSc(Hons), DIDA, Foundation degrees, HNC, HND, Nat AwardNVQs, Nat Dips/ Certs, PGCE

HULL COLLEGE
www.hull-college.ac.uk

Hull School of Art & Design
animation, architectural design, contemporary fine art practice, fashion and costume/textiles/design, games design, graphic design, interactive multimedia, jewellery and ceramics, lens-based photo media, television and film design, web design; BA(Hons), Foundation degrees, HNC

Business, Computing and Professional Development
business management, computing, education, IT & software design, retail, travel and tourism; BA(Hons), Foundation degrees

Construction and Engineering

construction/management, electrical/electronic, mechanical, and chemical engineering, engineering technology; BSc/BEng, FD, HNC, HND

Health and Science

biomedicine, chemistry, childcare and working with young people, counselling, criminology, health, social care; BSc(Hons), FD, HNC, HND

Performance and Media

acting, broadcast media, dance, music performance, music production and community performance, musical theatre, performing arts, stage management and technical theatre, touring and community theatre; BA, FD

Sport and Leisure

ICFT for travel and tourism, tourism planning and the environment, marketing and event management, travel and tourism travel operations; HNC, HND

NORTH LINDSEY COLLEGE
www.northlindsey.ac.uk

art, design & performing arts, business & computing/technology, childcare, construction, education & counselling, engineering, hair & beauty, health & social care, hospitality, interactive media, leisure & tourism, motor vehicle, social sciences & humanities, sports, recreation & land-based sustainability, teaching & learning, teaching in art, design and media; BA(Hons), Diplomas, FdA, FdSc, HNC, HND

UNIVERSITY OF LIVERPOOL
www.liv.ac.uk

Faculty of Arts; www.liv.ac.uk/arts

applied linguistics, classical Indian philosophy, classics, classical studies, communication, corpus linguistics, English/language and literature, English renaissance and romantic literature, European film, French, German, Hispanic studies, Irish studies, Italian, Latin American studies, Manx studies, mathematics, media, music, music industry studies, philosophy, politics, pure maths, science fiction studies, TESOL, Victorian literature, women and the word; BA(Hons), MA, MMus, MPhil, PhD

School of Medical Education; www.liv.ac.uk/sme

anatomy and human biology, child health and paediatrics, dental surgery, health studies, life sciences applicable to medicine, medicine, nursing, orthodontics, orthopaedic surgery, psychiatry, public health, surgery, tropical medicine, tropical paediatrics, veterinary science; BDS, BSc(Hons), BN, BVSc, MBChB, MChOrth, MCommH, MClinPsychol, MDS, MPH, MRCPsych, MTCH&CP, MTropMed, MTropPaed

Faculty of Engineering; www.liv.ac.uk/engfac

aerospace engineering, automation, avionics systems, civil engineering, computer science, electronics, electrical and electronic engineering, environmental engineering, intelligence engineering, laser and manufacturing engineering, medical electronics, maritime engineering, medical electronics and instrumentation, microelectronic systems and telecommunications, VLSI and free electron lasers; BEng, Deng, MEng, MPhil, MSc, PhD

Faculty of Science; www.liv.ac.uk/science

applied mathematics, artificial intelligence, astronomy, astrophysics, biochemistry, biological sciences, biosystems and informatics, chemistry, computer information systems, computer science, ecology, environmental biology, genetics, geology, geophysics, inorganic chemistry, internet computing, investigative & forensic psychology, marine biology, mathematical physics, mathematical sciences, mathematics, medical chemistry, microbiology, molecular biology, nuclear technology, ocean and earth sciences, organic chemistry, pharmacology, physical chemistry, physical geography, physics, psychology, pure mathematics, research methods in psychology, software development, statistics and probability, surface science, theoretical physics, zoology; BSc(Hons), MChem, MEng, MMath, MPhys, MESci, MRes, MSc, PhD

Faculty of Veterinary Science; www.liv. ac.uk/vets

animal reproduction, bioveterinary science, medicine, parasitology, veterinary infection and disease control, veterinary conservation; BSc(Hons), BVSc, DVSc, MSc

Faculty of Social and Environmental Studies; www.liv.ac.uk/ses

business studies, communication studies, consumer marketing, criminology, e-business strategy and systems, economics, entrepreneurship, environment, finance, football industries, geography, HRM, international business, international development, law/international business/medicine & healthcare, management, media & popular music, operations and supply chain management, philosophy, planning, politics, sociology research methodology, town and regional planning, urban regeneration; BA(Hons), BSc(Hons), CertHE, CPS, DipHE, DLitt, LlB, LlM, MA, MBA, MPA, MPhil, MPlan, MRes, PGDip/Cert, PhD

Degrees validated at the University of Liverpool offered by:

LIVERPOOL HOPE UNIVERSITY
www.hope.ac.uk

applied social science, business, childhood & youth studies, computing, dance, disability studies, drama & theatre studies, early childhood studies, education studies, English language/literature, environmental biology/management, film studies, fine art, geography, health, health therapies, history, human biology, inclusive education, information technology, law, leisure, media, ministry, music, nutrition, outdoor recreation, philosophy & ethics, police leadership, politics, psychology, sport development/studies, theology & religious studies, tourism; BA(Hons), BMin, BSc(Hons), BDes, FdA, FdSc, MA, MBA, MMin, MPhil, PGCE, PhD

LIVERPOOL JOHN MOORES UNIVERSITY
www.ljmu.ac.uk

Faculty of Business and Law; www.ljmu. ac.uk/BLW

accounting, applied languages (French/Chinese/Japanese/Spanish), business, business administration/management & information, commercial law, criminal justice, criminology, economics, finance, HRM, international business studies/commercial law, law and commerce, legal practice, marketing, personnel & development, PR, risk and crisis management, social enterprise management, strategic HRM, TESOL, tourism & leisure; BA(Hons), BSc(Hons), DBA, HND, LlB, LlM, MA, MBA, MPhil, MRes, MSc, PgDip/Cert

Faculty of Education, Community and Leisure; www.ljmu.ac.uk/ECL

CPD, educational practice,dyslexia/leadership and community nutrition, community, health and social welfare, dance studies, design & technology/modern languages, early childhood studies (0–8 years), education studies and English/early years/applied community studies/special and inclusive education, environmental adventure tourism, physical education, primary & secondary education, mathematics, science education, primary early years (primary French (TS)), psychology and sport science, school sport management/development, sport & physical activity, sport and dance/exercise science, sports technology, teacher training courses (primary, secondary), tourism & leisure management; BA(Hons), BSc(Hons), EdD, FD, MA, MPhil, MRes, PGCert, PgDip, PhD

Faculty of Media, Arts & Social Science; www.ljmu.ac.uk/MAS

American studies and imaginative writing/media and cultural studies/screen studies, applied community & social studies, architecture, broadcast engineering, communication, community, health and social welfare, computer aided design, computer animation and visualisation, creative writing, criminal justice, criminology, digital modelling, drama, early childhood studies, English/literature, imaginative writing/screen studies, fashion, film studies, fine art, graphic arts, history, history of art & museums, interactive media design, interior design, journalism, media, interactive media, television, popular music studies, product design & digital modelling, psychology, screen studies, screenwriting, criminology, social sciences, social work, sociology,textile design, urban design; BA(Foundation), BA(Hons), BDes, DipArch, DipHE, MA, MPhil, MRes, PG, PGCE, PhD

Faculty of Science; www.ljmu.ac.uk/faculties/scs

animal behaviour, applied psychology, astronomy, astrophysics, biochemistry, biological anthropology, biological chemistry, biology, biomedical sciences, clinical pharmacy, criminal justice, drug use and addiction, environmental sciences, food and nutrition, football, forensic anthropology, forensic science, geography, geology, health psychology, industrial/pharmaceutical science, medical biochemistry, medicinal and analytical chemistry, molecular biology with genetics, nutrition, occupational psychology, oncology, pharmaceutical analysis, pharmacy, physical geography, physics, psychology, science & secondary education), sport science, wildlife conservation, zoology; BSc(Hons), MPhil, MPhys, MRes, MSc, PGCE, PhD

Faculty of Technology & the Environment; www.ljmu.ac.uk/faculties/TAE

advanced manufacturing technology, architectural technology, automotive engineering, building surveying, built environment, business mathematics, civil engineering studies, civil engineering, commercial property development/management, computer-aided design, computer animation and visualisation/engineering/forensics/games technology/studies/ technology, construction management, control engineering/systems, design & technology, digital broadcast and media systems, earth science, e-business technology, electrical and electronic engineering, broadcast engineering, engineering, environmental planning, industrial electronics, information systems, information technology, IT and multimedia computing, machines and mechanisms, manufacturing engineering, manufacturing systems engineering, marine and offshore engineering, marine engineering,/technology, maritime business/studies, materials and fracture mechanics, mathematics, mechanical engineering, mechatronics, microelectronic systems design, multimedia computing, nautical science, navigation, neural computing, online computing, power and control engineering, power engineering, property and facilities management, quantity surveying, real estate management, software engineering, sports technology, statistics and computing, surveying (commercial buildings), transport and logistics, urban planning, web computing; BA(Hons), BSc(Hons), FdSc, HND/C, MPhil, MSc, PgC, PGCE, PgD, PhD

Faculty of Health & Applied Social Services; www.ljmu.ac.uk/faculties/HEA

assisting professional practice. acute care/ radiography) clinical case management, community public health nurse, psychological therapies, direct nursing or general practice nursing, health and social care, health sciences, health visiting or school nursing, midwifery, nursing (adult/child/mental health/paramedic practice), primary mental health care, social work, specialist community practitioner, traumatic death and loss, working with young people, children, their families and carers; BA(Hons), BSc, DNurs, DMidw, DPH, DipHE, Foundation degrees, FdA MPhil, MRes, MSc, PGDip/Cert

UNIVERSITY OF THE ARTS LONDON
www.artsac.uk

Camberwell College of Art & Design; www.camberwell.arts.ac.uk

3D design, art and design, book arts, book conservation, conservation, designer–maker, design practice, digital arts, drawing, graphic design, illustration, painting, photography, printmaking, sculpture, transnational arts; BA(Hons), Dip, FdA, MA, MPhil, PGDip, PhD

Central Saint Martins College of Art & Design; www.csm.arts.ac.uk

art & architecture, acting, architecture: spaces and objects, art & design, communication and curation:

fashion, menswear, womenswear, communication design, communication with promotion, creative practice for narrative environments, ceramics, furniture or jewellery, criticism, design for textile futures, design studies, European classical acting, fashion, fashion history and theory pathway, fine art, glass, graphic design, industrial design, innovation management, innovative pattern cutting, jewellery design, knitwear and print, marketing, orientation to art & design, performance design and practice, performance, photography, product design, screen: acting, directing, writing, textile design; BA(Hons), DipFndStudies, FdA, Foundation degree, GradDip, MA, MPhil, PGCert/Dip, PhD

Chelsea College of Art & Design; www. chelsea.arts.ac.uk

3D design (display design/flower design/interior design)/3D modelling, animation, art and design, book arts and design, broadcast media (sound design & music technology), creative advertising strategy, critical writing and curatorial practice, design for graphic communication, digital media design, digital origination, fashion marketing, fine art, graphic design communication, graphic design, interior design, photography, print production (print media), spatial design, textile design; BA(Hons), FdA, Foundation Dip, Grad Dip, MA, MPhil, PGCert/Dip, PhD

London College of Communication; www.lcc.arts.ac.uk

broadcast journalism, communication and critical practice, creative writing, creative writing theory, design/visual communication, design management, digital colour imaging, documentary film, events management, film, video, games design, graphic and media design – design for advertising/illustration/print/ information/typo/graphics, graphic branding and identity, graphic moving image/product innovation, information environments, innovation and creativity in industry, interactive media, interior design, international travel and tourism, journalism, magazine publishing, marketing and advertising, marketing communications, media and cultural studies/curating/practice, photography, photojournalism/and documentary, PR, print media management, production for live events and television, publishing, retail management, screenwriting, sound arts, sports journalism, surface design, writing criticism; BA(Hons), FdA, ABCDip, MA, MDes, MRes, MSc, PgDip

London College of Fashion; www. fashion.arts.ac.uk

active sportswear, art and design, bespoke tailoring, cordwainers accessories/footwear, cosmetic science, designer, fashion business/contour and development/design technology, menswear/womenswear/surface textiles, fashion design, fashion illustration/journalism/fashion management/marketing and promotion/media and communication/photography/PR/marketing/business/realisation/media, film and TV make up, image styling for performance, make up, prosthetics for performance, marketing and promotion, pattern cutter/knitwear/surface textiles, retail branding and visual merchandising, styling and photography, tailoring, technical effects for performance; BA(Hons), BSc(Hons), Diplomas, Foundation degrees, MA, PgDip/Cert

Wimbledon College of Art; www. wimbledon.arts.ac.uk

art and design, drawing, fine art: painting, print and time-based media, sculpture, visual language of performance theatre: costume design/theatre lighting design and practice/production for live events and television/costume interpretation/set design for stage and screen/design for performance/technical arts and special effects; BA(Hons), FdA, MA

LONDON METROPOLITAN UNIVERSITY
www.londonmet.ac.uk

Dept of Applied Social Sciences; www. londonmet.ac.uk/depts/dass

bioethics, city regeneration, community health/nursing/ sector management, crime, safety and security, criminology, health & social policy/social care management, housing and inclusion, individual and community empowerment, mental health and well-being, organisation and community development, practice nursing, prescribing, public health, return to nursing practice, school nursing

Media, Information and Communications

digital information management/media/media/management, information management, media and communications, media studies, mass communications

Sociology and Social Policy

applied sociology, cities, design & regeneration, community sector management, criminology, housing and inclusion, individual and community empowerment, organisation and community development, social anthropology, social development practice, social policy, social research/and evaluation, social statistics, social work, working with adults/children and young adults/people, specialist social work, sociology, labour and trades union studies, urban policy; BA(Hons), BSc(Hons), MA, MPhil, MRes, MSc, PGCert/Dip, PhD

Dept of Architecture and Spacial Design; www.londonmet.ac.uk/architecture

architectural history, architecture, cities, design and urban cultures, energy and sustainability, interior design/digital design systems; BA(Hons), MA, MSc, PhD, ProfDip

Faculty of Computing; www.londonmet.ac.uk/depts/cctm

Communications Technology

communications systems, computer networking/systems engineering, digital communications networks, electronics, electronics, communications engineering/computer engineering, embedded systems, information and communications technology support, mobile & satellite communication, network management & security, telecommunications and networks engineering,

Computing

business computing, business information technology, computer forensics, computer science, computing, internet computing, IT security, mobile computing, mining/distributed systems/mobile computing/advanced computing/software engineering

Mathematics

computer science/engineering applications, computing, decision science, financial mathematics, mathematical sciences, mathematics, statistics

Informatics & Multimedia Technology

computer animation/games/e-learning/games/internet, creative technology (e-learning/games/multimedia), consultancy, multimedia and cultural heritage; BSc(Hons), FdSc, MEng, MRes, MSc, PhD

Faculty of Humanities, Arts, Language and Education; www.londonmet.ac.uk/depts/hale

School of Humanities, Arts and Language; www.londonmet.ac.uk/depts/hale

American studies, applied translation studies, business English, Carribean studies, creative writing, ELT &ALS, English language studies/literature, film studies, filmmaking, game studies, history, interpreting/public service, journalism, modern performance, modern British women's history, performing arts, philosophy, professional writing, screenwriting, Spanish/and Latin American studies, teacher training, theatre studies

School of Education; www.londonmet.ac.uk/depts/hale/doed

early childhood studies, early years teaching, education international, Jewish education, leading and managing school development, learning and teaching in HE, music education with QTS, therapy and education; BA(Hons), BEd, FdA, MA, PGCE, PGDip/Cert

Dept of Law, Governance and International Relations; www.londonmet.ac.uk/depts/hale/lgr

advice work, Asia Pacific studies, business, business and law, business law, European family law and practice, European studies, governance and international relations/law, human rights and social justice, international development/economic law/law/politics/relations/relations/interdisciplinary international relations and globalisation/security studies, sustainable development/trade, law, peace and conflict, public administration (international), public services management, social justice, transport and maritime law; BA(Hons), BSc(Hons), FdG, LlB, LlM, MA, PGCE

Faculty of Life Sciences

School of Human Science; www.londonmet.ac.uk/depts/hhs

biochemistry, bioethics, biological and medicinal chemistry, biological sciences, biomedical sciences, chemistry, clinical nutrition, coaching, cosmetic science, dietetics, exercise and health, food and consumer studies, food science, forensic and bioanalytical science/industrial bioanalytical techniques/science, health promotion, herbal medicinal science, home economics, human biology/nutrition, public health/sports/dietetics, medical bioscience, medical genetics, nutrition, osteopathic medicine, osteopathy, personal training and fitness consultancy, pharmaceutical science, pharmacology, sports and exercise science, sports psychology and performance, fitness evaluation, sports therapy, sustainability in the food industry

School of Psychology; www.londonmet.ac.uk/depts/dops

counselling skills, forensic psychology, health psychology, psychology, sport & performance psychology; BSc(Hons), DipHE, FdSc, GradDip/Cert, MOst, MOstMed, MSc

London Metropolitan Business School; www.londonmet.ac.uk/lmb

accounting, advertising and marketing communication, arts and heritage management, finance, aviation management, banking, business, business economics/enterprise/information/ management/operations management/psychology, community sport coaching & management, computer systems, corporate finance and investment finance, corporate treasury management, economic studies, economics, events (marketing) management, fashion marketing, financial communications, financial economics, financial markets and derivatives/with information systems, financial regulation/and compliance management, HRM/development/strategy, insurance, international business and banking/finance/marketing, international business entrepreneurship/business/business finance/economics and finance/hospitality management/hotel and restaurant management/sustainable tourism/tourism management, trade and transport, investment, investment fund management, law, leadership, marketing, media and music management, music and media marketing/management/PR, music industry management, purchase and supply chain management, retail management, sports management, strategic management accounting, technology management, trade, travel management; BA(Hons), BSc(Hons), DipCass, DPS, FdSc, GradConv, HND, MA, MBA, MSc, PGDip,

Sir John Cass Dept of Art Media and Design; www.londonmet.ac.uk/jcmd

audio visual production, communications management, curating the contemporary, design, digital film and animation, fashion jewellery, film production, fine art, furniture design, furniture making, furniture and product design, graphic design, illustration, inclusive design, interior design, interior design and technology, jewellery and silversmithing design, manufacture and design for polymer products, plastic product design/with management/with marketing, polymer science and engineering, research for disability, textile design; BA(Hons), BSc(Hons), FdA, MA, MPhil, MSc, PhD

LONDON SOUTH BANK UNIVERSITY
www.lsbu.ac.uk

Faculty of Arts and Human Sciences; www.lsbu.ac.uk/#ahs

Arts, Media & English; www.lsbu.ac.uk/#ahsam

arts management, creative writing, digital film/media arts/photography, drama & performance studies, film studies, game cultures, media and cultural studies, media writing, new media, sonic media; BA(Hons), MA, MPhil, PhD

Education; www.lsbu.ac.uk/#ahsedu

early years, education for sustainability, graduate teacher programme (primary/secondary maths), higher education, initial teacher training, learning and teaching (FE and HE), secondary mathematics (ages 11–16); BA(Hons), Cert, FdA, MA, PgDip/Cert

Law; www.lsbu.ac.uk/#ahslaw

combined honours law field, common law, crime & litigation, international human rights and development, law, legal studies; Grad Dip, LlB(Hons), LLM

Psychology; www.lsbu.ac.uk/#ahspsycho

addiction psychology & counselling, investigative forensic psychology, psychology, psychology with criminology, psychology (clinical psychology/child development), sexual and relationship studies/therapy; BSc(Hons), Grad Dip, MSc, PhD

Social and Policy Studies; www.lsbu.ac.uk/#ahssps

childhood and family studies, criminology, development studies, European policy studies, international politics, refugee studies, social policy, social research methods, sociology; BA(Hons), BSc(Hons), MSc, PhD

Urban, Environmental & Leisure Studies; www.lsbu.ac.uk/#ahsuel

built environment studies, cities & local development, housing studies, international business tourism and hospitality management, planning policy and practice, spatial urban planning, sustainable communities, urban and environmental planning, urban regeneration and community development; BA(Hons), FdA, HNC, MA, MSc, PGCert/Dip

Faculty of Business; www.bus.lsbu.ac.uk

Accounting & Finance; accounting, banking, charity,finance, information management, international finance, investment; BA(Hons), FdA, MSc, PgDip

National Bakery School

baking technology management, craft studies, creative techniques, food manufacture, multi-skilled hospitality services; CGLI Dips/Certs, Diploma, FdSc

Business

accounting, business, business administration/information systems/& international studies/management/studies, economics, economics of international business, finance, HRM, international business, management, management science, marketing; BA(Hons), BSc(Hons), FdA, HNC, HND, MSc, PgDip

Business Information Technology & Computing

computing, e-business IT, health information systems, information assurance, information systems management/technology international finance & information management, internet & database systems, internet computing, managing wireless information systems, multimedia computing; BA(Hons), BSc(Hons), FdSc, HNC, HND, MSc

Human Resources

Certificate in personnel practice, Masters in human resources, Masters in international human resources,

Languages

Arabic, Chinese Mandarin, English IELTS, French, German, Greek, Hindi, Italian, Japanese, Polish, Portuguese, Russian and Spanish, Swedish and Urdu

Management

business administration, Eurasian business management, international management, management, managing in not-for-profit organisations, managing in the public sector, public administration, voluntary administration; Certs, Dips in Management Marketing, MA, MBA, Masters degrees in various subjects

Marketing

international marketing, international tourism marketing; BA(Hons), MA, MSc, PgCert, PgDip

Faculty of Engineering, Science & Built Environment; www.lsbuac.uk/esbe

Dept of Applied Science; www.lsbu.ac.uk/deparments/appsci

applied biology, applied science – food/ bioscience/ biochemistry/human biology/microbiology/nutrition, process engineering, chemical engineering, culinary art, engineering, food and nutrition, food design and technology, food safety and control, forensic science/ with criminology/law/psychology, integrated sciences, organic food studies, petroleum engineering, sport and exercise science; BA(Hons), BEng(Hons), BSc(Hons), FdSc, MSc/PgCert/PgDip

Architecture

architecture, engineering product design, product design/computing, professional practice, sports product design; BA(Hons), BSc(Hons), PgDip

Dept of Electrical, Computer & Communications Engineering

computer systems and networks, electrical and electronic engineering, embedded and distributed systems, internet and multimedia engineering, power distribution, systems for environmental services, telecommunications and computer networks engineering; BEng(Hons), BSc(Hons), FdEng, MRes, MSc, PgCert, PgDip

Dept of Engineering Systems

architectural engineering, building services engineering, civil engineering, computer-aided engineering, design and manufacturing management, manufacturing management, mechanical engineering/design, mechatronics, quality engineering management, railway civil engineering, structural design, sustainable energy systems; BEng(Hons), BSc(Hons), FdEng, HNC, HND, MSc, PgDip

Dept of Surveying, Property & Construction

architectural technology, building surveying, built environment, construction/management/project management, property development and planning, property management, quantity surveying, surveying; BSc(Hons), FdSc, HNC, MSc, PgDip

Faculty of Health & Social Care; www.lsbu.ac.uk/faculties/hsc

Adult and Mental Health and Learning Disabilities; Primary and Social Care; Traditional Chinese Medicine

acupuncture, acute and psychiatric intensive care, adult nursing, children's advanced nurse practitioner (strategic leadership and expert practice), children's nursing, Chinese medicine, diagnostic radiography, forensic mental health care, health protection, health studies (family planning and women's health), learning disability/nursing, mental health nursing, women's health, midwifery, non-medical prescribing, occupational therapy, operating department practice, physiotherapy, primary and social care, primary care (district nursing/public health and health promotion), primary care and mental health, professional development for allied health professions, professional midwifery practice, social work, specialist community public health nursing (health visiting/occupational health nursing/school nursing), therapeutic radiography; BSc, BSc(Hons), DipHE(Hons), MSc, PgDip/Cert, PhD, University AdvDip, Professional Doctorates; Allied Health Professions, MCMAc

UNIVERSITY OF LONDON; BIRKBECK
www.bbk.ac.uk

School of Arts; www.bbk.ac.uk/arts
English and humanities, European cultures and languages, history of art and screen media, media and cultural studies, Iberian and Latin American studies

School of Business, Economics and Informatics; www.bbk.ac.uk/business
computer science and information systems,economics, mathematics and management, organizational psychology

School of Law; www.bbk.ac.uk/law

School of Science; www.bbk.ac.uk
biological sciences, earth and planetary sciences, psychological sciences,

School of Social Sciences, History and Philosophy; www.bbk.ac.uk
applied linguistics and communication, geography, environment and development studies, history, classics and archaeology, philosophy, politics, psychosocial studies,social policy and education

UNIVERSITY OF LONDON; UNIVERSITY COLLEGE LONDON (UCL)
www.ucl.ac.uk

UCL School of Life and Medical Science (including UCL Medical School); www.ucl.ac.uk/slms

advanced paediatrics, ageing & mental health, anatomy and developmental biology, audiological science, biochemistry, biological sciences, biology of fertility and embryology development, biology of vision, biomedical science, brain and mind, cancer, cardiorespiratory, clinical & applied paediatrics, clinical biochemistry, clinical dental, clinical neuroscience, clinical ophthalmology, cognitive and decision sciences, cognitive neuropsychology, community child health, conservative dentistry, dental sedation & pain management, endodontics, environmental biology, genetics/ human diseases, global health & development, haemaglobinopathy, health informatics, health psychology, history of medicine, human genetics, human–computer interaction with ergonomics, immunology, implant dentistry, infection and immunity, international child health, language science, linguistics, medical mycology, medicine, molecular biology, molecular medicine, musculoskeletal science, neuroimaging, neuroscience, oral medicine, oral surgery, orthodontics, paediatric dentistry, periodontology, pharmacology, phonetics, phonology, physiology, pragmatics, prenatal genetics & fetal medicine, prosthodontics, psychiatric research, psychology, radiation biology, reproductive science and women's health, restorative dental practice, sexually transmitted infections and HIV, social epidemiology, special care dentistry, special needs dentistry, speech and hearing sciences, speech, language and cognition, sports & exercise medicine, surgical science,travel health & medicine, urology, voice pathology, zoology; BSc(Hons), DipCDSc, IbSc, MBBS, MClinDent, MD(Res), MPhil, MRes, MSc, MSci, PGCert/Dip, PhD

Faculty of the Built Environment

Built Environment; www.barlett.ucl.ac.uk

advanced architectural studies, architectural design, architectural history, architecture, building and urban design in development, built environment, environmental design and engineering/sustainable heritage, construction economics and management, development administration and planning, development planning, environment and sustainable development, European property development and planning, facility and environment management, international planning, planning studies, project and enterprise management, project management for construction, social development practice, strategic management of projects, town and country planning, town planning, urban design/development planning/economic development/studies; BSc(Hons), Diplomas, EngD, MA, MArch, MPhil, MSc, PhD

Faculty of Engineering Sciences; www. ucl.ac.uk/engineering

Civil, Environmental & Geomatic Engineering; www.rege.ucl.ac.uk

civil engineering, environmental engineering, environmental mapping, environmental systems engineering, GIS, hydrographic surveying, remote sensing, surveying, transport studies

Biochemical Engineering; www.ucl.ac.uk/biochemeng

biochemical engineering

Chemical Engineering; www.ucl.ac.uk/chemeng

chemical engineering, chemical process engineering

Computer Science; www.cs.ucl.ac.uk/

computer science, computational analysis, computational statistics and machine learning, computer graphics, vision and imaging, financial systems engineering, human–computer interaction with ergonomics, information security, machine learning, networked computer software systems

Electronic and Electrical Engineering; www.ee.ucl.ac.uk

communications engineering/computer science/nanotechnology, electronic engineering, nanotechnology, photonics systems, spacecraft technology and satellite communications, broadband communications, telecommunications/engineering

Management Science and Innovation; www.ucl.ac.uk/msi

information management for business, management , new ventures business, OR/decision analysis, project management, statistics, technical entrepreneurship/enterprise

Mechanical Engineering; www.ucl.ac.uk/mecheng

engineering with business finance, marine engineering, mechanical engineering, naval architecture, power engineering

Medical Physics & Bioengineering; www.ucl.ac.uk/medphys

biomedical engineering, medical imaging computing, medical physics/with physics, radiation physics

Crime Science; www.ucl.ac.uk/jdi

countering organised crime and terrorism, crime analysis, detection, crime prevention, community safety, detection of crime

Security & Crime Science; www.cscs.ucl.ac.uk

countering organised crime and terrorism; BEng, BSc, Certs, MEng, MPhil, MRes, MSc, PgDip, PhD

Faculty of Mathematical and Physical Sciences; www.ucl.ac.uk/maps-faculty

Chemistry; www.chem.ucl.ac.uk

chemistry, chemical physics, materials for energy and the environment, medicinal chemistry, molecular modelling and materials science

Earth Sciences; www.es.ucl.ac.uk

environmental geoscience, geology, geophysical hazards, geophysics, geosciences, natural hazards for insurers, palaeobiology (with biology), planetary science

Mathematics; www.ucl.ac.uk/mathematics

mathematics with mathematical physics/economics/modern languages/management studies/physics/statistical science, mathematical modelling, pure/applied mathematics

Physics and Astronomy; www.phys.ucl.ac.uk
astronomy, astrophysics, nanotechnology, physics, theoretical physics, ultra precision

Science and Technology Studies; www.ucl.ac.uk/sts
history & philosophy of science, science & technology studies

Space and Climate Physics; www.mssl.ucl.ac.uk
astrophysics, climate extremes, imaging, space plasma physics

Statistical Science; www.ucl.ac.uk/stats
applied stochastic modelling, biostatistics, economics, finance, financial mathematics, mathematics, statistical science, quantitative analysis for industry, quantitative decision making, statistics, statistics and management for business; BSc, BSc(Econ), EngD, MRes, MSc, MSci, PhD

Faculty of Arts & Humanities; www.ucl.ac.uk/ah
ancient and medieval languages, ancient world studies, comparative literature, Dutch, east European languages and culture, electronic communication & publishing, English language and literature, European social & political studies, film studies, fine art (Slade School), gender studies, Greek and Latin, Hebrew and Jewish studies, information science, language culture and history, language and culture, library, archive & information studies (SLAIS), library & information studies, modern languages, philosophy, publishing, records & archives management Scandinavian studies, Spanish and Latin American studies, translation theory and practice; BA(Hons), BFA, MA, MPhil, MRes, PhD, UCL

Faculty of Law; www.ucl.ac.uk/laws
alternative dispute resolution, banking law, carriage of goods by sea, children and their rights, civil and public litigation, company law, comparative contract law, comparative freedom of speech/human rights law, competition law and intellectual property rights competition law, constitutional and institutional law of the EU, corporate finance, corporate governance in the UK and US, corporate insolvency, liquidation, insolvent companies, criminal law doctrines, criminal procedure: doctrine and theory, designs and unfair competition, economic analysis of law, environmental governance and regulation, environmental law of the EU, EU administrative law/internal market/law and policy on climate change/migration law, European competition laws/equality and employment law and proof, family law and society: foreign relations law, insurance law, international and comparative competition law and policy insolvency law/copyright and related rights/trade marks, international and European refugee, international arbitration/criminal law/energy & natural resources law/environmental law/human rights law/law of foreign investment/law and policy on climate change/trade law/law of the sea, Japanese commercial law, judges, courts and judicial decision-making, judicial review, jurisprudence and legal theory, law and economics of regulated markets/industries, law and policy of international courts & tribunals, law with advanced studies/another legal system (Australia)/French law/German law/Hispanic studies/Italian law, secured transactions/commercial restitution LlB and Baccalaureus Legum, LlBHons, LlM, MPhil, PhD

Faculty of Historical and Social Sciences; www.ucl.ac.uk/shs

Anthropology; www.ucl.ac.uk/anthropology
archaeology, digital anthropology, environment and development, human evolution and behaviour, medical anthropology, material and visual culture; BA(Hons), BSc(Hons), MA, MPhil, MRes, MSc, PhD

Archaeology; www.ucl.ac.uk/archeology
African archaeology, archaeology of the eastern Mediterranean and the middle east, artefact studies, classical archaeology and classical civilisation, comparative art and archaeology, conservation for archaeology and museums, Egyptian archaeology, environmental archaeology, forensic archaeological science, GIS, maritime archaeology, palaeoanthropology and palaeolithic archaeology, principles of conservation, public archaeology, skeletal and dental bioarchaeology, social and cultural, technology and analysis of archaeological materials; BA(Hons), BSc(Hons), MA, MPhil, MSc, PhD

Economics; www.ucl.ac.uk/economics
advanced macroeconomic theory, business, econometric theory and methods, economics, economics and econometrics of policy evaluation, economics of development/ migration, game theory, health economics, industrial organisation, labour economics, macroeconomics, microeconometrics, microeconomics, money and finance, topics in enviromental

& resource, economics and environmental ethics; BSc(Hons), MSc, PhD

Geography; www.geog.ucl.ac.uk/
conservation, environment, GIS, geography, quaternary science, remote sensing, science and society, urban studies; BA(Hons), BSc(Hons), MSc, PhD

History; www.ucl.ac.uk/history
ancient history/Egyptology, European history, history (1500 to the present), history of political thought and intellectual history, history and culture of the Dutch golden age, medieval studies; BA(Hons), MA, MPhil, PhD

History of Art; www.ucl.ac.uk/art-history
history of art/with material studies/philosophy; BA(Hons), MA, MPhil, PhD

Political Science; www.ucl.ac.uk/ssp
democracy & democratisation, European public policy, global government & ethics, international public policy, legal & political theory; MA, MPhil, MSc, PhD

School of Slavonic and Eastern European Studies; www.ssees.ucl.ac.uk
central and south-east European Studies, East European languages and culture/studies, history 2008–2009, East European studies, identity, culture and power, politics and East European studies, institutions, development and globalisation, Russian and East European literature and culture, Russian studies; BA(Hons), Erasmus Mundus International Masters in Economy, State and Society, MA, MPhil, MRes, PhD

UNIVERSITY OF LONDON; COURTAULD INSTITUTE OF ART
www.courtald.ac.uk

conservation of easel paintings, curating the art museum, history of art, painting conservation (wall painting); BA(Hons), GradDip, MA, PGDip

UNIVERSITY OF LONDON; GOLDSMITHS
www.goldsmiths.ac.uk

Dept of Anthropology; www.gold.ac.uk/anthroplogy
anthropology, development & rights, cultural politics, history, sociology, social anthropology, visual anthropology; BA(Hons), MPhil, PhD, MRes

Dept of Art; www.gold.ac.uk/art
art practice, fine art and history of art, art writing, curating; BA(Hons), MFA, MPhil, PhD

Centre for Cultural Studies; www.gold.ac.uk/cultural-studies
cultural studies, culture industry, interactive media: critical theory and practice, post-colonial culture and global policy; MA, MPhil, PhD

Dept of Computing, Computing & Interaction Design; www.gold.ac.uk/computing
arts & computational technology, cognitive computing, computational studio arts, computer games & entertainment, computer science/nformation systems, creative computing, information technology, internet computing; music computing; BA(Hons), BA/BSc(Hons), MFA, MPhil, MSc, PhD

Dept of Design; www.gold.ac.uk/design
creative and cultural entrepreneurship, design, design & technology education: computing & interaction design, design & innovation/environment, design – critical practice/education/futures; BA(Hons), BA/BSc(Hons), BEng/MEng, MPhil, MRes, PhD

Dept of Drama; www.gold.ac.uk/drama
applied drama: theatre in educational, community & social contexts, arts administration & cultural policy, contemporary African theatre & performance, creative and cultural entrepreneurship, musical theatre, performance & culture, performance making, writing for performance BA(Hons), MA, MPhil, PhD

Dept of Educational Studies; www.gold.ac.uk/educational-studies
artist teachers, education, language & identity, public service professions, teacher training – primary/

secondary (art & design, design & technology, drama, English, geography, mathematics, modern languages, music, biology, chemistry, general science or physics); BA(Hons), DPS, MA, MPhil, PGCE, PhD

English and Comparative Literature; www. gold.ac.uk/ecl

American literature, applied linguistics, comparative literary studies, creative and life works, creative writing, drama, English, history media and modern literature; BA(Hons), MA, MPhil, MRes, PhD

Dept of History; www.gold.ac.uk/history

cultural history, history & anthropology/history of ideas/politics/sociology; BA (Hons), MA, MPhil, MRes, PhD

Centre for the Arts and Learning; www. gold.ac.uk/cal

creative cultural entrepreneurship, in creative and cultural entrepreneurship; MA, MPhil/PhD

Institute for Creative and Cultural Entrepreneurship; www.gold.ac.uk/ccl

creative and cultural entrepreneurship; MA, MPhil, PhD

Language Studies Centre; www.gold.ac.uk/ laguage-studies-centre

English language studies

Dept of Media and Communications; www. gold.ac.uk/media-communications

anthropology and media, media and communications/sociology/modern literature, media theory/ practice programmes

Dept of Music; www.gold.ac.uk/music

composition, creative practice, ethnomusicology, historical musicology, music, music computing, popular music performance and related studies, studio composition; BMus(Hons), BMus/BSc(Hons), MA, MMus, MPhil, PGCert, PhD

Dept of Politics; www.gold.ac.uk/politics

contemporary British politics, economics, politics & public policy, history, international studies, politics, political science, public service professions, sociology; BA(Hons), DPS, MA, MPhil, MRes, PhD

Dept of Professional and Community Education;

www.gold.ac.uk/pace

advanced social work, HE work, higher specialist social work, studies, psychotherapeutic practice education; BA(Hons), DipHE, Grad Dip, PGCert

Dept of Psychology; www.gold.ac.uk/ psychology

cognitive and clinical neuroscience, music, mind & brain, occupational psychology, organisational behaviour, psychology, research methods in psychology; FoundationCert, BSc(Hons), MPhil, MSc, PhD

Dept of Sociology; www.gold.ac.uk/ sociology

critical & creative analysis, gender & culture, photography & urban cultures, social research, sociology and anthropology/history/media/cultural studies/ politics, visual sociology, world cities and urban life; BA(Hons), MA, MPhil, PhD

Dept of Visual Cultures; www.gold.ac.uk/ visual-cultures

aural and visual cultures, contemporary art theory, fine art, history of art, research architecture; BA(Hons), MA, MPhil, PGDip, PhD

UNIVERSITY OF LONDON; HEYTHROP COLLEGE
www.heythrop.ac.uk

Abrahamic religions, biblical studies, canon law, Christian spirituality/theology, Christianity and interreligious relations, contemporary ethics, divinity, pastoral liturgy/mission/theology, philosophy, philosophy, religion and ethics/theology, psychology and philosophy/theology, study of religions, theology; BA, Certs, FD, GRAdDip, MA

UNIVERSITY OF LONDON; INSTITUTE IN PARIS
www.ulip.ac.uk

French studies, Paris studies – history and culture;
BA, MA, MPhil, PhD

UNIVERSITY OF LONDON; INSTITUTE OF EDUCATION
www.ioe.ac.uk

adult literacy, advanced educational practice, art and design in education, bilingual learners in urban educational settings, child development, citizenship, history and religious education, clinical education, comparative education, curriculum, development education, early years education, economics, economics of education, education and psychology/international development, education, educational planning, effective learning, English education, gender and international/ development/health promotion and international development, geography in education, higher and professional education, history of education, inclusive education, information and communications technology, leadership, language and numeracy, lifelong learning, literacy learning and literacy difficulties, mathematics education, media, culture and communication, museums and galleries in education, music education, pedagogy and assessment, PGCE primary/secondary/post-comp, philosophy of education, policy studies in education, primary education, psychology of education, psychosocial studies & education, school effectiveness and school improvement, science education, social justice and education, social pedagogy, sociology of childhood and children's rights/education, special education, teaching and learning in higher and professional education, TESOL technology in clinical practice; BEd, Certs, DedPsy, EdD, Grad Dip, MA, MBA, MPhil, MRes, MSc, MTg, PGCE, PhD

UNIVERSITY OF LONDON; KING'S COLLEGE LONDON
www.kcl.ac.uk

The School of Arts & Humanities; www.kcl.ac.uk/humanities
American studies, Australian studies, Byzantine and modern Greek, classics, comparative literature, computing in the humanities, culture, media & creative industries, eighteenth-century studies, English, European studies, film studies, French, German, history, humanities and academic English, linguistics, medieval studies, Middle East & Mediterranean studies, music, philosophy, Portuguese & Brazilian studies, Spanish & Spanish American studies, theology & religious studies; BA(Hons), MA, MMus, MRes, MSc

School of Biomedical & Health Sciences; www.kcl.ac.uk/biohealthbiochemistry
biomedical science, human sciences, molecular genetics, neuroscience, nutrition, dietetics, pharmacology, pharmacy, physiology,physiotherapy, medicine; BS, BSc(Hons), DHC, MB, MPH, MPharm, MRes, MSc

Dental Institute; www.kcl.ac.uk/dentistry
dentistry; general dental practice, aesthetic dentistry, dental public health, implant dentistry, oral surgery, orthodontics, paediatric dentistry, periodontology, sedation & special care dentistry; BDS, MClinDent, MOrth, MScDL, PGDip

Institute of Psychiatry; www.iop.kcl.ac.uk
addiction, advanced psychosocial practice, alcohol and drug use in the workplace, applied clinical neuropsychology, child and adolescent mental health, clinical forensic psychiatry/psychology/neuroscience, cognitive behavioural therapies, family therapy, forensic mental health science, medication management, mental health studies, neuroscience, neuropsychology, psychiatric research, psychology, social, genetic & developmental psychiatry; BSc, DClinPsy, Grad Cert, MSc, PGDip

School of Law; www.kcl.ac.uk/law

Australian law, construction law & dispute resolution, criminology & criminal justice, English law & French law/German law/American law, law, European Legal Studies, medical ethics & law; LlB, LLM, MA, MPhil, MSc, PhD

School of Medicine; www.kcl.ac.uk/ schools/medicine

clinical dermatology, immunology, medical immunology, medical engineering & physics, medical ultrasound, medicine, nuclear medicine, pallative care, primary health care, public health, rheumatology, translational cancer medicine, vascular ultrasound; MBBS, MPH, MSc, PDDip/Cert

Florence Nightingale School of Nursing & Midwifery; www.kcl.ac.uk/schools/nursing

advanced practice – cancer care/child care/critical care/education/leadership/midwifery/primary care, gastrointestinal nursing, nursing studies – adult nursing/child nursing/mental health nursing, midwifery studies, public health/women's health; BSc(Hons), DipHE, DHC, DPhil, MRes, MSc

School of Physical Sciences & Engineering; www.kcl.ac.uk /schools/pse

computational molecular biology, bioinformatics, biomolecular structure, genetics, molecular biology, protein structure predictions; MSc, PhD
computing, software engineering, computer science/with management/mathematics computing, computing and internet systems/security, IT law and management, web intelligence; BSc(Hons), MSc, MSci
electronic engineering, engineering with business management, mechanical engineering, mechatronics, nanotechnology engineering, telecommunication engineering; BEng, MEng, MPhil, MSc, PhD
financial mathematics, information processing and neural networks, mathematics, mathematics & philosophy/computer science/management & finance/physics/physics with astrophysics, theoretical physics; BA(Hons), BSc(Hons)

biophysics, materials and molecular modelling, mathematics and physics/with astrophysics, nanotechnology, physics and philosophy, physics with medical applications/astrophysics/computer science/management, solidstatephysics, theoretical and astroparticle physics, x-ray physics; BSc(Hons), MSci, PhD

School of Social Science and Public Policy; www.kcl.ac.uk/sspp

aquatic resource management, assessment in education, child studies, cities, creative arts in the classroom, disasters, adaptation and development, education and professional studies, education management/policy & society, e-inclusion, ELT & applied linguistics, English, English in education, English language and communication, environment and development, environment, politics and globalisation, environmental health/monitoring, modelling and management, geography with film studies/history/warstudies, geopolitics, territory and security, global environmental change, ICT education, ICT, Jewish education, language ethnicity & education, Latin American studies, mathematics, mathematics education, MFL with education, modern foreign languages education, PGCE in classics, RE, religious education, risk analysis, science, science education, society & change, sustainable cities, theology & geography, tourism, water; BA, BSc, MA, MSc, PhD
gerontology, global ageing, public policy and ageing; MSc, MRes, PGDip/Cert, PhD
business management, HRM, international management/marketing, management/and social science, public services policy & management; BSc(Hons), MRes, MSc
ageing, biomedicine and society, conflict, security & development, European public policy, gerontology, global ageing, history of warfare, intelligence & international security/conflict studies/peace & security/relations non-proliferation, public policy, public policy medicine, science and society, science & security, terrorism, security & society, war studies; BA(Hons), MA, MPhil, MRes, PhD

UNIVERSITY OF LONDON; LONDON SCHOOL OF ECONOMICS & POLITICAL SCIENCE
www.lse.ac.uk

Departments at LSE: Accounting, Anthropology, Economics, Finance, Geography and Environment, Government, International History, International Relations, Law, Management, Mathematics, Media and Communications, Philosophy, Logic and Scientific Method, Social Policy, Sociology, Statistics
accounting, anthropology, business, management, communications, development studies, economic history, economics, employment relations, environment, European studies, finance, gender, geography, government, history, international history, information systems and innovation, international history, international relations, languages, law, logic and scientific method, management, managerial economics, mathematics, media, methodology, operational research, organisational behaviour, philosophy, logic and scientific method, politics, public policy, risk and stochastics, social policy, social psychology, social research methodology, sociology, statistics, strategy and operational research; BA(Hons), BSc(Hons), Dips, EMBA, Ll, M, MBA, MPA, MPhil, MRes, MSc, PhD

UNIVERSITY OF LONDON; LONDON SCHOOL OF JEWISH STUDIES
www.lsjs.ac.uk

ethics, Jewish ethics, Jewish studies; MA

UNIVERSITY OF LONDON; QUEEN MARY
www.qmul.ac.uk

Humanities, Social Sciences and Law

School of Business & Management; www.busman.qmul.ac.uk
business management with/business computing/computer science/accounting/engineering/science/geography/mathematics/finance/politics/French/German/Hispanic Studies/Russian, corporate social responsibility, global business, governance and ethics, international financial management, international HRM and employment relations, management and organisational innovation, marketing; BA(Hons), BSc(Hons), MSc

Dept of Economics; www.econ.qmul.ac.uk
banking, business economics, econometrics, economics, finance, investment law, management, mathematics, mathematics, statistics and financial economics, statistics; BA(Hons), BSc(Econ), MPhil, MSc(Econ), PhD

Centre for Editing Lives and Letters; www.livesandletters.qmul.ac.uk
Renaissance and early modern studies; MRes, PhD

Centre for the Study of Migration; www.politics.qmul.ac.uk/migration
migration, migration and law; MA, MRes, MSc

School of English and Drama; www.sed.qmul.ac.uk
Dept of Drama
drama, drama and English/French/German/Hispanic studies/Russian/film studies, historiography and archives, performance research, theatre and performance theory
Dept of English
English/ and drama/film studies, history/modern language/French/German/Hispanic studies/Russian/linguistics, English literature, in renaissance and early modern studies, writing and society 1700–1820, writing in the modern age; BA(Hons), MA, MRes, PhD

School of Languages, Linguistics & Film; www.sllf.qmul.ac.uk
comparative literature/and language/film/linguistics, film studies and language/drama, drama and French/German/Hispanic studies/Russian, language with

139

business management/film studies/linguistics, linguistics and language; BA(Hons), MA, PhD

Dept of Geography; www.geog.qmul.ac.uk

cities, economies and social change, cities and cultures, environmental geography/science, business management, geography, global change: environment, economy and development, globalisation and development, human geography, London studies, physical geography; BA(Hons), BSc(Econ), BSc(Hons), MA, MSc, PhD

Dept of History; www.history.qmul.ac.uk

contemporary history, history, journalism, history and politics/film studies/history/French, German language, crusader studies, history of political thought and intellectual history, medieval history, Paris studies and twentieth-century history; BA(Hons), MA, PhD

School of Law; www.law.qmul.ac.uk law

banking and finance law, commercial and corporate law, comparative and international dispute resolution, competition law, computer and communications law, economic regulation, English and European law, environmental law, human rights law, intellectual property law, international business law, law and development, law and finance, legal theory and history, medical law, public international law, public law, tax law; Dips, LlB, LlM, MPhil, MSc, PGDip, PhD

Dept of Philosophy; www.philosophy.qmul.ac.uk

philosophy; BA(Hons), MPhil, PhD

Dept of Politics; www.politics.qmul.ac.uk

global and comparative politics, international relations, migration/and law, politics with business management/economics geography/modern languages; public policy, BA(Hons), MA, MPhil, MRes, PhD

School of Medicine & Dentistry; www.smd.qmul.ac.uk

Barts and The London School of Medicine and Dentistry; www.smd-edu.qmul.ac.uk/medicine/

biomedical engineering, community health sciences, experimental pathology, infection medicine, integrated clinical studies, medicine, molecular medicine, molecular therapeutics, neuroscience, preparation for clinical practice, psychology, psychiatry, surgery,systems in disease, systems in health;

Institute of Cancer

experimental cancer medicine, medical oncology, molecular oncology & imaging, tumour biology

Institute of Cell and Molecular Science

aesthetic surgery, burn care, clinical dermatology, clinical microbiology, gastroenterology

Institute of Dentistry

dental surgery, dentistry, caries, hard tissue and materials research, oral cancer research

Institute of Health Science and Education

primary care, public health, sports & exercise medicine

William Harvey Research Institute

clinical drug development, forensic human identification, healthcare research methods, mechanisms of vascular disease

Wolfson Institute of Preventative Medicine

mental health pathways: transcultural mental healthcare, psychological therapies, screening for Down's Syndrome; BDS, BMedSci, MBBS, MClinDent, MD, MRes, MPhil, MSc, NVQ, PGDip, Phd

Department of Science & Engineering

School of Biological and Chemical Sciences; www.sbcs.qmul.ac.uk

biochemistry, biology bioinformatics, biomedical sciences, chemistry, forensic science, freshwater and coastal sciences, genetics, marine ecology and environmental management, medical genetics, microbiology, molecular biology, pharmaceutical chemistry, psychology; BSc(Hons), Foundation degree, MPhil, MSci, PhD

School of Electronic Engineering & Computer Science; www.eecs.qmul.ac.uk

audio systems, communication engineering, computer engineering, digital music processing, digital signal processing, e-commerce engineering, electrical engineering, electronic engineering, information and communication technologies, interactive media design, internet computing, internet engineering, multimedia systems, networks, telecommunications, wireless networks; BEng, BSc(Eng), MEng, MSc, PhD

School of Engineering and Materials Science; www.sems.qmul.ac.uk

aerospace engineering/systems, avionics, biomedical engineering, engineering science, materials; clinical materials, biomedical materials science/and engineering, materials science and engineering, dental materials, environmemtal materials, materials engineering in medicine, biomaterials, mechanical engineering, medical electronics and physics, medical engineering, sports engineering, sustainable energy engineering/systems; BEng, BSc, MEng, MPhil, MRes, PhD

Interdisciplinary Research Centre in Biomedical Materials; www.materials. qmul.ac.uk

biomaterials in dentistry and for drug delivery; forming and processing technology, hard tissue replacement and biology, interfaces and sensors, orthopaedic cell and tissue engineering; PhD

School of Mathematical Sciences; www. maths.qmul.ac.uk

mathematics, pure mathematics, statistics & financial economics; BSc(Hons), MPhil, MSc, MSci, PGDip/Cert, PhD

Dept of Physics; www.phy.qmul.ac.uk

astrophysics, physics, theoretical physics and nanoscience; BSc(Hons), MSc, MSci, PGDip, PhD

Research Centre in Psychology; www. psychology.sbcs.qmul.ac.uk

applied psychology, biological and experimental psychology, biology with psychology, computational psychology, language and communication, psychology; BSc(Hons), MPhil, PhD

UNIVERSITY OF LONDON; ROYAL HOLLOWAY
www.rhul.ac.uk

Faculty of Arts; www.rhul.ac.uk/ departments/arts

Dept of Drama & Theatre; www.rhul.ac.uk/ drama

British theatre culture, classics/French/German/Italian/creative writing/music/philosophy, drama/and English, Greek theatre performance, theatre; BA(Hons), MPhil, PhD

Dept of Media Arts; www.rhul.ac.uk/ media-arts

documentary by practice, feature film screenwriting, media arts, film & television studies, screenwriting for TV & film; BA(Hons), MA, MPhil, PhD

Dept of Music; www.rhul.ac.uk/music

advanced musical studies, music, music with French/German/Italian/Spanish/management studies/political studies/social policy/philosophy/mathematics/psychology, performance studies; BA(Hons), BMus, MMus, MPhil, PhD

Faculty of History & Social Sciences; dev. 2008.rhul.ac.uk/departments/hss

Dept of Classics; www.rhul.ac.uk/classics

ancient history, classical archeology classical studies, Greek and Latin languages, literature & philosophy

Dept of Economics; www.rhul.ac.uk/ economics

applied microeconomics and political economy, economic history, economics, econometrics, experimental economics, financial & business economics, labour economics and the economics of education, microeconomic theory and game theory, macroeconomics, development and finance; BA(Hons), BSc(Econ)Hons, MPhil, MSc, PGDip, PhD

Dept of European Studies; www.rhul.ac.uk/ European-Studies

French/Spanish/Italian/German; management/history/ politics/international relations, economics, geography; classics/ computing/music, European integration, global security and international affairs; BA(Hons), MA, MPhil, PhD

Dept of Health and Social Care; www.rhul. ac.uk/Health and Social Care

criminology (youth justice, risk and violence), health (medical sociology, health, clinical and lifespan psychology), social care (social policy and social work), social work; BA(Hons), MA, MSc

Dept of History; www.rhul.ac.uk/History

crusader studies, culture 1450–1750, history/and French/German/Spanish/international relations, history of political thought and intellectual history late antique and Byzantine studies, modern history and politics; BA(Hons), MA, MPhil, PhD

School of Management; www.rhul.ac.uk/management

accounting & finance, entrepreneurship, European business, HR, information systems, international accounting/business/HRM management/management, leadership and management in health, marketing, organizations, leadership and change, Pacific business, production & operations, strategy, sustainability and management; BA(Hons), BSc(Hons), MA, MSc, PhD

Dept of Politics & International Relations; www.rhul.ac.uk/politics-and-IR

politics, and with international relations/philosophy, economics, European studies/history, politics and international geography/international relations; BA(Hons), MA, MBA, MSc

Faculty of Science; www.rhul.ac.uk/departments/science

School of Biological Sciences; www.rhul.ac.uk/biological-sciences

biochemistry, biology, evolution and behaviour, molecular biology and genetics, biomedical sciences, plant molecular sciences and ecology, BA(Hons), BSc(Hons), MSc, PhD

Dept of Computer Science; www.cs.rhul.ac.uk

computer science (information security AI), machine learning, constraints, discrete optimisation (languages and architectures); BSc(Hons), MPhil, MSc, PhD

Dept of Earth Sciences; www.gl.rhul.ac.uk

environmental geology, environmental geoscience, geology/ and geography/biology/mathematics/science communication, geoscience, planetary geology, petroleum geology

Dept of Geography; www.gg.rhul.ac.uk

cultural geography, geography, geology, human geography, physical geography, politics and international relations, practising sustainable development, sustainability & management

Dept of Mathematics; www.ma.rhul.ac.uk

information science, mathematics, mathematics for applications, maths of cryptology, statistics; BSc(Hons), MSc, MSci, PhD

Dept of Physics; www.rhul.ac.uk/physics

applied physics, astrophysics, low temperature physics, nanophysics & nanotechnology, particle physics, physics, theoretical physics, vision & signal processing; BSc(Hons), MPhil, MPhys, MSc, PhD

Dept of Psychology; www.pc.rhul.ac.uk

applied social psychology, human neuroscience, psychology; BSc(Hons), DClinPsych, MSc, PhD

UNIVERSITY OF LONDON; ROYAL VETERINARY COLLEGE
www.rvc.ac.uk

bioveterinary science, control of infectious diseases in animals, livestock health and production, veterinary epidemiology/and public health, veterinary nursing, veterinary pathology, veterinary physiotherapy, wild animal health, wild animal biology; BSc(Hons), BVetMed, FdSc, MPhilPhD, MRes, MSc, PGDip/Cert

UNIVERSITY OF LONDON; SCHOOL OF ORIENTAL AND AFRICAN STUDIES
www.soas.ac.uk

African language and culture, African literature, African politics, African studies, ancient Near Eastern languages/studies, anthropological research methods, anthropology of food/media, applied Japanese linguistics, applied linguistics and language pedagogy, Arabic cultural studies/ literature, Arabic/and Islamic studies, Asian politics, banking law, Chinese (modern and classical), Chinese law/ literature/studies, comparative literature (Africa/Asia), critical media and cultural studies, development and globalisation, development economics/studies, development studies/central Asia, dispute and conflict resolution, economics: Africa/south Asia/Asia Pacific region/Middle East, economics, environmental law, ethnomusicology, finance and development/financial law, gender studies, geography, Georgian, Bengal, Burmese (Myanmar), global cinemas and the transcultural, global media and postnational communication, Hausa, Hebrew and Israeli studies, Hindi, history of art/archaeology/Asia/Africa & Europe, history, history: Asia/Africa, human rights, conflict and justice, Indonesian, international and comparative legal studies, international and comparative/commercial law, international economic law, international management (China/Japan/Middle East and north Africa), international politics, Islamic law, Israeli studies, Japanese literature/studies, Japanese, Korean, Korean literature/studies, languages and cultures of south Asia, languages and literatures of south east Asia, law in the Middle East and north Africa, law, culture and society, development and governance, linguistics, medical anthropology, Middle East politics/ studies, migration and diaspora studies, migration mobility and development, music studies, Nepali, Pacific Asian studies, religions, performance, Persian, political economy of development, Sanskrit, Sinology, social anthropology, south Asian area studies/law/studies, state, society and development, study of religions, sustainable development, Swahili, Taiwan studies, Thai, Tibetan, translation (Asian and African languages), Turkish, Vietnamese international studies and diplomacy, violence, conflict & development; BA(Hons), LlB, LlM, MMus, MPhil, MSc, PGDip, PhD

UNIVERSITY OF LONDON; THE SCHOOL OF PHARMACY
www.pharmacy.ac.uk

clinical pharmacy, drug delivery, drug discovery, medicine management, pharmacognosy, pharmacy, pharmacy practice; Certs, MPharm, MSc, PGDip, PhD

UNIVERSITY OF LOUGHBOROUGH
www.lboro.ac.uk

Faculty of Engineering; www.lboro.ac. uk/eng

Aeronautical and Automotive Engineering; www.lboro.ac.uk/departments/tt/
aeronautical engineering, automotive engineering, automotive systems engineering

Chemical Engineering; www.lboro.ac.uk/ departments/cg
advanced chemical engineering, advanced process engineering, chemical engineering/with environmental protection/management, pharmaceutical engineering

Civil and Building Engineering; www.lboro. ac.uk/departments/cv
air transport management, architectural engineering and design management, civil engineering, commercial management and quantity surveying, construction engineering management, transport and business management

Electronic and Electrical Engineering; www.lboro.ac.uk/departments/el
advanced systems engineering, digital communication systems, electrical and renewable energy systems engineering,electronic and electrical engineering, electronics and computer systems engineering/software engineering, mechanical and manufacturing engineering, mobile communications, networked communications, renewable energy systems technology, systems engineering

Mechanical and Manufacturing; www. lboro.ac.uk/departments/mm
advanced manufacturing engineering and management, engineering design, manufacture, innovative manufacturing engineering, mechanical engineering, mechatronics, product design engineering, sports technology

Water Engineering and Development Centre (WEDC)
infrastructure in emergencies, sustainable infrastructure services management, sustainability in the built environment, water and environmental management,

143

water and waste engineering; BEng, BSc(Hons), MDes, MRes, MSc, PhD

Faculty of Science; www.lboro.ac.uk/sci

Faculty of Chemistry; www.lboro.ac.uk/departments/cm

analytical and pharmaceutical science, analytical chemistry, environmental science, chemistry, analytical chemistry/forensic analysis/sports science, chemistry and information technology, medicinal and pharmaceutical chemistry, medicinal chemistry

Dept of Computer Science; www.lboro.ac.uk/departments/co

applied computing/and maths, computer science/and artificial intelligence/e-business/maths, computing and management, digital imaging computer graphics and vision, information management and computing, information technology, mathematics and computing and network security, multimedia and internet computing, numbers computing

Dept of Human Sciences; www.lboro.ac.uk/departments/hu

ergonomics, psychology; BSc(Hons), MSc, PhD

Dept of Information Sciences; www.lboro.ac.uk/departments/is

information management & business studies/computing/ business technology, information and knowledge management, library management, publishing with English/e-business, web development and design; BSc(Hons), MPhil, PhD

Dept of Materials; www.lboro.ac.uk/departments/materials

automotive materials, design with engineering materials, materials engineering, materials for industry, packaging technology, polymer technology; BEng/MEng, BSc(Hons), Diploma in Industrial Studies, MSc, PG Dipl/Cert, PhD

Dept of Mathematics; www.lboro.ac.uk/departments/ma

financial mathematics, industrial mathematical modelling, IT and mathematics, mathematical processes in finance, mathematics, mathematics and accounting & financial management/management/sports science/computing, mathematics with economics, physics and mathematics; BSc(Hons), MSc, PhD

Dept of Physics; www.lboro.ac.uk/departments/ph

astrophysics and cosmology, engineering physics, materials physics and applications, nanoscience, physics, physics & maths/management/sports science, physics with cosmology, psychophysics, quantum information and computing, science of the internet, surface physics, theoretical condensed matter physics; BSc(Hons), MSc, PhD

Faculty of Social Sciences and Humanities; www.lboro.ac.uk/ssh

Loughborough University Business School; www.lboro.ac.uk/departments/bs

accounting and financial management, banking, finance and management, international business, management business analysis and management, management sciences, marketing and management, retailing; BSc(Hons), MBA, MPhil, MRes, MSc, PhD

Dept of Economics; www.lboro.ac.uk/departments/ec

banking and finance, business economics and finance, economics, economics with accounting, economics and finance, international banking, international economics, money, banking and finance; BSc(Hons), MSc, PhD

Dept of English & Drama; www.lboro.ac.uk/departments/ea

creative writing, drama, English, film, history, North American literature, performance and multi-media, sports science; BA(Hons), MA, PhD

Dept of Politics, International Relations & European Studies; www.lboro.ac.uk/departments/eu

European studies, history, international relations, politics, research methods (European and international); BSc(Hons), MPhil, MSc, PhD

Dept of Geography; www.lboro.ac.uk/departments/gy

environmental monitoring, geography, geography and management/sport management/sports science/economics, global transformations, globalization, human geography research, international financial & political relations, space & sport; BSc, MPhil, MSc, PhD

Dept of Sport, Exercise and Health Sciences; www.lboro.ac.uk/departments/ssehs

human biology, occupational health for safety professionals, physical activity and health, physical education/and sport pedagogy, psychology, sociology of sport, sport biomechanics, sport coaching, sport and exercise nutrition/psychology/exercise science, sport management/science; BSc(Hons), MPhil, MSc, PhD

School of Art & Design; www.lboro.ac.uk/departments/ac
2D and 3D visualisation, 3D design, fine art, studio ceramics, textiles, visual communication; BA(Hons), MA, MPhil, MSc, PhD

Dept of Social Sciences; www.lboro.ac.uk/departments/ss
communications and media studies, criminology and criminal justice/social policy, cultural sociology/

cultural analysis, media and cultural analysis, social science research, social psychology, sociology; BSc(Hons), MPhil, MSc, PhD

Teacher Education Unit; www.lboro.ac.uk/departments/teu
design and technology, education with qualified teacher status, physics enhancement, physical education, science; MSc, PGCE

UNIVERSITY OF MANCHESTER
www.manchester.ac.uk

Faculty of Engineering and Physical Sciences; www.eps.manchester.ac.uk

School of Chemical Engineering and Analytical Science; www.ceas.manchester.ac.uk
biotechnology, chemical engineering, chemical engineering with biotechnology/chemistry/environmental technology/industrial experience, chemical process design, colloids, crystals and interfaces, environmental technology/management, instrumentation and measurement science, process design for energy and the environment, product formulation, refinery design and operation, theory and modelling of fluids; BEng, MEng, MSc, PhD

School of Chemistry; www.chemistry.manchester.ac.uk
biological, inorganic, materials, chemistry, forensic & analytical chemistry, medicinal chemistry, organic, physical and theoretical chemistry, patent law; BSc(Hons), EngD, MChem, MEnt, MPhil, MSc, PhD

School of Computer Science; www.cs.manchester.ac.uk
advanced database management systems, advanced machine vision, artificial intelligence, automated reasoning, biohealth informatics, bioinformatics (e-learning), building web applications, computational biology, computational finite element methods, computer animation/science/ security/systems engineering, computing for business applications, databases and data modelling, distributed computing/systems and internet technology, e-business, Java: high performance execution, future multi-core computing, grid computing, HCI and web user interfaces, high-level programming (Java), information and knowledge management, interactive system design,

internet computing, IS strategy and enterprise systems, IT trends, knowledge representation and reasoning, machine learning, mobile computing, object oriented analysis and design with UML, semi-structured data and the web, software development in Java, software engineering, systems design and databases, the semantic web: ontologies and owl, visualisation for HPC; BSc(Hons), MEng, MEnt, MPhil, MSc, PhD

School of Earth, Atmospheric & Environmental Sciences; www.seas.manchester.ac.uk
earth sciences, environmental sciences/studies, geochemistry, geography, geology, planetary science, petroleum geoscience, pollution and environmental control, policy and management; BSc(Hons), MEarthSci, MEng, MSc, PhD

School of Electrical and Electronic Engineering; www.eee.manchester.ac.uk
communication engineering/systems engineering, computer systems engineering, control and systems engineering, electrical & electronic engineering, electronic systems engineering, electrical energy conversion systems, electrical power systems engineering, mechatronic engineering, nanoelectronics, sensors and electronic instrumentation; BEng(Hons), Dip, BSc(Hons), EngD, MEng(Hons), MPhil, MSc, PhD

School of Materials; www.materials.manchester.ac.uk
aerospace materials engineering, engineering materials, biomedical materials science, ceramics and glasses, composite materials, corrosion and protection, corrosion control engineering, international fashion retailing, materials science & engineering,

metallic materials, nanostructured materials, paper science, polymer materials, textile science & technology, textile design, fashion and management; BSc, MEng, MPhil, PhD

School of Mathematics; www.maths. manchester.ac.uk

actuarial science, applied maths, computer science, financial mathematics, mathematical finance, mathematics, numerical analysis, operational mathematics, pure maths, probability and statistics, quantitative finance and financial engineering, statistics, theoretical and applied fluid dynamics; BSc, MMath, MPhil, MSc, PhD

School of Mechanical, Aerospace and Civil Engineering; www.mace.manchester.ac.uk

advanced manufacturing technology & systems management, aerospace engineering, civil engineering, commercial project management, construction project management, engineering with management, engineering project management and IT, maintenance engineering & asset management, management of projects, mechanical engineering, structural engineering, thermal power & fluid engineering; BEng, EngD, MEng, MEnt, MPhil, MSc, PhD

School of Physics & Astronomy; www. physics.manchester.ac.uk

astronomy and astrophysics, biological physics, condensed matter physics, mathematics and physics, nuclear physics, particle physics, photon science (laser photonics), physics, theoretical physics; BSc, EngD, MMath & Phys, MPhys, MSc, PhD

Faculty of Humanities; www.humanities. manchester.ac.uk

School of Arts, Histories and Cultures; www.arts.manchester.ac.uk

ancient history, applied theatre, art gallery and museum studies, archeology, art history, arts management, policy and practice, biblical studies, classical studies, classics, comparative religion, composition, the holy and the supernatural, contemporary literature and culture, creative writing, cultural history, early modern history, economic and social history, electroacoustic music composition, English literature, gender, sexuality and culture, Greek, history of north west England, Islamic studies and Muslim societies, Latin and history, modern British history, modern European history, music, musicology, politics, post-1900 literatures, postcolonial literatures and cultures, religion and political life/society/

theology, screen studies, social anthropology, south Asian studies, biblical studies, Jewish studies, theology, culture and society, Victorian times, war, culture and history, world history

School of Education; www.education. manchester.ac.uk

communication and education, community and youth work, counselling, educational leadership and improvement/research/technology, HE, inclusive education, language, literacy & communication, leadership and school improvement, learning disability studies, management & leisure, PGCE primary/secondary business education/secondary/ design technology/secondary English/secondary mathematics/secondary modern languages/secondary science, profound & complex learning disability, process consultancy, psychology of education, supervision of counselling and the helping professions, TESOL; BA(Hons), DCons, DEd, EdD, MA, MEd, MPhil, MSc, PGCE, PGCert/Dip, PhD, UGCert/Dip

School of Environment and Development; www.sed.manchester.ac.uk

architecture, city & regional development, conflict and reconstruction, development economics/ finance/ management/ projects/informatics, environmental impact/management/monitoring, geography, geology, GIS, global urban development and planning, globalisation and development, human geography, industry, trade and development, international development, modelling and reconstruction/governance, planning and landscape, poverty, rural development, social policy and social development, town & country planning, urban development, urbanism; BSc, MA, MPlan, MSc, MTCP, PGDip, PhD

School of Languages, Linguistics and Cultures; www.llc.manchester.ac.uk

Arabic studies, Arabic, Chinese studies, contemporary China, English language, European languages and cultures, European studies, French, German studies, German, Hebrew studies, Hebrew, history, history of art, Islamic studies and Arabic, Italian studies, Italian, Japanese studies, Jewish studies, Latin American cultural studies Latin American studies, linguistics, Middle Eastern languages, Middle Eastern studies, modern Middle Eastern history, Persian, Portuguese, Russian, Russian and east European studies, screen studies, social anthropology, sociology, Spanish, Turkish; BA(Hons), MA, MML, MPhil, PhD

School of Law; www.law.manchester.ac.uk

bioethics and medical jurisprudence, crime, English law with French law, health care ethics, intellectual property law, international business & commercial law, international financial law, international trade transactions, law & economics/development/society/ criminology/politics, law, socio-legal studies; BA, LlB, LlM, MA, MPhil, MRes, PGDip, PhD

Manchester Business School; www.mbs. manchester.ac.uk

accounting, American business studies, business economics, business IT, Chinese business, corporate communications, decision science, e-business technology, economics, e-government, finance, financial markets and management, global business analysis, healthcare management, HR, industrial relations, information systems, information technology management, innovation management and entrepreneurship, international business, finance and economics/ studies/marketing/operations and technology/information systems, IT management for business, management, management accounting, management of science, technology and innovation, managerial psychology, marketing, mathematical finance, operations, project and supply chain management, organisational psychology, public administration, quantitative finance: financial engineering, reputation management, risk analysis, risk business administration; BA, BSc, MBA, MBus, MDA, MEnt, MPA, MRes, MSc, PhD

School of Social Sciences; www. socialsciences.manchester.ac.uk

anthropology, archaeology, criminology, development economics, development studies, econometrics, economic & social history, economics, environmental economics, European politics & policy, financial economics, gender politics and policy, governance and public policy, human rights, international development: international politics/relations, political economy/science/ theory, politics, social anthropology, social change, social research methods and statistics, social statistics and demography, sociological research, sociology, visual anthropology; BAEcon, BSc, MA, MRes, MSc, PGDip, PhD

Centre for Continuing Education, Centre for Educational Leadership; www.cel. manchester.ac.uk

educational leadership, process consultancy; MEd, PGCert

Faculty of Life Sciences; www.lf. manchester.ac.uk

anatomical sciences, biochemistry, bioinformatics, biology, biomechanics, biomedical and forensic studies in Egyptology, biomedical sciences, biotechnology, cell biology, cognitive neuroscience and psychology, computational neuroscience and neuroinformatics, genetics, history of science, technology and medicine, immunology and immunogenetics, life sciences, medical biochemistry, microbiology, neuroscience, optometry, pharmacology, physiology, plant science, structural biology and biophysics, zoology; BSc, MNeuroSci, MRes, MSc, PhD

Faculty of Medical & Human Sciences; www.mhs.manchester.ac.uk

School of Dentistry; www.dentistry. manchester.ac.uk

control of pain and anxiety, dental implantology, dental public health, dentistry, endodontics, fixed and removable prosthodontics, oral and maxillofacial surgery, oral health science, orthodontics; BDS, BSc, MDen, MDPH, MSc, MSc(Clin), PGDip/Cert, PhD

School of Medicine; www.medicine. manchester.ac.uk

cardiovascular sciences, maternal and fetal health, medical sciences, medicine, primary care, public health, tissue engineering for regenerative medicine, translational medicine: inter molecular medicine/ pharmaceutical cancer; ChB, MB, MD/ChM, MPH, MPhil, MRes, MSc, PGCert, PGDip, PhD

School of Nursing and Midwifery & Social Work; www.nursing.manchester.ac.uk

adult social work, advanced nursing studies, health and social care, midwifery, adult nursing/child nursing/mental health nursing, psychosocial interventions for psychosis, dementia, social work; BMidwif, BNurs, MA, MClinRes, MPhil, MRes, MSc, PgC, PgD, PGDip, PhD

School of Pharmacy & Pharmaceutical Sciences; www.pharmacy.manchester.ac.uk

clinical ad health services pharmacy, pharmaceutical industrial advanced training, pharmacy; MPharm, MPhil, MSc, PGCert/Dip, PhD

School of Psychological Sciences; www. psch-ci.manchester.ac.uk

audiology, clinical and health psychology, cognitive brain imaging, cognitive, neuroscience and

147

psychology, deaf education, pyschology, speech & language therapy; BSc, MPhil, MRes, MSc, PGDip, PhD

MANCHESTER METROPOLITAN UNIVERSITY
www.mmu.ac.uk

Faculty of Art & Design; www.artdes. mmu.ac.uk

acting, architecture, art and design, art direction, contemporary film and video, continuing professional practice for artists and designers, creative practice, design, design and art direction, embroidery, fashion, fashion design and technology, film and media studies, filmmaking, fine art, history of art and design, illustration with animation, interactive arts, interior design, international creative advertising, landscape architecture, media arts, photography, visual culture; BA(Hons), BArch, BL and Arch, MA, MEnterprise, MPhil, PGDip/Cert, PhD

Faculty of Health, Psychology & Social Care; www.hpsc.mmu.ac.uk

Health Professions

clinical counselling, health & social care, manual therapy, musculoskeletal physiotherapy, physiotherapy, psychology & speech, speech pathology and therapy, teaching speech reading; BSc(Hons), CertHE, FdA, MPhil, MSc, PhD

Nursing

community health, contemporary health practice, nursing/adult branch, practice development, health visiting, school nursing) BSc, BSc(Hons), MSc, PGDipPsychology, postgrad modular

Social Work and Social Change

social change/communication studies/community and society/health and social care/policy and management, social work; MA, MPhil, Msc, PGDip, PhD

Faculty of Humanities, Law & Social Science; www.hlss.mmu.ac.uk

Criminology

criminology; BA(Hons)

Economics; www.hlss.mmu.ac.uk/ economics

BA(Hons), BSc(Hons), MA/MPhil/PhD

English; www.hlss.mmu.ac.uk/english

creative writing, English, American Literature/creative writing/film, English Studies: contemporary literature and film/critical theory/the Gothic, teaching English as a foreign language; BA(Hons), MA, MPhil, PGDip, PhD

European Studies

European urban cultures, globalisation, societies and cultures; MA

History & Economic History; www.hlss. mmu.ac.uk/history

history, medieval and early modern history, modern history, social history; BA(Hons), MA, MPhil, PhD

Information & Communications

communications, digital media, information, information management, librarianship, library management, web development; BA(Hons), BSc(Hons), MA/MSc/MPhil/PhD

Islamic

Islamic and Middle Eastern studies, BA(Hons), CertHE

Languages

Arabic, Chinese or Japanese, EFL, French, French studies, German, Italian, linguistics, Spanish, BA(Hons), MA, MPhil, PhD

Law; www.hlss.mmu.ac.uk/law

law, legal practice (LPC), legal practice at the bar; PGDip, LLB(Hons), LLM, MPhil, PhD

Politics and philosophy; www.hlss.mmu.ac. uk/polphil

politics, public policy, public services, philosophy, European philosophy; BA(Hons), BSc(Hons), MA, MPhil, PhD

Sociology; www.hlss.soc.mmu.ac.uk/

criminology, European urban cultures, globalisation, societies and cultures, sociology; BA(Hons), MA, MPhil, PhD

Institute of Education; www.ioe.mmu.ac.uk

careers guidance, childhood studies and practice, childhood studies, design and technology/for industries, early childhood studies, early years practice, education business management, education studies, primary education/with MFL specialism, professional studies (early years education/careers education and guidance/education/special educational needs), school administration, school business management, secondary education, specific learning difficulties, supporting teaching and learning, teaching, urban education, youth & community work; BA(Hons), BA/BSc, Certs, EdD, Foundation degrees, MA, MPhil, MSc, PGDip/Cert, PhD

Faculty of Science & Engineering; www.sci-eng.mmu.ac.uk

School of Biology, Chemistry and Health Science Division of Biology; www.sci-eng.mmu.ac.uk/bchs/biology

animal behaviour, applied biological sciences, biology; cell and molecular biology, conservation biology, human behaviour ecology, microbiology, ornithology, tropical ecology, wildlife biology, zoo conservation biology, zoo studies; BSc(Hons), HNC, MPhil, MSc, PGDip/Cert, PhD

Division of Chemistry & Materials; www.sci-eng.mmu.ac.uk/chemistry

biomedical science, cellular pathology, chemistry, clinical chemistry, forensic chemistry, haematology, medical microbiology and transfusion science, medicinal and biological chemistry, pharmaceutical chemistry, pharmaceutical science; BSc(Hons), HNC, MChem(Hons), MSc, PGCert/Dip
biological and biomedical psychology, biomedical science, clinical physiology, dental technology, human biology, physiology with pharmacology; BSc(Hons), MPhil, MSc/PGDip/PgCert, PhD

Dept of Computing and Mathematics; www.sci-eng.docm.mmu.ac.uk

artificial intelligence, computer games technology, computer science, computing, digital media computing, enterprise computing, forensic computing, information systems, internet computing, mobile computing, multimedia computing, software engineering mathematics; financial mathematics; BSc, FdSc, MPhil, MSc, PhD

Department of Engineering & Technology; www.sci-eng.mmu.ac.uk/engtech

automation and control, automotive engineering, computer aided engineering, computer and communication engineering/network technology, electrical, electronic engineering, electronic systems design, mechanical design and technology, mechanical engineering, mechatronics, media technology, product design and technology, virtual product development, design and manufacture; BEng(Hons), BSc(Hons), HND, MSc, PhD

Dept of Environmental and Geographical Sciences; www.sci-eng.egs.mmu.ac.uk

climate change, the contemporary city, countryside management, ecological monitoring, ecology and conservation, environment & enterprise, environmental and climate change, environmental management and sustainability, environmental science, geography, GIS & spatial analysis, human geography, physical geography, sustainable aviation, urban regeneration; BSc(Hons), MPhil, MSc, PhD

Hollings Faculty; www.hollings.mmu.ac.uk

Department of Clothing Design & Technology

clothing, clothing technology, fashion buying/materials, fashion design, fashion marketing

Department of Food and Tourism Management

clothing/ product development, consumer marketing, environmental health, events management, food management/marketing, hospitality/and licensed retail management/business management/culinary arts/tourism, food and nutrition, food technology, human nutrition, international hospitality management, tourism management/and e-business, trading standards; BA(Hons), BSc(Hons), FdA, FdSc, HND, MA, MPhil, PhD

Business School; www.business.mmu.ac.uk

accounting, advertising management, brand management, business, business administration/enterprise/management, finance, business, health and social care management, digital marketing communications, entrepreneurial practice, finance, HRM, international business management/creative advertising/HRM, leadership, logistics and supply chain management, marketing, PR, professional accounting, project management, strategic financial, business information technology management; BA(Hons), MA, MBA, MPhil, MRes, MSc, PGDip/Cert, PhD

MMU Cheshire; *www.cheshire.mmu.ac.uk*

Dept of Business & Management Studies

business, business management, financial management, HRM, legal studies, marketing, marketing management, organisational change and development management, sports management, strategic leadership and change; BA/BSc, BA(Hons), FD, HNC, HND, MBA, MSc, MPhil, PhD

Dept of Contemporary Arts; *www.cheshire.mmu.ac.uk/dcu*

art media performance, community arts, contemporary arts, contemporary theatre & performance, creative music production, creative writing, dance, drama, music, popular music; BA(Hons), MA, MPhil, PhD

Dept of Exercise and Sports Science; *www.cheshire.mmu.ac.uk/exspsci*

coaching and sport development, coaching studies, sport development, exercise and physical activitiy, exercise & sport (biomechanics/coaching studies/physiology/psychology/sport development/sports injury), leisure management, sport & exercise science, psychology of sport and exercise; BA, BSc, Foundation degree, MA, MSc

---

MIDDLESEX UNIVERSITY
www.mdx.ac.uk

School of Arts and Education; *www.mdx.ac.uk/schools/arts*

Art & Design

animation, art & design, fashion/design, fashion textiles, fine art, graphic design, illustration, interactive media, interior architecture, jewellery and accessories, photography, product design, robotics moving image: film video interactive arts, sonic arts, sustainable design, design engineering, WBL, BA(Hons), FdA, MA, MSc

Dance, Music and the Theatre

choreography, dance, music and arts management, jazz, music composition/performance, popular music, technical theatre/performance/solo performance, theatre arts, theatre directing; BA(Hons), BMus, MA, MMus

English Literature and Language

business communication, creative and media writing, education studies with English/English literature /& media, TEFL

Film, Television & Media Arts

film and creative writing, media and cultural studies, film studies, film, video and interactive arts, sonics, television journalism, television production/technical arts; BA(Hons)

Media, Culture and Communication

advertising, PR and media, communications management, creative and media writing, English literature/journalism studies, journalism and communication studies/media and cultural studies/magazine publishing/and media/journalism and media/cultural studies, design for interactive media, moving image; BA(Hons), MA

Language and Translation Studies

international tourism management, TEFL, translation theory and practice of translation; BA(Hons), MA

Philosophy

aesthetics and art theory, contemporary critical theory, fine art and critical theory, modern European philosophy, philosophy, philosophy and religious studies; BA(Hons), MA

Teaching and Education

early childhood studies, early years, education studies/and religious studies/English language/English literature/philosophy, teaching studies; inclusive education, leadership management and change, professional practice; PGCE qualifications in range of subjects; BA(Hons), FdA, MA, PGCE, PGCert

Middlesex University Business School; *www.mdx.ac.uk/schools/bs*

Accounting and Finance

banking, business accounting, business and management, business economics, corporate accountability, economics, finance, financial management, HRM, international/finance, law, marketing and enterprise statistics, money, statistics; BA(Hons), BSc(Hons), MSc

Business and Management

business administration/and business economics/ enterprise/ business information/systems management/IT/management/studies, entrepreneurship, hospitality management, HRM, international business, international tourism, management, marketing, strategic management, tourism; BA(Hons), BSc(Hons), MSc

Economics

banking, business economics, economics, finance, international business, international finance, money, statistics; BSc(Hons), MA, MBA, MSc

Human Resource Management

personal and professional development, employment law, hospitality management, HRM, human resource development, international HRM and employment relations, recruitment practice, tourism; AdvDip, BA(Hons), FdA, PGCert, PGDip

Marketing and Enterprise

health and social marketing, international and cross cultural marketing, marketing, marketing communications/management, psychology with marketing, strategic management and marketing; BA(Hons), BSc(Hons), MA, MSc

Law

business law, employment law, international business law, law, law and business, minorities, rights and the law; BA(Hons), GradDip, LlBHons, LlM, MA, PGDip

The School of Engineering and Information Sciences; www.mdx.ac.uk/ schools/eis

Business Information Systems

business information systems/management/technology, data and knowledge, digital forensics, electronic security, enterprise management technologies, forensic computing, information security management and audit, web information management; BSc(Hons), MSc

Computer Communications

computer communication, digital inclusion, mobile computing, network programming, network management and security, networks, professional network engineering, telecommunication engineering; BEng, BSc(Hons), MSc

Computing and Multimedia Technology

biomedical modelling and informatics, computer science, computing, graphics and games, information technology, interactive systems design, internet application development, multimedia computing, networking, software engineering; BSc, MSc

Product Design and Engineering

design engineering, engineering management, engineering project management, interaction design, manufacturing management, product design, robotics; BA(Hons), BSc(Hons), MSc

School of Health & Social Sciences; www.mdx.ac.uk/schools/hssc

Biomedical and Biological Sciences

biomedical modelling and informatics, biomedical science, bioscience, clinical physiology, gynaecological science, medical microbiology, molecular pathology/obstetric, sports medicine; BSc(Hons), MSc

Complementary Health Sciences

Ayurvedic medicine, Chinese acupuncture, Chinese herbal formulae, traditional Chinese medicine; Adv Dip, BSc(Hons), MSc

Criminology & Sociology

community safety, criminal justice, criminology, criminology: crime, conflict and control, forensic computing, forensic psychology, policing, criminology, public protection, sociology with politics/psychology, youth justice; BA(Hons), BSc(Hons), MA, MSc

Environment, Development & Community

development, environmental health, environmental pollution control, social policy, sustainable development, sustainable environmental management; BSc(Hons), MA, MSc

Nursing and Midwifery

advanced nursing, child, adolescent and family mental health work, dual diagnosis mental health, health promotion, midwifery, nursing; AdvDip, BSc, BSc(Hons), Dip, MSc, PGCert

Social Science, Politics & Development

criminology, development studies with sociology, global social science, health and social care, housing practice in environmental health, housing studies, international political studies, international relations, international studies, psychoanalysis, social policy, sociology, politics, youth work; BA, BSc, CertHE, FdA, FdSc, MA

Social Work

social work; BA(Hons), MA

Psychology

applied psychology, criminology with forensic psychology, health psychology, psychology, psychology with criminology/sociology/counselling skills; BA(Hons), BSc(Hons), Grad Dip MSc

Public Health, Risk & Safety

environmental health, food premises inspection, health promotion, housing, occupational health, occupational safety and health management, public health, risk management, safety; BSc(Hons), CertHE, MSc

Sport & Exercise Science

coaching and sports development, foundation health and fitness, sport and exercise science/sports and exercise psychology/sports nutrition/clinical exercise, sport rehabilitation and injury prevention, strength and conditioning; BSc(Hons), FdSc, MSc

Tourism

hospitality management, international tourism management and marketing/languages/human resource management, tourism; BA(Hons), MA

Veterinary Nursing

veterinary nursing; BSc(Hons)

NAPIER UNIVERSITY
www.napier.ac.uk

The Business School; www.napier.ac.uk/ business-school

Accounting, Economics and Statistics

accounting, corporate strategy, economics, entrepreneurship, finance, financial services, HRM, international finance, investment promotion and economic development, management, marketing management, professional banking, wealth management; BA(Hons), DBA, MPhil, MSc, PhD

Management & Law

business & enterprise, business management, business studies, finance, criminal justice, entrepreneurship, health & social welfare law, HRM, international business management – international business studies, managerial leadership, marketing; BA/BA(Hons), BMA, LlB, LlM, MBA, MSc

Marketing Tourism and Languages

consumer studies, festival and event and hospitality management, heritage and cultural tourism/tourism management, international business languages, international event and festival management, languages and intercultural communication, marketing, tourism and airline management; BA, BA(Hons), MSc

Faculty of Engineering, Computing and Creative Industries; www.napier.ac.uk/ fecci

School of Computing

advanced networking, applied informatics, business information systems/technology, computer networks & distributed systems, computing security & forensics, computing, digital media/networking, embedded computer systems, enterprise web development, information systems for financial services, interactive media design/systems: user experience, multimedia systems, software engineering, software technology for the web, SWE computing; BEng, BSc, MPhil, MSc, PhD

Creative Industries

acting, film practice, advertising, PR, communication, creative writing, design and digital arts, English, film, graphic design, interaction design, interactive entertainment, interior architecture, journalism, music, music industries, music (popular), photography, product design, publishing, screen project development, screenwriting, sound production, television; BA/BA(Hons), BDes, BDes(Hons), BMus, BMus(Hons), MDes, MFA, MSc, PGCert/Dip

Engineering & the Built Environment

applied engineering, architectural technology & building performance, building surveying, built environment, timber engineering, civil engineering, communication engineering, computer aided engineering, construction/and project management, electronic/computer/electrical engineering, energy and environmental engineering, engineering design, environmental sustainability, facilities management, materials engineering, mechanical engineering, mechatronics, polymer engineering, product design engineering, product manufacture, project management, property and construction management, property development and valuation, investment quantity surveying, safety and environmental management, sports technology, structural engineering, timber industry management, transport management, transport planning and engineering, transportation engineering; BSc/BSs(Hons), BEng, BEng/Hons, MEng, MSc, MSci, PGCert/Dip

Faculty of Health, Life & Social Science; www.napier.ac.uk/fhlss

Health & Social Sciences

career guidance & development, complementary healthcare (aromatherapy/reflexology), complementary therapies practitioner, criminology, psychology, with sport & exercise science/sociology, social science, reflexology, social research; BA(Hons), MSc, PGCert/Dip

Life Sciences

biological science, biology, biomedical science, ecotourism, environmental biology, forensic biology, herbal medicine, immunology & toxicology, marine & freshwater biology, microbiology & biotechnology, sport and exercise medicine; BSc(Hons), MSc

School of Nursing, Midwifery and Social Care

adult nursing, child health, intellectual disability, mental health, midwifery; BMid, BN, DiplomaHE, MSc

UNIVERSITY OF NEWCASTLE UPON TYNE
www.ncl.ac.uk

Faculty of Humanities and Social Sciences; www.ncl.ac.uk/hass

School of Architectural Planning and Landscape; www.ncl.ac.uk/apl

architectural practice/studies, digital architecture, geography planning/and environment, planning practice, town planning, transportation planning & policy, urban design; BA, BArch, Cert, Dip, MA, MPhil, MSc, PGCert, PhD

School of Arts and Cultures; www.ncl.ac.uk/sacs

folk and traditional music, music, music and education, popular and contemporary music; BA, BMus, Diploma, MA, MLitt, MMus, MPhil, PhD

Fine Art

fine art, history of art; BA(Hons), MFA, MPhil, PhD

Digital Media

digital media; Diploma, MA, MRes

Museum, Gallery and Heritage Studies

art museum & gallery education/gallery studies, art as enterprise, heritage education & interpretation/management, museum studies; MA, MPhil, MPrac, PGCert, PGDip, PhD

Business School; www.ncl.ac.uk/nubs

accounting, arts, banking, business accounting, business management, e-business and information systems, economics, finance, financial & business economics, financial regulation, innovation, creativity and entrepreneurship, international business management/economics and finance/financial analysisi/huHR/ marketing, Islamic finance, law, management, marketing, operations management and logistics, strategic planning and investment; BA, BSc, DBA, MA, MBA, MSc, PhD

School of Education, Communication and Language Sciences; www.ncl.ac.uk/ecls

applied linguistics and TESOL, cross-cultural communication and applied linguistics/education/international management/marketing/international relations/media studies, education – primary/secondary, educational psychology, English literature, international development/multimedia, journalism, language and linguistics, media, communication and cultural studies, PR, speech and language sciences; BA(Hons), BSc(Hons), DedPsych, EdD, MA, MEd, MSc, PGCE, PhD

Combined Studies Centre

combined studies; BS(Hons)

School of English Literature, Language, Linguistics; www.ncl.ac.uk/elll

English language, literature, literary studies: writing, memory, culture, creative writing, language acquisition, modern and contemporary studies; BA(Hons), MA, MLitt, MPhil, PGCert, PhD

Geography, Politics and Sociology; www.ncl.ac.uk/gps

applied policy, critical geopolitics/global justice and ethics/globalisation, economics, European union studies, gender research, geography, government, health

153

research, human geography, international politics, international, local and regional development, physical geography, planning, politics, poverty and development, social research, social science, sociology; BA(Hons), BSc(Hons), MA, MSc, PhD

Global Urban Research Unit; www.ncl.ac. uk/guru

cities and international development, place and social cohesion, unit spatial planning and environment; MPhil, PhD

Institute of Health and Society

public health & health service; MSc, PGDip/Cert

School of Historical Studies; www.ncl.ac. uk/historical

ancient history, archaeology, archaeology of historic periods, British history, Byzantine archaeology, classical studies, classics, east Asian history, European history, Greek and Roman archaeology, history, history of medicine, history of the Americas, neolithic and bronze age Europe, politics, Roman frontier studies; BA(Hons), MA, MLitt, MPhil, PhD

Centre for History of Medicine; www.ncl. ac.uk/historical

history of medicine, medical history; BA(Hons), MLitt, MPhil, PhD

Centre for Knowledge, Innovation, Technology and Enterprise

economic development, older enterprise, enterprise education, innovation and economic development; DBA, MSc, PhD

Newcastle Law School; www.ncl.ac.uk/nuls

environmental law and policy, international trade law, international commercial law, law; LlB, LlM, MPhil, PhD

Centre for Learning and Teaching; www.ncl. ac.uk/cflat

educational leadership and management, educational research, information, communication and entertainment technology, inclusive education, international development and education, pedagogy and learning, practitioner enquiries; EdD, MA, MEd, PGCE

School of Modern Languages; www.ncl.ac. uk/sml

Chinese, cultural studies, French, German, international film, language acquisition, Latin American interdisciplinary studies, Latin American studies, linguistics, linguistics of European languages, Portuguese, professional translating for European

languages, Spanish, translating and interpreting – Chinese strand; BA(Hons), MA, MLitt, PhD

Newcastle Institute for the Arts, Social Sciences and Humanities

Policy, Ethics and Life Sciences Research Centre; www.ncl.ac.uk/peals

ageing, biosecurity, bioinformation and security studies, clinical ethics, disability, fertility, genetics, human stem cell research, public participation; PhD

Centre for Research in Linguistics and Language Science; www.ncl.ac.uk/ linguistics

applied lingustics and TESOL, cross-cultural communication, education (TESOL), English language, human communication sciences, language acquisition, language pathology, linguistics, linguistics of European languages; MA, MEd, MSc, PhD

Centre for Urban and Regional Development Studies; www.ncl.ac.uk/ curds

local and regional development; MA

Faculty of Medical Sciences; www.ncl. ac.uk/aboutpeoplestudies academic/ biosciences

Biomedical and Biomolecular Sciences & Medicine; www.ncl.ac.uk/biomed

ageing and health, biochemistry, biological sciences, biomedical sciences, biomedicine, biotechnology, cancer research, cancer studies, clinical education, clinical psychology, clinical research, experimental medicine and therapeutics, genetics, human genetics, immunobiology, immunology, medical and molecular biosciences, medical biotechnology, medical genetics, medical microbiology, medicine and surgery, nanomedicine, neuroscience, oncology and palliative care, pharmacology, physiological sciences, public health & health services, stem cells and regenerative medicine, systems biology, therapeutics, toxicology; BSc(Hons), DClinPsychol, MB, MClinEd, MClinRes, MD, MRes, MSc, MSci, PGCert, PGDip

Dental Sciences; www.ncl.ac.uk/dental

conscious sedation in dentistry, dental surgery, orthodontics, orthodontics integrated, restorative dentistry; BDS, DDS, MSc, PGDip, PhD

Faculty of Agriculture, Food and Rural Development; *www.ncl.ac.uk/ aboutpeoplestudies/academic/sage*

School of Agriculture, Food and Rural Development; www.ncl.ac.uk/afrd

advanced food marketing, agri-business management, agricultural and environmental science, agriculture, agronomy, animal science, countryside management, ecological farming and food production systems, environmental resource assessment/science, environmental, agricultural and wildlife conservation, farm business management, food and human nutrition, international agriculture, livestock technology, medicinal plants and functional foods, rural resource management, rural social science, rural studies; BSc(Hons), MPhil, MSc, PhD

School of Biology; www.ncl.ac.uk/biology

applied biology, biodiversity, conservation and ecotourism, biology, environmental consultancy, industrial and commercial biotechnology, zoology; BSc(Hons), MSC, PhD

Biopharmaceutical Bioprocessing Technology Centre; www.ncl.ac.uk/ceam

chemical engineering, intensified processing, material and process engineering, process control, sustainable engineering; BEngHons, MEngHons, MSc, PGDip

School of Chemical Engineering and Advanced Materials; www.ncl.ac.uk/ceam

bioprocess engineering, chemical engineering, clean technology, industrial quality technology, materials and process engineering, materials, design & engineering, process automation/ control/engineering, sustainable applied process control, sustainable chemical engineering; BEng(Hons), MEng(Hons), MSc, PGDip

School of Chemistry; www.ncl.ac.uk/ chemistry

chemistry, drug chemistry, medicinal chemistry; BSc(Hons), MChem, MPhil, MSc, PhD

Civil Engineering and Geosciences; www. cegsncl.ac.uk

applied hydrogeology, civil engineering, environmental engineering, geochemistry, geomatics, geoscience, geotechnical engineering, geotechnics and structures, resource engineering, structural engineering, transport, transport engineering, water environment; BEng, BSc(Hons), MEng, MPhil, MSc, PhD

Computing Science; www.cs.ncl.ac.uk/

computer game engineering, computer security and resilience, computing bioinformatics and computational systems biology, computing science, distributed systems/games and virtual environments/software engineering, e-business and information systems, information systems, internet technologies and enterprise computing; BSc(Hons), MPhil, MSc, PhD

Electrical, Electronic and Computer Engineering; www.ncl.ac.uk/eece

automation and control, communications and signal processing, electrical power, electronic communications, electronics & computer engineering, microelectronics, mobile and pervasive computing, power distribution; BEng, EngD, MEng, MPhil, PhD

Institute for Research on Environment and Sustainability; *www.ncl.ac.uk/ environment*

agriculture, food and environment, biological sciences, biosciences, engineering and science in the marine environment, environmental engineering, geography, rural development, rural social science, water resources engineering; MPhil, MRes, PhD

Informatics Research Institute; *www.ncl. ac.uk/iri*

research projects; PhD

Institute for Nanoscience and Technology; *www.ncl.ac.uk/irisat*

cell and molecular biosciences/medicine, chemical nanoscience, MEMS and smart materials, nano materials and electronics, nanoscience and nanotechnology, policy, ethics and life sciences, products and processes

Newcastle Centre for Railway Research; *www.ncl.ac.uk/newrail*

rail freight and logistics, rail infrastructure, rail systems, rail vehicles

School of Marine Science and Technology; *www.ncl.ac.uk/marine*

aquaculture enterprise and technology, international marine environmental consultancy, marine & offshore power systems/technology, marine biology, marine engineering/structures & integrity/transport & management, marine zoology, naval architecture, oceanography, offshore & environmental technology/

engineering, pipeline engineering, small craft technology/design, software reliability, subsea engineering & management, tropical coastal management; BEng, BSc(Hons), MEng, MRes MSc

Mathematics and Statistics; www.ncl.ac.uk/math

applied mathematics, financial mathematics, mathematical sciences, mathematics, pure mathematics, statistics; BSc(Hons), MMath and MMathStat, MPhil, PhD

School of Mechanical & Systems Engineering; www.ncl.ac.uk/mech

automotive engineering, design engineering, manufacturing engineering, materials engineering, mechanical engineering, mechanical engineering with mathematical modelling, mechatronics, microsystems engineering, railway engineering, scientific enterprise; BEng, MEng, MSc

Centre for Rural Economy; www.ncl.ac.uk/cre

consumption and marketing, food systems, rural development, rural social science, science and technology studies in food and environment; MPhil, MSc, PhD

Sir Joseph Swan Institute for Energy Research; www.ncl.ac.uk/energy

carbon neutral culture, energy biosciences, environmental impact characterisation, fuel cells and hydrogen, integrated systems, renewable electricity/energy, social aspects of energy; MPhil, MSc, PhD

Centre for Software Reliability; www.csr.ncl.ac.uk

dependability of computer-based systems, dependable computing systems centre

UNIVERSITY OF NORTHAMPTON
www.northampton.ac.uk

School of Applied Sciences; www.northampton.ac.uk/departments/applied science

Division of Computing; www2.northampton.ac.uk/appliedsciences/appliedscience/computing

computing, internet technology/computer networks engineering/computer systems engineering/graphics & visualisation; BA/BSc, BSc(Hons), HND, MSc, PhD

Division of Engineering; www2.northampton.ac.uk/appliedsciences/appliedscience/engineering

electrical and electronic engineering, engineering, lift and escalator technology/engineering, mechanical/production engineering, non-destructive testing; BSc(Hons), BTEC, FdSc, HNC, HND, MSc, Prof Cert

Environmental Science; www2.northampton.ac.uk/appliedsciences/appliedscience/geoenvsci

applied conservation biology, biology, cleaning enterprise & law, environmental cleaning management/management/science, geography, infection control, physical geography, pollution control, waste management; BA/B/Sc, BSc(Hons), FdSc, HNS, MBA, MSc, Univ Certs

British School of Leather Technology; www2.northampton.ac.uk/appliedsciences/appliedscience/bslt

leather studies, leather technology, materials technology (leather); BSc(Hons), BTEC National Certificate, Leathersellers Certificate, MSc, PhD/MPhil

The School of The Arts; www.northampton.ac.uk/departments/arts

Division of Design; www2.northampton.ac.uk/arts/home/Design

architectural technology, creative design, graphic communication, heritage management, illustration, interior design, interactive digital media, product design; BA(Hons), BSc(Hons)

Division of Fine Art; www2.northampton.ac.uk/arts/home/Fine%20Art

art and design, drawing, fine art, history of art & design, painting, photographic practice; BA(Hons), FD, MA

Division of Media, English and Culture; www2.northampton.ac.uk/arts/home/Media%20English%20Culture

American studies, creative writing, English, film and television studies, English language, gender studies, journalism, media production, modern English studies, popular music; BA(Hons), MA

Division of Performance Studies; www2. northampton.ac.uk/arts/home/ Performance%20Studies

acting, dance, drama, music production/practice, performance arts, popular music, theatre studies; BA(Hons), HND, MA, PhD

Division of Fashion; www2.northampton. ac.uk/arts/home/ Division%20of%20Fashion

School of Education; www. northampton.ac.uk/departments/ education

Teacher Education Division; www2. northampton.ac.uk/education/home1/ teacher-education

early childhood studies, early years education, education (early years & primary), graduate teacher programme (GTP), primary education, primary or early years/secondary in maths, science, English or design and technology, primary/early years, teacher training; BA(Hons), GTP, PGCE

Profession Development & Training Division; www2.northampton.ac.uk/ education/home1/teaching-assistants

learning and teaching, supporting learners higher level teaching assistant status; BA, CertHE, Foundation degree

Early Years & Educational Studies Division; www2.northampton.ac.uk/education/ home1/early-years

children and youth, early childhood studies, early years/sure start, early years education, GTP: early years primary and secondary routes; BA/BSc,FD

Special Needs and Inclusion Division;

boy friendly teaching, initial teacher training students, improving group dynamics to support learning and social inclusion, learning and support of primary school children with dyslexia, teacher training use of classroom support; PhD

School of Health; www.northampton.ac. uk/departments/health

adult nursing, children's nursing, dental nursing, health studies, learning disability, mental health, human bioscience, mental health studies, midwifery, occupational therapy, paramedic science, podiatry, social and community development, social care, social work, sport and exercise, BSc(Hons), MPhil, PGCert, PhD

Northampton Business School; www. northampton.ac.uk/departments/ business

accounting, advertising/with design or PR, applied management, business, business computing/systems/ entrepreneurship/studies, economics, EFL, enterprise (business development), entertainment marketing, events management, fashion marketing, finance, financial information/management, financial services, health and beauty marketing, HRM, international accounting/HRM/international logistics and trade finance, IT service management, marketing, office administration, retailing, social enterprise development, sports marketing, tourism marketing, tourism, travel & tourism management; BA(Hons), BA/ BscHons, CMS, DBA, DMS, FdA, HND, MA, MBA, MSc, PGDip(marketing), ProfDip

School of Social Sciences; www. northampton.ac.uk/departments/social sciences

History

18th-century research, history, public history, social and cultural history; BA(Hons), PhD

Law; www2.northampton.ac.uk/ socialsciences/sshome/law-2

international business law/ criminal law and security, law; LlB, LlM, PhD

Psychology

child and adolescent mental health, developmental and educational/sport and exercise psychology, psychology, transpersonal psychology and consciousness; BA/BSc, BSc(Hons), PhD

Sociology

criminology, international relations, offender management, sociology; BA(Hons), MA

UNIVERSITY OF NORTHUMBRIA AT NEWCASTLE
www.northumbria.ac.uk

Newcastle Business School; www. newcastlebusiness.ac.uk

accounting, business, business creation/management/ studies, corporate management, finance, global financial management, global logistics and supply chain management, hospitality and tourism management, HRM, international business administration/ business management,/hospitality & tourism management/HRM/management, investment management, logistics and supply chain management, marketing management, multidisciplinary design innovation, tourism, travel and tourism management; BA, DBA, MA, MBA, MSc, PhD

School of Applied Sciences; www. northumbria.ac.uk/sd/academic/sac

Biosciences
applied biology, applied biomedical sciences, biology with forensic biology, biomedical, biotechnology, human biosciences, medical biosciences, medical sciences, microbiology, molecular biology; BSc(Hons), MSc, PhD

Chemistry
analytical/applied chemistry, biomedical sciences, forensic chemistry, pharmaceutical chemistry; BSc, BSc(Hons), MChem, MRes, MSc

Food and Nutritional Sciences
food science, human nutrition, nutritional science, nutrition & psychological science; BS(Hons), MSc

Forensic and Crime Sciences
biology, crime science, criminology, forensic biology/ chemistry/science; BA(Hons), BSc(Hons), MSc, MSci

Geography and Environment
community wellbeing, environmental health/management, geography, human geography, physical geography

School of Arts & Social Sciences; www. northumbria.ac.uk/sd/academic/sass

English & CreativeWriting
creative writing, English language/literature, film studies, history, journalism, applied linguistics for TESOL

English Language Centre
media & communication, modern foreign languages, performing arts

Politics & History Division
sociology & criminology, TESOL, visual arts; BA(Hons), MA, MRes

Media & Communication
advertising & media, journalism, media production/ culture; BA(Hons), MA

Modern Foreign Languages
area studies, British Sign Language, French, German, Italian, Japanese, Mandarin Chinese, modern languages, Polish; BA(Hons), Dip

Performing Arts
choreograpy, dance, drama, performance, scripwriting; BA(Hons)

Politics & History
media culture and society, politics, public administration, regeneration, urban policy and renewal; BA(Hons), MA, MRes, MSc, PGDip/Cert

Sociology & Criminology
criminal justice, criminology, forensic science, international policing, psychology with criminology, sociology; BSc(Hons), BSc(Hons), MA, PGDip/Cert

Visual Arts
art & design, contemporary photographic practice, film and televison studies, fine art/and education, practice/conservation; cultural management, event & conference management, museum & heritage management, music management & promotion; BA(Hons), FdA, MA

School of Built Environment; www. northumbria.ac.uk/sd/academic/sobe

architectural technology, architecture, building design management/project management/services engineering/surveying, commercial/quantity surveying, construction, construction management/ project management, estate management, housing policy and management, housing sustainable communities, planning & development surveying, surveying (minerals), sustainable communities, sustainable development in the built environment; BA(Hons),

BSc(Hons), FdSc, MA, MSc, PGDip/Cert, PhD, ProfDip

Business Information Systems

business information management/systems/technology, business IT with entrepreneurship, IT management for business, technology, innovation & entrepreneurship; BSc(Hons), FdSc, MSc

School of Computing, Engineering & Information Science: northumbria.ac.uk/sd/academic/ceis

Computing

applied/ business computing, computer design & production, computer forensics/games software engineering/network/technology/science, computing and IT, computing studies, embedded computer systems engineering, informatics, IT, technical innovation & entrepreneurship

Engineering & Technology

communication & electronic engineering, computer aided production design, computer and network technology, electrical engineering, electrical power engineering, embedded computer systems engineering, mechanical design techniques, mechanical engineering, microelectronics and communication engineering, product design technology, technical innovation & entrepreneurship; BEng, BSc(Hons), MSc

Information and Communications Management

communication & PR, computing and IT, information & library management, librarianship, records management; BSc(Hons), MA, MSc

Mathematics & Statistics

mathematics, mathematics with business; BSc(Hons)

School of Design

3D design, design for industry/management, design professional practice, fashion, fashion communication/management and entrepreneurship/marketing, furniture and product design, graphic design, interactive media design, interior design, motion graphics & animation, transportation design; BA(Hons), Des, Doc, BSc(Hons), MA, MSc, Pract

School of Health, Community & Education Studies; www.northumbria.ac.uk/sd/academic/shes

health, midwifery studies, nursing studies/registered nurse/child/mental health, nursing studies/adv dip/higher education/registered nurse, nursing studies/registered nurse/adult/child/mental health, occupational therapy, physiotherapy; Adv Dip, BSc, MSc, PGDip

Northumbria Law School: northumbria.ac.uk/sd/academic/law

business law, child law, commercial property law, bar vocational course, commercial law, employment law, information rights law and practice, international commercial law, international trade law, legal practice, medical law, mental health law/mental health law policy and practice; BVC, GDL, Grad Cert, LlM, LLb, LPC, PGCert

School of Psychology and Sport Science; www.northumbria.ac.uk/sd/academic/psychsport

applied sport and exercise science, business psychology, coaching, criminology, exercise & nutrition, international sport management, nutrition & psychological sciences, occupational psychology, psychology/of sport & exercise behaviour, sport development/management; BSc(Hons), MSc

UNIVERSITY OF NOTTINGHAM
www.nottingham.ac.uk

Faculty of Arts; www.nottingham.ac.uk/arts

School of American and Canadian Studies (including the Institute of Film and Television Studies); www.nottingham.ac.uk/american

American & Canadian studies, Chinese studies, international study, Latin American studies/history/politics, art history, cultural sociology, film and television studies, Hispanic studies/; BA(Hons), MA, MRes, PhD

School of English Studies; www.nottingham.ac.uk/english

Anglo Saxon studies, applied linguistics, communication and entrepreneurship, early modern literature, English language and literature/language

159

teaching/studies, literary linguistics, the long 19th century, medieval English, Norse and Viking studies, old English studies, theatre research, 20th century and contemporary literature, Viking studies; BA(Hons), MA, MPhil, MSc, PGDip, PhD

School of History; www.nottingham.ac.uk/history

British history, east European civilisation, gender history, contemporary Chinese studies/ancient history/archaeology/art history/politics, Islamic and middle eastern history, medieval history, modern history, Robin Hood studies, Viking studies, warring societies; BA(Hons), MA, MPhil, PhD

Centre for English Language Education; www.cele.nottingham.ac.uk

foundation courses, courses for TESOL and postgraduate students

School of Humanities; www.nottingham.ac.uk/humanities

archaeological materials, archaeology, ancient history, classical civilisation, bioarchaeology, medieval archaeology, Mediterranean archaeology, Roman archaeology, underwater archaeology; BA(Hons), BSc(Hons), MA, MPhil

Art History; www.nottingham.ac.uk/art-history

art history, classical civilisation, English studies, history, visual culture; BA(Hons), MA
ancient drama/history, classical civilisation/literature, classics, Greek, Greek and Roman studies, Latin, visual culture of classical antiquity; BA(Hons), MPhil/PhD

Music; www.nottingham.ac.uk/music

composition, film and television studies, music, music and philosophy; BA(Hons), MPhil, PhD

Philosophy; www.nottingham.ac.uk/philosophy

psychology, philosophy, theology; BA(Hons), MA, MPhil/PhD

Theology and Religious Studies; www.nottingham.ac.uk/theology

biblical interpretation, middle eastern studies, philosophical theology, philosophy, philosophy and literature, religious conflict, religious studies, theology; BA(Hons), MA, MPhil/PhD

School of Modern Languages & Cultures; www.nottingham.ac.uk/modern-languages

20th & 21st century French thought, classical civilisation and French, contemporary Chinese studies, early modern French studies, francophone and post-colonial studies, French culture and politics, French studies, French with various modern European languages and Russian, international media communications studies, modern European studies, modern language studies; BA(Hons), MA, MPhil, PhD

German Studies; www.nottingham.ac.uk/german

Dutch, film, German, Germanic studies, modern and contemporary German studies, philosophy; BA(Hons), MA, MPhil, PhD

Spanish, Portuguese and Latin American Studies; www.nottingham.ac.uk/splas

Hispanic studies, international media communications studies, Portuguese (beginners), Spanish, Spanish and Latin American studies or Portuguese and Lusophone studies

Russian & Slavonic Studies; www.nottingham.ac.uk/slavonic

East European civilisations, modern language studies, Russian and East European civilisations, Russian and Serbian/Croatian studies, Russian; BA(Hons), MA, MPhil

Cultural Studies; www.nottingham.ac.uk/cultural-studies

cultural studies, entrepreneurship, international media communications studies; BA(Hons), MA, MPhil

Faculty of Science; www.nottingham.ac.uk/science

School of Biosciences; www.nottingham.ac.uk/biosciences

Agricultural and Environmental Sciences

agriculture, crop improvement, crop science, environmental science; BSc(Hons), MSc, PhD

Plant and Crop Sciences

agriculture and biotechnology, applied biology, crop biotechnology technology & entrepreneurship, environmental biology, genomic and proeonomic science, integrative biology, plant genetic manipulation, plant science; BSc(Hons), MSc, PhD

Animal Sciences

animal science, integrative systems biology, preveterinary science; BSc(Hons), Cert, MRes, MSc, PhD

Food Sciences

applied biomolecular technology, brewing science and food production management, food microbiology/science, industrial biochemistry, microbiology, nutrition and food science; BSc(Hons), MPhil, MRes, MSc, PGDip, PhD

Nutritional Sciences

advanced dietetic practice, food science, nutrition, nutritional biology; BSc(Hons), MPhil, MRes, MSc, PGDip, PhD

School of Chemistry; www.nottingham.ac.uk/chemistry

biochemistry, biological chemistry, chemistry, drug chemistry, molecular physics, medicinal chemistry; BSc(Hons), MChem, MPhil, MSc, MSci, PhD

School of Computer Science; www.nottingham.ac.uk/computerscience

advanced computing, artificial intelligence, computer science, computing and information systems, interactive systems design, management of information technology, scientific computation, software systems, technology; BSc(Hons), MPhil, MSc

School of Mathematical Sciences; www.maths.nottingham.ac.uk/

mathematical physics, mathematics, numerical techniques for finance, scientific computation/with electromagnetics/industrial mathematics/mathematical medicine and biology, statistics, statistics with biomedical applications/applied probability; BSc(Hons), MSc, PhD

School of Physics & Astronomy; www.nottingham.ac.uk/physics

astronomy, mathematical physics, medical physics, nanoscience, particle theory, physics, physics and philosophy, theoretical astrophysics, theoretical physics, chemistry and molecular physics; BSc(Hons), MSc, MSci, PhD

School of Psychology; www.nottingham.ac.uk/psychology

cognitive neuroscience and neuroimaging, psychology, psychology and cognitive neuroscience/philosophy; BSc(Hons), MSc, PhD

Faculty of Engineering; www.nottingham.ac.uk/engineering

Dept of Built Environment; www.nottingham.ac.uk/sbe

architectural environment engineering, architecture, architecture & critical theory, design, energy conversion and management, environmental design, renewable energy and architecture, sustainable built environment, sustainable tall buildings, technology, theory & design, urban design; BA(Hons), BArch (Hons), BEng (Hons), Dip Arch, MEng, MPhil, PhD

Dept of Chemical and Environmental Engineering; www.nottingham.ac.uk/scheme

chemical engineering, environmental engineering, petroleum and environmental process engineering, resource engineering; BEng(Hons), MEng(Hons), MPhil, MRes, MSc, PhD

Dept of Electrical & Electronic Engineering; www.nottingham.ac.uk/eee

biophotonics, computer engineering/communications engineering, electrical engineering, electrical technology for sustainable and renewable energy systems, electromagnetics design, electronic communications and computer engineering, electronic engineering, electronic and ultrasonic instrumentation, optical engineering techniques, photonic communications, power electronics, machines and drives, RF microelectronic design, renewable energy systems; BEng, MEng, MPhil, MRes, MSc, PGDip, PhD

Dept of Civil Engineering; www.nottingham.ac.uk/civil

civil engineering/mechanics, environmental engineering, environmental fluid mechanics, geotechnical engineering, infrastructure, pavement engineering, structural engineering, transportation; BEng(Hons), MEng(Hons), MPhil, MSc, PhD

Dept of Mechanical, Materials and Manufacturing Engineering; www.nottingham.ac.uk/schoolm3

advanced materials, applied ergonomics, automotive, bioengineering, design engineering, engineering materials failure and analysis, healthcare, human factors and ergonomics, manufacturing engineering, materials, mechanical engineering, product design and manufacture, systems design; BEng, MEng, MSc, PGCert, PhD

Faculty of Medicine & Health Science; *www.nottingham.ac.uk*

School of Biology; www.nottingham.ac.uk/ biology

biochemical genetics, biological photography and imaging, biology, human genetics; BSc, MSc, MSci, PhD

School of Biomedical Sciences; www. nottingham.ac.uk/biomedsci

biochemistry, biological chemistry, genetics, molecular medicine, neuroscience, sports medicine; BSc(Hons), MPhil, MRes, MSC, PhD

School for Clinical Sciences; www. nottingham.ac.uk/scs

assisted reproduction technology, management of the critically ill, medical sciences, stem cell technology, sports and exercise medicine; BMedSci, MMedSci, PhD

School of Community Health Sciences; www.nottingham.ac.uk/chs

applied epidemiology, applied genetics, behavioural sciences, clinical epidemiology, developmental psychiatry, forensic mental health, general adult psychiatry, health of older people, injury epidemiology and prevention, intellectual disabilities, long term neurological conditions, medical education, mental health studies, primary care, psychiatry, psychopharmacology, public health, rehabilitation and ageings, safe and effective uses of medicines, smoking cessation, stroke rehabilitation; MPH, MSc, PGDip/ Cert, PhD

School of Molecular Medical Sciences; www.moi1.nottingham.ac.uk/

human genetics, immunology, molecular and cellular bacteriology, translational cancer, virology; MSc, PhD

School of Nursing, Midwifery and Physiotherapy; www.nottingham.ac.uk/ nursing

adult critical care, advanced clinical practice, advanced clinical skills, advanced nursing, cognitive behaviour therapy, critical and high dependency care of neonates, health and social care, health communication, health sciences, infants & children, long term conditions, midwifery, neurorehabilitation physiotherapy, nursing – adult/mental health, physiotherapy manual therapy, psychological therapies; BMid(Hons), BSc(Hons), DHSci, MA, MNursSci, MPhil, MSc, PGDip/Cert, PhD

School of Pharmacy; www.nottingham.ac. uk/pharmacy

medicinal and biological chemistry, pharmacy; MPharm, MRes, MSc, MSci, PhD

School of Veterinary Medicine & Science; www.nottingham.ac.uk/vet

laboratory animal medicine, veterinary medicine & surgery; BVMBVS, BVMedSci, MPhil, MRes, PhD

Faculty of Social Sciences, Law, & Education; *www.nottingham.ac.uk*

Nottingham University Business School; www.nottingham.ac.uk/business

corporate social responsibility/strategy and governance, entrepreneurship, finance accounting and management, finance and investment, global supply chain management, industrial economics/with insurance, industrial engineering, international business, logistics and supply chain management, management studies, management with Asian studies/ Chinese studies, manufacturing systems, marketing, operations management, risk management, supply chain and operations management, tourism and travel management and marketing; BA(Hons), ExecMBA, MA, MBA, MSc

School of Contemporary Chinese Studies; www.nottingham.ac.uk/chinese

Chinese/English translation and interpreting, contemporary Chinese studies, management in contemporary China; BA, MSc, MSci, PhD

Economics; www.nottingham.ac.uk/ economics

applied economics, behavioural economics, economic development and policy analysis, economics, economics with modern languages, economics and international economics/development economics/ financial economics, econometrics, international economics, philosophy; BA(Hons), BSc(Hons), MPhil, PGDip, PhD

School of Education; www.nottingham.ac. uk/education

educational research methods, higher education, initial teacher education – secondary (English, geography, history, mathematics, modern languages, science, society, health), learning, technology and education, local and regional history , special needs, TESOL, trauma studies; BA(Hons), MA, MPhil,MRes, PGCE, PGCert/Dip, PhD, SCITT

School of Geography; www.nottingham.ac.uk/geography

geography, environmental management,GIS, human geography, landscape and culture

School of Law; www.nottingham.ac.uk/law

environmental law, European law, human rights law, international commercial law, international criminal justice and armed conflict, international law/and development, law and environmental science, law with French/German law/American law/Australian law/Chinese law/European law/New Zealand law/ South East Asian law, law, maritime law, public international law, public procurement and policy, senior status criminal justice, socio-legal and criminological research; BA(Hons), LlB, LlM, MA, MSc, PhD

Politics & International Relations; www.nottingham.ac.uk/politics

diplomacy, European and global politics, European politics, international relations/ and global issues, international security and terrorism, politics, politics and contemporary history/ and history/American studies/German/French, social and global justice; BA(Hons), MA, MPhil, MRes, PhD

School of Sociology and Social Policy; www.nottingham.ac.uk/sociology

administration, citizenship, identities and human rights, health communications, immigration and transnationalism, public administration, public policy, social and cultural studies, social policy, social work, social work studies, sociology, trauma studies; BA(Hons), MA, MPA, MPhil, MSWS, PhD

NOTTINGHAM TRENT UNIVERSITY
www.ntu.ac.uk

School of Animal, Rural and Environmental Sciences; www.ntu.ac.uk/ares

animal biology, biodiversity surveying, environmental conservation and countryside management/ design and management/science, equine sports science (equestrian psychology), equine health and welfare, geography/wildlife conservation, zoo biology; BSc(Hons), MSc/MRes/PGCert/PGDip, FdSc

School of Architecture, Design and Built Environment; www.ntu.ac.uk/adbe

art & design, civil engineering, product design, property construction & surveying/development investment, project management, real estate; BSc(Hons), MA, MSc, PGDip/Cert

School of Art & Design; www.ntu.ac.uk/art

art direction, computer aided product design, decorative arts, design for film and television, fashion/ and textile management/design/communication and promotion/knitwear design and knitted textiles/marketing and branding, fashion, knitwear and textiles, film, fine art, graphic design, innovation management, interaction design, international fashion business and textile design/illustration, knitwear business/marketing and communication, motion graphic design, multimedia, photography product design, product design, puppetry and digital animation, textile design and innovation, theatre design, visual communication. BA(Hons), GradDip, MA, MPhil, PhD

School of Arts & Humanities; www.ntu.ac.uk/hum

childhood, communication, English, the environment, geography, history, horticulture, international studies, journalism, language, linguistics, media, philosophy, politics, teacher training education, youth studies; BA(Hons), MA, PGDip, PhD

Nottingham Business School; www.ntu.ac.uk/nbs

accounting and finance, business and management, economics, HRM, information management and systems, marketing, strategic management and international business; BA(Hons), DBA, MBA, MSc

School of Education; www.ntu.ac.uk/edu

business and education development, childhood studies, design and technology education, early years, educational support, ICT and education, primary education, psychology and education/educational development/business and education, special and inclusive education, sport and leisure, teaching adult literacy, teaching adult numeracy/ literacy,TESOL, undergraduate teacher training; BA(Hons), MA, PGCE, PGCert, Prof Cert, Prof Doc

Nottingham Law School; www.ntu.ac.uk/nls

competition law, corporate law, criminal justice, employment law, Europe and the law, health law, human rights, insolvency law, intellectual property, international trade law, law, law and professional practice/business/criminology/psychology, sports law; GDL, GradDip, LlB, LlM, LPC, PhD

School of Science & Technology; www.ntu.ac.uk/sat

astrophysics, biological sciences, biomedical science, biosciences, biotechnology, chemical sciences, chemistry and forensics, coaching, computer science/ systems (networks, forensics and security), computing and technology, digital media, environmental management, financial mathematics, forensic science, games technology, geonomic and proteonomic science, healthcare science, information and communication techn, information systems, materials science, mathematics, molecular cell biology, multimedia engineering, neuroscience, nutrition and health, pharmaceutical and medicinal chemistry, pharmacology, physics and mathematics, software

engineering, sport sciences/ and management/exercise science, technological physics; BSc, FdSc, MChem, MRes, MSc, MSci, PhD

School of Social Sciences; www.ntu.ac.uk/soc

applied child psychology, career education/guidance, child care practice, children's services (education welfare, psychology), corporate responsibility, counselling, crime reduction, criminology, cyberpsychology, forensic mental health/psychology, health and environment/social care, health and safety risk management, politics, psychological well-being and mental health, psychology with criminology/sociology/sports science/philosophy, public health, safety and environment, safety, health and environmental management, social work, sociology, youth studies; BA(Hons), MA, MRes, MSC, Pfdip/Cert, PGDip/Cert, PhD, ProfDoc

Degrees validated by Nottingham Trent University offered at:

SOUTHAMPTON SOLENT UNIVERSITY
www.solent.ac.uk

Arts, Design and Media; www.solent.ac.uk/courses/artsandmedia

advertising/communications, animation, communication, computer & video games, digital music, English and advertising/film/magazine journalism/media/ professional writing/PR/screenwriting/writing contemporary fiction/journalism/magazine journalism and feature writing/screenwriting/sport writing/writing, fashion and culture, fashion graphics/styling, film and photography/ television studies, fine art, graphic design, illustration, industrial design, interior design, live performance, music, media communication/culture/ studies, music promotion, photography, popular music/record production/journalism/ performance, PR, product design, television production, urban and electronic music, video production; BA(Hons), HND, MA, MPhil, PhD

Business and Law; www.solent.ac.uk/courses/BusinessandLaw

accountancy, business finance, business management with commercial law/entrepreneurship/finance/business/human resource management/psychology, business, business management, business studies, management and finance/international business, international business management, law, management, marketing, advertising management/

entrepreneurship/event management/human resource management/international business/psychology/tourism studies; BA(Hons), Cert, CIM, FdA, GradDip, HND/C, LLM, MA, MBA, MProf, PGDip, ProfCert/Dip

Education

learner support and administration, learning and teaching (higher education), professional development; MProf, PGC

Human Resources/Personnel

HRM, personnel and development, personnel practice

Languages

English for business and cross-cultural communication, international business management and English, international language programme; BA(Hons), DipHE, FD, MPhil, PGD/C, PhD

Maritime and Environmental Science; www.solent.ac.uk/courses/MaritimeandEnvScience

Geography
geography with environmental studies/marine studies

Maritime Industry
management/shipping and commercial law/shipping and logistics/shipping ports and environment, maritime business, ship and port management, yacht and boat design/powercraft design, yacht production and surveying; BEng, BSc(Hons), MPhil, MSc, PhD

Social Sciences; www.solent.ac.uk/courses/SocialSciences
criminology; criminal investigation with psychology, criminology and psychology, housing, social housing, housing; psychology (counselling/criminal behaviour/education)
social work/adults; BA(Hons), BSc(Hons), DipHE, MPhil, PhD

Sports & Tourism; www.solent.ac.uk/courses
event management, health and fitness, personal training, exercise & physical activity, health promotion and fitness,outdoor and watersports, extreme sports management, outdoor adventure management, watersports studies, sport, football studies, sport and the media/recreation management, applied sport science football, tourism, business/cruise and travel operations, tourism studies; BA(Hons), BSc(Hons), HND, MPhil, MSc, PhD

Technology; www.solent.ac.uk/coursesTechnology

Architecture
architectural technology, architecture

Business IT
business information systems/technology, business information technology, information and communication technology,

Civil Engineering
building surveying, civil engineering, construction, construction management, property development, quantity surveying, surveying

Computer Networking
cisco network, computer games development, computer network management, web design, computer systems and networks, computing (including internet), software engineering, web design – and internet technology

Engineering
electrical engineering, electronic engineering, engineering (general), engineering with business (manufacture/service), interior design, mechanical engineering, manufacturiing engineering,

Media Technology
audio technology, live and studio sound, media technology, music studio technology

Music and Music Technology
sound engineering, sound for film, television and games

Outside Broadcast
outside broadcast/technology, BA(Hons), BEng(Hons), BSc(Hons), FdSc, HNC, HND, MPhil, MSc, PhD

UNIVERSITY FOR THE CREATIVE ARTS
www.ucreative.ac.uk (at Canterbury, Epsom, Farnham, Maidstone and Rochester)

animation, architecture, contemporary crafts, design management, digital game design, fashion, film and video, fine art, graphic design, interior design, photography, publishing, substainable product design, textiles; BA(Hons), FD, Grad Dip, MA, MPhil, PGCert, PhD

THE OPEN UNIVERSITY
www.open.ac.uk

Undergraduate subjects

Arts and Humanities Studies; www3.open.ac.uk/study/undergraduate/arts-and-humanities/index.htm

classical studies, creative writing, English language and literature, history, literature, modern language studies, music, philosophy and psychological studies, religious studies; BA(Hons), MA, PGDip

Business and Management; www3.open.ac.uk/study/undergraduate/business.and.management/index.htm

accounting, business, business studies, computing with business, delivering public services, financial services, leadership and management; BA/BSc, Diplomas, DipHE, FD, MA, MSc, PGDip

Childhood and Youth; www3.open.ac.uk/study/undergraduate/childhood.and-youth/index.htm

social care, working with young people, the early years: childhood and youth studies, early years, primary teaching and learning, youth justice, working with young people, effective practice (youth justice), youth: perspectives and practice; BA(Hons), Diplomas, DipHE, Certificates

Computing and ICT; www3.open.ac.uk/study/undergraduate/computing.and.ICT/index.htm

advanced networking, business information technology, computing, computing and design/commerce and industry/business, information and communication technologies, information systems; BSc(Hons), Certs, Diplomas, DipHE, FD, MSc, PgD

Education; www3.open.ac.uk/study/undergraduate/education/index.htm

academic practice, applied linguistics, child development, equality and diversity, childhood and youth studies, early years, language and literacy, mathematics education, online and distance education, primary teaching and learning, secondary education in physics, supporting learning in primary schools, working together for children, working with young people; BA/BSc, Certs, DipHE, FD, MA, PGCert

Engineering and Technology; www3.open.ac.uk/study/undergraduate/erngineering.and-technology/index.htm

advanced networking, computing and design/systems practice, engineering, exploring information systems, information systems, materials fabrication and engineering, technology management, technology strategy; BEng, FD, MBA, MEng, MSc, PGDip

Environment, Development and International Studies; www3.open.ac.uk/study/undergraduate/environment-development-and-international-studies/index.htm

environment and development, environmental decision making/policy/science/studies, geography and environment, global development management and international studies, international development and business innovation, pollution control; BSc(Hons), MSc, PGDip/Cert

Health and Social Care; www3.open.ac.uk/study/undergraduate/health.and.social.care/index.htm

adult nursing, childhood and youth studies, early years, health studies, managing care, mental health nursing, nursing healthcare, paramedic sciences, promoting public health, shortened health and social care, social work studies, sport and fitness, working with young people, youth justice, youth: perspectives and practice; BA(Hons), BA/BSc, CertHE, DipHE, FD

Language Sudies; www3.open.ac.uk/study/undergraduate/language.studies/index.htm

French, German, modern language studies, Spanish; BA(Hons), UGDip/Cert

Law; www3.open.ac.uk/study/undergraduate/law/index.htm

agreements, rights & responsibilities, businesss & consumer, company law, employment law, English law; Certificates, Diplomas, LlB(Hons), QLD

Mathematics and Statistics; www3.open.ac.uk/study/undergraduate/mathematics.and.statistics/index.htm

computing/economics and mathematical sciences, statistics, mathematics mathematics and its learning; BA/BSc, BSc(Hons), MMath, MSc, UGCert

Psychology; www3.open.ac.uk/study/ undergraduate/psychology/index.htm

forensic psychology and criminology, forensic psychological studies, investigating the psychological world, investigating the social world, psychology; BA/BSc, MSc, PgDip, UGDip

Science; www3.open.ac.uk/study/ undergraduate/science/index.htm

analytical sciences, astronomy, astronomy and planetary science, contemporary science, earth science, environmental studies, geosciences, health sciences, life sciences, medical physics, molecular science, natural sciences, operating department practice, paramedic sciences, physical science, secondary education in physics; BSc(Hons), DipHE, FD, MSc

Social Sciences; www3.open.ac.uk/study/ undergraduate/social.sciencess/index.htm

forensic psychology,criminology, psychological studies, social policy, social research methods, social sciences; BA(Hons), BA/BSc, FD, MA, PGDip

Postgraduate subjects

arts and humanities; business and management; childhood and youth; computing and ICT; education; engineering and technology; environment, development and international studies; health and social care; languages; law; mathematics and statistics; psychology; science; social sciences

UNIVERSITY OF OXFORD
www.ox.ac.uk

Division of Humanities; www.ox.ac.uk/ divisions/humanities

Rothermere American Institute; www.rai. ox.ac.uk/

English and American studies; MSt

Faculty of Classics; www.classics.ox.ac.uk

ancient and modern history, classical archaeology and ancient history, classical languages & literature, modern languages, Greek and/or Latin language and literature, literae humaniores; BA(Hons), MPhil, MSt

Ruskin School of Drawing and Fine Art; www.ruskin.ox.ac.uk

art history and theory, drawing, fine art, theoretical and practice led research; BFA, MLitt, DPhil

Faculty of English; www.english.ox.ac.uk

classics and English, English and modern languages, English language and literature, (650 to present), English and American studies, film aesthetics, history and English, medieval studies, women's studies; BA(Hons), DPhil, MLitt, MPhil, MSt

History of Art Department; www.hoa.ox.ac. uk

history of art, authenticity and replication in art and visual culture, media and modernity: art and mass culture, 1880–2000; BA(Hons), DPhil, MLitt, MSt

Faculty of History; www.history.ox.ac.uk

ancient and modern history, economic and social history, global and imperial history, history of art and visual culture, history of science, medicine, and technology, late antique and Byzantine studies, medieval history/studies, modern British and European history, US history; BA(Hons), DPhil, MPhil, MSc, MSt

Faculty of Linguistics, Philology and Phonetics; www.ling-phil.ox.ac.uk

comparative /historical and general philology, linguistics, philology and phonetics, modern languages and linguistics

Faculty of Medieval and Modern Languages; www.mod-langs.ox.uk

Celtic, comparative literature or medieval literature, cultural studies, Czech, French, German, linguistics, literature, modern Greek, Italian, medieval literature, language history, medieval & modern languages, European enlightenment, Polish, Portuguese, Russian, Russian, Spanish; BA(Hons), DPhil, MPhil, MSt

Faculty of Music; www.music.ox.ac.uk

aesthetics & criticism, chamber music, choral studies/ conducting performance, composition, analysis and criticism, dance music, ethnomusicology, historical musicology, jazz, musical history, orchestration, theory & analysis; BMus, DPhil, MA(Hons), MPhil, MSt

Faculty of Oriental Studies; www.orinst.ox. ac.uk

Buddhist studies, Chinese studies, eastern Christianity, Egyptology and ancient near east, south and inner Asia and East Asian studies, Hebrew and Jewish studies, Islamic world, Japanese studies, Korean studies; BA(Hons), DPhil, MPhil, MSt

Faculty of Philosophy; www.philosophy.ox. ac.uk

aesthetics, Aquinas, Aristotle, ethics, formal logic, Frege, history of philosophy, knowledge and reality, Kant, logic and language, mathematics, medieval philosophy, neuroscience, philosophy of mind, philosophy of physics, Plato, post-Kantian philosophy, religion, Russell, Wittgenstein; BA(Hons), BPhil, MPhil, PhD

Faculty of Theology; www.theology.ox.ac. uk

history, literature and theology of the old testament, the New Testament, development of early church doctrine/ from a contemporary perspective, history & doctrine, biblical studies, religious studies philosophical theology, eastern Christian studies, applied theology; BA(Hons), BTh, MTh, MSt, MLitt, MPhil, DPhil, PGDip/Cert

Division of Mathematical, Physical and Life Sciences; www.ox.ac.uk/divisions/ mpls

Dept of Chemistry; www.chemistry.ox.ac. uk

chemical biology, inorganic chemistry, mathematical techniques, medical chemistry, organic and chemical biology, organic reactions/synthesis, organometallic chemistry, physical and theoretical chemistry, quantum mechanics, reaction mechanisms, solid state chemistry, spectroscopy, theoretical chemistry, thermodynamics; DPhil, MChem, MSc

Oxford University Computing Laboratory; www.comlab.ox.ac.uk

computer science/ and mathematics, computional biology, foundations, logic & structures, information systems, numerical analysis, programming languages, software engineering; BA(Hons), MSc, DPhil

Dept of Engineering Science; www.eng.ox. ac.uk

biomedical engineering, chemical engineering, process engineering, civil and offshore engineering, electrical and opto-electronic engineering, electronic engineering, information engineering, control and vision engineering, materials engineering, mechanical/civil engineering; DPhil, MEng, MSc

Doctoral Training Centre

biological physics, mathematical geneticsand computational biology, medical imaging and signals; DPhil

Division of Materials; www.materials.ox.ac. uk

materials science, materials structures and mechanical properties of metals, nanoelectronics, non-metallic materials; composites, polymers, packaging materials, superconducting materials, semiconducting materials, etc; DPhil, MEng, MSc

Mathematical Institute; www.maths.ox.ac. uk

algebra, analysis, applied maths, statistics, geometry, pure maths, etc; BA(Hons), DPhil, MCF, MFoCS, MS, MSc

Dept of Physics; www.physics.ox.ac.uk

atmospheric oceanic and planetary physics, astrophysics, condensed matter physics, particle physics, physics, physics & philosophy, theoretical physics; BA(Hons), DPhil, MPhys, MPhysPhil

Dept of Plant Science; www.lps.plants.ox. ac.uk/plants

biochemistry and cell biology, biological science, biology, comparative developmental genetics, evolution, ecology and systematics, plant science; BA(Hons), DPhil, MRes, MSc

Dept of Statistics; www.stats.ox.ac.uk

applied statistics, bioinformatics, mathematics & statistics; BA(Hons), DPhil, MMath, MSc, PGDip

Dept of Zoology; www.zoo.ox.ac.uk

animal behaviour, biological science, biology, molecular biology and bioinformatics, ornithology; BA(Hons), DPhil, MRes, MSc

Division of Medical Science; www.oc.ac. uk/divisions/medical.science

Dept of Biochemistry; www.bioch.ox.ac.uk

biochemistry, cell biology, chromosome & developmental biology, genetics and molecular biology, infection, immunity and translational medicine, medical sciences, molecular biochemistry & chemical biology, structural biology; DPhil, MBiochem, MSc, PhD

Dept of Cardiovascular Medicine; www. cardiov.ox.ac.uk

cardiovascular science; DPhil

Nuffield Dept of Clinical Laboratory Services; www.ndcls.ox.ac.uk

cellular genetics, clinical laboratory services, radiation oncology radiobiology; DPhil, MSc

Dept of Clinical Neurology; www.clneuro.ox.ac.uk

autoimmune diseases of the nervous system, general and acute neurology, movement disorders, multiple sclerosis, neuropathology of degenerative disorders, stroke; PhD

Dept of Clinical Pharmacology; www.clinpharm.ox.ac.uk

cancer teatment, clinical pharmacology practical drug therapy; DPhil

Dept of Experimental Psychology; www.psy.ox.ac.uk

clinical/ experimental psychology, philosophy & physiology, psychological research; BA(Hons), DPhil, MSc

Wellcome Trust Centre for Human Genetics; www.well.ox.ac.uk

genomic medicine and statistics; PhD

Wetherall Institute of Molecular Medicine; www.imw.ox.ac.uk

cancer, haematology and single gene disorders, immunology and infection; DPhil

Nuffield Dept of Obstetrics & Gynaecology; www.obs-gyn.ox.ac.uk

clinical embryology, human reproduction, obstretics and gynaecology, womens' health; MSc

Nuffield Laboratory of Ophthalmology; www.eye.ox.ac.uk

cataract, diabetic retinopathy and oculoplastics, glaucoma, inherited retinal eye disease, retinal detachment, squint; DPhil, MSc

Nuffield Department of Orthopaedics, Rheumatology and Musculoskeletal Sciences; www.ndorms.ox.ac.uk

orthopaedics, rheumatology; MSc

Dept of Paediatrics Sir William Dunn School of Pathology; www.paediatrics.ox.ac.uk

medicine & physiological sciences infection, immunity and translational medicine chromosome and developmental biology: PhD

Dept of Pharmacology; www.pharm.ox.ac.uk

drug discovery/medicinal chemistry, cell signalling, molecular neuroscience and disease, pharmacology; DPhil, MSc

Dept of Physiology, Anatomy, and Genetics; www.dpag.ox.ac.uk

cardiac science, metabolic and respiratory control, cellular neuroscience, molecular neuroscience and disease, systems neuroscience, development and reproduction; MPhil, MSc

Dept of Psychiatry; www.pschiatry.ox.ac.uk

child & adolescent psychiatry, eating disorders, experimental psychopathology and cognitive therapy, forensic psychiatry, molecular neuropathology, old age psychiatry, psychopharmacology, suicide research; DPhil, MRCPsych

Division of Public Health & Primary Health Care; www.dphpc.ox.ac.uk

evidence-based healthcare, global health science; DPhil, MSc

Nuffield Dept of Surgery; www.surgery.ox.ac.uk

cardiothoracic surgery, diagnostic imaging, integrated immunology, interventional neuroradiology, orthopaedic surgery; DPhil, MCh, MSc

Divison of Social Sciences; www.socsci.ox.ac.uk

Oxford Institute of Ageing; www.ageing.ox.ac.uk

economic security, health, longevity and bio-demography and technology, intergenerational relationships and communities, work and retirement; DPhil, MPhil

School of Anthropology and Museum Ethnography, Institute of Social and Cultural Anthroplogy; www.anthro.ox.ac.uk

material anthropology and museum ethnography, medical anthropology, migration studies, social anthropology, visual anthropology; DPhil

Institute of Cognitive & Evolutionary Anthropology; www.iceq.ox.ac.uk

anthropology, cognitive and evolutionary anthropology: DPhil, MSc

Institute of Human Sciences; www.ihs.ox. ac.uk

human sciences; BA(Hons)

Centre for Anthropology and Mind, Centre on Migration, Policy & Society

civil society & everyday life, dynamics of migration, migrants /& labour markets, migration; DPhil, MPhil

PittRivers Museum; www.prm.ox.ac.uk

material anthropology and museum ethnography, visual anthropology; DPhil, MPhil, MSc

School of Archaeology; www.arch.ox.ac.uk

archeological science, archaeology & anthropology, classical archaeology & ancient history, European archaeology, landscape archaeology, world archaeology; BA(Hons), DPhil, MLitt, MSc, MSt

SAID Business School; www.sbs.ox.ac.uk

economics and management/ in materials/financial economics, financial economics, financial strategy, law and finance, management, management research, organisational leadership, public policy, strategy & innovation; BA(Hons), DPhil, MBA, MEng MSc, Oxford Dip

Dept of Economics; www.economics.ox.ac. uk

economics, economics for development, economics & management, engineering, economics and management, history & economics engineering, economics & management, financial economics, philosophy, politics & economics; BA(Hons), DPhil, MEng, MSc

Dept of Education; www.education.ox.ac. uk

applied linguistics and second language, child development and education, comparative & international education, e-learning, educational research methodology, HE, learning and teaching; DPhil, MSc, PGCE

School of Geography & the Environment; www.geog.ox.ac.uk

biodiversity, conservation & management, environmental change & management, nature, and practice of geography, nature, society & environmental policy, water science, policy & management; BA(Hons), DPhil, MSc

Dept of International Development; www. qeh.ox.ac.uk

development studies, diplomatic studies, economics for development, forced migration, global governance and diplomacy; Cert/Dip, DPhil, MPhil, MSc

Oxford Internet Institute; www.oil.ox.ac.uk

information, communication, social science of the internet; DPhil, MSc

Faculty of Law; www.law.ox.ac.uk

criminology and criminal justice, intellectual property law and practice, law, law and finance, law studies in Europe; BA(Hons), BCL, Dip, DPhil, MJur, MLitt, MPhil, MSc, MSt, PGDip

Dept of Politics & International Relations; www.politics.ox.ac.uk

comparative government, history and politics, international relations, philosophy, political theory, politics and economics, politics (comparative government/European politics and society/political theory); BA(Hons), DPhil, MLitt, MPhil, MSc

Dept of Social Policy & Social Work; www. spsw.ox.ac.uk

comparative social policy, evidence based social intervention, family policy, poverty, social security or demography; MPhil, MSc

Dept of Sociology; www.sociology.ox.ac.uk

political sociology, quantitative methods in politics and sociology, sociological theory, sociology, sociology of industrial societies; BA(Hons), DPhil, MPhil, MSc

OXFORD BROOKES UNIVERSITY
www.brookes.ac.uk

School of Arts & Humanities; www.ah. brookes.ac.uk

English and Drama; www.ah.brookes.ac. uk/english
contemporary literature, creative writing, drama, post-colonial literatures, Victorian popular theatre, women and modernism; BA(Hons), MA, PhD

Film Studies; www.ah.brookes.ac.uk/ filmstudies
film studies; BA (Hons), MA

Fine Art; www.ah.brookes.ac.uk;art
fine art, 3D design, fashon/textiles and graphic design composition; BA(Hons), MA

History; www.ah.brookes.ac.uk/history
history, history of art, history of medicine; BA(Hons), MA

Dept of Modern Languages; www.ah. brookes.ac.uk/languages
European business, culture and language, French studies, Japanese studies, Italian, Mandarin, Spanish; BA(Hons), MA

Dept of Music; www.ah.brookes.ac.uk/ music
contemporary practice in composition, music, music on stage and screen, popular culture; BA(Hons), BSc(Hons), MA

Oxford International Centre for Publishing Studies; www.ah.brookes.ac.uk/publishing
digital publishing, publishing – magazines, journals, books, language; BA(Hons), European Master in Publishing; MA

School of Built Environment; www. brookes.ac.uk/schools/be
advanced architectural design, architecture, building: performance and design, cities – environment, design and development, city and regional planning, construction project management, environmental assessment and management/technology, environmental impact assessment, historic conservation, interior architecture, international architectural regeneration, leisure planning, planning, project management, real estate, spatial planning, surveying and commercial management, tourism: development, transport planning, urban design; BA(Hons)/BSc(Hons), Cert, FBE, FdSc, MArch, MPhil, MPlan, MRes, MSc, PGCert, PGDip, PhD

Business School; www.business.brookes. ac.uk
accounting, management, enterprise, business information systems, business management economics, business and marketing, e-business, e-marketing, finance, information technology, innovation, creativity and enterprise, international HRM, international business economics/hospitality and tourism management/hotel and resort management, international business, hospitality management, tourism management, management economics, management for business; BA(Hons), BSc(Hons), Certs, DCaM, DBA, Dips, MA, MBA, MRes, MSc, PhD

School of Health and Social Care; www. shsc.brookes.ac.uk
adult nursing, cancer care, children & families, children's nursing, drugs and alcohol, health and social care, learning disability nursing, mental health nursing, midwifery, occupational therapy, operating department practice, physical rehabilitation & enablement, traditional acupuncture; BSc/BScHons, DipHE, Foundation degrees, MPhil, PhD

School of Life Sciences; www.brookes. ac.uk/lifesci
animal behaviour and welfare, applied human/sport and exercise nutrition, bioimaging with molecular technology, biological sciences, biomedical science, biotechnology, cell and molecular biology, conservation ecology, environmental management & technology, environmental sciences/conservation biology/ ecology / environmental / management / monitoring, equine science, exercise, nutrition and health, human biology, nutrition, public health nutrition, sport and exercise science; BA(Hons)/BSc(Hons), MSc, PGDip, PhD

School of Technology; www.tech. brookes.ac.uk
advanced engineering design, business informatics/ information systems/statistics, communication and network engineering, communication networks, computer-aided mechanical engineering, computer

networks and multimedia systems, computer science, computing, digital media production/music, ebusiness, electrical and electronic engineering, high speed networks & distributed systems, information systems, information technology management for business, mathematical sciences, mathematics and statistics, mechanical engineering, media technology, medical statistics, motorsport – performance & automotive technology/engineering, multimedia production, racing engine design, road and race car technology, software engineering, software engineering, sound & media technology, statistics, web technologies; BEng/MEng, FdSc, HNC, MPhil, MSc, PhD

Westmister School of Education; www. brookes.ac.uk

classroom support, communication, media and culture, early childhood studies, early years, education and human development, education for international schools, educational audiology, educational practice, ethics, hearing impairment, mind, brain and learning, performing arts, post compulsory education, practical and contextual theology, practice framework, primary teacher education/training, religion, religion, culture and ethics, secondary teacher training, sport and coaching studies, theology; BA(Hons), BA/BSSc(Hons), Cert Ed, FdA, MA, MPhil, PGCE, PGDip, PhD

UNIVERSITY OF PAISLEY
www.paisley.ac.uk

Faculty of Business & Creative Industries; www.paisley.ac.uk/schools/depts/business

Business School; www.uws.ac.uk/schoolsdepts/business

accounting, business analysis/economics/studies, corporate real estate management, enterprise, event management, HR management, information management, international business economics/financial management/marketing, law, management, tourism

School of Creative and Cultural Industries; www.uws.ac.uk/schoolsdepts/mlm

broadcast journalism/production, commercial music, creative media practice, digital art, film-making & screen writing, journalism, languages, music technology, performance, sports journalism; BA, BA(Hons), BAcc, ExecMBA, MA, MSc, PGDip, PhD

Faculty of Science & Technology; www. paisley.ac.uk/schools/depts/es

Biological Science; www.paisley.ac.uk/schools/depts/es/biol

applied bioscience and psychology/zoology/forensic investigation / immunology / microbiology / multimedia, biology, biomedical science, earth science, environment, environmental biology, forensic science, general science, health and lifestyle, health science; BSc(Hons), CertHE, DipHE, MSc, PhD

Centre for Environment & Waste Management; www.paisley.ac.uk/schools/depts/es/cewm

managing environmental responsibilities, occupational safety and health, waste management with environmental management, working with environmental responsibilities; BSc, IOSHCert, MSc, PGDip

Chemistry & Chemical Engineering; www. paisley.ac.uk/schools/depts/es/chemistry

chemical engineering, chemistry, forensic science, health science, medicinal chemistry, occupational safety and health, pharmaceutical science; BEng(Hons), BSc(Hons), MSc, PhD

Design & Engineering; www.paisley.ac.uk/schools/dept/es/eng

civil engineering, computer-aided design/engineering, design/with manufacturing systems/product development, engineering management, mechanical engineering, motorsport design engineering, product design & development, quality; BEng(Hons), GradDip, MSc

Earth Science; www.paisley.ac.uk/schools/dept/es/geology

earth science with applied bioscience/chemistry/physics/geology; BSc(Hons)

Mathematics & Statistics; www.paisley.ac.uk/schools/depts/es/maths

business analysis, computational methods/number theory, mathematical science/ education, simulation, statistics; BA(Hons), BSc(Hons), MSc, PhD

Physics; www.paisley.ac.uk/schools/depts/es/physics

medical technology, microscale sensors, physics, sensor design; BSc(Hons), Cert, MSc, PgD, PhD

Sports, Exercise & Therapy; www.paisley.ac.uk/schools/depts/es/sports-studies

sports therapy

School of Computing; www.paisley.ac.uk/schools/depts/computing

advanced computer systems development, business technology, computer animation/ames development/ames technology/networking, computing, information technology, management of ebusiness, multimedia and web authoring, multimedia technology; BA(Hons), BSc(Hons), MSc, PGDip

Faculty of Education, Health & Social Science; www.paisley.ac.uk/schools/depts

School of Education; www.paisley.ac.uk/schools/depts/education

chartered teacher & CPD for school teachers, childhood studies, education (secondary), inclusive education, primary education; BA, BEd MEd, PGCert/Dip

School of Health, Nursing & Midwifery; www.paisley.ac.uk/schools/depts/hnm

child protection, community mental health nursing, community nursing, gerontologics, health studies, independent and supplementary non-medical prescribing, midwifery, nursing studies, occupational health nursing, orthopaedic nursing, palliative care, perioperative nursing, public health nursing, unscheduled practice; BSc(Hons), MSc, PGCert

School of Social Sciences; www.paisley.ac.uk/schools/depts/socialsciences

alcohol and drug studies, careers guidance and development, criminal justice, economics, politics, psychology, race equality, social policy, social sciences, social work, sociology; BA(Hons), MSc, PGDip/Cert

UNIVERSITY OF PLYMOUTH
www.plymouth.ac.uk

Faculty of Arts; www.plymouth.ac.uk/arts

School of Architecture, Design, Building & Construction

architecture, design and structures, architectural conservation technology/ professional practice, 18th century: art, literature, identity, architectural history landscape; BA(Hons), Grad Dip, HND, MA, PhD

Archaeology

archaeology, heritage & archaeology, history; BSc(Hons), FdA, FdSc, PhD

Art, Design, Media & Performance

architecture, art, art history, crafts, dance, design (3D, graphic & illustration), drama, English and creative writing, fashion and textiles, film, fine art, media digital art and multimedia, photography, publishing & journalism, theatre; BA(Hons), BEd, BSc(Hons), FdA, HNC, MA, MRes, PGCE, PGDip, PhD,FD

Humanities & Languages

art, art history, eighteenth century: art, literature, identity, English and creative writing/media arts/modern languages/French, English: literature, culture and modernity, fine art, history, identity, journalism, modern languages, politics, social history, sociology, Spanish; BA(Hons), MA, MPhil, MRes, PhD

Faculty of Health & Social Work; www.plymouth.ac.uk/hsw

Health & Social Work

applied psychosocial sciences, biomedical sciences, criminology and criminal justice studies, food science, health care practice, health professions and therapies, mental health, midwifery, nursing, nutrition and dietetics, occupational therapy, psychology, social work and community work/law/politics/psychology, advanced occupational therapy: modules cognitive behavioural therapy: modules health and social care education: modules mental health: modules postgraduate modules: neurological rehabilitation, women's health: modules; BSc(Hons), FdA, FdSc, MA, MSc, PGCE, PGDip/Cert

Health Professions
dietetics, mental health, neurological rehabilitation, occupational therapy, physiotherapy, podiatry, women's health; BSc(Hons), DipHE, MSc, PGCert, PGDip

Nursing & Midwifery
adult/child health nursing, emergency care, health studies, midwifery, surgical care, specialist community public health nursing; BSc(Hons), DipHE

Faculty of Social Science & Business; www.plymouth.ac.uk/ssb
accounting, applied strategy and international security, banking, business, criminology and criminal justice studies, economics, EFL, finance, personnel and development, hospitality, international logistics, international relations, global security and development, international supply chain management/shipping, law, management and leadership, marketing, law, legal practice, maritime and marine law, organizational leadership, personnel and development, politics, port management, public management, public services, shipping and logistics, social research, sociology, sports, tourism and hospitality management; BA(Hons), BSc(Hons), GradDip, MA, MBM, MSc, LIM, PGDip, Masters in Business and Management

Faculty of Education; www.plymouth.ac.uk/education

School of Early Years and Primary Education Studies
early childhood studies, early years, Steiner Wardolf education; BA(Hons), BEd, PGCE

School of Secondary & Further Education Studies
PGCE secondary art and design/citizenship/ drama/ English/geography/mathematics/music, education and training, music, post-compulsory education and training, science (biology, chemistry, physics), teaching in the lifelong learning sector, teaching assistants; BA(Hons), FdA, PGCE

School of Partnership, Enterprise and Professional Studies
early childhood studies, early years & primary education studies, education, teacher training,

learning for sustainability, secondary & further education; EdD, MA, MSc PGCert, PGDip

Faculty of Science; www.plymouth.ac.uk/science

School of Biological Sciences
animal science, biomedicine, bioscience, environmental biology & conservation, marine biology; BSc(Hons), MRes, PGDip

School of Earth, Ocean & Environmental Sciences
chemistry, earth sciences, ecology and conservation, environmental sciences, environmental studies, geography, geology, geosciences, marine biology, marine sports science, marine studies, mechanical, marine and materials engineering, rural, resource and conservation management; BEng, BSc(Hons), FdSc, MGeol, MRes, MSc, PGCE, PGDip

School of Geography
enviromental management, geography, planning, sustainable environment, sustainable transport; BSc(Hons), MRes, MSc, PGDip

School of Psychology
applied psychology, psychology, criminology and criminal justice studies; BSc(Hons), MPhil, MSc/ PgDip, PhD

Faculty of Technology; www.plymouth.ac.uk/technology

School of Computing, Communications and Electronics
business computing, communication engineering, computer music/science, electrical and electronic engineering, electronic communication engineering, electronics & communications design, games and graphics, multimedia technology, network systems engineering, networks, new media design, security, software development, web applications and technologies; BSc(Hons), BA(Hons), BEng, MEng, MRes, MSc, PhD

School of Engineering
architecture, design and structures, building & construction engineering, building surveying and the environment, civil coastal & structural engineering – coastal engineering, civil engineering and computer aided design, construction management and the environment, environmental construction surveying, mechanical, marine and composite engineering – mechanical engineering, marine

technology, marine sports technology, mechanical design and manufacture, mechanical engineering and computer aided design; BEng(Hons), BSc(Hons), MEng(Hons), MRes, MSc, PGDip, PhD

School of Mathematics & Statistics

applied mathematics, applied statistics, epidemiology, industrial and engineering mathematics, mathematics, maths education, secondary mathematics, statistics; BSc(Hons), MMath, MStat, MSc, PhD

Peninsula College of Medicine and Dentistry; www.pcmd.ac.uk

Peninsula Dental School; www.pcmd.ac.uk/dentistry

Pensinsula School of Medicine; www.pcmd.ac.uk/pms

Peninsula Graduate School; www.pcmd.ac.uk/gradschool

Degrees validated by the University of Plymouth offered at:

SOUTH DEVON COLLEGE
www.southdevon.ac.uk

animal science, automotive master technician diploma, biosciences, building services engineering, business, computing, construction and building services, creative digital media, teaching in the lifelong learning sector, law, early years care and education, events and conference management, healthcare practice, hospitality management, mechanical engineering, electrical and electronic engineering, outdoor education, performance practice and events management, postgraduate certificate of education, 3D design, tourism and hospitality management, tourism management, visual studies, yacht operations, young people and community services; BA/BSc, BSc(Hons), FD, HNC, HND, PGCE

TRURO COLLEGE
www.trurocollege.ac.uk

applied geography, applied psychology, archaeology, art & design, biology, biomedical studies, communication & cultural studies, community studies, complementary therapies, computer technology, contemporary world jazz, counselling, dance, digital imaging/visualization, early childhood education, education/and training, hairdressing & salon management, history heritage, HRM, laboratory technology, law, literary studies, media advertising, music performance, outdoor educ, performance photography, popular music, public admininistration, public health, silversmithing & jewellery, sound engineering, sport performance, sports coaching & therapy, sports science, web technology; BA(Hons), BSc, FdA, FdSc, HNC, HND, PCET, PGCE, UnivCert/Dip

School of Engineering

Undergraduate courses, Postgraduate courses

UNIVERSITY OF PORTSMOUTH
www.port.ac.uk

Portsmouth Business School; www.port.ac.uk/departments/faculties/portsmouthbusinessschool

Department of Accounting and Finance; www.port.ac.uk/departments/academic/accountingandfinance

accountancy, business, business English, finance, financial decision analysis, financial management, forensic accounting, international finance and trade; BA(Hons), MSc

Department of Economics; www.port.ac.uk/departments/academic/economics

applied economics/with business law, banking, business economics, e-banking, cultural and tourism management, economic and business forecasting, economics, finance, international business and

English, marine resource economics; BA(Hons), BScEcon(Hons), MA, MSc, PgDip

Department of Human Resource and Marketing Management; www.port.ac.uk/departments/academic/hrmm

business administration/studies, coaching and development, hospitality management/with tourism, HR development/management, HRM, marketing, marketing/digital media, psychology, sales management, training management and consultancy; BA(Hons), MA, MPhil, PGCet/Dip, PhD

School of Law; www.port.ac.uk/departments/academic/law

corporate governance, criminology, employment law, European studies, forensic accounting, international business law, law; BA(Hons), LlB, LlM

Department of Strategy and Business Systems; www.port.ac.uk/academic/sbs

business/administration/enterprise systems/development, European business, international business studies, leadership & management, leadership in health and wellbeing, management, project management & leadership, risk management, strategic quality management; BA(Hons), FdA, HND, MB, MSc, PGDip/Cert

Faculty of Creative and Cultural Industries; www.port.ac.uk/departments/faculties/facultyofcreativeartsandindustries

Portsmouth School of Architecture; www.port.ac.uk/departments/academic/architecture/

architecture, interior design, professional practice, sustainable architecture, urban design; BA(Hons), MA, MArch

School of Art, Design and Media; www.port.ac.uk/departments/academic/adm

3D design for digital media, art, design, fashion and textile design with enterprise, fine art, graphic design, illustration, photography; BA(Hons), MA

School of Creative Arts, Film and Media; www.port.ac.uk/departments/academic/scafm

creative and performing arts, creative writing drama, drama, English, entertainment technology, film studies, media studies, television studies; BA(Hons), MA

School of Creative Technologies; www.port.ac.uk/departments/academic/ct

animation, computational sound, computer animation, computer games enterprise/technology, creative computing technologies, creative technologies and enterprise, digital media, entertainment technology, music and sound technology, television and film production, video and broadcasting; BA(Hons), BSc(Hons), FdSc, MSc

Portsmouth Centre for Enterprise, Institute for Industrial Research; www.port.ac.uk/departments/academic/pce

data analysis, image processing, monitoring systems and ambient, intelligent robotics, traffic analysis and resource management

Faculty of Humanities and Social Science; www.port.ac.uk/departments/faculties/facultyofhumanities

Institute of Criminal Justice Studies; www.port.ac.uk/departments/academic/icjs

counter fraud & criminal justice studies/counter corruption studies, crime and criminology, criminology and applied research/community safety/criminal justice/criminal psychology, forensic studies, criminology and criminal psychology, international criminal justice, investigation and evidence, police studies, policing, policy and leadership, risk and security management; BSc(Hons), FdA, LlB, MSc

School of Education and Continuing Studies; www.port.ac.uk/departments/academic/iecs

business studies, childhood and youth studies, early years care and education, education administration, education and training/management, English, geography, learning support, learning and teaching/in HE, mathematics, modern foreign languages, PGCE post compulsory education, practice and pedagogy in education, science learning and teaching in HE; BA(Hons), CertEd, FdA, MA, MSc, PGCE, PGCert

School of Languages and Area Studies; www.port.ac.uk/departments/academic/slas

American studies & history/English, applied languages, applied linguistics & TESOL, area studies, combined modern languages, communication & English studies/language skills, English language, European studies, French studies, German studies, international business English/development studies/ & languages/property development and languages/

relations and languages/trade, languages & international trade/American studies/European studies/law, logistics and business English, Spanish and Latin American studies, technical communication, translation studies; BA(Hons), MA

School of Social, Historical and Literary Studies; www.port.ac.uk/departments/academic/sshls
criminology/media studies/psychology, English & history/media/literature, English literature, English with psychology, European law & policy, European studies, government, history/& politics, history & heritage, history of war, culture & society, international journalism & languages, international relations/ & history/politics, journalism & English language/English literature/entertainment, local government, politics, sociology, literature, crime and culture/& identity, memory cultures, public administration, social research methods; BA(Hons), BSc(Hons), FdA, MPA, MSc

Faculty of Science; www.port.ac.uk/ departments/faculties/faculty of science

School of Biological Sciences; www.port.ac.uk/departments/academic/biology
aquatic environmental chemistry, biochemistry, biodiversity, biology, biotechnology, ecology and evolution, forensic biology, developmental biology, marine sciences, microbiology, molecular genetics and forensics, organisms and ecosystems; BSc(Hons), MPhil, PhD

School of Earth and Environmental Sciences; www.port.ac.uk/departments/academic/isees
crisis & disaster management, earth sciences, engineering geology & geotechnics, environmental forensics/hazards/environmental/environmental science, geological and environmental hazards, geological hazards, geology, marine environmental science, palaeobiology and evolution; BSc(Hons), MEng(Hons), MSc

Department of Geography; www.port.ac.uk/departments/academic/geography
environmental geography, geography, GIS, human geography, physical geography; BA(Hons), BSc(Hons), MSc

School of Professionals Complementary to Dentistry; www.port.ac.uk/departments/academic/dentistry
dental hygiene and dental therapy, dental nursing, science and dental therapy; BSc (Hons), CertHE, FdSc

School of Health Sciences and Social Work; www.port.ac.uk/departments/academic/shssw
healthcare, applied medical technology, child care social work, clinical health science, clinical physiology, diagnostic radiography, emergency care practice, medical imaging, operating department practice, paramedic science, social work, speech, language and communication science, therapeutic radiography; BSc(Hons), DipHE, FdSc, GradDip, MSc, PGDip

Faculty of Technology www.port.ac.uk/departments/faculties/facultyoftechnology

www.port.ac.uk/departments/academic/civils

www.port.ac.uk/departments/academic/comp

www.port.ac.uk/departments/academic/icg

www.port.ac.uk/departments/academic/ece

www.port.ac.uk/departments/academic/edam

www.port.ac.uk/departments/academic/learningatwork

www.port.ac.uk/departments/academic/maths

www.port.ac.uk/departments/academic/mde

QUEEN MARGARET UNIVERSITY COLLEGE
www.qmuc.ac.uk

School of Business, Enterprise and Management; www.qmuc.ac.uk/be
business management, consumer studies, entrepreneurship, events management, golf and country club

management, hospitality and tourism management, marketing, public services, retail business; BA/BA(Hons), MBA, PhD

The School of Drama and Creative Industries; www.qmuc.ac.u/facultiesschool/drama

arts and cultural management, costume design and construction, drama and performance, festival management; BA/BA(Hons), MA, MBA

The School of Health Sciences; www.qmuc.ac.uk/healthscience

applied pharmacology, dietetics, human biology, nursing, nutrition, occupational and arts therapies, physiotherapy, podiatry, public health nutrition, radiography

Institute for International Health and Development; www.qmuc.ac.uk/iild

health economics, health systems, human resources for health, sexual and reproductive health, social justice, development and health; BSc(Hons), MSc

The School of Social Sciences, Media and Communication; www.qmuc.ac.uk/schools/socialsciences

audiology, culture politics and economy, film, health psychology, marketing, media, PR, public health practice, psychology, screen studies, sociology, speech and language therapy; BSc, BSc(Hons), MSc, PhD

UNIVERSITY OF READING
www.reading.ac.uk

Faculty of Arts and Humanities; www.reading.ac.uk/fah

School of Arts, English and Communication, Design; www.reading.ac.uk/saed

children's literature, early modern literature and drama, English, English literature, European literature and culture/television/ film & theatre/philosophy/politics and international relations/French/German studies/history, history of art & architecture/Italian studies/culture, modern and contemporary writing, 19th-century literature; BA(Hons), MA, MA(Res), PhD

Film, Theatre and Television; www.reading.ac.uk/ftt

film, theatre & Italian/history of art/German/English literature, film studies, television, television & English literature/art, television studies, theatre studies; BA(Hons), MA, MPhil, PhD

Art

art, art and philosophy/psychology/history of art/film & theatre, fine art; BA(Hons), MFA, MPhil, PhD

Typography & Graphic Communication; www.reading.ac.uk/typography

book design, graphic communication, information design, typeface design, typography & graphic communication; BA(Hons), MA, MA(Res), MPhil, PhD

School of Continuing Education; www.reading.ac.uk/conted

archaeology and combined studies, English literature, history, history of art and architecture; Cert HE

School of Humanities; www.reading.ac.uk/humanities

ancient art, ancient history, history of art, the city of Rome, classical and medieval studies, classical studies, the classical tradition, classics; BA(Hons), MA, MPhil, PhD

History of Art; www.reading.ac.uk/arthistory

history of art and architecture/art, English/history/ancient history/ history of art; BA(Hons), MA, MPhil, PhD

Department of History; www.reading.ac.uk/history

early modern history, Franco-British history, history/history of art, medieval studies, modern history; BA(Hons), MARes, MPhil, PhD

Philosophy; www.reading.ac.uk/Phil

ethics, ethics & political theory, value and philosophy, philosophy; BA(Hons), MA, MPhil, PhD

French Studies; www.reading.ac.uk/languages/about/les-aboutfrench.aspx

French, French and Franco-British history, French studies; BA(Hons), MA, MPhil, PhD

Italian; www.reading.ac.uk/languages/about/les-aboutitalian

Italian, Italian and classical studies, Italian studies; BA(Hons), MA, MPhil, PhD

Faculty of Social Sciences; www.reading.ac.uk/internal/fss

Institute of Education; www.reading.ac.uk/education

children's development and learning, creative arts in education, education (art/English/music specialism), deaf studies, equity, inclusion and improvement, language and literacy in education, teaching and learning, theatre arts; BA(Hons), FdA, PGCE, PhD

School of Law; www.reading.ac.uk/law

advanced legal studies, European union law, international law & world order, law & society, law with legal studies in Europe, legal history; DPhil, LLM, MARes, PhD

School of Politics & International Relations; www.reading.ac.uk/spirs

diplomacy, economics, European studies, EU politics, French politics/German politics/history/Italian/philosophy, international law & world order, international security studies, philosophy and politics, politics, strategic studies, war, peace and international relations; BA(Hons), MA, MPhil, PhD

School of Health & Social Care; www.reading.ac.uk/hsc

advanced professional practice, children & young people, counselling, leadership & management, primary care nursing, public health nursing, social work (bursary/employment)/with children and young people, their families and carers/adults, social work practice education; BSc(Hons), Diploma, MSc/PG, PhD

Graduate School in Arts & Humanities

The School of Economics; www.reading.ac.uk/economics

banking and finance in emerging economies, business analysis, business and management in emerging markets, business economics, econometrics; accounting, economic development in emerging markets, economics, international banking and financial services/ business and economic development/finance/economic development/relations; BA(Hons), BSc(Hons), MSc, PhD

Henley Business School; www.henley.ac.uk as at School of Economics

Faculty of Life Sciences; www.reading.ac.uk/internal/lifesci

School of Agriculture, Policy & Development; www.reading.ac.uk/apd

agricultural business management/development economics, agricultural/food economics, agriculture and development agriculture, animal science, applied development studies, consumer behaviour and marketing, development finance/policy, environment and development, environmental and countryside management, food economics, food marketing and business economics, research agricultural and food economics, social development and sustainable livelihoods; BA(Hons), BSc(Hons), MPhil, PhD

School of Biological Sciences; www.reading.ac.uk/biologicalsciences

applied ecology and conservation, biochemistry, biological sciences, biomedical sciences, biometry, environmental biology, horticulture, environmental management, medical microbiology, plant diversity, wildlife management and conservation, zoology; BSc(Hons), MPhil, MSc, PhD

School of Chemistry, Food & Pharmacy; www.reading.ac.uk/fcfp

food science, food technology, nutrition, pharmacy, quality assurance; BSc(Hons), MPharm, MSc, PhD

School of Psychology & Clinical Language Science; www.reading.ac.uk/pcls

childhood and ageing, mental and physical health, neuroscience/of language, psychology/& mathematics/biology/philosophy, speech & language therapy; BSc(Hons), MSc, PhD

School of Systems Engineering; www.reading.ac.uk/sse

artificial intelligence, computational science, computer engineering, computer science and informatics/cybernetics, digital signal processing & communications, electronic engineering, information & communication technology, information technology with management/economics, network & e-business centered computing, robotics, systems engineering; BEng, BSc(Hons), FdSc, MEng, MPhil, MRes, MSc, PhD

School of Construction Management and Engineering; www.reading.ac.uk/CME

building construction and management, building surveying, construction, construction management and surveying, quantity surveying, renewable energy: technology and sustainability; BSc(Hons), MPhil, MSc, PGD, PhD

School of Mathematics, Metereology, & Physics; www.smmp.reading.ac.uk

applied meteorology, computational mathematics, mathematics, mathematics and economics/meterology/psychology/statistics/applied statistics, mathematics of scientific and industrial computation, meteorology, physics; lasers, microscopy, modelling, nanoscience & materials, polymers, remote sensing, surfaces; BSc(Hons), MMath, MPhil, MSc, PhD

ROBERT GORDON UNIVERSITY
www.rgu.ac.uk

Faculty of Health and Social Care

School of Applied Social Studies; www.rgu.ac.uk/social

applied social sciences, mental health, practice learning qualification, psychology, social care, social work, residential child care; BA(Hons), HNc, MSc, PgDip PhD

School of Health Sciences; www.rgu.ac.uk/health

diagnostic radiography, health improvement and health promotion, occupational therapy, physiotherapy, radiography, sport and exercise science, sports nutrition; BSc(Hons), CertHE, MPhil, MSc, PhD

School of Nursing & Midwifery; www.rgu.ac.uk/nursing

acute and mental health nursing, adult/children's/mental health/community, midwifery, nurse education; BN, DipHE, MPhil, MSc, PhD

School of Pharmacy; www.rgu.ac.uk/pharmacy

clinical pharmacy, prescribing science; MPharm, MSc, PGDip, PhD

Aberdeen Business School; www.rgu.ac.uk/abs

agribusiness/food business management, communication with PR, HRM, information studies, international business/marketing management, journalism, purchasing and supply chain management, management studies, marketing, media studies, oil and gas management, publishing, project management, quality management, fashion management, hospitality, international hospitality management/tourism management, law, law & management, retail management, corporate communication and public affairs, journalism, public administration, politics and research methods, construction law & abritration, employment law and practice, international commercial law/information technology law, trade, oil and gas law, information and library studies, information management, information science, knowledge management; BA/BA(Hons), DBA, DInfSc, LlB, LlM, MBA, MPA, MPhil, MSc, PGDip/Cert, PhD

Faculty of Design & Technology

School of Computing/ www.rgu.ac.uk/computing

business information systems, computer science, computing for business & e-commerce/graphics and animation/internet and multimedia, computing: information, information systems technology, multimedia development, software technology/with network management

School of Engineering; www.rgu.ac.uk/eng

computer network & design, electrical engineering, electronic engineering/systems, energy, enviromental technology, health and welfare, information technology management, the knowledge economy, materials and bioengineering/biomaterials, mechanical engineering, offshore engineering, robotics; BSc, BSc(Hons), MPhil, MSc, PhD

Gray's School of Art, Design & Craft; www.rgu.ac.uk/grays

3D design, art & design, design for digital media/industry, fashion design, fine art, graphic design, painting, photographic & electronic media, printmaking, product design, sculpture; BA/BA(Hons), BDes/BDes(Hons), MDes, MRes, PgDip/MA

The Scott Sunderland School of Architecture and Built Environment; www. rgu.ac.uk/sss

architecture design management, architectural technology, construction design and management, construction project management, environments for people, property development, surveying (building surveying/quantity surveying); Grad Dip, MArch, MSc, PhD

ROEHAMPTON UNIVERSITY
www.roehampton.ac.uk

School of Arts; www.roehampton.ac.uk/arts

art history, ballet studies, children's literature, classical civilisation, creative writing, dance anthropology/choreography, dance studies, documentary practices, drama, theatre and performance studies, early modern literature and culture (1500–1700), English language and linguistics/literature, film studies/and screen practice, historical research, history, journalism and news media, media and culture, modern languages, translating and interpreting, music, philosophy, photography, professional writing, religious studies, sociolinguistics, Spanish, TESOL, theology/and religious studies; BA(Hons), MA, MFA, MPhil, PGDip/Cert, PhD, PsychD

School of Business and Social Sciences; www.roehampton.ac.uk/bss

Business; www.roehampton.ac.uk/bss/business

business management/HRM/retail management, international business, international management information systems/finance, marketing; BSc(Hons), MBA, MSc, PGDip, PhD

Computing; www.roehampton.ac.uk/bss/computing

computing with database systems/web and multimedia/computing with information management, computing studies, international management of information systems, information system; BA/BSc, BSc(Hons), MSc/PGDip, PhD

Social Sciences; www.roehampton.ac.uk/bss/socialsciences

childhood & society, criminology, human rights/and society/international relations, social anthropology, sociology; BA/BSc, MA/PGDip/PGCert

School of Education; www.roehampton.ac.uk/education

applied music education, art, craft and design education, education leadership and management, English education, primary education, secondary education, social research methods, special education needs (erasmus mundus), special and inclusive education; BA(Hons), BA/BSc, EdD, FdA, Froebel Certificates and Graduate Certificate, MA, MPhil, PGCEPrimary, PGCESecondary, PhD

School of Human and Life Sciences; www.roehampton.ac.uk/hals

Biological Sciences; www.roehampton.ac.uk/hals/subjectareas/biologicalsciences

anthropology, biodiversity and conservation, biological anthropology, biological sciences, biology, biomedical sciences, conservation biology, ecology, environmental sciences, human biosciences, life sciences, neurobiology, primatology, zoology

Health Sciences; www.roehampton.ac.uk/hals/subjectareas/healthsciences

clinical neuroscience, clinical nutrition, diabetes, health & the community, health & social care/human sciences, health sciences, health studies, nutrition, nutrition & health, stress & health

Psychology; www.roehampton.ac.uk/hals/subjectareas/psychology

applied music psychology, counselling, counselling psychology, health, integrative counselling, psychological research methods, psychology, psychotherapy

Sport Sciences; www.roehampton.ac.uk/hals/subjectareas/psychotherapy

coaching, exercise, nutrition and health, sport & exercise biomechanics/exercise physiology/exercise science, sport psychology, sport science, sport studies; BA/BSc, BSc(Hons), MA, MPhil, MRes, MSc, PGDip/PGCert, PhD, PsychD

Arts and Play Therapies; www.roehampton. ac.uk/hals/subjectareas/ artsandplaytherapies

art therapy, arts & play therapies, dance movement psychotherapy, drama therapy, music therapy, play therapy; MA, MPhil, PGDip, PhD

ROYAL COLLEGE OF ART
www.rca.ac.uk

Departments

animation, architecture, art & design, ceramics & glass, communication, conservation, contemporary art, critical and historical studies, curating, design interactions, design products, drawing studio, fashion menswear, fashion womenswear, goldsmithing, history of design, innovation design engineering, metalwork & jewellery, painting, photography, printmaking, sculpture, silversmithing, textiles, vehicle design; MA, MPhil, PGCert, PhD

ROYAL SCOTTISH ACADEMY OF MUSIC & DRAMA
www.rsmad.ac.uk

acting, arts in social contexts, classical and contemporary text, composition, conducting, contemporary performance practice, digital film and television, modern ballet, musical theatre, opera, technical and production, performance, Scottish music; BA(Honours), BEd(Hons), BMus(Hons), MA, MA(Musical Theatre), MMus, MOpera, MPhil, PGDip, PhD

UNIVERSITY OF ST ANDREWS
www.st-andrews.ac.uk

Faculty of Arts

School of Art History; www-ah.st-andrews. ac.uk

art history, history of photography, mediaeval studies, museum & gallery studies; GradCert, GradDip, MA, MLitt, MPhil, PhD

School of Classics; www.st-andrews.ac.uk/ classics

ancient history, classical studies, Greek, Latin; MA, MLitt, MPhil, PGDip, PhD

School of Economics & Finance; www.st-andrews.ac.uk/economics

analytical finance, applied economics, applied quantitative finance, economics, international finance/ strategy & economics, money, banking & finance, sustainable development; BSc, MA, MSc, MPhil, PhD

School of English; www.st-andrews.ac.uk/ english

creative writing, English, mediaeval English, Romantic/Victorian studies, Shakespeare studies, TESOL, women, writing & gender; GradDip, MA, MLitt, MPhil, PhD

School of History; www.st-andrews.ac.uk/ history

Arabic, central & Eastern European studies, environmental history, history, international political theory/ relations/security studies, Iranian studies, mediaeval history/studies, Middle East studies, modern historiography/history/studies, peace & conflict studies, reformation studies, Scottish historical studies/history; GradDip, MA, DLitt, MPhil, PhD

School of International Relations; www.st-andrews.ac.uk/intrel

international relations, sustainable development; MA, MLitt, MPhil, MRes, PhD

School of Management; www.st-andrews.ac.uk/management

corporate social responsibility, finance & accounting/management, HRM, international business, management, managing in the creative industries, marketing, research (management studies); BSc, DipRes, MA, MLitt, MSc, MRes, PhD

School of Modern Languages; www.st-andrews.ac.uk/modlang

advanced language studies, European humanities, cultural identity studies, French studies, German, Italian studies, language /& linguistics, mediaeval studies, Russian, Russian, Central & Eastern European studies, Spanish, Spanish & Latin American studies; DLang, MA, MLitt, MPhil, PGDip, PhD

School of Philosophical, Anthropological & Film Studies; www.st-andrews.ac.uk/philosophy

film studies, logic & philosophy of science, philosophy, social anthropology; BSc, MA, MLitt, MPhil, MRes, PhD

Faculty of Divinity

School of Divinity; www.st-andrews.ac.uk/divinity

Bible & the contemporary world, biblical studies, divinity, Hebrew, New Testament, theological studies, theology; BD, MA, MLitt, MPhil, MTheol, PGDip, PhD

Faculty of Medicine

Bute Medical School; www.medicine.st-andrews.ac.uk

health psychology, medicine; BSc, MD, MPhil, MSc, PhD

Faculty of Science

School of Biology; www.biology.st-andrews.ac.uk

behavioural/cell/environmental/evolutionary/marine/molecular biology, biochemistry, biology, ecology & conservation, neuroscience, zoology; BSc, MPhil, MRes, PhD

School of Chemistry; www.ch.st-andrews.ac.uk

biomolecular/chemical sciences, chemistry, materials science; BSc, MChem, MSci, PgDip, PhD

School of Computer Science; www.cs.st-andrews.ac.uk

advanced computer science, artificial intelligence, computer science, information technology, internet computer, management & IT, networks & distributed systems, software engineering; BSc, MPhil, MSc, PhD

School of Geography & Geosciences; www.st-andrews.ac.uk/gg

environmental geoscience/history, geography, geoscience, managing environmental change, physical geography & geosciences, sustainable development; BSc, MA, MLitt, MPhil, MRes, MSc, PGCert, PGDip, PhD

School of Mathematics & Statistics; www-maths.mcs.st-andrews.ac.uk

applied mathematics, applied statistics & datamining, mathematics, pure mathematics, statistics; BSc, GradDip, MA, MLitt, MMath, MPhil, MSc, PhD

School of Physics & Astronomy; www.st-andrews.ac.uk/physics

astrophysics, physics, theoretical physics; BSc, EngDoc, MPhys, MSc, PhD

School of Psychology; www.psy.st-andrews.ac.uk

behavioural & neural sciences, evolutionary & comparative psychology, learning disabilities, neuroscience, psychology; BSc, MA, MPhil, MRes, MSc, PhD

UNIVERSITY OF SALFORD
www.salford.ac.uk

Faculty of Arts, Media & Social Sciences; www.famss.salford.ac.uk

School of Art & Design; www.artdes. salford.ac.uk

advertising design, animation, art & design, arts and museum management, communication design, computer and video games, contemporary fine art, creative games/technology, design for digital media, design management/for the creative industries, fashion, graphic design, heritage studies, interior design, journalism and design studies, museum & heritage exhibition design, product design, visual arts; BA(Hons), BSc(Hons), HND, MA, PGDip, PhD

School of English, Politics & Contemporary History; www.espach.salford.ac.uk

Creative Writing: innovation and experiment, drama and performance studies film studies/creative writing/linguistics/cultural studies/journalism, English, English language/literature

Sociology & Criminology

crime and criminal justice, criminology, cultural studies, human rights & ethics, journalism, law, politics, psychology, social sciences, sociology

Contemporary History

contemporary history, contemporary military & international history, east and west European political studies, intelligence & security studies, international relations and globalization/politics, journalism & politics, terrorism & security, war studies

School of Languages; www.languages. salford.ac.uk

Arabic/English translation and interpreting, Chinese/English, interpreting, linguistics & a modern language, modern language studies/with TESOL, translating and interpreting, translating for international business

School of Media, Music & Performance; www.smmp.salford.ac.uk

animation, compositional studies, computer & video games, contemporary theatre practice, critical musicology, English, fiction film production, film screenwriting/ studies, broadcasting, journalism, media & performance, media production/technology, mobile & internet television, music, performance, popular music & production/ & recording, popular musicology, radio production, social media, television & radio, television and radio scriptwriting, television documentary production, wildlife documentary production; BA(Hons), BSc(Hons), HND, MA, MPhil, MSc, PgCert, PgDip, PhD

Faculty of Business, Law & the Built Environment; www.flbe.salford.ac.uk

Salford Business School; www.business. salford.ac.uk

accounting, business and management studies/with law, business information technology/management/studies with financial management/HRM, corporate finance, events management, finance, financial services management, hospitality management, information security/technology, international banking and finance/business management/marketing management/tourism, investment banking, management, managing information technology, marketing, operational research and applied statistics, personnel practice, procurement, logistics and supply chain management, project management, sport and leisure management, tourism management; BA(Hons), BSc(Hons), CertHE, DipHE, Foundation degrees, Grad Cert, HNC, HND, MA, MBA, MPhil, ProfDip, ProfPGDip, PhD

School of the Built Environment; www. sobe.salford.ac.uk

advanced manufacturing in construction, architectural design and technology, building surveying, built environment for healthcare, construction & property, construction law & practice, construction management, construction project management, disaster mitigation & reconstruction, facilities management, project management in construction, property management and investment, quantity surveying, real estate development, real management, regeneration and urban renewal; BSc(Hons), DBEnv, DConst-Mangt, DRealEst, MSc, PGDip/Cert, PhD

Salford Law School; www.law.salford.ac.uk

construction law & practice, environmental law, health care law, health law, health and safety law, international business law and regulation, law; LlB, LLM, MA, MSc, PgCert, PgDip

Faculty of Health & Social Care; www.fhsc.salford.ac.uk

School of Social Work, Psychology & Public Health; www.swpph.salford.ac.uk
adult care, ageing, health and wellbeing, applied psychology (therapies), child care, complementary medicine, complementary therapy, counselling & psychotherapy, counselling, psychology/criminology, public health, social policy: protecting adults and children, social work; nursing, sociology; BA, MA, MPhil, MSc, PgCert, PgDip, PhD

School of Health, Sport & Rehabilitation Sciences; www.healthcare.salford.ac.uk
orthopaedics; management, prosthetics & orthotics, physiotherapy; podiatry, occupational therapy, radiography; advanced medical imaging, nuclear medicine, diagnostic radiography, sport and exercise; applied sports science, physical activity and health, sports development/injury rehabilitation/rehabilitation; BSc(Hons), MSc, PGDip/Cert

School of Nursing & Midwifery; www.nursing.salford.ac.uk
adult nursing, advanced nursing (education/practice/research), advanced practice (health and social care/neonatal), ageing, health and well-being, child and adolescent mental health, children's nursing, social care, leadership and management for health care practice, mental health nursing, midwifery, non-medical prescribing, nursing and social work (learning disabilities), public health; BSc, BSc(Hons), DipHE, DProfMed & Social Care, MSc, PGDip/Cert

Faculty of Science, Engineering & Environment; www.fsee.salford.ac.uk

School of Computing, Science & Engineering; www.cse.salford.ac.uk
advanced control systems, aeronautical engineering, aerospace business systems, aerospace design and manufacture/engineering, aerospace technology, aircraft engineering, audio acoustics, audio and video systems, audio production/technology, aviation technology, civil engineering, computer networks/science, creative games, data telecommunications and networks, databases and web-based systems, digital broadcast technology, energy and management/and waste, enterprise technology, gas engineering and management, industrial and commercial combustion engineering, information security, internet computing, manufacturing systems and management, materials physics, mechanical engineering, multimedia and internet technology, noise control, petroleum and gas engineering, physics, pilot studies, professional sound and video technology, robotics and automation, structural engineering, sustainable development, transport engineering and planning, vacuum engineering and applications; BEng, BSc(Hons), HND, MEng, MEnt(Tech), MPhys, MSc, PGDip, PG(Tech)

School of Environmental & Life Sciences; www.els.salford.ac.uk
Biosciences
analytical biosciences & drug design, biochemistry, biology, biomedical science, pharmaceutical science
Geography
applied GIS & remote sensing, aquatic environments, environmental geography, geographical information systems, geography
Environmental Studies
environmental assessment & management, environmental management
Environmental Health
environmental & public health, occupational safety & health, safety, health & environment
Housing & Regeneration
community governance, housing practice, regeneration (neighbourhood renewal), sustainable communities
Wildlife & Zoo Biology
biotechnology, molecular parasitology & vector biology, wildlife documentary production, drug design, wildlife & practical conservation, wildlife conservation with zoo biology, zoology; BSc(Hons), FD, MA, MSc, PhD

Degrees validated by University of Salford offered at:

RIVERSIDE COLLEGE, HALTON
www.haltoncollege.ac.uk
accounting, applied drama and creativity, business & management, dance, integrated children's practice/integrated young people's practice, laboratory operations and management; manufacturing technology,

mechanical technology, sports coaching, teaching in the lifelong learning sector, theatre; Dip, FD, FdSc, PGDip

UNIVERSITY OF SHEFFIELD
www.sheffield.ac.uk

Faculty of Arts & Humanities; www. sheffield.ac.uk/faculties/arts-and-humanities

Dept of Archaeology
Aegean archaeology, archaeological materials, archaeological science, archaeology, bible and ancient cultures, classical and historical archaeology, cognitive studies, environmental archaeology and palaeoeconomy, European historical archaeology, European prehistory, experimental archaeology, geoarchaeology, human osteology and funerary archaeology, landscape archaeology, material culture studies, palaeoanthropology; BA(Hons), BSc(Hons), MA, MPhil, MSc, PhD

School of English Literature, Language and Linguistics
19th-century studies, American literature, applied linguistics withTESOL, biblical studies and English, English literature, English language linguistics, international cinema, language acquisition, language, history and society, theatre and performance studies; BA(Hons), MA, MPhil, PhD

Dept of History
18th-century studies, 19th-century studies, 20th-century history, American early modern history, historical research, history, international history, medieval history, modern European history; BA(Hons), MA, MPhil, PhD

School of Modern Languages and Linguistics
Catalan, Chinese studies, Czech, Dutch, East Asian studies, French, German, Hispanic studies, intercultural communication, interpreting, Italian, Korean studies, linguistics, multilingual information management, Polish, Portuguese, Russian, Russian and Slavonic studies, screen translation, Spanish, Swedish, translation studies; BA(Hons), MA, MPhil, PhD

Department of Music
ethnomusicology, music, music management, music performance, music psychology in education, psychology of music, psychology for musicians, sonic arts, traditional musics with folklore studies, world music; BA(Hons), BMus(Hons), DPhil, MA, MMus, PhD

Dept of Philosophy
philosophy, metaphysics and epistemology, language and the mind, politics and value; BA(Hons), MA, MPhil, PhD

Faculty of Engineering; www.sheffield. ac.uk/faculties/engineering

Dept of Aerospace Engineering
aerospace, aerospace engineering, aerospace engineering with private pilot instruction; BEng, MEng, MPhil, MSc, PhD

Dept of Materials
aerodynamics and aerostructures, aerospace materials, avionic systems; BEng, MEng, MPhil, MRes, MSc(Eng), PhD

Dept of Automatic Control & Systems Engineering
business skills & management, control systems, control and systems, gas turbine control, computer systems engineering, electronic, mechanical systems engineering, mechatronics, medical systems engineering, systems & control engineering; BEng, MEng, MPhil, MSc, PhD

Dept of Chemical & Process Engineering
biological and bioprocess engineering, chemical & process engineering, environmental and energy engineering, fuel technology, process safety and loss prevention; BEng, MEng, MPhil, MSc, MSc(Eng), PhD

Dept of Civil & Structural Engineering
architectural engineering design, civil and structural engineering, civil engineering with a modern language/business management, civil structures, contaminant hydrogeology, earthquake and civil engineering dynamics, engineering (civil and mechanical), engineering, environmental management of urban land and water, groundwater and water engineering, steel construction, structural and concrete engineering, structural engineering and architecture/architectural studies, urban water

engineering and management; BEng, MEng, MPhil, MSc, PGDip/Cert, PhD

Dept of Computer Science

advanced computer science, advanced software engineering, computer science, computer science with maths/French/German/software engineering/artificial intelligence, computer science with speech and language processing, data communications information systems, information technology management for business, software systems and internet technology; BEng, BSc, MComp, MEng, MPhil, MSc, MSc(Eng), PhD

Dept of Electrical & Electronic Engineering

avionic systems, data communications, digital electronics, electrical engineering with a modern language/foundation year/management, electrical engineering, electronic and communications engineering with management, electronic and communications engineering, electronic engineering with a modern language/management, electronic engineering, microelectronics; Eng, MEng, MPhil, MSc, PhD

Dept of Engineering Materials

aerospace materials, biomaterial science and tissue engineering, biomedical engineering, materials science and engineering, materials science & engineering with modern language/industrial management, metallurgy; BEng, EngD, MEng, MPhil, MSc, PhD

Dept of Mechanical Engineering

advanced mechanical engineering, aerodynamics and aerostructures, automotive engineering, computational biomechanics, mechanical engineering, mechanical engineering with French, German, Italian or Spanish/industrial management/foundation year, motor sports engineering management, sports engineering, structural integrity; BEng, MEng, MPhil, MSc, MSc(Res), PhD

Faculty of Medicine, Dentistry & Health; www.sheffield.ac.uk/faculties/medicine-dentistry-health

Dept Cardiovascular Science

cell biology, coronary artery disease, haemostasis, medical physics, non-mammalian models, vascular biology; MPhil, PhD

School of Clinical Dentistry

adult dental care, dental hygiene and therapy, dental implantology, dental public health, dentistry, oral & maxillofacial surgery and oral pathology, oral health and development, oral pathology, orthodontics, periodontics, restorative dentistry; BDS, ClinDent, Diploma, MDPH, MMedSci, MPhil, PhD

Dept of Human Communication Sciences

cleft palate studies, clinical communication studies, human communication sciences, language and communication impairment in children, speech, speech difficulties; AdvCert, BMedSci(Hons), BSc(Hons), MMedSci, MPhil, MSc, PGCert/Dip, PhD

The Medical School

cardiovascular science, endocrinology & reproduction, human metabolism, human nutrition, infection & immunity, medicine, molecular and genetic medicine, molecular medicine, musculoskeletal science, nephrology, neuroscience, orthoptics, surgery; BMedSci, ChB, MB, MD, PhD

School of Nursing & Midwifery

advanced nursing studies, maternity care, midwifery studies, nursing studies, occupational health nursing; BMedSci, MMedSci, MMid, MPhil, PGCert, PhD

The Faculty of Science; www.sheffield.ac.uk/faculties/science

Dept of Animal and Plant Science

animal behaviour, biology, conservation and biodiversity, ecology, plant sciences; evolution and behaviour, global change biology, plant molecular science, population and community ecology, zoology; MBiolSci, PhD, Phil, Sc

Dept of Biomedical Science

developmental and cell biology, medical sciences, molecular and cellular basis of human disease, neuroscience, physiology with pharmacology, stem cell and regenerative medicine, tissue engineering and functional genomics and stem cell science; BSc(Hons), MSc, PhD

Dept of Chemistry

biological chemistry, chemistry, chemistry with mathematics, polymers for advanced technologies; BSc, MChem, MPhil, MPhys, PhD

Dept of Molecular Biology & Biotechnology

biochemistry, genetics, medical biochemistry, medical genetics, medical microbiology, microbiology, molecular cell biology, biology; genomics, cell biology, molecular microbiology, structural biology; BSc(Hons), MBiolSci, PhD

Dept of Physics & Astronomy
astronomy, astrophysics, medical physics, nanoscale science and technology, physics, theoretical physics; BS(Hons), MPhys, MSc, PhD

Dept of Psychology
cognitive studies, cognitive and computational neuroscience, occupational psychology, philosophy & psychology, psychology, psychological research; BA(Hons), BSc(Hons), DClinPsych, MA, MPhil, MSc, PhD

Faculty of Social Science; www.sheffield. ac.uk/faculty/social-science

School of Architecture
architectural design, architecture, architecture and landscape, computer aided environmental design, structural engineering, sustainable architectural, urban design; BA(Hons), MArch, MPhil, MSc, PhD

School of East Asian Studies
Chinese studies, East Asian studies, Japanese studies, Korean studies; BA(Hons), MA, PhD

Dept of Economics
business analysis and economics, development economics and policy, economics, economics and mathematics/politics/economics/sociology/social policy, finance, financial economics, health economics, international finance and economics, money, banking and finance; Adv Cert, BA(Hons), BSc(Hons), MSc, PhD

Sheffield Law School
biotechnological law and ethics, commercial law, conflict and security law, European law, global politics and law, international criminology, international legal studies, law, law (European and international), politics and governance, socio-legal research; LlB, LlM, MAPhil, PhD

Sheffield Management School
financial management, business management, accounting, economics, information management, above subjects with mathematics/Japanese studies/Chinese studies/Korean studies/East Asian studies/French/German/Hispanic studies/Russian; BA(Hons), BSc(Hons), MSc, MPhil, PhD, SheffieldMBA, ExecMBA

Dept of Politics
economics, European governance and politics, European law, governance and politics, geography, global politics and law, global security, globalisation and development, governance and public policy, history, international history/east Asian studies, international political economy, international politics, international relations, philosophy, political theory, politics, sociology; BA, MA, MPhil, PhD

Dept of Sociological Studies
childhood studies, children and their families, criminology, economics, social policy, social work, sociology; BA(Hons), MA, MPhil, PhD

Dept of Town & Regional Planning
commercial property, European development and planning, geography, international development and planning, planning, planning and development, planning research, town and regional planning, urban studies; BA(Hons), MA, MPlan, PhD

The School of Education
PGCEs in applied professional studies in education, early childhood education, education policy and practice, educational research, English, geography, history, mathematics, modern languages and science, new literacies, teaching and learning in higher education, working with communities: identities, regeneration and change; EdD, MA, MEd, MPhil, PhD

Dept of Geography
economics/planning/politics/sociology, environmental mathematics, environmental science, geography and archaeology, human geography, physical geography; BA(Hons), BSc(Hons), MEnvSci, PhD

Dept of Information Studies
business management, electronic and digital library management, health informatics, informatics, information literacy, information management, information systems, information systems management, librarianship, multilingual information management; MA, MChem, MSc, MSc(Res), PhD/MPhil

Dept of Journalism Studies
broadcast journalism, journalism, magazine journalism studies/with a modern language, political communication, print journalism, web journalism; BA, MPhil, PhD

Dept of Landscape
landscape architecture with ecology/planning, landscape management, landscape research, landscape studies; BA(Hons), BSc(Hons), MA, PGDip, PhD

SHEFFIELD HALLAM UNIVERSITY
www.shu.ac.uk

Faculty of Arts, Computing, Engineering & Science; *www.shu.ac.uk/faculties/aces*

Business Systems and ICT; www.shu.ac.uk/systems

business information systems, computing, grid-based computing, internet and business technologies, IT management, requirements engineering, soft computing and intelligent systems; BSc(Hons), FdSc

Communication, Media & Journalism; www.shu.ac.uk/media

corporate communication, international broadcast/sports journalism, media, PR/and communication/media, online communication, professional communication, sports journalism, technical communication; BA(Hons), MA, MPhil, PhD

Computing, Computer and Electronic Systems; www.shu.ac.uk/computing

business information systems/technology, computer and information security/network engineering, computer graphics and visualisation, computer networks, computer studies, computing & IT/information systems, databases, enterprise systems, forensic and security technologies, games design/software development, information technology networks/software, interactive media with animation, internet and business technologies, multimedia technologies, network technologies, software engineering, web information systems and services; BEng, BSc(Hons), FdSc, GradDip, HND, MComp, MSc

Engineering & Technology; www.shu.ac.uk/engineering

advanced engineering, aerospace technology, automotive design technology, computer and network engineering, computer-aided engineering and design/technology, design engineering /technology, electronics and information technology, forensic engineering, industrial management, logistics and supply chain management, manufacturing engineering materials and product design, software engineering, sport technology/engineering, telecommunication and electronic engineering; BSc(Hons), FdSc, MBA, MSc, PhD

Mathematics & Statistics; www.shu.ac.uk/mathematics

applied statistics, business intelligence, mathematics, statistics; BSc(Hons), MSc, PhD

Sheffield Institute of the Arts; www.shu.ac.uk/art

arts and cultural management, creative media practice, design, fine art; BA(Hons), MA, MArt, PhD

Faculty of Development & Society; *www.shu.ac.uk/faculties/ds*

Built Environment; www.shu.ac.uk/built

architectural technology, architecture, environmental design, building surveying, building studies, built environment, business property management, construction and real estate, construction engineering/management, estate construction and development, estate agency, planning and property development, project management, quantity surveying, real estate investment and management, technical architecture, urban land economics; BSc(Hons), HNC, HND, MPhil, MSc, PGDip/Cert, PhD

Counselling; www.shu.ac.uk/counselling

brief therapy, counselling, counselling supervision, couple counselling, hypnotherapy, professional development in counselling and psychotherapy; BA(Hons), Cert, DipHE, MA, PGDip/Cert

Criminology & Community Justice; www.shu.ac.uk/justice

criminology and psychology/forensic and analytical science, forensic biosciences/criminology/engineering/ security technologies, international criminal justice; BEng, BSc(Hons), FdSc, MA/PgDip/PgCert, MSc

Education; www.shu.ac.uk/education

Asperger's syndrome, autism, childhood studies, children and playwork, compulsory education and training, design and technology education/mathematics/science with education and qualified teacher status, disability studies, early childhood studies, early years/education, earning and teaching/in HE, education and disability studies/learning support/education and specialist learning support, education for international students, education studies and sociology/TESOL/psychology and counselling/

English, ESOL or numeracy learning and skills, inclusion, business education/citizenship/design and technology/English/information and communication technology/mathematics/modern foreign languages/ physical education/religious education/science, integrated working, learning and skills, literacy, managing school design and technology, mentoring, primary education, science education, secondary 14–19, TESOL, young people's services, youth work; BA(Hons), CertE, EdD, FdA, MA, MPhil, MSc, PGCert/Dip, PhD

Environment; www.shu.ac.uk/environment

corporate social responsibility/international resource management and climate care/people and communities/rural development/wildlife and landscape conservation/sustainable communities and environm, environmental conservation, environmental management/ studies, planning, planning and transport; BA(Hons), BSc(Hons), MPlan, MSc/PGDip/PGCert

English & History; www.shu.ac www.shu.ac.uk/english

academic English, criminology and history, English/ language, historical research: imperialism and culture, history, film and television, humanities, politics; BA(Hons), MA, PgDip

Film, Theatre, & Performance; www.shu.ac.uk/performance

film studies, film, drama, dance and music, performance and professional practice, screen studies/with scriptwriting/English; BA(Hons), FdA, MA, MA/ PGDip/PGCert, PGCert, PGDip

Geography; www.shu.ac.uk/geography

geography/with planning, GIS, international relations; BA(Hons), BSc(Hons), MSc, PGDip/Cert

Forensic; www.shu.ac.uk/forensic

forensic accounting, analytical science, biosciences/ criminology/engineering psychology, intelligence and forensics management, forensic and security technologies; BSc(Hons), FdSc, MSc

Law; www.shu.ac.uk/law

business law, corporate law and strategy, forensic accounting/criminology/psychology/science, law, law and criminology, maîtrise en droit Français; GradDip, LlB, LLM, MSc, PGCert, PGDip

Planning Regeneration & Housing; www.shu.ac.uk/planning

geography with planning, GIS, housing for environmental health, housing policy and practice, housing practice, local and regional economic development,

neighbourhood renewal, planning studies sustainable communities/and environments, transport/planning and management, urban land economics, urban and regional planning, urban regeneration; BA(Hons), BSc(Hons), MPlanning and Transport, MSc/PGDip

Psychology; www.shu.ac.uk/psychology

applied cognitive neuroscience, corporate management psychology, criminology, developmental psychology, forensic, sexual and relationship psychotherapy; BSc(Hons), MRes/PGDip/PGCert, MSc

Social Sciences; www.shu.ac.uk/social

applied social science, criminology, sociology, education, international relations, politics, psychology, public health, social sciences, social work, planning and policy, youth work; BA(Hons), Graduate Diploma, MA, MPhil/PhD, MRes/PgDip/PgCert,

Faculty of Health & Wellbeing; www.shu.ac.uk/faculties/hwb

Sport and Active Lifestyles; www.shu.ac.uk/active

sport business/event management, PE, youth sport, coaching, physical activity, exercise science/psychology, sport injury management and therapy, sport business management, sports engineering; BSc(Hons), MA, MSc, PGDip/Cert, ProfDoc

Biosciences; www.shu.ac.uk/bio

biochemistry, biology, biomedical sciences, biosciences, cardiovascular medicine, forensic and analytical science, forensic biosciences, human biology, international and travel health, pathological sciences, pharmaceutical analysis/sciences, pharmacology and biotechnology; BSc(Hons), MSc/PGDip/PGCert, ProfDocBiomedSci

Diagnostic Radiography; www.shu.ac.uk/radiography

breast imaging and diagnosis, diagnostic radiography, medical imaging programme, medical ultrasound programme; BSc(Hons), DocProf Studies (Health and Social Care), MSc/PGDip/PGCert

Management and Leadership; www.shu.ac.uk/faculties/hwb/cpod

health and social care leadership/management/services management; BA(Hons), DipHE, MSc, PhD

Nursing & Midwifery; www.shu.ac.uk/midwifery/nursing

acute and critical care, advancing paediatric practice, clinical education, health and social care, health care education, international and travel health, maternal health care, nursing; nursing/midwifery, adult, child or mental health nursing, supportive and palliative care, primary care nursing/district nursing, health visiting and school nursing; AdvDip, AdvProfDev Framework, BA(Hons), BSc(Hons), DocProfStud, Foundation degree, MSc/PGDip/PGCert

Occupational Therapy; www.shu.ac.uk/occupational

occupational therapy, paediatric practice, vocational rehabilitation; BSc(Hons), DocProf, MSc/PGDip/PGCert,

Operating Department Practice; www.shu.ac.uk/opd

advanced professional development, operating department practice; BA(Hons), BSc(Hons), DipHE, DoctProfStud, MSc/PGDip, PGCert

Paramedic Studies; www.shu.ac.uk/paramedic

paramedic practice; BSc(Hons), DipHE

Physiotherapy; www.shu.ac.uk/physio

advancing paediatric practice, physiotherapy, sport injury management and therapy, supportive and palliative care; BA(Hons), BSc(Hons), MSc, PGCert, PGDip

Radiotherapy and Oncology; www.shu.ac.uk/radiotherapy

psychological aspects, radiotherapy and oncology practice, supportive and palliative care; BA(Hons), BSc(Hons), DipHE, MSc/PGDip/PGCert

Social Work; www.shu.ac.uk/socialwork

applied nursing and social work (learning disability), safeguarding and caring for children and young people, social work, specialist mental health practice/practitioner, working with children young people and families, youth and community work; BA(Hons), GradDip, MScPgDip, MSW, PGCert

Sheffield Business School; www.shu.ac.uk/faculties/sbs

Accounting, Banking & Finance

accounting and finance, audit management and consultancy, banking, business accounting, financial management, forensic accounting, risk management; BA(Hons), MA, MSc, PGDip/Cert

Business & Management

business and management, charity resource management, coaching and mentoring, corporate management psychology, global business/strategic marketing, HRM/HR development, leadership, industrial management, international business and management/HRM/marketing, leadership and management, organisation development and consultancy, property management, sport business management, total quality management, tourism, hospitality and facilities management; BSc(Hons), DBA, FD, GradDip, HNC, HND, MBA, MPhil, MSc, PGCert, PGDip, PhD

Facilities Management

food management, nutrition with public health management, tourism, hospitality and facilities management; BA(Hons), BSc(Hons), Cert Food and Nutrition, FD, MA, MPhil, MSc, PGCert, PGDip, PhD

Languages

business and English, English for academic purposes/international students, teaching English for academic purposes; GradDip/Cert, MPhil, PGCert, PhD

Tourism, Hospitality & Events Management

international events and conference management, international hospitality and tourism management, tourism for international development; BSc(Hons), FdSc, HND, MA, MPhil, MSc, PGCert, PGDip, PhD

UNIVERSITY OF SOUTHAMPTON
www.soton.ac.uk

The Faculty of Engineering, Science and Mathematics; www.soton.ac.uk/about/academicschools/esm

School of Chemistry; www.soton.ac.uk/chemistry

chemical biology, chemistry, chemistry with medicinal science/entrepreneurship, electrochemistry & surface science, structural & materials chemistry, synthesis; BSc(Hons), MChem, MPhil, PhD

School of Civil Engineering and the Environment; www.civil.soton.ac.uk

civil engineering, environmental engineering, environmental sciences; BEng, BSc(Hons), EngD, MEng, MenvSci, MRes, MSc, PhD

School of Electronics & Computer Science; www.ecs.soton.ac.uk

computer science, electrical engineering, electromechanical engineering, electronic engineering, software engineering; BEng, BSc, EngD, MConp, MEng, PhD

Information Technology

artificial intelligence, bionanotechnology, microelectronic systems design microelectromechanical systems, nanoelectronics, nanotechnology, radio frequency communications systems, system-on-chip, web science/technology; BSc, BEng, EngD, MEng, MSc, PhD,

School of Engineering Sciences; www.soton.ac.uk/ses

advanced material, advanced mechanical engineering science, aerodynamics & computation, aerospace, automotive, bioengineering, engineering management, marine technology, maritime engineering science, mechanical engineering, mechatronics, naval engineering, race car aerodynamics, sustainable energy technologies; EngD, European Master, MPhil, MSc, PhD

School of Geography; www.soton.ac.uk/geography

creative cities, geography, geology, oceanography, physical geography, remote sensing and spatial analysis; BA(Hons), BSc(Hons), MA, MSc, PhD

School of Mathematics; www.soton.ac.uk/maths

applied mathematics, mathematical studies, mathematics, maths with actuarial studies/astronomy/biology/computer science/economics/finance/management science/music/operational research/physics/statistics, OR in finance; BSc(Hons), MMath, MPhil, MSc PgDip, PhD

School of Ocean & Earth Sciences; www.soton.ac.uk/soes

climate science, engineering in the coastal environment, geology, geophysics, marine biology, marine environment and resources, marine geology and geophysics, marine resource management, marine science, policy and law, ocean and earth system science, oceanography, ocean remote sensing; BSc(Hons), MRes, MSc, PhD; see also National Oceanic Centre, Southampton

Dept of Physics and Astronomy; www.phys.soton.ac.uk/

nanophotonics, optoelectronics, particle physics, physics with astronomy/nanotechnology/space science/ photonics/astronomy/mathematics, quantum, light & matter, space environment physics; BSc(Hons), MPhys, MSc, PhD

Institute of Sound and Vibration Research; www.isvr.soton.ac.uk

acoustical engineering, acoustics & music, applied digital signal processing, audiology, biomedical signals and systems, biomedical signal processing, engineering acoustics, sound and vibration studies, structural dynamics; DClinPract, European Doctorate, MSc, PhD

Optioelectronic Research Centre; www.soton.ac.uk/orc

biophotonic microsystems, fundamental photonics, high-power, high energy laser, nanophotonics and meta-materials, optical fibres and materials, optical networks and systems, planar lightwave integration, ultrafast lasers and applications; MPhil, PhD

Faculty of Law, Arts and Social Sciences; www.lass.soton.ac.ak/academicschools/lass

Centre for Contemporary China; www.soton.ac.uk/ccc

international comparative studies; MSc

School of Art (Winchester School of Art); www.wsa.soton.ac.uk

graphic arts; advertising design, graphic design, illustration & digital animation, photography & digital media, fine art; fashion & fibre, fashion design, fashion promotion & marketing, new media, painting, printmaking, sculpture, textile, textile design; BA(Hons), MA, MPhil, PhD

School of Education; www.education.soton.ac.uk

computer based learning and training, education, education and training (primary) with qualified teacher status/PCET training, educational practice and innovation, higher education management and policy, institutional management and leadership in mathematics education/professional development, management, leadership and innovation, mathematics education, social justice and inclusive education, specific learning difficulties (dyslexia), sport studies, sports management & development, teacher training; BA, BA(Hons), EdD, MA, MA(Ed), MPhil, MSc, PhD

School of Humanities; www.soton.ac.uk/humanities

archaeology, English, film studies, history, medieval & renaissance studies, modern languages/contemporary Europe/English language studies/French studies/German studies/linguistic studies, music, philosophy, Spanish, Portugese & Latin American Studies; BA(Hons), BSc(Hons), CertHE, GradDip, MA, MSc, MPhil, PhD

School of Law; www.soton.ac.uk/law

commercial and corporate law, European and comparative property law, European law, European legal studies, information technology and commerce, international business law, international law, international legal studies, law, maritime law; LlB, LlM, MPhil, PhD

School of Management; www.management.soton.ac.uk/

accounting, business administration, corporate risk & security management, economics, entrepreneurship, finance, global supply chain management, higher education management, higher education management and policy, HRM, human resource strategies, international banking & financial studies, international financial markets, knowledge and information systems management, management, management sciences, marketing analytics, marketing management, mathematics, risk management, strategic entrepreneurship; BSc(Hons), DBA, MBA, MSc, PhD

School of Social Sciences; www.soton.ac.uk/socsci

home ageing, gerontology, applied social sciences, economics, politics & international relations, social statistics, social work studies, sociology BSc(hons)MSc,Grad Dip

School of International Relations

international relations, sustainable development; MA, MLitt, MPhil, MRes, PhD

School of Health Sciences; www.soton.ac.uk/healthsciences

health and social care, midwifery, nursing, occupational therapy, physiotherapy, podiatry

Statistical Science Research Institute; www.soton.ac.uk/ssri

Faculty of Medicine, Health & Life Sciences; www.soton.ac.uk/academicschools/mhls

School of Biological Sciences; www.sbs.soton.ac.uk

biochemistry, biology, biomedical sciences, cellular & molecular biology, neuroscience, pharmacology, zoology, ecology & the environment; BSc(Hons), CertHE, DipHE, MPhil, PhD

School of Psychology; www.psychology.soton.ac.uk

canine assistance, clinical psychology, cognitive therapy for severe mental health problems, companion animal counselling, educational psychology, health psychology, psychology; BSc(Hons), DocClinPsych, MPhil, MSc, PgDip, PhD

School of Medicine; www.som.soton.ac.uk

advanced clinical practice, allergy, cancer sciences, developmental origins of health and disease, health and rehabilitation, human genetics, leaders and management, medicine, mental health practitioner, mental health studies, nursing, podiatry, public health, public health nutrition; BM, MSc, PgDip/Cert, PhD

STAFFORDSHIRE UNIVERSITY
www.staffs.ac.uk

Staffordshire UniversityBusiness School; www.staffs.ac.uk/business

accounting, business studies, e-business, economics, events management, finance, HRM, international business/marketing/supply chain management, internet business development, management studies, mentoring & coaching, multimedia marketing, tourism management; BA, BSc, HNC, HND, MA, MBA, MPhil, MSc, PGCert, PGDip, PhD

Faculty of Arts, Media & Design; www.staffs.ac.uk/faculties/artand.design

advertising & brand management, animation, arts, media & design, journalism, ceramic design, creative arts, creative writing, crime, dance & theatre arts, design, digital media production, drama, performance & theatre arts, English/literature, ethics, philosophy & society, European interactive multimedia, film production, film, TV & radio studies, fine art, graphic design, graphics & digital design, heritage & culture, history, illustration, interactive advertising/animation/design, international history/ policy & diplomacy/relations, journalism, literature & contemporary culture, media management/production/studies, broadcasting, photography, product design/innovation, scriptwriting, sociology, sports journalism, sustainable design: product/transport design, theatre studies, transnational organized crime, transport design, VFX: visual effects & concept design; BA, FdA, MA, MFA, MPhil, MSc, PhD

Faculty of Computing, Engineering & Technology; www.staffs.ac.uk/faculties comp.eng.tech

3D games modelling, computing/technology, aeronautical technology, applied computing/information technology/internet commerce/multimedia systems/ network management, automotive electronics/engineering, autosport engineering, broadcast technology, business computing/data analysis/informatics/ information technology, computer game design & programming/graphics/networks & security/science/ systems, computing science, creative music technology, database administration & management/technology, design technology, digital feature film production/3D animation technology, educational software development, electrical engineering, electronic engineering, electronic & broadcast engineering, environmental engineering, film production & music technology, forensic computing/engineering, logistics technology, mathematics & applied statistics, mechanical engineering, mechatronics, medical engineering, computer systems/computing, motorsport technology, multimedia computing/systems, music production/technology, network computing/engineering/systems management, product design engineering/technology, robotics/software engineering, sports technology, technology for teaching & learning, telecommunications engineering, user support systems, web development; BA, BEng, BSc, FdSc,

HND, MEng, MSc, MPhil, MRes, PGCE, PGCert, PGDip, PhD

Faculty of Health; www.staffs.ac.uk/ faculties/health

ageing, social studies, sport & exercise psychology/ science, mental health, clinical biomechanics/practice, death, coaching science, exercise & lifestyle management, health management & policy/social care, medical education, mental health nursing, midwifery practice, nursing practice: adult nursing/children's nursing, district nursing/specialist practice/specialist practice (public health nursing – health visiting), palliative & end of life care, PE & youth sport coaching, physical activity, public health, social care/ work ,sport & exercise nutrition/psychology/science, sport studies/ therapy; BSc, MA, MPhil, MSc, PGCE, PGCert, PGDip, PhD

Faculty of Sciences; www.staffs.ac.uk/ faculties/sciences

animal biology & conservation, applied sport & exercise psychology, biochemistry & microbiology, biology, biomedical science, clinical psychology, early childhood studies, environment & sustainability, environmental conservation/forensics/management & protection, forensic biology/investigation/psychology/science, geography,health psychology, human biology, human & environmental geography, molecular biology, policing & criminal investigation, psychology, psychotherapeutic counselling, sustainable communities, water & sustainable development; BA, BSc, DClinPsy, DHealthPsy, FdSc, MA, MSc, MPhil, PGCert, PGDip, PhD

Law School; www.staffs.ac.u/faculties/ law

business law, criminology, HRM, human rights law, law, legal practice, sports law; LLB, LLM, MPhil, PhD

UNIVERSITY OF STIRLING
www.external.stir.ac.uk

Dept of Applied Social Science; www.dass. stir.ac.uk

applied social research, child welfare & protection/ management & leadership in social services, crime & society, dementia studies, European social policy, housing studies, social services management, social

work studies, sociology & social policy; BA, GradCert, MSc, PGCert, PGDip, PhD

Dept of Computing Science & Mathematics; www.cs.stir.ac.uk

advanced computing, business computing, computing for e-business/financial markets, computing science, information systems/technology, mathematics & its applications, software engineering; BSc, MSc, PhD

Dept of English Studies; www.english.stir. ac.uk

EFL, English language teaching/studies, humanities, linguistics, modern Scottish writing, post-colonial studies, publishing studies, renaissance studies, TESOL, textual culture; BA, MLitt, MPhil, MRes, MSc, PhD

Dept of Film, Media & Journalism; www. fmj.stir.ac.uk

film & media studies, financial journalism, global cinema, journalism studies, media & culture/management, public communications management, PR; BA, MLitt, MPhil, MSc, PGDip, PhD

Dept of Nursing & Midwifery; www.nm.stir. ac.uk

advanced practice, health research, midwifery studies, nursing studies; BM, BN, BSc, DAHP, DM, DN, MPhil, MRes, MSc, PGDip, PhD

Dept of Philosophy; www.philosophy.stir. ac.uk

philosophy; BA, MLitt, MPhil, PhD

Dept of Psychology; www.psychology.stir. ac.uk

child development: early years, evolution & behaviour, health psychology, psychology, psychological research methods/therapy & primary care; BA, BSc, MSc, PGDip, PhD

Dept of Sports Studies; www.sports.stir.ac. uk

sport & exercise science, sports coaching/management/studies, physical education & professional education; BA, BSc, MPhil, MSc, PGDip, PhD

Institute of Aquaculture; www.aqua.stir.ac. uk

aquaculture, aquaculture business management/nutrition/systems, veterinary studies, marine biology, sustainable aquaculture; BSc, MPhil, MSc, PGCert, PGDip, PhD

School of Biological & Environmental Sciences; www.sbes.stir.ac.uk

animal biology, biology, cell biology, conservation biology & management, ecology, environmental geography, environmental history, management/science & outdoor education, river basin management, sports & exercise science; BSc, MPhil, MRes, MSc, PGCert, PGDip, PhD

School of History & Politics; www. historyandpolitics.stir.ac.uk

environmental history, history, international conflict & cooperation, politics, revolution & counter-revolution; BA, MLitt, MPhil, MRes, MSc, PhD

School of Languages, Culture and Regions; www.slcr.stir.ac.uk

hermeneutics, humanities, international management studies with European studies & society/intercultural studies, professional education (primary) with specialism in modern languages, professional education (secondary), religion, Spanish; BA, MLitt, MRes, PhD

School of Law; www.law.stir.ac.uk

business/commercial law, law; BA, LLB, LLM, PhD

Stirling Institute of Education; www.ioe.stir. ac.uk

academic practice, EFL, English language teaching, international policing, professional enquiry, TESOL; BA, BSc, EdD, MEd, MPhil, MRes, MSc, PGCert, PGDip, PhD

Stirling Management School; www. management.stir.ac.uk

Accounting & Finance Division

accountancy, finance, international accounting & finance, investment analysis; BA, BAcc, MPhil, MSc, PhD

Business & Organization Division

business & management, business studies, HRM, international business, management science, public management & administration, public service management; BA, BSc, MBA, MPhil, MRes, MSc, PhD

Division of Economics

banking & finance, economics, energy management, environmental finance, money, politics, philosophy & economics; BA, MSc, PhD

Division of Marketing

international tourism management, marketing, retail marketing, retaining, tourism management; BA, MBA, MSc, PhD

STOCKPORT COLLEGE
www.stockport.ac.uk

business & IT management/marketing, childcare: early years senior practitioner/working with children & young people, childhood studies; early childhood studies, commercial photography, computer systems management, computing, design & visual arts – pathway in graphic design/illustration/moving image/surface design, engineering, forensic science, graphic communication, media studies: TV production, photography, social work; BA, FdA, FDSc

UNIVERSITY OF STRATHCLYDE
www.strath.ac.uk

Faculty of Education; www.strath.ac.uk/ education

Dept of Childhood & Primary Studies; www.strath.co.uk/cps
autism, careers guidance & vocational development, childhood practice, early childhood studies, education & social services, primary education; BA, BEd, MSc, PGCE, PGCert, PGDip

Dept of Creative & Aesthetic Studies; www.strath.ac.uk/caasl
applied music, creative & aesthetic studies; BA, MPhil, PhD

Dept of Curricular Studies; www.strath.ac.uk/curricularstudies
computing/design & technology education, education (secondary), language/ mathematics/science & technology/social studies education; DBA, MPhil, MSc, PGDE, PGCert, PGDip, PhD

Dept of Educational & Professional Studies; www.strath.ac.uk/eps
adult guidance/literacies, advanced academic studies/professional studies, applied educational research, community education, counselling/psychology, educational & professional studies, educational support, equality & discrimination, management & leadership in education, philosophy safety & risk management, school leadership & management, speech & language pathology; BA, BSc, EdD, MEd, MPhil, MSc, PGCert, PGDE, PGDip, PhD

Dept of Sport, Culture & the Arts; www.strath.ac.uk/scu
community arts, sport & physical activity; BA, BSc, MPhil, PGDE, PhD

Glasgow School of Social Work; www.strath.ac.uk/gssw
advanced residential childcare, community care, social work, social work management; BA, MPhil, MSc, MSW, PGCert, PhD

Faculty of Engineering; www.strath.ac.uk/engineering

Bioengineering Unit; www.strath.ac.uk/bioeng
bioengineering, medical devices, biomedical engineering, medical technology; EngD, MPhil, MRes, MSc, PGCert, PGDip, PhD

Dept of Architecture; www.strath.ac.uk/architecture
aarchitectural design/studies, building design & management for sustainability, lean design & practice management, urban design; MArch, MRes, MSc, PGCert, PGDip

Dept of Chemical & Process Engineering; www.strath.ac.uk/chemeng
applied chemistry & chemical engineering, chemical engineering/technology & management, process technology & management, mechanical engineering, sustainable engineering: chemical processing; BEng, MEng, MSc, PGCert, PGDip

Dept of Civil Engineering; www.strath.ac.uk/civeng
architectural/civil/environmental engineering, forensics/health/science/studies, geo-environmental engineering, geotechnics, global water sustainability, integrated pollution prevention & control, science, technology & sustainability, supply chain & operations management, sustainable construction & infrastructure; BEng, BSc, MEng, MPhil, MRes, MSc, PhD

Dept of Design, Manufacture & Engineering Management; www.strath.ac.uk/dmen

computer aided engineering design, digital creativity, engineering design, integrated product development, management of competitive manufacturing, operations management in engineering, product design engineering/design & innovation, production engineering & management, sports engineering, supply chain management, technology management; BEng, BSc, MEng, MSc, PGCert, PGDip

Dept of Electronic & Electrical Engineering; www.strath.ac.uk/eee

communications, computer & electronic systems, digital multimedia & communication systems, electrical energy systems, electrical & mechanical engineering, electrical power engineering with business, electronic & digital systems, electronic engineering; BEng, MEng, MSc, PGCert, PGDip

Dept of Mechanical Engineering; www.strath.ac.uk/mecheng

aero-mechanical/enviro-mechanical/mechanical engineering, power plant engineering/technologies, sustainable engineering: energy systems & the environment; BEng, MEng, MPhil, PGCert, PGDip, PhD

Dept of Naval Architectural & Marine Engineering; www.strath.ac.uk/na-me

marine engineering/technology, naval architecture, naval marine engineering, ocean engineering/small craft engineering, subsea engineering, sustainable energy: offshore renewable energy, technical management of ship operations; BEng, MEng, MPhil, MSc, PGCert, PGDip, PhD

National Centre for Prosthetics & Orthotics; www.strath.ac.uk/prosthetics

prosthetics & orthotics, rehabilitation studies; BSc, MPhil, MSc, PGCert, PGDip, PhD

Faculty of Law, Arts & Social Sciences; www.strath.ac.uk/arts

Dept of English Studies; www.strath.ac.uk/english

English, journalism, literature, culture & place, Renaissance studies; BA, MLitt, MPhil, MRes, MSc, PGDip, PhD

Dept of Geography & Sociology; www.gs.strath.ac.uk

geography, human ecology, media & communication research, refugee & migration studies, social research, sociology; BA, MRes, MSc, PGCert, PGDip, PhD

Dept of Government; www.strath.ac.uk/goverment

European/international public policy, political research, politics, public policy; BA, MSc, PhD

Dept of History; www.strath.ac.uk/history

historical studies, history, social history; BA, MPhil, MRes, MSc, PGCert, PGDip, PhD

Dept of Modern Languages; www.strath.ac.uk/modlang

French, German, Italian, Spanish, Russian; BA, MPhil, MRes, PhD

Dept of Psychology; www.strath.ac.uk/psychology

educational psychology, psychology; BA, MRes, MSc, PhD

The Law School; www.law.strath.ac.uk

construction law, criminology & criminal justice, human rights law, international economic law, international law & sustainable development, IT & telecommunications law, Scots law; BA, LLB, LLM, PGCert, PGDip

Faculty of Science; www.strath.ac.uk/science

Centre for Forensic Science

forensic & analytical chemistry, forensic biology/informatics/science; BSc, MSc, PGDip

Dept of Pure & Applied Chemistry; www.chem.strath.ac.uk

applied chemistry, chemical engineering, chemistry, forensic & analytical chemistry, forensic chemistry/informatics/science; BSc, MChem, MSc, PGDip, PhD

Dept of Computer & Information Sciences; www.strath.ac.uk/cis

business information systems/technology systems, computer & electronic systems,internet technologies, computer science, forensic informatics, information & library studies, information management, software engineering; BEng, BSc, MEng, MPhil, MRes, MSc, PGCert, PGDip

Dept of Mathematics & Statistics; www.mathstat.strath.ac.uk

mathematics, mathematics & computer science/physics/statistics, statistics & accounting/economics/finance/management science/teaching; BSc, MSc, PhD

Dept of Physics; www.strath.ac.uk/physics

high power radio frequency science & engineering, physics, physics with teaching; BSc, MPhys, MSc, PhD

Strathclyde Institute of Pharmacy & Biomedical Sciences; www.strath.ac.uk/sibs

biochemistry & immunology/microbiology, biological/biomedical sciences, clinical pharmacy, food biotechnology/science & microbiology, forensic biology, immunology & microbiology/pharmacology, pharmaceutical analysis, pharmacy, sport & exercise science; BSc, MPharm, MPhil, MSc, PGCert, PGDip, PhD

Strathclyde Business School; www.strath.ac.uk/business

Dept of Accounting & Finance; www.strath.ac.uk/accfin

accounting, business enterprise/law/technology, economics, finance, hospitality & tourism,HRM, international accounting & finance/banking & finance, investment & finance, management, management science, marketing; BA, MSc

Dept of Economics; www.strath.ac.uk/economics

economics economic management & policy, research methodology in business & management; BA, BSc, DBA, MPhil, MRes, MSc, PhD

Dept of Human Resource Management; www.strath.ac.ukhrm

HRM; BA, DBA, MRes, MSc, PGCert, PGDip, PhD

Dept of Management; www.strath.ac.uk/management

business administration, business & management, business IT systems, hospitality & tourism management, international management, management; BA, MBA, MBM, MSc

Dept of Management Science; www.strath.ac.uk/mansci

business analysis & consulting, operational research; DBA, MSc, DPhil, PhD

Dept of Marketing; www.strath.ac.uk/marketing

international marketing, marketing & French/German/Spanish/psychology/tourism; DBA, MPhil, MRes, MSc, PhD

UNIVERSITY CAMPUS SUFFOLK
www.ucs.ac.uk

School of Arts & Humanities; www.ucs.ac.uk/study/SchoolsAndCentres/SchoolOfArtsAndHumanities

computer games design, creative music, design crafts, graphic & typographic design, English, history, family, local & community history, fashion & textiles, film & media studies, fine art, football development & coaching, graphic communication/design, graphic graphic illustration/motion graphics, interior design, landscape & garden design, music production, photographic & digital media, photography, visual media production; BA, FdA, MA, PGCert, PGDip

School of Health, Science & Social Care; www.ucs.ac.uk/study/SchoolsAndCentres/SchoolOfHealthScienceAndSocialCare

animal science & welfare, applied computing, architectural technology, building control/services engineering/surveying, civil engineering, clinical practice, computing, construction management, counselling, diagnostic radiography, education for health & social care   electrical/electronic/mechanical/operations engineering, holistic therapies, leadership & innovation in health & social care, nutrition & human health, oncology & radiotherapy technology, operating department practice, person-centred counselling, personal training with sports massage therapy, social care practice, social work, specialist community public health nursing, exercise science, sport, health & exercise, physical activity development; BA, BSc, DipHE, FdA, FdSc, MA, PGCert, PGDip

School of Nursing & Midwifery; www.ucs.ac.uk/study/SchoolsAndCentres/SchoolOfArtsAndHumanities/events/events

adult/child health nursing, health administration, health & wellbeing, health care practice, health sciences (diagnostic imaging)/(radiotherapy & oncology), mental health nursing, public health practice; BSc, DipHE, FdA, FdSc

School of Social Science & Business; www. ucs.ac.uk/study/SchoolsAndCentres/ SchoolOfSocialScienceAndBusiness
business administration/management, children's care, criminology, youth studies, early childhood studies/learning, employment law, event management, human resource strategy, leadership & development/management, learning & development, leisure/tourism management, management/uniformed public services, network & communication technologies, personnel management, psychology & business management/criminology/sociology/youth studies, sustainable land use management, teaching, training & development in the FE & skills sector, wildlife management & conservation; BA, BSc, CertEd, FdA, FdSc, GradCert, MA, MBA, PGCert, PGDip

UNIVERSITY OF SUNDERLAND
www.sunderland.ac.uk

Faculty of Applied Sciences; www. sunderland.ac.uk/faculties/apsc

Dept of Computing, Engineering & Technology; www.sunderland.ac.uk/ faculties/apsc/ourfaculty/ ourdepartments/cet
applied business/forensic/network computing, automotive/electronic & electrical/manufacturing/ mechanical/software/telecommunications engineering, business computing, computer applications/ science/systems engineering, health information management, information & communications technologies, IT applications multimedia games, network systems, operational excellence, project management, sound & music technology; BA, BEng, BSc, FdSc, MSc

Dept of Pharmacy, Health & Well-being; www.sunderland.ac.uk/faculties/apsc/ ourfaculty/ourdepartments/phw
advanced clinical practice, biomedical sciences, biotechnology, chemical & pharmaceutical science, clinical pharmacy/prescribing sciences, clinical physiology, community health, drug discovery & development, environment, geography, health & safety/ social care, nursing, pharmacotherapy & medicines management, pharmacy; BA, BSc, FdA, MPharm, MSc, PGCE

Dept of Psychology; www.sunderland.ac. uk/faculties/apsc/ourfaculty/ ourdepartments/psychology
counselling, psychology, sport & exercise psychology; BA, FdA, MA, MSc

Dept of Sport & Exercise Sciences; www. sunderland.ac.uk/faculties/apsc/ ourfaculty/ourdepartments/sport
exercise, health & fitness, outdoor & adventure education, sport & exercise development/psychology/sciences, sport studies, sports coaching/development; BA, BSc, FdA MSc

Faculty of Arts, Design & Media; www. sunderland.ac.uk/faculties/adm/

Dept of Arts & Design; www.sunderland.ac. uk/faculties/adm/ourfaculty/ ourdepartments/departmentofartsdesign
advertising & design, animation & design, applied art/music practice, art & design, ceramics, contemporary performance practice, curating, dance, design: graphics, design studies, drama, fashion, textiles & promotion, fine art, glass, graphic communication/ illustration, interior design, jewellery & silversmithing, music, performing arts, photography, video & digital imaging; BA, BSc, FdA, MA

Dept of Media; www.sunderland.ac.uk/ faculties/adm/ourfaculty/ourdepartments/ departmentofmedia
film & cultural studies/media, journalism, media & cultural studies/production (TV radio, video, new media) writing (film, TV & radio), news journalism, PR, radio (production & management), screenwriting, sports journalism, video, television studies; BA, BSc, FdA, MA

Faculty of Business & Law; www. sunderland.ac.uk/faculties/bl
accountancy & financial/business & enterprise/financial management, HRM, marketing /operations/retail management, business education, law, leadership &

management, legal studies, leisure management, marketing, tourism, tourism & events/hospitality, travel & tourism; BA, CertHE, FdA, GradDip, LLB, LLM, MA, MBS, MSc, PGDip

Faculty of Education & Society

Dept of Education; www.sunderland.ac.uk/faculties/es/ourfaculty/ourdepartments/departmentofeducation

advanced professional practice (primary)/(primary/secondary)/(secondary), advancing pedagogy, primary education, professional learning & guidance, secondary education (various subjects), special needs & inclusive education, teaching & learning in HE/with ICT, TESOL; BA, BSc, MA, PGCE

Dept of Culture; www.sunderland.ac.uk/faculties/es/ourfaculty/ourdepartments/departmentofculture

American studies, Buddhist studies, contemporary history & politics, English/creative writing/drama/

film/ education (11–18 years)/language & linguistics/secondary education, French, German, history, politics, Spanish, world literatures; BA, BSc, MA, PGCE

Dept of Social Sciences; www.sunderland.ac.uk/faculties/es/ourfaculty/ourdepartments/departmentofsocialsciences/

applied family studies, career guidance, childhood studies, community & youth work studies, criminology, education & care/curriculum studies, health & social care, interprofessional practice education, social work, sociology, working with young people; BA, FdA, MA

BA(Hons), BEng(Hons), BSc(Hons), EdEng, FdA, FdSc, LLM, MA, MBA, MSc, PGCE, PGCert

Degrees validated by University of Sunderland offered at:

CITY OF SUNDERLAND COLLEGE
www.citysun.ac.uk

accountancy, art and design, beauty therapy, business administration, business and management, care, catering and hairdressing, childcare, construction, planning and the built environment, counselling and

health, education, training and teaching assistants, engineering and motor vehicle, English courses, horticulture, ICT and computing, media and performing arts, science and mathematics

UNIVERSITY OF SURREY
www.surrey.ac.uk

Faculty of Arts & Human Sciences; www2.surrey.ac.uk/fahs/

Dept of Dance, Film & Theatre; www.surrey.ac.uk/dance

dance, dance cultures, film studies, theatre studies; BA, MA, MPhil, PGDip, PhD

Dept of Economics; www.econ,surrey.ac.uk

business economics, finance, economics, energy economics & policy, international economics, finance & development; BSc, MSc, PhD

Dept of English; wwwr.english.surrey.ac.uk

communication & international marketing, cultural studies, English literature, creative writing,

intercultural communication with international business; BA, MA, MPhil, PGDip, PhD

Dept of Languages & Translation Studies; www.surrey.ac.uk/languages

audiovisual translation, French/German/Spanish, languages & contemporary cultures, translation; BA, BSc, MA, MSc, PGDip

Dept of Music & Sound Recording; www.surrey.ac.uk/music

creative music technology, music, music & sound recording; BMus, BSc, MMus, MPhil, MRes, PGDip, PhD

Dept of Political, International & Policy Studies; www2.surrey.ac.uk/politics

European politics/ business & law, international politics, law with international politics, politics/ & languages; BA, LLB, MA, MPhil, PhD

Dept of Psychology; www.psy.surrey.ac.uk

applied psychology & sociology, clinical/environmental/forensic/health/occupational & organizational/psychotherapeutic & counselling/social psychology, psychology, social research; BSc, MSc, PhD, PsychD

Dept of Sociology; www.soc.surrey.ac.uk

criminology, criminal justice & criminal research, media studies, social research methods, sociology, culture & media; BSc, MSc, PhD

Faculty of Engineering & Physical Sciences; www.surrey.ac.uk/feps

Dept of Computing; www2,surrey.ac.uk/computing

computer science/ & engineering, computing & information technology, information systems, internet computing, security technologies & applications; BSc, MSc, PhD

Dept of Electronic Engineering; www.ee.surrey.ac.uk

audio & digital media/communications/electronic/ satellite communications engineering/networks & software, electronics & computer/satellite engineering, mobile communication systems, multimedia technology & systems, nanotechnology & nanoelectronic devices, signal processing & machine intelligence, space technology & planetary exploration; BEng, MEng, MPhil, MSc, PhD

Dept of Mathematics; www2.maths.surrey.ac.uk

financial mathematics, mathematics; BSc, MMath, MSc, PhD

Dept of Physics; www2.surrey.ac.uk/physics

medical physics, physics, radiation detection & instrumentation, radiation & environmental protection; BSc, MSc, MPhys

Division of Civil, Chemical & Environmental Engineering; www.surrey.ac.uk/cce

chemical & bio-systems, civil/information & business systems, information & process systems, process & environmental systems, structural/water & environmental engineering, corporate environmental management,strategy, sustainable development, technology management, transport planning & practice, water regulation & management; BEng, MEng, MSc, PGCert, PGDip

Division of Mechanical, Medical, & Aerospace Engineering; www.surrey.ac.uk/mma

advanced materials/aerospace/biomedical/mechanical/medical engineering, entrepreneurship in technology, IT & business; BEng, MEng, MSc, PGCert, PGDip

Faculty of Health & Medical Sciences; www2.surrey.ac.uk/fhms

Division of Biochemical Sciences; www2.surrey.ac.uk/biochem

applied/genetic toxicology, biochemistry, clinical biochemistry/pharmacology, toxicology; BSc, MSc

Division of Chemical Sciences; www2.surrey.ac.uk/chemistry

chemistry, chemistry with forensic investigation, medicinal chemistry, natural drug discovery & design; BSc, MChem, MRes, MSc, PGDip, PhD

Division of Health & Social Care; www2.surrey.ac.uk/healthandsocialcare

advanced/clinical practice, health ergonomics, health & social care, learning & teaching for professional practice, mental health (primary care), midwifery studies, nursing studies:adult/child/mental health, occupational health & safety, operating department practice paramedic practice, public health practice, safety & ergonomics; BSc, DipHE, MSc, PGCert, PGDip

Division of Microbial Sciences; www2.surrey.ac.uk/microbial

biotechnology, food science & microbiology, microbial genetics, microbiology, veterinary biosciences; BSc, MSc

Division of Nutritional Sciences; www.surrey.ac.uk/nutrition

nutrition, food science, dietetics, nutritional medicine; BSc, MSc, PGCert, PGDip

Faculty of Management & Law; www.surrey.ac.uk/fml

School of Management; www.som.surrey.ac.uk

accounting & financial management, business management, entrepreneurship, financial services, food / health care management, HRM, international business/event/financial/hospitality/tourism/hotel marketing/retail marketing management, management information systems, marketing management, operations & logistics management, retail management, tourism development/management/marketing; BSc, DBA, MBA, MSc, PhD

School of Law; www2.surrey.ac.uk/law

employment/environmental health/European/international/international commercial law, justice, law, law with criminology/French law/German law/international studies/Spanish law; LLB, LLM, MA, PhD

Degrees validated by the University of Surrey offered at:

FARNBOROUGH COLLEGE OF TECHNOLOGY
www.farn-ct.ac.uk

accounting, aero engineering, business, childcare, computing, education, holistic therapies, hospitality management, learning support, media, motorsport, music, performing arts, photography, salon & spa management, sports performance, tourism & event management; BA, BSc

NESCOT
www.nescot.ac.uk

acoustics & noise control, animal management, applied biological science, biomedical science, healthcare science, business, computing, counselling, early years, health & social care, media (moving image), music production, osteopathy, performing arts, photo imaging, sports therapy, teaching in the lifelong learning sector, travel & tourism management; BA(Hons), BSc(Hons), DipHE, FdA, FdSc, HNC, HND, MSc, PGDip

ST MARY'S COLLEGE
www.smuc.ac.uk

advanced health studies, linguistics, ELT, sport & exercise physiology, sport psychology, bioethics, business law, Catholic school leadership, charity management, clinical hypnosis, creative & professional writing/writing studies, drama, applied theatre, drama & physical theatre/theatre arts, education, leading innovation & change/pedagogy & professional values & practice, education & social science, English, employment & corporate law, film & popular culture/television, geography, health & exercise, history, culture & belief, international business practice, Irish studies, management studies, media arts, nutrition, physical activity for public health, pastoral theology, philosophy, physical education, sport education, physical theatre, primary education, psychology, sociology, sport & exercise rehabilitation,, sport science/ coaching science/ journalism, strength & conditioning science, theatre directing, theology & religious studies, tourism; BA, BSc, FdA, LLM, MA, MPhil, MSc, PGCE, PGCert, PGDip, PhD

UNIVERSITY OF SUSSEX
www.sussex.ac.uk

Brighton & Sussex Medical School; www. bsms.sussex.ac.uk

cardiology, clinical education, health or social care, diabetes, leadership & management in health care, medical education, medicine, nephrology, professional development in health & social care, public health, surgery, trauma & orthopaedics; MA, MD, MPhil, PGCert, PGDip, PhD

School of Business, Management & Economics; www.sussex.ac.uk/aboutus/ schoolsdepartments/bmec

Dept of Business & Management; www. sussex.ac.uk/Units/spru/bams

business (finance/international business/marketing), business & management/with development studies, corporate & financial risk management, economics & management studies, finance & business, financial mathematics, international accounting, finance & strategy/finance/management, management & entrepreneurship/finance, managing knowledge & intellectual property, science & technology policy, technology & innovation management; BA, BSc, MSc, PGDip

Dept of Economics; www.sussex.ac.uk/ economics

economics/and development studies/international relations/politics, development economics, international economics/finance; BA, BSc, GradDip, MSc

Dept of Science & Technology Policy Research (SPRU); www.sussex.ac.uk/spru

international management, management & entrepreneurship/finance, international accounting, finance & strategy, public policies for science, technology & innovation, science & technology policy/for sustainability, technology & innovation management; BA, BSc, DPhil, MPhil, MSc

School of Education & Social Work; www.sussex.ac.uk/aboutus/ schoolsdepartments/esw

Dept of Education; www.sussex.ac.uk/ education

education, English or mathematics education studies, international education & development, social research methods (education); BA, PGCE, PGCert, PGDip, MA

Dept of Social Work; www.sussex.ac.uk/ socialwork

integrated children's services, leadership & management in integrated children's services/with children, young people, their families & carers, practice education, practice with children, young people, social research methods social work/with children & young people, their families & carers; BA, DPhil, MA, MPhil, MSc, PGCert

School of Engineering & Design; www. sussex.ac.uk/aboutus/ schoolsdepartments/engdes

advanced mechanical engineering, aerospace technology, automotive engineering, computer systems engineering, creative design, digital communications & embedded systems, electrical engineering, communication engineering, electronic engineering, mechanical engineering, product design, robotics, satellite communications & space systems, security technologies & systems, turbomachinery; BEng, BSc, DPhil, MEng, MPhil, MSc

School of English; www.sussex.ac.uk/ aboutus/schoolsdepartments/english

applied linguistics, drama studies, English, English language, ELT & French/German/Italian/Spanish, linguistics, linguistics; BA, DPhil, MA, MPhil

School of Global Studies; www.sussex. ac.uk/aboutus/schoolsdepartments/ global

Dept of Anthropology; www.sussex.ac.uk/ anthroplogy

anthropology/(Africa/Europe/South Asia), anthropology of conflict, violence & conciliation/development & social transformation, comparative & cross-cultural research methods (anthropology), medical/social anthropology; BA, DPhil, MA, MSc

Dept of Geography; www.sussex.ac.uk/ geography

human geography, development studies, environment, development & policy, globalization, ethnicity & culture, human geography, human rights, migration studies, rural development, social development; BA, BSc, DPhil, MA, MPhil, MSc

Dept of International Relations; www.sussex.ac.uk/ir

conflict, security & development, geopolitics & grand strategy, global political economy, international relations/security; BA, DPhil, MA

School of History, Art History & Philosophy; *www.sussex.ac.uk/aboutus/schoolsdepartments/hahp*

Dept of American Studies; www.sussex.ac.uk/americanstudies

American literature: critical reading, American studies; BA

Dept of Art History; www.sussex.ac.uk/arthistory

art history; BA

Dept of History; www.sussex.ac.uk/history

contemporary history/& politics, early modern history, history, intellectual history, modern European history; BA

Dept of Philosophy; www.sussex.ac.uk/philosophy: philosphy, philosophy & cognitive science; BA

School of Informatics; *www.sussex.ac.uk/aboutus/schoolsdepartments/informatics*

computer science, computing & artificial intelligence, creative systems, e-learning design, evolutionary & adaptive systems, games & multimedia environments, human-centred computer systems, human-computer interaction design, information technology for e-commerce, intelligent systems, internet computing, multimedia & digital systems, music informatics, philosophy of cognitive science; BA, BSc, DPhil, MA, MComp, MPhil, MSc, PGCert

School of Law, Politics & Sociology; *www.sussex.ac.uk/aboutus/schoolsdepartments/lps*

Dept of Politics & Contemporary European Studies; www.sussex.ac.uk/polces

contemporary European studies, European politics, politics; BA, DPhil, MPhil

Sussex Law School; www.sussex.ac.uk/law

European law, family & child law, international criminal law, international law: international trade law, law/& business/international security; DPhil, GradDip, LLB, LLM, MPhil, MSc

Dept of Sociology; www.sussex.ac.uk/sociology

comparative & cross-cultural research methods (sociology), gender & development, gender studies, social & political thought, social research in health & medicine, sociology; BA, DPhil, MA, MPhil, MSc

School of Mathematical & Physical Sciences; *www.sussex.ac.uk/aboutus/schoolsdepartments/mps*

Dept of Mathematics; www.sussex.ac.uk/maths

corporate & financial risk management, financial mathematics with computer science/economics, scientific computation; BSc, DPhil, MMath, MPhil, MSc

School of Physics & Astronomy; *www.sussex.ac.uk/physics*

astronomy, astrophysics, cosmology, physics, astronomy, astrophysics, theoretical physics, theoretical particle physics; BSc, DPhil, MPhil, MPhys

School of Life Sciences; *www.sussex.ac.uk/aboutus/schoolsdepartments/lifesci*

Dept of Biology & Environmental Science; www.sussex.ac.uk/biology

biology, biosciences, cellular & molecular neuroscience, cognitive neuroscience, developmental cell biology, ecology & conservation, environmental science, human sciences, medical neuroscience, neuroscience, plant conservation; BSc, DPhil, MPhil, MSc, PGDip

Dept of Biochemistry & Biomedical Science; *www.sussex.ac.uk/biochemistry*

biochemistry, bioinformatics, biological sciences, biomedical science, genetic manipulation & molecular bell biology, molecular genetics, molecular medicine; BSc, DPhil, MPhil, MSc

Dept of Chemistry; www.sussex.ac.uk/chemistry

chemical biology, chemistry; BSc, DPhil, MPhil, MChem, MSc

School of Media, Film & Music; www. sussex.ac.uk/aboutus/ schoolsdepartments/mfm

Dept of Media & Film; www.sussex.ac.uk/ studywithus/ug/degrees/subjects/Media

creative media practice, digital documentary/media, film studies, gender & media, media & cultural studies, media practice & theory, media studies; BA, MA, PGDip

Dept of Music; www.sussex.ac.uk/ studywithus/ug/degrees/subjects/Music

music, music informatics, opera & music theatre, professional musicianship; BA, BSc, DPhil, MA, MPhil

School of Psychology; www.sussex.ac. uk/aboutus/schoolsdepartments/ psychology

applied social psychology, experimental psychology, clinical psychology & mental health, health psychology, psychological methods, psychology, substance misuse; BSc, MRes, MSc, PGDip

---

SWANSEA UNIVERSITY
www.swansea.ac.uk

School of Arts & Humanities; www. swansea.ac.uk/artsandhumanities

Arts: applied linguistics, classics, English language studies, English literature, finance, French, German, Italian,language & communication, language studies, Latin, media studies, public & media relations, screen studies, Spanish, TEFL, translation, Welsh

Humanities: American studies, ancient Egyptian culture/history, ancient & medieval history, child welfare, childhood studies, classical archaeology/ civilization, classics, ancient history & Egyptology, contemporary conflict & violence, early childhood, early modern history, economic & social history, European history, global politics & intercultural studies, Greek, history, international communication/relations/security, maritime & imperial history, medieval studies, modern Celtic studies/history, philosophy, politics & economics, political communications/theory, politics, social history & social policy, social research, war & society; BA, MA, MPhil, MSC, MScEcon, PhD

School of Business & Economics; www. swansea.ac.uk/business

accounting and finance, actuarial studies, business economics/management, business management with law, economics, finance, financial economics, international business management, international management science, management, management science, marketing; BA, BSc, MBA, MPhil, MSc, MScEcon, PhD

School of Engineering; www.swansea. ac.uk/engineering

aerospace engineering, chemical engineering, chemical & biochemical engineering/bioprocess engineering, computational engineering, civil engineering, communication systems, computer modelling in engineering, electronic & electrical engineering, electronic systems design engineering, electronics with computer science, electronics for sustainable energy, environmental engineering/management, integrated aerospace engineering/chemical & bioprocess engineering, internet technology, materials engineering/science/mechanical engineering, medical engineering, medical radiation physics, mobile communication & internet technology, nanoscience, nanotechnology, product design,engineering/technology, recycling technology, sports materials, steel technology, telecommunication engineering, water technology & management; BEng, EngD, MEng, MPhil, MRes, MSc

School of the Environment & Society; www.swansea.ac.uk/ environmentsociety

aquaculture & the environment, aquatic ecology & conservation, biochemistry, biological sciences/& geography/psychology, biology, environmental biology: conservation & resource management, environmental dynamics & climate change, geography, human geography, marine biology, medical biochemistry, migration & international development, social development & communication/conflict, social

205

research, sustainable aquaculture & fisheries, zoology; BA, BSc, MA, MPhil, MSc, PhD

School of Health Science; www. swansea.ac.uk/health.science

adult nursing, audiology, advanced clinical practice/(infection control/nurse practitioner), chronic condition management, clinical physiology with cardiology/respiratory physiology, clinical technology (medical physics), community health studies, ethics of health care/law/management, health informatics/science, infection prevention & control, medical humanities/sciences & humanities, mental health nursing, midwifery, nursing (adult/child/mental health), public health & health promotion/partnerships in care/specialist community public health nursing; BMid, BN, BSc, DipHE, MA, MPhil, MSc, PGCert, PGDip, PhD

School of Human Sciences; www. swansea.ac.uk/human-sciences

abnormal & clinical psychology, applied criminal justice & criminology, behavioural analysis, child welfare, childhood studies, criminology & criminal justice/psychology/social policy, law & criminology, psychology, social history, social policy, social policy, social work, sports science; BA, BSc, HND, LLB, MA, MPhil, MSc, MScEcon, PhD

School of Law; www.swansea.ac.uk/law

global legal orders & law, international commercial law/commercial & maritime law/maritime law/trade law, law, law & globalization, law with business, legal practice & advanced drafting; GradDip, LLB, LLM, MA, MPhil, PGDip, PhD

School of Medicine; www.swansea.ac. uk/medicine

genetics, biochemistry/marine biology/zoology, medical genetics, medicine, trauma surgery; BSc, MBBCh, MD, MPhil, MSc, PhD

School of Physical Sciences; www. swansea.ac.uk/physical.sciences

applied mathematics, computer graphics, computer science, computing, computing & communications/future interaction technologies/software technology, computing with finance, logic & computation, mathematics, mathematics (information & communications technology), physics, physics with nanotechnology/particle physics & cosmology, pure mathematics, stochastic processes, theoretical physics; BSc, MEng, MMath, MPhil, MPhys, MRes, MSc, PhD

UNIVERSITY OF TEESSIDE
www.tees.ac.uk

School of Arts & Media; www.tees.ac.uk/schools/sam

broadcast media production, creative writing, dance, design, digital arts, e-media, English & cultural studies/media studies/history, European history, fine art, future arts/design, graphic arts/(advertising/illustration/multimedia & web publishing), history, interior architecture/design, journalism, local & regional history, media studies, modern & contemporary European history, music & animation/computer games design/digital media, music creation/technology, performance & events production, product design (contemporary lifestyle & furniture,industrial & transportation/marketing, social & cultural history, television & film production; BA, FdA, MA, MPhil, MSc, PhD

School of Computing; www.tees.ac.uk/schools/scm

applied computing, business computing/systems design, computer animation/character animation/games animation/games art/(character/environment/vehicle)/games design/games programming/graphics programming/networks/science/studies, computing, computing (information technology/networking, concept art for games & animation, creative digital media, digital animation, sound & visual media, i-computing, information & communication technologies, international business information technology,IT/management, network systems/& communications, software development/engineering, web & multimedia design/e-publishing; BA, BSc, DProf, FdSc, HNC, HND, MA, MPhil, MProf, MSc, PGDip, PhD

School of Health & Social Care; www.tees.ac.uk/schools/soh

advanced clinical practice, management of long-term health conditions, neurological rehabilitation/occupational performance & mental health, cinical psychology, diagnostic radiography, evidence-based medicine/(anaesthesia, orthopaedics/ophthalmology), health & social care, end of life care/generic pathway/public health, leadership in health & social care, management of long-term health conditions, midwifery, nursing studies/(adult/child/learning disability/mental health), occupational performance & mental health, occupational therapy, operating department practice, physiotherapy, primary care practitioner, social work, nursing studies (learning disabilities/mental health); BA, BSc, DipHE, FdSc, HND, MA, MPhil, MSc, PGCert, PGDip, PhD

School of Science & Technology; www.tees.ac.uk/schools/sse

advanced manufacturing systems, analytical chemistry, applied chemistry, biological sciences, biotechnology, chemical engineering, civil engineering, disaster management, computer-aided design engineering, control & electronics, crime & investigation, crime scene science, death investigation, digital forensics, disaster management, electrical & electronic engineering, electronics & communications, engineering, environmental sustainability/technology, fabrication & welding, fire & major incident response, food & consumer safety/nutrition & health science, forensic bology/chemistry/computing/investigation/instrumentation & control engineering, mechanical engineering, nanotechnology & microsystems, petroleum technology, process manufacturing management, project management, sustainable design & technology, trading standards & consumer protection; BEng, BSc, FdEng, HNC, HND, MPhil, MRes, MSc, PGDip, PhD

School of Social Sciences & Law; www.tees.ac.uk/schools/sss

advanced sports therapy & rehabilitation science, counselling psychology, criminal investigation/law, criminology, digital technologies for learning, early childhood studies, education, forensic /psychology, human rights, international law, law, criminology, psychology & counselling/criminology/education studies, social research methods, social sciences, sociology, sociology & politics/with psychology/youth studies, sport & exercise, sport science/coaching science/psychology, youth & childhood studies, youth studies,youth work, youth studies with criminology/psychology; BA, BSc, DProf, FdA, FdSc, FdSocSc, GradCert, HNC, HND, LLB, LLM, MA, MPhil, MProf, MSc, PhD

Teeside Business School; www.tees.ac.uk/schools/tubs/

accounting & finance, business administration/finance/management, business management (international business/tourism), business with law, economic crime, fraud management, HRM, international management, management, marketing, public services, sport management, transport & logistics/tourism; BA, BSc, DBA, FdA, FdSc, HND, MA, MBA, MSc, PGDip

THAMES VALLEY UNIVERSITY
www.tvu.ac.uk

Faculty of the Arts; www.tvu.ac.uk/the.university/faculties.and.schools/Faculty.of.the.Arts

London College of Music; www.tvu.ac.uk/music/london college of music

applied sound engineering, audio technology, composing concert music, music (performance & composition)/industry management & artist development/performance/technology, record production; BA, BMus, BSc, DipHE, FdA, FdMus, MA, MMus, PGCert, PGDip

School of Art & Design; www.tvu.ac.uk/artdesign/school.of.art.and.design

digital animation/media production, fashion & textiles, games development (games art/games design), graphic design (visual communication & interaction design), illustration, interaction design, new media art & design, photography, digital imaging, web design; BA, DipHE, FdA, MA

School of Media; www.tvu.ac.uk/media/school.of.media

advertising, broadcast journalism, broadcasting, community radio, event management, media studies, music & media, practical filmmaking, PR, video production & film studies; BA, FdA, MA

Faculty of Health & Human Studies; www.tvu.ac.uk/the_university/faculties_and_schools/Faculty_of_Health_and_Human_Sciences

School of Community Health & Social Care

substance use & misuse studies; BSc, FdSc, MSc

School of Human & Psychological Studies

advanced nutritional practice, complementary approaches to health: body massage, reflexology & aromatherapy, complementary medicine, criminology with psychology, forensic sciences, health promotion & public health, health psychology, homeopathy, human sciences, nutritional therapy, performance & health, performance, health & personal development, psychology, sport, health & exercise science; BSc, CertHE, DipHE, FdSc, MA, MPhil, MSc, PGCert, PGDip, PhD

School of Nursing & Midwifery

learning disability nursing, midwifery; BSc, DipHE, MA, MM, MPhil, PGDip, PhD

Faculty of Professional Studies

Business School; www.tvu.ac.uk/businessschool/Business_School.jsp

accounting & finance, business administration/management/studies/travel & tourism, credit management, enterprise & entrepreneurship: business start-up, further & HE management, hospitality management, food studies, HRM, HR, international hotel management/marketing, library & information management, logistics management, management studies, marketing, project management, PR, public service management, purchasing & supply, retail operations & people management, third (voluntary) sector management; DMS, FdA, GradCert, GradDip, HND, MA, MBA, MPhil, MSc, PGDip, PhD

Ealing Law School; www.tvu.ac.uk/law/Ealing_Law_School.jsp

applied law, criminology, criminology & law/ forensic science/psychology/substance use & misuse, international business & commercial law/finance law, law, legal practice; GradDip, LLB, LLM

London School of Hospitality & Tourism; www.tvu.ac.uk/London_School_of_Hospitality_and_tourism

airline & airport management, business travel & tourism, culinary arts/management, event design/ management, food & professional cookery, hospitality/ management, international culinary arts/hotel management, travel & tourism/management; BA, DipHE, FdA, GradCert, HND, MA, MPhil, PGDip, PhD

School of Computing; www.tvu.ac.uk/School_of_Computing

business information systems, computer network management, computing, information systems, computing interaction design, computing science, information management, information systems; BSc, FdSc, HND, MSc

School of Education; www.tvu.ac.uk/higher-education

UNIVERSITY OF ULSTER
www.ulster.ac.uk

Faculty of Art, Design & the Built Environment; www.adbe.ulster.ac.uk

School of Architecture & Design; www.adbe.ulster.ac.uk/schools/archi.design

3D design (interior, product & furniture design), architectural studies/technology & management, architecture, interior design, landscape architecture; BA, BDes, BSc, CertHE, MArch, MLA, MSc

School of Art & Design; www.adbe.ulster.ac.uk/schools/art.design

art & design, design for visual communication, fine & applied arts, fine art, interactive multimedia design, photography, textile material product, textiles & fashion design; BA, BDes, BSc, MA, MDes, MFA, PGDip

School of the Built Environment; www.adbe.ulster.ac.uk/schools/built.environment

building engineering & materials, building services & energy engineering, building surveying, civil engineering, construction engineering, construction & project management, energy & building services engineering, environmental health, fire safety engineering, housing management/studies, infrastructure engineering, occupational therapy, property investment & development/ planning,quantity surveying, renewable engineering & energy management, transportation;BEng, BSc, MEng, MPhil, MSc, PGCert, PGDip, PhD

Faculty of Arts; www.arts.ulster.ac.uk

School of Creative Arts; www.ulster.ac.uk/schools/creative.arts
art & design, arts, computing & design, multimedia, dance, design & communication, drama, music; BA, BDes, BMus, BSc, MDes, MMus, MPhil, MRes, MSc, PGDip, PhD

School of History, English and Politics; www.adbe.ulster.ac.uk/schools/history.intern
American studies, English,cultural heritage, history, history & politics, international politics, Irish history & politics, peace & conflict studies, philosophy; BA, MA, MRes, PGDip, PhD

School of Languages, Literatures & Cultures; www.adbe.ulster.ac.uk/schools/lanlit
Celtic studies, English, European studies (with options), film studies, American studies/English/European studies/French/German/history/international development/Irish/journalism/media studies/Spanish, French, German, Irish, languages, business & computing, Spanish; BA, CertHE, MA, MPhil, PGDip, PhD

School of Media, Film & Journalism; www.adbe.ulster.ac.uk/schools/media.film
documentary practice, film studies (with options), film & TV management & policy, interactive media arts, international media studies, journalism (with options), media studies; BA, MA, MPhil, PGDip, PhD

Faculty of Computing & Engineering; www.compeng.ulster.ac.uk

School of Computing & Information Engineering; www.compeng.ulster.ac.uk/cie
computing, computing (artificial intelligence/digital games development/internet systems), financial engineering, telecommunications & internet systems; BSc, MSc, PGDip, PhD

School of Computing & Intelligent Systems; www.scis.ulster.ac.uk
computer games development, computer science, computing & creative technologies/e-business/intelligent systems/financial services, electronics & computer systems, mobile robotics, multimedia computing & design, multimedia computer games; BEng, BSc, MSc, PGDip, PhD

School of Computing & Mathematics; www.infj.ulst.ac.uk/cm/
computing & information systems, computing science, computing, information & communication technologies, industrial practice, interactive multimedia design, interactive teaching technologies, software engineering; BSc, MSc, PGCert, PGDip, PhD

Faculty of Engineering; www.seng.ulster.ac.uk/eme
biomedical engineering, electronics, communications & software, engineering (electrical/electronic)/management, mechanical engineering, sports technology, technology with design; BSc, BEng, MEng, MSc, PGDip, PhD

Faculty of Life & Health Sciences; www.science.ulster.ac.uk

School of Biomedical Sciences; www.biomed.science.ulster.ac.uk
applied biosciences, biology, biomedical science, biotechnology, dietetics, European food regulatory affairs, food & nutrition, forensic & legal medicine, forensic studies, human nutrition, medical science, optometry, pharmaceutical sciences, pharmacology, pharmacy, veterinary public health; BSc, DMedSc, GradCert, MPharm, MSc, PGCert, PGDip

School of Environmental Sciences; www.science.uster.ac.uk/envsci
coastal zone management, environmental management/science/studies/toxicology & pollution monitoring, geographic information systems, geography, marine science; AB, BSc, DEnvSci, MPhil, MRes, MSc, PGCert, PGDip, PhD

School of Health Sciences; www.science.uster.ac.uk/health
clinical physiology/research, health science, occupational therapy, physiotherapy, podiatry, radiography

(diagnostic/therapeutic), speech & language therapy; BSc, MClinRes, MSc

School of Nursing; www.science.ulster.ac.uk/nursing

community & public health nursing, dementia studies, education for nurses, midwifes health promotion & population health, health & social care, independent & supplementary nurse prescribing, midwifery sciences, nursing (adult/mental health), nursing sciences, palliative care & cancer healthcare, specialist midwifery/nursing practice; BSc, CertHE, MSc, PGCert, PGDip

School of Psychology; www.science.ulster.ac.uk/psychology

applied behaviour analysis, applied psychology (mental health), psychology; BSc, MSc, PGDip

School of Sports Studies; www.science.ulsportsster.ac.uk

physical activity & population health, sport & exercise sciences/management/coaching/studies/technology, sports-related studies; BSc, FdSc, MPhil, MSc, DPhil, PGDip, PhD

Faculty of Social Sciences; www.socsci.ulster.ac.uk

School of Communication; www.comms.ulster.ac.uk

communication, language & linguistics, linguistics; BSc, MPhil, MSc, PGCert, PGDip, PhD

School of Economics; www.socsci.ulster.ac.uk/ecompolitics

applied/ business economics, economics, economics with accounting/marketing/politics; BSc, MSc, PGDip

School of Education; www.socsci.ulster.ac.uk/education

art & design, education (primary), English with drama & media studies, further & HE, geography, history, home economics, library & information management, music, physical education, (TESOL), technology & design; MA, MEd, PGCE, PGCert, PGDip

School of Law; www.socsci.ulster.ac.uk/law

law, human rights law; LLB, LLM

School of Criminology, Politics & Social Policy; www.socsci.ulster.ac.uk/policy

criminology & criminal justice, health & social care policy, politics, public administration, social policy, social policy with procurement; BSc, MPA, PGCert, PGDip

School of Sociology & Applied Social Sciences; www.socsci.ulster.ac.uk/sociology

cognitive therapy, community development/youth work, restorative practices, social work, sociology; BSc, MSc, PGCert, PGDip

Graduate School of Professional Legal Education; www.socsci.ulster.ac.uk/gsple

legal practice; PGDip

Ulster Business School; www.business.ulster.ac.uk

accounting, advertising, applied management, business & management, business administration/development & innovation/improvement/studies, consumer studies, culinary arts management, cultural management, executive leadership, finance & investment analysis, financial services, HRM, international business/hospitality management/hotel & tourism management/travel & tourism management, leisure & events management, management & corporate governance/leadership, marketing, sport management; BSc, CertHE, GradDip, HND, MBA, MBS, MSc, PGDip

UNIVERSITY OF WALES INSTITUTE, CARDIFF
www.uwic.ac.uk

Cardiff School of Art & Design; www.csad.uwic.ac.uk

advanced product design, architectural design technology, building maintenance & management, building technology & management, ceramics, contemporary textile practice, fine art, graphic communication, illustration, interior architecture, media studies with visual cultures, product design, web & game design, music production & technology; BA, BSc, HNC, HND, MA, MFA, MPhil, MSc, PGCert, PhD

Cardiff School of Education; www3. uwic.ac.uk/English/education

Dept of Humanities; www3.uwic.ac.uk/English/education/humanities

educational studies & early childhood studies/English/humanities/psychology/sport & physical activity/Welsh, English & creative writing/drama/modern history/popular culture, modern history & educational studies/politics, sociology & criminology/popular culture; BA, MA, PGCert, PGDip

Dept of Professional Development; www3. uwic.ac.uk/English/education/profdevelopment

education, learning support, management in the community professions, preparing to teach, youth & community education; BA, MA, MPhil, MSc, PhD

Dept of Teacher Education & Training; www3.uwic.ac.uk/English/education/teachedu

primary; secondary: art & design, design & technology, drama, English with drama, French, history, ICT, mathematics, modern foreign languages (French, German, Italian &/or Spanish), music, physical education, science (biology/chemistry/physics), Welsh; BA, PGCE

Cardiff School of Health Sciences; www3.uwic.ac.uk/English/health

Centre for Applied Social Sciences; www3. uwic.ac.uk/English/health/ass

health & social care, housing: policy & practice/supported housing, interprofessional studies (health/quality assurance/learning disability/regulation/supported housing/working with children), social work; BA, BSc, FdSc, GradCert, GradDip, HNC, HND, MRes, MSc PGCert, PGDip

Centre for Biomedical Science; www3.uwic. ac.uk/English/health/cbs

biomedical science, (applied biomedical sciences/forensic toxicology, molecular biology), health sciences; BSc, FdSc, HNC, HND, MSc, PGCert, PGDip

Centre for Complementary Therapies; www3.uwic.ac.uk/English/health/cct

complementary therapies; BSc

Centre for Dental Technology; www3.uwic. ac.uk/English/health/cdt

dental technology; BSc, FdSc, MSc, PGCert, PGDip

Centre for Nutrition, Dietetics & Food Sciences; www3.uwic.ac.uk/English/health/cnfc

applied public health, consumer & trading standards, dietetics, food safety management, food science & technology, human nutrition, public health nutrition, sports & exercise nutrition/ biomedicine; BSc, FdSc, HNC, MSc, PGDip

Centre for Psychology; www3.uwic.ac.uk/English/health/cp

forensic psychology, health psychology, lifestyle psychology, psychology, psychology & human biology; BSc, FdSc, MSc

Centre for Public Protection; www3.uwic. ac.uk/English/health/cpp

applied public health, environmental health, environmental risk management, occupational health & safety, waste management; BSc, FdSc, HNC, MSc, PGDip

Centre for Speech & Language Therapy; www3.uwic.ac.uk/English/health/cslt

speech & language therapy; BSc

Wales Centre for Podiatric Studies; www3. uwic.ac.uk/English/health/wcps

musculoskeletal studies, podiatry, therapeutic footware; BSc, MSc, PGCert, PGDip

Cardiff School of Management; www3. uwic.ac.uk/English/management

Business & Management Department; www3.uwic.ac.uk/English/management/dbm

business administration/studies, management studies, health sector management, international business management/ management, management, management consultancy, marketing, product design, project management, retail management, social entrepreneurship; BA, HND, MBA, MSc

Dept of Accounting, Economics & Finance; www3.uwic.ac.uk/English/management/dafe

accounting, finance, economics, financial management/services; BA, BSc, FdA, MSc

Information Systems Department; www3. uwic.ac.uk/English/management/dis

business information systems/ technology, computer studies, information systems management, software development; BSc, HNC, HND, MSc

Dept for International Studies & Learning Support; www3.uwic.ac.uk/English/management/disls

international business administration/management, management with finance/marketing; BA, MSc

Tourism, Leisure & Events Management Dept; www3.uwic.ac.uk/English/management/dthem

events management, hospitality management, international tourism & hospitality management, tourism

management; BA, FdA, HNC, HND, MSc, PGCert, PGDip

Cardiff School of Sport; www3.uwic.ac.uk/English/sport

dance, sports coaching/development, sport & exercise science, PE, sport management/massage; BA(Hons), BSc(Hons), MA, MSc, PGDip/Cert

UNIVERSITY OF WALES: GLYNDWR UNIVERSITY
www.newi.ac.uk

North Wales School of Art & Design; www.newi.ac.uk/en/Academicschools/ArtandDesign

animation, applied arts, art & design/for landscape, computer-generated imagery, contemporary applied arts, design: animation/creative lens media/digital art for computer games/fashion & textiles/graphic design/illustration/illustration for children's publishing/illustration for graphic novels, interactive multimedia design, design for decorative arts, digital media design & production, fine art, illustration for publishing; BA, FdA, MA, MPhil, PhD

School of Business; www.newi.ac.uk/en/Academicschools/ArtandDesign/

accounting & financial management, business & management, business accounting/management, business management with accounting/marketing, festival & events management, international management, leadership & management, legal/logistics operations management, marketing/tourism management; BA, FdA, HNC, MBA, MSc, MPhil, PhD

School of Computing & Communications Technology; www.newi.ac.uk/en/Academicschools/ComputingandCommunicationsTechnology/

applied computing, communications technology, computer game development/network management & security, computing, creative industries/media computing, information management, IT support, mobile computing, music technology, radio production & communication, studio technology, television; BA, BSc, FdEng, FdSc, HNC, HND, MPhil, MSc, PhD

School of Education & Community; www.newi.ac.uk/en/Academicschools/EducationandCommunity

community studies, early childhood studies, education studies, e-learning: learning & development of babies & young children, learning support, play & playwork, post-compulsory education & training, primary education with QTS, professional development in HE, youth & communitystudies; BA, DipHE, FdA, MA, MA(Ed), MPhil, PGCert, PGDip, PhD

School of Health, Social Care, Sport & Exercise Studies; www.newi.ac.uk/en/Academicschools/EducationandCommunity

advanced clinical nursing practice, Chinese medicine, community specialist practice (community children's nursing/district nursing/general practice nursing), community sport development, complementary & criminal justice, equestrian psychology, health & care studies, interdisciplinary palliative care, leadership in health & social care, occupational health, safety & environmental management, occupational therapy, public health, professional education, psychology, public & social policy, social work, specialist community public health nursing (health visiting/occupational health nursing/school nursing), sport & exercise sciences, sports coaching, therapeutic childcare, nursing (pre-registration) with adult nursing mental health; BA, BN, BSc, CertHE, DipHE, FdA, FdSc, MA, MPH, MPhil, MSc, PGCert, PhD

School of Humanities; www.newi.ac.uk/en/Academicschools/Humanities

broadcasting, journalism & creative writing/media communications/screen, history, English, broadcasting & journalism, media communications/ screen studies, English literary culture: 1880–1920, history & screen studies/Welsh language studies, local history, media communications, print journalism, theatre, television & performance, Welsh translation; BA, CertHE, FdA, MA, MPhil, PhD

School of Science & Technology; www. newi.ac.uk/en/Academicschools/ ScienceandTechnology

advanced electronic techniques, aeronautical & electronic engineering (avionics)/mechanical engineering/mechanical manufacturing, aircraft maintenance, animal studies, architectural design technology, automation, instrumentation & control, automotive electronic technology, building studies (construction management/maintenance management), digital sound & vision processing, electrical engineering/technology, electrical & electronic systems & digital technologies, environmental science, estate agency/management, forensic science, horticulture production management, housing studies, landscape design & management, mechanical technology, medical electronics, organic horticulture management, polymer science & technology, renewable energy & sustainable technologies, renewable energy systems, sound & broadcast engineering, sports surface management, sustainable development, supported housing; BEng, BSc, FdEng, FdSc, HNC, HND, MPhil, MRes, PhD

UNIVERSITY OF WALES: LAMPETER
www.lamp.ac.uk

Dept of Archaeology & Anthropology; www.lamp.ac.uk/archanth

anthropology, anthrozoology, archaeology, archaeology (environmental/practice), archaeology/theology, ancient history, civilizations of the Mediterranean, cultural astronomy & astrology, cultural heritage, death studies, environmental anthropology, nature, social anthropology/archaeology; BA, DipHE, MA, PgCert, PGDip, MPhil, PhD

Centre for Chinese Studies; www.lamp. ac.uk/chinese/

Chinese studies, culture in society: East & West; BA, MA, MPhil, PhD

Dept of Classics; www.lamp.ac.uk/ classics

ancient history, classical studies, medieval history, ancient myth & society/narrative literature, classical language & literature, classics, Greek, Latin; BA, MA, MPhil, PhD

Dept of English; www.lamp.ac.uk/ english

creative & script writing, English, modern literatures,creative writing/TEFL; BA, MA

Dept of Film & Media; www.lamp.ac.uk/ fm

film & media, film studies, media production/studies, screen studies; BA, MA, MPhil, PhD

Dept of History; www.lamp.ac.uk/ history

Arthurian studies, historical studies, history, medieval studies; BA, MA, MBA, PGDip, MPhil, PhD

Dept of Management & Information Technology; www.lamp.ac.uk/mit

business information technology/management, e-commerce, entrepreneurial management, leadership, small business management; BA, MA, MSc, MPhil, PhD

Dept of Philosophy; www.lamp.ac.uk/ philosophy

applied philosophy, Eastern & Western perspectives, ethics of life & death, European philosophy, medical ethics, nature, philosophy, religion, ethics; BA, MA, MPhil, PhD

Dept of Theology & Religious Studies; www.lamp.ac.uk/trs

Biblical interpretation, Celtic christianity, Church history, death & immortality, divinity, Indian religions, Islamic studies, liturgical studies, Marian studies, medical ethics, monastic studies, orthodox studies, religion, ethics & society, religious history/studies, systematic & philosophical theology, theology, the world's religions; BA, DMin, DPT, LTh, MA, MMin, MTh

Dept of Welsh; www.welsh.lamp.ac.uk/ Department/English

Welsh studies, Celtic studies; BA(Hons), MPhil, PhD

Dept of Voluntary Sector Studies; www. volstudy.ac.uk

voluntary sector studies, interpersonal skills for volunteers, intergeneration practice; MA, Univ Cert

UNIVERSITY OF WALES: NEWPORT
www.newport.ac.uk

Centre for Community & Lifelong Learning; www.ccll.newport.ac.uk

combined open studies; CertHE

Newport Business School; www.nbs. newport.ac.uk

accounting, economics/finance/financial management/law, building studies, HRM, law, management, marketing, business information studies business leadership/enterprise development/studies, construction engineering, civil engineering, computing, electrical engineering, electronic & communication engineering, engineering, fire safety engineering, forensic computing, games development & artificial intelligence, information security, IT management, mechanical & manufacturing engineering, networks & web development, project management, robotic & intelligent systems engineering, strategic management, technology management, telecommunications with management; BA, BSc, BEng, FdSc, HNC, HND, MBA, MSc

School of Art, Media & Design; www. amd.newport.ac.uk

advertising design, animation, computer games design, creative music practice/sound & music, design by practice, documentary film & television/ photography, fashion design, film, video, fine art, graphic design, interactive media, performing arts, photographic art, photography for fashion & advertising, printmaking; BA, MA, MFA

School of Education; www.education. newport.ac.uk

adult literacy/numeracy, applied drama, autism, child & adolescent mental health, childhood studies, creative therapies in education, creative writing, critical & creative thinking, early years, education & ICT, education leadership & management, education studies, English/literature: health promotion & education, history, learning support (secondary & further education), inclusive practice health & education, post-compulsory education/& training, primary studies, regional history, religious education/studies, secondary design & technology, secondary teaching mathematics & science with ICT, SEN specific learning difficulties/visual impairment, teaching English as an additional language, tTESOL; BA, BSc, FdA, MA, PGCE, PGCert, PGDip

School of Health & Social Sciences; www.hss.newport.ac.uk

community health & community social care, counselling, criminology & criminal justice, health, exercise & nutrition, interprofessional practice, psychology, social ethics & public advocacy, social welfare, social work, sociology, sport and youth & community studies/ youth justice, sports coaching, sports studies, youth & community studies, youth justice; BA, BSc, MA, PGCert, PGDip

UNIVERSITY OF WALES: SWANSEA METROPOLITAN UNIVERSITY
www.smu.ac.uk

Faculty of Applied Design & Engineering; www.smu.ac.uk/index.php/potential-students/faculty-of-applied-design-and-engineering

School of Applied Computing; www.smu.ac.uk/index.php/potential-students/faculty-of-applied-design-and-engineering/school-ofapplied-computing

business information technology, computer games development, computer networks/systems & electronics, computing & information systems, electronic engineering, software engineering, web development; BEng, BSc, HND, MSc

School of Automotive Engineering; www.smu.ac.uk/index.php/potential-students/faculty-of-applied-design-and-engineering/school of automotive engineering

automotive engineering, computer networks, e-commerce, motorcycle engineering, motorsport & automotive electronic systems, motorsport engineering & design/technology; BEng, BSc, HND

School of Built & Natural Environment; www.smu.ac.uk/index.php/potential-students/faculty-of-applied-design-and-engineering/school- of-natural-environment

building conservation, building studies, civil engineering & environmental management, civil engineering studies, construction management, environmental conservation/& management, facilities management, project & construction management, quantity surveying; BSc, HNC, HND, MSc

School of Digital Media; www.smu.ac.uk/index.php/potential-students/faculty-of-applied-design-and-engineering/school-of digital-media

computer animation, creative computer games design, interactive digital media, multimedia, music technology; BA, BSc, HND, MA, MSc

School of Industrial Design; www.smu.ac.uk/index.php/potential-students/faculty-of-applied-design-and-engineering/school-of-industrial-design

automotive design, industrial design, product design /& innovation, transportation design; BA, BSc, MA, MSc

School of Logistics & Manufacturing Engineering; www.smu.ac.uk/index.php/potential-students/faculty-of-applied-design-and-engineering/school-of-logistics-a-manufacturing

logistics & supply chain management, manufacturing systems engineering, mechanical & manufacturing engineering, motorsport management/manufacturing engineering, transport management; BSc, BEng, HND

Welsh School of Architectural Glass; www.smu.ac.uk/index.php/faculty-of-applied-design-a-engineering/welsh-school-of-architectural-glass

architectural glass, glass, stained glass restoration & conservation; BA, MA

Faculty of Art & Design; www.smu.ac.uk/index.php/potential-students/faculty-of-art-and-design

School of Contextual Studies & Visual Communication; www.smu.ac.uk/index.php/potential-students/faculty-of-art-and-design/csvc

art history & English studies/psychology/visual arts practice, design for advertising, graphic design, general illustration; BA, HND

School of Fine & Applied Arts; www.smu.ac.uk/index.php/potential-students/faculty-of-art-and-design/school-of-fine-a-applied-arts

fine arts (ceramics/combined media/painting & drawing), surface pattern design (contemporary applied arts practice/textiles for fashion/textiles for interiors); BA, FdA

School of Photography & Video; www.smu. ac.uk/index.php/potential-students/ faculty-of-art-and-design/school-of-photography-video

documentary video, photography in the arts, photo-journalism, video arts; BA

School of Research & Postgraduate Studies; www.smu.ac.uk/index.php/potential-students/faculty-of-art-and-design/rps-art

fine art, photography, textiles, visual communication; MA

Faculty of Humanities

Centre for Leisure, Tourism & Sport; www. smu.ac.uk/index.php/faculty-of-humanities/clts

events management, international tourism/travel & tourism management, leisure management, sports management, watersports & adventure activities management; BA, HND, MBA

Swansea Business School; www.smu.ac.uk/ index.php/faculty-of-humanities/ swansea-business-schools

accounting, business & finance, business studies /& psychology, HRM, management, marketing; BA, FdA, GradDip, HND, MA, MA(Ed), MRes, PGCE

Swansea School of Education; www.smu.ac. uk/index.php/faculty-of-humanities/ swansea-school-of-education

counselling & educational studies, educational studies, English studies, post compulsory education & training, primary education, professional development (education), education & training, secondary education, youth & community studies; BA, PGCE, PGCert, PGDip

School of Performance & Literature; www. smu.ac.uk/index.php/faculty-of-humanities/school-of-performance-a-literatuture

art history & English studies, English & counselling/ education studies/psychology, performing arts, technical theatre; BA, HNC, HND

School of Psychology & Counselling; www. smu.ac.uk/index.php/faculty-of-humanities/school-of-psychology-a-counselling

business studies & psychology, counselling & educational studies/psychology, educational studies & psychology, English studies & counselling/psychology; BA, MPhil, PhD

School of Public Service Leadership; www. smu.ac.uk/index.php/faculty-of-humanities/school-of-public-service-leadership

health & social care, public administration, public services; BA, MPhil, PhD

UNIVERSITY OF WALES: TRINITY COLLEGE, CARMARTHEN
www.trinity-cm.ac.uk

Faculty of Arts & Social Sciences; www. trinity-cm.ac.uk/en/fac.arts

School of Computing, Business & Tourism; www.trinity-cm.ac.uk/en/fac.arts/sch.cbt

business information technology, business & management, community development, computing, heritage tourism, information systems management, local history, management (heritage), management /& sustainability, tourism; BA, BSc, FdA, FdSc, MA, MBA

School of Creative Arts & Humanities; www.trinity-cm.ac.uk/en/fac.arts/sch.cah

arts management, creative writing, educational studies, English, film studies, fine art, media studies; BA, MBA

School of Sport, Health & Outdoor Education; www.trinity-cm.ac.uk/en/ fac.arts/sch.shoe

health & exercise, sports studies, health, nutrition & lifestyle, outdoor education, physical education; BA, MA

School of Theatre & Performance; www. trinity-cm.ac.uk/en/fac.arts/sch.tp

acting, educational drama, theatre design & production; BA, MA

Faculty of Education & Training; www. trinity-cm.ac.uk/en/fac.edu

School of Education Studies & Social Inclusion; www.trinity-cm.ac.uk/en/ fac.edu/essi

community support, early years education & social inclusion education studies & English/religious studies/social inclusion, inclusive studies, primary education studies, psychology, religious studies & social inclusion, social inclusion, special educational needs, youth & community work; BA, BSc, CertHE, DipHE, FdA, GradCert, MA

School of Initial Teacher Education Training; www.trinity-cm.ac.uk/en/fac.edu/tet

education, primary education, professional development, religious education; BA, GradCert, GradDip, MA, PGCEBA

School of Early Years Education; www. trinity-cm.ac.uk/en/fac.edu/eye

early years education, nursery management; BA, CertHE, MA, PGDip

School of Theology and Religious Studies; www.trinity-cm.ac.uk/en/ fac.edu/trs

religious studies, religion in society, religious education, Christianity & community studies; education studies/social inclusion; BA

UNIVERSITY OF WARWICK
www.warwick.ac.uk

Faculty of Arts; www2.warwick.ac.uk/ fac/arts

Dept of Classics & Ancient History; www2. warwick.ac.uk/fac/arts/classics

ancient history & classical archaeology, classical civilization/with philosophy, classics, English & Latin literature; BA, MA, MPhil, PhD

Dept of English & Comparative Literary Studies; www2.warwick.ac.uk/fac/arts/ english

English literature, creative writing, English & theatre studies, pan-romanticisms, writing; BA, MA, MPhil, PhD

Dept of Film & TV Studies; www2.warwick. ac.uk/fac/arts/film

film & literature/TV studies; BA, MA, MPhil, PhD

Dept of French Studies; www2.warwick.ac. uk/fac/arts/french

English & French, French/French studies with German/history/international studies/Italian/politics, French culture & thought; BA, MA, MPhil, PGDip, PhD

Dept of German Studies; www2.warwick. ac.uk/fac/arts/german

English & German literature, German cultural studies, German/German studies with business studies/ French/international studies/Italian/Spanish; BA, MA, MPhil, PGDip, PhD

Dept of History; www2.warwick.ac.uk/fac/ arts/history

18th-century studies, global history, history, history & culture/politics/sociology, history of race in the Americas, modern history, religious & social history, 1500-1700; BA, MA, MPhil, PhD

Dept of History of Art; www2.warwick.ac. uk/fac/arts/arthistory

art history with Italian, history of art, history of art & French; BA, MA, MPhil, PGDip, PhD

Dept of Italian; www2.warwick.ac.uk/fac/ arts/italian

English & Italian literature, Italian, Italian culture & communication, writing & cultural difference; BA, MA, MPhil, PGDip, PhD

School of Comparative American Studies; www2.warwick.ac.uk/fac/arts/cas

history, literature & culture of the Americas, history of race in the Americas; BA, MA, PhD

School of Theatre, Performance & Cultural Policy Studies; www2.warwick.ac.uk/fac/ arts/Theatres

English & theatre, European cultural policy & administration, theatre & performance studies; BA, MA, MPhil, PhD

Faculty of Medicine; www2.warwick.ac. uk/fac/med

Warwick Medical School

child health, diabetes, health sciences, medical education/leadership, medicine & surgery, orthodontics, philosophy & ethics of mental health, prehospital critical care, public health, sexual & reproductive health care, trauma & orthopaedic surgery; MBChB, MD, MMedSci, MPhil, MSc, PhD

Faculty of Science; www2.warwick.ac. uk/fac/sci

Dept of Biological Sciences; www2. warwick.ac.uk/fac/sci/bio

biochemistry, biomedical science, biological sciences, bioprocessing & business management, biotechnology, cardiovascular risk, clinical oncology,microbiology & virology, renal transplantation, techniques & applications of molecular biology, virology; BSc, MD, MPhil, MSc, PhD

Dept of Chemistry; www2.warwick.ac.uk/ fac/sci/chemistry

biomedical chemistry, chemical biology, chemistry, chemistry with management/medicinal chemistry; BSc, MChem, MSc, PhD

Dept of Computer Science; www2.warwick. ac.uk/fac/sci/dcs

computer & business studies/management sciences, computer science/applications, computing systems, discrete mathematics; BSc, MEng, MPhil, MSc, PhD

School of Engineering; www2.warwick.ac. uk/fac/sci/eng

automotive engineering, biomedical engineering, civil engineering, computer & information engineering, electronic engineering/systems, electronic systems with communications/sensor technology, energy & power electronic systems, engineering with/automotive engineering/computer engineering/instrumentation/robotics/sustainability/systems engineering, engineering business management, manufacturing & mechanical engineering/systems, systems engineering; BEng, BSc, EngD, MPhil, MSc, PhD

Dept of Mathematics/Warwick Mathematics Institute; www2.warwick.ac. uk/fac/sci/maths

financial mathematics, interdisciplinary mathematics, mathematics, mathematics & business studies/economics/philosophy/physics/statistics; BSc, MMath, MSc, PhD

Dept of Physics; www2.warwick.ac.uk/fac/ sci/physics

mathematics & physics, physics; BSc, MPhys, MSc, PhD

Dept of Psychology; www2.warwick.ac.uk/ fac/sci/psych

philosophy with psychology, psychology; BSc, MPhil, MSc, PhD

Dept of Statistics; www2.warwick.ac.uk/ fac/sci/statistics

statistics, mathematics, operational research, statistics & economics (MORSE); BSc, MMathStat, MPhil, MSc, PgDip, PhD

Warwick HRI; www2.warwick.ac.uk/fac/ sci/whri

enterprise in horticulture, environmental biology/bioscience in a changing climate, plant bioscience for crop production; BSc, MSc, MPhil, PhD

Faculty of Social Studies; www2. warwick.ac.uk/fac/soc

Centre for Applied Linguistics; www2. warwick.ac.uk/fac/soc/al

English language teaching/for young learners, English language teaching (studies & methods); EdD, MA, MPhil, PGCert, PGDip, PhD

Dept of Economics; www2.warwick.ac.uk/ fac/soc/economics

economics, economic history/industrial organization/international financial economics, politics & international studies; BA, BSc, MSc, PGDip, PhD

Dept of Philosophy; www2.warwick.ac.uk/ fac/soc/philosophy

continental philosophy, philosophy, philosophy & literature, philosophy of mind, philosophy, politics & economics; BA, BSc, MA, MPhil, PGDip, PhD

Dept of Politics & International Studies; www2.warwick.ac.uk/fac/soc/pais

economics, politics & international studies, French/German with international studies, globalization & development, history & politics, international political economy, international politics & East Asia/Europe, international relations, international security, politics/ & sociology/international studies; BA, MA, MPhil, PhD

Dept of Sociology; www2.warwick.ac.uk/fac/soc/sociology

gender & international development, postcolonialism, racism & global order, social & political thought, social research, gender & international development/interdisciplinary gender studies, sociology; BA, MA, MPhil, PGDip, PhD

School of Health & Social Sciences; www2.warwick.ac.uk/fac/soc/shss

applied social research with health studies, Islam in contemporary societies, social work; MA, MPhil, PGDip, PhD

Warwick Business School; www2.wbs.warwick.ac.uk/fac/soc/

accounting & finance, computer & business studies, finance & economics, financial mathematics, industrial relations & managing human resources, information systems & management, international business, international & European employment relations, international management, law & business studies, management & organizational analysis,

management science & operational research, marketing & strategy, physics & business studies; BA, BSc, MA, MBA, MPA, MPhil, MSc, PGDip, PhD

Warwick Institute of Education; www2.warwick.ac.uk/fac/soc/wie

applied education & training, business & enterprise education, childhood in society, early childhood studies, drama & theatre education, educational assessment/leadership & innovation research methods/studies, learning & teaching, mathematics education/subject leadership, religious education, teaching advanced mathematics; BA, EdD, FdA, MA, MPhil, MSc, PGCE, PhD

Warwick School of Law; www2.warwick.ac.uk/fac/soc/law

advanced legal studies, European law, international corporate governance & financial regulation law, international economic law, international development law & human rights, law & business/sociology, socio-legal studies; BA, LLB, LLM, MPhil, PhD, PGCert, PGDip

THE UNIVERSITY OF WESTMINSTER
www.westminster.ac.uk

School of Architecture & the Built Environment; www.westminster.ac.uk/schools/architecture

architectural technology, architecture, building engineering/surveying, business management & urban development, commercial management, conference & events management, construction commercial management, management/project management, construction & surveying, domestic violence studies, housing law & policy/practice, interior design, leisure property, logistics & supply chain management, property with business/urban development, quantity surveying, real estate development, street design & management, tourism with business, tourism management, tourism & planning, transport planning & management, travel & tourism, urban design, urban estate management, urban regeneration, urban & regional planning; BA, BSc, MA, MPhil, MSc, PGCert, PGDip, PhD

School of Electronics & Computer Science; www.westminster.ac.uk/schools/computing

advanced information technology, advanced software engineering, biometrics information systems, broadband & high-speed communication networks, business computing/information systems, computer animation/ forensics/ games development/ games programming/network security/networks & communications/science/systems engineering, data mining, database systems, decision sciences, DSP for multimedia communications, e-commerce with online databases, electronic engineering, embedded systems, enterprise information systems, information & knowledge management/quality/systems, interactive multimedia, IT security, media technology, mobile computing, mobile & web computing/wireless computing, multimedia computing/computing & animation/systems for cultural heritage/systems for museums & libraries, software engineering; BEng, BSc, MEng, MPhil, MSc, PhD

School of Law; *ww.westminster.ac.uk/schools/law*

commercial law, corporate finance law, dispute prevention & resolution, entertainment law, EU law, European legal studies, international & commercial dispute resolution, international commercial law, international law, law, legal practice; GradDip, LLB, LLM, LPC

School of Life Sciences; *www.westminster.ac.uk/schools/science*

advanced social work, applied biomedical science/microbiology & biotechnology, biochemistry, biological sciences, biomedical sciences, biotechnology, cellular pathology, Chinese herbal medicine/acupuncture, clinical chemistry, community development, complementary therapies, drug discovery & development, environmental biotechnology, forensic biology, health sciences: complementary sciences/herbal medicine/naturopathy/nutritional therapy, haematology, human nutrition, medical biotechnology/microbiology/molecular biology, microbiology, molecular biology & genetics, nutrition & exercise science, physiology & pharmacology, psychology with neuroscience, health promotion public health practice, teachers in primary care; BSc, FdSc, MA, MPhil, MSc, PGCert, PhD

School of Media, Arts & Design; *www.westminster.ac.uk/schools/media*

animation, art & media practice, audio production, ceramics, clinical photography, commercial music, contemporary media practice, design for communication, digital & photographic imaging, fashion business management/design/merchandise management, film & TV directing/production/theory, global media, graphic information design, illustration, journalism, media management, mixed media fine art, music business management/informatics, photographic arts/studies, photography & digital imaging, photojournalism, popular musician, PR, radio production, screenwriting; BA, BMus, BSc, FdA, Grad-Dip, MA, PGDip

School of Social Sciences, Humanities & Languages; *www.westminster.ac.uk/schools/humanities*

Dept of English, Linguistics & Cultural Studies

creative writing, cultural & critical studies, English language/literature, language teaching, linguistics, London studies, TESOL, visual culture; modern & applied languages, Arabic, bilingual translation, Chinese, conference interpreting, French, German, Russian, Spanish, technical & specialized translation, translation & linguisticss; BA, MA, MPhil, PhD

Westminster Business School; www.westminster.ac.uk/schools/business

accounting, business, business administration/coaching & mentoring at work/economics/management/studies, employment & diversity law, digital enterprise management, European management, finance & accounting, financial management, global marketing, human resource development/management, information management & finance, international business, international development management/finance, investment & quantitative finance, management, managing health & social care, marketing communications/management, personnel & development, purchasing & supply chain management, strategic HRM; BA, MA, MBA, MPhil, MSc, PGCert, PhD

THE UNIVERSITY OF WINCHESTER
www.winchester.ac.uk

Faculty of Arts; *www.winchester.ac.uk/?page=5033*

American literature/studies, applied theatre, arts management, choreography & dance, contemporary literature, creative industries/writing, critical writing, cultural & arts management, design for digital media, drama, English/literature & language, film & cinema technologies, film studies, journalism, media studies, performance management/arts, rhetoric stage management, street arts, theatre & media for development, writing for children; BA, FdA, MA, PGCert, PGDip, PhD

Faculty of Humanities and Social Sciences; www.winchester.ac.uk/?page=2989

Dept of Archaeology
ancient and medieval archaeology spirituality, rhetoric & rituals of death

Dept of History
history, regional and local history &/or archaeology

Dept of Psychology
psychological research methods, psychology; BA, BSc, MA, MPhil, MRes, MSc, PGCert, PGDip, PhD

Faculty of Education,Health and Social Care; www.winchester.ac.uk/?page=2989

educational studies, childhood studies, childhood, youth & community studies, education: education studies, primary education; community development, heath and wellbeing,health and social care, primary health care, social care studies,social work; BA, FdA, MA(Ed), MPhil, PGCE, PhD

Faculty of Business, Law & Sport; www.winchester.ac.uk/?page=9734

Winchester Business School
accounting & finance/law/management, business administration/management, event management, human resources, management, managing contemporary global issues, marketing, politics & global studies; BA, FdA, MBA, MSc, PGCert, PGDip

Dept of Law
law; BA/LLB, LLB

Dept of Sports Studies
sports coaching & development, sports management, sports science, sports studies; BA, BSc, FdA

UNIVERSITY OF WOLVERHAMPTON
www.wlv.ac.uk

School of Applied Sciences; www.wlv.ac.uk/default.aspx?page=6878
agricultural biotechnology, amenity horticulture, animal behaviour & wildlife conservation, animal management, biochemistry, biomedical sciences, biotechnology, clinical physiology, cognitive behaviour therapy, counselling psychology, environmental fieldwork practice/health/management/science & management/technology, equine sports science, forensic science, genetics, geography, human biology/physiology, life sciences, microbiology, molecular biology, pharmaceutical science, pharmacology, pharmacy, psychology, rehabilitation studies, science & technology; BA, BSc, DBMS, FdSc, GradDip, HND, MPharm, MSc, PGDip

School of Art & Design; www.wlv.ac.uk/default.aspx?page=6963
animation, art & design, computer games design, commercial video production, design & applied arts (3D design/ceramics/glass), design for advertising, digital media, fashion, fashion accessories, fine art, graphic communication, illustration, interactive media, interior design, journalism & editorial design, photography, product design, textile design, video & film production; BA, FdA, HND, MA

School of Computing & IT; www.wlv.ac.uk/default.aspx?page=6964
business information systems/technology, computer science /web development, information systems, IT, multimedia applications development, statistical sciences, strategic information technology management, web computing; BSc, FdSc, HNC, HND, MSc, PGCert

School of Education; www.wlv.ac.uk/default.aspx?page=6965
childhood & family studies, conductive education, early years services, education studies, ESOL, literacy, numeracy, post-compulsory education, primary education, special needs & inclusion studies; BA, EdD, FdA, MA, PGCert, PGDip, PhD

School of Engineering & Built Environment; www.wlv.ac.uk/default.aspx?page=6966
advanced technology management, architectural studies, auctioneering & valuation, automotive systems engineering, building surveying, civil engineering, environmental engineering, commercial management & quantity surveying, computer-aided design & construction, construction, construction law/management/project management, design technology, electronics & communications engineering, engineering design management, interior architecture & property

development, mechanical engineering, mechatronics, polymer engineering, product design & innovation, property management, quantity surveying, real estate, transport & environmental management, transport & infrastructure management; BDes, BEng, BSc, FdSc, HNC, MEng, MSc, PGCert

School of Health & Wellbeing; www.wlv.ac.uk/default.aspx?page=6067

acute care (high-dependency/ophthalmic/orthopaedic), advancing clinical practice, community health & social care, complementary therapies, critical care, health studies, integrated children & young people's services, learning disabilities, long-term care, mental health & psychosocial care, public health, social care, social studies (mental health), social work, specialist community nursing/public health nursing, specialist social work (adults/children, young people, their families & carers/mental health); BA, BSc, DipHE, FdA, GradDip, MA, MPH, MSc, PGCert, PGDip

School of Law, Social Sciences & Communications

applied social studies, broadcasting & journalism, conflict studies, consumer protection, contemporary media, corporate & financial law, creative & professional writing, criminology & criminal justice, English, film studies, French, German, history, international corporate & financial law, interpreting, law, linguistics, media & communication/cultural studies, philosophy, policing, politics, popular culture, practice management, PR,public sector, religious studies, social policy, sociology, Spanish, TESOL, trade union studies, voluntary & public sectors: policy & practice, war studies; BA, FdA, LLB, LLM, MA

School of Sport, Performing Arts & Leisure; www.wlv.ac.uk/default.aspx?page=6970

applied sport & exercise science, composition & songwriting, dance practice & performance/science, drama & performance, entertainment industries management, event & venue management, hospitality management, music, musicology, exercise & health/education, popular music, professional licensed retailing, sport & exercise science, sports coaching/management, tourism management, travel operations management; BA, BSc, FdA, FdSc, MA, MSc

University of Wolverhampton Business School; www.wlv.ac.uk/default.aspx?page=6971

accounting, business, business economics, coaching & mentoring, enterprise, finance, health service management, healthcare leadership, HRD/M, information systems & networking, integrated children's services, law, management, marketing, medical education, project management; BA, FdA, HND

UNIVERSITY COLLEGE WORCESTER
www.worc.ac.uk

Institute of Education; www.worc.ac.uk/departments/661.html

early childhood studies, education, educational management & leadership, higher education, improving practice in education, ITT for teachers in lifelong learning, learning & teaching,early years practice, learning support, teaching & learning English/ESOL/maths, mentoring & coaching, primary initial teacher education, special & inclusive education, teaching & learning in HE, teaching primary modern foreign languages; BA, CertHE, FdA, MA, MSc, PGCE, PGCert, PGDip

Institute of Health & Safety; www.worc.ac.uk/departments/659.html

advanced social & health care studies, applied health sciences, business psychology, changing health behaviours, child & adolescent mental health, counselling, counselling psychology, health & complementary therapies/social care/well-being, health management, health psychology, health sciences, midwifery, nursing studies, nutritional therapy, pre-hospital, unscheduled & emergency care, psychology, social welfare, social work, spa & salon management, sports therapy, young people services, youth & community services; BSc, DipHE, FdA, FdSc, GradDip, MA, MSc, PGCert, PGDip

Institute of Humanities & Creative Arts; www.worc.ac.uk/departments/663.html

American studies, animation, art & design/professional practice, creative digital media, dance, digital film production, drama & performance, English language studies/literary studies/literature: politics & identity, film making/studies, fine art practice, graphic design & multimedia, history, illustration, journalism, media & cultural studies, performance (costume & make-up), politics (people & power), screenwriting, sociology, urban & electronic music production; BA, HND, MA, MSc

Science & the Environment; www.worc.ac.uk/departments/652.html

animal biology/care science/welfare & management, applied nutrition for professional practice, archaeology & heritage studies/landscape studies, biology, ecology, environmental management/science, food safety & quality management, garden design, geography, horticulture, human nutrition, professional gardening, sustainable woodland management, water & environmental management; BSc, FdSc, HNC, HND, MSc, PGCert, PGDip

Institute of Sport & Exercise Science; www.worc.ac.uk/departments/652.html

applied sport science, outdoor adventure leadership & managemen/education, physical education, sport & exercise psychology/science, sports coaching/management/performance & coaching/therapy; BSc, HND, MSc

Worcester Business School; www.worc.ac.uk/departments/655.html

accountancy, advertising, business IT/management, computing, economics, finance, HRM, innovation, international business, IT for education & training, leadership, management, marketing, networks & information security, PR, public services, web design/development; BA, BSc, DMS, GradCert, MBA, MSc

UNIVERSITY OF YORK
www.york.ac.uk

Dept of Archaeology; www.york.ac.uk/depts/arch

archaeology, history, bioarchaeology, conservation studies, cultural heritage management, historic landscape studies, historical archaeology; BA, BSc, MA, MPhil, MSc, PhD

Dept of Biology; www.york.ac.uk/depts/biol

biology, bioscience technology, ecology, conservation & environment, functional genomics, genetics, molecular cell biology; BSc, MPhil, MRes, MSc, PhD

Dept of Chemistry; www.york.ac.uk/depts/chemistry

chemistry, chemistry with biological & medicinal chemistry/management & industry/resources & the environment; BSc, MChem, MPhil, MSc, PhD

Dept of Computer Science & Engineering; www.cs.york.ac.uk/depts

computer science/with artificial intelligence/business enterprise systems/embedded systems/mathematics/software engineering, human-centred interactive technologies, information technology, safety critical systems engineering; BEng, BSc, MEng, MMath, MPhil, MSc, PGCert, PGDip

Dept of Economics & Related Studies; www.york.ac.uk/depts/econ

economics, econometrics & finance/economic history/education/mathematics/sociology, mathematics & finance, project analysis, finance & investment; BA, BSc, MSc, PGCert, PGDip, PhD

Dept of Educational Studies; www.york.ac.uk/depts/educ

educational studies, language & literature in education, TESOL, young learners, teaching studies; BA, MA, MPhil, PhD

Dept of Electronics; www.york.ac.uk/depts/elec

avionics, digital systems engineering, electronic engineering, media technology/music technology systems/nanotechnology, electronic & communication engineering/computer engineering, media technology; BEng, MEng, MSc, MPhil, PhD

Dept of English & Related Literature; www.york.ac.uk/depts/engl

English, English & history/history of art/linguistics/philosophy/politics, English literary studies, film & literature; BA, MA, MPhil, PhD

Dept of Environment; www.york.ac.uk/depts/eeem

environmental economics & environmental management, environmental geography, environmental science; BSc, MPhil, MSc, PGDip, PhD

Dept of Health Sciences; www.york.ac.uk/depts/healthsciences

haematopathology, health sciences, midwifery practice, nursing, evidence-based practice/nursing studies (adult/child/learning disability/mental health); BA, BSc, DipHE, MPhil, MSc, PGCert, PGDip, PhD

Dept of History; www.york.ac.uk/depts/hist

history, history with archaeology/economics/English/education/French/history of art/philosophy/politics/sociology, medieval studies, railway studies; BA, GradCert, MA, MPhil, PhD

Dept of History of Art; www.york.ac.uk/depts/histart

history of art/with English/history, stained glass conservation & heritage management; BA, MA, MPhil, PhD

Dept of Language & Linguistic Science; www.york.ac.uk/depts/lang

English language, forensic speech science, linguistics /with education/literature/modern languages/philosophy, phonetics & phonology, psycholinguistics, sociolinguistics; BA, MA, MPhil, MSc, PhD

Dept of Law; www.york.ac.uk/depts/law

law; LLB, LLM. MPhil, PhD

Dept of Mathematics; www.york.ac.uk/depts/maths

mathematics, chemoinformatics, mathematics with computer science/economics/education/finance/linguistics/philosophy/physics/statistics; BA, BSc, MMath, MPhil, MRes. MSc, PGCert, PGDip, PhD

Dept of Music; www.york.ac.uk/depts/music

music, music with education, music technology; BA, MA, MPhil, PhD

Dept of Philosophy; www.york.ac.uk/depts/phil

philosophy, philosophy with education/English/history/linguistics/mathematics/sociology, theology & ethics; BA, BSc, GradDip, MA, MPhil, PGCert, PGDip, PhD

Dept of Physics; www.york.ac.uk/depts/physics

physics, physics with astrophysics/business management/education/mathematics/philosophy, theoretical physics; BA, BSc, MMath, MPhil, MPhys, MSc, PhD

Dept of Politics; www.york.ac.uk/depts/poli

applied human rights, conflict, governance & development, politics/with English/history/international relations/social policy/sociology, postwar recovery, public administration; BA, MA, PGDip, PhD

Dept of Psychology; www.york.ac.uk/depts/psych

cognitive neuroscience, forensic psychology, psychology; BSc, MPhil, MRes, MSc, PhD

Dept of Social Policy & Social Work; www.york.ac.uk/depts/spsw

applied social science (children & young people/crime/health), demography, social policy, social work, sociology; BA, MA, MPhil, MRes, PGCert, PhD

Dept of Sociology; www.york.ac.uk/depts/soci

communication studies, sociology /with criminology/economics/education/history/philosophy/politics/social policy/social psychology, social research, women's studies (in Centre for Women's Studies); BA, MA, MPhil, MSc, PhD

Dept of Theatre, Film & Television; www.york.ac.uk/depts/tft

cinema, television & society, post-production, theatre, film & television, writing, directing & performance; BA, MA, MPhil, MSc, PhD

Hull York Medical School; www.york.ac.uk/depts/hyms

medicine; BMBS, MD, MPhil, MSc, PGCert, PhD

School of Politics, Economics & Philosophy; www.york.ac.uk/depts/poli

economics, philosophy, politics; BA, MA, MRes, PGCert, PhD

York Management School; www.york.ac.uk/depts/management

accounting, business finance & management, management; BA, BSc, MA, MPhil, MRes, MSc, PhD

YORKSHIRE COAST COLLEGE
www.yorkshirecoastcollege.ac.uk

Higher education

applied digital media (design), business & management, costume, fine art, sport & leisure management; BA, FdA

Part 5

Qualifications Awarded by Professional and Trade Associations

THE FUNCTIONS OF PROFESSIONAL ASSOCIATIONS

Qualifications

Some associations qualify individuals to act in a certain professional capacity. They also try to safeguard high standards of professional conduct. Few associations have complete control over the profession with which they are concerned. Some professions are regulated by the law, and their associations act as the central registration authority. Entry to others is directly controlled by associations which alone award the requisite qualifications. If a profession is required to be registered by the law and is controlled by the representative council, a practitioner found guilty by his or her council of misconduct may be suspended from practice or completely debarred by the removal of his or her name from the register of qualified practitioners. In other professions the consequence of misdemeanour may not be so serious, because the profession does not exercise the same degree of control. The professions registered by statute, and therefore subject to restrictions on entry and loss of either privileges or the right to practise on erasure, are listed in Table 5.1. Certain other professions are closed. Admission to the Bar is controlled by the Inns of Court, although their powers have never been confirmed by Statute. Merchant Navy Officers and Mine Managers are certificated by the Department for Business, Enterprise and Regulatory Reform and the Health and Safety Executive respectively.

Table 5.1 Professions registered by statute

Profession	Statutory committee controlling professional conduct
Architects	Architects Registration Board
Dentists	General Dental Council
Doctors	General Medical Council
Professions supplementary to medicine: chiropodists; dieticians; medical laboratory technicians; occupational therapists; orthoptists, physiotherapists; radiographers	Health Professions Council
Nurses and midwives	Nursing and Midwifery Council
Opticians	General Optical Council
Patent agents	Chartered Institute of Patent Agents
Social workers	General Social Care Council Social Care Register
Teachers	General Teaching Councils for England, Wales and Scotland

Study

Some associations give their members an opportunity to keep abreast of a particular discipline or to undertake further study in it. Such associations are especially numerous in medicine, science and applied science. Many qualifying associations also provide an information and study service for their members. Some of the more famous learned societies confer added status upon distinguished practitioners by electing them to membership or honorary membership.

Protection of Members' Interests

Some associations exist mainly to look after the interests of individual practitioners and the group. A small number are directly concerned with negotiations over salary and working conditions.

MEMBERSHIP OF PROFESSIONAL ASSOCIATIONS

Qualifying Associations

The principal function of qualifying associations is to examine and qualify persons who wish to become practitioners in the field with which they are concerned. As already indicated, some regulate professional conduct and many offer opportunities for further study. Membership is divided into grades, usually classified as corporate and non-corporate. Non-corporate members are those not yet admitted to full membership, mainly students; they are divided from corporate membership by barriers of age and levels of responsibility and experience. The principal requirement for admission to membership is the knowledge and ability to pass the association's exams; candidates may be exempted from the association's exams if they have acceptable alternative qualifications.

Non-Corporate or Affiliated Members

Non-corporate members are those who are as yet unqualified or only partly qualified. They are accorded limited rights and privileges, but may not vote at meetings of the corporate body. Most associations have a student membership grade. Students are those who are preparing for the exams which qualify them for admission to corporate membership. Some associations have licentiate and graduate membership grades, which are senior to the student grade. Graduates are those who have passed the qualifying exams but lack other requirements, such as age and experience, for admission to corporate membership.

Corporate or Full Members

Corporate members are the fully qualified, constituent members of incorporated associations. They are accorded full rights and privileges and may vote at meetings of the corporate body. Corporate membership is often divided into 2 grades, a senior grade of members or fellows and a general grade of associate members or associates.

Honorary Members

Some associations have a special class of honorary members or fellows for distinguished members or individuals who have made an outstanding contribution to the profession in question.

Examinations and Requirements

Professionals normally become corporate members by exam or exemption, with or without additional requirements. Many final professional exams are of degree standard, and a number of professional qualifications are accepted as evidence of competence at operational level by employers. Ongoing professional development is encouraged by most associations to ensure members' skills and knowledge are up to date and relevant.

The transition from the general grade of membership to the senior can be automatic in some associations (for instance, on reaching a prescribed age), but in others the higher grade is reached only after the submission of evidence of research or progress in the profession.

Qualifying exams are usually conducted in two or more stages. The first stage leads to an Intermediate or Part I qualification. The second stage leads to a Final or Part II or Part III qualification, which is about the standard of a degree.

Gaining Professional Qualifications

Prospective students can study by any of the following means:

- correspondence courses (distance learning and/or online support);
- personal attendance at the schools maintained by some associations (eg the Architectural Association School of Architecture);
- further and higher education institutions.

ACCOUNTANCY

Membership of Professional Institutions and Associations

ASSOCIATION OF ACCOUNTING TECHNICIANS

140 Aldersgate Street
London EC1A 4HY
Tel: 0845 863 0802
Fax: 020 7397 3009
E-mail: aat@aat.org.uk
Website: www.aat.org.uk

The AAT is the UK's leading qualification and membership body for accounting professionals. We have over 120,000 members, including students, people working in accountancy, and self-employed business owners, in more than 90 countries worldwide. Established in 1980 to ensure consistent training and regulation for accounting support staff, our qualifications provide a vocation progression route to the UK's senior accountancy qualifications: ACCA, CIMA, CIPFA, ICAS, ICAEW.

MEMBERSHIP
Student Member
Affiliate Member

Full Member (MAAT)
Fellow Member

QUALIFICATION/EXAMINATIONS
Accounting Qualification – offered via the NVQ/SVQ or Diploma pathway
NVQ/SVQ in Payroll Administration
Award in Bookkeeping (QCF) (Level 2)

DESIGNATORY LETTERS
MAAT

ASSOCIATION OF CHARITY INDEPENDENT EXAMINERS

The Gatehouse
White Cross
South Road
Lancaster
Lancashire LA1 4XQ
Tel: 01524 348920
E-mail: info@acie.org.uk
Website: www.acie.org.uk

ACIE provides support, training and qualifications for anyone acting as an independent examiner of charity accounts (subscriptions apply).

MEMBERSHIP
Associate

Full Member (with category of Licentiate, Member or Fellow)

QUALIFICATION/EXAMINATIONS
Licentiate (Receipts & Payments Accounts only): LCIE

THE ASSOCIATION OF CHARTERED CERTIFIED ACCOUNTANTS

London WC2A 3EE
Tel: 020 7059 5000
Fax: 020 7059 5050
E-mail: info@accaglobal.com
Website: www.accaglobal.com

The ACCA is the global body for professional accountants, with 131,500 members and 362,00 students in 170 countries. Our aim is to support our members throughout their career in accounting, business or finance so that they achieve the highest professional, ethical and governance standards.

MEMBERSHIP
Associate (ACCA)
Fellow (FCCA)

QUALIFICATION/EXAMINATIONS
Diploma in Financial Management (DipFM)
Certified Accounting Technician (CAT) qualification
ACCA Qualification
BSc in Applied Accounting (awarded by Oxford Brookes University)
MBA (awarded by Oxford Brookes University; accredited by the Association of MBAs)

DESIGNATORY LETTERS
ACCA, FCCA

THE ASSOCIATION OF CORPORATE TREASURERS

51 Moorgate
London EC2R 6BH
Tel: 020 7847 2540
Fax: 020 7374 8744
E-mail: enquiries@treasurers.co.uk
Website: www.treasurers.org

The ACT is the international body for professionals working in treasury, risk and corporate finance. We are the leading examining body for international treasury, providing the widest scope of benchmark qualifications and continuing development through training, conferences and publications – including *The Treasurer* magazine.

MEMBERSHIP
Student Member
Faculty Member
Associate Member (AMCT)
Member (MCT)
Fellow (FCT)
Corporate Member
International Affiliate

QUALIFICATION/EXAMINATIONS
Advanced Diploma in Treasury, Risk and Corporate Finance (MCT)

Diploma in Treasury (AMCT)
Certificate in Corporate Finance and Funding (CertCFF)
Certificate in Financial Mathematics and Modelling (CertFMM)
Certificate in International Cash Management (CertICM)
Certificate in International Treasury Management (CertITM)
Certificate in International Treasury Management – Public Finance (CertITM-PF)
Certificate in Risk Management (CertRM)
Diploma in Treasury (AMCT)
Advanced Diploma in Treasury, Risk and Corporate Finance (MCT)

DESIGNATORY LETTERS
AMCT, MCT, FCT

THE ASSOCIATION OF INTERNATIONAL ACCOUNTANTS

Staithes 3
The Watermark
Metro Riverside
Newcastle upon Tyne NE11 9SN
Tel: 0191 493 0277
Fax: 0191 493 0278
E-mail: aia@aiaworldwide.com
Website: www.aiaworldwide.com

The AIA was founded in the UK in 1928 as a professional accountancy body and from conception has promoted the concept of 'international accounting' to create a global network of accountants in over 85 countries worldwide. We are recognised by the UK government as a Recognized Qualifying Body (RQB) for statutory auditors.

MEMBERSHIP
Student Member
Graduate Member
Affiliate Member (AMIA)
Academic Member
Associate (AAIA)
Fellow (FAIA)
Honorary Member
Retired Member

QUALIFICATION/EXAMINATIONS
Professional Accountancy Qualification
Statutory Audit Qualification
Audit Diploma
Corporate Finance Diploma
IFRS Diploma
Islamic Accounting & Compliance Diploma
Management Accounting & Costing Diploma

DESIGNATORY LETTERS
AMIA, AAIA, FAIA

THE CHARTERED INSTITUTE OF PUBLIC FINANCE AND ACCOUNTANCY

3 Robert Street
London WC2N 6RL
Tel: 020 7543 5656
Fax: 020 7543 5700
E-mail: students@cipfa.org.uk
Website: www.cipfa.org.uk

The CIPFA is the professional body for people in public finance. Our 14,000 members work throughout the public services and as the only UK professional accountancy body to specialize in public services, CIPFA's qualifications are the foundation for a career in public finance.

MEMBERSHIP
Student Member
Affiliate
Associate
Full Member

QUALIFICATION/EXAMINATIONS
CIPFA Professional Qualification
Certificate in Charity Finance and Accountancy
Certificate in International Treasury Management – Public Finance

THE INSTITUTE OF CERTIFIED BOOKKEEPERS

1 Northumberland Avenue
Trafalgar Square
London WC2N 5BW
Tel: 0845 060 2345
Fax: 01635 298960
E-mail: info@bookkeepers.org.uk
Website: www.bookkeepers.org.uk

The ICB is the largest bookkeeping institute in the world. Our aims are to promote bookkeeping as a profession, to improve training in the principles of bookkeeping, and to establish qualifications and the award of grades of membership that recognize academic attainment, work experience and professional competence, and thereby enable qualified bookkeepers to gain recognition as an integral part of the financial world.

MEMBERSHIP
Registered Student
Affiliate
Associate Member (AICB)
Member (MICB)
Fellow (FICB)

QUALIFICATION/EXAMINATIONS
Level 1: Certificate in Basic Bookkeeping
Level 2 (Intermediate): Certificate in Computerized Bookkeeping
Level 2 (Intermediate): Certificate in Manual Bookkeeping
Level 3 (Advanced): Diploma in Computerized Bookkeeping
Level 3 (Advanced): Diploma in Manual Bookkeeping
Level 3 (Advanced): Diploma in Payroll Management
Level 3 (Advanced): Diploma in Self-Assessment Tax Returns

DESIGNATORY LETTERS
AICB, MICB, FICB

THE INSTITUTE OF CHARTERED ACCOUNTANTS IN ENGLAND AND WALES

Metropolitan House
321 Avebury Boulevard
Milton Keynes MK9 2FZ
Tel: 01908 248100
Fax: 01908 248088
E-mail: careers@icaew.com
Website: www.icaew.com/careers

The ICAEW is the largest professional accountancy body in Europe, with more than 132,000 members in 165 countries. We provide our members with knowledge and guidance based on the highest ethical and technical standards, and we shape opinion, understanding and delivery to ensure the highest standards in business and in the public interest.

MEMBERSHIP
Associate Chartered Accountant (ACA)
Fellow Chartered Accountant (FCA)

QUALIFICATION/EXAMINATIONS
Please see the ICAEW website.

DESIGNATORY LETTERS
ACA, FCA

THE INSTITUTE OF CHARTERED ACCOUNTANTS OF SCOTLAND

CA House
Edinburgh EH12 5BH
Tel: 01313 470161
Fax: 01313 470112
E-mail: catraining@icas.org.uk
Website: www.icas.org.uk

The ICAS was the world's first professional body of accountants, receiving its Royal Charter in 1854. It was also the first to adopt the designation 'Chartered Accountant' and the designatory letters CA.

MEMBERSHIP
To qualify as a Chartered Accountant (CA) students must secure a training contract with an organization authorized to train CA students. The 3-year training programme comprises supervised work experience in the training office, completion of a competency-based Achievement Log, and participation in the ICAS education programme in preparation for the professional examinations. For further information please see the ICAS's website.

QUALIFICATION/EXAMINATIONS
Test of Competence: Financial Accounting, Principles of Auditing and Reporting, Finance, Business Management, Business Law.
Test of Professional Skills: Taxation, Advanced Finance, Financial Reporting, Assurance and Business Systems.
Test of Professional Expertise: one multidisciplinary case study designed to test candidates' ability to apply their theoretical knowledge and practical skills to problems likely to be encountered by the newly qualified accountant. Additional material includes Corporate Planning, Corporate Strategies and Management, Business Improvement, Management of Financial Structures, and Ethics.

DESIGNATORY LETTERS
CA

ACOUSTICS
Membership of Professional Institutions and Associations

INSTITUTE OF ACOUSTICS

77A St Peter's Street
St Albans
Hertfordshire AL1 3BN
Tel: 01727 848195
Fax: 01727 850553
E-mail: ioa@ioa.org.uk
Website: www.ioa.org.uk

The IOA is the UK's professional body for those working in acoustics, noise and vibration, and has more than 3,000 members in research, educational, environmental, government and industrial organizations. We offer a range of professionally recognized courses and are licensed by the Engineering Research Council to offer registration at Chartered and Incorporated Engineer levels.

MEMBERSHIP
Student
Affiliate
Technician Member (TechIOA)
Associate Member (AMIOA)
Member (MIOA)
Fellow (FIOA)
Honorary Fellow (HonFIOA)
Incorporated Engineer (IEng)

Chartered Engineer (CEng)
Sponsor

QUALIFICATION/EXAMINATIONS
Certificate of Competence in Environmental Noise
Measurement
Certificate of Competence in Workplace Noise Risk
Assessment

Certificate Course in the Management of Occupational Exposure to Hand–Arm Vibration
Diploma in Acoustics and Noise Control

DESIGNATORY LETTERS
TechIOA, AMIOA, MIOA, FIOA, HonFIOA, IEng,
CEng

ADVERTISING AND PUBLIC RELATIONS
Membership of Professional Institutions and Associations

CHARTERED INSTITUTE OF PUBLIC RELATIONS

52--53 Russell Square
London WC1B 4HP
Tel: 020 7631 6900
Fax: 020 7631 6944
E-mail: info@cipr.co.uk
Website: www.cipr.co.uk

The CIPR, founded in 1948, is the professional body for PR practitioners and has more than 9,000 members, to whom it offers information, advice, support and training. Our aim is to raise standards within the profession through the promotion of best practice and our members abide by our strict code of professional conduct.

MEMBERSHIP
Student
Affiliate
Associate (ACIPR)

Member (MCIPR)
Fellow (FCIPR)
Honorary Fellow (Hon FCIPR)

QUALIFICATION/EXAMINATIONS
Foundation Award in Public Relations
Advanced Certificate
Diploma

DESIGNATORY LETTERS
ACIPR, MCIPR, FCIPR

INSTITUTE OF PRACTITIONERS IN ADVERTISING

44 Belgrave Square
London SW1X 8QS
Tel: 020 7235 7020
Fax: 020 7245 9904
E-mail: training@ipa.co.uk
Website: www.ipa.co.uk

The IPA is the UK's leading professional body for advertising, media and marketing communications agencies. We promote the services of our member agencies, which have access to a range of services and benefits, including a Legal Department, Information Centre and training courses provided by our Professional Development Department.

MEMBERSHIP
Personal Member (MIPA)
Fellow/Honorary Fellow (FIPA)
Member Agency

QUALIFICATION/EXAMINATIONS
Foundation Certificate
Advanced Certificate

LegRes Certificate
Excellence Diploma

DESIGNATORY LETTERS
MIPA, FIPA

INSTITUTE OF SALES PROMOTION

Arena House
66/68 Pentonville Road
Islington
London N1 9HS
Tel: 020 7837 5340
Fax: 020 7837 5326
E-mail: enquiries@isp.co.uk
Website: www.isp.org.uk

The Institute of Sales Promotion represents promoters, agencies and service partners engaged in promotional marketing in the UK by protecting, promoting and progressing effective sales promotion across all media channels through its education, legal advice, awards, and other products and services.

MEMBERSHIP
Personal Member (MISP)
Corporate Member

QUALIFICATION/EXAMINATIONS
Certificate in Digital Promotions
Certificate in Experiential Marketing
Diploma in Motivation
Certificate in Promotional & Interactive Marketing
Diploma in Promotional & Interactive Marketing

DESIGNATORY LETTERS
MISP

LONDON SCHOOL OF PUBLIC RELATIONS

David Game House
69 Notting Hill Gate
London W11 3JS
Tel: 020 7221 3399
Fax: 020 7243 1730
E-mail: info@lspr-education.com
Website: www.pr-school-london.com

The LSPR provides up-to-date training for those wishing to enter public relations as a career or for those already in PR or an information/communications job who require some formal training. Our Diploma, *An Integrated Approach to Public Relations for the 21st Century,* is awarded to students upon successful completion of a 2-week full-time intensive course or 3-month part-time evening course.

QUALIFICATION/EXAMINATIONS
Diploma

AGRICULTURE AND HORTICULTURE
Membership of Professional Institutions and Associations

INSTITUTE OF HORTICULTURE

Capel Manor College
Bullsmoor Lane
Enfield
Middlesex EN1 4RQ
Tel: 01992 707025
Website: www.horticulture.org.uk

The IoH represents all those professionally engaged in horticulture in the UK and the Republic of Ireland. Our main aim is to promote the profession and its importance in food and ornamental plant production, improving the environment, providing employment and as the leisure pursuit of gardening. We are also developing CPD and mentoring schemes for our members and liaise with government and other bodies on matters of interest or concern.

MEMBERSHIP
Student Member
Affiliate
Associate (AI Hort)
Member (MI Hort)
Fellow (FI Hort)
Group Membership

DESIGNATORY LETTERS
AI Hort, MI Hort, FI Hort

ROYAL HORTICULTURAL SOCIETY

RHS Qualifications
RHS Garden Wisley
Woking
Surrey GU23 6QB
Tel: 0845 260 9000
E-mail: qualifications@rhs.org.uk
Website: www.rhs.org.uk

RHS Qualifications is a nationally recognized awarding body offering a range of qualifications to provide recognition of horticultural knowledge and skills. Part-time courses leading to RHS qualifications are offered by colleges and other approved centres throughout the UK and Ireland, and by distance-learning providers.

QUALIFICATION/EXAMINATIONS
Certificate in Horticulture (Level 2)
Advanced Certificate in Horticulture (Level 3)
Diploma in Horticulture (Level 4)
Master of Horticulture (RHS)

THE ROYAL BOTANIC GARDEN EDINBURGH

20A Inverleith Row
Edinburgh EH3 5LR
Tel: 01312 482825
Fax: 01312 482901
E-mail: education@rbge.org.uk
Website: www.rbge.org.uk

The RBGE was founded in the 17th century as a physic garden, growing medicinal plants. Now it extends over four Gardens boasting a rich living collection of plants, and is a world-renowned centre for plant science and education.

QUALIFICATION/EXAMINATIONS
Certificate in Practical Field Botany

Certificate in Practical Horticulture
Diploma in Botanical Illustration
Diploma in Garden Design
Diploma in Herbology
HND/BSc in Horticulture with Plantsmanship

MSc in The Biodiversity and Taxonomy of Plants

AMBULANCE SERVICE
Membership of Professional Institutions and Associations

AMBULANCE SERVICE INSTITUTE

Suite 183
Maddison House
226 High Street
Croydon CR9 1DF
E-mail: enquiries@asi-international.com
Website: www.asi-international.com

The ASI is a non-union, non-political, independent institute whose membership is dedicated to raising the standards and quality of ambulance provision and thereby improving the professionalism and quality of care available to patients. Membership is open to non-NHS personnel as well as to employees of NHS Ambulance Services.

MEMBERSHIP
Student
Member (MASI)
Licentiate (LASI)
Associate (AASI)

Graduate (GASI)
Fellow (FASI)

QUALIFICATION/EXAMINATIONS
The Institute offers professional examinations and qualifications in the areas of Pre-Hospital Care, Control and Communications, and Management, for those who desire a career in the ambulance service.

DESIGNATORY LETTERS
MASI, LASI, AASI, GASI, FASI

ARBITRATION

Membership of Professional Institutions and Associations

THE CHARTERED INSTITUTE OF ARBITRATORS

12 Bloomsbury Square
London WC1A 2LP
Tel: 020 7421 7444
Fax: 020 7404 4023
E-mail: info@ciarb.org
Website: www.ciarb.org

The CIArb is a not-for-profit, UK-registered charity with 12,000 members worldwide that exists to promote and facilitate the settlement of private disputes by arbitration and alternative dispute resolution. We provide training for arbitrators, mediators and adjudicators and act as an international centre for practitioners, policy-makers, academics and those in business concerned with the cost-effective and early settlement of disputes.

MEMBERSHIP
Associate (ACIArb)

Member (MCIArb)
Fellow (FCIArb)

QUALIFICATION/EXAMINATIONS
Introductory Certificate
Advanced Certificate
Diploma

DESIGNATORY LETTERS
ACIArb, MCIArb, FCIArb

ARCHAEOLOGY

Membership of Professional Institutions and Associations

THE INSTITUTE FOR ARCHAEOLOGISTS

SHES
University of Reading
Whiteknights
PO Box 227
Reading RG6 6AB
Tel: 0118 378 6446
Fax: 0118 378 6448
E-mail: admin@archaeologists.net
Website: www.archaeologists.net

The IfA is a professional organization for all archaeologists and others involved in protecting and understanding the historic environment, with more than 2,700 members. We advance the practice of archaeology and allied disciplines by promoting professional standards and ethics for conserving, managing, understanding and enjoying our heritage.

MEMBERSHIP
Student
Affiliate
Practitioner (PIfA)
Associate (AIfA)
Member (MIfA)
Registered Organization

ARCHITECTURE

Membership of Professional Institutions and Associations

ARCHITECTS REGISTRATION BOARD

8 Weymouth Street
London W1W 5BU
Tel: 020 7580 5861
Fax: 020 7436 5269
E-mail: info@arb.org.uk
Website: www.arb.org.uk

The ARB is the regulatory body for architects in the UK. Only individuals registered with the Board can use the title 'architect'. Applicants must have passed the recognized exams at a school of architecture in the UK (or have an equivalent non-UK professional qualification) and have at least 2 years' practical experience working under the supervision of an architect.

CHARTERED INSTITUTE OF ARCHITECTURAL TECHNOLOGISTS

397 City Road
London EC1V 1NH
Tel: 020 7278 2206
Fax: 020 7837 3194
E-mail: info@ciat.org.uk
Website: www.ciat.org.uk

The CIAT represents over 9,000 professionals working and studying in the field of Architectural Technology. We are internationally recognized as the qualifying body for Chartered Architectural Technologists (MCIAT) and Architectural Technicians (TCIAT).

MEMBERSHIP
Student Member
Profile Candidate
Associate (ACIAT)
Architectural Technician (TCIAT)
Chartered Architectural Technologist (MCIAT)
Honorary Member

DESIGNATORY LETTERS
ACIAT, TCIAT, MCIAT

ROYAL INSTITUTE OF BRITISH ARCHITECTS

60 Portland Place
London W1B 1AD
Tel: 020 7580 5533
Fax: 020 7255 1541
E-mail: info@inst.riba.org
Website: www.architecture.com

The Royal Institute of British Architects is the UK body for architecture and the architectural profession. We provide support for our 40,500 members worldwide in the form of training, technical services, publications and events, and set standards for the education of architects, both in the UK and overseas. We also work with government to improve the design quality of public buildings, new homes and new communities.

MEMBERSHIP
Student Member
Affiliate Member

Associate Member
Chartered Member
Chartered Practice

ART AND DESIGN
Membership of Professional Institutions and Associations

BRITISH ASSOCIATION OF ART THERAPISTS

Claremont
24–27 White Lion Street
London N1 9PD
Tel: 020 7686 4216
E-mail: info@baat.org
Website: www.baat.org

The BAAT is the professional organization for art therapists in the UK and has its own Code of Ethics of Professional Practice. We maintain a comprehensive directory of qualified art therapists and work to promote art therapy in the UK through 20 regional groups. We also have a European section and an international section.

MEMBERSHIP
Trainee Member

Associate Member
Full Member
Honorary Member
Fellow
Corporate Member

QUALIFICATION/EXAMINATIONS
The BAAT organizes a programme of CPD courses for Art Therapists. For details see the website.

BRITISH ASSOCIATION OF PAINTINGS CONSERVATOR-RESTORERS

PO Box 258
Norwich NR13 4WY
Tel: 01603 516237
Fax: 01603 510985
E-mail: office@bapcr.org.uk
Website: www.bapcr.org.uk

The BAPCR (founded in 1943 as the Association of British Picture Restorers) is the professional association for conservator-restorers of paintings and has more than 400 members worldwide. Our aims are to advance the profession by providing means for CPD to our members and thereby a service to the public.

MEMBERSHIP
Associate (Student)
Associate
Fellow

D&AD (BRITISH DESIGN & ART DIRECTION)

9 Graphite Square
Vauxhall Walk
London SE11 5EE
Tel: 020 7840 1111
Fax: 020 7840 0840
E-mail: info@dandad.co uk
Website: www.dandad.org

Founded in 1962, D&AD is a professional association and educational charity with a membership of more than 2,000, working on behalf of the design and advertising communities. Our mission is to set creative standards, educate and inspire the next creative generation, and promote the importance of good design and advertising to business as a whole.

MEMBERSHIP
StudentNew Creative
Elected Associate
Associate
Member

SOCIETY OF DESIGNER CRAFTSMEN

24 Rivington Street
London EC2A 3DU
Tel: 020 7739 3663
E-mail: info@societyofdesignercrafstmen.org.uk
Website: www.societyofdesignercraftsmen.org.uk

The Society, which was founded in 1887 as the Arts and Crafts Exhibition Society, is the largest and oldest multi-craft society in the UK. Our aim is to emphasize designer-making where innovation, originality and quality are important, and we provide promotional services and exhibiting opportunities to members.

MEMBERSHIP
Associate
Licentiate (LSDC)
Member (MSDC)
Fellow (FSDC)

DESIGNATORY LETTERS
LSDC, MSDC, FSDC

THE CHARTERED SOCIETY OF DESIGNERS

1 Cedar Court
Royal Oak Yard
Bermondsey Street
London SE1 3GA
Tel: 020 7357 8088
Fax: 020 7407 9878
E-mail: info@csd.org.uk
Website: www.csd.org.uk

The CSD, which was founded in 1930, is the professional body for designers and has more than 3,000 members. We promote sound principles of design in all areas in which design considerations apply, further design practice and encourage the study of design techniques for the benefit of the community.

MEMBERSHIP
Student Member

Graduate Member
Member (MCSD)
Fellow (FCSD)

DESIGNATORY LETTERS
MCSD, FCSD

THE INDEX OF PROFESSIONAL MASTER DESIGNERS

Kensington House
33 Imperial Square
Cheltenham Spa
Gloucestershire GL50 1QZ
Tel: 08701 161823
Fax: 08702 626146
E-mail: masterdesigners@kensington-house.com

The Index was formed to provide a register of designers practising in all areas of design. Our objectives are to enable designers to achieve recognition and attain qualifications and also to accredit schools and training organizations offering suitable courses.

MEMBERSHIP
Student

Professional Designer (IPMD (DIP))
Master Designer (IPMD (MAS))

QUALIFICATION/EXAMINATIONS
Certificate of Excellence – Interior Design Students

DESIGNATORY LETTERS
IPMD (DIP), IPMD (MAS)

ASTRONOMY AND SPACE SCIENCE
Membership of Professional Institutions and Associations

THE BRITISH INTERPLANETARY SOCIETY

27/29 South Lambeth Road
London SW8 1SZ
Tel: 020 7735 3160
Fax: 020 7820 1504
E-mail: mail@bis-spaceflight.com
Website: www.bis-spaceflight.com

The BIS was formed in 1933 and has been at the forefront of actively promoting new ideas on space exploration at technical, educational and popular levels for almost 70 years. We serve the interests of those professionally involved with space, promote fundamental space research, technology and applications, encourage technical and scientific space studies, and undertake educational activities on space topics.

MEMBERSHIP
Member
Fellow (FBIS)

DESIGNATORY LETTERS
FBIS

AUDIOLOGY
Membership of Professional Institutions and Associations

HEARING AID COUNCIL

70 St Mary Axe
London EC3A 8BE
Tel: 020 3102 4030
Fax: 020 3102 4476
E-mail: hac@thehearingaidcouncil.org.uk
Website: www.thehearingaidcouncil.org.uk

HAC is the statutory regulator for the sale of hearing aids in the UK. It is illegal for anyone to sell hearing aids unless they are registered with us. To join the register, dispensers must be educated to a certain level. Once on our register, they must meet our standards of conduct and CPD.

AVIATION
Membership of Professional Institutions and Associations

CIVIL AVIATION AUTHORITY

CAA House
London WC2B 6TE
Tel: 020 7379 7311
Website: www.caa.co.uk

The CAA grants licences to pilots, aircraft maintenance engineers and air traffic controllers. Applicants must meet appropriate requirements in respect of age, knowledge, experience and skill, and in most cases medical fitness. In addition, we advise the government on aviation issues, represent consumer interests, conduct scientific and economic research, produce statistical data and provide specialist services.

THE GUILD OF AIR PILOTS AND AIR NAVIGATORS

Cobham House
9 Warwick Court
London WC1R 5DJ
Tel: 020 7404 4032
Fax: 020 7404 4035
E-mail: gapan@gapan.org
Website: www.gapan.org

The Guild, an active Livery Company of the City of London, represents pilot and navigator interests within all areas of aviation. Most of our members are, or have been, professional licence holders, or hold a private licence. Our aims include promoting the highest standards of air safety, liaising with all authorities connected with licensing, training and legislation, providing advice and facilitating exchange of information.

MEMBERSHIP
Associate
Freeman
Upper Freeman

QUALIFICATION/EXAMINATIONS
Master Air Pilot Certificate

Master Air Navigator Certificate

THE GUILD OF AIR TRAFFIC CONTROL OFFICERS

4 St Mary's Road
Bingham
Nottingham
Nottinghamshire NG13 8DW
Tel: 01949 876405
Fax: 01949 876405
E-mail: caf@gatco.org
Website: www.gatco.org

Founded in 1954, GATCO is an independent professional organization that exists to promote honourable practice and the highest standards in all aspects of aviation. It is dedicated to the safety of all who seek their livelihood or pleasure in the air.

MEMBERSHIP
Student Member
Associate Non-Operational Member

Associate Operational Member
Full Member
Corporate Member

QUALIFICATION/EXAMINATIONS
Qualifying criteria apply to all memberships categories. Further information should be sought from GATCO Ltd, Central Administrative Facility (CAF).

BANKING
Membership of Professional Institutions and Associations

IFS SCHOOL OF FINANCE

8th Floor
Peninsular House
36 Monument Street
London EC3R 8LJ
Tel: 01227 818609
Fax: 01227 784331/786030
E-mail: customerservices@ifslearning.ac.uk
Website: www.ifslearning.ac.uk

The ifs School of Finance is a world-class provider of financial learning, and has more than 50,000 students in over 90 countries. Having built a reputation for excellence in learning, all the qualifications it provides combine innovation and quality, and draw from over 130 years of educational experience.

MEMBERSHIP
Member
Affiliate
Associate

Fellow
Chartered Associate
Adviser Membership (for financial and mortgage advisers)

QUALIFICATION/EXAMINATIONS
The ifs offer a wide range of qualifications for those employed or aspiring to a career in the financial services industry, and for consumers. For details see; www.ifslearning.ac.uk

THE CHARTERED INSTITUTE OF BANKERS IN SCOTLAND

Drumsheugh House
38B Drumsheugh Gardens
Edinburgh EH3 7SW
Tel: 0131 473 7777
Fax: 0131 473 7788
E-mail: info@charteredbanker.com
Website: www.charteredbanker.com

The Chartered Institute of Bankers in Scotland provides world-class professional qualifications for both the UK and international markets. Our vision for the financial services industry is one of professionalism. We are the only organization in the world entitled to award the designation 'Chartered Banker' to its members.

MEMBERSHIP
Student
Affiliate
Associate (ACIBS)
Member (MCIBS)
Fellow (FCIBS)

QUALIFICATION/EXAMINATIONS
Certificate
Diploma
Advanced Diploma
Chartered Banker

DESIGNATORY LETTERS
ACIBS, MCIBS, FCIBS

BEAUTY THERAPY AND BEAUTY CULTURE
Membership of Professional Institutions and Associations

ASSOCIATION OF THERAPY LECTURERS

18 Shakespeare Business Centre
Hathaway Close
Eastleigh
Hampshire SO50 4SR
Tel: 0844 875 2022
Fax: 023 8062 4399
E-mail: info@fht.org.uk
Website: www.fht.org.uk

(Part of the Federation of Holistic Therapists)

The ATL began in 1963 as the Society of Beauty Teachers, when Beauty Therapy teaching was still in its infancy. In the 1990s it amalgamated with the National Beauty Teachers and Lecturers Association (NBTLA) and today it represents Lecturers in a wide range of therapies.

MEMBERSHIP
Student
Associate
Member
Ireland Member

QUALIFICATION/EXAMINATIONS
Please see www.fht.org.uk for details.

BRITISH ASSOCIATION OF BEAUTY THERAPY AND COSMETOLOGY LTD

BABTAC Limited
Ambrose House, Meteor Court
Barnett Way
Barnwood
Gloucester GL4 3GG
Tel: 0845 065 9000
Fax: 0845 065 9001
E-mail: enquries@babtac.com
Website: www.babtac.com

BABTAC was formed in 1977 and is a non-profit-making organization for beauticians and therapists in the UK. Members work to a rigorous code of ethics and good practice, both in terms of the treatments and therapies they offer and the way they conduct their relationships with their clients. CIBTAC, an international, educational awarding body that works closely with BABTAC, offers over 30 internationally recognized diplomas in beauty and complementary therapies to accredited colleges and students in the UK and abroad.

MEMBERSHIP
Student Member
Associate Member
Nail Technician
Full Member
Overseas Member
SalonPlan Member

QUALIFICATION/EXAMINATIONS
BABTAC offers a programme of short courses. For details see the BABTAC website. For CIBTAC diplomas see http:/ www.cibtac.com/courses_home. htm

BRITISH INSTITUTE AND ASSOCIATION OF ELECTROLYSIS LTD

40 Parkfield Road
Ickenham
Middlesex UB10 BLW
Tel: 08445 441373
E-mail: sec@electrolysis.co.uk
Website: www.electrolysis.co.uk

The BIAE is a non-profit-making organization that demands a high standard of skill and ethical conduct from its members, who are spread throughout the UK and overseas. Candidate Electrolysists must complete the rigorous assessments, both theoretical and practical, of the BIAE Examining Board before being accepted onto the Register.

MEMBERSHIP
Member

QUALIFICATION/EXAMINATIONS
Certificate in Remedial Electrolysis (CRE)

FEDERATION OF HOLISTIC THERAPISTS

18 Shakespeare Business Centre
Hathaway Close
Eastleigh
Hampshire SO50 4SR
Tel: 0844 875 2022
Fax: 023 8062 4399
E-mail: info@fht.org.uk
Website: www.fht.org.uk

The FHT is the largest professional beauty, sports and complementary therapy organization in the UK, with more than 21,000 members and a 45-year history of representing the interests of holistic therapists. We have a comprehensive CPD programme for our members and require them to abide by our code of ethics and professional practice.

MEMBERSHIP
Student
Associate
Member
Ireland Member

QUALIFICATION/EXAMINATIONS
Please see the FHT's website.

INTERNATIONAL COUNCIL OF HEALTH, FITNESS AND SPORTS THERAPISTS

18 Shakespeare Business Centre
Hathaway Close
Eastleigh
Hampshire SO50 4SR
Tel: 0844 875 2022
Fax: 023 8062 4399
E-mail: info@fht.org.uk
Website: www.fht.org.uk

(Part of the Federation of Holistic Therapists)

This professional association supports therapists in the health and fitness industry. Membership is open to those qualified through awarding bodies such as IIST, NVQ/SVQ and C&G.

INTERNATIONAL FEDERATION OF HEALTH AND BEAUTY THERAPISTS

18 Shakespeare Business Centre
Hathaway Close
Eastleigh
Hampshire SO50 4SR
Tel: 0844 875 20 22
Fax: 023 8062 4399
E-mail: info@fht.org.uk
Website: www.fht.org.uk

(Part of the Federation of Holistic Therapists)

This professional association supports therapists in the health and beauty industry. Membership is open only to those qualified through awarding bodies such as VTCT, NVQ/SVQ, BTEC and C&G. Exemptions are granted only for those who have other acceptable qualifications and experience.

ITEC

2nd Floor, Chiswick Gate
598--608 Chiswick High Road
London W4 5RT
Tel: 020 8994 4141
Fax: 020 8994 7880
E-mail: info@itecworld.co.uk
Website: www.itecworld.co.uk

ITEC is an international examination board offering a variety of qualifications in the beauty therapy, complementary therapy and sports therapy sectors worldwide. We also offer teacher training courses in: Skincare; Make-up; Manicure and Pedicure; Waxing; Holistic Massage; Aromatherapy; Reflexology; Body Treatments; and other areas as required.

QUALIFICATION/EXAMINATIONS
Please see the ITEC website.

BIOLOGICAL SCIENCES
Membership of Professional Institutions and Associations

INSTITUTE OF BIOMEDICAL SCIENCE

12 Coldbath Square
London EC1R 5HL
Tel: 020 7713 0214
Fax: 020 7837 9658
E-mail: mail@ibms.org
Website: www.ibms.org

The IBMS is the professional body for biomedical scientists in the UK. We aim to promote and develop the role of biomedical science within healthcare to deliver the best possible service for patient care and safety.

MEMBERSHIP
Associate
Licentiate (LIBMS)
Member (MIBMS)
Fellow (FIBMS)
Company member

QUALIFICATION/EXAMINATIONS
Certificate of Competence

Specialist Diploma in:
Cellular Pathology, Clinical Biochemistry, Clinical Immunology, Cytopathology, Haematology & Transfusion Science, Histocompatibility & Immunogenetics (developed in conjunction with BSHI), Medical Microbiology, Transfusion Science, Virology.
Diploma of Specialist Practice
Higher Specialist Diploma
Diploma of Higher Specialist Practice

DESIGNATORY LETTERS
LIBMS, MIBMS, FIBMS

SOCIETY OF BIOLOGY

9 Red Lion Court
London EC4A 3EF
Tel: 020 7936 5900
Fax: 020 7936 5901
E-mail: info@societyofbiology.org
Website: www.societyofbiology.org

The Society of Biology aims to be a single unified voice for biology: advising government and influencing policy; advancing education and professional development; supporting members, and engaging and encouraging public interest in the life sciences.

MEMBERSHIP
Associate Member (AMSB)
Member (MSB)
Fellow (FSB)
Chartered Biologist (CBiol)

DESIGNATORY LETTERS
AMSB, MSB, FSB, CBiol

BREWING
Membership of Professional Institutions and Associations

INSTITUTE OF BREWING & DISTILLING

33 Clarges Street
Mayfair
London W1J 7EE
Tel: 020 7499 8144
Fax: 020 7499 1156
E-mail: enquiries@ibd.org.uk
Website: www.ibd.org.uk

The IBD is a members' organization dedicated to the education and training needs of brewers and distillers and those in related industries. We do this by offering a range of internationally recognized qualifications and the training to support them, through either direct instruction or distance learning.

MEMBERSHIP
Member
Honorary Member
Senior Member
Fellow (FIBD)
Honorary Fellow
Corporate Member

QUALIFICATION/EXAMINATIONS
Certificate in the Fundamentals of Brewing and Packaging of Beer (FBPB)
General Certificate in Brewing (GCB) (Level 3)
General Certificate in Distilling (GCD) (Level 3)
General Certificate in Packaging (GCP) (Level 3)
Diploma in Beverage Packaging (Beer) (Dipl Pack) (Level 4)
Diploma in Brewing (DiplBrew) (Level 4)
Diploma in Distilling (DiplDistill) (Level 4)
Master Brewer(MBrew)

DESIGNATORY LETTERS
FIBD, Hon FIBD

BUILDING
Membership of Professional Institutions and Associations

INSTITUTE OF ASPHALT TECHNOLOGY

Paper Mews Place
280 High Street
Dorking
Surrey RH4 1QT
Tel: 01306 742792
Fax: 01306 888902
E-mail: secretary@instofasphalt.org
Website: www.instofasphalt.org

The IAT is the UK's professional body for persons working in asphalt technology and those interested in aspects of the manufacture, placing, technology and uses of materials containing asphalt or bitumen. A fully audited CPD system for members has been available since 1994 and is now also offered in computerized format for ease of data entry and auditing, via members' own PCs.

MEMBERSHIP
Student
Technician (Tech IAT)
Affiliate (AIAT)
Member (MIAT)
Fellow (FIAT)

DESIGNATORY LETTERS
Tech IAT, AIAT, MIAT, FIAT

THE CHARTERED INSTITUTE OF BUILDING

Englemere
Kings Ride
Ascot
Berkshire SL5 7TB
Tel: 01344 630700
Fax: 01344 630777
E-mail: reception@ciob.org.uk
Website: www.ciob.org

The CIOB represents for the public benefit the most diverse set of professionals in the construction industry. Our mission is to contribute to the creation of a modern, progressive, and responsible construction industry, able to meet the economic, environmental and social challenges faced in the 21st century.

MEMBERSHIP
Student Member
Associate (ACIOB)

QUALIFICATION/EXAMINATIONS
Chartered Member status is recognised internationally as the mark of a true, skilled professional in the construction industry and CIOB members have a common commitment to achieving and maintaining the highest possible standards within the built environment. To find out more about our qualifications and joining the CIOB just visit our website www.ciob.org.

DESIGNATORY LETTERS
ACIOB, ICIOB, MCIOB, FCIOB

THE INSTITUTE OF CARPENTERS

3rd Floor D
Carpenters' Hall
1 Throgmorton Avenue
London EC2N 2BY
Tel: 020 7256 2700
Fax: 020 7256 2701
E-mail: info@instituteofcarpenters.com
Website: www.instituteofcarpenters.com

The IOC was founded in 1890 to oversee training for carpenters and joiners and maintain high professional standards at a time when many feared that traditional skills were being lost. Today, while remaining committed to our original aims, we embrace many other wood craftsmen, such as shopfitters, furniture and cabinetmakers, boat builders (woodworking skills), structural post & beam carpenters (heavy structural timber framers), wheelwrights, wood carvers and wood turners, and offer professional status to those holding recognized qualifications.

MEMBERSHIP
Student
Mature Student
Affiliate

Licentiate (LIOC)
Member (MIOC)
Fellow (FIOC)
College Member
Corporate Member
Corporate Associate

QUALIFICATION/EXAMINATIONS
Certificate of Competence in Joinery & Shopfitting
Setting-Out
Foundation Certificate in Carpentry and Joinery
Intermediate Examination
Advanced Craft Examination
Fellowship Examination

DESIGNATORY LETTERS
LIOC, MIOC, FIOC

THE INSTITUTE OF CLERKS OF WORKS AND CONSTRUCTION INSPECTORATE OF GREAT BRITAIN INC

28 Commerce Road
Lynch Wood
Peterborough PE2 6LR
Tel: 01733 405160
Fax: 01733 405161
E-mail: info@icwgb.co.uk
Website: www.icwgb.org

The ICWCI is the professional body that supports quality construction through inspection. As a membership organization, we provide a support network of meeting centres, technical advice, publications and events to help keep our members up to date with the ever-changing construction industry.

MEMBERSHIP
Student
Licentiate (LICWCI)
Member (MICWCI)
Fellow (FICWCI)

DESIGNATORY LETTERS
LICWCI, MICWCI, FICWCI

BUSINESS STUDIES
Membership of Professional Institutions and Associations

ASSOCIATION OF BUSINESS RECOVERY PROFESSIONALS (R3)

8th Floor
120 Aldersgate Street
London EC1A 4JQ
Tel: 020 7566 4200
Fax: 020 7566 4224
E-mail: association@r3.org.uk
Website: www.r3.org.uk

The Association of Business Recovery Professionals (known by its brand name 'R3') is the leading professional association for insolvency, business recovery and turnaround specialists in the UK. A not-for-profit organization, it promotes best practice for professionals working with financially troubled individuals and businesses, and provides a forum for debate on key issues facing the profession.

MEMBERSHIP
Student Member
Networking Member

Associate Member (AABRP)
Full Member (MABRP)
Fellow (FABRP)

QUALIFICATION/EXAMINATIONS
R3 provides comprehensive Continuing Professional Education in the field of Insolvency and Restructuring. For details of courses see R3's website.

DESIGNATORY LETTERS
AABRP, MABRP, FABRP)

INSTITUTE OF ASSESSORS AND INTERNAL VERIFIERS

PO Box 148
Wirral CH62 7WB
Tel: 01925 485 786
E-mail: office@iavltd.co.uk

The IAV is the professional organization representing assessors and internal verifiers in the UK in vocational training and assessment.

MEMBERSHIP
Affiliate Member
Associate Member
Licentiate Member

THE FACULTY OF SECRETARIES AND ADMINISTRATORS (1930) WITH THE ASSOCIATION OF CORPORATE SECRETARIES

Brightstowe
Catteshall Lane
Godalming
Surrey GU7 1LL
Tel: 01483 427323

The Faculty and Association is a professional body for company and corporate secretaries whose prime qualified designation is that of Certified Public or Corporate Secretary.

MEMBERSHIP
Membership Fellows (FFCS)
Associates (AFCS)
Member (MACS)
Ordinary Member
Student Member

QUALIFICATION/EXAMINATIONS
Part 1 The Generic Business Assessment to ONC/D Level

Part 2 Professional Papers in Company Secretarial Practice, Company Law and Management, Secretarial and Administrative Practice, Commercial Law
Part 3 Professional Meetings Law and Procedure, Company Taxation, Accountancy and Finance, Company Law

DESIGNATORY LETTERS
FFCS, AFCS, MACS

THE INSTITUTE OF CHARTERED SECRETARIES AND ADMINISTRATORS

16 Park Crescent
London W1B 1AH
Tel: 020 7580 4741
Fax: 020 7323 1132
E-mail: info@icsa.co.uk
Website: www.icsa.org.uk

ICSA is the body through which Chartered Secretaries are qualified and supported. The Institute provides a broad-based professional qualification focusing on business practice, law, accountancy, finance and regulation. Members are employed in a variety of sectors, including business, local government and charities, with the core membership employed as Company Secretaries.

MEMBERSHIP
Affiliate
Member (Grad.ICSA)
Associate (ACIS)
Fellow (FCIS)

QUALIFICATION/EXAMINATIONS
Certificate in Business Practice
Certificate in Company Secretarial Practice and Share

Registration Practice
Certificate in Employee Share Plans
Certificate in Further Education Governance
Certificate in Irish Company Secretarial Practice and Share Registration Practice
Certificate in Offshore Finance and Administration
Postgraduate Certificate in Charity Management
Diploma in Business Practice
Diploma in Offshore Finance and Administration
Professional Programme Part 1
Professional Programme Part 2

DESIGNATORY LETTERS
Grad.ICSA, ACIS, FCIS

CATERING AND INSTITUTIONAL MANAGEMENT
Membership of Professional Institutions and Associations

BII

Wessex House
80 Park Street
Camberley
Surrey GU15 3PT
Tel: 01276 684449
E-mail: info@bii.org
Website: www.bii.org

Founded in 1981, BII is the professional body for the licensed retail sector with a remit to raise standards throughout the industry. BIIAB, the wholly owned awarding body of BII, does this through offering qualifications specifically tailored to, and designed in conjunction with, the industry.

MEMBERSHIP

There is a wide range of membership grades available, from those who have just started their careers in licensed retailing to those who have been in the industry for many years. The grade of membership awarded depends on both experience and qualifications and is determined by a points system.

QUALIFICATION/EXAMINATIONS
Qualifications for licensing
National Certificate for Personal Licence Holders (Level 2)
Scottish Certificate for Personal Licence Holders
Scottish Certificate for Licensed Premises Staff
National Certificate for Door Supervisors (Level 2)
National Certificate for Door Supervisors (Scotland)
National Certificate for Door Supervisors (Northern Ireland) (Level 2)
Certificate in Physical Interventions (in conjunction with Maybo)
National Certificate for CCTV Operators (Public Space Surveillance) (Level 2)
National Certificate for Security Guards (Level 2)
National Certificate for Security Guards (Scotland)
National Certificate for Licensees (Drugs Awareness) (Level 2)
Scottish Licensee's Certificate in Drug Awareness
National Certificate for Designated Premises Supervisors (Level 2)

Qualifications for new licensed retail managers
National Certificate in Licensed Retailing (Level 2)
Award in Beer and Cellar Quality

Qualifications for staff development
Award in Responsible Alcohol Retailing (Level 1)
Award in Conflict Management
Award in Essentials of Catering (Level 1)
Award in Cooking Theory and Practice (Level 2)
Certificate in Kitchen Management (Level 3)
Award in Customer and Drinks Service (Licensed Hospitality) (Level 1)
Scottish Award in Customer and Drinks Service (Licensed Hospitality
Qualifications for management development
Profitable Business Portfolio (professional development programme)
Advanced Certificate in Licensed Hospitality (Level 3)
Diploma in Licensed Hospitality (Level 3)
Qualifications for personal and social responsibility
Certificate in Alcohol Awareness (Level 1)
Scottish Certificate in Alcohol Awareness
Award for Music Promoters (Level 2)

CONFEDERATION OF TOURISM AND HOSPITALITY

13–16 Manchester Street
London W1U 4DJ
Tel: 020 7258 9850
Fax: 020 7258 9869
E-mail: info@cthawards.com
Website: www.cthawards.com

The CTH was established in 1982 to provide recognized standards of management and vocational training appropriate to the needs of the hotel and travel industries, via its syllabuses, examinations and awards. We work with approved centres worldwide and are acknowledged by leading hotel and travel industry organizations.

MEMBERSHIP
Student Member
Associate Member (AMCTH)
Member (MCTH)
Fellow (FCTH)

QUALIFICATION/EXAMINATIONS
Diploma in Hotel Management
Advanced Diploma in Hotel Management
Diploma in Hotel and Casino Management
Diploma in Tourism Management
Advanced Diploma in Tourism Management
Diploma in Travel Agency Management

DESIGNATORY LETTERS
AMCTH, MCTH, FCTH

GUILD OF INTERNATIONAL PROFESSIONAL TOASTMASTERS

Life President: Ivor Spencer
12 Little Bornes
Alleyn Park
London SE21 8SE
Tel: 020 8670 5585
Fax: 020 8670 0055
Website: www.guildoftoastmasters.co.uk

The Guild of Professional Toastmasters was established over 30 years ago to improve standards in the profession and support its members. A 5-day course is offered to prospective members, who may apply for membership upon successful completion of the course. Applications are considered by the Fellows of the Guild.

MEMBERSHIP
Fellow (FGIntPT)

DESIGNATORY LETTERS
FGIntPT

INSTITUTE OF HOSPITALITY

Trinity Court
34 West Street
Sutton
Surrey SM1 1SH
Tel: 020 8661 4900
Fax: 020 8661 4901
E-mail: awardingbody@instituteofhospitality.org
Website: www.instituteofhospitality.org

The Institute of Hospitality is the professional body for managers and aspiring managers in the hospitality, leisure and tourism industries. We are an accredited awarding body in the UK and have more than 10,000 members worldwide, whose professional and career development we promote to ensure the highest standards.

MEMBERSHIP
Student Member
Affiliate
Associate (AIH)
Member (MIH)
Fellow (FIH)

DESIGNATORY LETTERS
AIH, MIH, FIH

CHEMISTRY
Membership of Professional Institutions and Associations

SOCIETY OF COSMETIC SCIENTISTS

Suite 6
Langham House East
Mill Street
Luton
Bedfordshire LU1 2NA
Tel: 01582 726661
Fax: 01582 405217
E-mail: ifscc.scs@btinternet.com
Website: www.scs.org.uk

The main object of the Society, which was formed in 1948, is to advance the science of cosmetics. We endeavour to do this by attracting highly qualified scientists with both academic and industrial experience in cosmetics or a related science to our membership of around 900 members, and by means of our publications, educational programmes and scientific meetings.

MEMBERSHIP
Student

Affiliate
Associate Member
Member – B Grade
Member – A Grade
Honorary Member

QUALIFICATION/EXAMINATIONS
Diploma in Cosmetic Science (validated by De Montfort University)

THE OIL AND COLOUR CHEMISTS' ASSOCIATION

1st Floor
3 Eden Court
Eden Way
Leighton Buzzard
Bedfordshire LU7 4FY
Tel: 01525 372530
Fax: 01525 372600
E-mail: membership@occa.org.uk
Website: www.occa.org.uk

OCCA, founded in 1918, is a learned society comprising individual qualified persons employed in, or associated with, the worldwide surface coatings industries. Most of our members work in a technical capacity, but there are senior personnel from throughout the surface coating industries. The word 'oil' in our title refers to vegetable oils, which once formed a major part of surface coatings' formulations.

MEMBERSHIP
Student Member
Ordinary Member
Honorary Member
Licentiate (LTSC)
Associate (ATSC)
Fellow (FTSC)

DESIGNATORY LETTERS
LTSC, ATSC, FTSC

THE ROYAL SOCIETY OF CHEMISTRY

Thomas Graham House
Science Park
Milton Road
Cambridge CB4 0WF
Tel: 01223 420066
Fax: 01223 423623
E-mail: membership@rsc.org
Website: www.rsc.org

The RSC is the UK professional body for chemical scientists and an international learned society for advancing the chemical sciences. With over 46,000 members worldwide and an internationally acclaimed publishing business, our activities span education and training, conferences, science policy and the promotion of the chemical sciences to the public.

MEMBERSHIP
Affiliate
Associate Member (AMRSC)
Member (MRSC)
Fellow (FRSC)

QUALIFICATION/EXAMINATIONS
NVQ Analytical Chemistry (Level 5)
Qualified Person (QP) for the Pharmaceutical Industry
Mastership in Chemical Analysis (MChemA)
Chartered Chemist (CChem)
Chartered Scientist (CSci)

DESIGNATORY LETTERS
AMRSC, MRSC, FRSC

CHIROPODY

Membership of Professional Institutions and Associations

BRITISH CHIROPODY AND PODIATRY ASSOCIATION

New Hall
149 Bath Road
Maidenhead
Berkshire SL6 4LA
Tel: 01628 632440
Fax: 01628 674483
E-mail: membership@bcha-uk.org
Website: www.bcha-uk.org

The BCPA, formed in 1959, is the largest professional organization in the UK representing the interests of independent private chiropodists and podiatrists. We have about 7,000 members, most of whom work mainly in private practice, together with some who work in the NHS or in education.

MEMBERSHIP
Member (MSSCh & MBChA)

Fellow (FSSCh)

QUALIFICATION/EXAMINATIONS
Diploma in Podiatric Medicine (DipPodMed)

DESIGNATORY LETTERS
MSSCh, MBChA, FSSCh

THE INSTITUTE OF CHIROPODISTS AND PODIATRISTS

27 Wright Street
Southport
Merseyside PR9 0TL
Tel: 01704 546141
Fax: 01704 500477
E-mail: secretary@iocp.org.uk
Website: www.inst-chiropodist.org.uk

The IOCP represents all levels of the profession and our CPD is open to both members and non-members, as by elevating professional standards we aim to improve public safety. We have branches throughout the UK and the Republic of Ireland, and members overseas, and hold lectures, seminars and workshops to enable members to keep up to date.

MEMBERSHIP
Full Member
Fellow

THE SOCIETY OF CHIROPODISTS AND PODIATRISTS

1 Fellmongers Path
Tower Bridge Road
London SE1 3LY
Tel: 020 7234 8620
Fax: 0845 450 3721
E-mail: enq@scpod.org
Website: www.feetforlife.org

The SCP is the professional body and trade union for registered podiatrists. Membership is restricted to those qualified for registration and the Society represents around 10,000 NHS podiatrists, private practitioners and students. We monitor standards of undergraduate education and provide opportunities for CPD for our members.

MEMBERSHIP
Member (MChS)
Fellow (FChS)

DESIGNATORY LETTERS
MChS, FChS

CHIROPRACTIC
Membership of Professional Institutions and Associations

BRITISH CHIROPRACTIC ASSOCIATION

59 Castle Street
Reading
Berkshire RG1 7SN
Tel: 01189 505950
Fax: 01189 588946
E-mail: enquiries@chiropractic-uk.co.uk
Website: www.chiropractic-uk.co.uk

The BCA was the first professional association for chiropractors in the UK and is the largest, representing well over 50 per cent of registered UK chiropractors. We provide a wide range of member services as well as promoting the chiropractic profession in the UK.

MEMBERSHIP
The BCA only accepts into membership those chiropractors who are registered with the regulator, have completed a chiropractic qualification at an internationally recognized college of education and have completed a post-registration training scheme.

GENERAL CHIROPRACTIC COUNCIL

44 Wicklow Street
London WC1X 9HL
Tel: 020 7713 5155
Fax: 020 7713 5844
E-mail: enquiries@gcc-uk.org
Website: www.gcc-uk.org

The GCC is the statutory regulatory body for chiropractors and its functions and powers are defined in the Chiropractors Act 1994. Its main responsibilities are to protect patients, to set standards of conduct, practice and education, and to develop the practice of chiropractic. All applicants wishing to practise chiropractic in the UK must must have completed a recognized courses and be registered with the GCC prior to commencing practice.

MCTIMONEY CHIROPRACTIC ASSOCIATION

Crowmarsh Gifford
Wallingford
Oxfordshire OX10 8DJ
Tel: 01491 829211
Fax: 01491 829494
E-mail: admin@mctimoney-chiropractic.org
Website: www.mctimoneychiropractic.org

The McTimoney Chiropractic Association is the professional body for McTimoney chiropractors, who in the UK are registered with the General Chiropractic Council.

MEMBERSHIP
Provisional Member
Full Member
Fellow

SCOTTISH CHIROPRACTIC ASSOCIATION

1 Chisholm Avenue
Bishopton
Renfrewshire PA7 5JH
Tel: 0141 404 0260
Fax: 0)141 404 0260
E-mail: admin@sca-chiropractic.org
Website: www.sca-chiropractic.org

The SCA was formed in 1979 and now has more than 60 members practising in Scotland and over 120 associated members elsewhere in the UK and abroad. Our aims are to enhance the chiropractic profession in the UK, maintain high standards of professional practice, and provide advice and support to our members.

MEMBERSHIP
Member

UNITED CHIROPRACTIC ASSOCIATION

1st Floor
45 North Hill
Plymouth
Devon PL4 8EZ
Tel: 01752 658785
Fax: 01752 658786
E-mail: admin@united-chiropractic.org
Website: www.united-chiropractic.org

The UCA is a UK-based organization for qualified, professional, principal-based chiropractors, associates and students. Full membership is open to qualified, GCC registered Chiropractors from any recognized school of chiropractic.

MEMBERSHIP
Student
Associate
Affiliate
1st Year Graduate

2nd Year Graduate
Full Member
Overseas Member

THE CHURCHES
Membership of Professional Institutions and Associations

BAPTIST UNION OF SCOTLAND

Baptist House
14 Aytoun Road
Glasgow G41 5RT
Tel: 0141 423 6169
Fax: 0141 424 1422
E-mail: admin@scottishbaptist.org.uk
Website: www.scottishbaptist.org.uk

The Baptist Union of Scotland was formed in 1869, when 51 churches with a total congregation of about 3,500 united. Today, with 142 churches and about 14,000 members, the Union strives for simplicity in organizational structure and promotes increasing contact between the local churches and Council-appointed Core Leaders, who function under the overall direction of the General Director.

QUALIFICATION/EXAMINATIONS
Certificate/Diploma of Higher Learning in Theology
BD in Theology & Pastoral Studies
Graduate Diploma in Applied Theology through Work Based Learning
Graduate Diploma in Pastoral Studies
(awarded by the Scottish Baptist College, Paisley, and validated by the University of Paisley)

BRISTOL BAPTIST COLLEGE

The Promenade
Clifton Down
Clifton
Bristol BS8 3NJ
Tel: 0117 946 7050
Fax: 0117 946 7787
E-mail: admin@bristol-baptist.ac.uk
Website: www.bristol-baptist.ac.uk

The central aim of the College is to train men and women for ministry in the Church and in the world. We do this by enabling critical reflection upon the Bible and Christian theological tradition and on the contexts from which we come and within which we are placed.

QUALIFICATION/EXAMINATIONS
Certificate in Theological Studies
Diploma in Theological Studies
BA in Theological Studies
MA in Biblical Studies
MA in Mission Studies
(all validated by the University of Bristol)

METHODIST CHURCH IN IRELAND

Board of Examiners
Secretary: Rev Peter D Murray, BA, BD
28 Windermere Drive
Bangor
Co Down BT20 4QF

MEMBERSHIP
Candidates for training must normally have the standard of general education for university entrance. They must be accredited Local Preachers of the Methodist Church, and are examined by written papers in Biblical Studies and Theology and by oral aptitude and personality tests. After admission to training, candidates normally spend 3 years at Edgehill Theological College, Belfast, studying for a diploma or degree of Queen's University, Belfast, in New Testament Greek, Hebrew, the English Bible, Theology, Church History, Pastoral Psychology, or Homiletics. This is followed by 3 years as a probationer Minister working under a superintendent Minister. During probation the candidate continues study within a tutorial system and is examined by continuous assessment.

THE CHURCH OF ENGLAND

Ministry Division of The Archbishops' Council
Church House
Great Smith Street
London SW1P 3AZ
Tel: 020 7898 1404
Fax: 020 7898 1421
E-mail: david.way@c-of-e.org.uk (ordination training) susan.hart@c-or-e.org.uk (Reader training)
Website: www.cofe.anglican.org www.archbishopofcanterbury.org/1027

The Church of England's Ministry Division issues certificates for successful completion of training for ordination and for Reader ministry. Enquiries about entry into training should be directed to the candidate's own diocese. In addition, The Archbishop's Examination in Theology offers means of study at three postgraduate levels.

QUALIFICATION/EXAMINATIONS
Archbishop's Examination:
PG Diploma of Student of Theology
Master of Philosophy
Doctor of Philosophy

THE CHURCH OF SCOTLAND

Church of Scotland Offices
121 George Street
Edinburgh EH2 4YN
Tel: 0131 225 5722
Fax: 0131 220 3113
Website: www.churchofscotland.org.uk

The Ministries Council runs an enquiry process to help those who sense a call to any of the ministries within the Church of Scotland to consider it in a supportive environment. Attendance at one of our enquirers' conferences, which are held twice each year, is the first stage of the enquiry process. For more information see; www.churchofscotland.org.uk/councils/ministries/mintraining.htm

THE METHODIST CHURCH

Formation in Ministry Office (Initial Development of Ministries)
25 Marylebone Road
London NW1 5JR
Tel: 020 7486 5502

Candidates for Diaconal or Presbyteral Ministry in the Methodist Church must have been members of the Methodist Church at least 2 years and are expected to offer at least 10 yrs of ministerial service. The first stage of preparation is Foundation Training, which requires 1 year (FT) or 2 years (PT) to complete, during which a person may apply to become a candidate for ordained ministry. The process of selection takes 6 months. To enter into training for Presbyteral Ministry, a candidate must be a trained Local Preacher, which involves taking the Methodist Local Preachers' Training Course, Faith & Worship. Deacons become members of the Methodist Diaconal and are not required to be preachers. Accepted candidates for either order receive 1 or 2 years of further theological training, which in most cases leads to a degree or diploma in Theology or Ministry. Upon completion of training, a candidate serves as a Methodist Minister for 2 years on probation before ordination. For Presbyters, the appointment may be to an itinerant appointment (stipendiary) or to a local appointment (usually non-stipendiary) or as licensed to minister in secular employment. Deacons are always itinerant.

THE MORAVIAN CHURCH IN GREAT BRITAIN AND IRELAND

Moravian Church House
5--7 Muswell Hill
London N10 3TJ
Tel: 020 8883 3409
Fax: 020 8365 3371
E-mail: moravianchurchhouse@btinternet.com
Website: www.moravian.org.uk

Candidates for Moravian Church Service must be members of the Moravian Church and would normally have completed the Lay Training Course and have the support of their local church committee. They should make an initial application to the Provincial Board of the Moravian Church. Their qualifications are examined by the Church Service Advisory Board, which reports on them to the Provincial Board, with whom the final decision rests. Normally the standard of education required for the work of the Ministry is a university Divinity degree or Certificate together with a thorough acquaintance with the history, principles and methods of the Moravian Church. Candidates receive guidance for the Ministry during a period of supervised service under the direction of experienced Ministers. A class of non-stipendiary Ministers has been established for those who wish to serve on a non-maintained basis. Training varies according to candidates' needs. In all cases applications should be made to the address given above.

THE PRESBYTERIAN CHURCH IN IRELAND

The Director of Ministerial Studies
Union Theological College
108 Botanic Avenue
Belfast BT7 1JT
Tel: 02890 205088
Fax: 02890 205099

Qualifications required: Under 30 – a non-theological degree; over 30 but under 40 (as reckoned on 1 October following application) – either a non-theological degree or 2 years non-graduating Arts or 4 modules of PT BD study or 6 modules of PT study in Humanities acceptable to the Board of Studies; over 40 – not normally accepted, except in exceptional circumstances, where candidate is already possessed of good educational background and/or professional experience.

THE PRESBYTERIAN CHURCH OF WALES

Tabernacle Chapel
81 Merthyr Road
Whitchurch
Cardiff CF14 1DD
Tel: 02920 627465
Fax: 02920 616188
E-mail: swyddfa.office@ebcpcw.org.uk
Website: www.ebcpw.org.uk

The Presbyterian Church of Wales (PCW) is a Protestant non-conformist denomination. Ordination is dependent on successful application through the local church and Presbytery to the Candidates and Training Department.

MEMBERSHIP
Ministers are ordained to the full-time, part-time or non-stipendary ministry.

QUALIFICATION/EXAMINATIONS
Pastoral Studies course

THE ROMAN CATHOLIC CHURCH

Candidates for the priesthood in the RC Church attend a residential seminary course of at least 6 years. Among subjects studied are Philosophy, Psychology, Dogmatic and Moral Theology, Scripture, Church History, Canon Law, Liturgy, Catechetics, Communications and Pastoral Theology. Each College/Seminary has its own arrangements for the university education of its students. Those who do not attend university take a final internal exam.

THE SALVATION ARMY

UK Headquarters
101 Newington Causeway
London SE1 6BN
Tel: 020 7367 4500
E-mail: thq@salvationarmy.org.uk
Website: www.salvationarmy.org.uk

Salvation Army officers engaged in FT service are ordained ministers of religion, and are commissioned following a 2-year period of residential training at the William Booth College, Denmark Hill, London SE5 8BQ. This course – an HE Diploma in Salvation Army Officer Training – may now be undertaken by distance learning, and a mixture of residential and distance learning. Officers may be appointed to corps (church) work, to social services centres (for which additional professional qualifications are required) or to administrative posts.

THE SCOTTISH EPISCOPAL CHURCH

Theological Institute of the Scottish Episcopal Church
Forbes House
21 Grosvenor Crescent
Edinburgh EH12 5EE
Tel: 0131 225 6357
Fax: 0131 346 7247
E-mail: tisec@scotland.anglican.org
Website: www.scotland.anglican.org

Candidates are trained for lay and ordained, stipendiary and non-stipendiary ministries in the Scottish Episcopal Church and Methodist Church. Training may be undertaken on an FT or PT basis. The curriculum is delivered centrally through residential sessions and regionally through diocesan groups. The Diploma in Theology for Ministry course run by the Institute is validated by York St John's University. Some students undertake further studies through universities, leading to degree qualifications.

THE SCOTTISH UNITED REFORMED AND CONGREGATIONAL COLLEGE

The Principal
Glasgow G1 2BQ
Tel: 0141 332 7667
E-mail: Scottishcollege@urcscotland.org.uk
Website: www.scotland.urc.org.uk

The College is recognized as a resource centre for learning by the General Assembly of the United Reformed Church and is one of the institutions charged with responsibility for initial ministerial education.

QUALIFICATION/EXAMINATIONS
The College awards only its own certificate, which is part of the process of accreditation of ordinands as ministers of the United Reformed Church. Students, however, are normally concurrently matriculated for a degree, normally in Theology or Religious Studies, at a university.

THE UNITARIAN AND FREE CHRISTIAN CHURCHES

Essex Hall
London WC2R 3HY
Tel: 020 7240 2384
Fax: 020 7240 3089
E-mail: info@unitarian.org.uk
Website: www.unitarian.org.uk

Candidates accepted for training for the ministry in the Unitarian and Free Christian Churches take courses of training either at Manchester Academy & Harris College, Oxford (2 to 4 years study for an Oxford degree in Theology/or Theology & Philosophy or an Oxford Certificate in Theology/Religious Studies), or at the Unitarian College (Luther King House, Brighton Grove, Rusholme, Manchester; an individually designed contextual theology course of the Partnership for Theological Education which may lead to a degree or other academic qualification validated by Chester or Manchester University). Alternative arrangements can be made for candidates wishing to study through the Welsh language. Placement work and Unitarian studies are also integral to ministerial preparation. Training normally takes 2 or more years.

THE UNITED REFORMED CHURCH

Church House
86 Tavistock Place
London WC1H 9RT
Tel: 020 7916 2020
Fax: 020 7916 2021
E-mail: training@urc.org.uk
Website: www.urc.org.uk

Stipendiary Ministry: URC Ministers are usually trained in the Church's theological colleges. All training is ecumenical. Candidates must been a member of the URC for at least 2 years and most then take a 3- or 4-year degree in Theology or a diploma of the university to which their college is attached. They then go through a candidating process in the other Councils of the Church to decide whether they should be sponsored for training. In certain cases it is possible to train PT on an ecumenical course. The minimum requirement on training completion is a Theology diploma and 800 hrs placement in a church.

Non-Stipendiary: A training programme of PT study usually over 4 years is open to committed members of the URC. Candidates must be recommended by their local church and go though the process indicated above. A Director of Training guides the student. Most students study PT on a recognized ecumenical course, with an additional programme to study Reformed History Ethics and Worship, but some train FT in a college. A Leaving Certificate for a call to the ordained ministry is granted. Training is arranged by the Board of Studies of the Training Committee.

Church-related Community Workers: They help lead and strengthen the local church's mission through community development in an area where specialist help is required to meet unusual needs. Candidates must be members of the URC and show capabilities for leadership. They are required to obtain at least a Diploma in Theology and a Diploma in Community Work before being commissioned.

Lay Preacher's Certificate: Training for Learning & Serving is the qualifying course for this. The course takes 3 years. Work is done in local groups and there are five residential weekend courses each year. Candidates are also expected to undertake some practical work in churches.

THE WESLEYAN REFORM UNION

Wesleyan Reform Church House
123 Queen Street
Sheffield S1 2DU
Tel: 0114 272 1938
E-mail: admin@thewru.co.uk
Website: www.thewru.com

The Wesleyan Reform Union has no training college of its own and encourages candidates for its Ministry to enter a Bible College for 2 or 3 years. All candidates are, however, under the personal supervision of a Union Tutor, who directs a Biblical Studies & Training Department offering fairly extensive courses. Candidates attend Headquarters once a year for an oral exam in Theology conducted by the Tutor in the presence of the Union Examination Committee; they also take written exams.

UNITED FREE CHURCH OF SCOTLAND

11 Newton Place
Glasgow G3 7PR
Tel: 01413 323435
Fax: 01413 331973
E-mail: ufcos@tiscali.co.uk
Website: www.ufcos.org.uk

The United Free Church of Scotland is Presbyterian and Evangelical. It came into being in 1929 with the union of the United Free Church (which itself had been formed in 1900 from a union of the Free Church and the United Presbyterian Church) and the Church of Scotland, following problems caused by state interference in the life of the Church and in particular the issue of patronage.

THE CHURCH IN WALES

St Michael's College
Llandaff
Cardiff CF5 2YJ
Tel: 029 205 63379
Fax: 029 208 38088

The Church in Wales expects candidates for ordination to satisfy the requirements of recognized theological courses. University graduates usually spend at least 2 years at a theological college, and if they are non-theological graduates, they are encouraged to study for a university degree or diploma in Theology. Non-graduate candidates must have at least 5 passes at GCSE and normally study for a university diploma in Theology or a degree in Theology if they have obtained the necessary grades at A level. These requirements may be modified in the case of older candidates.

CINEMA, FILM AND TELEVISION
Membership of Professional Institutions and Associations

BRITISH KINEMATOGRAPH SOUND AND TELEVISION SOCIETY (BKSTS)/ THE MOVING IMAGE SOCIETY

Pinewood Studios
Pinewood Road
Iver Heath
Buckinghamshire SL0 0NH
Tel: 01753 656656
Fax: 01753 656618
E-mail: info@bksts.com
Website: www.bksts.com

The BKSTS was founded in 1931 to serve the growing film industry and today arranges meetings, presentations, seminars, international exhibitions and conferences, as well as organizing an extensive programme of training courses, lectures, workshops and special events. We ensure that our members remain up to date with the latest techniques through master classes and our print and electronic publications.

MEMBERSHIP
Student Member
Intermediate Member
Associate Member
Full Member (MBKS)
Retired Member
Fellow (FBKS)

DESIGNATORY LETTERS
MBKS, FBKS

THE LONDON FILM SCHOOL

24 Shelton Street
Covent Garden
London WC2H 9UB
Tel: 020 7836 9642
Fax: 020 7497 3718
E-mail: info@lfs.org.uk
Website: www.lfs.org.uk

The LFS is one of the foremost independent film schools in Europe and is recognized by Skillset as a Centre of Excellence. It is a registered charity and a non-profit-making company, limited by guarantee. Since 1956 we have trained thousands of directors, cinematographers, editors and other film professionals from around the world.

QUALIFICATION/EXAMINATIONS
MA in Filmmaking (validated by London Metropolitan University)
MA in Screenwriting (validated by London Metropolitan University)

THE NATIONAL FILM AND TELEVISION SCHOOL

Beaconsfield Studios
Station Road
Beaconsfield
Buckinghamshire HP9 1LG
Tel: 01494 671234
Fax: 01494 674042
E-mail: info@nfts.co.uk
Website: www.nfts.co.uk

A Skillset Screen & Media Academy, the UK's leading film and television school offers full-time MA and Diploma courses in all the key film and television disciplines, from Animation to VFX. Purpose-built studios include two film stages, a large television studio, and post-production facilities rivalling those of many professional companies.

QUALIFICATION/EXAMINATIONS
Diploma (in one of three disciplines)
MA in Film and Television (specializing in 1 of 13 disciplines)

CLEANING, LAUNDRY AND DRY CLEANING
Membership of Professional Institutions and Associations

BRITISH INSTITUTE OF CLEANING SCIENCE

9 Premier Court
Boarden Close
Moulton Park
Northampton NN3 6LF
Tel: 01604 678710
Fax: 01604 645988
E-mail: info@bics.org.uk
Website: www.bics.org.uk

The BICSc is the largest independent professional and educational body within the cleaning industry. Our aim is to raise the status and standards of the cleaning industry through training and education. We offer our 5,000 members a range of assessment schemes and training courses, together with a telephone and e-mail helpline.

MEMBERSHIP
Practitioner
Associate
Member
Corporate Member

THE GUILD OF CLEANERS AND LAUNDERERS

5 Portland Place
London W1B 1PW
Tel: 0845 600 1838
E-mail: enquiries@gcl.org.uk
Website: www.gcl.org.uk

The Guild, formed in 1949, is a technical and professional society whose aim is to further knowledge and skill in all branches of the industry. We keep out members up to date through lectures, seminars and written reports, exchange information of mutual benefit with other organizations in the industry, and voice our opinion in relevant forums.

MEMBERSHIP
Young Guilder

Member
Associate (AGCL)
Advanced Member (AdGCL)
Licentiate (LGCL)
Fellow (FGCL)

DESIGNATORY LETTERS
AGCL, AdGCL, LGCL, FGCL

COLOUR TECHNOLOGY
Membership of Professional Institutions and Associations

PAINTING AND DECORATING ASSOCIATION

32 Coton Road
Nuneaton
Warwickshire CV11 5TW
Tel: 024 7635 3776
Fax: 024 7635 4513
E-mail: info@paintingdecoratingassociation.co.uk
Website: www.paintingdecoratingassociation.co.uk

The PDA is a registered trade and employers' organization, catering exclusively for the needs of professional painting and decorating trade employers. The Association conducts no examinations, but all membership applications are scrutinized at Branch level to ensure that only bona fide firms who agree to abide by our code of conduct are admitted.

MEMBERSHIP
Full Member
Associate

THE SOCIETY OF DYERS AND COLOURISTS

Perkin House
82 Grattan Road
Bradford BD1 2JB
Tel: 01274 761773
Fax: 01274 392888
E-mail: colour.education@sdc.org.uk
Website: www.sdc.org.uk

The SDC is recognized globally as the authority for colour science and technology, delivering high-quality, international qualifications and training programmes. An educational charity, professional body and chartered society, it serves the global textile supply chain through the knowledgeable and enthu-siastic involvement of its professional members and industry partners.

MEMBERSHIP
Non-Corporate Member
Corporate Member
Licentiate (LSDC)

Associate (CCol ASDC)
Fellow (CCol FSDC)
Patron Supporter

QUALIFICATION/EXAMINATIONS
Colour Management Diploma
Certificate of Licentiateship
Diploma of Associateship
Diploma of Fellowship

DESIGNATORY LETTERS
LSDC, CCol ASDC, CCol FSDC

COMMUNICATIONS AND MEDIA
Membership of Professional Institutions and Associations

THE PICTURE RESEARCH ASSOCIATION

Box 105 Hampstead House
176 Finchley Road
London NW3 6BP
Tel: 07771 982308
Website: www.picture-research.org.uk

The PRA, founded in 1977, is a professional organization for picture researchers, picture editors and anyone specifically involved in the research, management and supply of visual material to the media industry. Our aims are to provide information and give support to our members, and to promote their interests and specific skills to potential employers.

MEMBERSHIP
Introductory Member
Associate Member
Full Member

273

COMPUTING AND INFORMATION TECHNOLOGY
Membership of Professional Institutions and Associations

ASSOCIATION OF COMPUTER PROFESSIONALS

ACP
Chilverbridge House
Arlington
East Sussex BN26 6SB
Tel: 01323 871874
Fax: 01323 871875
E-mail: admin@acpexamboard.com
Website: www.acpexamboard.com

The ACP is an independent professional examining body, founded in 1984 to set and maintain standards of education that reflect the constantly changing requirements of the computer industry, both in the UK and overseas. We do so through the provision of course syllabuses and examinations to our carefully vetted training centres around the world.

MEMBERSHIP
Student
Practitioner

Graduate (GradACP)
Licentiate (LACP)
Associate (AACP)
Member (MACP)
Fellow (FACP)

QUALIFICATION/EXAMINATIONS
Please see the ACP's website.

DESIGNATORY LETTERS
GradACP, LACP, AACP, MACP, FACP

BRITISH COMPUTER SOCIETY

1st Floor, Block D
North Star House
North Star Avenue
Swindon
Wiltshire SN2 1FA
Tel: 01793 417417
Fax: 01793 417444
E-mail: customerservices@hq.bcs.org.uk
Website: www.bcs.org.uk

The BCS is the professional membership and accreditation body for IT and has more than 70,000 members, including practitioners, businesses, academics and students, in the UK and internationally. Our aim is to promote the academic study and professional practice of computing and to show the public that IT is about far more than simply using a PC.

MEMBERSHIP
Student
Affiliate
Associate Member (AMBCS)

Professional Fellow (FBCS)
Honorary Fellow
Distinguished Fellow
Incorporated Engineer (IEng)
Chartered Engineer (CEng)
Chartered IT Professional (MBCS CITP)
Chartered Fellow (FBCS CITP)
Chartered Scientist (CSci)
Education Affiliate (institutional member)

QUALIFICATION/EXAMINATIONS
Certificate in IT

Certificate in IT for Insurance Professionals (developed jointly with The Chartered Insurance Institute)

Diploma in IT

Professional GradDip in IT

See the BCS website for details of other qualifications.

INSTITUTE FOR THE MANAGEMENT OF INFORMATION SYSTEMS

5 Kingfisher House
New Mill Road
Orpington
Kent BR5 3QG
Tel: 07000 023456
Fax: 07000 023023
E-mail: central@imis.org.uk
Website: www.imis.org.uk

IMIS is one of the leading professional associations in the IT sector. A registered charity, it plays a prominent role in fostering greater understanding of IS management, in working to enhance the status of those engaged in the profession, and in promoting higher standards through better education and training worldwide.

MEMBERSHIP
Student Member
Practitioner Member
Licentiate Member (LIMIS)

Associate Member (AIMIS)
Full Member (MIMIS)
Fellow (FIMIS)

QUALIFICATION/EXAMINATIONS
Foundation
Diploma
Higher Diploma

DESIGNATORY LETTERS
LIMIS, AIMIS, MIMIS, FIMIS

INSTITUTION OF ANALYSTS AND PROGRAMMERS

Charles House
36 Culmington Road
London W13 9NH
Tel: 020 8567 2118
Fax: 020 8567 4379
E-mail: dg@iap.org.uk
Website: www.iap.org.uk

The IAP is a professional organization for people who work in the development, installation and testing of business systems and computer software. Our aim is to promote high standards of competence and conduct among our members, to encourage them to develop their skills and progress their career, and to facilitate the advancement and spreading of knowledge within the profession.

MEMBERSHIP
Licentiate
Graduate (GradIAP)
Associate Member (AIAP)
Member (MIAP)
Fellow (FIAP)

DESIGNATORY LETTERS
GradIAP, AIAP, MIAP, FIAP

CONFERENCE EXECUTIVES
Membership of Professional Institutions and Associations

ASSOCIATION FOR CONFERENCES AND EVENTS — ACE INTERNATIONAL

Riverside House
High Street
Huntingdon
Cambridgeshire PE29 3SG
Tel: 01480 457595
Fax: 01480 412863
E-mail: ace@aceinternational.org
Website: www.aceinternational.org

Established in 1971, ACE acts as a forum and information centre for member organizations involved in all facets of the industry. These include corporate companies, professional institutions, charities, societies, local authorities, trade associations and educational bodies, together with supplier members such as hotels, universities, conference centres and event venues.

COUNSELLING
Membership of Professional Institutions and Associations

COUNSELLING LTD

Registered Office
5 Pear Tree Walk
Wakefield
West Yorkshire WF2 0HW
E-mail: E-mail via the website
Website: www.counselling.ltd.uk

Counselling, a registered charity founded in 1998, is a membership organization for counsellors and psychotherapists in the UK that has established a network of about 2,700 affiliated CCC Registered Counsellors, many of whom are able to provide occasional free or discounted face-to-face counselling with clients on low incomes.

MEMBERSHIP
Affiliate

COUNSELLORS AND PSYCHOTHERAPISTS IN PRIMARY CARE

Queensway House
Queensway
Bognor Regis
West Sussex PO21 1QT
Tel: 01243 870701
Fax: 01243 870702
E-mail: cpc@cpc-online.co.uk
Website: www.cpc-online.co.uk

CPC is a professional membership association for individual practitioners, whose names are entered in a Register of Members. The aims of the Association are to represent counsellors and psychotherapists working in an NHS setting and to lead the way in establishing national standards and guidelines for further development of professional and effective counselling throughout the NHS.

MEMBERSHIP
Student
Subscriber
Intermediate Member
Registered Member
Supervisor
Organizational Member

QUALIFICATION/EXAMINATIONS
PGDip in Supervision for the Primary Care Setting

CSCT COUNSELLING TRAINING

13 Coleshill Street
Sutton Coldfield
West Midlands B72 1SD
Tel: 0121 321 1396/0870 1
Fax: 0121 355 5581
E-mail: info@counsellingtraining.com
Website: www.counsellingtraining.com

CSCT has been producing counselling training courses for over 25 years, during which time we have trained over 50,000 students. Our courses are offered PT via a network of colleges and private providers throughout the UK. Our training materials are written to the specifications of the appropriate awarding body and we provide 24-hour e-mail and telephone support from Client Services and the Academic Team.

QUALIFICATION/EXAMINATIONS
Please see the CSCT's website.

CREDIT MANAGEMENT
Membership of Professional Institutions and Associations

THE INSTITUTE OF CREDIT MANAGEMENT

The Water Mill
Station Road
South Luffenham
Oakham
Leicestershire LE15 8NB
Tel: 01780 722900
Fax: 01780 721333
E-mail: info@icm.org.uk
Website: www.icm.org.uk

The ICM is the largest professional credit management organization in Europe and the only one accredited by the Qualifications and Curriculum Authority (QCA) as an awarding body. We represent the credit profession across trade, consumer and export credit, as well as in related activities such as collections, credit reporting, credit insurance and insolvency, promote excellence in credit management and raise awareness of its vital role in business and the community.

MEMBERSHIP
Affiliate
Asociate Member (AICM)

Graduate Member (MICM(Grad))
Member (MICM)
Fellow (FICM)

QUALIFICATION/EXAMINATIONS
Diploma in Credit Management (Level 2)
Diploma in Credit Management (Level 3)
Diploma in Credit Management(Level 5)

DESIGNATORY LETTERS
AICM. MICM(Grad), MICM, FICM

DANCING
Membership of Professional Institutions and Associations

BRITISH BALLET ORGANIZATION

Woolborough House
39 Lonsdale Road
Barnes
London SW13 9JP
Tel: 020 8748 1241
Fax: 020 8748 1301
E-mail: info@bbo.org.uk
Website: www.bbo.org.uk

The BBO, founded in 1930, is an awarding body offering teacher training and examinations in classical ballet, tap, modern dance and jazz. We have schools throughout the UK and in several other countries.

MEMBERSHIP
Student Member
Senior Student Member
Affiliated Member
Student Teacher Member
Teacher Member

QUALIFICATION/EXAMINATIONS
Please see the BBO website for details.

IMPERIAL SOCIETY OF TEACHERS OF DANCING

Imperial House
22/26 Paul Street
London EC2A 4QE
Tel: 020 7377 1577
Fax: 020 7247 8309
E-mail: education@istd.org
Website: www.istd.org

The ISTD is a registered educational charity and examinations board. Our aims are to promote knowledge of dance, to maintain and improve teaching standards, and to qualify (by examination) teachers of dancing. Our dance techniques cover all forms of dancing and are taught by our 10,000 members in our Approved Dance Centres throughout the world.

MEMBERSHIP
Student Member
Professional Member

QUALIFICATION/EXAMINATIONS
Please see the ISTD website.

INTERNATIONAL DANCE TEACHERS' ASSOCIATION LIMITED

International House
76 Bennett Road
Brighton BN2 5JL
Tel: 01273 685652
Fax: 01273 674388
E-mail: info@idta.co.uk
Website: www.idta.co.uk

The IDTA is one of the world's largest dance examination boards, with more than 7,000 members in 55 countries. Our aims are to promote knowledge and foster the art of dance in all its forms, to maintain and improve dancing standards, and to offer a comprehensive range of professional qualifications in all dance genres.

MEMBERSHIP
Associate (AIDTA)
Licentiate (LIDTA)
Fellow (FIDTA)

DESIGNATORY LETTERS
AIDTA, LIDTA, FIDTA

LONDON CONTEMPORARY DANCE SCHOOL

17 Duke's Road
London WC1H 9PY
Tel: 020 7121 1111
Fax: 020 7121 1145
E-mail: lcds@theplace.org.uk
Website: www.theplace.org.uk

The BA (Hons) Contemporary Dance involves rigorous daily training in contemporary technique and ballet alongside choreography, improvisation, performance studies and a range of contextual studies that place dance in a wider cultural and historical context. Postgraduate programmes are vocationally relevant and professionally focused and include specialisms in choreography, performance and dance training.

QUALIFICATION/EXAMINATIONS
BA in Contemporary Dance
PG Dip in Contemporary Dance (pathways in Choreography, Performance, Dance Training and Education, and Advanced Dance Studies)

ROYAL BALLET SCHOOL

46 Floral Street
Covent Garden
London WC2E 9DA
Tel: 020 7836 8899
Fax: 020 7845 7080
E-mail: enquiries@royalballetschool.co.uk
Website: www.royalballetschool.co.uk

The Royal Ballet School is one of the world's leading vocational classical ballet schools, providing full academic studies to A level. The Lower School is for students aged 11–15 years; the Upper School is for students aged 16–19 years. The School is co-educational and entry is by audition only, with the main intakes at 11 and 16 years of age.

THE BENESH INSTITUTE

36 Battersea Square
London SW11 3RA
Tel: 020 7326 8031
Fax: 020 7326 8033
E-mail: beneshinstitute@rad.org.uk
Website: www.benesh.org

The Benesh Institute is the international centre for Benesh Movement Notation (BMN) founded in 1962 to promote, develop and offer education in BMN. We also function as an examining body and professional centre, and are responsible for coordinating technical developments. Since 1997 The Benesh Institute has been incorporated within the Royal Academy of Dance.

MEMBERSHIP
Fellow (FI Chor)

QUALIFICATION/EXAMINATIONS
Certificate in Benesh Movement Notation (CBMN) (validated by the Royal Academy of Dance)
Diploma for Professional Benesh Movement Notators (DPBMN) (validated by the Royal Academy of Dance)

DESIGNATORY LETTERS
FI Chor

THE ROYAL ACADEMY OF DANCE

36 Battersea Square
London SW11 3RA
Tel: 020 7326 8000
Fax: 020 7924 3129
E-mail: info@rad.org.uk
Website: www.rad.org.uk

The Royal Academy of Dance is one of the world's largest and most influential dance education, training and membership organisations. With over 13,000 members worldwide it is both a leading provider of dance teacher training and an awarding body for classical ballet examinations.

MEMBERSHIP
Full Member
Affiliate Member
Registered Teacher Member
Teacher Recognised by Mutual Agreement
Friend of the Academy

QUALIFICATION/EXAMINATIONS
BA (Hons) Ballet Education (validated by the University of Surrey)
BA (Hons) Dance Education (validated by the University of Surrey)
Professional Dancer's Teaching Diploma
Certificate in Ballet Teaching Studies
Postgraduate Certificate in Education: Dance Teaching
Graded examinations – for children from the age of 5, starting at Pre-Primary and Primary and progressing through 8 grades. Vocational graded examinations – For students who study classical ballet. Five levels: Intermediate Foundation, Intermediate, Advanced Foundation, Advanced 1, Advanced 2 and Solo Seal Award.

DENTISTRY
Membership of Professional Institutions and Associations

GENERAL DENTAL COUNCIL

37 Wimpole Street
London W1G 8DQ
Tel: 0845 222 4141
Fax: 020 7224 3294
E-mail: information@gdc-uk.org
Website: www.gdc-uk.org

The GDC regulates dental professionals in the UK. All dentists, clinical dental technicians, dental hygienists, dental nurses, dental technicians, dental therapists and orthodontic therapists must be registered with the GDC in order to work in the UK.

THE BRITISH DENTAL ASSOCIATION

64 Wimpole Street
London W1G 8YS
Tel: 020 7935 0875
Fax: 020 7487 5232
E-mail: enquiries@bda.org
Website: www.bda.org

The BDA, which was founded in 1880, is the professional association and trade union for dentists in the UK. Our aims are to advance the science, arts and ethics of dentistry, improve in UK's oral health, and promote the interests of our members. Membership, which is voluntary, stands at around 23,000, mostly in general practice.

MEMBERSHIP
Student member
(Recently) Qualified member
Ordinary Member
Retired member
Overseas member

BRITISH SOCIETY OF DENTAL HYGIENE AND THERAPY

3 Kestrel Court
Waterwells Business Park
Gloucester GL2 2AT
Tel: 01452 886365
Fax: 01452 886468
E-mail: enquiries@bsdht.org.uk
Website: www.bsdht.org.uk

The BSDHT is the only nationally recognized body that represents dental hygienists, dental hygienist-therapists and students of dental hygiene. We have a membership of more than 3,500 in the UK and beyond, and look after their interests through liaising with the Department of Health, General Dental Council, British Dental Association and other organizations.

MEMBERSHIP
Member

BRITISH ASSOCIATION OF DENTAL NURSES

PO Box 4, Room 200
Hillhouse International Business Centre
Thornton-Cleveleys
Lancashire FY5 4QD
Tel: 01253 338360
Fax: 01253 773266
E-mail: admin@badn.org.uk
Website: www.badn.org.uk

The BADN represents dental nurses, whether qualified or unqualified, working in general practice, hospital, the community, the armed forces, industry, practice management or reception, and has representation on the National Examining Board, the Dental Nurses Standards and Training Advisory Board and its Registration Committee, the Joint Consultative Committee, and other bodies.

MEMBERSHIP
Associate Member
Full Member

CLINICAL DENTAL TECHNICIANS ASSOCIATION

Room 3b, Ground Floor
Tower House Business Centre
Fishergate
York YO10 4UA
Tel: 01904 625130
Fax: 01904 658361
Website: www.cdta.org.uk

The CDTA provides political and educational representation for its members, who are registered with the General Dental Council and trained in designing, creating, constructing, repairing and rebasing removable appliances to ensure optimal fit, maximum comfort and general well-being of patients. We are committed to team dentistry and ensure that our members work to the highest professional standards.

MEMBERSHIP
Member

DENTAL TECHNOLOGISTS ASSOCIATION

3 Kestral Court
Waterwells Drive
Waterwells Business Park
Gloucester GL2 2AT
Tel: 0870 243 0753
E-mail: sueadams@dta-uk.org
Website: www.dta-uk.org/

The DTA is an organization that supports the development of the dental technology profession by encouraging and promoting education, including CPD, and for the exchange of views between dental technicians. We advise, develop and support dental technicians and maintain links with the government, other dental organizations, service providers and the public.

MEMBERSHIP
Member

BRITISH ASSOCIATION OF DENTAL THERAPISTS

E-mail: secretary@badt.org.uk
Website: www.badt.org.uk

The BADT promotes the development of dental therapy thoughout the UK and the interests and well-being of its qualified and trainee members.

DIETETICS
Membership of Professional Institutions and Associations

THE BRITISH DIETETIC ASSOCIATION

5th Floor
Charles House
Queensway
Birmingham B3 3HT
Tel: 0121 200 8080
Fax: 0121 200 8081
E-mail: info@bda.uk.com
Website: www.bda.uk.com

The BDA, established in 1936, is the professional association and trade union for dietitians. Our aims are to advance the science and practice of dietetics and associated subjects, to promote education and training in the science and practice of dietetics and associated subjects, and to regulate relations betweens our more than 6,500 members and their employers.

MEMBERSHIP
Student Member
Associate Member
Affiliate Member
Full Member

DISTRIBUTION
Membership of Professional Institutions and Associations

THE CHARTERED INSTITUTE OF LOGISTICS AND TRANSPORT (UK)

Earlstrees Court
Earlstrees Road
Corby
Northamptonshire NN17 4AX
Tel: 01536 740104
E-mail: membership@ciltuk.org.uk
Website: www.ciltuk.org.uk

The CILT(UK) is the professional body for transport, logistics and integrated supply chain management and has more than 20,000 members in manufacturing, distribution, passenger transport, retail, import and export, national and local government, purchase and supply, warehousing, education, research and the armed forces. Our aim is to promote professional excellence and the development of modern techniques, and to encourage the adoption of efficient and sustainable policies.

MEMBERSHIP
Part-time Student
Full-time Student

Affiliate
Member (MILT)
Chartered Member (CMILT)
Chartered Fellow (CFILT)

QUALIFICATION/EXAMINATIONS
Certificate (Level 2)
Certificate (Level 3)
Professional Diploma (Level 5)
Advanced Diploma in Logistics and Transport (Level 6)
MSc in International Transport and Logistics *or* International Logistics and Supply Chain Management

DESIGNATORY LETTERS
MILT, CMILT, CFILT

DIVING

Membership of Professional Institutions and Associations

DIVING CERTIFICATES

Health & Safety Executive, Diving Operations Strategy Team
Wren House, Hedgerows Business Park
Colchester Road, Springfield
Chelmsford
Essex CM2 5PF
Tel: 01245 706256
Fax: 01245 706222
E-mail: cathy.uprichard@hse.gsi.gov.uk
Website: www.hse.gov.uk/diving

The Health and Safety Executive (HSE) issues diver competence certificates to divers who have been assessed as competent by an HSE-recognized diver-training organization (a list of which can be obtained from the HSE) for the following competencies: SCUBA, Surface Supplied, Surface Supplied (top-up) and Closed Bell.

DRAMATIC AND PERFORMING ARTS

Membership of Professional Institutions and Associations

EQUITY

Guild House
Upper St Martins Lane
London WC2H 9EG
Tel: 020 7379 6000
Fax: 020 7379 7001
E-mail: info@equity.org.uk
Website: www.equity.org.uk

Equity is the UK trade union representing professional performers and other creative workers from across the entertainment, creative and cultural industries. The main function of Equity is to negotiate minimum terms and conditions of employment for its members and to represent its members interests to the government and other bodies.

MEMBERSHIP
Youth Member
Student Member
Graduate Member
Full Member

NATIONAL COUNCIL FOR DRAMA TRAINING

249 Tooley Street
London SE1 2JX
Tel: 020 7407 3686
Fax: 020 7387 3860
E-mail: info@ncdt.co.uk
Website: www.ncdt.co.uk

The NCDT is a partnership of employers in the theatre, broadcast and media industries, employee representatives and training providers. We accredit vocational courses, act as a champion for the sector and work to optimize support for professional drama training and education in acting, stage management and technical theatre, embracing change and development.

ROYAL ACADEMY OF DRAMATIC ART

62–64 Gower Street
London WC1E 6ED
Tel: 020 7636 7076
Fax: 020 7323 3865
E-mail: enquiries@rada.ac.uk
Website: www.rada.org

RADA, established in 1904, is one of the world's leading drama schools. We offer a range of courses designed to teach the highest possible levels of skill to the most talented young actors, designers, directors, stage managers and technicians, in the best possible facilities.

QUALIFICATION/EXAMINATIONS
Foundation Course in Acting
Foundation Degree in Technical Theatre and Stage Management
BA in Acting
PGDip in Property Making
PGDip in Scenic Art
PGDip in Scenic Construction
PGDip in Stage Electrics and Lighting Design
PGDip in Theatre Costume
PGDip in Theatre Design
MA in Theatre Directing

A number of short courses are also available – see the RADA website for details.

THE BRITISH (THEATRICAL) ARTS

12 Deveron Way
Rise Park
Romford
Essex RM1 4UL
Tel: 01708 756263
Website: www.britisharts.org

The British Arts is a non-profit-making organization dedicated to maintaining and where necessary raising the standard of the teaching of Performing Arts subjects. We work to encourage a strong technical foundation combined with an understanding of professional theatrical presentation and conduct exams in Dramatic Art, Classical, Stage Ballet, Mime, Tap, Musical Theatre and Modern Dance.

MEMBERSHIP
Student Member

Companion
Associate (Teaching and Non-teaching)
Member (Teaching and Non-teaching)
Advanced Teacher Member

Fellow

QUALIFICATION/EXAMINATIONS
Please see the British Arts website.

TRINITY COLLEGE LONDON

89 Albert Embankment
London SE1 7TP
Tel: 020 7820 6100
Fax: 020 7820 6161
E-mail: info@trinitycollege.co.uk
Website: www.trinitycollege.co.uk

Trinity College London is a charity and a company limited by guarantee. Its principal activities are to promote education and instruction in the study and appreciation of Music, the English Language and the Performing Arts throughout the world by the provision of examinations and teaching qualifications in each of these subject areas.

QUALIFICATION/EXAMINATIONS
For details please see the College's website or Part 4.

DESIGNATORY LETTERS
ATCL, LTCL, FTCL, AMusTCL, LMusTCL, FMusTCL, Cert TCL, Dip TCL, Cert TESOL, Dip TESOL

DRIVING INSTRUCTORS
Membership of Professional Institutions and Associations

REGISTER OF APPROVED DRIVING INSTRUCTORS

The Axis Building
112 Upper Parliament Street
Nottingham NG1 6LP
Tel: 0300 200 1122
E-mail: ADIReg@dsa.gsi.gov.uk

The Register of Approved Driving Instructors (ADI) and the licensing scheme for trainee instructors (PDI) are administered under the provisions of the Road Traffic Act 1988 by the Department for Transport (DfT). It is an offence for anyone to give professional instruction (that is instruction paid for by or in respect of the pupil) in driving a motor car unless: (a) his or her name is on the Register of Approved Driving Instructors; or (b) he or she holds a 'trainee's licence to give instruction' issued by the Registrar.

QUALIFICATION/EXAMINATIONS
Please see the Transport Office's website (www. transportoffice.gov.uk) for details of the qualifying exam.

DRIVING INSTRUCTORS ASSOCIATION

Safety House
Beddington Farm Road
Croydon
Surrey CR0 4XZ
Tel: 020 8665 5151
Fax: 020 8665 5565
E-mail: dia@driving.org
Website: www.driving.org

The DIA was founded in 1978 to represent the interests of the Professional Driving Instructor. It is regularly consulted by the relevant government bodies, has representation in Parliament and enjoys influence in Europe and throughout the world. Members enjoy a host of benefits, business advice and career development opportunities.

EMBALMING

Membership of Professional Institutions and Associations

INTERNATIONAL EXAMINATIONS BOARD OF EMBALMERS

39 Poplar Grove
Kennington
Oxford OX1 5QN
Tel: 01865 735788
Fax: 01865 730941

The Board examines candidates who wish to become qualified members of the British Institute of Embalmers (qv), which is not itself an examining body but can provide information packs (also available from the above address) that contain lists of approved schools and accredited tutors.

THE BRITISH INSTITUTE OF EMBALMERS

Anubis House
21c Station Road
Knowle
Solihull
West Midlands B93 0HL
Tel: 01564 778991
Fax: 01564 770812
E-mail: enquiries@bioe.co.uk
Website: www.bioe.co.uk

The BIE, founded in 1927, is an organization for professional embalmers. Its objectives include supporting and protecting the status, character and interests of embalmers, promoting the efficient tuition of persons seeking to become embalmers, and encouraging the study and practice of improved methods of embalming.

MEMBERSHIP
Member (MBIE)
Fellow (FBIE)

DESIGNATORY LETTERS
MBIE, FBIE

EMPLOYMENT AND CAREERS SERVICES
Membership of Professional Institutions and Associations

RECRUITMENT AND EMPLOYMENT CONFEDERATION

4th Floor
Albion House
Chertsey Road
Woking
Surrey GU21 6BT
Tel: 020 7009 2100
Fax: 01483 714979
E-mail: info@rec.uk.com
Website: www.rec.uk.com

The REC is the representative body for the UK's £27 billion private recruitment and staffing industry, with a membership of more than 8,000 Corporate Members comprising agencies and businesses from all sectors, and 6,000 members of the Institute of Recruitment Professionals (IRP) made up of recruitment consultants and other industry professionals.

MEMBERSHIP
Affiliate (AIRP)
Member (MIRP)
Fellow (FIRP)

QUALIFICATION/EXAMINATIONS
Certificate in Recruitment Practice (CertRP)
Diploma in Recruitment Practice (DipRP)
BA in Recruitment Practice (run jointly with Middlesex University Business School)
MA in Recruitment Practice (run jointly with Middlesex University Business School)

DESIGNATORY LETTERS
AIRP, MIRP, FIRP

THE INSTITUTE OF CAREER GUIDANCE

Ground Floor
Copthall House
1 New Road
Stourbridge
West Midlands DY8 1PH
Tel: 01384 376464
Fax: 01384 440830
E-mail: hq@icg-uk.org
Website: www.icg-uk.org

The ICG is the oldest and largest professional association for career guidance practitioners in the UK. Our aim is to promote access to high-quality guidance services, delivered by professionally qualified staff working within an appropriate ethical framework, and to underpin this our members adhere to a strict code of ethics.

MEMBERSHIP
Student Member
Full Member
Fellow
Honorary Fellow
School Member
Organizational Member

QUALIFICATION/EXAMINATIONS
Qualification in Career Guidance (QCG)

ENGINEERING, AERONAUTICAL
Membership of Professional Institutions and Associations

ROYAL AERONAUTICAL SOCIETY

4 Hamilton Place
Hyde Park Corner
London W1J 7BQ
Tel: 020 7670 4300
Fax: 020 7670 4309
E-mail: raes@aerosociety.com
Website: www.aerosociety.com

The RAeS, founded in 1866 to further the science of aeronautics, is a multidisciplinary professional institution dedicated to the global aerospace community. We work on our members' behalf to promote the highest professional standards in all aerospace disciplines, to provide specialist information and act as a central forum for the exchange of ideas, and to play a leading role in influencing opinion on aviation matters.

MEMBERSHIP
Student Affiliate
Affiliate
Associate (ARAeS)
Associate Member (AMRAeS)
Member (MRAeS)
Companion (CRAeS)
Fellow (FRAeS)
Engineering Technician (EngTech)
Incorporated Engineer (IEng)
Chartered Engineer (CEng)

ENGINEERING, AGRICULTURAL
Membership of Professional Institutions and Associations

BRITISH AGRICULTURAL AND GARDEN MACHINERY ASSOCIATION

Entrance B, Level 1
Salamander Quay West
Park Lane
Harefield
Middlesex UB9 6NZ
Tel: 0870 205 2834
Fax: 0870 205 2835
E-mail: info@bagma.com
Website: www.bagma.com

BAGMA is the trade association representing agricultural and garden machinery dealers in the UK. We have some 850 dealer members and 75 affiliated suppliers and allied industry companies. We offer a range of training and assessment courses through our online learning package and at approved Training and Assessment Centres.

QUALIFICATION/EXAMINATIONS
Please see the BAGMA website.

THE INSTITUTION OF AGRICULTURAL ENGINEERS

Barton Road
Silsoe
Bedford MK45 4FH
Tel: 01525 861096
Fax: 01525 861660
E-mail: secretary@iagre.org
Website: www.iagre.org

The IAgrE is the professional body for engineers, scientists, technologists and managers in agricultural and allied land-based industries, including forestry, food engineering and technology, amenity, renewable energy, horticulture and the environment.

MEMBERSHIP
Student

Associate (AIAgrE)
Associate Member (AMIAgrE)
Member (MIAgrE)
Fellow (FIAgrE)
Honorary Fellow

DESIGNATORY LETTERS
AIAgrE, AMIAgrE, MIAgrE, FIAgrE

ENGINEERING, AUTOMOBILE
Membership of Professional Institutions and Associations

INSTITUTE OF AUTOMOTIVE ENGINEER ASSESSORS

Brooke House
24 Dam Street
Lichfield
Staffordshire WS13 6AA
Tel: 01543 266906
Fax: 01543 257848
E-mail: secretary@iaea-online.co.uk
Website: www.iaea-online.org

The IAEA, a Professional Affiliate of the Engineering Council, was founded in 1932 and now represents more than 1,500 automotive engineer assessors responsible for activities such as vehicle damage assessment, accident reconstruction, investigation of mechanical failures, electrical failures and vehicle fires, providing expert witness testimony, repair assessment, car fleet surveys, and conciliation and arbitration.

MEMBERSHIP
Student
Graduate
Associate
Licensed Estimator

Incorporated Member (IMInstAEA)
Member (MInstAEA)
Fellow (FInstAEA)

QUALIFICATION/EXAMINATIONS
Basic Principles of Maths & Physics Application to Accident Reconstruction
Motor Vehicle Legislation as related to Insurance Principles
Principles and Practice of Vehicle Damage Assessment
Motor Insurance

DESIGNATORY LETTERS
IMInstAEA, MInstAEA, FInstAEA

SOCIETY OF AUTOMOTIVE ENGINEERS

PO Box 13312
Birmingham B28 1BG
E-mail: info@sae-uk.org
Website: www.sae-uk.org

SAE-UK is the only professional society dedicated solely to the vehicle and component manufacturing industries and has more than 2,000 members. Our aims are to improve the standards of design, use of materials, methods of manufacturing and safety, to encourage the development and continuous updating of automotive technology, and to improve the status of our members.

MEMBERSHIP
Personal Member
Corporate Member

THE INSTITUTE OF THE MOTOR INDUSTRY

Fanshaws
Brickendon
Hertford SG13 8PQ
Tel: 01992 511521
Fax: 01992 511548
E-mail: imi@motor.org.uk
Website: www.motor.org.uk and www.automotivetechnician.org.uk

The IMI is the professional association for individuals working in the motor industry and exists to help individuals and employers improve professional standards and performance by qualifying, recognizing and developing people. We are the Sector Skills Council for the automotive retail industry, a Licensed Member of the Engineering Council and the governing body for Automotive Technician Accreditation (ATA) -- the UK's first national voluntary assessment system for vehicle technicians.

MEMBERSHIP
Affiliate (AffIMI)
Licentiate (LIMI)
Associate (AMIMI)
Member (MIMI)
Fellow (FIMI)
For technicians only, there are two special IMI awards recognizing technical qualifications and experience:
AAE (Advanced Automotive Engineer)
CAE (Certificated Automotive Engineer)

DESIGNATORY LETTERS
AffIMI, LIMI, AMIMI, MIMI, FIMI, AAE, CAE

ENGINEERING, BUILDING SERVICES
Membership of Professional Institutions and Associations

THE CHARTERED INSTITUTION OF BUILDING SERVICES ENGINEERS

222 Balham High Road
London SW12 9BS
Tel: 020 8675 5211
Fax: 020 8675 5449
Website: www.cibse.org

The CIBSE is the professional body for people involved in the design, construction, operation and maintenance of the engineering elements of the built environment (other than its structure), as well as with heating, ventilation, air conditioning, refrigeration, lighting, electrical power and its utilization, lifts and passenger conveyors, fire protection, gas utilization, fuel efficiency and energy conservation.

MEMBERSHIP
Student Affiliate
Affiliate
Graduate
Companion
Licentiate (LCIBSE)
Associate (ACIBSE)
Member (MCIBSE)
Fellow (FCIBSE)

QUALIFICATION/EXAMINATIONS
Please see the CIBSE website.

DESIGNATORY LETTERS
LCIBSE, ACIBSE, MCIBSE, FCIBSE

ENGINEERING, CHEMICAL
Membership of Professional Institutions and Associations

THE INSTITUTION OF CHEMICAL ENGINEERS

Davis Building
Railway Terrace
Rugby
Warwickshire CV21 3HQ
Tel: 01788 578214
Fax: 01788 560833
E-mail: onlineassistance@icheme.org
Website: www.icheme.org

The IChemE, founded in 1922, is an international professional membership organization for chemical, biochemical and process engineers, and we have some 30,000 members in more than 113 countries. We promote competence and a commitment to sustainable development, advance the discipline for the benefit of society, and support the professional development of our members.

MEMBERSHIP
Student
Affiliate
Associate Member (AMIChemE)
Member (MIChemE)
Fellow {FIChemE)
Chartered Chemical Engineer (CEng MIChemE)
Chartered Engineer (CEng)
Chartered Scientist (CSci)
Chartered Environmentalist (CEnv)

DESIGNATORY LETTERS
AMIChemE, MIChemE, FIChemE, CEng MIChemE,
CEng, CSci, CEnv

ENGINEERING, CIVIL
Membership of Professional Institutions and Associations

INSTITUTION OF CIVIL ENGINEERS

1 Great George Street
Westminster
London SW1P 3AA
Tel: 020 7222 7722
Fax: 020 7233 0515
E-mail: membership@ice.org.uk
Website: www.ice.org.uk

The ICE is a UK-based international organization with 80,000 members that strives to promote and progress civil engineering around the world. Our purpose is to quality professionals engaged in civil engineering, exchange knowledge and best practice, and support our members, and in the UK liaise we with government and publish reports on civil engineering issues.

MEMBERSHIP
Student
Graduate
Affiliate
Technician Member
Associate Member (AMICE)
Member (MICE)
Companion
Fellow (FICE)

ENGINEERING, ELECTRICAL, ELECTRONIC AND MANUFACTURING
Membership of Professional Institutions and Associations

INSTITUTION OF LIGHTING ENGINEERS

Regent House
Regent Place
Rugby
Warwickshire CV21 2PN
Tel: 01788 576492
Fax: 01788 540145
E-mail: info@ile.org.uk
Website: www.ile.co.uk

The ILE is a professional lighting association with about 2,200 members, including lighting designers, consultants and engineers. We are dedicated to excellence in lighting and to raising awareness about the important contribution of lighting in road safety, crime prevention and the environment. We support members by providing technical advice and encourage their CPD through our bimonthly journal and by holding a wide range of conferences, regional meetings, seminars and courses.

MEMBERSHIP
Student
Affiliate
Associate Member (AMILE)
Member (MILE)
Fellow (FILE)
Siver Group Member
Gold Group Member
Engineering Technician (EngTech)
Incorporated Engineer (IEng)
Chartered Engineer (CEng)

QUALIFICATION/EXAMINATIONS
Exterior Lighting Diploma

DESIGNATORY LETTERS
AMILE, MILE, FILE, EngTech, IEng, CEng

THE INSTITUTION OF ENGINEERING AND TECHNOLOGY

Michael Faraday House
Stevenage
Hertfordshire SG1 2AY
Tel: 01438 313311
Fax: 01438 765526
E-mail: postmaster@theiet.org
Website: www.theiet.org

The IET was formed in 2006 by the amalgamation of the Institution of Electrical Engineers and the Institution of Incorporated Engineers and has more than 150,000 members in 127 countries worldwide. We provide a global knowledge network to facilitate the exchange of ideas and promote the positive role of science, engineering and technology in the world.

Member
Fellow (FIET)
Honorary Fellow
ICT Technician (ICTTech)
Engineering Technician (EngTech)
Incorporated Engineer (IEng)
Chartered Engineer (CEng)

MEMBERSHIP
Student
Associate

DESIGNATORY LETTERS
FIET, ICTech, EngTech, IEng, CEng

ENGINEERING, ENERGY
Membership of Professional Institutions and Associations

ENERGY INSTITUTE

61 New Cavendish Street
London W1G 7AR
Tel: 020 7467 7100
Fax: 020 7255 1472
E-mail: info@energyinst.org.uk
Website: www.energyinst.org.uk

The EI is the leading professional body for the energy industries, supporting almost 13,500 professionals internationally. A Royal Charter membership organization, we are licensed to offer Chartered, Incorporated and Engineering Technician status to engineers, and to award Chartered Scientist and Chartered Environmentalist status.

Graduate Member (Grad EI)
Member (MEI)
Fellow (FEI)
Engineering Technician (EngTech)
Incorporated Engineer (IEng)
Chartered Engineer (CEng)
Chartered Scientist (CSci)
Chartered Environmentalist (CEnv)

MEMBERSHIP
Student Member
Affiliate

DESIGNATORY LETTERS
GradEI, MEI, FEI, EngTech, IEng, CEng

ENGINEERING, ENVIRONMENTAL

Membership of Professional Institutions and Associations

INSTITUTE OF ENVIRONMENTAL MANAGEMENT AND ASSESSMENT

St Nicholas House
Lincoln LN1 3DP
Tel: 01522 540069
Fax: 01522 540090
E-mail: info@iema.net
Website: www.iema.net

The IEMA is a not-for-profit membership organization that provides recognition and support to environmental professionals and promotes sustainable development through improved environmental practice and performance. We have about 15,000 individual and corporate members in 87 countries, in the public, private and non-governmental sectors.

MEMBERSHIP
Student Member
Affiliate Member
Graduate Member
Associate (AIEMA)

Full Member (MIEMA)
Fellow (FIEMA)
Chartered Environmentalist (CEnv)
Corporate Member

QUALIFICATION/EXAMINATIONS
Foundation Certificate in Environmental Management
Associate Certificate in Environmental Management
Diploma

DESIGNATORY LETTERS
AIEMA, MIEMA, FIEMA, CEnv

THE CHARTERED INSTITUTION OF WATER AND ENVIRONMENTAL MANAGEMENT

15 John Street
London WC1N 2EB
Tel: 020 7831 3110
Fax: 020 7405 4967
E-mail: admin@ciwem.org
Website: www.ciwem.org

Founded in 1895, CIWEM is an independent professional body and registered charity with 12,000 members that advances the science and practice of water and environmental management for a clean, green and sustainable world by promoting environmental excellence and professional development, supplying independent advice and evidence-based opinion, and providing a forum for debate through conferences, technical meetings and its publications.

MEMBERSHIP
Student

Affiliate
Associate
Graduate
Member
Fellow
Environmental Partner
Chartered Engineer (CEng)
Chartered Environmentalist (CEnv)
Chartered Scientist (CSci)

DESIGNATORY LETTERS
CEng, CEnv, CSi

THE SOCIETY OF ENVIRONMENTAL ENGINEERS

The Manor House
High Street
Buntingford
Buntingford
Hertfordshire SG9 9AB
Tel: 01763 271209
Fax: 01763 273255
E-mail: office@environmental.org.uk
Website: www.environmental.org.uk

The SEE, founded in 1959, is a professional society that promotes awareness of the discipline of environmental engineering (the measurement, modelling, control and simulation of all types of environment). We provide members with information, training and representation within this field and encourage communication and good practice in quality, reliability, and cost-effective product development and manufacture.

MEMBERSHIP
Student
Member
Corporate Member
Engineering Technician (EngTech)
Incorporated Engineer (IEng)
Chartered Engineer (CEng)

DESIGNATORY LETTERS
EngTech, IEng, CEng

ENGINEERING, FIRE
Membership of Professional Institutions and Associations

ASSOCIATION OF PRINCIPAL FIRE OFFICERS

10/11 Pebble Close
Amington
Tamworth
Staffordshire B77 4RD
Tel: 01827 302300
Fax: 01827 302399
E-mail: enquiries@apfo.org.uk
Website: www.apfo.org.uk

The APFO is the staff association of the most senior Fire Officers in the UK. Our objectives are: to represent and promote the interests of members in conditions of service and legal and employment matters; to negotiate and promote the settlement of disputes involving members; to provide assistance to members and their dependents in exceptional circumstances; and to provide support to members in matters concerning employment or a work-related injury.

MEMBERSHIP
Associate Member
Lifetime Past Member

CHIEF FIRE OFFICERS' ASSOCIATION

9–11 Pebble Close
Amington
Tamworth
Staffordshire B77 4RD
Tel: 01827 302300
Fax: 01827 302399
Website: www.cfoa.org.uk

The CFOA is a professional membership association of the most senior fire officers in the UK. We provide independent advice to the government, local authorities and others. Our aim is to reduce loss of life, personal injury and damage to property by improving the quality of fire fighting, rescue, fire protection and fire prevention in the UK.

MEMBERSHIP
Member

THE INSTITUTION OF FIRE ENGINEERS

London Road
Moreton-in-March
Gloucestershire GL56 0RH
Tel: 01608 812580
Fax: 01608 812581
E-mail: info@ife.org.uk
Website: www.ife.org.uk

The IFE, founded in 1918, is a non-profit-making professional body for fire professionals and has more than 12,000 members worldwide. Our aim is to encourage and improve the science and practice of fire extinction, fire prevention and fire engineering, to enhance technical networks, and to give advice and support to our members for the benefit of the community at large.

MEMBERSHIP
Student
Affiliate Member
Technician (TIFireE)
Graduate (GIFireE)
Associate (AIFireE)
Member (MIFireE)
Fellow (FIFireE)
Engineering Technician (EngTech)
Incorporated Engineer (IEng)
Chartered Engineer (CEng) Affiliate Organization

QUALIFICATION/EXAMINATIONS
Level 2 Certificate Level 3 Certificate
Level 3 Diploma Level 4 Certificate

DESIGNATORY LETTERS
TIFireE, GIFireE, AIFireE, MIFireE, FIFireE, EngTech, IEng, CEng

ENGINEERING, GAS

Membership of Professional Institutions and Associations

THE INSTITUTION OF GAS ENGINEERS AND MANAGERS

IGEM House
High Street
Kegworth
Derbyshire DE74 2DA
Tel: 0844 375 4436
Fax: 01509 678198
Website: www.igem.org.uk

IGEM is licenced by EC(UK) and serves a wide range of professionals in the UK and international gas industry through membership and technical standards, having a diverse membership ranging from university students to qualified professionals. Anyone working or interested in the gas industry can form positive connections to enhance their career through IGEM.

MEMBERSHIP
Student Member
Associate (AIGEM)

Associate Member (AMIGEM)
Graduate Member (GradIGEM)
Member Manager (MIGEM)
Technician Member (Eng Tech (MIGEM))
Incorporated Member (I Eng (MIGEM))
Chartered Member (C Eng (MIGEM))
Fellow (C Eng (FIGEM))
Industrial Affiliate (company membership)

DESIGNATORY LETTERS
MIGEM, Eng Tech (MIGEM), I Eng (MIGEM), C ENG (MIGEM), C Eng (FIGEM)

ENGINEERING, GENERAL

Membership of Professional Institutions and Associations

ASSOCIATION OF COST ENGINEERS

Lea House
Sandbach
Cheshire CW11 1XL
Tel: 01270 764798
Fax: 01270 766180
E-mail: enquiries@acoste.org.uk
Website: www.acoste.org.uk

The ACostE represents the professional interests of those with responsibility for the prediction, planning and control of resources for engineering, manufacturing and construction. As a Professional Affiliate of The Engineering Council, we can propose suitably qualified members for the award of the titles of Chartered Engineer (CEng) and Incorporated Engineer (IEng).

MEMBERSHIP
Student

Associate (AA Cost E)
Companion (Companion A Cost E)
Graduate (Grad A Cost E)
Member (MA Cost E)
Fellow (FA Cost E)
Honorary Fellow (Hon FA Cost E)
Certified Cost Engineer (CCE)
Engineering Technician (EngTech)
Incorporated Engineer (IEng)
Chartered Engineer (CEng)

DESIGNATORY LETTERS
AA Cost E, Companion A Cost E, Grad A Cost E, MA
Cost E, FA Cost E, CCE, EngTech, IEng, CEng

INSTITUTE OF MEASUREMENT AND CONTROL

87 Gower Street
London WC1E 6AF
Tel: 020 7387 4949
Fax: 020 7388 8431
E-mail: membership@instmc.org.uk
Website: www.instmc.org.uk

The IMC is a multidisciplinary body that brings together thinkers and practitioners from the many disciplines that have a common interest in measurement and control. Our object is to promote for the public benefit, by all available means, the general advancement of the science and practice of measurement and control technology and its application.

MEMBERSHIP
Student Member
Affiliate Member
Associate Member
Member (MemInstMC)
Fellow (FInstMC)
Honorary Fellow (HonFInstMC)

SEMTA – THE SECTOR SKILLS COUNCIL FOR SCIENCE, ENGINEERING AND MANUFACTURING TECHNOLOGIES

14 Upton Road
Watford
Hertfordshire WD18 0JT
Tel: 01923 238441
Fax: 01923 256086
E-mail: customerservices@semta.org.uk
Website: www.semta.org.uk

Semta is part of the Skills for Business network of 25 employer-led Sector Skills Councils in the UK and works with employers in the aerospace, automotive, electrical, electronics, marine, mechanical, metals and science & bioscience sectors to ascertain their current and future skills needs and provide short- and long-term solutions to meet those needs.

THE ENGINEERING COUNCIL

2nd Floor
246 High Holborn
London WC1V 7EX
Tel: 020 3206 0500
Fax: 020 3206 0501
Website: www.engc.org.uk

The Engineering Council holds the national registers of Chartered Engineers (CEng), Incorporated Engineers (IEng), Engineering Technicians (EngTech) and Information and Communication Technology Technicians (ICTTech). We set and maintain internationally recognized standards of competence and ethics, ensuring that employers, government and society can have confidence in registrants' skills and commitment.

THE INSTITUTION OF BRITISH ENGINEERS

Clifford Hill Court
Clifford Chambers
Stratford upon Avon
Warwickshire CV37 8AA
Tel: 01789 298739
Fax: 01789 294442
E-mail: info@britishengineers.com
Website: www.britishengineers.com

MEMBERSHIP
Vice President
Fellow (FIBE)
Member (MIBE)
Associate Member (AMIBE)
Graduate Member (GradIBE)
Qualified Sales Engineer (SEng)

Bi-Lingual Engineer (BLEng)
Diploma in Business Engineering (DBE)
Certificate of Competence in Engineering

DESIGNATORY LETTERS
FIBE, MIBE, AMIBE, GradIBE, SEng, BLEng, DBE

WOMEN'S ENGINEERING SOCIETY

Michael Faraday House
Six Hills Way
Stevenage
Herts SG1 2AY
Tel: 01438 765506
E-mail: info@wes.org.uk
Website: www.wes.org.uk

The WES, founded in 1919, is a professional, not-for-profit network of women engineers, scientists and technologists, who offer inspiration, support and professional development. Working in partnership, we campaign to encourage women to participate and achieve as engineers, scientists and as leaders.

MEMBERSHIP
Student Member

Associate
Member (MWES)
Group Member
Corporate Member

DESIGNATORY LETTERS
MWES

ENGINEERING, MARINE
Membership of Professional Institutions and Associations

THE INSTITUTE OF MARINE ENGINEERING, SCIENCE AND TECHNOLOGY

80 Coleman Street
London EC2R 5BJ
Tel: 020 7382 2600
Fax: 020 7382 2670
E-mail: membership@imarest.org
Website: www.imarest.org

The IMarEST, established in 1889, is the leading international membership body and learned society for marine professionals and has more than 15,000 members worldwide. We have a strong international presence, with a network of 50 international branches, affiliations with major marine societies around the world, representation on the key marine technical committees and non-governmental status at the International Maritime Organization.

MEMBERSHIP
Student (SIMarEST)
Affiliate
Elective Member

Associate Member (AMIMarEST)
Member (MIMarEST)
Fellow (FIMarEST)
Marine Engineering Technician (MarEngTech)
Incorporated Marine Engineer (IMarEng)
Chartered Marine Engineer (CMarEng)
Engineering Technician (EngTech)
Incorporated Engineer (IEng)
Chartered Engineer (CEng)

DESIGNATORY LETTERS
SIMarEST, AMIMarEST, MIMarEST, FIMarEST, MarEngTech, IMarEng, CMarEng, EngTech, IEng, CEng

ENGINEERING, MECHANICAL
Membership of Professional Institutions and Associations

INSTITUTION OF MECHANICAL ENGINEERS

1 Birdcage Walk
Westminster
London SW1H 9JJ
Tel: 020 7304 6999
E-mail: membership@imeche.org
Website: www.imeche.org

The IMechE is a professional engineering body with about 80,000 members. Our aims are to promote sustainable energy and engineering sustainable supply, economic growth while mitigating and adapting to climate change and the depletion of natural resources, and safe, efficient transport systems to ensure less congestion and emissions, and to inspire, prepare and support tomorrow's engineers so we can respond to society's changes.

MEMBERSHIP
Affiliate
Associate Member (AMIMechE)
Member (MIMechE)
Fellow (FIMechE)
Engineering Technician (EngTech)
Incorporated Engineer (IEng)
Chartered Engineer (CEng)

DESIGNATORY LETTERS
AMIMechE, MIMechE, FIMechE, EngTech, IEng,
CEng

ENGINEERING, MINING

Membership of Professional Institutions and Associations

INSTITUTE OF EXPLOSIVES ENGINEERS

Wellington Hall 289
Cranfield University
Defence Academy of the UK
Shrivenham, Swindon
Wiltshire SN6 8LA
Tel: 01793 785322
Fax: 01793 785772
E-mail: iexpe@cranfield.ac.uk
Website: www.iexpe.org

The Insitute of Explosives Engineers promotes the occupational competency, education and professional standing of those who work with explosives and provides consultative facilities for organizations and government departments within the explosives field.

MEMBERSHIP
Student

Associate (AIExpE)
Member (MIExpE)
Fellow (FIExpE)
Company

DESIGNATORY LETTERS
AIExpE, MIExpE, FIExpE

THE INSTITUTE OF MATERIALS, MINERALS AND MINING (IOM^3)

1 Carlton House Terrace
London SW1Y 5DB
Tel: 020 7451 7300
Fax: 020 7839 1702
Website: www.iom3.org

IOM^3 is a major UK engineering institution whose activities encompass the whole materials cycle, from exploration and extraction, through characterization, processing, forming, finishing and application, to product recycling and land reuse. We promote and develop all aspects of materials science and engineering, geology, mining and associated technologies, mineral and petroleum engineering and extraction metallurgy, as a leading authority in the worldwide materials and mining community.

MEMBERSHIP
Student
Graduate
Affiliate
Member (MIMMM)
Fellow (FIMMM)

DESIGNATORY LETTERS
MIMMM, FIMMM

THE INSTITUTE OF QUARRYING

7 Regent Street
Nottingham NG1 5BS
Tel: 0115 945 3880
Fax: 0115 948 4035
E-mail: mail@quarrying.org
Website: www.quarrying.org

The Institute of Quarrying, which dates from 1917, is the international professional body for quarrying, construction materials and related extractive and processing industries, and has 6,000 members in some 50 countries. Our aim is to improve all aspects of operational performance through education and training at supervisory and management level.

MEMBERSHIP
Student

Associate
Member (MIQ)
Fellow (FIQ)

QUALIFICATION/EXAMINATIONS
Professional Examination

DESIGNATORY LETTERS
MIQ, FIQ

ENGINEERING, NUCLEAR
Membership of Professional Institutions and Associations

THE NUCLEAR INSTITUTE

Allan House
1 Penerley Road
London SE6 2LQ
Tel: 020 8695 8220
Fax: 020 8695 8229
E-mail: admin@nuclearinst.com
Website: www.nuclearinst.com

The NI (a Nominated Body of the Engineering Council) is a registered charity established to support the nuclear sector. We organize lectures, seminars and events at a regional and national level, and can award EngTech, IEng and CEng to suitably qualified individuals.

MEMBERSHIP
Student Member
Learned Member

Graduate Member
Technician Member (TNucI)
Associate Member (AMNucI)
Member (MNucI)
Fellow (FNucI)
Honorary Fellow

DESIGNATORY LETTERS
TNucI, AMNucI, MNucI, FNucI

ENGINEERING, PRODUCTION
Membership of Professional Institutions and Associations

THE INSTITUTE OF OPERATIONS MANAGEMENT

CILT(UK)
Earlstrees Court
Earlstrees Road
Corby
Northamptonshire NN17 4AX
Tel: 01536 740105
E-mail: info@iomnet.org.uk
Website: www.iomnet.org.uk

The IOM is the professional body for persons involved in operations and production management in the manufacturing and service industries and in the public sector in the UK. Our object is to equip operations professionals with the skills and resources they need to maximize individual potential and organizational success.

MEMBERSHIP
Student
Associate
Member (MIOM)

Fellow (FIOM)
Group Member
Corporate Member

QUALIFICATION/EXAMINATIONS
Certificate in Operations Management (COM)
Diploma in Operations Management (DOM)
Advanced Diploma in Operations Management

DESIGNATORY LETTERS
MION, FIOM

ENGINEERING, REFRACTORIES
Membership of Professional Institutions and Associations

INSTITUTE OF REFRACTORIES ENGINEERING

25 Woodland Way
Long Newton
Stockton-on-Tees
Co Durham TS21 1DJ
Tel: 01642 583840
Fax: 01642 589397
E-mail: secretary@ireng.org
Website: www.ireng.org

The IRE is a non-profit-making organization dedicated to fostering the science, technology and skills of refractories engineering and to serving the needs of refractories engineers worldwide. Our members have a background in R&D, design, engineering, manufacturing and installation contracting in the iron & steel, cement, non-ferrous, glass, chemical/petrochemical incineration, power generation, ceramics/bricks and similar industries.

MEMBERSHIP
Student
Associate Member (AMI Ref Eng)
Member (MI Ref Eng)
Fellow (FI Ref Eng)

DESIGNATORY LETTERS
AMI Ref Eng, MI Ref Eng, FI Ref Eng

ENGINEERING, REFRIGERATION
Membership of Professional Institutions and Associations

H.A.L. TRAINING SERVICES

Transport Building
Doncaster Road
Kirk Sandall
Doncaster DN3 1HT
Tel: 01302 883276
Fax: 01302 812887
E-mail: info@hal-training.co.uk
Website: www.hal-training.co.uk

H.A.L. (Heat, Air, Liquids) are City & Guilds & Construction Skills (CITB) approved and have been providing training in the refrigeration and air conditioning sector since 1993. We offer a range of courses for personnel entering the field and assessments for persons who already have a sound knowledge of refrigeration and air conditioning systems.

QUALIFICATION/EXAMINATIONS
Please see the H.A.L. website.

THE INSTITUTE OF REFRIGERATION

Kelvin House
76 Mill Lane
76 Mill Lane
Carshalton
Surrey SM5 2JR
Tel: 020 8647 7033
Fax: 020 8773 0165
E-mail: ior@ior.org.uk
Website: www.ior.org.uk

The IOR is the professional body for the refrigeration and air conditioning industries. We promote the technical advancement and perfection of refrigeration, and the minimization of its effects on the environment, encourage the extension of refrigeration, air conditioning and heat pump services for the benefit of the community, and provide advice, CPD and support to our members.

MEMBERSHIP
Student
Affiliate
Associate Member (AMInstR)
Member (MInstR)
Fellow (FInstR)
Engineering Technician (EngTech)
Incorporated Engineer (IEng)
Chartered Engineer (CEng)

DESIGNATORY LETTERS
AMInstR, MInstR, FInstR

ENGINEERING, ROAD, RAIL AND TRANSPORT
Membership of Professional Institutions and Associations

INSTITUTE OF HIGHWAY INCORPORATED ENGINEERS

De Morgan House
58 Russell Square
London WC1B 4HS
Tel: 020 7436 7487
Fax: 020 7436 7488
E-mail: secretary@ihie.org.uk
Website: www.ihie.org.uk

The IHIE is the professional body for highway and traffic professionals and is part of the NVQ awarding body for Transportation qualifications. We are run by engineers for engineers and technicians, and work to keep the standards of the profession high, to safeguard the interests of our members, and to ensure that their contribution is recognized.

MEMBERSHIP
Student Member
Graduate Member
Associate Member (AMIHE)
Member (MIHE)

Fellow (FIHE)
Engineering Technician (EngTech)
Incorporated Engineer (IEng)
Chartered Engineer (CEng)

QUALIFICATION/EXAMINATIONS
Prof Cert in Traffic Sign Design
Prof Cert in Traffic Signal Control
Prof Cert in Transport Development Control

DESIGNATORY LETTERS
AMIHE, MIHE, FIHE, EngTech, IEng, CEng

INSTITUTION OF RAILWAY SIGNAL ENGINEERS

4th Floor
1 Birdcage Walk
Westminster
London SW1H 9JJ
Tel: 020 7808 1180
Fax: 020 7808 1196
E-mail: hq@irse.org
Website: www.irse.org

The Institution of Railway Signal Engineers, known more usually as the IRSE, is an international organization, active throughout the world. It is the professional institution for all those engaged or interested in railway signalling and telecommunications and allied disciplines. Membership is open to anyone engaged or interested in the management, planning, design, installation, telecommunications or associated equipment.

MEMBERSHIP
Student

Associate
Accredited Technician
Associate Member
Member
Fellow
Companion

QUALIFICATION/EXAMINATIONS
Professional Examination

DESIGNATORY LETTERS
AMIRSE, MIRSE, FIRSE, CompIRSE

SOCIETY OF OPERATIONS ENGINEERS

22 Greencoat Place
London SW1P 1PR
Tel: 020 7630 1111
Fax: 020 7630 6677
E-mail: soe@soe.org.uk
Website: www.soe.org.uk

The SOE is a professional membership organization that represents more than 18,000 individuals and companies in the engineering industry. It was formed in 2000 by the merger of the Institute of Road Transport Engineers (IRTE) and the Institution of Plant Engineers (IPlantE). The Society's third professional sector, the Bureau of Engineer Surveyors (BES), joined us in 2004.

MEMBERSHIP
Associate Member (AMSOE)
Member (MSOE)
Fellow (FSOE)
Honorary Fellow (HonFSOE)
Companion (CompanionSOE)
Engineering Technician (EngTech)
Incorporated Engineer (IEng)
Chartered Engineer (CEng)

THE INSTITUTION OF HIGHWAYS AND TRANSPORTATION

119 Britannia Walk
London N1 7JE
Tel: 020 7336 1555
Fax: 020 7336 1556
E-mail: info@iht.org
Website: www.iht.org

The IHT is a learned society concerned specifically with the planning, design, construction, maintenance and operation of land-based transport systems and infrastructure. We provide support and networking opportunities to members, with routes to qualifications, cutting-edge technical seminars and conferences, and exciting social events.

MEMBERSHIP
Student
Associate Member (AMIHT)
Member (MIHT)

Fellow (FIHT)
Incorporated Engineer (IEng)
Chartered Engineer (CEng)

QUALIFICATION/EXAMINATIONS
Transport Planning Professional (TPP) status (awarded jointly with the Transport Planning Society (TPS))

DESIGNATORY LETTERS
AMIHT, MIHT, FIHT, IEng, CEng

ENGINEERING, SHEET METAL
Membership of Professional Institutions and Associations

INSTITUTE OF SHEET METAL ENGINEERING

PO Box 5493
Wolverhampton WV6 6EU
Tel: 07891499146
E-mail: ismesec@googlemail.com
Website: www.isme.org.uk

The ISME is a learned body with individual membership open to those employed in the sheet metal and associated industries and corporate membership open to relevant companies. Our aims are to promote the science of working and using sheet metal by providing opportunities for the exchange of ideas and information, and to encourage the professional development of our members.

MEMBERSHIP
Student Member
Member (MISME)
Fellow (FISME)
Corporate Member

DESIGNATORY LETTERS
MISME, FISME

ENGINEERING, STRUCTURAL
Membership of Professional Institutions and Associations

THE INSTITUTION OF STRUCTURAL ENGINEERS

11 Upper Belgrave Street
London SW1X 8BH
Tel: 020 7235 4535
Fax: 020 7235 4294
E-mail: membership@istructe.org
Website: www.istructe.org

The Institution of Structural Engineers, founded in 1908, is the world's largest membership organization dedicated to the art and science of structural engineering. Our aims include: maintaining professional standards for structural engineering; ensuring continued technical excellence; advancing safety, creativity and innovation; and promoting a sustainable approach to both the structural engineering profession and the built environment.

MEMBERSHIP
Student
Affiliate

Graduate
Technician (TIStructE)
Associate-member (AMIStructE)
Associate (AIStructE)
Chartered member (MIStructE)
Fellow (FIStructE)
Engineering Technician (EngTech)
Incorporated Engineer (IEng)
Chartered Engineer (CEng)

DESIGNATORY LETTERS
TIStructE, AMIStructE, AIStructE. MIStructE, FIStructE, EngTech, IEng, CEng

ENGINEERING, WATER
Membership of Professional Institutions and Associations

INSTITUTE OF WATER

4 Carlton Court
Team Valley
Gateshead
Tyne and Wear NE11 0AZ
Tel: 0191 422 0088
Fax: 0191 422 0087
E-mail: info@instituteofwater.org.uk
Website: www.instituteofwater.org.uk

The IW is the only institute concerned with the UK water industry. Our aim is to promote high standards of integrity, conduct and ethics, and to provide our members with an opportunity for CPD and growth through sharing knowledge, experience and networking opportunities.

MEMBERSHIP
Student Member
Associate Member
Full Member
Fellow
Honorary Member
Engineering Technician (EngTech)
Incorporated Engineer (IEng)
Chartered Engineer (CEng)
Chartered Environmentalist (CEnv)
Company Member

DESIGNATORY LETTERS
EngTech, IEng, CEng, CEnv

ENGINEERING DESIGN
Membership of Professional Institutions and Associations

THE INSTITUTION OF ENGINEERING DESIGNERS

Courtleigh
Westbury Leigh
Westbury
Wiltshire BA13 3TA
Tel: 01373 822801
Fax: 01373 858085
E-mail: ied@ied.org.uk
Website: www.ied.org.uk

Established in 1945, the IED represents 4,000 members worldwide working in engineering design, product design and CAD. Benefits include a bimonthly journal, access to an extensive library, legal advice helpline, local branch activities, and guidance and support to registration with the EC(UK) for suitably qualified members.

MEMBERSHIP
IED membership has two divisions; Engineering Design, and Product Design and Technology.
Each division has a range of membership grades; Student Member (StudIED), Graduate/Diplomate Member (GradIED/DipIED), Competent Draughting Associate (CDAIED), Associate (AIED), Member (MIED), Fellow (FIED).

QUALIFICATION/EXAMINATIONS
Registration with EC(UK) for suitably qualified members

DESIGNATORY LETTERS
AIED, MIED, FIED

ENVIRONMENTAL SCIENCES
Membership of Professional Institutions and Associations

INSTITUTE OF ECOLOGY AND ENVIRONMENTAL MANAGEMENT

43 Southgate Street
Winchester
Hampshire SO23 9EH
Tel: 01962 868626
Fax: 01962 868625
E-mail: enquiries@ieem.net
Website: www.ieem.net

The IEEM was founded in 1991 to advance the science, technology and practice of ecology, environmental management and sustainable development to further conservation and the enhancement of biodiversity through education, training, study and research. We now have more than 3,800 members drawn from local authorities, government agencies, industry, environmental consultancy, teaching/research and NGOs.

MEMBERSHIP
Student Mamber
Affiliate Member
Graduate Member
Associate Member (AIEEM)
Full Member (FMIEEM)
Fellow (FIEEM)

DESIGNATORY LETTERS
AIEEM, FMIEEM, FIEEM

EXPORT
Membership of Professional Institutions and Associations

IOE INTERNATIONAL (INSTITUTE OF EXPORT)

Export House
Lynch Wood
Peterborough PE2 6FT
Tel: 01733 404400
E-mail: enquiries@export.org.uk
Website: www.export.org.uk

Established since 1935 offering training and professional qualifications to those working within international trade. We are the only professional institiute in the UK offering qualifications ranging from the new 14–19 Diploma up to a level 5 Diploma as well as standard and bespoke training courses for individuals and companies.

MEMBERSHIP
Affiliate
Student
Associate
Member MIEx (Grad)
Member MIEx
Fellow
Business
Corporate

ACIT – Advanced Certificate in International Trade
DIT – Diploma in International Trade

FISHERIES MANAGEMENT

Membership of Professional Institutions and Associations

INSTITUTE OF FISHERIES MANAGEMENT

22 Rushworth Avenue
West Bridgford
Nottingham NG2 7LF
Tel: 01159 822317
Fax: 01159 826150
E-mail: info@ifm.org.uk
Website: www.ifm.org.uk

The Institute of Fisheries Management is an international organization of persons sharing a common interest in the modern and sustainable management of recreational and commercial fisheries. It is a non-profit-making body and is a constituent body of the Society for the Environment.

MEMBERSHIP
Subscriber
Student Member
Associate Member (AMIFM)

Registered Member (MIFM)
Fellow (FIFM)
Honorary Fellow (Hon FIFM)
Corporate Member

QUALIFICATION/EXAMINATIONS
Certificate
Diploma (accredited by The Open University)

DESIGNATORY LETTERS
AMIRM, MIFM, FIFM, Hon FIFM

FLORISTRY

Membership of Professional Institutions and Associations

SOCIETY OF FLORISTRY LTD

Tel: 07896 639520
E-mail: info@societyoffloristry.org
Website: www.societyoffloristry.org

The SOF, founded in 1951, is an awarding body that promotes the highest standards in professional floristry. We are responsible for preparing and setting the highest floristry qualifications and for designing programmes for the training of SOF judges and examiners. We provide help, advice and information to our more than 1,000 members, who include business owners, florists, training providers, and students.

MEMBERSHIP
Member
Corporate Member

QUALIFICATION/EXAMINATIONS
Level 4 Higher Diploma in Floristry (ICSF)
Level 5 Master Diploma in Professional Floristry (NDSF)

FOOD SCIENCE AND NUTRITION
Membership of Professional Institutions and Associations

INSTITUTE OF FOOD SCIENCE AND TECHNOLOGY

5 Cambridge Court
210 Shepherd's Bush Road
London W6 7NJ
Tel: 020 7603 6316
Fax: 020 7602 9936
E-mail: info@ifst.org
Website: www.ifst.org

The IFST is a leading independent qualifying body for food professionals in Europe and the only professional body in the UK concerned with all aspects of food science and technology. We aim to promote standards of competence, integrity and ethical behaviour among our members and to improve public knowledge and awareness of important issues relating to the supply, production and quality of food.

MEMBERSHIP
Associate
Member (MIFST)
Fellow (FIFST)
Chartered Scientist (CSci)

DESIGNATORY LETTERS
MIFST, FIFST, CSci

FORESTRY AND ARBORICULTURE
Membership of Professional Institutions and Associations

INSTITUTE OF CHARTERED FORESTERS

59 George Street
Edinburgh EH2 2JG
Tel: 0131 240 1425
Fax: 0131 240 1424
E-mail: icf@charteredforesters.org
Website: www.charteredforesters.org

The ICF is the Royal Chartered body for foresters and arboriculturists in the UK. We have over 1,000 members, to whom we offer advice, guidance and support. We also strive to foster a greater public understanding and awareness of the profession, as the environment and its management become more relevant to everyone.

MEMBERSHIP
Student Member

Supporter
Associate Member
Professional Member (MICFor)
Fellow (FICFor)

QUALIFICATION/EXAMINATIONS
Professional Membership Entry (PME) exam

DESIGNATORY LETTERS
MICFor, FICFor

THE ARBORICULTURAL ASSOCIATION

Ullenwood Court
Ullenwood
Cheltenham
Gloucestershire GL53 9QS
Tel: 01242 522152
Fax: 01242 577766
E-mail: admin@trees.org.uk
Website: www.trees.org.uk

The Arboricultural Association, founded in 1964, is the leading body in the UK for the amenity tree care professional in either civic or commercial employment at craft, technical, supervisory, managerial or consultancy level. There are currently over 2,000 members of The Arboricultural Association in a variety of membership classes.

MEMBERSHIP
Individual Membership
Student Member
Ordinary Member
Associate Member
Technician Member
Professional Member
Fellow
Corporate Membership
Corporate Member
Corporate Gold Member

THE ROYAL FORESTRY SOCIETY

102 High Street
Tring
Hertfordshire HP23 4AF
Tel: 01442 822028
Fax: 01442 890395
E-mail: rfshq@rfs.org.uk
Website: www.rfs.org.uk

The RFS was founded in 1882 and now has over 4,000 members. We are dedicated to promoting the wise management of trees and woodlands, and to increasing people's understanding of forestry. We publish a popular magazine, the *Quarterly Journal of Forestry*, arrange outdoor meetings, organize woodland study tours in the UK and overseas, run exams in arboriculture and manage model woodlands.

MEMBERSHIP
Member

QUALIFICATION/EXAMINATIONS
Certificate in Arboriculture (Level 2)
Professional Diploma in Arboriculture (DipArb(RFS)) (Level 6)

FOUNDRY TECHNOLOGY AND PATTERN MAKING
Membership of Professional Institutions and Associations

THE INSTITUTE OF CAST METALS ENGINEERS

National Metalforming Centre
47 Birmingham Road
West Bromwich
West Midlands B70 6PY
Tel: 01216 016979
Fax: 01216 016981
E-mail: info@icme.org.uk
Website: www.icme.org.uk

The ICME is the professional body for those in the Castings and associated industry. It was formed in 1904, granted its first Royal Charter in 1921, a Third Supplemental Charter in 1994 and changed its name in 2001. The granting of the Third Supplemental Charter aligned its membership requirements with those of the ECUK.

MEMBERSHIP
Student
Member (MICME)

Professional Member (Prof MICME)
Fellow (FICME)
Engineering Technician (EngTech)
Incorporated Engineer (IEng)
Chartered Engineer (CEng)
European Engineer (EurIng)

DESIGNATORY LETTERS
MICME, Prof MICME, FICME, EngTech, IEng, CEng, EurIng

FREIGHT FORWARDING
Membership of Professional Institutions and Associations

BRITISH INTERNATIONAL FREIGHT ASSOCIATION

Redfern House
Browells Lane
Feltham
Middlesex TW13 7EP
Tel: 020 8844 2266
Fax: 020 8890 5546
E-mail: bifa@bifa.org
Website: www.bifa.org

BIFA is the principal trade association providing representation and support to British companies engaged in the international movement of freight to and from the UK by air, rail, road and sea. It is a not-for-profit organization. Members are encouraged to contribute to the running of the Association.

MEMBERSHIP
Associate Member
Trade Member

FUNDRAISING
Membership of Professional Institutions and Associations

INSTITUTE OF FUNDRAISING

12--14 Park Place
Lawn Lane
London SW8 1UD
Tel: 020 7840 1000
Fax: 020 7840 1001
E-mail: training@institute-of-fundraising.org.uk
Website: www.institute-of-fundraising.org.uk

The Institute of Fundraising is the professional body for fundraisers in the UK. We offer professional support, act as a voice for fundraisers and promote best practice. We run a number of training courses and the annual National Convention, the largest fundraising conference of its type in the UK.

MEMBERSHIP
Associate
Full Member (MInstF)

Full Certificated Member (MInstF(Cert))
Fellow (FInstF)
Organizational Member
Corporate Member

QUALIFICATION/EXAMINATIONS
Certificate in Fundraising Management

DESIGNATORY LETTERS
MInstF, MInstF(Cert), FInstF

FUNERAL DIRECTING, BURIAL AND CREMATION ADMINISTRATION
Membership of Professional Institutions and Associations

NATIONAL ASSOCIATION OF FUNERAL DIRECTORS

618 Warwick Road
Solihull
West Midlands B91 1AA
Tel: 0845 230 1343
Fax: 0121 711 1351
E-mail: info@nafd.org.uk
Website: www.nafd.org.uk

The NAFD, founded in 1905, is an independent trade association whose members include more than 3,200 funeral homes throughout the UK, suppliers to the profession, and overseas funeral directing businesses. We provide support to our members and offer informed opinion to government.

MEMBERSHIP
Funeral Director (Category A) Member
Supplier (Category B) Member

Overseas Member

QUALIFICATION/EXAMINATIONS
Foundation Certificate in Funeral Service
Advanced Certificate in Funeral Services
Diploma in Funeral Directing (DipFD)
Diploma in Funeral Service Management (DipFSM)
Advanced Diploma in Funeral Arranging and Administration

NATIONAL ASSOCIATION OF MEMORIAL MASONS

1 Castle Mews
Rugby
Warwickshire CV21 2AL
Tel: 01788 542264
Fax: 01788 542276
E-mail: enquiries@namm.org.uk
Website: www.namm.org.uk

The NAMM was formed in 1907 to promote excellence and craftsmanship within the memorial masonry trade. Our services to members include training, business advice, technical advice, promotion, a legal helpline, a conciliation and arbitration service, trade exhibitions and a conference. We protect members' interests through representation to the British Standards Institution (BSI) and the Burial & Cemeteries Advisory Group (BCAG).

MEMBERSHIP
Individual Associate Member
Affiliate Retail Member
Full Retail and Wholesale Members
Company Associate Member
Corporate Associate Member

THE INSTITUTE OF BURIAL AND CREMATION ADMINISTRATION

Kelham Hall
Newark
Nottinghamshire NG23 5QX
Tel: 01636 708311
Fax: 01636 706311

MEMBERSHIP
Student
Registered Licentiate (LInstBCA)
Associate Member (AInstBCA)
Member (MInstBCA)
Fellow (FInstBCA)

QUALIFICATION/EXAMINATIONS
Diploma
Final Diploma

DESIGNATORY LETTERS
LInstBCA, AInstBCA, MInstBCA, FInstBCA

FURNISHING AND FURNITURE
Membership of Professional Institutions and Associations

FLOORING INDUSTRY TRAINING ASSOCIATION

4c St Marys Place
The Lace Market
Nottingham NG1 1PH
Tel: 0115 9506836
E-mail: info@fita.co.uk
Website: www.fita.co.uk

The FITA was set up and is fully supported by the CFA and NICF to provide training for the floor-covering industry. We have a fully equipped training centre at Loughborough, where the majority courses are run, and the use of a training facility in

Manchester. We also offer tailor-made courses to suit individual specifications and requirements.

QUALIFICATION/EXAMINATIONS
FITA standard courses are:
Basic carpet – 5 days
Intermediate carpet – 5 days
Advanced carpet – 4 days
Essential (basic) wood – 3 days
Intermediate wood – 3 days

Solid wood sanding and finishing – 2 days
Laminate and floating wood – 2 days
Domestic vinyl – 2 days
Safety and smooth vinyl (commercial) – 4 days
Luxury vinyl tile – 4 days
Estimating and planning – 2 days
Damp testing floors – 1 day
Sub-floor preparation – 2 days

NATIONAL INSTITUTE OF CARPET AND FLOORLAYERS

4c St Marys Place
The Lace Market
Nottingham NG1 1PH
Tel: 0115 9583077
Fax: 0115 9412238
E-mail: info@nicfltd.org.uk
Website: www.nicfltd.org.uk

The NICF furthers the interests of its members by promoting excellence in the field of carpet and floorlaying and providing a range of benefits, products and services.

MEMBERSHIP
Associate Member
Trainee Fitter

Approved Fitter
Master Fitter
Retailer Member

QUALIFICATION/EXAMINATIONS
Master Fitter qualification assessment

GEMMOLOGY AND JEWELLERY
Membership of Professional Institutions and Associations

THE GEMMOLOGICAL ASSOCIATION OF GREAT BRITAIN

27 Greville Street
London EC1N 8TN
Tel: 020 7404 3334
Fax: 020 7404 8843
E-mail: edu@gem-a.com
Website: www.gem-a.com

The Gemmological Association of Great Britain (Gem-A), a UK registered charity, is the world's longest established provider of gem and jewellery education, our first diploma having been awarded in 1913. We are committed to promoting the study of gemmology and to providing CPD to our members – an international community of gem professionals and enthusiasts.

MEMBERSHIP
Member
Fellow (FGA)
Diamond Member (DGA)
Corporate Member

QUALIFICATION/EXAMINATIONS
Foundation Certificate in Gemmology
Diploma in Gemmology
Gem Diamond Diploma

DESIGNATORY LETTERS
FGA, DGA

THE NATIONAL ASSOCIATION OF GOLDSMITHS

78A Luke Street
London EC2A 4XG
Tel: 020 7613 4445
Fax: 020 7613 4450
E-mail: nag@jewellers-online.org
Website: www.jewellers-online.org

The NAG, established in 1894, serves and supports the jewellery industry of Great Britain and Ireland. We promote high professional standards among our members, who must adhere to a code of professional practice. In return, we offer them advice, support and CPD in the form of distance learning courses, seminars and tutorials.

MEMBERSHIP
Alumni Member

Allied Member
Affiliate Member
Ordinary Member

QUALIFICATION/EXAMINATIONS
Professional Jewellers' Diploma
Professional Jewellers' Gemstone Diploma
Professional Jewellers' Management Diploma
Professional Jewellers' Valuation Diploma

GENEALOGY
Membership of Professional Institutions and Associations

SOCIETY OF GENEALOGISTS

14 Charterhouse Buildings
Goswell Road
London EC1M 7BA
Tel: 020 7251 8799
Fax: 020 7250 1800
E-mail: info@sog.org.uk
Website: www.sog.org.uk

The Society (founded 1911) is the National Library and Education Centre for Family History. A registered educational charity, it was founded to encourage and foster the study, science and knowledge of genealogy. This it does chiefly through its library, publications and extensive education programme of courses and events. It currently does not hold exams.

MEMBERSHIP
Member
Fellow (FSG)
Honorary Fellow (FSG-Hon)

DESIGNATORY LETTERS
FSG, FSG Hon

THE HERALDRY SOCIETY

PO Box 772
Guildford GU3 3ZX
Tel: 01438 237373
Fax: 01483 237375
Website: www.theheraldrysociety.com

The Heraldry Society is a registered charity that aims to encourage interest in heraldry through publications, lectures, visits and related activities. Members receive *The Heraldry Gazette*, which contains heraldic news and comment and Society information quarterly. We maintain contact with heraldic societies in many parts of the UK and abroad.

MEMBERSHIP
Associate Member
Ordinary Member
Fellow (FHS)

Honorary Fellow (Hon FHS)
Institutional Member

QUALIFICATION/EXAMINATIONS
Elementary Certificate
Intermediate Certificate
Advanced Certificate
Diploma (DipHS)

DESIGNATORY LETTERS
FHS, Hon FHS

THE INSTITUTE OF HERALDIC AND GENEALOGICAL STUDIES

79–82 Northgate
Canterbury
Kent CT1 1BA
Tel: 01227 768664
Fax: 01227 765617
E-mail: ihgs@ihgs.ac.uk
Website: www.ihgs.ac.uk

The IHGS, founded in 1961, is an independent educational charitable trust that offers a wide range of courses on family history, heraldry and related historical subjects, and has an extensive library, archive and research facilities. We also public a monthy e-mail newsletter and a quarterly journal, *Family History*.

MEMBERSHIP
Associate Member
Graduate Member

Licentiate (LHG)
Fellow (FHG)

QUALIFICATION/EXAMINATIONS
Correspondence Course in Genealogy
Higher Certificate in Genealogy
Diploma in Genealogy

DESIGNATORY LETTERS
LHG, FHG

GEOGRAPHY
Membership of Professional Institutions and Associations

ROYAL GEOGRAPHICAL SOCIETY (WITH THE INSTITUTE OF BRITISH GEOGRAPHERS)

1 Kensington Gore
London SW7 2AR
Tel: 020 7591 3000
Fax: 020 7591 3001
E-mail: info@rgs.org
Website: www.rgs.org

The Society is the learned society and professional body for geography. We aim to foster an understanding and informed enjoyment of our world: developing, supporting and promoting geographical research, expeditions and fieldwork, education, public engagement, and geography input to policy; and hold the world's largest private geographical collection.

MEMBERSHIP
Young Geographer
Member
Postgraduate Fellow
Fellow
Chartered Geographer (CGeog)
Corporate Member

DESIGNATORY LETTERS
FRGS, CGeog

GEOLOGY
Membership of Professional Institutions and Associations

THE GEOLOGICAL SOCIETY

Burlington House
Piccadilly
London W1J 0BG
Tel: 020 7434 9944
Fax: 020 7439 8975
E-mail: enquiries@geolsoc.org.uk
Website: www.geolsoc.org.uk

The Geological Society, which was founded in 1807, is the UK's national organization for professional Earth scientists.

MEMBERSHIP
Fellow

Chartered Geologist

DESIGNATORY LETTERS
FGS, CGeol

GLASS TECHNOLOGY
Membership of Professional Institutions and Associations

BRITISH SOCIETY OF SCIENTIFIC GLASSBLOWERS

Unit W1, MK2 Business Centre
Barton Road
Bletchley
Milton Keynes
Buckinghamshire MK2 3HU
Tel: 01908 821191
Fax: 01908 821195
E-mail: batwillow@hotmail.com
Website: www.bssg.co.uk

The Society was founded in 1960 for the benefit of those engaged in Scientific Glassblowing and its associated professions, and to uphold and further the status of Scientific Glassblowers. We welcome written submissions to our quarterly journal, which is circulated to members.

MEMBERSHIP
Associate

Student Member
Craft Member
Full Member
Master
Honorary Member
Retired Member
Overseas Member

SOCIETY OF GLASS TECHNOLOGY

Unit 9
Twelve O'clock Court
21 Attercliffe Road
Sheffield
South Yorkshire S4 7WW
Tel: 01142 634455
Fax: 01142 634411
E-mail: info@sgt.org
Website: www.sgt.org

The objects of the Society of Glass Technology are to encourage and advance the study of the history, art, science, design, manufacture, after treatment, distribution and end use of glass of any and every kind.

MEMBERSHIP
Personal Member
Fellow (FSGT)
Fellow Emeritus

Honorary Fellow (HonFSGT)
Corporate Member

QUALIFICATION/EXAMINATIONS
Peer review by the Board of Fellows

DESIGNATORY LETTERS
FSGT, HonFSGT

HAIRDRESSING

Membership of Professional Institutions and Associations

HABIA

Oxford House
Sixth Avenue
Sky Business Park, Robin Hood Airport
Doncaster
South Yorkshire DN9 3GG
Tel: 0845 2 306080
Fax: 01302 774949
E-mail: info@habia.org
Website: www.habia.org

Habia is the government appointed standards-setting body for hair, beauty, nails, spa therapy, barbering and African type hair, and creates the standards that form the basis of all qualifications, including NVQs, SVQs, apprenticeships, diplomas and foundation degrees, as well as industry codes of practice.

THE GUILD OF HAIRDRESSERS

Archway House
Barnsley S71 1AQ
Tel: 01226 786555
Fax: 01226 786555

The Guild of Hairdressers dates back to 1340, when it was part of the Guild of Barbers and Surgeons. Then in the late 16th century, when the surgeons split off, it became the Guild of Hairdressers, Wigmakers and Perfumers. Today it still exists for the benefit of its members, who adhere to a code of ethics and to whom it provides help and advice.

HEALTH AND HEALTH SERVICES

Membership of Professional Institutions and Associations

BRITISH OCCUPATIONAL HYGIENE SOCIETY – FACULTY OF OCCUPATIONAL HYGIENE

5/6 Melbourne Business Court
Millennium Way
Pride Park
Derby DE24 8LZ
Tel: 01332 298101
Fax: 01332 298099
E-mail: admin@bohs.org
Website: www.bohs.org

The BOHS promotes public and professional awareness, good practice and high standards to help reduce work-related ill-health. The Faculty is our professional arm and examining board, and administers examinations and awards qualifications in Occupational Hygiene and allied subjects.

MEMBERSHIP
Individual
Student
Affiliate
Retired
Licentiate (LFOH)

Member (MFOH)
Specialist Member (MFOH(S))
Fellow (FFOH)

QUALIFICATION/EXAMINATIONS
Please see the BOHS's website.

DESIGNATORY LETTERS
LFOH, MFOH, FFOH, MFOH(S)

CHARTERED INSTITUTE OF ENVIRONMENTAL HEALTH

Chadwick Court
15 Hatfields
London SE1 8DJ
Tel: 020 7827 5800
Fax: 020 7827 5832
E-mail: customerservices@cieh.org
Website: www.cieh.org

The CIEH is a professional, awarding and campaigning body at the forefront of environmental and public health and safety.

MEMBERSHIP
Student member
Associate
Accredited Associate
Graduate member

Fellow

QUALIFICATION/EXAMINATIONS
The CIEH offers a range of QCA accredited qualifications at four levels in health and safety, food safety and environmental protection.

ERGONOMICS SOCIETY

Elms Court
Elms Grove
Loughborough
Leicestershire LE11 1RG
Tel: 01509 234904
Fax: 01509 235666
E-mail: ergsoc@ergonomics.org.uk
Website: www.ergonomics.org.uk

The Ergonomics Society, founded in 1949, is a UK-based professional society for ergonomists world-wide. We encourage and maintain high standards of professional practice through education, accreditation and development, promote the interests of our members across government, academia, business and industry, and raise awareness of ergonomics in general.

MEMBERSHIP
Student Member
Associate Member
Graduate Member
Registered Member (MErgS)
Fellow (FErgS)

INSTITUTE OF HEALTH PROMOTION AND EDUCATION

c/o Helen Draper, Secretary IHPE
School of Dentistry, University of Manchester
Higher Cambridge Street
Manchester M15 6FH
Tel: 01612 756610
Fax: 01612 756299
E-mail: honsec@ihpe.org.uk
Website: www.ihpe.org.uk

The IHPE was established 40 years ago to bring together professionals with a common interest in health education and promotion to share their experience, ideas and information. Our members come from a diverse range of backgrounds, including nursing, midwifery, health visiting, medicine, dentistry, public health, stress management, psychology and teaching.

MEMBERSHIP
Student Member
Affiliate Member
Associate Member (AIHPE)
Member (MIHPE)
Fellow (FIHPE)
Hon Fellow (FIHPE (Hon))
Corporate Member

DESIGNATORY LETTERS
AIHPE, FIHPE, FIHPE (Hon)

INSTITUTE OF HEALTH RECORD INFORMATION AND MANAGEMENT

141 Leander Drive
Rochdale
Lancashire OL11 2XE
Tel: 01706 868481
Fax: 01706 868481
E-mail: ihrim@zen.co.uk
Website: www.ihrim.co.uk

The IHRIM was founded in 1948, primarily as an educational body to provide qualifications as well as career and professional assistance to members. We encourage professionalism and high standards among our members, who work in the fields of health records, information management, clinical coding and information governance.

MEMBERSHIP
Student
Affiliate
Licentiate
Certificated Member (CHRIM)
Associate (AHRIM)
Fellow (FHRIM)
Corporate Affiliate

QUALIFICATION/EXAMINATIONS
Foundation exam
Certificate
Certificate of Technical Competence
Diploma
National Clinical Coding Qualification

DESIGNATORY LETTERS
CHRIM, AHRIM, FHRIM

INSTITUTE OF HEALTHCARE ENGINEERING AND ESTATE MANAGEMENT

2 Abingdon House
Cumberland Business Centre
Northumberland Road
Portsmouth PO5 1DS
Tel: 023 92 823186
Fax: 023 92 815927
E-mail: office@iheem.org.uk
Website: www.iheem.org.uk

IHEEM is the learned society and professional body for those working in healthcare engineering, estates and facilities management. Our members are architects, builders, engineers, estate managers, surveyors, medical engineers and other related professionals. Our aim is to promote the art and science of Healthcare Engineering and Estate Management and to advance research, education and training.

MEMBERSHIP
Graduate
Associate Member
Member (MIHEEM)
Fellow (FIHEEM)

DESIGNATORY LETTERS
MIHEEM, FIHEEM

INSTITUTE OF HEALTHCARE MANAGEMENT

18--21 Morely Street
London SE1 7QZ
Tel: 020 7620 1030
Fax: 020 7620 1040
E-mail: enquiries@ihm.org.uk
Website: www.ihm.org.uk

The IHM is the professional organization for managers throughout healthcare, including the NHS, independent providers, healthcare consultants and the armed forces. Our focus is on improving patient/user care by publishing standards of management practice, promoting the IHM Code (which covers behavioural and ethical aspects of management practice) and establishing a CPD framework for our members.

MEMBERSHIP
Associate Member
Full Member (MIHM)
Fellow (FIHM)

Companion (CIHM)

QUALIFICATION/EXAMINATIONS
Certificate in Health Management Studies (CertHMS)
Certificate in Health Services Management (CertHSM)
Certificate in Managing Health Services (CertMHS)
Certificate in Managing Health & Social Care (CertMHSC)
Diploma in Health Services Management (DipHSM)

DESIGNATORY LETTERS
MIHM, FIHM, CIHM

THE ROYAL SOCIETY FOR PUBLIC HEALTH

3rd Floor
Market Towers
1 Nine Elms Lane
London SW8 5NQ
Tel: 020 3177 1600
Fax: 020 3177 1601
E-mail: info@rsph.org.uk
Website: www.rsph.org.uk

The RSPH was formed in October 2008 by the merger of the Royal Society for the Promotion of Health (RSPH/RSH) and the Royal Institute of Public Health (RIPH). We offer a wide range of vocationally related qualifications in the fields of food safety and nutrition, hygiene, health and safety, pest control, health promotion and the built environment.

MEMBERSHIP
Associate (ARSPH)

Licentiate (LRSPH)
Member (MRSPH)
Fellow (FRSPH)

QUALIFICATION/EXAMINATIONS
Please see the RSPH's website.

DESIGNATORY LETTERS
ARSPH, LRSPH, MRSPH, FRSPH

HORSES AND HORSE RIDING
Membership of Professional Institutions and Associations

THE BRITISH HORSE SOCIETY

Contact: Equestrian Qualifications GB Limited
c/o The British Horse Society
Stoneleigh Deer Park
Kenilworth CV8 2XZ
Tel: 01926 707700
E-mail: exams@bhs.org.uk
Website: www.bhs.org.uk

The British Horse Society offers vocational and work-based examinations for grooms, stable managers, riding instructors and coaches. Founded in 1947, the BHS exams system is world renowned as credible and rigorous, producing competent, practical people who follow safe practices. We also offer competency certificates for the recreational rider.

MEMBERSHIP
Individual Member
Trade Member
Corporate Member

QUALIFICATION/EXAMINATIONS
Equestrian Qualifications GB Limited awards examinations and qualifications for grooms, stable managers, riding instructors and coaches on behalf of the British Horse Society and British Equestrian Federation. Please see the BHS's website for details.

HOUSING
Membership of Professional Institutions and Associations

THE CHARTERED INSTITUTE OF HOUSING

Octavia House
Westwood Way
Coventry CV4 8JP
Tel: 02476 851700
Fax: 02476 695110
E-mail: customer.services@cih.org
Website: www.cih.org

The CIH is the professional body for people involved in housing and communities. We are a registered charity and not-for-profit organization. We have a diverse and growing membership of over 22,000 people – both in the public and private sectors – living and working in over 20 countries on five continents across the world.

MEMBERSHIP
Student
Affiliate
Housing Practitioner (Cert. CIH)
Associate Member (ACIH)
Corporate Member (MCIH)
Fellow (FCIH)

QUALIFICATION/EXAMINATIONS
Certificate Courses
The CIH offers a range of Certificated courses at Levels 2, 3 and 4 delivered at various centres across the UK. They are also available by distance learning. We also offer, jointly with the Chartered Institute of Building (CIOB), a suite of Certificated courses in repairs and maintenance, also at Levels 2, 3 and 4.
Professional Qualifications
The CIH Professional Qualification can be achieved at either undergraduate or postgraduate level, FT or PT.
 Please see the CIH's website for details.

DESIGNATORY LETTERS
Cert. CIH, ACIH, MCIH, FCIH

INDEXING
Membership of Professional Institutions and Associations

SOCIETY OF INDEXERS

Woodbourn Business Centre
10 Jessell Street
Sheffield S9 3HY
Tel: 01142 449561
E-mail: admin@indexers.org.uk
Website: www.indexers.org.uk

The Society of Indexers is the professional body for indexing in the UK and Ireland, and exists to promote indexing, the quality of indexes and the profession of indexing. We offer information to publishers and other organizations on commissioning indexes and our online directory 'Indexers Available' provides an up-to-date guide to indexers currently working in a wide range of fields.

MEMBERSHIP
Student Member
Member (MSocInd)
Professional Member MSocInd(Adv)
Advanced Professional Member
Fellow (FSocInd)
Corporate Member

INDUSTRIAL SAFETY

Membership of Professional Institutions and Associations

BRITISH SAFETY COUNCIL

70 Chancellors Road
London W6 9RS
Tel: 020 8741 1231
Fax: 020 8741 4555
E-mail: mail@britsafe.org
Website: www.britsafe.org

The BSC is one of the world's leading health and safety organizations. Our mission is to keep people healthy and safe at work. Our range of charitable initiatives, such as free health and safety qualifications for school children, is supported by a broad mix of commercial activities centred on membership, training, auditing and qualifications.

MEMBERSHIP
UK Member
International Member

QUALIFICATION/EXAMINATIONS
Certificate in Process Safety
Certificate in COSHH Risk Assessment (Level 2)
Certificate in DSE Risk Assessment (Level 2)
Certificate in Fire Risk Assessment (Level 2)
Certificate in Manual Handling Risk Assessment (Level 2)
Certificate in Risk Assessment (Level 2)
Certificate in Supervising Staff Safely (Level 2)
Certificate in Occupational Health and Safety (Level 3)
Diploma in Occupational Health and Safety Level 6)
Diploma in Environmental Management (DipEM)
International Certificate in Occupational Health and Safety
International Diploma in Environmental Management
International Diploma in Occupational Health and Safety

HEALTH & SAFETY EXECUTIVE APPROVED MINING QUALIFICATIONS

Mining Qualifications, The Health & Safety Executive
3rd Floor, Edgar Allen House
241 Glossop Road
Sheffield
South Yorkshire S10 2GW
Tel: 0114 291 2394
Fax: 0114 291 2399
E-mail: sarah.johnson@hse.gsi.gov.uk
Website: www.hse.gov.uk/mining

The HSE issues First and Second Class Qualification of Competency certificates as required under the Management and Administration of Safety and Health at Mines Regulations (MASHAM) 1993 for the appointment of a manager and undermanager, respectively, in mines of coal, shale and fireclay in the UK. It also issues certificates to Mining Mechanical and Mining Electrical Engineers and Mechanics, Electricians Class I and Class II, and the Mines Surveyor and Deputy Mines Surveyor. For details see; www.hse.gov.uk/mining

HM TRAINEE INSPECTORATE OF HEALTH AND SAFETY

Rose Court
2 Southwark Bridge
London SE1 9HS
Tel: 01519 513366
Website: www.hse.gov.uk

Health and Safety Executive (HSE) inspectors inspect a variety of workplaces to ensure the maintenance and improvement of health and safety standards. Trainee inspectors receive initial basic on-the-job training over 2 years, underpinned by formal study towards a PG qualification in Occupational Health and Safety.

INTERNATIONAL INSTITUTE OF RISK AND SAFETY MANAGEMENT

Suite 7a
77 Fulham Palace Road
London W6 8JA
Tel: 020 8741 9100
Fax: 020 8741 1349
E-mail: info@iirsm.org
Website: www.iirsm.org

The IIRSM is a professional body for health & safety practitioners and specialists in associated professions. Our aim is to advance professional standards in accident prevention and occupational health throughout the world. We have more than 8,100 members, in the UK and over 70 other countries, to whom we provide support and offer advice via a technical helpline.

MEMBERSHIP
Student
Affiliate
Associate (AIIRSM)
Member (MIIRSM)
Specialist Member (SIIRSM)
Fellow (FIIRSM)

DESIGNATORY LETTERS
AIIRSM, MIIRSM, SIIRSM, FIIRSM

NEBOSH (THE NATIONAL EXAMINATION BOARD IN OCCUPATIONAL SAFETY AND HEALTH)

Dominus Way
Meridian Business Park
Leicester LE19 1QW
Tel: 0116 263 4700
Fax: 0116 282 4000
E-mail: info@nebosh.org.uk
Website: www.nebosh.org.uk

NEBOSH offers globally recognized qualifications designed to meet the health, safety, environmental and risk management needs of all places of work. Courses leading to NEBOSH qualifications attract over 30,000 candidates annually in nearly 80 countries around the world. NEBOSH also offers qualifications in Oil and Gas, and Health and Well-being.

MEMBERSHIP

NEBOSH's National General Certificate, National Certificate in Fire Safety and Risk Management, The National Certificate in Construction Health and Safety and the International General Certificate are all accepted as meeting the academic requirements to apply for Technician Membership (Tech IOSH) of the Institution of Occupational Safety and Health (IOSH), and Associate Membership (AIIRSM) of the International Institute of Risk and Safety Management (IIRSM).

NEBOSH's National Diploma and International Diploma are accepted as meeting the requirements to apply for Graduate Membership (Grad IOSH) of the Institution of Occupational Safety and Health (IOSH). Diplomates may also apply to become full Members (MIIRSM) of the International Institute of Risk and Safety Management (IIRSM). The National Diploma provides a sound basis for progression to MSc level: a number of UK universities offer MSc programs that accept the National Diploma as a full or partial entry requirement.

The NEBOSH Environmental Diploma fulfils the academic requirements for both Associate Membership (AIEMA) of the Institute of Environmental Management and Assessment (IEMA) and Associate Membership (AIIRSM) of the International Institute of Risk and Safety Management (IIRSM).

QUALIFICATION/EXAMINATIONS

Award in Health and Safety at Work (Pilot)
National Certificate in Construction Health and Safety (Level 3)
National Certificate in Environmental Management
National Certificate in Fire Safety and Risk Management (Level 3)
NEBOSH National General Certificate in Occupational Health and Safety (Level 3)
International General Certificate in Occupational Health and Safety
NEBOSH National Diploma in Environmental Management (Level 6) (EnvDipNEBOSH)
NEBOSH National Diploma in Occupational Health and Safety (Level 6) (DipNEBOSH)
International Diploma in Occupational Health and Safety (IDipNEBOSH)
NEBOSH International Technical Certificate in Oil and Gas Process Safety (Pilot)

THE INSTITUTION OF OCCUPATIONAL SAFETY AND HEALTH

The Grange
Highfield Drive
Wigston
Leicestershire LE18 1NN
Tel: 0116 257 3100
Fax: 0116 257 3101
E-mail: membership@iosh.co.uk
Website: www.iosh.co.uk

IOSH is world's largest organization for health and safety professionals, with more than 36,000 members worldwide, including 13,000 Chartered Safety and Health Practitioners. The Institution was founded in 1945 and is an independent, not-for-profit organization that sets professional standards, supports and develops members, and provides authoritative advice and guidance on health and safety issues.

MEMBERSHIP

Affiliate Member
Technician Member (Tech IOSH)
Graduate Member (Grad IOSH)
Chartered Member (CMIOSH)
Chartered Fellow (CFIOSH)

DESIGNATORY LETTERS

Tech IOSH, Grad IOSH, CMIOSH, CFIOSH

INSURANCE AND ACTUARIAL WORK
Membership of Professional Institutions and Associations

ASSOCIATION OF AVERAGE ADJUSTERS

Secretariat: The Baltic Exchange
St Mary Axe
London EC3A 8BH
Tel: 020 7623 5501
Fax: 020 7369 1623
E-mail: aaa@balticexchange.com
Website: www.average-adjusters.com

The AAA was founded in 1869 to promote correct principles in the adjustment of marine insurance claims and general average, uniformity of practice among average adjusters and the maintenance of good professional conduct. It ensures the independence and impartiality of its members by imposing a strict code of conduct and has close links with other international associations and insurance markets.

MEMBERSHIP
Subscriber
Associate
Fellow

QUALIFICATION/EXAMINATIONS
The Association's examination consists of six modules. Passes in Modules 1 & 2 are required for Associateship, passes in Modules 3–6 for Fellowship. For details see the Association's website.

THE CHARTERED INSTITUTE OF LOSS ADJUSTERS

Warwick House
65/66 Queen Street
London EC4R 1EB
Tel: 020 7337 9960
Fax: 020 7929 3082
E-mail: info@cila.co.uk
Website: www.cila.co.uk

The CILA, which was founded in 1941, is the professional body representing the claims specialists who investigate, negotiate and agree the conclusion of insurance and other claims on behalf of insurers and policyholders. We safeguard the interests of our members and maintain the high standards of the profession by requiring them to abide by our code of professional conduct.

MEMBERSHIP
Student Member

Ordinary Member
Associate (ACILA)
Fellow (FCILA)
Honorary Member

QUALIFICATION/EXAMINATIONS
CILA examination

DESIGNATORY LETTERS
ACILA, FCILA

THE CHARTERED INSURANCE INSTITUTE

42--48 High Road
South Woodford
London E18 2JP
Tel: 020 8989 8464
Fax: 020 8530 3052
E-mail: customer.serv@cii.co.uk
Website: www.cii.co.uk

The CII is the premier professional body for those working in the insurance and financial services industry. We are dedicated to promoting higher standards of competence and integrity through the provision of relevant qualifications for employees at all levels across all sectors of the industry.

MEMBERSHIP
Ordinary Member
Qualified Member
Associate Member (ACII)
Fellow (FCII)

QUALIFICATION/EXAMINATIONS
Award in Financial Planning
Award in Insurance

Certificate in Equity Release
Certificate in Financial Administration
Certificate in Financial Planning
Certificate in Insurance
Certificate in Life and Pensions
Certificate in Mortgage Advice
Diploma in Financial Planning
Diploma in Insurance
Advanced Diploma in Financial Planning
Advanced Diploma in Insurance
MSc in Insurance and Risk Planning (in association with Cass Business School)

DESIGNATORY LETTERS
ACII, FCII

THE FACULTY AND INSTITUTE OF ACTUARIES

Faculty of Actuaries
Maclaurin House
18 Dublin Street
Edinburgh EH1 3PP
Tel: 0131 240 1313
Fax: faculty@actuaries.or
Website: www.actuaries.org.uk

Institute of Actuaries
Staple Inn Hall
High Holborn
London WC1V 7QJ
Tel: 020 7632 2111
E-mail: institute@actuaries.org.uk

Napier House
4 Worcester Street
Oxford OX1 2AW
Tel: 01865 268211
E-mail: institute@actuaries.org.uk

Actuaries are experts in assessing the financial impact of tomorrow's uncertain events. They enable financial decisions to be made with more confidence by analysing the past, modelling the future, assessing the risks involved, and communicating what the results mean in financial terms.

MEMBERSHIP
Student Member
Affiliate Member

Associate (AFA or AIA)
Fellow (FFA or FIA)
Honorary Fellow

QUALIFICATION/EXAMINATIONS
Certificate in Financial Mathematics

DESIGNATORY LETTERS
AFA, AIA, FFA, FIA

JOURNALISM

Membership of Professional Institutions and Associations

BROADCAST JOURNALISM TRAINING COUNCIL

18 Miller's Close
Rippingale
Nr Bourne
Lincolnshire PE10 0TH
Tel: 01778 440025
E-mail: sec@bjtc.org.uk
Website: www.bjtc.org.uk

The BJTC is a registered charity composed of representatives from all sides of industry: employers, National Union of Journalists and educational institutions offering courses in broadcast journalism. The Council visits courses and grants recognition to those that have reached and are maintaining the Council's published standards. It offers guidance for institutions seeking BJTC recognition and some careers advice, through its website.

NATIONAL COUNCIL FOR THE TRAINING OF JOURNALISTS

NCTJ Training Ltd
The New Granary
Newport
Saffron Walden
Essex CB11 3PL
Tel: 01799 544014
Fax: 01799 544015
E-mail: info@nctj.com
Website: www.nctj.com

The NCTJ provides a range of journalism training products and services in the UK, including: accredited courses; qualifications and examinations; awards; careers information; distance learning; short courses and CPD; information and research; publications and events. We play an influential role in all areas of journalism education and training.

QUALIFICATION/EXAMINATIONS
Certificate in Journalism
National Certificate Examination (NCE) for Press photographers and photo-journalists
National Certificate Examination (NCE) for Reporters
National Certificate Examination (NCE) for Sub-editors

THE CHARTERED INSTITUTE OF JOURNALISTS

2 Dock Offices
Surrey Quays Road
London SE16 2XU
Tel: 020 7252 1187
Fax: 020 7232 2302
E-mail: memberservices@cioj.co.uk
Website: www.cioj.co.uk

The CIoJ, which dates back to 1884, is a professional body and trade union for journalists. We expect our members to uphold high standards in the way they work and to adhere to a strict code of conduct, and in return we champion journalistic freedom, protect their interests in the workplace and campaign for better working conditions.

MEMBERSHIP
Student Member
Affiliate Member
Trainee Member
Full Member
International Member

LAND AND PROPERTY

Membership of Professional Institutions and Associations

RICS (ROYAL INSTITUTION OF CHARTERED SURVEYORS)

12 Great George Street
Parliament Square
London SW1P 3AD
Tel: 0870 333 1600
Fax: 020 7334 3811
E-mail: contactrics@rics.org
Website: www.rics.org/careers

RICS, an independent, not-for-profit organization, has around 100,000 qualified members and more than 50,000 students and trainees in some 140 countries, and provides the world's leading professional qualification in land, property, construction and associated environmental issues. We accredit over 600 courses at leading universities worldwide and provide impartial, authoritative advice on key issues for business, society and governments.

MEMBERSHIP
Student
Associate (AssocRICS)
Technical Surveyor (TechRICS)
Member (MRICS)
Fellow (FRICS)

DESIGNATORY LETTERS
AssocRICS, TechRICS, MRICS, FRICS

THE COLLEGE OF ESTATE MANAGEMENT

Whiteknights
Reading
Berkshire RG6 6AW
Tel: 0118 921 4696
Fax: 01189 921 4620
E-mail: courses@cem.ac.uk
Website: www.cem.ac.uk

The CEM is an independent organization dedicated to helping professionals working in the property and construction industries achieve career success through supported distance learning. We cover almost every conceivable aspect of real estate and the built environment at diploma, undergraduate and postgraduate level.

QUALIFICATION/EXAMINATIONS
Diploma in Construction Practice
Diploma in Shopping Centre Management
Diploma in Surveying Practice
BSC in Building Services Quantity Surveying
BSc in Building Surveying
BSc in Construction Management
BSC in Estate Management
BSc in Property Management
BSc in Quantity Surveying
Graduate Development Programme
Graduate Development Programme (Construction Management Route)
MBA in Construction and Real Estate
MSc in Real Estate
Postgraduate Diploma in Ajudication
Postgraduate Dipoma in Arbitration
Postgraduate Diploma in Project Management
Postgraduate Diploma/MSc in Conservation of the Historic Environment
Postgraduate Diploma/MSc in Facilities Management
Postgraduate Diploma/MSc in Property Investment
RICS Professional Membership Graduate Route – Adaptation 1

THE INSTITUTE OF REVENUES, RATING AND VALUATION

41 Doughty Street
London WC1N 2LF
Tel: 020 7831 3505
Fax: 020 7831 2048
Website: www.irrv.org.uk

The Institute offers professional and technical qualifications for all those whose professional work is concerned with local authority revenues and benefits, valuation for rating, property taxation and the appeals procedure. Our qualifications are widely recognized throughout the profession.

MEMBERSHIP
Student Member
Affiliate Member
Graduate Member
Technician Member (Tech IRRV)
Honorary Member
Fellow (FIRRV)

QUALIFICATION/EXAMINATIONS
Level 3 Certificate
NVQ Level 3/SVQ Level 3
Diploma

DESIGNATORY LETTERS
Tech IRRV, IRRV (Dip), IRRV (Hons), FIRRV

THE NATIONAL FEDERATION OF PROPERTY PROFESSIONALS

Arbon House
6 Tournament Court
Edgehill Drive
Warwick CV34 6LG
Tel: 01926 417794
Fax: 01926 417789
E-mail: quals@nfopp.co.uk
Website: www.nfopp.co.uk

The NFOPP Awarding Body is committed to raising standards within agency through the provision of accredited, nationally recognized qualifications. We are recognized by the Qualifications and Examinations Regulator (Ofqual) and have to follow strict guidelines and maintain quality standards in the provision of all our qualifications.

MEMBERSHIP
For membership details of the following organizations please refer to the relevant website:
APIP; www.apip.co.uk
ARLA; www.arla.co.uk
ICBA; www.icba.uk.com
NAEA; www.naea.co.uk
NAVA; www.nava.org.uk

QUALIFICATION/EXAMINATIONS
Technical Award in Commercial Property Agency (Level 3)
Technical Award in Real Property Auctioneering (Level 3)
Technical Award in Residential Letting and Property Management (Level 3)
Technical Award in Sale of Residential Property (Level 3)
Diploma in Commercial Property Agency (DipCPA) (Level 5)
Diploma in Commercial Property Agency (DipREA) (Level 5)
Diploma in Residential Letting and Management (DipRLM) (Level 5)

THE PLANNING INSPECTORATE

Temple Quay House
2 The Square
Temple Quay
Bristol BS1 6PN
Tel: 0117 372 6372
E-mail: enquiries@planning-inspectorate.gsi.gov.uk
Website: www.planning-inspectorate.gov.uk

The main work of The Planning Inspectorate is processing planning and enforcement appeals and examining 'regional spatial strategies' (eg the scale and distribution of new housing and employment premises) and local development plans. Candidates for Planning Inspectors, who, working largely from home, conduct local inquiries, carry out site inspections, etc, are selected on the basis of an assessment and interview.

THE PROPERTY CONSULTANTS SOCIETY

Basement Office
Surrey Court
1 Surrey Street
Arundel
West Sussex BN18 9DT
Tel: 01903 883787
E-mail: info@propertyconsultantssociety.org
Website: www.propertyconsultantssociety.org

The Property Consultants Society is a non-profit-making organization that offers advice to qualified surveyors, architects, valuers, auctioneers, land and estate agents, master builders, construction engineers, accountants and members of the legal profession to help them to undertake their property consultancy in a competent, legitimate and publicly acceptable way.

MEMBERSHIP
Student (SPCS)
Licentiate (LPCS)
Associate (APCS)
Fellow (FPCS)
Honorary Member

DESIGNATORY LETTERS
SPCS, LPCS, APCS, FPCS

LANDSCAPE ARCHITECTURE
Membership of Professional Institutions and Associations

LANDSCAPE INSTITUTE

33 Great Portland Street
London W1W 8QG
Tel: 020 7299 4500
Fax: 020 7299 4501
E-mail: membership@landscapeinstitute.org
Website: www.landscapeinstitute.org

The LI is an educational charity and chartered body responsible for protecting, conserving and enhancing the natural and built environment for the benefit of the public. We champion well-designed and well-managed urban and rural landscape. Our 6,000 members include chartered landscape architects, academics and scientists working for local authorities, government agencies and in private practice, and students.

MEMBERSHIP
Student Member
Affiliate Member
Licentiate Member
Chartered Member (CMLI)
Fellow (FLI)
Academic Fellow (FLI)

DESIGNATORY LETTERS
CMLI, FLI

LANGUAGES, LINGUISTICS AND TRANSLATION
Membership of Professional Institutions and Associations

INSTITUTE OF TRANSLATION & INTERPRETING

Fortuna House
South Fifth Street
Milton Keynes MK9 2EU
Tel: 01908 325250
Fax: 01908 325259
E-mail: info@iti.org.uk
Website: www.iti.org.uk

The Institute of Translation & Interpreting is one of the primary sources of information on these services to government, industry, the media and the general public. We promote the highest standards, providing guidance to those entering the profession and advice to those who offer language services and their customers.

MEMBERSHIP
Student Associate
Associate Member
Academic Member
Corporate Member

THE CHARTERED INSTITUTE OF LINGUISTS

Saxon House
48 Southwark Street
London SE1 1UN
Tel: 020 7940 3100
Fax: 020 7940 3101
E-mail: info@iol.org.uk
Website: www.iol.org.uk

The Chartered Institute of Linguistics, founded in 1910, is a respected language assessment and accredited awarding body, with about 6,500 members. Our aims include promoting the learning and use of modern languages, improving the status of all professional linguistics, and ensuring the maintenance of high professional standards through adherence to our code of conduct.

MEMBERSHIP
Registered Student
Associate Member (ACIL)

Member (MCIL)
Fellow (FCIL)
Chartered Linguist (CL)

QUALIFICATION/EXAMINATIONS
Certificate in Bilingual Skills (CBS)
Diploma in Public Service Interpreting (DPSI)
International Diploma in Bilingual Translation (IDBT)
Diploma in Translation (DipTrans)

DESIGNATORY LETTERS
ACIL, MCIL, FCIL, CL

THE GREEK INSTITUTE

34 Bush Hill Road
London N21 2DS
Tel: 020 8360 7968
Fax: 020 8360 7968
E-mail: info@greekinstitute.co.uk
Website: www.greekinstitute.co.uk

The Greek Institute, which was founded in 1969, is a non-profit-making cultural organization that promotes Modern Greek studies and culture through lectures, publications, literary competitions, Greek cultural evenings and the award of Certificates and a Diploma which are recognized by many UK universities as equivalent to GCSE and GCE A level Modern Greek.

MEMBERSHIP
Member
Associate (AGI)
Fellow (FGI)

QUALIFICATION/EXAMINATIONS
Certificate in Greek Conversation – Basic Stage: Levels 1 and 2
Certificate in Greek Conversation – Intermediate Stage: Levels 3 and 4
Certificate in Greek Conversation – Higher Stage: Levels 5 and 6
Preliminary Certificate
Intermediate Certificate
Advanced Certificate
Diploma in Greek Translation (DipGrTrans)

DESIGNATORY LETTERS
AGI, FGI

TRINITY COLLEGE LONDON

89 Albert Embankment
London SE1 7TP
Tel: 020 7820 6100
Fax: 020 7820 6161
E-mail: info@trinitycollege.co.uk
Website: www.trinitycollege.co.uk

Trinity College London is a charity and a company limited by guarantee. Its principal activities are to promote education and instruction in the study and appreciation of Music, the English Language and the Performing Arts throughout the world by the provision of examinations and teaching qualifications in each of these subject areas.

QUALIFICATION/EXAMINATIONS
For details please see the College's website or Part 4.

DESIGNATORY LETTERS
ATCL, LTCL, FTCL, AMusTCL, LMusTCL, FMusTCL, Cert TCL, Dip TCL, Cert TESOL, Dip TESOL

LAW

ENGLAND AND WALES

MAGISTRATES
Following the Constitutional Reform Act 2005, which came into force in April 2006, the Lord Chief Justice has become head of the Judiciary. He is responsible for the welfare, training and deployment of magistrates, for approving the names of the candidates recommended for appointment and for disciplinary action, short of removal. The Lord Chancellor also has responsibility for the protection for judicial independence and for working to endure that the magistracy reflects the diversity of society as a whole.

There are six key qualities that a magistrate must possess: good character, social awareness, maturity and sound temperament, sound judgement, commitment and reliability. Political views are no longer sought and considered.

Before sitting in court, magistrates must undertake some basic training which includes structured observations in court. This covers practice and procedure in court, structured decision making, sentencing etc. New magistrates are assigned a mentor for their first two years. Consolidation training takes place about 18 months to two years after appointment, followed by appraisals. Magistrates only sit in adult courts when first appointed. Having got that experience they may apply to sit in youth courts and family courts and have to undertake more training before they can sit.

JUDGES

As the courts are the Queen's Courts, the Crown makes all appointments to the judiciary, acting on the advice of Ministers. Since 2006 candidates for judicial appointment in England and Wales have been selected by the independent Judicial Appointments Commission, which passes its selections to the Lord Chancellor for approval; he in turn formally advises The Queen. The most senior appointments – the Lords of Appeal in Ordinary (who from October 2009 will be the Justices of the new Supreme Court), the Lord Chief Justice and other Heads of Division, and the Lords Justices who are the judges of the Court of Appeal – are approved by the Lord Chancellor and then passed to The Queen via the Prime Minister. The Lord Chancellor makes the recommendations for the High Court and Circuit Judges, Masters, Registrars and District Judges, District Judges (Magistrates' Courts) and Recorders. The Lord Chancellor himself appoints Deputy District Judges and most members of tribunals. He also appoints the 30,000 unpaid magistrates (who are selected by local Advisory Committees, not by the Judicial Appointments Commission).

Appointments to salaried or fee-paid judicial posts are made from among judges or practising lawyers. In general the requirement for appointment is that the candidate must have been a practising barrister or solicitor for 7 years (for appointment to the Circuit Bench or above) or for 5 years (appointments to the District Bench and to most tribunal posts). Certain posts are also open to legal executives, patent agents and trade mark agents of the required seniority. Candidates for appointment as Law Lords (who will

become Justices of the Supreme Court) must be existing holders of high judicial office or must have been practising barristers or solicitors for 15 years.

Scotland and Northern Ireland have their own separate court systems, with their own arrangements for appointing members of the judiciary.

OFFICERS OF THE COURT

Officers of the Court include judicial and administrative staff; the former include Masters and Registrars, the latter secretaries and clerks to the judges and the staff who administer the court service. Details are given in 'The English Legal System 2009–2010' (Routledge Cavendish). Qualifications for the judicial offices vary somewhat, but most appointments are limited to established barristers and solicitors.

THE LEGAL PROFESSION

The legal profession consists of two branches. Each performs distinct duties, although there is a degree of overlap in some aspects of their work.

Solicitors undertake all ordinary legal business for their clients (with whom they are in direct contact). They may also appear on behalf of a client in the magistrates' and county courts and in some circumstances in the Crown Court.

Barristers (known collectively as the 'Bar' and collectively and individually as 'Counsel') advise on legal problems submitted by solicitors and conduct cases in court; in the High Court advocacy may be practised only by barristers.

CORONERS

Coroners must be barristers, solicitors or legally qualified medical practitioners of not less than 5 years' standing. They are appointed by local authorities. There are approximately 110 coroners' jurisdictions in England and Wales. Coroners are independent judicial officers. When not engaged in coronal duties, coroners (apart from 'whole-time' coroners) continue in their legal or medical practices. Further information from the Coroners' Society of England and Wales, website; www.coronersociety.org.uk.

Qualification as a Barrister at the Bar of England and Wales

There are three stages that must be completed in order to qualify as a barrister. The Academic Stage consists of an undergraduate degree in law or an undergraduate degree in any other subject with a minimum of a 2ii. For those with an undergraduate degree in a subject other than law a one year conversion course (CPE) must be completed. Before commencing the Vocational Stage candidates must join one of the four Inns and then undertake the Bar Vocational Course which is either one year full-time or two years part-time as well as undertaking twelve qualifying sessions. Once these have been successfully completed candidates are 'Called to the Bar' by their Inn. The Pupillage Stage consists of one year spent in an authorised pupillage training organisation.

To find out more about all three stages of qualification as a barrister visit www.barcouncil.org.uk.

Qualification as a Solicitor in England and Wales

To practise as a solicitor in England and Wales a person must have been admitted as a solicitor, his or her name having been entered on the Roll of Solicitors, and must hold a practising certificate issued by **The Solicitors Regulation Authority (SRA)**, Ipsley Court, Berrington Close, Redditch, Worcestershire B98 0TD, Tel: 0870 666 2555. The SRA is the independent regulatory body of the Law Society of England and Wales. Persons will be admitted as solicitors only if they have passed the appropriate academic and vocational course and have completed a training contract and Professional Skills Course, or have transferred from another jurisdiction or the Bar. The SRA controls the training of solicitors. Most solicitors become members of the Law Society, but membership is not compulsory. Intending solicitors other than Fellows of the Institute of Legal Executives and Justices' Clerk's Assistants, and qualified lawyers from other jurisdictions, are required to serve a period of training with a practising solicitor after they have completed the Legal Practice Course.

All new entrants to the profession are required to complete a Criminal Records Bureau standard disclosure prior to admission. A candidate who wishes to start training must enrol as a student with the SRA and satisfy them that they have successfully completed the academic stage of training and have no issues which may call their character and suitability into question.

THE COMMON PROFESSIONAL EXAM/ POSTGRADU-ATE DIPLOMA IN LAW

Subjects: the foundations of legal knowledge: Public Law, including Constitutional Law, Administrative Law and Human Rights, Law of the European Union, Criminal Law, Obligations including Contract, Restitution and Tort, Property Law, and Equity and the Law of Trusts.

For an up-to-date list of course providers for the CPE, visit the SRA website at www.sra.org.uk/students/conversion-courses.

THE LEGAL PRACTICE COURSE

Compulsory subjects: Litigation & Advocacy, Business Law & Practice.

Three elective subjects: from a range of Corporate Client or Private Client topics (the range of elective available can differ from institution to institution).

Persuasive subjects: Accounts, Professional Conduct and Client Care, Land Accounts, Human Rights, European Union Law, Revenue Law. These areas pervade the compulsory and elective subjects of the course.

Legal Skills: Practical legal research, writing and drafting, interviewing and advising, advocacy. These skills form an integral part of the compulsory and elective subjects.

New courses are being phased in from September 2009 to September 2010. From 2010, all courses will have to comply with new underpinning outcomes and structural requirements, as follows: *Compulsory subjects* (called 'Stage 1'): Professional Conduct and Regulation, Wills and Administration of Estates, and Taxation; *Core Practice areas*: Business Law and Practice, Property Law and Practice, and Litigation; *Course Skills*: Practical Legal Research, Writing, Drafting, Interviewing and Advising, and Advocacy; *Three Elective subjects* (called 'Stage 2'): from a range of Corporate Client or Private Client topics (the range of elective available differs from institution to institution). An up-to-date list of course providers for the LPC, in its current and new forms, is available from the SRA website at www.sra.org.uk/students/lpc.page.

TRAINING CONTRACT

The training contract to be served by all intending solicitors, other than Fellows of the Institute of Legal Executives and Justices' Clerk's Assistants is 2 years. The training contract can also be delivered on a PT basis, lasting 4 years.

The PT course can be taken following the LPC or at the same time as a PT LPC. The law graduate who holds a qualifying law degree must complete the Legal Practice Course at a recognized institution, and then serve under the training contract for 2 years. The non-law graduate must first pass the Common Professional Exam (CPE) or the Postgraduate Diploma in Law, having attended either a 1-year FT or 2-year PT preparatory course. He or she may then serve under the training contract for 2 years after completion of a Legal Practice Course. Fellows of the Institute of Legal Executives and Justices' Clerk's Assistants may obtain up to 8 exemptions from the CPE by virtue of similar subjects passed in their Fellowship exams. After passing or being exempted from the CPE, the Fellow/Justices' Clerk's Assistant may be exempt from serving under a training contract following successful completion of an LPC. A Professional Skills Course must be taken prior to application for admission.

THE PROFESSIONAL SKILLS COURSE

The aim of the Professional Skills Course is to build on the foundations laid in the LPC so as to develop a trainee's professional skills. Providers of the course, trainees and their employers are encouraged to regard the course as the first stage of a trainee's lifetime professional development.

Built upon the LPC, the course provides training in three subject areas, *viz:* Financial and Business Skills; Advocacy and Communication Skills; Client Care and Professional Standards. Elective topics will also be chosen which fall within one or more of these three core areas.

All trainees have to complete all sections of the course satisfactorily before being admitted. The course consists of a minimum of 48 hours' face-to-face instruction on the core subjects and 24 hours on the elective subjects, and must be taken during the training contract. Subject to the Law Society being satisfied that the syllabuses will be properly covered and that appropriate tutors and teaching material will be used, it should be possible for the course to be provided by firms in-house, or by local law societies as well as by approved teaching institutions and commercial organizations.

QUALIFIED LAWYERS FROM OTHER JURISDICTIONS

UK lawyers together with lawyers from certain foreign jurisdictions and EU lawyers can apply for admission under the Qualified Lawyers Transfer Regulations 1990.

Under the European Communities Directive No 2005/36/EC, lawyers from EU jurisdictions may apply for admission following successful completion of an aptitude test – the Qualified Lawyers Transfer Test. The test covers Property, Litigation, Professional Conduct and Accounts, and Principles of Common Law. Lawyers from other jurisdictions are required to pass such aptitude tests as well as completing at least 2 years experience in common law jurisdiction with at least 12 months practising in English and Welsh law. All transferees are required to prove their character and suitability to be a solicitor.

European lawyers can apply to be a Registered European Lawyer (REL) under the Establishment of Lawyers Directive 98/5/EC. RELs can apply for admission as a solicitor after 3 years, with an expected minimum of 2 years practice in UK law. For information on any of the routes to qualification, contact Information Services at the SRA. Tel 0870 606 2555.

SCOTLAND

The Court of Session, High Courts, Sheriff Courts and Justice of the Peace Courts are administered by the Scottish Court service, an Executive Agency of the Scottish Government. For further information on Scottish Courts go to www.scotcourts.gov.uk.

THE LEGAL PROFESSION
The profession consists of **Solicitors** and **Advocates.**

Qualification as a Solicitor in Scotland
Solicitors in Scotland have their names inserted in a Roll of Solicitors and are granted annual **Certificates** entitling them to practise by **The Law Society of Scotland**, 26 Drumsheugh Gardens, Edinburgh EH3 7YR, Tel: 01312 267411 Fax: 01312 252934 E-mail: lawscot@lawscot.org.uk Website: www.lawscot.org.uk. A Certificate is granted to candidates who have completed a term of practical training and passed approved exams. (The Law Society will be happy to provide copies of its 'Careers Information' booklet on request.).

THE QUALIFYING EXAMINATIONS
Scots Law (the LLB) can be studied as a first degree in ten higher education institutions in Scotland. Admission requirements to the LLB degree are high, typically four A grades and one B at Higher. The only preferred subject is English. Students with a background in science and those who have studied

modern languages and/or history, geography and modern studies are equally acceptable.

At each university there are compulsory professional subjects for anybody who wishes to enter the legal profession. These subjects reflect the requirements of the syllabus for the Society's professional exams, which are detailed on the Law Society website.

An alternate route to qualifying as a solicitor in Scotland is by a combination of the Law Society's own examinations, three years pre-Diploma training and the Diploma in Legal Practice, followed by two years post-Diploma training. In order to be eligible to sit the Law Society's examinations, non-law graduates must find full time employment as a pre-Diploma trainee with a qualified solicitor practising in Scotland. A pre- Diploma training contract lasts for three years and during that time training must be given in the three prescribed areas of conveyancing, litigation, and either trusts and executries or the legal work of a public authority. To be eligible to enter into a pre-Diploma training contract, non-law graduates must fulfil certain educational requirements as outlined in Appendix 1 of the leaflet 'pre-Diploma training' found on the Law Society of Scotland website http:// www.lawscot.org.uk/training/default.aspx. During the period of the training contract, a pre-Diploma trainee will study for the Law Society's examinations (having four years from commencement of the first examination) in which to complete eight core subjects (Public Law & the Legal System, Conveyancing, Scots Private Law I and II, Evidence, Scots Criminal Law, Taxation, European Community Law and Scots Commercial Law I and II) before proceeding to the Diploma in Legal Practice. Upon successful completion of the Diploma the graduate will enter into a two year post-Diploma training contract with a qualified solicitor practicing in Scotland.

Please note, legal education and training in Scotland has undergone a major review, and the changes resulting from this will be implemented from 2011. The LLB will be replaced with a new 'Foundation programme', which will be offered at the same level as the LLB with the benefits of more flexibility in the programme to deliver subjects outside the professional subjects. The Diploma will be replaced by PEAT 1; that is Professional Education and Training Stage, incorporating a Diploma with increased choice and flexibility around electives. The introduction of PEAT 1 to replace the Diploma means that entry selection criteria and process for entry onto the PEAT 1 stage will be reviewed in due course. The Law Society of Scotland's website will continue to detail these changes as they are updated. The final stage of qualification – the 'Traineeship' will be replaced with Professional Education and Training Stage 2 from 2011, which will follow on from PEAT 1. The alternative route to qualification has also been reviewed and there is a commitment to retain it until a replacement can be found. However, it is likely that within the next few years details will emerge on how this route is to be phased out, with other flexible options for qualifying being phased in.

Qualification as an Advocate in Scotland

Barristers in Scotland are called Advocates. Scottish Advocates are not only members of the **Faculty of Advocates**, but also members of the College of Justice and officers of the Court. The procedure for the admission of Intrants is subject in part to the control of the Court and in part to the control of the Faculty; the Court is responsible for most of the formal procedures and the Faculty for the exams and periods of professional training. In order to become an Intrant, applicants must produce evidence that they hold one of the following standard of degree, a degree with Honours, Second Class (Division 2) or above, in Scottish Law at a Scottish university, or a degree in Scottish Law at a Scottish university together with a degree with Honours, Second Class (Division 2) or above, in another subject at a United Kingdom university or an ordinary degree with distinction in Scottish Law at a Scottish university. A Diploma in Legal Practice from a Scottish University is also required, although in exceptional cases this requirement may be waived. Once this evidence is provided and the relevant references obtained, a notice is posted outside Parliament House for a period of 21 days declaring the candidate's intention to present a Petition. At the end of this period the Petition is presented to the Court. After the Petition has been remitted by the Court to the Faculty, and it is signed off by the Clerk of Faculty and Dean of Faculty the candidate is considered to have **Matriculated** as an Intrant. An Intrant must also comply with the professional training required by the Faculty, wihch consists of a period of 21 months' training in a Solicitors office (in some cases 12 months). The Faculty **Exams in Legal Scholarship** are conducted on the standard known as the 'LLB standard' at the Scottish universities. Subject-for-subject exemptions are granted to Intrants who have passed exams at this standard in the course of a curriculum for a law degree at a Scottish university. Every Intrant must pass or be exempted from exams in 9 compulsory subjects and 2 optional subjects. The compulsory subjects include Roman Law of Property and Obligations, Jurisprudence, Constitutional and Administrative Law, Scottish Criminal Law, Scottish Private Law, Commercial Law and Business Institutions, Evidence, International Private Law and European Law and Institutions. In addition, and prior to the commencement of pupillage (also known as devilling) every Intrant must sit the Faculty's entrant examination in Evidence, Practice and Procedure. If successfully passed the Intrant can then commence their pupillage.

During the first 5 or 6 weeks of pupillage pupils undertake the Foundation Course. Intrants who have passed all the necessary exams and undergone the necessary professional training as well as successfully completing their pupillage may apply to be admitted to membership of the Faculty and are admitted at a public meeting of the Faculty. Once admitted to the Faculty, Intrants are introduced to the Court by the Dean of Faculty, make a Declaration of Allegiance to the Sovereign in open Court and are then admitted by the Court to the public office of Advocate. For further information on becoming an advocate contact Scott Brownidge, Secretariat Administrator, Faculty of Advocates, Parliament House, Edinburgh, EH1 1RF, Tel: 0131 260 5765.

NORTHERN IRELAND

As in England and Wales, the **superior courts** are the Court of Appeal, the High Court and the Crown Court. The latter is an exclusively criminal court. The Court of Appeal hears appeals in civil cases from the High Court and in criminal cases from the Crown Court and cases stated on a point of law from, *inter alia*, the County Court and the Magistrates' Courts. Appeals lie from the Court of Appeal to the House of Lords.

Inferior Courts: As in England and Wales, the **county courts** are principally civil courts, but in Northern Ireland they also hear appeals from conviction in the Magistrates' Courts for summary offences.

Magistrates' Courts: Magistrates' Courts deal principally with minor criminal offences (summary offences) and are presided over by Resident Magistrates (stipendiaries). Resident Magistrates are appointed by the Crown on the advice of the Lord Chancellor.

Coroners: Coroners must be barristers or solicitors of not less than 5 years standing practising in Northern Ireland.

THE LEGAL PROFESSION
The legal profession in Northern Ireland consists of barristers and solicitors belonging to professional bodies organized on similar lines to those in England and Wales.

Qualification as a Barrister in Northern Ireland

To qualify for practice as a barrister in Northern Ireland a candidate must be admitted to the degree of Barrister-at-Law by the **Honorable Society of the Inn**

of Court of Northern Ireland, enquiries to Under Treasurer, Bar Council Office, Bar Library, 91 Chichester Street, Belfast BT1 3JQ, Tel: Belfast 028 9056 2349.

A candidate must be at least 21, hold a degree conferred by a university of the United Kingdom or the Republic of Ireland or by the Council for National Academic Awards of not lower than 2nd class honours and have obtained their Certificate of Professional Legal Studies or otherwise be qualified to Call to the Bar of Northern Ireland.

Qualification as a Solicitor in Northern Ireland

The solicitors' professional body in Northern Ireland is the **Law Society of Northern Ireland**, Law Society House, 98 Victoria Street, Belfast BT1 3GN, Tel 028 9023 1614. It has overall responsibility for education and admission to the profession.

Admission to training is generally dependent upon possession of a recognised law degree from a university. Details of the recognised law degrees are available on the website of the Institute of Professional Legal Studies; www.qub.ac.uk/ips, see the Admissions section. Law graduates must attend a 2-year vocational apprenticeship course at the Institute of Professional Legal Studies, The Queen's University of Belfast, or the Graduate School of Professional Legal Education at the University of Ulster's Magee Campus after which they may be admitted as solicitors, but they are restricted from practising on their own account until they have served for 3 years as the qualified assistant of a practising solicitor.

Non-law graduates must complete a 2-year FT academic course in law at the Law Faculty at Queen's University, followed by the 2-year vocational apprenticeship course, and may then be admitted on the same conditions as indicated above.

Membership of Professional Institutions and Associations

COUNCIL FOR LICENSED CONVEYANCERS

16 Glebe Road
Chelmsford
Chelmsford
Essex CM1 1QG
Tel: 01245 349599
Fax: 01245 341300
E-mail: clc@clc-uk.org
Website: www.conveyancer.org.uk/

The CLC was established under the provisions of the Administration of Justice Act 1985 as the Regulatory Body for Licensed Conveyancers. Our purpose is to set entry standards and regulate the profession of Licensed Conveyancers effectively.

MEMBERSHIP
Student
Licensed Conveyancer
Probate Practitioner

QUALIFICATION/EXAMINATIONS
Foundation
Finals
Practical Training

THE LAW SOCIETY OF SCOTLAND

26 Drumsheugh Gardens
Edinburgh EH3 7YR
Tel: 0131 226 7411
Fax: 0131 225 2934
E-mail: lawscot@lawscot.org.uk
Website: www.lawscot.org.uk

The Law Society of Scotland is the membership organization of Scottish solicitors. We promote the interests of the profession and of the public in relation to the profession. Our services include providing initial career advice, overseeing legal education in Scotland, handling admissions to the profession, monitoring trainees, providing post-qualifying legal education, and administering courses and examinations for the Society of Law Accountants in Scotland.

MEMBERSHIP
All practising solicitors in Scotland must be members of the Society and must hold a current Practising Certificate which is issued by the Society.

QUALIFICATION/EXAMINATIONS
Please see the Law Society of Scotland's website.

INSTITUTE OF LEGAL EXECUTIVES

Kempston Manor
Kempston
Bedford MK42 7AB
Tel: 01234 841000
E-mail: info@ilex.org.uk
Website: www.ilex.org.uk

ILEX, founded in 1892, is a professional body representing around 22,000 practising and trainee legal executives (qualified lawyers who specialize in a particular area of law). Our objectives are to provide for the education, training and development of our Fellows, to advance and protect their interests, and to promote cooperation among everyone engaged in legal work.

MEMBERSHIP
Student Member
Affiliate Member
Associate Member (AInstLEX)

Graduate Member (GInstLEX)
Fellow (FInstLEX)

QUALIFICATION/EXAMINATIONS
Level 3 Certificate in Law and Practice
Level 3 Professional Diploma in Law and Practice
Level 6 Certificate in Law
Level 6 Professional Higher Diploma in Law and Practice
Graduate Fast Track Diploma (Level 6)

DESIGNATORY LETTERS
AInstLEX, GInstLEX, FInstLEX

THE ACADEMY OF EXPERTS

3 Gray's Inn Square
Gray's Inn
London WC1R 5AH
Tel: 020 7430 0333
Fax: 020 7430 0666
E-mail: admin@academy-experts.org
Website: www.academy-experts.org

The Academy of Experts is a multidisciplinary body established in 1987 to establish and promote high objective standards for those acting as expert witnesses. We act as an accrediting and professional body, offering training, technical guidance and representation. In addition we promote cost-efficient dispute resolution, maintaining a register of qualified dispute resolvers.

MEMBERSHIP
Non-Practising Subscriber

Associate Member
Associate Member (AMAE)
Full Member (MAE)
Fellow (FAE)
Practising Corporate Member

QUALIFICATION/EXAMINATIONS
There are examinations for upgrade.

DESIGNATORY LETTERS
AMAE, MAE, FAE

THE INSTITUTE OF LEGAL CASHIERS AND ADMINISTRATORS (ILCA)

2nd Floor
Marlowe House
109 Station Road
Sidcup
Kent DA15 7ET
Tel: 020 8302 2867
Fax: 020 8302 7481
E-mail: info@ilca.org.uk
Website: www.ilca.org.uk

The ILCA, which was founded in 1978, is a non-profit-making professional body dedicated to the education and support of specialist financial and administrative personnel working within the legal community. We encourage the development of our members' skills through educational courses, training workshops, seminars, conferences and our bimonthly magazine, *Legal Abacus*.

MEMBERSHIP
Ordinary Member

Diploma Member (ILCA (Dip))
Associate Member (AILCA)
Fellow Member (FILCA)
Affiliated Professional Member

QUALIFICATION/EXAMINATIONS
Diploma
Associateship examination

DESIGNATORY LETTERS
ILCA (Dip), AILCA, FILCA

LEISURE AND RECREATION MANAGEMENT
Membership of Professional Institutions and Associations

INSTITUTE FOR SPORT, PARKS AND LEISURE

Abbey Business Centre
1650 Arlington Business Park
Theale
Reading RG7 4SA
Tel: 0844 418 0077
Fax: 0118 929 8001
E-mail: infocentre@ispal.org.uk
Website: www.ispal.org.uk

ISPAL is the membership body for sport, parks and leisure industry professionals. We promote high standards and provide CPD as well as a wide range of training courses to our members in-house and at venues across the UK. We also work hard to influence government policy on behalf of our members.

MEMBERSHIP
Student
Studying Member
Full Member
Retiree
Local Authority Member
Corporate Member

INSTITUTE OF GROUNDSMANSHIP

28 Stratford Office Village
Walker Avenue
Wolverton Mill East
Milton Keynes MK12 5TW
Tel: 01908 312511
Fax: 01908 311140
E-mail: iog@iog.org
Website: www.iog.org

The Institute of Groundsmanship is the only membership organization supporting the whole of the grounds care industry. Serving the industry for 75 years, we provide a range of quality products, services and events including education, training and membership services, exhibitions, local information days, an annual conference and awards programme.

MEMBERSHIP
Junior Member
Student Member
Amateur Associate
Professional Associate
Full Individual Member
Affiliate Member
Corporate Member

QUALIFICATION/EXAMINATIONS
For details see; www.iog.org/training-training-courses.asp

INSTITUTE OF SPORT AND RECREATION MANAGEMENT (ISRM)

Sir John Beckwith Centre for Sport
Loughborough University
Loughborough
Leicestershire LE11 3TU
Tel: 01509 226474
Fax: 01509 226475
E-mail: info@isrm.co.uk
Website: www.isrm.co.uk

ISRM is the only national professional body for those involved exclusively in providing, managing, operating and developing sport and recreation services in the UK. Our aim is to ensure that the benefits of sport and physical activity are delivered effectively through the professional, safe and efficient management and development of facilities and services.

MEMBERSHIP
Associate Member
Member
Diploma Member
Companion (CInstSRM)
Fellow (FInstSRM/FInstSRM(Hons))
Corporate Affiliate
Further & Higher Education Corporate Affiliate
Commercial Affiliate

QUALIFICATION/EXAMINATIONS
National Pool Plant Operators Foundation Certificate
National Spa Pool Foundation Certificate
National Spa Pool Operators Certificate
National Pool Carers Certificate (Level 2)
Operations Certificate (Level 2)
Events Management Certificate (Level 3)
Fitness Management Certificate (Level 3)
Food and Beverage Management Certificate (Level 3)
Health & Safety Management Certificate (Level 3)
National Pool Plant Operators Certificate (Level 3)
Supervisory Management Certificate (Level 3)
National Pool Lifeguard Qualification (NPLQ)
Pool Technical Management Diploma

DESIGNATORY LETTERS
CInstSRM, FInstSRM, FInstSRM(Hons)

LIBRARIANSHIP AND INFORMATION WORK
Membership of Professional Institutions and Associations

CHARTERED INSTITUTE OF LIBRARY AND INFORMATION PROFESSIONALS

7 Ridgmount Street
London WC1E 7AE
Tel: 020 7255 0500
Fax: 020 7255 0501
E-mail: quals@cilip.org.uk
Website: www.cilip.org.uk

CILIP is the professional body representing those working within libraries and the information profession in the UK.

MEMBERSHIP
Certified Affiliate (ACLIP)
Chartered Member (MCLIP)
Chartered Fellow (FCLIP)
Revalidated Chartered Member or Fellow

QUALIFICATION/EXAMINATIONS
Application for membership qualifications is through the submission of a portfolio of evidence meeting published criteria. Please contact the Institute for further information.

DESIGNATORY LETTERS
ACLIP, MCLIP, FCLIP

MANAGEMENT
Membership of Professional Institutions and Associations

ASSOCIATION FOR COLLEGE MANAGEMENT

35 The Point
Market Harborough
Leicestershire LE16 7QU
Tel: 01858 464171
Fax: 01858 461366
E-mail: helpline@acm.uk.com
Website: www.acm.uk.com

ACM is a trade union and professional association representing managers in post-16 education. It was formed in the early 1990s and now has some 4,000 members.

ASSOCIATION FOR PROJECT MANAGEMENT

Ibis House, Regent Park
Summerleys Road
Princes Risborough
Buckinghamshire HP27 9LE
Tel: 0845 458 1944
Fax: 0845 458 8807
E-mail: info@apm.org.uk
Website: www.apm.org.uk

APM is the largest independent professional body of its kind in Europe. We have over 17,500 individual and 500 corporate members throughout the UK and abroad. Our aim is to develop and promote project management across all sectors of industry and beyond.

MEMBERSHIP
Student Member
Associate Member
Full Member (MAPM)

Fellow (FAPM)
Corporate Member

QUALIFICATION/EXAMINATIONS
Introductory Certificate in Project Management
APMP
APM Practitioner
Certified Project Manager

DESIGNATORY LETTERS
MAPM, FAPM

ASSOCIATION OF CERTIFIED COMMERCIAL DIPLOMATS

The Chartered Commercial Diplomats
ACCD Global Headquarters
PO Box 50561, Docklands
London E16 3WY
Tel: 08445 864249
Fax: 08445 864252 /087032
E-mail: enquiries@commercialdiplomats.eu
Website: www.commercialdiplomats.eu

ACCD is the first independent, not-for-profit, global professional body regulating and providing training and accreditation for commercial diplomats, ie trade negotiators, and commercial diplomacy practitioners, negotiators of foreign investment agreements, policy-makers and officials involved in investment issues, IIA experts, academia, private sector and NGO representatives, and officials in government ministries, parastatals, corporations and academic, public and private institutions worldwide.

MEMBERSHIP
Graduate Member
Associate (ACDipl)
Associate Fellow (AFCDipl)

Fellow (FCDipl)
Institutional Member

QUALIFICATION/EXAMINATIONS
Certificate of Competency
Advanced Certificate of Competency (ACertCD)
Advanced Dipolma of Professional Competence (ADiplCD)
Master Certificate of Competency (MCertCD)
Mastership in Commercial Diplomacy (MCDipl)
Qualified Certified Diplomat (QCD)
Chartered Diplomat (CDipl)

DESIGNATORY LETTERS
ACDipl, AFCDipl, FCDipl

351

ASSOCIATION OF UNIVERSITY ADMINISTRATORS

AUA National Office
University of Manchester
Oxford Road
Manchester M13 9PL
Tel: 0161 275 2063
Fax: 0161 175 2036
E-mail: aua@manchester.ac.uk
Website: www.aua.ac.uk

AUA is a provider of professional development opportunities for higher education managers and administrators, including academic and senior clerical/secretarial staff, with around 4,000 members. We organize an annual programme of seminars, workshops and conferences, publish 'Good Practice Guides', a quarterly journal and a quarterly newsletter, and have established a number of Special Interest Groups and e-mail discussion groups.

MEMBERSHIP
Associate Member

Member
Fellow (FAUA)
International Associate Member

QUALIFICATION/EXAMINATIONS
Postgraduate Certificate in Professional Practice (Higher Education Administration and Management) (validated by The Open University)

DESIGNATORY LETTERS
FAUA

BRITISH INSTITUTE OF FACILITIES MANAGEMENT

Number One Building
The Causeway
Bishop's Stortford
Hertfordshire CM23 2ER
Tel: 0845 058 1356
Fax: 01279 712669
E-mail: info@bifm.org.uk
Website: www.bifm.org.uk

The BIFM is the 'natural home' of facilities management (FM) in the UK. Founded in 1993, the Institute provides information, education, training and networking services for nearly 13,000 members – both individual professionals and organizations. The BIFM's mission is to advance the profession – to consolidate FM as a vital management discipline.

MEMBERSHIP
Associate
Member (MBIFM)
Certified Member (CBIFM)
Fellow (FBIFM)

Corporate Member

QUALIFICATION/EXAMINATIONS
Award in Facilities Mangement (Level 4)
Certificate in Facilities Management (Level 4)
Diploma in Facilities Management (Level 4)
Certificate in Facilities Management (Level 5)
Diploma in Facilities Management (Level 5)
Diploma in Facilities Management (Level 6)

DESIGNATORY LETTERS
MBIFM, CBIFM, FBIFM

BUSINESS MANAGEMENT ASSOCIATION

Coborn House
3 Coborn Road
Docklands
London E3 2DA
Tel: 0871 231 1869
Fax: 02075 441499
E-mail: enquiries@businessmanagement.org.uk
Website: www.businessmanagement.org.uk

The Business Management Association is an independent association of small businesses, operating on an international basis. We promote the aims and interests of the small business sector, provide information and advice to our members, encourage networking between members, and run courses aimed at equipping members with advanced knowledge, skill and accreditation in several aspects of management.

MEMBERSHIP
Affiliate (AffBMA) Associate (ABMA)
Member (MBMA)
Fellow (FBMA)
Companion (CBMA)
Certified Manager (CertMgr)
Certified Master of Management (CMMgt)

Certified Master of Business Administration (CMBA)
Certified Doctor of Business Administration (CDBA)
Member Certified Business Management Accountant (MCBMA)
Fellow Certified Business Management Accountant (FCBMA)

QUALIFICATION/EXAMINATIONS
Certificate in Business Start-up
Certificate in Management Studies (CMS)
Diploma In Business Management (DipBMA)
Diploma in International Business (DIB)
Diploma in Management Studies (DMS)

DESIGNATORY LETTERS
AffBMA, ABMA, MBMA, FBMA, CBMA, CertMgr, CMMgt, CMBA, CDBA, MCBMA, FCBMA

DIPLOMATIC ACADEMY OF EUROPE AND THE ATLANTIC

Central Administration Office
Docklands
Greater London E16 3WY
Tel: 08445 857027
Fax: 08445 857077
E-mail: enquiries@eatcd.org
Website: www.eatcd.org

The Diplomatic Academy of Europe and the Atlantic is an independent, membership-driven, diplomatic and professional organization founded to improve knowledge, understanding and professional practice in commercial diplomacy, the prevention of corruption and organized crime, international security and defence, human rights and related issues.

MEMBERSHIP
Associate
Associate Fellow

Fellow

QUALIFICATION/EXAMINATIONS
Master Certificate of Competency (MCert)
Mastership in Anti-Corruption Policy and Strategy (MACor)
Mastership in Commercial Diplomacy (MCDipl)
Mastership in International Diplomatic Affairs
Mastership in International Human Rights (MIHR)
Mastership in International Security and Defence Policy (MIPol)

INSTITUTE OF ADMINISTRATIVE MANAGEMENT

6 Graphite Square
Vauxhall Walk
London SE11 5EE
Tel: 020 7091 9620
Fax: 020 7091 7340
E-mail: info@instam.org
Website: www.instam.org

The IAM is the leading professional body and UK government recognized awarding body for those involved in the administration and management of business. We offer a range of qualifications, from an introduction to the subject up to a full BA Hons degree.

MEMBERSHIP
Student Member
Associate (AInstAM)
Member (MInstAM)
Fellow (FInstAM)

QUALIFICATION/EXAMINATIONS
Introductory Award in Administrative Management (Level 2)
Certificate in Administrative Management (Level 3)
Diploma in Administrative Management (Level 4)
Advanced Diploma in Administrative Management (Level 5)
(BA Hons degree in Business Management, from The Open University, Sheffield Hallam University or The University of Teeside)

DESIGNATORY LETTERS
AInstAM, MInstAM, FInstAM

INSTITUTE OF BUSINESS CONSULTING

4th Floor
2 Savoy Court
Strand
London WC2R 0EZ
Tel: 020 7497 0580
Fax: 020 7497 0463
E-mail: ibc@ibconsulting.org.uk
Website: www.ibconsulting.org.uk

The Institute of Business Consulting was formed in 2007 by the merger of the Institute of Business Advisers and the Institute of Management Consultancy, and we are the professional body for business consultants and advisers. Our aim is to raise the standards of professional practice in support of better business performance.

MEMBERSHIP
Student
Affiliate
Associate (AIBC)
Member (MIBC)
Fellow (FIBC)

Certified Business Advisor (CBA)
Certified Management Consultant (CMC)
Practice Member (corporate membership)

QUALIFICATION/EXAMINATIONS
Certificate in Business Support
Certificate in Management Consulting Essentials
Diploma in Business Support
Diploma in Management Consultancy (in conjunction with the Chartered Management Institute)

DESIGNATORY LETTERS
AIBC, MIBC, FIBC

INSTITUTE OF DIRECTORS

116 Pall Mall
London SW1Y 5ED
Tel: 020 7766 2601
Fax: 020 7930 1949
E-mail: professionaldev@iod.com
Website: www.iod.com/development

The IoD is the UK's largest organization representing professional leaders, with individual members ranging from entrepreneurs of start-up companies to CEOs of multinational organizations. The Institute's principal objectives are to advance the interests of its members as company directors, and to provide them with business facilities and a variety of services.

MEMBERSHIP
Associate Member

Member (MIoD)
Fellow (FIoD)
Chartered Director (C Dir)

QUALIFICATION/EXAMINATIONS
Certificate in Company Direction (CertIoD)
Diploma in Company Direction (DipIoD)

DESIGNATORY LETTERS
MIoD, FIoD, C Dir

INSTITUTE OF LEADERSHIP & MANAGEMENT

Stowe House
Netherstowe
Lichfield
Staffordshire WS13 6TJ
Tel: 01543 266867
Fax: 01543 266893
E-mail: customer@i-l-m.com
Website: www.i-l-m.com

The ILM supports, develops and informs leaders and managers at every stage of their career. With our broad range of industry-leading qualifications, membership services and learning resources, the ILM provides flexible development solutions that can be blended to meet the specific needs of employers and learners.

MEMBERSHIP
Studying Member
Professional Member

QUALIFICATION/EXAMINATIONS
Management
Award in Effective Team Skills (Level 2)
Award and Certificate in Team Leading (Level 2)
Award, Certificate and Diploma in First Line Management (Level 3)
Award, Certificate and Diploma in Management (Level 4)

Award, Certificate and Diploma in Management (Level 5)
Award in Management (Level 6)
Award, Certificate and Diploma in Executive Management (Level 7)
Leadership
Award and Certificate in Leadership (Level 3)
Award in Leadership (Level 4)
Award and Certificate in Leadership (Level 5)
Award, Certificate and Diploma in Strategic Leadership (Level 7)
Leadership and management
Award, Certificate and Diploma in Leadership and Management (Level 3)
Award, Certificate and Diploma in Leadership and Management (Level 5)
Award, Certificate and Diploma in Strategic Leadership and Executive Management (Level 7)
Coaching and mentoring

Award and Certificate in Workplace Coaching for Team Leaders and First Line Managers (Level 3)

Certificate in Workplace Coaching and Mentoring (Level 3)

Certificate in Coaching and Mentoring in Management (Level 5)

Diploma for Professional Management Coaches and Mentors (Level 5)

Certificate in Executive Coaching and Leadership Mentoring (Level 7)

Diploma for Professional Executive Coaches and Leadership Mentors (Level 7)

Specialist management qualifications

Environmental Management

Facilities Management

Managing Equality and Diversity

Managing Volunteers

Sales Management

Site Waste Management

INSTITUTE OF MANAGEMENT SERVICES

Brooke House
Lichfield
Staffordshire WS13 6AA
Tel: 01543 266909
Fax: 01543 257848
E-mail: admin@ims-stowe.fsnet.co.uk
Website: www.ims-productivity.com

The IMS is the primary body in the UK concerned with the promotion, practice and development of methods and techniques for the improvement of productivity and quality. We act as the qualifying body for the management services profession in the UK, focusing developments in practice and knowledge and acting as a forum for information exchange.

MEMBERSHIP
Affiliate

Associate (AMS)
Member (MMS)
Fellow (FMS)

QUALIFICATION/EXAMINATIONS
Management Services Certificate
Management Services Diploma

DESIGNATORY LETTERS
AMS, MMS, FMS

INSTITUTE OF VALUE MANAGEMENT

Westminster
London SW1H 9JJ
Tel: 08709 020905
E-mail: secretary@irm.org.uk
Website: www.ivm.org.uk

The Institute aims to establish Value Management as a process for achieving value in every sector of the economy and to provide support in the innovative use of value management techniques.

MEMBERSHIP
Corporate Membership: Open to any company or organization practising or promoting value techniques. Each corporate member may nominate up to 10 members of their organization as representatives to the Institute. A member nominated by a corporate body can hold executive office and has full voting rights.

Ordinary Membership: Open to any professional person who has an interest in and can demonstrate an involvement in practising value techniques.

Student Membership: Open to students who have an interest in value management and who are registered FT students possessing a valid student card.

Fellow: Awarded to a member as a special honour for outstanding contribution to the field of value management.

QUALIFICATION/EXAMINATIONS
Certificate and Training: The Institute has worked closely with the Commission of the European Communities to establish a European Training System and Certification Procedure.

Roll of Practitioners: The Institute maintains an authorized list of value practitioners who are members of the Institute.

It launched its European Training and Certification System in 1998. This European Commission funded initiative offers, through the IVM's Certification Board, certification in the following categories: Certificated Value Analyst (CVA); Professional in Value Management (PVM); Certificated Value Manager (CVM); Trainer in Value Management (TVM). The Certification Board also approves basic and advanced courses in value management that have been designed by trainers in value management. The Institute provides a list of trainers.

INTERNATIONAL PROFESSIONAL MANAGERS ASSOCIATION

5 Starnes Court
Union Street
Maidstone
Kent ME14 1EB
Tel: 01622 672867
Fax: 01622 755149
E-mail: admin@ipma.co.uk
Website: www.ipma.co.uk

The IPMA is an international examining, licensing and regulatory professional body, which, through its qualifications, enables practising managers to participate in and be part of the process of improving managerial performance and effectiveness in all areas of business, industry and public administration.

MEMBERSHIP
Student member
Graduate Member (GRD PMA)
Licentiate Member (LMPMA)
Certified Associate (AMPMA)

Certified Member (MPMA)
Certified Fellow (FPMA)
Honorary Member (MPMA)
Honorary Fellow (FPMA)

QUALIFICATION/EXAMINATIONS
Certified International Professional Manager (CIPM) examination

DESIGNATORY LETTERS
GRD PMA, LMPMA, AMPMA, MPMA, FPMA

PROFESSIONAL BUSINESS & TECHNICAL MANAGEMENT

Head Office
Warwick Corner
42 Warwick Road
Kenilworth
Warwickshire CV8 1HE
Tel: 01926 855498
E-mail: info@group-ims.com
Website: www.group-ims.com

PBTM was founded in 1983 to forge the link between business and technology. We give professional recognition to the knowledge and skills of managers in business and technology, supporting lifelong learning to help members fulfil their career ambitions and develop their potential.

MEMBERSHIP
Student Member (StudProfBTM)

Associate Member (AMProfBTM)
Member (MProfBTM)
Fellow (FProfBTM)
Companion (CProfBTM)

Diploma of Merit

THE ASSOCIATION OF BUSINESS EXECUTIVES

5th Floor, CI Tower
St Georges Square
New Malden
Surrey KT3 4TE
Tel: 020 8329 2930
Fax: 020 8329 2945
E-mail: info@abeuk.com
Website: www.abeuk.com

The ABE is a professional membership body and examination board. We develop business and management qualifications at Certificate, Diploma, Advanced Diploma and Postgraduate Diploma levels. ABE qualifications provide progression routes to degree and Master's programmes worldwide.

MEMBERSHIP
Student Member
Associate Member (AMABE)
Member (MABE)
Fellow (FABE)

QUALIFICATION/EXAMINATIONS
Certificate, Diploma and Advanced Diploma (Levels 3, 5 and 6) in:
Business Information Systems
Business Management
Financial Management
Human Resource Management
Marketing
Travel, Tourism and Hospitality Management
and Postgraduate Diploma (Level 7) in Business Management

DESIGNATORY LETTERS
AMABE, MABE, FABE

THE CAMBRIDGE ACADEMY OF MANAGEMENT

Wellington House
Cambridge CB1 1BH
E-mail: info@cambridge-uk.org
Website: www.businessmanagement.org.uk

The Cambridge Academy of Management (CAM) is a professional, autonomous, not-for-profit institution established in to foster the concept of UK management education made available to all internationally. CAM is built on the foundation to promote state-of-the-art knowledge and expertise in all facets of management education, training and development for the global educational arena.

MEMBERSHIP
Associate Category (ACAM)
Member Category (MCAM)
Fellowship Category (FCAM)

QUALIFICATION/EXAMINATIONS
All programmes offered by Cambridge Academy of Management are accredited by Quality Assurance Commission UK. Programmes Offered:
CAM International Foundation Diploma CAM International
Certificate in Restaurant & Catering Management CAM
International Diploma in Business Management CAM International
Diploma in Business (Restaurant & Catering Management)

CAM International Diploma in Business (Tourism Management)

CAM International Advanced Diploma in Business Management

CAM International Advanced Diploma in Business (Restaurant & Catering Management)

CAM International Advanced Diploma in Business (Tourism Management)

CAM International Postgraduate Diploma in Hospitality Management

CAM International Postgraduate Diploma in Business

CAM International Postgraduate Diploma in Business with Specialization in: Marketing Finance Human Resource

THE CHARTERED MANAGEMENT INSTITUTE

Membership Department
Management House
Cottingham Road
Corby
Northants NN17 1TT
Tel: 01536 207307
Fax: 01536 400388
E-mail: membership@managers.org.uk
Website: www.managers.org.uk

The CMI is the only chartered professional body dedicated to managers and leaders, and the organizations they work in. As guardian of the National Occupational Standards for Management and Leadership excellence, we set the standards that others follow. As a membership organization we give our members the tools they need to make a genuine impact on business in the UK.

MEMBERSHIP
Associate (ACMI)
Member (MCMI)
Fellow (FCMI)
Chartered Manager (CMgr)

DESIGNATORY LETTERS
ACMI, MCMI, FCMI, CMgr

THE INSTITUTE OF COMMERCIAL MANAGEMENT

ICM House
Castleman Way
20A Bargates Christchurch
Ringwood
Hampshire BH24 3BA
Tel: 01202 490555
Fax: 01202 490666
E-mail: info@icm.ac.uk
Website: www.icm.ac.uk

The Institute is the leading professional body for Commercial and Business Development Managers. It is also a fully accredited UK Examining and Awarding Board for those undertaking business and management studies, and offers in excess of 200 programmes at HND, first degree, and Master's levels. It works with education and training providers and government agencies in more than 100 countries.

MEMBERSHIP
Student
Associate Member (AMInstCM)
Graduate Member (GradDipCM)
Member (MInstCM)
Fellow (FInstCM)

QUALIFICATION/EXAMINATIONS
ICM Awards cover the following areas: Accounting & Finance; Business Studies; Commercial Management; Hospitality Management; Human Resource Development; Journalism; Legal Studies; Management Studies; Maritime Management; Marketing Management; Sales Management; Travel & Tourism.

DESIGNATORY LETTERS
AMInstCM, MInstCM, FInstCM

THE SOCIETY OF BUSINESS PRACTITIONERS

PO Box 11
Sandbach
Cheshire CW11 3GE
Tel: 01270 526339
Fax: 01270 526339
E-mail: info@mamsasbp.org.uk
Website: wow.mamsasbp.org.uk

The SBP is a professional body for business practitioners and business students. Our objective is sharing knowledge, skill and experience with our members, with the aim of furthering and protecting their success.

MEMBERSHIP
Student (StuSBP)
Member (MSBP)
Fellow (FSBP)
Certified Professional Manager (CPMSBP)
Honorary Fellow (HonFSBP)

A CPD programme is also offered, together with a special Diploma syllabus for the Asia Division.

QUALIFICATION/EXAMINATIONS
Diploma in Business Administration
Advanced Diploma in Business Administration
PGDip in Business Administration
PGDip in International Marketing
Diploma in Computer Studies
Advanced Diploma in Computer Studies
GradDip in IT & E-Commerce
GradDip in Entrepreneurship
Advanced Diploma in Accounting
Joint Diploma in Marketing Management and MAMSA Diploma in Sales & Marketing Practices
Joint Advanced Diploma in Marketing Management and MAMSA Advanced Diploma in Sales Management

MARKETING AND SALES
Membership of Professional Institutions and Associations

LONDON CENTRE OF MARKETING

Buckingham House East
Stanmore
London HA7 4EB
Tel: 020 8385 7766
Fax: 020 8385 7755
E-mail: info@lcmuk.com
Website: www.lcmuk.com

The London Centre of Marketing is an accredited, non-political, non-profit-making institution based in London, which exists with the sole aim of providing internationally recognized professional qualifications in marketing and marketing management.

QUALIFICATION/EXAMINATIONS
Diploma, Higher Diploma, Professional Diploma and
Advanced Diploma in:
Business Management & Marketing

Human Resource Development & Marketing
Sales & Marketing Management
Travel & Tourism Marketing

MANAGING AND MARKETING SALES ASSOCIATION EXAMINATION BOARD

PO Box 11
Sandbach
Cheshire CW11 3GE
Tel: 01270 526339
Fax: 01270 526339
E-mail: info@mamsasbp.org.uk
Website: www.mamsasbp.org.uk

MAMSA is an international organization offering
qualifications in marketing and business practice and
services to members through representatives in
Europe, the Middle East, Africa and the Far East.

MEMBERSHIP
Graduate (GradMAMSA)
Graduate Affiliate (GradAfMAMSA)
Professional (MMAMSA)
Fellow (FMAMSA)

QUALIFICATION/EXAMINATIONS
Standard Diploma in Salesmanship

Certificate in Sales Marketing
Higher Diploma in Marketing
Advanced Diploma in Sales Management
Certificate in Marketing Strategy
Diploma in Marketing Strategy & Management
(Hypothesis/Thesis)
Diploma in Sales and Marketing Practices
A CPD programme is also offered.

DESIGNATORY LETTERS
GradMAMSA,   GradAfMAMSA,   MMAMSA,
FMAMSA

MRS (THE MARKET RESEARCH SOCIETY)

15 Northburgh Street
London EC1V 0JR
Tel: 020 7490 4911
Fax: 020 7490 0608
E-mail: profdevelopment@mrs.org.uk
Website: www.mrs.org.uk

With members in more than 70 countries, MRS is the
world's largest association serving those with professional equity in the provision or use of market, social
and opinion research. We offer various qualifications
and membership grades, and are an awarding body
for vocationally related qualifications in market and
social research.

MEMBERSHIP
Affiliate
Studying Affiliate
Associate Member (AMRS)

Full Member (MMRS)
Fellow (FMRS)
Honorary Member

QUALIFICATION/EXAMINATIONS
Certificate in Market and Social Reseach
Certificate in Interviewing Skills in Market and Social
Research
Advanced Certificate in Market and Social Research
Practice
Diploma in Market and Social Research Practice

DESIGNATORY LETTERS
AMRS, MMRS, FMRS

THE CHARTERED INSTITUTE OF MARKETING

Moor Hall
Maidenhead
Berkshire SL6 9QH
Tel: 01628 427120
Fax: 01628 427158
E-mail: qualifications@cim.co.uk
Website: www.cim.co.uk/learningzone

The Chartered Institute of Marketing is the leading international professional marketing body, with 47,000 members worldwide. We aim to improve the skills of marketing practitioners, enabling them to deliver exceptional results for their organization. Qualifications from Introductory to Chartered postgraduate level are offered to anyone wanting to develop their career in marketing.

MEMBERSHIP
Affiliate (Studying/Professional)
Associate (ACIM)
Member (MCIM)
Fellow (FCIM)

Chartered Marketer

QUALIFICATION/EXAMINATIONS
Introductory Certificate in Marketing
Professional Certificate in Marketing
Professional Diploma in Marketing
Chartered Postgraduate Diploma in Marketing
Diploma in Marketing Communications
Diploma in Managing Digital Media
Diploma in Digital Marketing
Diploma in Hospitality and Tourism Marketing

DESIGNATORY LETTERS
ACIM, MCIM, FCIM

THE INSTITUTE OF DIRECT MARKETING

1 Park Road
Teddington
Middlesex TW11 0AR
Tel: 020 8977 5705
Fax: 020 8943 2535
E-mail: enquiries@theidm.com
Website: www.theidm.com

The IDM is Europe's leading professional development body for direct, data and digital marketing. Founded in 1987, we are an educational trust and registered charity. We advocate lifelong learning and maintain an up-to-date education portfolio designed to meet the needs of marketing practitioners throughout their career.

MEMBERSHIP
Affiliate Member
Associate Member
Member
Fellow

Corporate Member

QUALIFICATION/EXAMINATIONS
Certificate in B2B Marketing (Cert BusM)
Certificate in Digital Marketing (Cert DigM)
Certificate in Direct and Interactive Marketing (Cert IDM)
Diploma in B2B Marketing (Dip BusM)
Diploma in Digital Marketing (Dip DigM)
Diploma in Direct and Interactive Marketing (Dip IDM)
Diploma in Integrated Marketing Communications (Dip IMC)

THE INSTITUTE OF SALES AND MARKETING MANAGEMENT

Harrier Court
Woodside Road
Lower Woodside
Bedfordshire LU1 4DQ
Tel: 01582 843260
Fax: 01582 849142
E-mail: education@ismm.co.uk
Website: www.ismm.co.uk

The ISSM offers professional qualifications in sales and marketing. The qualifications are accredited by the Qualification and Curriculum Authority, the body set up by the government to regulate qualifications. The programmes are available through ISMM accredited centres.

MEMBERSHIP
Student
Associate (AInstSMM)
Member
Fellow

QUALIFICATION/EXAMINATIONS
Award in Basic Sales Skills (Level 1)

Award and Certificate in Sales and Marketing (Level 2)
Award, Certificate and Diploma in Advanced Sales and Marketing (Level 3)
Award, Certificate and Diploma in Operational Sales and Marketing (Level 4)
Award, Certificate and Diploma in Account Management/Sales Management (Level 5)
Diploma in Sales and Account Management (Level 5)
Executive Award, Executive Certificate and Executive Diploma in Strategic Sales and Account Management (Level 6)

DESIGNATORY LETTERS
AInstSMM, MInstSMM, FInstSMM

THE SOCIETY OF SALES & MARKETING

40 Archdale Road
East Dulwich
London SE22 9HJ
Tel: 0845 643 6832
Fax: 0845 643 6834
E-mail: info@ssm.org.uk
Website: www.ssm.org.uk

The Society is the only professional examining body that awards Certificates and Diplomas in all the four areas of selling, namely selling and sales management, marketing, retail management, and international trade and services. The Society celebrated its Silver Jubilee in style in 2005 at Imperial College London.

MEMBERSHIP
Graduate (GSSM)
Associate (ASSM)
Fellow (FSSM)

QUALIFICATION/EXAMINATIONS
Candidates for the Certificate, Advanced Certificate or Diploma choose any one of the following: (A) Selling & Sales Management, (B) Marketing, (C) Retail Management and (D) International Trade & Services.
(A) Selling & Sales Management subjects:
Certificate: (1) Business Communication, (2) Bookkeeping & Accounts, (3) Selling & Sales Management, (4) Fundamentals of Marketing
Advanced Certificate: (5) Marketing Research Management, (6) Consumer Behaviour, (7) Principles of Selling, (8) Consumer Law

Diploma: (9) Management Information Systems, (10) Consumerism, Ethics & Social Responsibility, (11) Marketing Planning & Control, (12) Marketing Communication

(B) Marketing subjects:

Certificate: (1) Business Communication (2) Book-keeping & Accounts, (3) Selling & Sales Management, (4) Fundamentals of Marketing

Advanced Certificate: (5) Marketing Research Management, (6) Consumer Behaviour, (7) Principles of Selling, (8) Consumer Law

Diploma: (9) Management Information Systems, (10) Consumerism, Ethics & Social Responsibility, (11) Marketing Planning & Control, (12) Marketing Communication

(C) Retail Management subjects:

Certificate: (1) Business Communication, (2) Book-keeping & Accounts, (3) Selling & Sales Management, (4) Retail Management

Advanced Certificate: (5) Marketing Research Management,(6) Consumer Behaviour, (7) Principles of Selling, (8) Consumer Law

Diploma: (9) Management Information Systems, (10) Consumerism, Ethics & Social Responsibility, (11) Fundamentals of Marketing, (12) Marketing Communication

(D) International Trade & Services:

Certificate: (1) Business Communication, (2) Book-keeping & Accounts, (3) International Trade & Services, (4) Fundamentals of Marketing

Advanced Certificate: (5) Marketing Research Management, (6) Import & Export Management, (7) Finance for Export, (8) Consumer Law

Diploma: (9) Management Information Systems, (10) Consumerism, Ethics & Social Responsibility, (11) Marketing Planning & Control, (12) Marketing Communication

DESIGNATORY LETTERS
GSSM, ASSM, FSSM

MARTIAL ARTS

Membership of Professional Institutions and Associations

INSTITUTE OF MARTIAL ARTS AND SCIENCES

1 Henrietta Street
Bolton
Lancashire BL3 4HL
Tel: 01942 212378
Fax: 01942 211650
E-mail: admin@institute-of-martialarts-and- sciences.com
Website: www.institute-of-martialarts-and-sciences.com

The IMAS was formed by a group of high-ranking martial arts instructors, educators, researchers and academics to encourage education and research in martial arts, promote professionalism among martial arts instructors, afford martial artists the opportunity of obtaining recognized and accredited qualifications, and to act as a platform to encourage academic debate.

MEMBERSHIP
Associate (AIMAS)
Member (MIMAS)
Fellow (FIMAS)

MASSAGE AND ALLIED THERAPIES
Membership of Professional Institutions and Associations

BRITISH MEDICAL ACUPUNCTURE SOCIETY

BMAS House
3 Winnington Court
Winnington Street
Northwich
Cheshire CW8 1AQ
Tel: 01606 786782
Fax: 01606 786783
E-mail: admin@medical-acupuncture.co.uk
Website: www.medical-acupuncture.co.uk

The BMAS was formed in 1980 as an association of medical practitioners interested in acupuncture and we now have a membership of more than 2,700 registered doctors and allied health professionals who practise acupuncture alongside more conventional techniques. We believe that acupuncture has an important role to play in healthcare and promote its use as a therapy following orthodox medical diagnosis by suitably trained practitioners. We run training programmes in the UK for doctors, dentists and other healthcare professionals.

MEMBERSHIP
Affiliated Member
Member
Accredited Member
Dental/Veterinary Member
Retired Member
Honorary Member
Overseas Member

QUALIFICATION/EXAMINATIONS
Certificate of Basic Competence (CoBC)
Diploma of Medical Acupuncture (DipMedAc)

INTERNATIONAL COUNCIL OF HOLISTIC THERAPISTS

18 Shakespeare Business Centre
Hathaway Close
Eastleigh
Hampshire SO50 4SR
Tel: 0844 875 2022
Fax: 023 8062 4399
Website: www.fht.org.uk

(Part of the Federation of Holistic Therapists)

This professional association supports therapists in holistic therapies, including aromatherapy, reflexology, Indian head massage, body massage, and many more. Membership is open only to those qualified through awarding bodies such as the IIHHT, VTCT, NVQ/SVQ, BTEC and C&G. Exemptions from these requirements are granted only for those who have other acceptable qualifications and experience.

INTERNATIONAL REGISTER OF MASSAGE THERAPISTS

PO Box 5537
Hatfield Peverel
Essex CM3 2QN
Tel: 06626 713867
Fax: 01323 440282
E-mail: irmt-eb@yahoo.co.uk
Website: www.irmt.co.uk

The IRMT is a professional trade association that provides courses, through external tutors, for anyone serious about a career in the complementary or physical therapy professions. We offer courses in: Massage/Anatomy & Physiology; Remedial Back Therapy; Sports Therapy; Aromatherapy; Reflexology; Reiki; Skin Care; Head Massage; and On-site Massage.

MEMBERSHIP
Associate (AIRMT)
Member (MIRMT)
Fellow (FIRMT)

QUALIFICATION/EXAMINATIONS
Diploma

DESIGNATORY LETTERS
AIRMT, MIRMT, FIRMT

LCSP REGISTER OF REMEDIAL MASSEURS AND MANIPULATIVE THERAPISTS

38A High Street
Lowestoft
Suffolk NR32 1HY
Tel: 01502 563344
Fax: 01502 582220
E-mail: lcsp@btconnect.com
Website: www.lcsp.uk.com

The Register accepts practitioners who currently work in Massage, Remedial Massage or Manipulative Therapy. Applicants must have completed a course of education at an establishment whose training meets or exceeds the National Occupational Standards. The Register offers heavily discounted comprehensive medical malpractice insurance, business support, regular communications and CPD opportunities.

MEMBERSHIP
Student Member
Associate Member (LCSP (Assoc))
Full Member (LSCP (Phys))
Affiliate
Fellow (FLCSP)
Honorary Member

DESIGNATORY LETTERS
LCSP (Assoc), LCSP (Phys), FLCSP

NORTHERN INSTITUTE OF MASSAGE LTD

14–16 St Mary's Place
Bury
Greater Manchester BL9 0DZ
Tel: 0161 797 1800
E-mail: information@nim.co.uk
Website: www.nim.co.uk

The NIM was founded in 1924 and offers professional training in Remedial Massage, Advanced Remedial Massage, and Manipulative Therapy. We also offer a number of CPD seminars and short courses to supplement our main training programme. Research is carried out mostly by therapists on patients from their own clinics or by students completing university courses.

QUALIFICATION/EXAMINATIONS
Diploma in Remedial Massage
Advanced Remedial Massage Diploma
Manipulative Therapy Diploma

SOCIETY OF HOMEOPATHS

11 Brookfield Duncan Close
Moulton Park
Northampton NN3 6WL
Tel: 08454 506611
Fax: 08454 506622
E-mail: info@homeopathy-soh.org
Website: www.homeopathy-soh.org

The Society of Homeopaths was established in 1978 and is now the largest organization registering professional homeopaths in Europe. Our vision is 'homeopathy for all' and we aim to achieve this both by supporting our members and by raising the profile of homeopathy in general.

MEMBERSHIP
Subscriber
Student Member
Student Clinical Member
Registered Member (RSHom)
International Affiliate

DESIGNATORY LETTERS
RSHom

MATHEMATICS
Membership of Professional Institutions and Associations

EDINBURGH MATHEMATICAL SOCIETY

School of Mathematics, Edinburgh University
James Clerk Maxwell Building
Mayfield Road
Edinburgh EH9 3JZ
Tel: 01316 505040
Fax: 01316 506553
E-mail: edmathsoc@maths.ed.ac.uk
Website: www.maths.ed.ac.uk

The EMS, founded in 1883, is the principal mathematical society for the academic community in Scotland as well as mathematicians in industry and commerce. We organize meetings, publish a journal and support mathematical activities through various funds.

MEMBERSHIP
Ordinary Member
Reciprocal Member
Honorary Member

THE INSTITUTE OF MATHEMATICS AND ITS APPLICATIONS

Catherine Richards House
16 Nelson Street
Southend-on-Sea
Essex SS1 1EF
Tel: 01702 354020
Fax: 01702 354111
E-mail: post@ima.org.uk
Website: www.ima.org.uk

The IMA, founded in 1964, is the UK's learned society for mathematics and its applications. We promote mathematical research, education and careers, and the use of mathematics in business, industry and commerce. In 1990 the Institute was incorporated by Royal Charter and subsequently granted the right to award the status of Chartered Mathematician, Chartered Scientist and Chartered Mathematics Teacher.

MEMBERSHIP
Student

Affiliate
Associate Member (AMIMA)
Member (MIMA)
Fellow (FIMA)
Chartered Mathematician (CMath)
Chartered Mathematics Teacher (CMathTeach)
Chartered Scientist (CSci)

DESIGNATORY LETTERS
AMIMA, MIMA, FIMA, CMath, CMathTeach, CSci

THE MATHEMATICAL ASSOCIATION

259 London Road
Leicester LE2 3BE
Tel: 01162 210013
Fax: 01162 122835
E-mail: office@m-a.org.uk
Website: www.m-a.org.uk

The MA dates from 1871 and supports and improves the teaching and learning of mathematics and its applications, and provides opportunities for communication and collaboration between teachers and students of mathematics. We publish a number of books, journals and magazines, hold an annual conference and regional meetings, and organize CPD events for our members. We also confer with government re the curriculum and assessment.

MEMBERSHIP
Student Member
Personal Member
Institutional Member

MEDICAL HERBALISM
Membership of Professional Institutions and Associations

THE NATIONAL INSTITUTE OF MEDICAL HERBALISTS

Elm House
54 Mary Arches Street
Exeter
Devon EX4 3BA
Tel: 01392 426022
Fax: 01392 498963
E-mail: info@nimh.org.uk
Website: www.nimh.org.uk

The NIMH is the UK's leading professional organization of herbal practitioners. We maintain high standards of practice and patient care, and work to promote the benefits of herbal medicine. We also provide codes of conduct, ethics and practice, and represent the profession, patients and the public through participation in external processes.

MEMBERSHIP
Member (MNIMH) Membership is open to graduates holding a BSc(Hons) degree in Herbal Medicine from: Edinburgh Napier University, Middlesex University, Scottish School of Herbal Medicine, University of East London, University of Lincoln or University of Westminster. There is also a student affiliate membership scheme for those who are undergraduates of any of the above schools.
Fellow (FNIMH)

DESIGNATORY LETTERS
MNIMH, FNIMH

MEDICAL SECRETARIES
Membership of Professional Institutions and Associations

ASSOCIATION OF MEDICAL SECRETARIES, PRACTICE MANAGERS, ADMINISTRATORS AND RECEPTIONISTS

Tavistock House North
Tavistock Square
London WC1H 9LN
Tel: 020 7387 6005
Fax: 020 7388 2648
E-mail: info@amspar.co.uk
Website: www.amspar.com

AMSPAR is a registered, nationally recognized awarding body and membership organization. We work with City & Guilds to provide non-clinical qualifications within the National Qualifications Framework. We aim to promote quality and coherence in the delivery of qualifications, and encourage and support standards of excellence in the pursuit of continuous professional development and lifelong learning.

MEMBERSHIP
Associate Member (AAMS)
Member (MAMS)
Fellow (FAMS)

QUALIFICATION/EXAMINATIONS
Certificate in Health Service Administration
Advanced Certificate in Continuing Professional Development
Award in Medical Terminology Certificate in Continuing Professional Development (Level 2)
Certificate in Medical Administration (Level 2)
Diploma in Medical Administration (Level 2)
Certificate in Medical Administration (Level 3)
Certificate in Medical Terminology (Level 3)
Diploma for Medical Secretaries (Level 3)
Certificate/Diploma in Primary Care Management (Level 5)

DESIGNATORY LETTERS
AAMS, MAMS, FAMS

MEDICINE

A student who wishes to qualify as a doctor in the UK must first obtain a primary qualification. He/she is then entitled to apply for provisional registration by the General Medical Council and, after satisfactorily completing training for provisionally registered doctors he or she is eligible for consideration for full registration. The **General Medical Council**, 350 Euston Road, London, NW1 3JN, Tel: 0161 923 6602, e-mail: gmc@gmc-uk.org, website; www.gmc-uk.org is charged with the responsibility under the Medical Act 1983 of keeping a Register of all duly qualified medical practitioners.

Primary qualifications
A qualifying examination for the purposes of Part II of the Medical Act is an examination held for the purpose of granting one or more primary qualifications by any one of the bodies or combinations of bodies in the United Kingdom which are included in a list maintained by the GMC and published on the GMC's website. Subject to the provisions of the Act any persons whose fitness to practice is not impaired and who –

(a) hold one or more primary United Kingdom qualifications and has satisfactorily completed as acceptable programme for provisionally registered doctors; or

(b) being a national of any relevant European State, holds one or more primary European qualifications,

is entitled to be registered as a fully registered medical practitioner.

Membership of Professional Institutions and Associations

BRITISH MEDICAL ASSOCIATION (BMA)

BMA House
Tavistock Square
London WC1H 9JP
Tel: 020 7387 4499
Fax: 020 7383 6400
E-mail: info.web@bma.org.uk
Website: www.bma.org.uk

The BMA is the independent trade union and professional association for doctors and medical students, with over 140,000 members worldwide.

COLLEGE OF OPERATING DEPARTMENT PRACTITIONERS

197–199 City Road
London EC1V 1JN
Tel: 0870 746 0984
Fax: 0870 746 0985
E-mail: office@aodp.org
Website: www.aodp.org

The CODP is the professional body for Operating Department Practitioners. It is a membership, not-for-profit organization that sets standards of education for the pre-registration aspect of the profession and promotes the enhancement of knowledge and skills, in the context of the multidisciplinary team, through regional, national and international networks.

MEMBERSHIP
Student Member
Association Member
Full College Member

HEALTH PROFESSIONS COUNCIL

Park House
184 Kennington Park Road
London SE11 4BU
Tel: 020 7582 0866
Fax: 020 7820 9684
E-mail: registrations@hpc-uk.org
Website: www.hpc-uk.org

The HPC is a health regulator that was set up to protect the public. We currently maintain a register of health professionals who meet our standards for their training, skills, behaviour and health in 14 health professions. It is a criminal offence for anyone not registered with us to use a professional title or to claim that they are registered with us.

ROYAL COLLEGE OF OBSTETRICIANS AND GYNAECOLOGISTS

27 Sussex Place
London NW1 4RG
Tel: 020 7772 6200
Fax: 020 7723 0575
E-mail: services@rcog.org.uk
Website: www.rcog.org.uk

The RCOG encourages the study and advancement of the science and practice of obstetrics and gynaecology. We do this through postgraduate medical education and training development, and the publication of clinical guidelines and reports on aspects of the specialty and service provision. The RCOG International Office works with other international organizations to help lower maternal morbidity and mortality in under-resourced countries.

MEMBERSHIP
Junior Affiliate
Affiliate
Associate
Diplomate
Trainee – pre-membership
Member without Examination (MRCOG)
Member (MRCOG)
Fellow (FRCOG)
Fellow *honoris causa*
Fellow *ad eumdem* (FRCOG)
Honorary Fellow (FRCOG)

QUALIFICATION/EXAMINATIONS
Membership Examination

DESIGNATORY LETTERS
MRCOG, FRCOG

ROYAL SOCIETY OF MEDICINE

1 Wimpole Street
London W1G 0AE
Tel: 020 7290 2900
Fax: 020 7290 2989
E-mail: membership@rsm.ac.uk
Website: www.rsm.ac.uk

The RSM, founded in 1805, is a medical charity that promotes the exchange of information and ideas in medical science. We provide a broad range of educational activities and opportunities for doctors, dentists, veterinary surgeons, students of these disciplines and allied healthcare professionals, organize conferences, and publish books and journals through our publishing division, RSM Press.

MEMBERSHIP
Student
Associate
Fellow

THE FEDERATION OF THE ROYAL COLLEGES OF PHYSICIANS OF THE UNITED KINGDOM

MRCP(UK) Central Office
11 St Andrews Place
Regent's Park
London NW1 4LE
Tel: +44 (0)20 7935 1174
Fax: +44 (0)20 7935 4143
E-mail: part1@mrcpuk.org
Website: www.mrcpuk.org

The three Royal Colleges of Physicians of the United Kingdom share a common membership examination in general medicine: this is the examination for the Diploma of Membership of the Royal Colleges of Physicians of the United Kingdom (MRCP(UK)). Successful candidates will also take a compulsory Speciality Certificate Examination as part of their assessment for Certificate of Completion of Training (CCT).

MEMBERSHIP
Member of the Royal Colleges of Physicians (MRCP(UK))

QUALIFICATION/EXAMINATIONS
MRCP(UK) Diploma (Membership of the Royal Colleges of Physicians of the United Kingdom)
Speciality Certificate Examination (in Acute Medicine; Dermatology; Endocrinology and Diabetes; Gastroenterology, Geriatric Medicine; Infectious Diseases; Medical Oncology; Nephrology; Neurology; Respiratory Medicine; or Rheumatology)

DESIGNATORY LETTERS
MRCP(UK)

THE INSTITUTE OF CLINICAL RESEARCH

Institute House
Boston Drive
Bourne End
Buckinghamshire SL8 5YS
Tel: 0845 521 0056/01628
Fax: 01628 530641
E-mail: info@icr-global.org
Website: www.icr-global.org

The ICR was founded in 1978 and is now the largest professional clinical research body in Europe and India. Our aim is to promote knowledge and understanding by engaging with the healthcare community and the general public, to support and facilitate communication between our members, and to provide opportunities for learning and development to enhance professional competence.

MEMBERSHIP
Affiliate

Registered Member (RICR)
Professional Member (MICR)
Fellow (FICR)
Honorary Fellow (Hon FICR)

QUALIFICATION/EXAMINATIONS
Please see the ICR's website.

DESIGNATORY LETTERS
RICR, MICR, FICR, HonFICR

THE ROYAL COLLEGE OF ANAESTHETISTS

Churchill House
35 Red Lion Square
London WC1R 4SG
Tel: 020 7092 1500
Fax: 020 7092 1730
E-mail: info@rcoa.ac.uk
Website: www.rcoa.ac.uk

The RCA, which dates from 1948, is the professional body responsible for the specialty of anaesthesia throughout the UK. Our principal responsibility is to ensure the quality of patient care through the maintenance of standards in anaesthesia, pain management and intensive care. We set and run examinations, and provide CPD for all practising anaesthetists.

MEMBERSHIP
Trainee
Affiliate

Associate Member
Member (MRCA)
Associate Fellow
Fellow *ad eundem* (FRCA)
Fellow (FRCA)
Honorary Fellow (FRCA)

QUALIFICATION/EXAMINATIONS
FRCA Examinations

DESIGNATORY LETTERS
MRCA, FRCA

THE ROYAL COLLEGE OF GENERAL PRACTITIONERS

14 Princes Gate
Hyde Park
London SW7 1PU
Tel: 020 7581 3232
Fax: 020 7225 3047
E-mail: info@rcgp.org.uk
Website: www.rcgp.org.uk

The aims of the College are to encourage, foster and maintain the highest possible standards in general medical practice. Full entry to the College is by exam undertaken whilst in training for General Practice, or assessment as a qualified GP.

MEMBERSHIP
Associate in Training
Associate
Member (MRCGP)
Fellow (FRCGP)

Undergraduate medical students and Foundation programme students may register with the College's Student Forum, which exposes the students to life in general practice.

QUALIFICATION/EXAMINATIONS
Assessment for Membership of the RCGP (nMRGGP)

DESIGNATORY LETTERS
MRCGP, FRCGP

THE ROYAL COLLEGE OF PATHOLOGISTS

2 Carlton House Terrace
London SW1Y 5AF
Tel: 020 7451 6700
Fax: 020 7451 6701
E-mail: info@rcpath.org
Website: www.rcpath.org

The College aims to advance the science and practice of pathology, to provide public education, to promote research in pathology and to disseminate the results.

MEMBERSHIP
Affiliate Member
Associate
Diplomate Member (DipRCPath)
Fellow (FRCPath)

QUALIFICATION/EXAMINATIONS
Training programmes are approved for all pathology specialities and sub-specialities. The exact examination arrangements vary for each speciality but they will all involve a Part 1 and a Part 2 which include, inter alia, written, practical and oral components. In addition the College offers a Diploma in Cytopathology, a Diploma in Dermatopathology and a Diploma in Forensic Pathology. Further details may be obtained from the Examinations Department or the College's website.

DESIGNATORY LETTERS
DipRCPath, FRCPath

THE ROYAL COLLEGE OF PHYSICIANS AND SURGEONS OF GLASGOW

232–242 St Vincent Street
Glasgow G2 5RJ
Tel: 01412 216072
Fax: 01412 211804
Website: www.rcpsg.ac.uk

Granted a Charter from James V1 in 1599 and the honorific 'Royal' in 1910, the College welcomes professionals from a diverse range of disciplines. Our collegiate body includes physicians, surgeons, and professionals in dentistry and travel medicine, as well as professions allied to medicine.

MEMBERSHIP
Associate Member
Member (MRCPS(Glasg))
Fellow (FRCP(Glasg)/FRCP(Glas)/FDS RCPS(Glasg))

QUALIFICATION/EXAMINATIONS
Diploma in Child Health (DCH) Diploma in Dermatology (Dip Derm)
Diploma in Geriatric Medicine (DGM)
Diploma in Travel Medicine (DTM)
Diploma of Membership of the Royal College of Physicians of the United Kingdom (MRCP(UK)) (see RCP(UK) website)
Diploma of Membership of the Royal College of Surgeons (MRCS (Intercollegiate))
Diploma of Fellowship of the Royal College of Physicians and Surgeons of Glasgow in Opthalmology (FRCS (Opthalmology))
MSc in Clinical Leadership (offered jointly with the University of Glasgow Business School (UGBS))

DESIGNATORY LETTERS
MRCPS(Glasg), FRCP(Glasg)/FRCS(Glasg)/FDS FRCPS(Glasg)

THE ROYAL COLLEGE OF PHYSICIANS OF EDINBURGH

9 Queen Street
Edinburgh EH2 1JQ
Tel: 01312 257324
Fax: 01312 266124
E-mail: l.tedford@rcpe.ac.uk
Website: www.rcpe.ac.uk

The RCPE promotes the highest standards in internal medicine internationally. Along with our sister Colleges in Glasgow and London we oversee the Member of the Royal College of Physicians (MRCP(UK)) examination enabling doctors to enter higher specialist training, leading eventually to a Certificate of Completion of Specialist Training (CCST).

MEMBERSHIP
e-Associate

Associate
Collegiate Member (MRCPE)
Fellow (FRCPE)

QUALIFICATION/EXAMINATIONS
MRCP(UK)
Specialty Certificate Examinations

DESIGNATORY LETTERS
MRCPE, FRCPE

THE ROYAL COLLEGE OF PHYSICIANS OF LONDON

11 St Andrews Place
Regent's Park
London NW1 4LE
Tel: 020 7224 1539
Fax: 020 7487 5218
E-mail: infocentre@rcplondon.ac.uk
Website: www.rcplondon.ac.uk

The RCP is a professional body representing more than 20,000 physicians that aims to improve the quality of patient care by continually raising medical standards. We set standards in clinical practice and education & training, conduct assessments and examinations, quality assure external audit programmes, support doctors in their practice of medicine, and advise the government, the public and the profession on healthcare issues.

MEMBERSHIP
Associate member
Collegiate member (MRCP(UK))
Affiliate member
Fellow (FRCP)

QUALIFICATION/EXAMINATIONS
MRCP(UK) Examination
Speciality Certificate Examinations in: Acute Medicine; Dermatology; Endocrinology and Diabetes; Gastroenterology; Geriatric Medicine; Infectious Diseases; Medical Oncology; Nephrology; Neurology; Respiratory Medicine; Rheumatology
Diploma in Geriatric Medicine (DGM)
Diploma in Tropical Medicine and Hygiene (DTM&H)
PGCert/PGDip/MSc in Medical Education
PGCert/PGDip/MSc in Medical Leadership

DESIGNATORY LETTERS
MRCP(UK), FRCP

THE ROYAL COLLEGE OF PSYCHIATRISTS

17 Belgrave Square
London SW1X 8PG
Tel: 020 7235 2351
Fax: 020 7245 1231
E-mail: latkinson@rcpsych.ac.uk
Website: www.rcpsych.ac.uk

The RCPsych is the professional and educational body for psychiatrists in the UK and Ireland. We are committed to improving the understanding of psychiatry and mental health, and are at the forefront in setting and achieving the highest standards through education, training and research. We actively promote psychiatry as a career, and provide guidance and support to our members and associates.

MEMBERSHIP
Pre-Membership Psychiatric Trainee
New Associate
Corresponding Associate
Affiliate
Specialist Associate
Member (MRCPsych)
Fellow (FRCPsych)
Honorary Fellow
International Associate

QUALIFICATION/EXAMINATIONS
MRCPsych qualifying exams
FRCPsych qualifying exams

DESIGNATORY LETTERS
MRCPsych, FRCPsych

THE ROYAL COLLEGE OF RADIOLOGISTS

38 Portland Place
London W1B 1JQ
Tel: 020 7636 4432
Fax: 020 7323 3100
E-mail: enquiries@rcr.ac.uk
Website: www.rcr.ac.uk

The RCR is a professional body representing nearly 8,000 medical and dental practitioners worldwide that aims to advance the science and practice of clinical radiology and clinical oncology. We promote the highest standards of professional competence, undertake regular audits of training and practice, conduct examinations for Certificates and Diplomas, encourage CPD among our members, and provide information for the public.

MEMBERSHIP
Junior Member
Associate
Member
Fellow (FRCR)
Honorary Member/Fellow (Hon MRCR/Hon FRCR)

QUALIFICATION/EXAMINATIONS
Certificate of Completion of Training (in Clinical Radiology or Clinical Oncology)
First FRCR Examination
Final FRCR Examination
Diploma in Dental Radiology (DDR)

DESIGNATORY LETTERS
FRCR, Hon MRCR, Hon FRCR

THE ROYAL COLLEGE OF SURGEONS OF EDINBURGH

Nicolson Street
Edinburgh EH8 9DW
Tel: 0131 527 1600
Fax: 0131 557 6406
E-mail: information@rcsed.ac.uk
Website: www.rcsed.ac.uk

The Royal College of Surgeons of Edinburgh, which dates from 1505, is dedicated to the maintenance and promotion of the highest standards of surgical practice, through education, training and rigorous examination, and its liaison with external medical bodies. Today, with more than 17,000 Fellows and Members, we pride ourselves also on our innovation and adaptability.

MEMBERSHIP
Affiliate
Surgical Associate Member
Member (MRCSEd)
Fellow (FRCSEd)

QUALIFICATION/EXAMINATIONS
Please see the Royal College of Surgeons of Edinburgh website.

DESIGNATORY LETTERS
MRCSEd, FRCSEd

THE ROYAL COLLEGE OF SURGEONS OF ENGLAND

35–43 Lincoln's Inn Fields
London WC2A 3PE
Tel: 020 7405 3474
Fax: 020 7831 9438
E-mail: exams@rcseng.ac.uk
Website: www.rcseng.ac.uk

The Royal College of Surgeons of England is committed to enabling surgeons to achieve and maintain the highest standards of surgical practice and patient care. We examine trainees, supervise the training of and provide support and advice for surgeons, promote and support surgical research in the UK, and liaise with the DoH, health authorities, Trusts and hospitals in the UK and other medical and academic organizations worldwide.

MEMBERSHIP
Intercollegiate Member

QUALIFICATION/EXAMINATIONS
Please see the Royal College of Surgeons of England website.

THE SOCIETY OF APOTHECARIES OF LONDON

Black Friars Lane
London EC4V 6EJ
Tel: 020 7236 1180
Fax: 020 7329 3177
E-mail: registrar@apothecaries.org
Website: www.apothecaries.org

The Society of Apothecaries of London was incorporated by Royal Charter in 1617 and allowed to prepare and sell drugs for medicinal purposes, laying the foundations of the British pharmaceutical industry. Later, apothecaries were permitted to prescribe and dispense medicines, becoming the forerunners of today's GPs. Now the Society is primarily an examining body.

QUALIFICATION/EXAMINATIONS
PGDip in the Forensic and Clinical Aspects of Sexual Assault (DFCASA)

PGDip in Forensic Human Identification (DipFHID)
PGDip in Forensic Medical Sciences (DFMS)
PGDip in Genitourinary Medicine (DGUM)
PGDip in the History of Medicine (DHMSA)
PGDip in HIV Medicine
PGDip in the Medical Care of Catastrophes (DMCC)
PGDip in Medical Jurisprudence (DMJ)
PGDip in the Philosophy of Medicine (DPMSA)

METALLURGY
Membership of Professional Institutions and Associations

INSTITUTE OF CORROSION

7B High Street Mews
High Street
Vimy Road
Leighton Buzzard
Bedfordshire LU7 1EA
Tel: 01525 851771
Fax: 01525 376690
E-mail: admin@icorr.org
Website: www.icorr.org

The Institute of Corrosion has since 1959 been serving the corrosion science, technology and engineering community in the fight against corrosion, which costs the UK around 4 per cent of GNP per annum. We promote the establishment and promotion of sound corrosion management practice, the advancement of cost-effective corrosion control measures, and a sustained effort to raise corrosion awareness at all stages of design, fabrication and operation.

MEMBERSHIP
Student Member
Ordinary Member

Technical Member (TICorr)
Professional Member (MICorr)
Engineering Technician (EngTech)
Incorporated Engineer (IEng)
Chartered Engineer (CEng)
Chartered Scientist (CSci)

QUALIFICATION/EXAMINATIONS
Please see the Institute of Corrosion website.

DESIGNATORY LETTERS
TICorr, MICorr, EngTech, IEng, CEng

THE INSTITUTE OF METAL FINISHING

Exeter House
48 Holloway Head
Birmingham B1 1NQ
Tel: 01216 227387
Fax: 01216 666316
E-mail: exeterhouse@instituteofmetalfinishing.org
Website: www.uk-finishing.org.uk

The IMF, founded in 1925, provides a focus for surface engineering and finishing activities worldwide through the fulfilment of technical, educational and professional needs at all levels for individuals and companies involved in the coatings industry. We promote R&D within the industry and CPD for our members, cooperate with other institutes, and liaise with legislative bodies to influence decision-making.

MEMBERSHIP
Student
Affiliate
Associate (AssocIMF)
Technician (TechIMF)

Licentiate (LIMF)
Member (MIMF)
Fellow (FIMF)
Engineering Technician (EngTech)
Sustaining Member (company)

QUALIFICATION/EXAMINATIONS
Foundation Certificate
Technician Certificate
Advanced Technician Certificate

DESIGNATORY LETTERS
AssocIMF, TechIMF, LIMF, MIMF, FIMF, EngTech

METEOROLOGY AND CLIMATOLOGY
Membership of Professional Institutions and Associations

MET OFFICE COLLEGE

Met Office
Fitzroy Road
Exeter
Devon EX1 3PB
Tel: 01392 885680
Fax: 01392 885681
E-mail: met-training@metoffice.gov.uk
Website: www.metoffice.gov.uk

The Meteorological Office College is part of the Met Office and is located in Exeter, Devon. We provide meteorological training for our own staff and to meteorological services worldwide, as places become available on a fee-paying basis.

QUALIFICATION/EXAMINATIONS
NVQ in Meteorological Observing (Level 3)
NVQ in Meteorological Weather Forecasting (Level 4)
Forecaster Foundation Training Programme
Professional Development Programme
Specialist Forecaster Programme

ROYAL METEOROLOGICAL SOCIETY

104 Oxford Road
Reading RG1 7LL
Tel: 0118 956 8500
Fax: 0118 956 8571
E-mail: info@rmets.org
Website: www.rmets.org

The RMetS is the learned and professional society for anyone whose profession or interests are connected with weather and climate. It administers the NVQs of the profession and is the accreditation body for the status of Chartered Meteorologist. Its principal aim is the advancement of the understanding of weather and climate for the benefit of everyone.

Associate Fellow
Fellow (FRMetS)
Honorary Member
Chartered Meteorologist (CMet)
Chartered Environmentalist (CEnv)
School Member
Corporate Member

MEMBERSHIP
Student

DESIGNATORY LETTERS
FRMetS, CMet, CEnv

MICROSCOPY
Membership of Professional Institutions and Associations

THE ROYAL MICROSCOPICAL SOCIETY

Oxford OX4 1AJ
Tel: 01865 254760
Fax: 01865 791237
E-mail: info@rms.org.uk
Website: www.rms.org.uk

The RMS, which dates from 1839, is an international scientific society dedicated to advancing the science of microscopy and the interests of its 1,400 members, who range from individuals interested in microscopy to scientists and company members representing manufacturers and suppliers of microscopes, other equipment and services.

MEMBERSHIP
Ordinary Member
Fellow (FRMS)
Corporate Member

DESIGNATORY LETTERS
FRMS

MUSEUM AND RELATED WORK
Membership of Professional Institutions and Associations

MUSEUMS ASSOCIATION

24 Calvin Street
London E1 6NW
Tel: 020 7426 6955
Fax: 020 7426 6962
E-mail: cpd@museumsassociation.org
Website: www.museumsassociation.org

The MA is the oldest museums association in the world, set up in 1889 to guard the interests of museums and galleries. Today, we have 5,200 individual members, 600 institutional members and 250 corporate members. Our aim is to enhance the value of museums to society by sharing knowledge, developing skills, inspiring innovation and providing leadership.

MEMBERSHIP
Student
Volunteer
Professional member
Associate (AMA)
Commercial member
Institutional member

DESIGNATORY LETTERS
AMA

MUSIC

Musical Education and Training

Most children and young people before the age of entry to further and higher education to study music-related courses take graded written and practical exams in musicianship, singing and instruments. Graded exams for individual instruments, singing and theory are accredited by the regulatory authorities in England, Wales and Northern Ireland and are part of the National Qualifications Framework (NQF). The Universities and Colleges Admissions Service (UCAS) includes Grades VI–VIII in the tariff for UK university and college entrance. Grades VII and VIII are sometimes used to indicate the minimum standard required of entrants by colleges training professional musicians. Graded exams for those learning various instruments are conducted by the ABRS, Trinity College of Music, Guildhall LCMM and Rockschool. Further music courses may be taken at Birmingham School of Music, The Royal Academy of Music, The Royal College of Music, The Royal Northern College of Music and The Royal Scottish Academy of Music and Drama. The Royal Welsh College of Music and Drama and The Royal College of Organists also award diplomas.

PERFORMERS

Music colleges, such as Brighton Institute of Modern Music offer courses for intending performers. Here the emphasis is on practical work, rehearsal and performance. They also provide courses which, while still demanding a high standard in practical work, give more time for an all-round training in general musicianship.

TEACHERS

Awards made by the various colleges of music are not accepted by the DCSF as offering Qualified Teacher Status (QTS). Graduates and other students must also take a course of initial teacher training leading to QTS in order to teach in maintained schools and non-maintained special schools in England. Some peripatetic music teachers without QTS are generally paid on the unqualified teacher scale.

In Scotland the BE (Music) awarded by the Royal Scottish Academy of Music and Drama carries QTS and allows graduates immediate entry to the teaching profession; graduates of other degree courses (eg BMus) must take a one-year course of professional training.

Membership of Professional Institutions and Associations

ASSOCIATED BOARD OF THE ROYAL SCHOOLS OF MUSIC

24 Portland Place
London W1B 1LU
Tel: 020 7636 5400

Fax: 020 7637 0234
E-mail: abrsm@abrsm.org
Website: www.abrsm.org

ABRSM is the world's leading authority on musical assessment, actively supporting and encouraging music learning for all. We offer a rich and immersive programme of courses and seminars to instrumental and vocal teachers throughout the world, and provide a flexible range of exams and assessments that inspire and motivate music learners worldwide.
MEMBERSHIP
Licentiate (LRSM)
Fellow (FRSM)

QUALIFICATION/EXAMINATIONS
Diploma in Instrumental/Vocal Teaching (DipABRSM)
Diploma in Music Direction (DipABRSM)
Diploma in Music Performance (DipABRSM)

Please see the ABRSM website for details of other examinations and awards.
DESIGNATORY LETTERS
DipARSM, LRSM, FRSM

INCORPORATED SOCIETY OF MUSICIANS

10 Stratford Place
London WIC 1AA
Tel: 020 7629 4413
Fax: 020 7408 1538
E-mail: membership@ism.org
Website: www.ism.org

The ISM, a non-profit-making organization founded in 1882, is the UK's professional body for musicians. We promote the art of music and the interests of musicians through campaigns, support and practical advice. Members also receive our monthly in-house magazine, *Music Journal*, which includes news and information on CPD.

MEMBERSHIP
Student Member
Associate Member
Full Member
Corporate Member

ROYAL COLLEGE OF MUSIC

Prince Consort Road
South Kensington
London SW7 2BS
Tel: 020 7589 3643
Fax: 020 7589 7740
E-mail: info@rcm.ac.uk
Website: www.rcm.ac.uk

The RCM, founded in 1882, is one of the world's leading conservatoires. We train gifted musicians from all over the world for an international career as a performer, conductor or composer. Our professors are musicians with a worldwide reputation, accustomed to working with the most talented students of each generation to unlock their artistic potential.

Many of our graduates are at the forefront of the international music scene.

QUALIFICATION/EXAMINATIONS
DipRCM(Performer)
BMus
BSc in Physics with Studies in Musical Performance (jointly with Imperial College London)
PGDip in Performance/Advanced Performance
MMus in Advanced Performance

GradDip in Vocal Studies
PGDip/MMus in Advanced Vocal Performance
Artist Diploma in Opera
PGDip/MMus in Composition and Composition for Screen
Artist Diploma in Performance (instrumentalists and singers)
PGDip in Creative Leadership
DMus

ROYAL NORTHERN COLLEGE OF MUSIC

124 Oxford Road
Manchester M13 9RD
Tel: 0161 907 5200
Fax: 0161 273 7611
E-mail: info@rncm.ac.uk
Website: www.rncm.ac.uk

The RNCM was formed in 1973 by the merger of the Royal Manchester College of Music (founded in 1893) and the Northern School of Music (founded in 1920). We offer undergraduate and postgraduate courses, as well as holding concerts, recitals, operas and other events.

QUALIFICATION/EXAMINATIONS
Foundation Degree in Popular Music Practice
BMus
PGCert in Performing Arts Education
PGCE in Music with Specialist Instrumental Teaching (Wind, Brass, Percussion and Strings)
PGDip in Instrumental Teaching
PGDip in Performing Arts Leadership (delivered by ARTIS)
PGDip/MMus in Chamber Music

PGDip/MMus in Composition
PGDip/MMus in Orchestral Studies
PGDip/MMus in Solo Performance (including Conducting)
MPhil/PhD in Composition
MPhil/PhD in Music Psychology
MPhil/PhD in Musicology
MPhil/PhD in Performance
International Artist Diploma in Chamber Music
International Artist Diploma in Opera Studies
International Artist Diploma in Solo Performance
Hallé/RNCM String Leadership Diploma (UK nationals only)

MPhil and PhD degrees are validated by Manchester Metropolitan University.

THE ROYAL COLLEGE OF ORGANISTS

PO Box 56357
London SE16 7XL
Tel: 05600 767208
E-mail: admin@rco.org.uk
Website: www.rco.org.uk

The RCO is a charity and membership organization for the promotion and advancement of organ playing and choral directing, with 3,000 members in 40 countries around the world. We are also a professional examining body and through our Academy place education and outreach at the heart of our work to maintain the highest standards in musical performance and music teaching.

MEMBERSHIP
Student Member
Member
Associate (ARCO)
Fellow (FRCO)
Corporate Member

Associateship Diploma of the Royal College of Organists (ARCO)
Fellowship Diploma of the Royal College of Organists (FRCO)
Licentiateship in Teaching (LTRCO)
Diploma in Choral Directing (DipCHD)

QUALIFICATION/EXAMINATIONS
Certificate of the Royal College of Organists (CertRCO)

DESIGNATORY LETTERS
ARCO, FRCO

MUSICAL INSTRUMENT TECHNOLOGY
Membership of Professional Institutions and Associations

INCORPORATED SOCIETY OF ORGAN BUILDERS

Smithy Steads
Cragg Vale
Hebden Bridge
West Yorkshire HX7 5SQ
Fax: 0870 139 3645
E-mail: admin1@isob.co.uk
Website: www.isob.co.uk/

The ISOB was founded in 1947 to advance the science and practice of organ building, to provide a central organization for organ builders, and to provide for the better definition and protection of the profession by a system of examinations and the issue of certificates and distinctions. We hold regular meetings and conferences around the UK and overseas.

MEMBERSHIP
Student Member

Ordinary Member (MISOB)
Associate Member (AISOB)
Fellow (FISOB)
Councillor (CISOB)

DESIGNATORY LETTERS
MISOB, AISOB, FISOB, CISOB

PIANOFORTE TUNERS' ASSOCIATION

PO Box 1312
Lightwater
Woking
Surrey GU18 5UB
Tel: 0845 602 8796
E-mail: secretary@pianotuner.org.uk
Website: www.pianotuner.org.uk

The PTA is a professional body committed to improving standards, and applicants for membership must pass a theoretical and practical examination to prove their ability as a qualified piano tuner or technician. We publish a regular newsletter and hold an Annual Convention and General Meeting in different towns around Britain, to which members and aspiring non-members are invited.

MEMBERSHIP
Student
Patron
Associate
Technician Member
Member

NAVAL ARCHITECTURE
Membership of Professional Institutions and Associations

THE ROYAL INSTITUTION OF NAVAL ARCHITECTS

10 Upper Belgrave Street
London SW1X 8BQ
Tel: 020 7235 4622
Fax: 020 7259 5912
E-mail: membership@rina.org.uk
Website: www.rina.org.uk

The RINA is an internationally renowned professional institution whose members are involved at all levels in the design, construction, maintenance and operation of marine vessels and structures. Our members are widely represented in industry, universities and colleges, and maritime organizations in over 90 countries.

MEMBERSHIP
Student Member
Associate (AssocRINA)
Associate Member (AMRINA)
Member (MRINA)
Fellow (FRINA)

DESIGNATORY LETTERS
AssocRINA, AMRINA, MRINA. FRINA

NAVIGATION, SEAMANSHIP AND MARINE QUALIFICATIONS
Membership of Professional Institutions and Associations

THE NAUTICAL INSTITUTE

202 Lambeth Road
London SE1 7LQ
Tel: 020 7928 1351
Fax: 020 7401 2817
E-mail: sec@nautinst.org
Website: www.nautinst.org

The NI is an international professional body for qualified seafarers and others with an interest in nautical matters, with 40 branches worldwide and more than 6,500 members in over 100 countries. Our aims are to improve the standards of competence and knowledge of persons in control of seagoing craft, to cooperate with government departments and other bodies concerned with statutory and other qualifications, and to encourage the exchange and publication of information and research on nautical science.

MEMBERSHIP
Student Member

Companion (CNI)
Associate Member (ASNI)
Member (MNI)
Fellow
Honorary Fellow

QUALIFICATION/EXAMINATIONS
Harbour Master's Certificate
Pilotage Certificate
Command Diploma

DESIGNATORY LETTERS
CNI, ASNI, MNI

THE ROYAL INSTITUTE OF NAVIGATION

1 Kensington Gore
London SW7 2AT
Tel: 020 7591 3130
Fax: 020 7591 3131
E-mail: info@rin.org.uk
Website: www.rin.org.uk

The RIN is a learned society with charitable status. Our aims are: to unite those with a professional or personal interest in any aspect of navigation in one unique body; to further the development of navigation in every sphere; and to increase public awareness of both the art and science of navigation, how it has shaped the past, how it impacts our world today, and how it will affect the future.

MEMBERSHIP
Junior Associate Member
Student
Associate
Member (MRIN)
Associate Fellow (AFRIN)
Fellow (FRIN)
Affiliate Club
Affiliate College or University
Corporate Member

DESIGNATORY LETTERS
MRIN, AFRIN, FRIN

NON-DESTRUCTIVE TESTING
Membership of Professional Institutions and Associations

THE BRITISH INSTITUTE OF NON-DESTRUCTIVE TESTING

1 Spencer Parade
Northampton NN1 5AA
Tel: 01604 630124
Fax: 01604 231489
E-mail: info@bindt.org
Website: www.bindt.org

The BINDT was formed in 1976 from the merger of the Society of Non-Destructive Examination (SONDE) and the Society of Industrial Radiology and Allied Methods of Non-Destructive Testing, later renamed the NDT Society of Great Britain (NDTS), both formed in 1954. Our aim is to promote and advance the science and practice of non-destructive testing, condition monitoring, diagnostic engineering and all other materials and quality testing disciplines.

MEMBERSHIP
Student Member
Affiliate

Practitioner Member (PInstNDT)
Graduate Member (GInstNDT)
Member (MInstNDT)
Fellow (FInstNDT)
Engineering Technician (EngTech)
Incorporated Engineer (IEng)
Chartered Engineer (CEng)
Associate Member (corporate)

DESIGNATORY LETTERS
PInstNDT, GInstNDT, MInstNDT, FInstNDT, EngTech, IEng, CEng

NURSERY NURSING

Membership of Professional Institutions and Associations

COUNCIL FOR AWARDS IN CHILDREN'S CARE AND EDUCATION

Apex House
81 Camp Road
St Albans
Hertfordshire AL1 5GB
Tel: 0845 347 2123
Fax: 01727 818618
E-mail: info@cache.org.uk
Website: www.cache.org.uk

CACHE is an Awarding Body that designs courses and qualifications in the care and education of children and young people. Our courses, which are widely available, range from entry level to advanced qualifications for sector professionals. We regularly lobby the government and other agencies to raise the quality and professionalism of child care.

QUALIFICATION/EXAMINATIONS
Please see the CACHE website.

NURSING AND MIDWIFERY

Membership of Professional Institutions and Associations

THE NURSING & MIDWIFERY COUNCIL

23 Portland Place
London W1B 1PZ
Tel: 020 7333 9333
E-mail: advice@nmc-uk.org
Website: www.nmc-uk.org

The core function of the NMC is to establish standards of education, training, conduct and performance for nursing and midwifery, and to ensure that those standards are maintained, thereby safeguarding the health and well-being of the public. We work closely with partner organizations to provide quality assurance of nursing and midwifery education in the UK.

OCCUPATIONAL THERAPY
Membership of Professional Institutions and Associations

BRITISH ASSOCIATION OF OCCUPATIONAL THERAPISTS

106--114 Borough High Street
Southwark
London SE1 1LB
Tel: 020 7357 6480
Fax: 020 7450 2299
E-mail: membership@cot.co.uk
Website: www.cot.org.uk

The British Association and College of Occupational Therapists is the professional body for occupational therapy in the UK. The College has 28,000 members and represents the profession nationally and internationally.

MEMBERSHIP
Student Member
Associate
Discounted Associate
Professional Member
Discounted Professional Member
Self-employed Member
Retired Member
Overseas Member

QUALIFICATION/EXAMINATIONS
Diploma (DipCOT)

OPTICIANS (DISPENSING)

Dispensing opticians need to be registered with the General Optical Council (GOC; 41 Harley Street, London W1G 8DJ E-mail: goc@optical.org Website: www.optical.org). Qualification takes three years in total, and can be completed by combining a distance learning course or day release while working as a trainee under the supervision of a qualified and GOC-registered optician. Alternatively students can do a two-year FT course followed by one year of supervised practise with a qualified and registered optician. In the UK you can study at six GOC-approved training establishments: Association of British Dispensing Opticians (ABDO), Anglia Ruskin University, Bradford College, City and Islington College, City University and Glasgow Caledonian University. All routes are assessed by final ABDO examinations. On successful completion of training you must register with the GOC in order to practise in the UK. If you qualify as a dispensing optician and have completed training to fit contact lenses, the University of Bradford offers a career progression course that enables you to graduate with a degree in optometry in one calendar year.

ENTRY REQUIREMENTS
You will normally need to have 5 GCSEs (or equivalent) at grades C or above, including English, maths and science. For mature students and overseas/alternative/vocational courses, admission requirements will vary and may be more flexible. For further details contact the admissions tutor at the university you wish to apply to.

Membership of Professional Institutions and Associations

ASSOCIATION OF BRITISH DISPENSING OPTICIANS

199 Gloucester Terrace
London W2 6LD
Tel: 020 7298 5100
Fax: 020 7298 5111
E-mail: general@abdolondon.org.uk
Website: www.abdo.org.uk

The ABDO is the qualifying body for dispensing opticians in the UK. Our aims are to advance the science and art of dispensing optics, to further the education and training of dispensing opticians, and to support and promote the interests of the profession.

MEMBERSHIP
Student Member
Associate Member
Full Member
Fellow (FBDO)

QUALIFICATION/EXAMINATIONS
Certificate in Contact Lens Practice (Level 6)
Diploma in The Assessment & Management of Low Vision (Level 6)
Diploma in Ophthalmic Dispensing (Level 6)
Diploma in Advanced Contact Lens Practice (Level 7)
Diploma in Spectacle Lens Design (Level 7)

DESIGNATORY LETTERS
FBDO

ASSOCIATION OF CONTACT LENS MANUFACTURERS

PO Box 735
Devizes
Wiltshire SN10 3TQ
Tel: 01380 860418
Fax: 01380 860863
E-mail: secgen@aclm.org.uk
Website: www.aclm.org.uk

The ACLM was founded in 1962 to publicize the work of UK contact lens manufacturers, to develop new products and to raise standards. Today we represent the manufacturers of over 95 per cent of prescription contact lenses and lens care products in the UK, and provide a cohesive voice for our members.

MEMBERSHIP
Member

BRITISH CONTACT LENS ASSOCIATION

Walmar House
288/292 Regent Street
London W1B 3AL
Tel: 020 7580 6661
Fax: 020 7580 6669
Website: www.bcla.org.uk

The BCLA is the UK's leading supplier of information and education on contact lenses and the anterior eye, with a membership of around 1,800 in more than 40 countries. Our mission is to promote excellence in the research, manufacture and clinical practice of contact lenses and related areas. Our annual Clinical Conference and Exhibition, the world's largest, attracts more than 1,000 visitors.

MEMBERSHIP
Student Member
Member
Fellow (FBCLA)

QUALIFICATION/EXAMINATIONS
Educational activities include approved Continuing Education and Training courses and evening meetings. For details see the website.

DESIGNATORY LETTERS
FBCLA

OPTOMETRY

Careers in optometry are overseen by the General Optical Council (41 Harley Street, London W1G 8DJ E-mail: goc@optical.org Website: www.optical.org). You can study for an undergraduate optometry degree from one of eight GOC-approved institutions in the UK: Anglia Ruskin University, Aston University, the University of Bradford, Cardiff University, City University, Glasgow Caledonian University, the University of Manchester and the University of Ulster.

LENGTH OF COURSE
Usually 4 years in total (Scotland 5 years): an FT 3-yr (in Scotland 4-yr) degree course, followed by one yr's salaried pre-registration training with a practice under the guidance of a GOC-registered optometrist. This includes a series of assessments throughout the placement, which are set by the College of Optometrists.

ENTRY REQUIREMENTS
You will normally need 5 GCSEs (or equivalent) at grade C or above, one of which should be in English. You will normally be required to have 3 A Level passes/ approx. 320 UCAS tariff points from the following subjects: physics, biology, chemistry or mathematics.

Requirements vary between universities, so be sure to check the university's prospectus and/or consult the relevant admission tutors.

Membership of Professional Institutions and Associations

ASSOCIATION OF OPTOMETRISTS

61 Southwark Street
London SE1 0HL
Tel: 020 7261 9661
Fax: 020 7261 0228
E-mail: postbox@aop.org.uk
Website: www.aop.org.uk

The AOP serves its members by promoting and protecting them, providing them with relevant services, representing and supporting them, enhancing their professional and business effectiveness, and expanding the role of optometry in primary and secondary eyecare.

MEMBERSHIP
Student Member
Honorary Member
Dispensing Associate
Full Member

ORTHOPTICS
Membership of Professional Institutions and Associations

BRITISH AND IRISH ORTHOPTIC SOCIETY

Tavistock House North
Tavistock Square
London WC1H 9HX
Tel: 020 7387 7992
Fax: 020 7383 2584
E-mail: bios@orthoptics.org.uk
Website: www.orthoptics.org.uk

MEMBERSHIP
Student Members
Members

QUALIFICATION/EXAMINATIONS
Degrees in orthoptics are offered by Liverpool University and Sheffield University.

OSTEOPATHY AND NATUROPATHY
Membership of Professional Institutions and Associations

BRITISH OSTEOPATHIC ASSOCIATION

3 Park Terrace
Manor Road
Luton
Bedfordshire LU1 3HN
Tel: 01582 488455
Fax: 01582 481533
E-mail: enquiries@osteopathy.org
Website: www.osteopathy.org

The BOA was formed in 1998 as a result of the merger of the British Osteopathic Association, the Osteopathic Association of Great Britain and the Guild of Osteopaths. We provide opportunities for individual and professional development in osteopathic practice and promote the highest standards of osteopathic education and research.

MEMBERSHIP
Student Member
1st/2nd/3rd Year Graduate Member
Full Member
Overseas Member

THE LONDON SCHOOL OF OSTEOPATHY

First Floor
56–60 Nelson Street
London E1 2DE
Tel: 020 7265 9333
Fax: 020 7265 8877
E-mail: info@lso.ac.uk
Website: www.lso.ac.uk

The London School of Osteopathy is based in Whitechapel and offers a 5-year modified attendance programme in the principles and clinical practice of osteopathy. Practical tuition is given throughout and students gain their clinical experience under supervision in the School's in-house Outpatient Clinic. Students successfully completing the course are awarded an undergraduate Master's in Osteopathy (MOst), validated by Anglia Ruskin University.

QUALIFICATION/EXAMINATIONS
Master's in Osteopathy (MOst) (validated by Anglia Ruskin University)

PATENT AGENCY
Membership of Professional Institutions and Associations

THE CHARTERED INSTITUTE OF PATENT ATTORNEYS

95 Chancery Lane
London WC2A 1DT
Tel: 020 7405 9450
Fax: 020 7430 0471
E-mail: mail@cipa.org.uk
Website: www.cipa.org.uk

The CIPA is the professional, training and examining body for patent attorneys in the UK. From 2010 the IP Regulation Board, an independent body within the CIPA, will set the standards for regulation of the profession. Trainees, all technical graduates, also study for the qualification to practise before the European Patent Office.

MEMBERSHIP
Student Member
Associate
Fellow
Registered Patent Attorney (RPA)
Chartered Patent Attorney (CPA)

QUALIFICATION/EXAMINATIONS
Qualifying examination for registration as a Patent Attorney

DESIGNATORY LETTERS
RPA, CPA

PENSION MANAGEMENT
Membership of Professional Institutions and Associations

THE PENSIONS MANAGEMENT INSTITUTE

PMI House
4–10 Artillery Lane
London E1 7LS
Tel: 020 7247 1452
Fax: 020 7375 0603
E-mail: education@pensions-pmi.org.uk
Website: www.pensions-pmi.org.uk

The Pensions Management Institute is the professional body that promotes standards of excellence and lifetime learning for pensions professionals and trustees through its qualifications, membership and ongoing support services. For further details please visit our website.

MEMBERSHIP
Student Member
Ordinary Member (MPMI)
Associate Member (APMI)
Fellow (FPMI)

QUALIFICATION/EXAMINATIONS
Retirement Provision Certificate (RPC)

Advanced Diploma in Retirement Provision
Qualification in Pensions Administration (QPA)
Diploma in Pension Calculations (DPC)
Qualification in Public Sector Pensions Administration (QPSPA)
Diploma in Member Directed Pension Scheme Administration (MDPSA)
Diploma in International Employee Benefits (Dip. IEB)
The Awards in Pensions Trusteeship

DESIGNATORY LETTERS
MPMI, APMI, FPMI

PERSONNEL MANAGEMENT
Membership of Professional Institutions and Associations

CHARTERED INSTITUTE OF PERSONNEL AND DEVELOPMENT

151 The Broadway
London SW19 1JQ
Tel: 020 8612 6208
Fax: 020 8612 6201
E-mail: membershipenquiry@cipd.co.uk
Website: www.cipd.co.uk

The CIPD is Europe's largest HR and development professional body. As a globally recognized brand with over 135,000 members, we pride ourselves on supporting and developing those responsible for the management and development of people within organizations.

MEMBERSHIP
Affiliate Member

Studying Affiliate Member
Associate Member
Licentiate Member
Graduate Member
Chartered Member (MCIPD)
Chartered Fellow (FCIPD)
Chartered Companion (CCIPD)
For further information see; www.cipd.co.uk/membership

QUALIFICATION/EXAMINATIONS
We are launching a new qualifications structure in January 2010. For details of current courses see; www.cipd.co.uk/qualifications

DESIGNATORY LETTERS
MCIPD, FCIPD, CCIPD

THE INSTITUTE OF CONTINUING PROFESSIONAL DEVELOPMENT

Grosvenor Gardens House
35/37 Grosvenor Gardens
London SW1W 0BS
Tel: 020 7828 1965
Fax: 020 7828 1967
E-mail: info@cpdinstitute.org
Website: www.cpdinstitute.org

The Institute of Continuing Professional Development is part of the Continuing Professional Development Foundation, an educational charitable trust providing high-quality and broad-ranging CPD since 1981. We serve the public interest by helping to raise the effectiveness of professionals through the promotion of CPD as an important and integral element of lifelong learning.

MEMBERSHIP
Member (MInstCPD)
Fellow (FInstCPD)

DESIGNATORY LETTERS
MInstCPD, FInstCPD

UK EMPLOYEES ASSISTANCE PROFESSIONALS ASSOCIATION

3 Moors Close
Ducklington
Witney
Oxfordshire OX29 7TW
Tel: 07770 924615
Fax: 01993 772765
E-mail: info@eapa.org.uk
Website: www.eapa.org.uk

The EAPA is the professional body for Employee Assistance Programmes (EAPs). It represents the interests of professionals concerned with employee assistance, psychological health and well-being in the UK. EAPA members include external and internal EAP providers, purchasers, counsellors, consultants and trainers.

MEMBERSHIP
Individual Member
Associate Member
Retiree Member
Organizational Member
Registered External/Internal Provider

PHARMACY

Membership of Professional Institutions and Associations

ROYAL PHARMACEUTICAL SOCIETY OF GREAT BRITAIN

1 Lambeth High Street
London SE1 7JN
Tel: 020 7735 9141
Fax: 020 7735 7629
E-mail: enquiries@rpsgb.org
Website: www.rpsgb.org

The RPSGB, which dates from 1841, is the professional body for pharmacists and pharmacy technicians in England, Scotland and Wales. Our primary objectives are to lead, regulate, develop and represent the profession. We promote advancement of the science and practice of pharmacy, and pharmaceutical education and knowledge, and liaise with government and other bodies in the interests of our members.

MEMBERSHIP
Pharmacy Technician
Member (MRPharmS)
Fellow (FRPharmS)

DESIGNATORY LETTERS
MRPharmS, FRPharmS

THE COLLEGE OF PHARMACY PRACTICE

28 Warwick Row
Coventry CV1 1EY
Tel: 024 762 21359
Fax: 024 765 21110
E-mail: info@collpharm.org.uk
Website: www.collpharm.org.uk

The College of Pharmacy Practice, set up in 1981 by the Pharmaceutical Society of Great Britain, is an organization of pharmacists who share the aim of promoting and maintaining a high standard of pharmacy practice. Its mission is to promote professional and personal development through education, examination, practice and research, benefiting both patients and healthcare provision.

MEMBERSHIP
Student Member
Associate (ACPP)
Member (MCPP)
Fellow (FCPP)
Member Emeritus

DESIGNATORY LETTERS
ACPP, MCPP, FCPP

THE PHARMACEUTICAL SOCIETY OF NORTHERN IRELAND

73 University Street
Belfast BT7 1HL
Tel: 028 9032 6927
Fax: 028 9043 9919
Website: www.psni.org.uk

The Pharmaceutical Society of Northern Ireland, founded in 1925, is the regulatory and professional body for pharmacists in Northern Ireland. It maintains a register of more than 2,000 pharmacists and over 500 pharmacy premises, and sets and promotes the standards for pharmacists' admission to and remaining on the register, thereby protecting public safety.

MEMBERSHIP
Trainee
Member

QUALIFICATION/EXAMINATIONS
Registration Examination

PHOTOGRAPHY
Membership of Professional Institutions and Associations

ASSOCIATION OF PHOTOGRAPHERS (AOP)

81 Leonard Street
London EC2A 4QS
Tel: 020 7739 6669
Fax: 020 7739 8707
E-mail: general@aophoto.co.uk
Website: www.the-aop.org

The AOP was founded in 1968 to promote the highest standards throughout the industry and to improve the rights of all professional photographers based in the UK. Our membership currently comprises 1,800 photographers and photographic assistants, and we are supported by photographers' agents, printers, and manufacturers and suppliers of photographic equipment.

MEMBERSHIP
Student Member
Assistant Member
Provisional Member
Photographer (full) Member
Agent Member
College Member
Affiliated Company

BRITISH INSTITUTE OF PROFESSIONAL PHOTOGRAPHY

1 Prebendal Court
Oxford Road
Aylesbury
Buckinghamshire HP19 8EY
Tel: 01296 718530
Fax: 01296 336367
E-mail: info@bipp.com
Website: www.bipp.com

The BIPP is the qualifying body for professional photographers in the UK. We provide support, training and qualifications for photographers across all types of photography, and organize a number of regional activities and events. A not-for-profit organization, we ensure that professional standards are met and maintained.

MEMBERSHIP
Open to full- or part-time professional photographers. Join as an Affiliate (maximum of 3 years) and work towards gaining a professional qualification. Student membership is also available.

QUALIFICATION/EXAMINATIONS
Three tiers of qualification:
Licentiateship (entry level) (LBIPP)
Associateship (ABIPP)
Fellowship (FBIPP)
Full details of the qualifications criteria may be found at www.bipp.com

DESIGNATORY LETTERS
LBIPP, ABIPP, FBIPP

MASTER PHOTOGRAPHERS ASSOCIATION

Jubilee House
1 Chancery Lane
Darlington
Co Durham DL1 5QP
Tel: 01325 356555
Fax: 01325 357813
E-mail: general@mpauk.com
Website: www.mpauk.com

The MPA was founded in 1952 and is now the UK's only organization for FT, qualified professional photographers. We have more than 2,000 members, who enjoy a range of benefits, including education, qualifications, informative regional meetings, business building promotions and marketing support, and abide by the Association's Code of Conduct.

MEMBERSHIP
Licentiate (LMPA)
Associate (AMPA)
Fellow (FMPA)

DESIGNATORY LETTERS
LMPA, AMPA, FMPA

THE ROYAL PHOTOGRAPHIC SOCIETY

Fenton House
122 Wells Road
Bath BA2 3AH
Tel: 01225 325733
Fax: 01225 448688
E-mail: reception@rps.org
Website: www.rps.org

The RPS, which dates from 1853, is an educational charity whose aim is to promote the art and science of photography. Membership is open to anyone and we provide information, training and advice, hold workshops on a variety of photographic topics and stage three major touring exhibitions, as well as a monthly exhibition of members' work at our headquarters in Bath.

MEMBERSHIP
Student Member
Member
Licentiate (LRPS)
Associate (ARPS)

Fellow (FRPS)

QUALIFICATION/EXAMINATIONS
Qualified Imaging Scientist and Licentiate (QIS LRPS)
Graduate Imaging Scientist and Associate (GIS ARPS)
Accredited Imaging Scientist and Associate (AIS ARPS)
Accredited Senior Imaging Scientist and Fellow (ASIS FRPS)

DESIGNATORY LETTERS
LRPS, ARPS, FRPS

PHYSICS
Membership of Professional Institutions and Associations

INSTITUTE OF PHYSICS AND ENGINEERING IN MEDICINE

Fairmount House
230 Tadcaster Road
York YO24 1ES
Tel: 01904 610821
Fax: 01904 612279
E-mail: office@ipem.org.uk
Website: www.ipem.ac.uk

The IPEM is dedicated to bringing together physical science, engineering and clinical professionals in academia, healthcare services and industry to share knowledge, advance science and technology, and inform and educate the public, with the purpose of improving the understanding, detection and treatment of disease and the management of patients.

MEMBERSHIP
Student Member
Affiliate

Associate
Medical Member (MedMIPEM)
Medical Fellow (MedFIPEM)
Incorporated Member (IIPEM)
Corporate Member (MIPEM)
Fellow (FIPEM)
Overseas Affiliate
Company Member

DESIGNATORY LETTERS
MedMIPEM, MedFIPEM, IIPEM, MIPEM, FIPEM

THE INSTITUTE OF PHYSICS

76 Portland Place
London W1B 1NT
Tel: 020 7470 4800
Fax: 020 7470 4848
E-mail: physics@iop.org
Website: www.iop.org

The IOP is a scientific charity devoted to increasing the practice, understanding and application of physics. We have a worldwide membership of over 36,000 and are a leading communicator of physics-related science to all audiences, from specialists through to government and the general public. Our publishing company, IOP Publishing, is a world leader in scientific publishing and the electronic dissemination of physics.

MEMBERSHIP
Student Member
Affiliate
Associate Member (AMInstP)
Member (MInstP)
Fellow (FInstP)
Chartered Physicist (CPhys)

DESIGNATORY LETTERS
AMInstP, MInstP, FInstP, CPhys

PHYSIOTHERAPY
Membership of Professional Institutions and Associations

THE CHARTERED SOCIETY OF PHYSIOTHERAPY

14 Bedford Row
London WC1R 4ED
Tel: 0207 306 6666
Fax: 0207 306 6611
E-mail: enquiries@csp.org.uk
Website: www.csp.org.uk

The CSP is the professional, educational and trade union body for the UK's 48,000 chartered physiotherapists, physiotherapy students and assistants. In order to become a member of the CSP it is necessary to have undertaken a qualification recognized by the Health Professions Council (HPC) – see; www.hpc-uk.org.

MEMBERSHIP
Student Member
Associate
Member (MCSP)
Fellow (FCSP)

DESIGNATORY LETTERS
MCSP, FCSP

PLASTICS AND RUBBER
Membership of Professional Institutions and Associations

LONDON METROPOLITAN POLYMER CENTRE

London Metropolitan University
166–220 Holloway Road
London N7 8DB
Tel: 020 7133 2248
Fax: 020 7133 2184
E-mail: polymers@londonmet.ac.uk
Website: www.londonmet.ac.uk/depts/polymers/

The London Metropolitan Polymer Centre is a leading UK centre for education, research and consultancy in polymer engineering, science and technology. We have a comprehensive range of modern equipment for polymer processing, testing, characterization, etc, offer courses from technician to postgraduate level, and work closely with industry, contributing to its continuing technical and commercial success.

QUALIFICATION/EXAMINATIONS
NC in Polymer Technology

HNC in Polymer Engineering
HND in Polymer Science and Engineering
BEng in Polymer Engineering
BSc in Sports Product Design
MSc in Manufacture and Design for Polymer Products
MSc in Plastics Product Design
MSc in Plastics Product Design with Management
MSc in Plastics Product Design with Marketing
MSc in Polymer Science and Engineering
MRes in Polymer Trecnology

PLUMBING
Membership of Professional Institutions and Associations

CHARTERED INSTITUTE OF PLUMBING AND HEATING ENGINEERING

64 Station Lane
Hornchurch
Essex RM12 6NB
Tel: 01708 472791
Fax: 01708 448987
E-mail: linfo@ciphe.org.uk
Website: www.ciphe.org.uk

The CIPHE, founded in 1906, is the professional body for the UK plumbing and heating industry. Our membership of around 12,000 is made up of individuals from a wide range of backgrounds and includes consultants, specifiers, designers, public health engineers, lecturers, trainers, trainees and practitioners, as well as manufacturers and distributors.

MEMBERSHIP
Trainee

Affiliate
Companion (CompCIPHE)
Associate (ACIPHE)
Member (MCIPHE)
Fellow (FCIPHE)

QUALIFICATION/EXAMINATIONS
Master Plumber Certificate (awarded jointly with the Worshipful Company of Plumbers and the City & Guilds of London Institute)

DESIGNATORY LETTERS
CompCIPHE, ACIPHE, MCIPHE, FCIPHE

PRINTING

Membership of Professional Institutions and Associations

PROSKILLS UK

Centurion Court
85b Milton Park
Abingdon
Oxfordshire OX14 4RY
Tel: 01235 833844
E-mail: info@proskills.co.uk
Website: www.proskills.co.uk

Proskills UK is an employer-led organization that represents the interests of the industries that make up the process and manufacturing sector to government, ie: building products & refractories; coatings; ceramics; extractive & mineral processing; furniture, furnishings & interiors; glass and related industries; paper; and printing. We develop industry-relevant standards and qualifications in response to industry need in collaboration with employers, training providers and awarding bodies.

QUALIFICATION/EXAMINATIONS
Please see the Proskills UK website.

THE INSTITUTE OF PAPER, PRINTING AND PUBLISHING (IP3)

Runnymede Malthouse
off Hummer Road
Egham
Surrey TW20 9BD
Tel: 0870 330 8625
Fax: 0870 330 8615
E-mail: info@ip3.org.uk
Website: www.ip3.org.uk

IP3 is the professional body representing the interests of individuals within the paper, printing and publishing sector. It was formed in 2005 from the merger of the Institute of Paper, the Institute of Printing and the Institute of Publishing, and brought together more than 2,000 members and a wealth of knowledge.

MEMBERSHIP
Student

Associate (AIP3)
Member (MIP3)
Fellow (FIP3)

QUALIFICATION/EXAMINATIONS
Certificate

DESIGNATORY LETTERS
AIP3, MIP3, FIP3

PROFESSIONAL INVESTIGATION
Membership of Professional Institutions and Associations

THE INSTITUTE OF PROFESSIONAL INVESTIGATORS

Runnymede Malthouse
off Hummer Road
Egham
Surrey TW20 (BD
Tel: 0870 330 8622
Fax: 0870 330 8612
E-mail: admin@ipi.org.uk
Website: www.ipi.org.uk

The IPI was founded in 1976 as a professional body, catering primarily for the work and educational needs of professional investigators of all types and all specializations. We encourage members' CPD and require them to adhere to the Institute's strict code of ethics, and we promote the recognition of professional investigation as a profession by government, legislative bodies and the public.

MEMBERSHIP
Affiliate
Associate
Member (MIPI)
Fellow (FIPI)

DESIGNATORY LETTERS
MIPI, FIPI

PSYCHOANALYSIS
Membership of Professional Institutions and Associations

THE BRITISH PSYCHOANALYTICAL SOCIETY

Byron House
112a Shirland Road
London W9 2EQ
Tel: 020 7563 5000
Fax: 020 7563 5001
Website: www.psychoanalysis.org.uk

The British Psychoanalytical Society was founded in 1913 and now has 438 members and 46 candidates for membership. Our aims include: to support the development of psychoanalytical knowledge as a general theory of mind, to further the clinical and scientific standards of psychoanalysis, and to train high-quality psychoanalytical professionals in sufficient numbers to develop the profession.

MEMBERSHIP
Associate Member
Full Member

PSYCHOLOGY
Membership of Professional Institutions and Associations

BRITISH PSYCHOLOGICAL SOCIETY

St Andrews House
48 Princess Road East
Leicester LE1 7DR
Tel: 0116 254 9568
Fax: 0116 247 1314
E-mail: enquiries@bps.org.uk
Website: www.bps.org.uk

The British Psychological Society is the representative body for psychology and psychologists in the UK. Formed in 1901, it has more than 47,000 members. Through its Royal Charter, the Society has responsibility for the development, promotion and application of pure and applied psychology for the public good.

MEMBERSHIP
Student Member
Affiliate
Graduate Member
Associate Fellow (AFBPsS)
Fellow (FBPsS)
Honorary Fellow
Foreign Affiliate

Chartered Membership (CPsychol)

QUALIFICATION/EXAMINATIONS
Award in Educational Psychology (Scotland)
Diploma in Forensic Psychology
Practioner Full Membership Qualification (PFMQ) in Clinical Neuopsychology
Qualification in Counselling Psychology (QCoP)
Qualification in Health Psychology (Stages 1 & 2)
Qualification in Occupational Psychology (QOccP-sych)
Qualification in Sport & Exercise Psychology (QSEP)

DESIGNATORY LETTERS
AFBPsS, FBPsS, CPsychol

PSYCHOTHERAPY
Membership of Professional Institutions and Associations

ASSOCIATION OF CHILD PSYCHOTHERAPISTS

120 West Heath Road
London NW3 7TU
Tel: 020 8458 1609
Fax: 020 8458 1482
E-mail: contactus@childpsychotherapy.org.uk
Website: www.childpsychotherapy.org.uk

The ACP is the main professional body for psycho-analytic child and adolescent psychotherapists in the UK. Our members work with children and young people as well as their parents, families and wider networks, treating a wide range of difficulties ranging from problems with sleeping and bed-wetting to eating disorders, self-harm, depression and anxiety.

MEMBERSHIP
Member

BRITISH ASSOCIATION FOR COUNSELLING AND PSYCHOTHERAPY

15 St John's Business Park
Lutterworth
Leicestershire LE17 4HB
Tel: 01455 883300
Fax: 01455 550243
E-mail: bacp@bacp.co.uk
Website: www.bacp.co.uk

The British Association for Counselling and Psychotherapy welcomes applications from qualified and experienced counsellors who wish to become BACP Accredited. BACP Accreditation as a counsellor offers a direct route to Registration as an independent practitioner with the United Kingdom Register of Counsellors.

MEMBERSHIP
Student
Associate

Member (MBACP)
Fellow (FBACP)

QUALIFICATION/EXAMINATIONS
SEAs Certificate
SEAs Diploma
SEAs Professional Qualification

DESIGNATORY LETTERS
MBACP, MBACP(Accred), FBACP

BRITISH ASSOCIATION FOR THE PERSON CENTRED APPROACH

BAPCA
PO Box 143
Ross-on-Wye
Herefordshire HR9 9AH
Tel: 01989 763863
E-mail: enquires@bapca.org.uk
Website: www.bapca.org.uk

The BAPCA was founded in 1989 as a non-religious, non-profit-making organization with the aim of advancing education in Client-Centred Psychotherapy and Counselling and the Person-Centred Approach through its publications and website, and cooperation with other national and international organizations with similar goals.

MEMBERSHIP
Individual Member
Joint Member
International Member
Institutional Member

BRITISH ASSOCIATION OF PSYCHOTHERAPISTS

37 Mapesbury Road
London NW2 4HJ
Tel: 020 8452 9823
Fax: 020 8452 5182
E-mail: mail@bap-psychotherapy.org
Website: www.bap-psychotherapy.org

The BAP is one of the longest established and largest independent providers of Jungian analytic and psychoanalytic psychotherapy for adults and children in the UK. We have been training psychoanalytic and Jungian psychotherapists for nearly 60 years, and our members work in the NHS, the corporate and voluntary sectors and as private practitioners.

MEMBERSHIP
Member

QUALIFICATION/EXAMINATIONS
Certificate/Diploma/MSc in Psychodynamics of Human Development (jointly with Birkbeck College, University of London)
DPsych in Child and Adolescent Psychotherapy (jointly with Birkbeck College, University of London)

CAMBRIDGE COLLEGE OF HYPNOTHERAPY

24 Milton Road
Impington
Cambridge CB24 9NF
Tel: 01223 235127
E-mail: j.teague@ntlworld.com
Website: www.hypnotherapytraining.org.uk

The CCH offers training to become a professional hypntherapist. The course is accredited by the NCH, HA, APHP and NRAH. No formal qualifications are required to enrol on the course.

QUALIFICATION/EXAMINATIONS
Diploma in Hypnotherapy

NATIONAL COLLEGE OF HYPNOSIS AND PSYCHOTHERAPY

PO Box 5779
Loughborough
Leicestershire LE12 5ZF
Tel: 0845 257 8735
E-mail: enquiries@nchp,org,uk
Website: www.hypnotherapyuk.net

The NCHP is a not-for-profit organization founded in 1977 and now offers accredited hypnotherapy training, hypnosis training and psychotherapy training at weekends in Leeds, Leicester, Liverpool, London, Manchester, Newcastle, Oxford, Glasgow and South Wales. We also provide a programme of one- and two-day workshops and seminars, and (where appropriate) distance-learning courses.

QUALIFICATION/EXAMINATIONS
Foundation Course
Certificate in Hypno-Psychotherapy (CHP(NC))
Diploma in Hypno-Psychotherapy (DHP(NC))
Advanced Diploma in Hypno-Psychotherapy (ADHP(NC))
European Certificate of Clinical Hypnosis (through the European Association for Hypno-Psychotherapy)
Hypnotherapy Practitioner Diploma

NATIONAL COUNCIL OF PSYCHOTHERAPISTS

PO Box 7219
Heanor
Derbyshire DE75 9AG
Tel: 08452 306072
Fax: 01773 711031
E-mail: ncphq@btinternet.com
Website: www.ncphq.co.uk

The National Council is a registering and accrediting body for psychotherapists, counsellors and coaches within the UK and also, through the International Council, the rest of the world.

Members can join the Council regardless of which discipline and where they completed their training.

MEMBERSHIP
Affiliate (ANCP)
Licentiate (LNCP)
Full Member (MNCP)
Fellow (FNCP)

DESIGNATORY LETTERS
ANCP, LNCP, MNCP, FNCP

THE FOUNDATION FOR PSYCHOTHERAPY AND COUNSELLING

Tel: 020 7378 2090
E-mail: office@thefoundation-uk.org
Website: www.thefoundation-uk.org

The Foundation for Psychotherapy and Counselling was formed during the 1970s as the graduate body of WPF Therapy (the largest charitable provider of counselling and psychotherapy in England) and now has some 700 fully trained and qualified members, most of whom are in private practice.

MEMBERSHIP
Member

THE NATIONAL REGISTER OF HYPNOTHERAPISTS AND PSYCHOTHERAPISTS

1st Floor
18 Carr Road
Nelson
Lancashire BB9 7JS
Tel: 01282 716839
E-mail: admin@nrhp.co.uk
Website: www.nrhp.co.uk

The NRHP (est 1985) is a professional association of qualified therapists who trained with a UKCP accredited training organization. Members are required to adhere to a code of ethics and carry appropriate insurance. We publish a Directory of Practitioners and offer a referral service for the public via our website and the office. We are a member of the UKCP.

MEMBERSHIP
Student
Associate 1 (NRHP(Assoc 1))
Associate 2 (NRHP(Assoc 2))
Associate 3 (NRHP(Assoc 3))
Full Member (MNRHP)
Fellow (FNRHP)

DESIGNATORY LETTERS
NRHP(Assoc 1), NRHP(Assoc 2), NRHP(Assoc 3),
MNRHP. FNRHP

UK COUNCIL FOR PSYCHOTHERAPY

2nd Floor Edward House
2 Wakley Street
London EC1V 7LT
Tel: 020 7014 9955
Fax: 020 7014 9977
E-mail: ukcp@psychotherapy.org.uk
Website: www.psychotherapy.org.uk

The UKCP's purpose is to promote the art and science of psychotherapy for the public benefit; to promote research and education in psychotherapy and disseminate the results of any such research; and to promote (or assist in the promotion, preservation and protection of public health by encouraging) high standards of training and practice in psychotherapy and the wider provision of psychotherapy for the public. The *National Register of Psychotherapists* is published annually, and only psychotherapists who meet the training requirements of UKCP and abide by its ethical guidelines are included.

PUBLIC ADMINISTRATION
Membership of Professional Institutions and Associations

THE INSTITUTE OF PUBLIC SECTOR MANAGEMENT

45 Cherry Tree Road
Axminster
Devon EX13 5GG
Tel: 01297 35423
Fax: 01297 35423
E-mail: info@ipsm.org.uk
Website: www.ipsm.org.uk

The IPSM is the only membership body exclusively dedicated to managers working in the public, voluntary and not-for-profit sectors. We encourage the sharing of knowledge, skills and experience between our members, provide advice and support ourselves, and as a campaigning body seek to raise public awareness and respect for public services and the role of the manager in those services.

MEMBERSHIP
Student Member
Individual (Full) Member (MIPSM)
Fellow (FIPSM)
Corporate Member

PUBLISHING
Membership of Professional Institutions and Associations

LONDON SCHOOL OF PUBLISHING

David Game House
London W11 3JS
Tel: 020 7221 3399
Fax: 020 7243 1730
E-mail: lsp@easynet.co.uk
Website: www.publishing-school.co.uk

The LSP offers a range of courses in traditional areas of publishing such as copy-editing, proofreading and picture research, alongside aspects of electronic publishing, such as using QuarkXPress, InDesign and Photoshop. All courses are practical and provide an overview of a particular publishing skill. Upon successful completion of a course, students are awarded a Certificate.

QUALIFICATION/EXAMINATIONS
Certificate in: Editorial & Proofreading, Advanced Editorial/Feature & Corporate Writing, Magazine Sub-editing, Picture Research, QuarkXPress, InDesign, Photoshop, Illustrator, PageMaker, Dreamweaver, Flash, HTML, FrontPage, Writing for Web

PURCHASING AND SUPPLY
Membership of Professional Institutions and Associations

THE CHARTERED INSTITUTE OF PURCHASING & SUPPLY

Easton House
Easton on the Hill
Stamford
Lincolnshire PE9 3NZ
Tel: 01780 756777
Fax: 01780 751610
E-mail: info@cips.org
Website: www.cips.org

The CIPS is the leading international body representing purchasing and supply management professionals and is dedicated to promoting good practice. We have over 54,000 members in 150 different countries, including senior business people, high-ranking civil servants and leading academics.

MEMBERSHIP
Student Member
Affiliate
Certificate Member

Diploma Member
Associate Member
Full Member (MCIPS)
Fellow (FCIPS)

QUALIFICATION/EXAMINATIONS
Please see the CIPS's website.

DESIGNATORY LETTERS
MCIPS, FCIPS

QUALITY ASSURANCE
Membership of Professional Institutions and Associations

THE CHARTERED QUALITY INSTITUTE

12 Grosvenor Crescent
London SW1X 7EE
Tel: 020 7245 6722
Fax: 020 7245 6788
E-mail: info@thecqi.org
Website: www.thecqi.org

The CQI is the chartered body for quality manage-ment professionals. Established in 1919, we gained a Royal Charter in 2006 and became the CQI shortly afterwards. Our vision is to place quality at the heart of every organization: we promote the benefits of quality management to industry, disseminate quality knowledge and resources, provide qualifications and training, and assess quality competence.

MEMBERSHIP
Student
Associate Member (ACQI)

Member, Chartered Quality Professional (MCQI, CQP)
Fellow, Chartered Quality Professional (FCQI, CQP)
Company member

QUALIFICATION/EXAMINATIONS
Certificate in Quality
Diploma in Quality

DESIGNATORY LETTERS
MCQI, CQP; FCQI, CQP

RADIOGRAPHY
Membership of Professional Institutions and Associations

THE SOCIETY OF RADIOGRAPHERS

207 Providence Square
Mill Street
London SE1 2EW
Tel: 020 7740 7200
Fax: 020 7740 7204
E-mail: info@sor.org
Website: www.sor.org

The Society of Radiographers, founded in 1920, represents more than 90 per cent of the diagnostic and therapeutic radiographers in the UK. It is responsible for their professional, educational, public and workplace interests. Together with the College of Radiographers, our charitable subsidiary, our efforts are directed towards education, research and other activities in support of the science and practice of radiography.

MEMBERSHIP
Student Member
Radiographic Assistant
Assistant Practitioner
Member

RETAIL

Membership of Professional Institutions and Associations

BOSS (BRITISH OFFICE SYSTEMS AND SUPPLIES) FEDERATION

Farringdon Point
29--35 Farringdon Road
London EC1M 3JF
Tel: 0845 450 1565
Fax: Fax: 020 7405 7784
E-mail: info@bossfederation.co.uk
Website: www.bossfederation.com

BOSS is a non-profit-making organization that supports, promotes and protects all businesses along the distribution chain in the office products industry, covering stationery, office machines and supplies, office furniture, office systems and related product areas. We have over 80 manufacturing members and over 1,200 dealer and reseller members from all of the major buying and marketing groups.

QUALIFICATION/EXAMINATIONS
The BOSS Federation, in association with the British Printing Industries Federation & Vision in Print, offer numerous generic and specific training courses to companies and individuals working in or wishing to work in these industries. See the BOSS website for details.

IGD

Grange Lane
Letchmore Heath
Watford
Hertfordshire WD25 8GD
Tel: 01923 857141
Fax: 01923 852531
E-mail: igd@igd.com
Website: www.igd.com

IGD (the Institute of Grocery Distribution) was formed in 1972 from the merger of the Institute of Charted Grocers and the Institute of Food Distribution. We provide information and practical training to the industry and now have more than 700 corporate members, covering a broad spectrum of companies and organizations across the world.

MEMBERSHIP
Corporate Member

QUALIFICATION/EXAMINATIONS
PG Cert in Food & Grocery Industry Management (validated by the University of Edinburgh)

INSTITUTE OF MASTERS OF WINE

2/3 Philpot Lane
London EC3M 8AN
Tel: 020 7621 2830
Fax: 020 7929 2302
Website: www.mastersofwine.org

The Institute of Masters of Wine is a membership body that represents the interests of its members (Masters of Wine), administers the MW Examination, and runs an education programme in preparation for the examination. We also hold a number of events throughout the year, including seminars and tastings, master classes, discussions, and, every 4 years, a symposium, most of which are open to the public.

MEMBERSHIP
Master of Wine (MW)

QUALIFICATION/EXAMINATIONS
Master of Wine Examination

DESIGNATORY LETTERS
MW

MEAT TRAINING COUNCIL

PO Box 141
Winterhill House
Snowdon Drive
Milton Keynes MK6 1YY
Tel: 01908 231062
Fax: 01908 231063
E-mail: info@meattraining.org.uk
Website: www.meattraining.org.uk

The MTC is a registered charity, limited by guarantee, working for, and with, the UK meat industry. We provide information about jobs, careers and the qualifications required to work in the red meat and poultry sector of the food business. Professional membership is administered by the Worshipful Company of Butchers via its Guild of Freemen. The qualifications awarding body is now the Food and Drink Qualifications Awarding Body (FDQ Ltd) (www.fdq.org.uk).

MEMBERSHIP
Affiliate (AffInstM)
Associate (AInstM)
Graduate Member (GMInstM)

QUALIFICATION/EXAMINATIONS
Please see the Meat Training Council's website.

DESIGNATORY LETTERS
AffInstM, AInstM, GMInstM

THE BRITISH ANTIQUE DEALERS' ASSOCIATION

20 Rutland Gate
London SW7 1BD
Tel: 020 7589 4128
Fax: 020 7581 9083
E-mail: info@bada.org
Website: www.bada.org

BADA, which was founded in 1918, is the trade association for antique dealers in Britain. Our vetted members are elected for their high business standards and expertise, and adhere to a strict code of practice; we provide safeguards for members of the public who deal with our members, including independent arbitration if a dispute arises.

MEMBERSHIP
Member

THE GUILD OF ARCHITECTURAL IRONMONGERS

8 Stepney Green
London E1 3JU
Tel: 020 7790 3431
Fax: 020 7790 8517
E-mail: info@gai.org.uk
Website: www.gai.org.uk

The GAI represents the interests of architectural ironmongers and manufacturers of architectural ironmongery. We develop, promote and protect standards of integrity and excellence, and encourage academic study relating to the industry, operating an Institute for individual members to facilitate their continuous professional development. We liaise with various bodies on matters affecting the industry.

MEMBERSHIP
Affiliate Member
Associate Member
Full Member

Registered Architectural Ironmonger (Reg AI)

QUALIFICATION/EXAMINATIONS
The GAI provides a 3-year incremental training programme. Students are examined each year and must pass each year in turn before progressing to the next. A Certificate is awarded to successful students each year, culminating in the GAI Diploma (Dip GAI) on successful completion of year 3.

DESIGNATORY LETTERS
Reg AI

THE INSTITUTE OF BUILDERS MERCHANTS

Touchwood
Oak View Rise
Harlow Wood
Mansfield
Nottinghamshire NG18 4UT
Tel: 01623 427693
E-mail: admin@instbm.co.uk
Website: www.instbm.co.uk

To improve through seminars and website articles, the technical and general knowledge of persons engaged in builders' merchants; to verify management training courses with providers; to acknowledge personal achievements and award diplomas, certificates and other distinctions; to encourage the need for knowledge, integrity and efficiency in the builders' merchants industry.

MEMBERSHIP
Student
Associate
Member
Fellow
Corporate Supporter

QUALIFICATION/EXAMINATIONS
University Degree
The Institute of Builders Merchants Business Studies Course
The Builders Merchants Federation Diploma in Merchanting
Higher National Certificate (HNC) in Business Studies
Higher National Diploma (HND) in Business Studies
NVQ Level 4
Company management programmes as approved by the Board of Governors

THE SOCIETY OF SHOE FITTERS

c/o The Anchorage
28 Admirals Walk
Hingham
Norfolk NR9 4JL
Tel: 01953 851171
Fax: 01953 851190
E-mail: secretary@shoefitters-uk.org
Website: www.shoefitters-uk.org

The Society of Shoe Fitters is a not-for-profit organization in our 50th year, set up to assist the trade and public. We disseminate shoe fitting/footwear knowledge via courses and an examination, and in turn endeavour to keep shoe fitting advice available via our website, leaflets and a helpline.

MEMBERSHIP
Student Member
Member (MSSF)
Fellow (FSSF)

Associate Member (corporate membership)

QUALIFICATION/EXAMINATIONS
One-day on-site courses – certificate only
Five- or 10-month course leading to membership qualification
Entrance examination for experienced shoe fitters leading to qualification

DESIGNATORY LETTERS
MSSF, FSSF

SECRETARIAL AND OFFICE WORK
Membership of Professional Institutions and Associations

INSTITUTE OF PROFESSIONAL ADMINISTRATORS

6 Graphite Square
Vauxhall Walk
London SE11 5EE
Tel: 020 7091 2606
Fax: 020 7091 7340
E-mail: info@inprad.org
Website: www.inprad.org

The IPA was founded in 1957 as the Institute of Qualified Professional Secretaries and is today the leading membership body for administration and office professionals. We provide our members with information, advice and guidance on suitable training and development to advance their career as well as a CPD scheme designed to meet their individual needs.

MEMBERSHIP
Student Member
Affiliate (AffIPA)
Member (MIPA)
Fellow (FIPA)
Corporate Member

DESIGNATORY LETTERS
AffIPA, MIPA, FIPA

SECURITY
Membership of Professional Institutions and Associations

THE SECURITY INSTITUTE

1 The Courtyard
Caldecote
Warwickshire CV10 0AS
E-mail: info@security-institute.org
Website: www.security-institute.org

The Institute promotes professionalism in the security world and encourages a proper understanding of the value of the security function by management. The Institute has declared its intention to progress towards chartered status. Membership of the Institute is now recognized as an employment prerequisite by many companies and government departments.

MEMBERSHIP
Affiliate/Student
Graduate

Associate
Member
Fellow (FSyI)

QUALIFICATION/EXAMINATIONS
Certificate in Security Management
Diploma in Security Management

DESIGNATORY LETTERS
FSyI

SOCIAL WORK AND PROBATION

SOCIAL WORK
The General Social Care Council (GSCC) is responsible for regulating and supporting social work education and training in England. The GSCC accredits universities who offer social work qualifications at both qualifying and post-qualifying levels, and quality-assures all social work courses. In 2003, professional qualifying training for social workers in the United Kingdom changed to a degree in social work. The diploma in social work (DipSW) and all other 'predecessor' social work qualifications will continue to be recognized as valid social work qualifications.

For further details contact the General Social Care Council: Tel: 0845 070 063; Website: www.gscc.org.uk.

For information about social work training in Scotland, contact Scottish Social Services Council: Tel: 08456 030891; Website: www.sssc.uk.com.

For information about social work training in Wales, contact Care Council for Wales: Tel: 02920 226257; Website: www.ccwales.org.uk.

For information about social work training in Northern Ireland, contact Northern Ireland Social Care Council: Tel: 02890 417600; Website: www.niscc.n-i.nhs.uk.

Membership of Professional Institutions and Associations

THE BRITISH ASSOCIATION OF SOCIAL WORKERS

16 Kent Street
Birmingham B5 6RD
Tel: 0121 6223911

Fax: 0121 6224860
Website: www.basw.co.uk

The BASW is the largest professional association representing social work and social workers in the UK. Whether you are qualified or not, experienced or just entering the profession, we are here to help, support, advise and campaign on your behalf.
MEMBERSHIP

Student Member
Affiliate
Member (4 categories)

Retired Member
Overseas Member

SOCIOLOGY
Membership of Professional Institutions and Associations

BRITISH SOCIOLOGICAL ASSOCIATION

Bailey Suite, Palatine House
Belmont Business Park
Belmont
Durham DH1 1TW
Tel: 0191 383 0839
Fax: 0191 383 0782
E-mail: enquiries@britsoc.org.uk
Website: www.britsoc.co.uk

The BSA was founded in 1951 to represent the intellectual and sociological interests of sociologists in the UK. Our members include researchers, teachers, students and practitioners in a variety of fields. We provide a network of communication to all who are concerned with the promotion and use of sociology and sociological research.

SPEECH AND LANGUAGE THERAPY
Membership of Professional Institutions and Associations

ROYAL COLLEGE OF SPEECH AND LANGUAGE THERAPISTS

2 White Hart Yard
London SE1 1NX
Tel: 020 7378 1200
Fax: 020 7378 7254
E-mail: postmaster@rcslt.org
Website: www.rcslt.org

The RCSLT is the professional body for speech and language therapists and support workers. We set, promote and maintain high standards in education, clinical practice and ethical conduct. Our national campaigning work aims to improve services for people with speech, language, communication and swallowing needs and to influence health, education and social care policies.

MEMBERSHIP
Student Member
Newly Qualified Member
Full Member
Fellow (FRCSLT)
Honorary Fellow (Hon FRCSLT)

DESIGNATORY LETTERS
FRCSLT, Hon FRCSLT

SPORTS SCIENCE
Membership of Professional Institutions and Associations

LONDON SCHOOL OF SPORTS MASSAGE

28 Station Parade
Willesden Green
London NW2 4NX
Tel: 020 8452 8855
Fax: 020 8452 4524
E-mail: admin@lssm.com
Website: www.lssm.com

The LSSM, founded in 1989, was the first to provide specialist training in Sport & Remedial Massage. We offer vocational training for those who want to develop a professional career in massage therapy and were instrumental in setting up the Institute of Sport & Remedial Massage (ISRM), which is the professional body promoting our needs and aspirations as clinical therapists.

MEMBERSHIP
Member

QUALIFICATION/EXAMINATIONS
Introductory Massage Workshop
Professional Diploma in Clinical Sport & Remedial Massage Therapy (Level 5)

STATISTICS
Membership of Professional Institutions and Associations

THE ROYAL STATISTICAL SOCIETY

12 Errol Street
London EC1Y 8LX
Tel: 020 7638 8998
Fax: 020 7614 3905
E-mail: rss@rss.org.uk
Website: www.rss.org.uk

The RSS is the learned society and professional body for statistics and statisticians in the UK. We have over 7,000 members worldwide, and are active in a wide range of areas both directly and indirectly relating to the study and application of statistics.

MEMBERSHIP
Student Member
Fellow

Graduate Statistician (GradStat)
Chartered Statistician (CStat)

QUALIFICATION/EXAMINATIONS
Ordinary Certificate in Statistics
Higher Certificate in Statistics
Graduate Diploma in Statistics

DESIGNATORY LETTERS
GradStat, CStat

STOCKBROKING AND SECURITIES
Membership of Professional Institutions and Associations

CFA SOCIETY OF THE UK

2nd Floor
135 Canon Street
London EC4N 5BP
Tel: 020 7280 9620
Fax: 020 7280 9636
E-mail: info@cfauk.org
Website: www.cfauk.org

The CFA Society of the UK was formerly the UK Society of Investment Professionals (UKSIP) and was renamed in 2007. Our aim is to promote the development of the investment profession in the UK through the promotion of the highest standards of ethical behaviour and the provision of education, professional development, information, career support and advocacy to our members.

MEMBERSHIP
IMC Member
Candidate Member
Affiliate Member
Regular Member

QUALIFICATION/EXAMINATIONS
Investment Management Certificate (IMC)

THE CHARTERED INSTITUTE FOR SECURITIES & INVESTMENT

8 Eastcheap
London EC3M 1AE
Tel: 020 7645 0600
Fax: 020 7645 0601
Website: www.cisi.org.uk

The Chartered Institute for Securities & Investment is the largest professional body for practitioners in stockbroking, derivatives markets, investment management, corporate finance, operations and related activities, having over 38,000 members.

MEMBERSHIP
Student Member
Affiliate (ASI)
Member (MSI)
Fellow (FSI)

QUALIFICATION/EXAMINATIONS
Introduction to Investment
Islamic Finance Qualification
IT in Investment Operations
Risk in Financial Services
Investment Administration Qualification (IAQ™)
Certificate in Corporate Finance
Certificate in Investment Management (CertIM)
International Certificate in Wealth Management
Advanced Certificate in Global Securities Operations
Advanced Certificate in Investment Schemes Administration
Advanced Certificate in Operational Risk
Diploma in Investment Compliance
Diploma in Investment Operations
Master's programme

DESIGNATORY LETTERS
ASI, MSI, FSI

SURGICAL, DENTAL AND CARDIOLOGICAL TECHNICIANS
Membership of Professional Institutions and Associations

THE BRITISH INSTITUTE OF DENTAL AND SURGICAL TECHNOLOGISTS

4 Thompson Green
Shipley
West Yorkshire BD17 7PR
Tel: 0845 644 3726
E-mail: secretary@bidst.org
Website: www.bidst.org

The BIDST has been established for over 70 years and exists to provide a vehicle for the continuing education of technicians within the spheres of dental and surgical technology. It is our aim to make membership of the Institute an aspiration for all technicians, raising standards and portraying an image of professionalism which professional technicians deserve.

MEMBERSHIP
Student Associate
Associate
Licentiate (LBIDST)
Life Member
Fellow (FBIDST)

DESIGNATORY LETTERS
LBIDST, FBIDST

SURVEYING
Membership of Professional Institutions and Associations

ASSOCIATION OF BUILDING ENGINEERS

Lutyens House
Billing Brook Road
Weston Favell
Northampton NN3 8NW
Tel: 0845 126 1058
Fax: 01604 784220
E-mail: building.engineers@abe.org.uk
Website: www.abe.org.uk

The ABE is the professional body for those specializing in the technology of building, providing the prime qualification Building Engineer. Our objectives are to promote and advance the planning, design, construction, maintenance and repair of the built environment, to maintain a high standard of professional practice, and to encourage cooperation between construction professionals.

MEMBERSHIP
Student
Technician
Associate Member (ABEng)
Graduate Member (GradBEng)

Member (MBEng)
Fellow (FBEng)
Honorary Fellow (HonFBEng)

QUALIFICATION/EXAMINATIONS
Certificate in Valuation for Secured Lending (CertValSL)
Diploma in Home Inspection (DipHI)
Diploma in Domestic Energy Assessment (DipDEA) (Level 3)
Diploma in Energy Display Certificates (Level 3)
Diploma in Non-Domestic Energy Assessment (Level 3)

Top-Up Diploma in Domestic Energy Assessment
(Level 4)

DESIGNATORY LETTERS
ABEng, GradBEng, MBEng, FBEng

SWIMMING INSTRUCTION
Membership of Professional Institutions and Associations

HALLIWICK AST

c/o ADKC Centre
Whitstable House
Silchester Road
London W10 6SB
Tel: 01727 825524
E-mail: patrick.hastings@btopenworld.com
Website: www.halliwick.org.uk

The Halliwick Association of Swimming Therapy in the UK, founded in 1952, teaches people with disabilities swimming and safety in the water using the Halliwick Concept. We operate through a network of more than 90 affiliated swimming clubs and groups in the UK, plus personal and overseas affiliates. We produce a range of publications, videos and teaching resources.

THE SWIMMING TEACHERS' ASSOCIATION

Anchor House
Birch Street
Walsall
West Midlands WS2 8HZ
Tel: 01922 645097
Fax: 01922 720628
E-mail: sta@sta.co.uk
Website: www.sta.co.uk

The STA is dedicated to the preservation of human life by the teaching of swimming, lifesaving and survival techniques to as many people as possible, both in the UK and internationally. We offer a range of specialist training programmes and qualifications, which are used in more than 25 countries worldwide, and liaise with other organizations concerned with swimming teaching and water safety.

MEMBERSHIP
Junior Member
Associate Member (ASTA)
Qualified Member (MSTA)
Corporate Member

QUALIFICATION/EXAMINATIONS
Certificate in Teaching Swimming – Beginners (STC[B]) Certificate in Teaching Swimming – Full (STC[F])
Certificate in Teaching Swimming – Primary Teacher (STC[PT])
Certificate in Teaching Swimming – Secondary Teacher (STC[ST])
Level 2 Certificate in Aquatic Teaching – Aquacise (ATA)
Level 2 Certificate in Aquatic Teaching – Baby & Pre-school (BPC)
Level 2 Certificate in Aquatic Teaching – Special Needs
Level 1 Certificate in Aquatic Teaching – Special Needs Teaching – Assistant
Student Teacher Certificate

Level 2 Certificate for the National Rescue Standard – Pool Attendant

Level 2 Certificate for the National Rescue Standard – Pool Lifeguard

Level 2 Certificate for the National Rescue Standard – Poolside Helper

Level 1 Foundation Certificate in Swimming Pool and Spa Water Treatment

Level 2 Certificate in Swimming Pool and Spa Water Treatment

DESIGNATORY LETTERS
ASTA, MSTA

TAXATION
Membership of Professional Institutions and Associations

SOCIETY OF TRUST & ESTATE PRACTITIONERS

Artillery House (South)
11–19 Artillery Row
London SW1P 1RT
Tel: +44 (0)20 7340 0500
Fax: +44 (0)20 7340 0501
E-mail: step@step.org
Website: www.step.org

The Society of Trust and Estate Practitioners (STEP) is a unique professional body providing members with a local, national and international learning and business network focusing on the responsible stewardship of assets today and across the generations.

MEMBERSHIP
Full members of STEP are the most experienced and senior practitioners in the field of trusts and estates.

QUALIFICATION/EXAMINATIONS
STEP Diplomas and Foundation Certificates are recognised as essential qualifications and TEP's are sought after by employers. A portfolio of courses have been designed to enhance your career. STEP qualifications include the STEP Diploma for England & Wales (Trusts and Estates), STEP Diploma for Ireland, STEP Diploma for Scotland, STEP Diploma in International Trust Management, STEP Certificate for Financial Services (Trusts and Estate Planning) and many more.

DESIGNATORY LETTERS
TEP

THE ASSOCIATION OF TAXATION TECHNICIANS

1st Floor
Artillery House
11–19 Artillery Row
London SW1P 1RT
Tel: 0844 251 0830
Fax: 0844 251 0831
E-mail: info@att.org.uk
Website: www.att.org.uk

The AAT was founded in 1989 in recognition of the increasing demand for tax services and the development of tax practice as a professional activity in its own right. Our primary aim is to provide an appropriate qualification for individuals who undertake such work, and we now have more than 10,500 members, affiliates and registered students.

MEMBERSHIP
Student

Affiliate

Member

QUALIFICATION/EXAMINATIONS
Certificate of Competency in Business Compliance

Certificate of Competency in Business Taxation and Accounting Principles

DESIGNATORY LETTERS
ATT

THE CHARTERED INSTITUTE OF TAXATION

First Floor
11–19 Artillery Row
London SW1P 1RT
Tel: 020 7340 0550
Fax: 0844 579 6701
E-mail: post@tax.org.uk
Website: www.tax.org.uk

The CIOT, which dates from 1930, is the professional body for Chartered Tax Advisers and has 14,300 members. Our aims are to promote education in and the study of the administration and practice of taxation, and to achieve a better, more efficient, tax system for all affected by it – taxpayers, advisers and the authorities.

MEMBERSHIP
Associate (CTA or ATII)

Fellow (CTA or FTII)

QUALIFICATION/EXAMINATIONS
Chartered Tax Adviser (CTA) examination
Advanced Diploma in International Taxation (ADIT)

DESIGNATORY LETTERS
CTA, ATII, FTII

THE INSTITUTE OF INDIRECT TAXATION

The Stables
Station Road West
Oxted
Surrey RH8 9EE
Tel: 01883 730658
Fax: 01883 717778
E-mail: enquiries@theiit.org.uk
Website: www.theiit.org.uk

The Institute was founded in 1991 to establish a professional body of indirect tax practitioners to regulate and support its members. Membership is worldwide and includes barristers, solicitors, accountants, sole practitioners and tax specialists in commerce, the professions and government. The Institute is a member of the Confederation Fiscale Europeenne.

MEMBERSHIP
Student
Affiliate

Associate (AIIT)
Honorary Associate (AIIT(Hon))
Fellow (FIIT)
Honorary Fellow (FII(Hon))

QUALIFICATION/EXAMINATIONS
Associate Examination – two routes: VAT and Customs
VAT Compliance Diploma (IIT (Dip))

DESIGNATORY LETTERS
AIIT, AIIT (Hon), FIIT, FIIT (Hon)

TAXI DRIVERS

Membership of Professional Institutions and Associations

TAXI DRIVERS (LONDON)

Cab drivers and cab proprietors in the Metropolitan Police District and City of London are licensed by an Assistant Commissioner of the Metropolitan Police, through the Public Carriage Office at 15 Penton Street, Islington N1 9PU. A cab driver's licence is valid for 3 years and a cab proprietor's licence for 1 year.

TEACHING/EDUCATION

Initial Qualifications in the UK

RECOGNITION

To obtain a teaching appointment as a qualified teacher in maintained schools in England and Wales, it is necessary to have **Qualified Teacher Status (QTS)**. In order to be qualified, teachers must have satisfactorily completed an approved course of initial training, and to be able to teach in maintained schools in England must have successfully completed their induction period (there are similar arrangements for teaching in Scotland, Wales and Northern Ireland).

APPROVED COURSES OF TRAINING IN ENGLAND AND WALES

Initial teacher training courses in England and Wales are provided by Colleges and University Departments of Education. The main courses available are Bachelor of Education (BEd) degrees Bachelor of Arts with QTS and Bachelor of Science with QTS for non-graduates, and Postgraduate Certificates of Education (PGCEs) for graduates at accredited institutions.

BEd degrees usually last 4 years for an honours degree and PGCEs generally last 1 year FT. There are also some employment-based routes into teaching. The Graduate Teacher Programme is for mature, well-qualified people who need to earn money while they train and are able to take on responsibilities quickly, and the Registered Teacher Programme is for those without a degree but with at least two years of higher education. These employment-based routes now account for around 15 per cent of all teacher training places. In addition, *Teach First* is a programme enabling graduates to spend two years working in challenging secondary schools in London, Manchester and the Midlands. The programme enables trainees to qualify as a teacher while also completing leadership training.

OTHER APPROVED COURSES OF TRAINING

Courses of initial teacher training (ITT, sometimes referred to as initial teacher education or ITE) at institutions providing teacher training: a course of training leading to registration as a primary or secondary school teacher in Scotland. A course of training in Northern Ireland, approved by the Department of Education Northern Ireland, leading to **recognition as a school teacher**.

QUALIFICATIONS FOR ADMISSION TO TRAINING

Students entering 4 year BEdHons courses will normally be expected to have at the very least 3 GCSE/O levels at grade C or above, and 2 GCE A levels (or equivalent qualifications) while entrants to PGCE courses require a UK degree or a recognized equivalent and a GCE (or recognised equivalent) in English Grade C or above; a GCSE (or recognised equivalent) in mathematics, Grade C or above; and a GSCE (or recognised equivalent) in a science subject if you want to teach primary of key stage 2/3, Grade C or above. A requirement of QTS in England is passing Skills Tests in numeracy, literacy and ICT. These tests cover core skills that teachers need in their jobs and QTS cannot be awarded until they are passed.

THE GENERAL TEACHING COUNCILS OF THE UK

The General Teaching Council for England (GTCE) is an independent professional council for teachers in England. Similar councils exist in Wales (GTCW), Scotland (GTCS) and Northern Ireland (GTCNI). These councils hold registers of qualified teachers and also act as disciplinary bodies. You can find out more from their respective websites:

GTCE; www.gtce.org.uk
GTCW; www.gtcw.org.uk
GTCS; www.gtcs.org.uk
GTCNI; www.gtcni.org.uk

APPLICATIONS
Applications for undergraduate courses are made through the University and Colleges Admission Services (UCAS) and postgraduate applications through the Graduate Teacher Training Registry (GTTR).

You can find out more about training to teach from the following websites: GTTR; www.gttr.ac.uk; UCAS; www.ucas.ac.uk; Training and Development Agency for Schools (TDA); www.tda.gov.uk and www.teach.gov.uk/talent. You can also call the TDA's Teaching Information Line in England and Wales on 0845 6000 991–992 for Welsh speakers (minicom 0117 915 8161).

TECHNICAL COMMUNICATIONS
Membership of Professional Institutions and Associations

THE INSTITUTE OF SCIENTIFIC AND TECHNICAL COMMUNICATORS (ISTC LTD)

Airport House
Purley Way
Croydon CR0 0XZ
Tel: 020 8253 4506
Fax: 020 8253 4510
E-mail: istc@istc.org.uk
Website: www.istc.org.uk

The ISTC is a non-profit-making organization and the largest UK body representing professional communicators and information designers. Our aims include improving standards of scientific and technical communication, promoting scientific and technical communication as a career, supporting our members, and consulting, cooperating and collaborating with other bodies that share out ideals.

MEMBERSHIP
Student
Associate
Member (MISTC)
Fellow (FISTC)
Business Affiliate

DESIGNATORY LETTERS
MISTC, FISTC

TEXTILES
Membership of Professional Institutions and Associations

THE TEXTILE INSTITUTE

1st Floor
Oxford Street
Manchester M1 6FQ
Tel: 01612 371188
Fax: 01612 361991
E-mail: tiihq@textileinst.org.uk
Website: www.textileinstitute.org

The Textile Institute covers all disciplines – from technology and production to design, development and marketing – relating to fibres, fabrics, clothing, footwear, and interior and technical textiles.

MEMBERSHIP
Student
Individual
Licentiate (LTI)
Associate (CText ATI)
Fellow (CText FTI)

Companion
Honorary Fellow
Corporate

DESIGNATORY LETTERS
LTI, CText ATI, CText FTI

TIMBER TECHNOLOGY
Membership of Professional Institutions and Associations

WOOD TECHNOLOGY SOCIETY

Third Floor D
Carpenters' Hall
1 Throgmorton Avenue
London EC2N 2BY
Tel: 020 7256 2700
Fax: 020 7256 2701
E-mail: info@iwsc.org.uk
Website: www.iwsc.org.uk

The Wood Technology Society (IWSc – a Division of the Institute of Materials, Minerals and Mining), formerly the Institute of Wood Science, is the professional body for the timber and allied industries. We promote and encourage a better understanding of timber, wood-based materials and associated timber processes, and are the UK examining body, awarding qualifications at Foundation, Certificate and Diploma level.

MEMBERSHIP
Student Member
Affiliate Member

Technician (TIWSc)
Licentiate (LIWSc)
Member (MIWSc)
Fellow (FIWSc)
Corporate Member

QUALIFICATION/EXAMINATIONS
Timber Studies Award (Foundation course)
Certificate
Diploma

DESIGNATORY LETTERS
TIWSc, LIWSc, MIWSc, FIWSc

TOWN AND COUNTRY PLANNING
Membership of Professional Institutions and Associations

ROYAL TOWN PLANNING INSTITUTE

41 Botolph Lane
London EC3R 8DL
Tel: 020 7929 9494
E-mail: membership@rtpi.org.uk
Website: www.rtpi.org.uk

The RTPI is the largest professional institute for planners in Europe, with over 22,000 members. As well as promoting spatial planning, we develop and shape policy affecting the built environment, work to raise professional standards and support members through continuous education, training and development.

MEMBERSHIP
Student Member
Licentiate Member
Associate Member
Legal Associate Member (LARTPI)
Technical Member (TechRTPI)
Retired Member

Honorary Member (HonMRTPI)
Chartered Member (MRTPI)
Chartered Fellow (FRTPI)

QUALIFICATION/EXAMINATIONS
Please see www.rtpi.org.uk/item/178/23/5/3 for a list of accredited training providers

DESIGNATORY LETTERS
LARTPI, TechRTPI, HonMRTPI, MRTPI, FRTPI

TRADING STANDARDS
Membership of Professional Institutions and Associations

THE TRADING STANDARDS INSTITUTE

1 Sylvan Court
Sylvan Way
Southfields Business Park
Basildon
Essex SS15 6TH
Tel: 0845 608 9400
Fax: 0845 608 9425
E-mail: institute@tsi.org.uk
Website: www.tsi.org.uk

The TSI, formed in 1881, is a not-for-profit membership association representing trading standards professionals in both the public and private sectors in the UK and overseas. We encourage honest enterprise and business, and help safeguard the economic, environmental, health and social well-being of consumers.

MEMBERSHIP
Student Member
Affiliate Member
Associate Member (ASTI)
Full Member (MSTI)
Fellow (FSTI)

Corporate Affiliate

QUALIFICATION/EXAMINATIONS
Certificate of Competence
Foundation Certificate in Consumer Affairs and Trading Standards
Module Certificate in Consumer Affairs and Trading Standards
Diploma in Consumer Affairs and Trading Standards
Higher Diploma in Consumer Affairs and Trading Standards

DESIGNATORY LETTERS
ASTI, MSTI, FSTI

TRANSPORT
Membership of Professional Institutions and Associations

INSTITUTE OF TRANSPORT ADMINISTRATION

The Old Studio
25 Greenfield Road
Westoning
Bedfordshire MK45 5JD
Tel: 01525 634940
Fax: 01525 750016
E-mail: director@iota.org.uk
Website: www.iota.org.uk

The primary aim of IoTA is to broaden and improve the knowledge, skills and experience of its members in the practice of efficient road, rail, air and sea transport. We are one of the few professional bodies still recognized within the terms of the Road Traffic 1968 (Statutory Instrument 78), wherein it is permitted to proffer qualified opinion as to the professional competence of its members.

MEMBERSHIP
Individual
Student
Associate (AInstTA)
Honorary Member
Corporate
Associate Member (AMInstTA)
Member (MInstTA)
Fellow (FInstTA)

DESIGNATORY LETTERS
AInstTA, AMInstTA, MInstTA, FInstTA

THE INSTITUTE OF TRAFFIC ACCIDENT INVESTIGATORS

Column House
London Road
Shrewsbury
Shropshire SY2 6NN
Tel: 08456 212066
Fax: 08456 212077
E-mail: gensec@itai.org
Website: www.itai.org

The Institute provides a means of communication, education, representation and regulation in the field of Traffic Accident Investigation. Our main aim is to provide a forum for spreading knowledge and enhancing expertise among those engaged in the discipline. Members include police officers, lecturers in higher education and private practitioners.

MEMBERSHIP
Affiliate
Associate (AITAI)
Member (MITAI)

DESIGNATORY LETTERS
AITAI, MITAI

TRAVEL AND TOURISM
Membership of Professional Institutions and Associations

CONFEDERATION OF TOURISM AND HOSPITALITY

11-16 Manchester Street
London W1U 4DJ
Tel: 020 7258 9850
Fax: 020 7258 9869
E-mail: info@cthawards.com
Website: www.cthawards.com

The Confederation of Tourism and Hospitality is an awarding body approved by Ofqual, and registered on the QCA's National Qualifications Framework. We were established in 1982 to provide recognized standards of management and vocational training appropriate to the needs of the hotel and travel industries, via our syllabuses, examinations and awards.

MEMBERSHIP
Student Member
Associate Member (AMCTH)
Member (MCTH)
Fellow (FCTH)

QUALIFICATION/EXAMINATIONS
Diploma in Hospitality and Tourism Management
Diploma in Hotel Management
Diploms in Hotel and Casino Management
Diploma in Tourism Management
Diploma in Travel Agency Management
Advanced Diploma in Hotel and Event Management
Advanced Diploma in Tourism Management
Advanced Diploma in Travel Agency Management
Postgraduate Diploma in Hotel Management

DESIGNATORY LETTERS
AMCTH, MCTH, FCTH

INSTITUTE OF TRAVEL AND TOURISM

PO Box 217
Ware
Hertfordshire SG12 8WY
Tel: 0844 4995 653
Fax: 0844 4995 654
E-mail: enquiries@itt.co.uk
Website: www.itt.co.uk

The ITT, founded in 1956, is a professional membership body for individuals employed in the travel and tourism industry. We provide support and guidance for our members throughout their career and offer them CPD and training to maintain standards for the benefit of the industry as a whole.

MEMBERSHIP
Student Member
Introductory Member
Affiliate Member
Member
Member (MInstTT)
Fellow
Fellow (FInstTT)
University/College Member
Group Member
Corporate Member

DESIGNATORY LETTERS
MInstTT, FInstTT

THE TOURISM MANAGEMENT INSTITUTE

c/o CPD Co-ordinator, Cathy Guthrie, PhD, FTMI, FTS
18 Cuninghill Avenue
Inverurie
Aberdeenshire AB51 3TZ
Tel: 01467 620769
E-mail: secretary@tmi.org.uk
Website: www.tmi.org.uk

Part of the Tourism Society, the TMI is the professional body for tourism destination managers. Its network of over 300 professionals shares information via the website, conferences, seminars, working groups, e-mails and newsletters. Committed to excellence, the TMI/Tourism Society run a Continuing Professional Development programme to support destination management and tourism professionals.

MEMBERSHIP
Student
Affiliate
Associate (ATMI)
Member (MTMI)

Fellow (FTMI)

QUALIFICATION/EXAMINATIONS
Postgraduate Certificate
Postgraduate Diploma
MSc in Destination Management (awarded by Leeds Metropolitan University and delivered in partnership with Bournemouth and Lancaster Universities; available as online distance learning so busy professionals can fit study around their existing schedules)

DESIGNATORY LETTERS
ATMI, MTMI, FTMI

THE TOURISM SOCIETY

Trinity Court
34 West Street
Sutton
Surrey SM1 1SH
Tel: 020 8661 4636
Fax: 020 8661 4637
E-mail: admin@tourismsociety.org
Website: www.tourismsociety.org

The Tourism Society, founded in 1977, is the professional membership body for people working in all sectors of tourism. We strive to drive up standards of professionalism and act as an advocate of tourism to the government and the public and private sectors, and liaise with other tourism professionals worldwide. We also provide advice, support and networking opportunities to our 1,000 or so members.

MEMBERSHIP
Student
Full Member (MTS)
Fellow (FTS)
Overseas/Retired Member
Group Member
Corporate Member

DESIGNATORY LETTERS
MTS, FTS

VETERINARY SCIENCE
Membership of Professional Institutions and Associations

BRITISH VETERINARY ASSOCIATION

7 Mansfield Street
London W1G 9NQ
Tel: 020 7636 6541
Fax: 020 7908 6349
E-mail: bvahq@bva.co.uk
Website: www.bva.co.uk

The BVA is the representative body for the veterinary profession in the UK and has more than 11,500 members. We promote and support the interests of our members and the animals under their care, liaise with the government and are the leading provider of veterinary information to the media and general public.

MEMBERSHIP
Student Member
Associate Member
Full Member
Overseas Member
Organizational Member

SOCIETY OF PRACTISING VETERINARY SURGEONS

The Governor's House
Cape Road
Warwick CV34 5DJ
Tel: 01926 410454
Fax: 01926 411350
E-mail: office@spvs.org.uk
Website: www.spvs.org.uk

The SPVS was founded in 1933 with the aim of promoting the interests of veterinary surgeons in private practice. We are a non-territorial division of the British Veterinary Association. Our remit is to advise on all aspects of managing the business of a clinical veterinary practice, and we hold one-day, weekend and week-long courses and an annual congress.

MEMBERSHIP
Student Member
Associate Member
Full Member
Retired Member

THE ROYAL COLLEGE OF VETERINARY SURGEONS

Belgravia House
62–64 Horseferry Road
London SW1P 2AF
Tel: 020 7222 2001
Fax: 020 7222 2004
E-mail: admin@rcvs.org.uk
Website: www.rcvs.org.uk

The RCVS is the regulatory body for veterinary surgeons in the UK. It role is to safeguard the health and welfare of animals committed to veterinary care through the regulation of the educational, ethical and clinical standards of the veterinary profession, and to act as an impartial source of informed opinion on animal health and welfare issues and their interaction with human health.

MEMBERSHIP
Member (MRCVS)

Fellow (FRCVS)

QUALIFICATION/EXAMINATIONS
Certificate in Advanced Veterinary Practice (CertAVP)
Diploma in Advanced Veterinary Nursing
Diploma of Fellowship (FRCVS)

DESIGNATORY LETTERS
MRCVS, FRCVS

WASTES MANAGEMENT
Membership of Professional Institutions and Associations

CHARTERED INSTITUTION OF WASTES MANAGEMENT

9 Saxon Court
St Peter's Gardens
Marefair
Northampton NN1 1SX
Tel: 01604 620426
Fax: 01604 621339
E-mail: education@ciwm.co.uk
Website: www.ciwm.co.uk

The CIWM represents more than 6,000 waste management professionals – predominantly in the UK but also overseas. We promote education, training and research in the scientific, technical and practical aspects of waste management for the safeguarding of the environment, and set and strive to maintain high standards for individuals working in the waste management industry.

MEMBERSHIP
Student Member
Technician Member (TechMCIWM)
Associate Member (AssocMCIWM)
Graduate Member (GradMCIWM)
Licentiate (LCIWM)

Member (MCIWM)
Fellow (FCIWM)
Affiliated Organization

QUALIFICATION/EXAMINATIONS
CIWM Training Services specializes in developing and providing waste management training for individuals & organizations. Each year we organize more than 70 courses. For details see the website.

DESIGNATORY LETTERS
TechMCIWM, AssocMCIWM, GradMCIWM, LCIWM, MCIWM, FCIWM

WATCH AND CLOCK MAKING AND REPAIRING
Membership of Professional Institutions and Associations

THE BRITISH HOROLOGICAL INSTITUTE LIMITED

Upton Hall
Upton
Newark
Nottinghamshire NG23 5TE
Tel: 01636 813795
Fax: 01636 812258
E-mail: clock@bhi.co.uk
Website: www.bhi.co.uk

The BHI, which was formed in 1858 to promote horology, is a professional body with about 3,000 members worldwide. We provide education and specialist training, set recognized standards of excellence in workmanship and professional conduct, and support our members in their work making, repairing and servicing clocks and watches.

MEMBERSHIP
Student
Associate

Graduate (GradBHI)
Member (MBHI)
Fellow (FBHI)

QUALIFICATION/EXAMINATIONS
Certificate in Clock and Watch Servicing (Level 2)
Certificate in the Repair, Restoration and Conservation of Clocks/Watches (Level 3)

DESIGNATORY LETTERS
GradBHI, MBHI, FBHI

WELDING
Membership of Professional Institutions and Associations

THE WELDING INSTITUTE

Granta Park
Great Abington
Cambridge CB21 6AL
Tel: 01223 899000
Fax: 01223 894219
E-mail: twi_professional@twi.co.uk
Website: www.twiprofessional.com

The Welding Institute is the engineering institution for welding and joining professionals. We are committed to promoting the importance of welding/materials joining technology, given its importance as a key industrial technology governing the reliability and safety of many products, and to the advancement of education, training and CPD for our members.

MEMBERSHIP
Graduate (GradWeldI)

Technician (TechWeldI)
Senior Associate (SenAWeldI)
Incorporated Member (IncMWeldI)
Member (MWeldI)
Senior Member (SenMWeldI)
Fellow (FWeldI)
Honorary Fellow (HonFWeldI)
Engineering Technician (EngTech)
Incorporated Engineer (IEng)
Chartered Engineer (CEng)

QUALIFICATION/EXAMINATIONS
Certificate in Welding and Joining Technology for Students in Materials and Engineering

DESIGNATORY LETTERS
GradWeldI, TechWeldI, SenAWeldI, IncMWeldI, MWeldI, SenMWeldI, FWeldI, HonFWeldI, EngTech, IEng, CEng

WELFARE

Membership of Professional Institutions and Associations

INSTITUTE OF WELFARE

PO Box 5570
Stourbridge
West Midlands DY8 9BA
Tel: 01214 548883
Fax: 01214 547873
E-mail: info@instituteofwelfare.co.uk
Website: www.instituteofwelfare.co.uk

The Institute of Welfare was founded in 1945 and exists to promote the highest possible standards in the delivery of welfare to those who need it. We make representations to government, undertake research on welfare issues, encourage and facilitate the exchange of information, and provide opportunities for those engaged in welfare work to pursue CPD.

MEMBERSHIP
Associate Member (AMIW)
Member (MIW)
Fellow (FIW)
Companion (CIW)

DESIGNATORY LETTERS
AMIW, MIW, FIW, CIW

Part 6

Bodies Accrediting Independent Institutions

THE BRITISH ACCREDITATION COUNCIL FOR INDEPENDENT FURTHER AND HIGHER EDUCATION (BAC)

BAC is a registered charity that was established in 1984 to act as the national accrediting body for independent further and higher education. It is independent both of government and of the colleges it accredits.

A college that is accredited by BAC undergoes a thorough inspection every four years, with an interim visit after two years. Until 2000, BAC accreditation was only available to colleges in the United Kingdom, but there are now accredited colleges in Bulgaria, the Czech Republic, France, Germany, Greece, India, Pakistan, Spain, Switzerland and the UAE. At present BAC accredits 230 colleges in the United Kingdom and 27 overseas. Lists of accredited colleges are published each year, but full details can be viewed on the BAC website.

BAC's Council includes nominees of a number of the major bodies concerned with the maintenance of standards in British education, including the Open University Validation Service, the Council of Validating Universities, Universities UK, the Association of Learning Providers, the Quality Assurance Agency for Higher Education and the United Kingdom Council for Overseas Student Affairs (UKCOSA), and observers from the Federation of Awarding Bodies, the Joint Council for Qualifications, GuildHE, the Home Office and the DfES.

Further details of the work of the BAC and a current list of accredited institutions may be obtained from The Chief Executive, BAC, 44 Bedford Row, London WC1R 4LL; tel 020 7447 2584, fax 020 7447 2585, e-mail info@the-bac.org, website www.the-bac.org.

THE BRITISH COUNCIL

The British Council runs the Accreditation UK scheme in partnership with English UK for the inspection and accreditation of organizations that provide courses in English as a Foreign Language (EFL) in Britain. The scheme is managed jointly by the British Council and English UK. One of its aims is to effectively promote accredited UK ELT through the British Council's network of overseas offices.

Under the terms of the scheme, institutions are inspected rigorously every four years in the areas of management, resources and environment, teaching and learning, and welfare and student services. The scheme also includes a system of random spot-checking. The management and policy of the scheme is conducted by an independent board while a separate independent committee reviews inspectors' reports.

Some 86 per cent of recognized schools are also members of English UK, which insists on British Council accreditation as a criterion for membership. In addition, all English UK members, of which there are 357, are required to abide by the Association's Code of Practice and Regulations. English UK exists to raise the high standards of its members even further through conferences, training courses and publications. The association also represents the interests of members and students to government bodies, and promotes the teaching of English in Britain at home and overseas.

Further information on the Accreditation UK scheme may be obtained from the Accreditation Unit, British Council, Bridgewater House, 58 Whitworth Street, Manchester M1 6BB; Tel: 01619 577692, Fax: 01619 517074, e-mail: accreditation.unit@britishcouncil.org, Website: www. britishcouncil.org/accreditation. Further information on English UK may be obtained from

English UK, 56 Buckingham Gate, London SW1E 6AG; Tel: 020 7802 9200, Fax: 020 7802 9201, e-mail: info@englishuk.com, Website: www.englishuk.com.

THE OPEN AND DISTANCE LEARNING QUALITY COUNCIL (ODL QC)

ODL QC was established in 1969 as the Council for the Accreditation of Correspondence Colleges, a joint initiative of the then Labour government and representatives of the sector. It is the principal accrediting body for a wide variety of providers of open and distance learning in the UK, from commercial colleges to professional and public-sector institutions. Now independent, it nevertheless continues to have the informal support of government.

ODL QC promotes quality by:

- establishing standards of education and training in open and distance learning;
- recognizing good quality provision, wherever it occurs;
- supporting and protecting the interests of learners;
- encouraging the improvement of existing methods and the development of new ones;
- linking open and distance learning with other forms of education and training;
- promoting wider recognition of the value of open and distance learning.

Accreditation includes a rigorous assessment of an educational provision, including materials, tutorial support, publicity, contractual arrangements with learners and general administrative procedures, each of which is measured against the council's published benchmark standards. If accredited, the provider is monitored on a regular basis and reassessed at least once every three years.

The council promotes those colleges that it accredits, which are by definition quality providers of ODL, and acts as honest broker in matching accredited colleges to potential markets. A list of courses offered by accredited providers is circulated widely, both in the UK and abroad, and is also included on the council's website, www.odlqc.org.uk.

The council also seeks to protect the interests of learners by promoting the importance of accreditation, and by offering advice and support directly to learners. At the same time, knowledge of good practice is disseminated more widely, and quality encouraged wherever open and distance learning occurs.

The council consists of members nominated by professional and public bodies involved in education, as well as representatives of accredited providers, and has strong links with other bodies in the sector, both in the UK and abroad.

All enquiries should be addressed to the Chief Executive, ODL QC; Tel: 020 7612 7090, Fax: 020 7612 7092, e-mail: info@odlqc.org.uk, Website: www. odlqc.org.uk.

THE CONFERENCE FOR INDEPENDENT FURTHER EDUCATION (CIFE)

CIFE was founded in 1973 to promote strict adherence by independent sixth-form and tutorial colleges to the highest standards of academic and professional integrity. All member colleges must be accredited by the British Accreditation Council for Independent Further and Higher Education (BAC), or optionally or as well as the Independent Schools Joint Council (ISJC) if they are registered by the Department for Education and Employment (DfEE) as schools. Candidate membership is available for up to three years for colleges that are seeking BAC or ISJC accreditation and otherwise satisfy CIFE's own exacting membership criteria. All colleges must also abide by stringent codes of conduct and practice, the character and presentation of their published exam results are subject to regulation, and the accuracy of the information must be validated by BAC as academic auditor to CIFE. Full members are subject to reinspection by their accrediting bodies. There are 17 colleges in full or candidate membership of CIFE at present, spread throughout England but with concentrations in London, Oxford and Cambridge.

CIFE colleges offer a wide range of GCSE, A and AS level courses. In addition some CIFE colleges offer English language tuition for students from overseas, and degree-level tuition. A number of the colleges offer summer holiday academic courses, and most of them also provide A level and GCSE revision courses during the Christmas and/or Easter holidays. Further information on CIFE may be obtained from the CIFE website: www.cife.org.uk, Tel: 0207 656 7777, e-mail: enquiries@cife.org.uk.

Part 7

Study Associations and the 'Learned Societies'

Study associations consist of persons who wish to increase their knowledge of a particular subject or range of subjects; they may be professionals or amateurs. Some associations consist almost entirely of specialists (eg, the Royal Statistical Society); others (eg, the Royal Geographical Society and the Zoological Society of London) have a more general membership. The learned societies usually have two grades of membership, fellows or members. Some also admit group members (such as schools or libraries), which are known as corporate members, and junior associate, corresponding and overseas members, who pay lower subscriptions. Some also elect honorary fellows or members. The members of some societies may use designatory letters, but this does not mean that the holder is 'qualified' in the same sense as a doctor or a chartered accountant.

Membership of some learned societies is by election, and is commonly accepted as distinguishing the candidate by admission to an exclusive group. Candidates may be selected in respect of pre-eminence in their subject or in the public service. The chief associations of this type are the Royal Society (founded 1660 and granted Royal Charters in 1662 and 1663), the Royal Academy of Arts (founded 1768) and the British Academy (granted the Royal Charter in 1902).

The **Royal Society** was established to improve 'natural knowledge' and is mainly concerned with pure and applied science and technology. Election to Fellowship (FRS) is regarded as one of the highest distinctions. The society elects Royal Fellows, Fellows and Foreign Members.

The **Royal Academy** was established to cultivate and improve the arts of painting, sculpture and architecture. There are two main grades of membership: Academicians (RA), including Senior Academicians, and Associates (ARA); there are also a small number of Honorary Academicians.

The **British Academy** is the national academy for the humanities and the social sciences. It is the counterpart to the Royal Society that exists to serve the natural sciences. The Academy has Fellows (FBA), Corresponding Fellows and a small number of Honorary Fellows.

A list of Learned Societies and Study Associations can be found below.

OCCUPATIONAL ASSOCIATIONS

The occupational associations do not qualify practitioners but organize them. Some coordinate the activities of specialists (eg, the Society of Medical Officers of Health) and others promote the individual and collective interests of professionals working in a wider area. Both also seek to safeguard the public interest and to offer an educational service to their members. The latter type of association is especially numerous among teachers, who have over 20 associations (eg, the National Union of Teachers, the Educational Institute of Scotland, the National Association of Schoolmasters/Union of Women Teachers and the National Association of Head Teachers), and is represented in the medical profession by the British Medical Association. Both types of association usually have only one grade of membership.

LIST OF STUDY ASSOCIATIONS AND LEARNED SOCIETIES

This list largely excludes qualifying bodies, which are covered in Part 5. The date on the left is that of foundation or adoption of title.

Agriculture and Related Subjects

1926	Agricultural Economics Society	1882	Royal Forestry Society of England, Wales and N Ireland
1952	British Agricultural History Society		
1945	British Grassland Society	1784	Royal Highland and Agricultural Society of Scotland
1944	British Society of Animal Production		
1947	British Society of Soil Science	1804	Royal Horticultural Society
1921	Commonwealth Forestry Association	1854	Royal Scottish Forestry Society
1947	Fertiliser Society	1904	Royal Welsh Agricultural Society
1927	Herb Society of Great Britain	1931	Society for Applied Bacteriology
1925	Institute of Foresters	1943	Society of Dairy Technology
1938	Institution of Agricultural Engineers	1945	The Soil Association
1839	Royal Agricultural Society of England		

Anthropology and Related Subjects

1963	African Studies Association of the UK	1891	Japan Society
1883	Alliance Francaise	1921	National Institute of Industrial Psychology
1974	Association for the Study of German Politics		
		1865	Palestine Exploration Fund
1979	Association for the Study of Modern and Contemporary France	1843	Royal Anthropological Institute of Great Britain and Ireland
1982	Association for the Study of Modern Italy	1823	Royal Asiatic Society of Great Britain and Ireland
1946	Association of Social Anthropologists of the UK and Commonwealth	1868	Royal Commonwealth Society
		1901	Royal Society for Asian Affairs
1985	British Association for Irish Studies	1936	Saltire Society
1974	British Association for Japanese Studies	1977	Society for Caribbean Studies
		1964	Society for Latin American Studies
1961	British Institute of Persian Studies	1969	Society for Libyan Studies
1973	British Society for Middle Eastern Studies	1972	Society for South Asian Studies
		1983	Society for the Promotion of Byzantine Studies
1951	British Sociological Association		
	Board of Celtic Studies	1879	Society for the Promotion of Hellenic Studies
1907	Eugenics Society		
1981	European Association for Jewish Studies	1910	Society for the Promotion of Roman Studies
1878	Folklore Society	1969	University Association for Contemporary European Studies
1931	Institute for the Study and Treatment of Delinquency		
		1892	Viking Society for Northern Research
1991	Instituto Cervantes	1988	Women in German Studies
1972	Japan Foundation	2005	The Young Foundation

Archaeology

1924	Ancient Monuments Society	1846	Cambrian Archaeological Association
1979	Association for Environmental Archaeology	1944	Council for British Archaeology
		1882	Egypt Exploration Society
1843	British Archaeological Association	1855	London and Middlesex Archeological Society
1996	British Epigraphy Society		
1948	British Institute of Archaeology at Ankara	1865	Palestine Exploration Fund
		1908	Prehistorical Society

| 1843 | Royal Archaeological Institute |
| 1967 | Society for Post-Medieval Archaeology |

Art

1974	Association of Art Historians	1904	Royal Society of British Sculptors
1910	Contemporary Art Society	1904	Royal Society of Marine Artists
1936	Faculty of Royal Designers for Industry	1895	Royal Society of Miniature Painters, Sculptors and Gravers
1950	International Institute for Conservation of Historic and Artistic Works	1884	Royal Society of Painter-Etchers and Engravers
1888	National Society for Art Education	1804	Royal Society of Painters in Watercolours
1899	Pastel Society	1891	Royal Society of Portrait Painters
1768	Royal Academy of Arts	1919	Society of Graphic Artists
1814	Royal Birmingham Society of Artists	1952	Society of Portrait Sculptors
1883	Royal Institute of Oil-Painters	1952	United Society of Artists
1831	Royal Institute of Painters in Watercolours	1955	William Morris Society
1826	Royal Scottish Academy of Painting, Sculpture and Architecture		

Biology and related subjects

1904	Association of Applied Biologists	1913	The British Ecological Society
1960	Biological Engineering Society	1896	The British Mycological Society
1836	The Botanical Society of the British Isles	1858	The British Ornithologists' Union
1836	The Botanical Society of Edinburgh	1959	British Society for Cell Biology
1896	British Bryological Society	1933	The British Trust for Ornithology
		1929	Freshwater Biological Association

Human Biology

| 1937 | The Systematics Association | 1826 | The Zoological Society of London |

Chemistry

1911	The Biochemical Society	1881	Society of the Chemical Industry
1841	The Chemical Society	1897	Society of Leather Technologists and Chemists
1913	The Institute of Petroleum		
1918	Oil and Colour Chemists' Association		

Economics, Philosophy and related subjects

1992	Association of Business Schools	1955	Institute of Economic Affairs
1987	Conference of Heads of University Departments of Economics	1915	Philosophical Society of England
		1920	Royal Institute of International Affairs
1927	Economic History Society	1834	Royal Statistical Society
2003	Economic Research Institute of Northern Ireland	1953	Scottish Economic Society

Engineering

1847	The Architectural Association	1920	Newcomen Society for the Study of the History of Engineering and Technology
1966	Concrete Society		
1946	Faculty of Building		
1976	Fellowship of Engineering	1916	Royal Incorporation of Architects in Scotland
1881	Institute of British Carriage and Automobile Manufacturers		
		1860	Royal Institution of Naval Architects
1978	Institute of Concrete Technology	1927	Royal Television Society
1899	Institute of Refrigeration	1854	Society of Engineers
1959	Institution of Nuclear Engineers	1958	Society of Environmental Engineers

Geography, Geology and related subjects

1963	British Cartographic Society	1858	Geologists Association
1949	British Geotechnical Society	1846	Hakluyt Society
1940	British Society of Rheology	1933	Institute of British Geographers
1968	Council for Environmental Education	1971	Institution of Environmental Sciences
1988	Council of British Geography	1876	Mineralogical Society of Great Britain and Ireland
1923	English Place-Name Society		
1931	Gemmological Association of Great Britain	1847	Palaeontographical Society
		1957	Paleontological Association
1893	Geographical Association	1830	Royal Geographical Society
1807	Geological Society of London	1884	Royal Scottish Geographical Society

History and related subjects

1981	Association of Chief Archivists in Local Government	1986	Institute of Contemporary British History
1908	Baptist Historical Society	1961	Institute of Heraldic and Genealogical Studies
1902	British Academy for the Promotion of Historical, Philosophical, and Philological Studies		
		1921	Institute of Historical Research
		1893	Jewish Historical Society of England
1952	British Agricultural History Society	1964	London Record Society
1932	British Records Association	1981	Maghreb Studies Association
1888	British Record Society	2000	Museums, Libraries and Archives Council
1947	British Society for the History of Science		
		1969	Napoleonic Society (of Great Britain)
1904	Canterbury and York Society	1920	Newcomen Society for the Study of the History of Engineering and Technology
1904	Catholic Record Society		
1988	Centre for Metropolitan History		
1864	Early English Texts Society	1921	Oriental Ceramic Society
1839	Ecclesiological Society	1868	Royal Historical Society
1923	English Place-Name Society	1836	Royal Numismatic Society
1903	Friends Historical Society	1953	Scottish Genealogy Society
1964	Furniture History Society	1886	Scottish History Society
1869	Harleian Society	1897	Scottish Record Society
1906	The Historical Association	1976	Social History Society
1885	Huguenot Society of Great Britain and Ireland	1921	Society for Army Historical Research
		1910	Society for Nautical Research

1967	Society for Renaissance Studies	1947	Society of Archivists
1970	Society for the Social History of Medicine	1911	Society of Genealogists
1707	Society of Antiquaries of London	1958	Victorian Society
1780	Society of Antiquaries of Scotland	2005	The Young Foundation
1956	Society of Architectural Historians in Great Britain		

Languages

1883	Alliance Française	1910	Institute of Linguists
1891	An Comunn Gaidhealach	1991	Instituto Cervantes
1981	Association for French Language Studies	1964	National Association for the Teaching of English
1990	Association for Language Learning	1993	University Council of Modern Languages
2003	Centre for Information and Language Teaching and Research	1988	Women in German Studies
1932	Conference of University Teachers of German in Great Britain and Ireland		

Law

1958	British Institute of International and Comparative Law	1949	Law Society of Scotland
		1920	Royal Institute of International Affairs
1972	Intellectual Property Bar Association	1965	Scottish Law Commission
1922	Law Society of Northern Ireland	1887	The Selden Society

Literature and Arts

1959	Academi – Yr Academi Gymreig	1915	Design and Industries Association
1973	Alliance of Literary Societies	1902	Dickens Fellowship
1969	Art Libraries Society of UK and Ireland	1890	Edinburgh Bibliographical Society
		1906	English Association
1970	Association for Scottish Literary Studies	1886	Francis Bacon Society Inc
		1997	Historical Novel Society
1989	Association of Independent Libraries	1973	Joseph Conrad Society
1892	Bibliographical Society	1997	Leeds Philosophical and Literary Society
1992	British Association for Information and Library Education and Research	1906	Malone Society
		1781	Manchester Literary and Philosophical Society
1975	British Comparative Literature Association	1995	Philip Larkin Society
1933	British Film Institute	1842	Philological Society
1960	British Society of Aesthetics	1909	Poetry Society
1893	Bronte Society	1874	Royal Musical Association
1949	Cambridge Bibliographical Society	1820	Royal Society of Literature of the United Kingdom
1935	Charles Lamb Society		
1904	Classical Association	1884	Society of Authors

2004	Society of College, National and University Libraries	1968	Thomas Hardy Society
1984	Standing Conference for the Arts and Social Sciences	1960	H. G. Wells, Society

Management

1986	British Academy of Management

Mathematics and Physics

1924	Astronomical Society of Edinburgh	1930	The Institution of Electronics
1890	The British Astronomical Association	1871	The Mathematical Association
1966	British Biophysical Society	1820	The Royal Astronomical Society
1927	The British Institute of Radiology	1850	The Royal Meteorological Society
1933	The British Interplanetary Society		

Medicine

1887	The Anatomical Society of GB and Ireland	1945	British Association of Urological Surgeons
1957	Association for Child Psychology and Psychiatry	1934	The British Diabetic Association
1957	The Association for the Study of Medical Education	1948	The British Geriatric Society
		1832	British Medical Association
1932	Association of Anaesthetists of GB and Ireland	1950	The British Neuropathological Society
1933	Association of British Neurologists	1953	The British Occupational Hygiene Society
1953	The Association of Clinical Bio-chemists	1918	The British Orthopaedic Association
		1928	The British Paediatric Association
1927	The Association of Clinical Pathologists	1931	The British Pharmaceutical Society
		1913	The British Psycho-Analytical Society
1972	Association of Psychiatrists in Training	1901	British Psychological Society
1920	Association of Surgeons of GB and Ireland	1948	British Society for Allergy and Clinical Immunology
1959	The British Academy for Forensic Sciences	1962	British Society for Clinical Cytology
		1960	British Society for Haematology
		1947	The British Society for Research on Ageing
1977	British Association of Clinical Anatomists	1937	The British Society of Gastro-enterology
1950	British Association of Forensic Medicine	1965	Chiropractic Advancement Association
1962	British Association of Oral Surgeons	1947	Ergonomics Society
1965	British Association of Orthodontists	1946	Experimental Psychology Society
1943	British Association of Otolaryngologists	1950	The Faculty of Homeopathy
		1959	The Forensic Science Society
1954	British Association of Paediatric Surgeons	1813	Harveian Society of London
		1936	The Heberden Society
1964	British Association of Social Psychiatry	1819	The Hunterian Society
		1969	Institute of Occupational Medicine
1973	British Association of Surgical Oncology	1964	Institute of Pharmacy Management International

1922	The Medical Society for the Study of Venereal Diseases	1805	The Royal Society of Medicine
1773	The Medical Society of London	1907	The Royal Society of Tropical Medicine and Hygiene
1901	The Medico-Legal Society	1884	The Society for the Study of Addiction (to Alcohol and Other Drugs)
1941	The Nutrition Society		
1880	The Ophthalmological Society of the UK	1950	Society for the Study of Fertility
1925	Osteopathic Association of Great Britain	1926	The Society of British Neurological Surgeons
1906	Pathological Society of Great Britain and Ireland	1946	The Society of Endocrinology
		1933	The Society of Thoracic and Cardiovascular Surgeons of Great Britain and Ireland
1734	Royal Medical Society		
1875	The Royal Sanitary Association of Scotland	1945	The Thoracic Society

Music

1977	Alkan Society	1882	Incorporated Society of Musicians
1979	British Music Society	1888	Plainsong and Medieval Music Society
1971	Chopin Society	1874	Royal Musical Association
1932	English Folk Dance and Song Society	1955	Welsh Music Guild

Philosophy

1870	Aristotelian Society	1990	Nietzsche Society of Great Britain
2003	British Philosophical Association	1913	Philosophical Society of England
1984	British Society for the History of Philosophy	1925	Royal Institute of Philosophy
1819	Cambridge Philosophical Society	1802	Royal Philosophical Society of Glasgow
1979	Hegel Society of Great Britain	1967	Society for Renaissance Studies
1781	Manchester Literary and Philosophical Society	1865	Victoria Institute, or Philosophical Society of Great Britain

Politics

1974	Association for the Study of German Politics	1884	Electoral Reform Society
1975	British International Studies Association	1945	Federal Trust for Education and Research
1951	David Davies Memorial Institute of International Studies	1943	Hispanic and Luso Brazilian Council
		1987	Institute of Welsh Affairs
		1969	Politics Association
2003	Economic Research Institute of Northern Ireland	1868	Royal Commonwealth Society

Science general

1924	ASLIB	1956	The British Society for the History of Science
1831	The British Association for the Advancement of Science	1960	The British Society for the Philosophy of Science
1901	The British Psychological Society		

449

1925	The Royal Institute of Philosophy	1754	The Royal Society of Arts
1799	The Royal Institution of Great Britain	1783	The Royal Society of Edinburgh
1660	The Royal Society		

Theology and Religious Studies

1908	Baptist Historical Society	1981	European Association for Jewish Studies
1954	British Association for the Study of Religions	1903	Friends Historical Society
1904	Canterbury and York Society	1972	United Reformed Church History Society
1904	Catholic Record Society	1893	Wesley Historical Society
1961	Ecclesiastical History Society		
1839	Ecclesiological Society		

Town and Country Planning

1899	Town and Country Planning Association

General Index

Note: In addition to the abbreviations listed at the beginning of the book, the following are used throughout the index; FE – Further Education; HE – Higher Education. Universities are listed under locations eg: Aberdeen, University of

INDEX OF ADVERTISERS